Boundary Politics
and
International Boundaries of Iran

*With Afghanistan, Armenia, Azerbaijan Republic,
Bahrain, (the autonomous republic of Ganjah) Iraq,
Kazakhstan, Kuwait, Oman, Pakistan, Qatar,
Russia, Saudi Arabia, Turkey, Turkmenistan,
and the United Arab Emirates*

Author and Editor
Pirouz Mojtahed-Zadeh

Universal Publishers
Boca Raton, Florida
USA • 2006

Boundary Politics and International Boundaries of Iran:
With Afghanistan, Armenia, Azerbaijan Republic, Bahrain, (the autonomous republic of Ganjah)
Iraq, Kazakhstan, Kuwait, Oman, Pakistan, Qatar, Russia, Saudi Arabia, Turkey, Turkmenistan,
and the United Arab Emirates

Copyright © 2006 Pirouz Mojtahed-Zadeh
All rights reserved.

Universal Publishers
Boca Raton, Florida • USA
2006

ISBN: 1-58112-933-5

www.universal-publishers.com

ACKNOWLEDGEMENTS

Preparation and presentation of this work has been inspired by the success of an international symposium on boundaries of modern Iran (London University, 9 and 10 October 2002) attended by many experts in the field, including the contributors to this volume. The chapters of this book that might have started on the basis of the papers presented in that symposium have subsequently been researched and prepared for this work. Early versions of the articles prepared by the author/editor have appeared in various publications. That is to say, the versions appearing in this volume have evolved over a considerable period of time and have gone through various stages of improvement.

However, my sincere thanks are first and foremost to the Society for Contemporary Iranian Studies, especially its president Dr. M. A. Ala, its treasurer Dr. Nasser Rahimi, and to Mr. Hormuz Nafisi, its member of the board of directors, for agreeing to allocate the necessary funds for the preparation of this book. Similarly, I would like to thank the Iranian Ministry of Foreign Affairs for providing some assistance in paving the way for some of the symposium participants to travel from Iran to London.

I thank the efforts of Dr. Bruce Ingham, Chairman, Dr. Sarah Stewart, administrator, and her colleagues, especially Ms. Anna Cormak of the Centre for Near and Middle Eastern Studies at the University of London School of Oriental and African Studies (SOAS) in guaranteeing a smooth and efficient organization of the symposium. Similarly, my sincere thanks are due to Miss Margaret Davis, secretary, and Miss Pamela Davis, treasurer, of the Urosevic Research Foundation of London for their assistance in the organization of the symposium and for their assistance in editing the text of this book.

Those that participated in the symposium and contributed to this volume have been admirably helpful in making this project a reality. The list includes a number of respectable and reputable experts in the field such as (in alphabetical order): Dr. Kaveh Afrasiabi, Dr. Hamid Ahmadi, Dr. Bahram Amirahmadian, Dr. Sohrab Asgari, Dr. Davood Hermitas Bavand, Professor Mohammad Hassan Ganji, Dr. Mohammad Reza Hafeznia, Dr. Bruce Ingham, Dr. Masud Moradi, Dr. Richard Schofield, and Ms. Narges Taghavi. I owe them all much gratitude. Not only has Mr. Farzad Sharifi-Yazdi contributed to this volume by undertaking to research and prepare a chapter on the Western Iranian boundaries, but he has also assisted editing this book diligently, for which I am most grateful.

During the course of my research for the chapters that I have contributed to this book, I exchanged views with and received information from a number of academics and government officials in the United Kingdom, Iran, France, Pakistan, Afghanistan and the Arab states of the Persian Gulf. Similarly, a number of academics and interested friends have seen these works in their evolutionary stages and have made a number of valuable suggestions, which undoubtedly improved the text. I am very grateful to all of them, specially (in alphabetic order); Amir Parviz Khozeimeh Alam, Mr. Mehdi Besharat editor of *Persian* monthly *Ettelaat Siasi va Eqtesadi* of Tehran, Dr. Hassan Shahbaz editor of *Rahavard* quarterly of Los Angeles, Dr. Mahmood

Sariolghalam, editor of *Discurse* quarterly journal of Tehran, and Amir Masud Ejtehadi, managing editor of the *Iranian Journal of International Affairs*.

The controllers of the India Office Library and Records, the Public Record Office, the document centre of the Iranian Ministry of Foreign Affairs, the Library of the School of Oriental and African Studies, the (UN) Office and Library in London, the National Document Organization of Iran and the document centre of the Cultural Studies Centre of Tehran have kindly permitted me to use and helped me to find and photocopy masses of relevant documents. My sincere thanks are due to all of them.

Last, but not least, I am most grateful to my family for their patience with me and the endless hours that I worked at home in preparing this book. Moreover, I am particularly grateful to my beloved daughter Tosca Nayereh for assisting me in typing some of the chapters of this volume.

Pirouz Mojtahed-Zadeh
London – Summer 2006

TABLE OF CONTENTS

PREFACE 9
INTRODUCTION
The Concept of Boundary and Its Origin in the Ancient Persian Tradition
Pirouz Mojtahed-Zadeh 13
CHAPTER I
Traditional Regions and National Frontiers of Iran: A General Overview
Keith S. McLachlan 29
    SECTION A
    IRAN'S NORTHERN BOUNDARIES 39
    Section A1– Iran's Boundaries in the Caucasus 39
CHAPTER II
Stages in the Shaping of Iran's North-Western Boundaries
Mohammad Hassan Ganji 41
CHAPTER III
Evolution of Russo-Iranian Boundaries in the Caucasus
Bahram Amirahmadian 51
    Section A2 – Iran's Boundaries in the Caspian Sea 67
CHAPTER IV
A Review of the Oil and Gas Prospects of the Iranian Sector of the Caspian Sea and the Surrounding Areas
Mohammad Ali Ala 69
CHAPTER V
Perspectives on the Caspian Sea Dilemma: An Iranian Construct
Pirouz Mojtahed-Zadeh and Mohammad Reza Hafeznia 73
CHAPTER VI
Iran's Caspian Oil and Gas Dilemma
Hossein Askari and Roshanak Taghavi* 85
    Section A3- Iran's North-Eastern Boundaries 101
CHAPTER VII
Emergence and Evolution of Iran's North-Eastern Boundaries
Pirouz Mojtahed-Zadeh 103
    SECTION B
    EMERGENCE AND EVOLUTION OF WESTERN BOUNDARIES OF IRAN 121
A General Introduction Western Boundaries of Iran
Pirouz Mojtahed-Zadeh 123
CHAPTER VIII
The Borders of the Persian and the Ottoman Empires:
An Analysis of Persian Sovereignty over the District of Qotur
Masud Moradi 127

CHAPTER IX
Evolution of Iran's Western Boundaries
Farzad Cyrus Sharifi-Yazdi 135
CHAPTER X
Evolution of the Shatt al-Arab Dispute after the 1913 Protocol
Pirouz Mojtahed-Zadeh 149
Appendix to Chapter X 156
   SECTION C
   EMERGENCE AND EVOLUTION OF EASTERN IRANIAN BOUNDARIES **159**
CHAPTER XI
The Partitioning of Eastern Provinces of Iran
Pirouz Mojtahed-Zadeh 161
CHAPTER XII
Emergence of Khorasan and Baluchistan Boundaries
Pirouz Mojtahed-Zadeh 187
CHAPTER XIII
Emergence and Evolution of Sistan Boundaries
Pirouz Mojtahed-Zadeh 213
CHAPTER XIV
Hydropolitics of Hirmand and Hamun
Pirouz Mojtahed-Zadeh 245
CHAPTER XV
Behavioral Analysis of Iran-Afghanistan Boundary
Mohammad Reza Hafeznia 253
   SECTION D
   IRAN'S SOUTHERN BOUNDARIES **261**
CHAPTER XVI
Maritime Boundaries in the Persian Gulf
Pirouz Mojtahed-Zadeh 263
CHAPTER XVII
The Unfinished Case of Iran - Kuwait Maritime Boundary Delimitation
Sohrab Asghari 295
CHAPTER XVIII
Disputes over Tunbs and Abu Musa
Pirouz Mojtahed-Zadeh 305
CHAPTER XIX
Legal and Historical Arguments on Tunbs & Abu Musa 319
Pirouz Mojtahed-Zadeh 319
CHAPTER XX
Seizure of the Two Tunbs and Restoration of Sovereignty in Abu Musa
Pirouz Mojtahed-Zadeh 341
CHAPTER XXI
A Look at Some of the More Recently Propagated UAE Arguments
Pirouz Mojtahed-Zadeh 349
Appendix to Chapter XXI **366**
Contributors 369

TABLE OF ILLUSTRATIONS

Figure 1
Iran and neighboring states 29

Figure 2
Map showing Iranian territories ceded to
Russia in terms of Golestan and Turkmenchai treaties 47

Figure 3
Iran 1, Azerbaijan Republic 2, and Turkmenistan 3, sectors in the Caspian Sea 71

Figure 4
Imaginary Astara-Hassangholi line 77

Figure 5
Boundaries in the Caspian based upon an equal division
of the sea surface, seabed, and subsoil. 78

Figure 6
Formula for delineation of the Caspian 79

Figure 7
The North-Eastern Boundaries of Iran: Boundaries of Iran and Turkmenistan 115

Figure 8
A topographic profile of Qotur district 129

Figure 9
The break up of the Ottoman Empire and final developments
in the evolution of Western Iranian boundary 141

Figure 10
Iran's Thalweg boundary with Iraq in Shatt al-Arab 153

Figure 11
Hashtadan and Hari-rud boundaries of northern Khorasan 191

Figure 12
The Musa-Abad, Namakzar, and Qaenat boundaries (the Altay Line) 198

Figure 13
The Iran-Pakistan boundaries of 1871, 1872, 1903 and 1905 205

Figure 14
Iran - Saudi Arabian Continental Shelf Boundaries 269

Figure 15
Iran - Qatar Continental Shelf Boundary 272

Figure 16
Iran - Bahrain Continental Shelf Boundary 275

Figure 17
Iran-Oman Continental Shelf Boundaries and shipping lanes in the Strait of Hormuz 278

Figure 18
Iran-Dubai Continental Shelf Boundaries in the Persian Gulf 281

Figure 19
Geographical position of the Islands of Tunb and Abu Musa
near the Strait of Hormuz 306

Figure 20
Letter of 1 Jamadi al-Akhar 1301 (29 March 1884) 323
Figure 21
Approximate limits of Iranian dominions on the southern side of the Persian Gulf 355
Figure 22
H. H. Sheikh Saqar Bin Mohammad al-Qassemi, is welcomed on board the Iranian naval vessel at anchor in Abu Musa waters. 360

PREFACE

Boundary and territoriality have often been the cause of conflicts and erosion of security in international relations, and Iran is no exception in this respect. In fact, with at least fifteen neighbours, Iran has the largest number of neighbours in the world, and that is the reason for the existence around Iran of arguably the most varied and complex boundary issues in the world. Cross-border issues here greatly influence the regional economic and political life of the country. For example, determining Iran's territorial sovereignty and her boundary delimitation in the Caspian Sea extensively influenced her national interests and foreign relations in the 1990s, especially considering that the United States was trying to neutralize her extremely important geopolitical and geo-strategic position between the Persian Gulf and Caspian Sea energy depots: territorial challenges to Iran in the south by the United Arab Emirates in respect of the islands of Abu Musa and the two Tunbs and to the west by former Baath regime of Iraq in Shatt al-Arab and Khuzestan have had a major impact on Iran's political life over the past three decades.

In spite of this situation, Iran is one of a handful of the world's major nations that has not systematically studied, catalogued, and analyzed information about its boundaries. This is mainly because Iran's boundaries have not, as yet, been systematically and comprehensively studied by scholars and academics. This shortcoming is particularly noticeable when remembering the fact that although such concepts as *state, territory,* and *boundary* have been formulated in Europe of 19th century, they are rooted in the ancient Persian civilization.

Apart from legendary Arash the Archer, the range of whose arrows determined Iran's frontiers, historical documents confirm that the Achaemenids of 500 BC founded the first empire of global aspiration and fashioned the concepts of "state", "territory" and "frontiers." About a thousand years later the Persian concept of frontier developed into the concept of "boundary" similar to the modern sense of the term *"a line in space that separated"* Iran from her neighbours. 10th century epic *Shahnameh* of Ferdosi reports that the Sassanid Bahram IV (420 – 438 AD) commissioned construction of boundary pillars between Iran and Turan to its east. He decided that River Oxus (Jeyhun) would form a river boundary between the two sides.

This is indeed creation of a boundary line within the modern forms of the concept. This is Ferdosi saying, a thousand years ago, that boundary pillars were erected six hundred years earlier, and people were prohibited from going beyond them unless permitted by the king himself, which must have amounted to the early form of a passport from the Sassanid State.

The territorial inheritance of the nation state of Iran from the Qajar dynasty in 1921 was much reduced from earlier periods and weakly defined in international practice. In this volume, attempts will be made to examine the evolution of the international boundaries of the country in the contemporary epoch during which Iran has been buffeted by an apparently unending series of international and regional crises. It is against this background that Iran today needs to compile and catalogue not only historical data about the evolution of its concept of territoriality and boundary, but also is in need of seriously studying its boundaries with her neighbours in order to reduce the causes of friction with the outside world.

In this volume Iran's boundaries will be studied by the author/editor and a number of other experts in the field. This study will be divided into four sections each including a number of chapters in the following:

A- Iran's Boundaries in the North: the Caucasus, the Caspian, and Central Asia

Two experts from Iranian universities will examine Iran's boundaries in the Caucasus, which began to take shape in the wake of the conclusion of the treaties of Golestan (1813) and Turkmenchai (1828). These boundaries were first defined with Russia largely against Iran's territorial rights and interests. The Khanats and local chiefs played an important role throughout history in shaping the political geography of the border regions between Iran and Russia. The Soviets, especially under Stalin, introduced serious changes to the regional political geography by moving the population around and turning occupied territories into a number of new republics. In some instances, they changed the historical names of geographical localities for questionable reasons.

Improved Soviet-Iranian relations in the 1960s allowed the two sides to consolidate existing boundaries in most cases and began cross-border co-operation in various fields. The fall of the Soviet Union and the emergence of the independent or autonomous republics of Armenia, Karabakh, Nakhjevan, and the Republic of Azerbaijan have brought territorial and boundary sensitivities into the open once again. These territorial and border sensitivities have led to new conflicts, but they could also precipitate cooperation in the region.

A number of Iranian experts will state that, with the disintegration of the Soviet Union and emergence of the US geopolitics of the New World Order, a combination of the Caspian Sea and Central Asia have emerged as one geo-strategic 'region' with enormous geopolitical significance. US oil and gas companies have invaded this region and, with the signing of many oil and gas agreements, the United States has been able to claim substantial 'interest' in this region. The US's strategy of neutralizing Iran's unique position between the Caspian Sea and the Persian Gulf has influenced Iran's relations with many of her neighbours, including Russia, Turkey, and the Republic of Azerbaijan. Diverting oil and gas pipelines of the Caspian Sea from the Iranian routes, on the other hand, has had far reaching consequences for Iran's national interests in the region and has put Iran at a disadvantage in the geo-economic rivalries with her neighbours. Meanwhile, this strategy has substantially increased tension in the Iran-US relationship, with major security implications for the rest of West Asia. Though Iran prefers the Caspian Sea to be declared as a condominium or a sea of common use for the five littoral states, it realizes that, even in the case of full condominium, no country can define its boundaries on the coastline. That is to say that any legal regime division of at least coastal waters among the littoral states is inevitable. Yet, the fact is that bilateral agreements on coastal curve, though legally allowed, cannot replace a comprehensive legal regime decided by the five and satisfactory to the five.

At the end of this section, attention will be paid to a brief study of Iran's north-eastern boundaries that is the boundary line between Iran and Turkmenistan.

B- Iran's Western Boundaries

In this section, Iran's boundaries in the west will be studied by three experts from Iran and the United Kingdom, as well as the editor. They will state that Iran's western boundaries began to emerge in the 17th century, predating the emergence of the European concept of 'boundary'. Some of these borders were settled by war, and others through negotiation, mediation, or arbitration, and even as a result of international decision at the Berlin Congress. Cross-border tribes have influenced the formation of the boundaries between Iran and Turkey, which are amongst Iran's most stable with no major differences between the two countries.

The emergence of Iran's boundaries with Iraq also dates back to the time of the Ottoman Empire. Local tribes have had a significant role in shaping the political geography of western Iranian boundaries. Some of these tribes consider themselves 'Arab', although they are from Mesopotamia, which, for more than two thousand years, had been part of Iranian realm.

Land and river boundaries in Mesopotamia have been the cause of much controversy between Iran and Iraq, with a catalogue of political and military ups and downs; pacts and protocols; and a major war that lasted for eight years. These controversies have expanded over several decades to include almost all aspects of political relations between the two countries. Even the war has not settled these controversies and there are still many instances of territorial and boundary issues that prevent peace and cooperation between the two neighbours. Today's crisis in Iraq is bound to influence Iranian borderlands. Even if the United States employed the utmost care in preserving Iraq's territorial integrity, its war on Iraq is bound to cause the influx of new waves of terrorism. Iran, like any other nation, was and is naturally opposed to any pre-emptive or unilateral military intervention in Iraq or any other country. This is not to overlook the fact that Iraq of Baath Party was indeed a serious threat to the peace and security of West Asia. Iraq has invaded Iran and Kuwait and has used chemical and biological weapons against Iranians and its own citizens in the past.

C- Iran's Eastern Boundaries

Nowhere in Iran has the role of autonomous local Amirs or Khans in shaping territorial and border arrangements been as significant as that played in eastern Iranian borderlands. Though the eastern frontiers of Iran have long been settled, there are still areas of uncertainty that need to be addressed. This is particularly true in the case of boundaries with Afghanistan, where civil wars have negatively influenced Iran's border areas. The influx of about two million Afghan refugees has left its permanent mark on the demography and human geography of Iran's eastern borderlands, while the traffic of illicit drugs has escalated dangerously. The hope in this context is that these developments may attract attention in both capitals to the urgency of a return to normalcy and re-establishment of security of border areas between the two countries.

More urgent, however, are the case of Hirmand River boundary and the issue of water distribution between Afghanistan and Iran. Previous agreements have failed to settle this problem, but they provide the necessary background information and useful bases on which a permanent and equitable solution can be found. Furthermore, the meeting in 2002 of the presidents of the two countries seems to have resulted in new agreements on the water use of Hirmand River. No detailed information has been made available as yet, but the two neighbours seem to have decided to settle boundary issues in a technical manner away from the sentimentalities of the past.

E- Iran's Boundaries in the Persian Gulf

Iran's maritime boundaries in the Persian Gulf have all been settled except in two areas: one is with UAE where territorial claims on islands of Tunbs and Abu Musa by the United Arab Emirates have prevented delimitation of relevant maritime areas. The other area is the north-western end of the Persian Gulf where Iran, Iraq and Kuwait have not been able to define their realms and boundaries. This is mainly because Iraq is unable to define a starting point for maritime division, owing to its continued claims on Iranian and Kuwaiti border areas.

Although some measures have been foreseen in the existing boundary arrangements to prevent horizontal drilling for extraction from cross-border oil fields, no measures exist to regulate the use of energy from the newly discovered cross-border gas fields. Sizeable gas fields, such as south Pars and Arash between Iran on the one hand and Qatar and Kuwait on the other, are the subject of controversies between Iran and these states. However, unlike some areas mentioned previously, cross-border cooperation here can lead to a just and equitable settlement of these controversies.

INTRODUCTION

The Concept of Boundary and Its Origin in the Ancient Persian Tradition
Pirouz Mojtahed-Zadeh

Whither Boundary?

Boundary can be described as a line in space drawn to manifest the ultimate peripheries of the state and/or a line in space to show the ultimate limitations of the territory.

Boundaries can also be described as lines demarcating the outer limits of territory under the Sovereign jurisdiction of a nation-state (Dikshit, 1995: 54).

Whereas man was preoccupied, in the ancient world, with the idea of establishing the "frontiers" of his realm, the modern man's main concern regarding the peripheries of his dominion is to define its "boundaries". Boundary, in the modern sense of the word, did not exist until the nineteenth century. Ancient man considered the end of his conquest as the frontier. Frontier is, therefore, ancient and boundary is new. Endeavouring to distinguish frontiers from boundaries, geographers have used various etymologies. Having quoted Kristof (1959) that the etymology of each term derives their essential difference; that frontier comes from the notion of 'in front' as the "spearhead of the civilisation" and boundary comes from 'bounds' implying territorial limits, Taylor (1989) observes that: *"Frontier is therefore outward-oriented and boundary inward-oriented. Whereas a boundary is a definite line of separation, a frontier is a zone of contact."* (1)

A frontier, therefore, functioned in the more ancient times as a zone of contact between two socially and politically united entities on its two extremes and can safely be described as the embodiment of the outer limits of a state's power and influence, and/or it can be described as the embodiment of the edges of the political push of one power against another. Boundaries in the Persian Gulf, for instance, are, on the whole, the manifestation of political push between the Persian and Ottoman empires in the beginning, and later between British and Iranian powers in the 19th and 20th centuries. Best examples of frontier zones in the ancient world were those between the Persian and Roman empires in the areas now known as Iraq and Syria.

With the emergence of the world-economy in the nineteenth century, which in turn was caused by the development of imperialism of global aspirations of the earlier periods, and with the development of the inherent structural phenomena of the new world economic order, such as trade and communication systems, the need for defining precise points of contacts between states, through their political and economic agents, and establishing customs houses gave birth to the idea of creating border lines or "boundaries". The new border-lines were defined first in North America, Europe, Australia, South Africa and boundaries between Iran and British India – now Pakistan.

The functions or practices of boundaries change overtime. These function can be economic, defensive or military, separating of the sovereign jurisdiction of two countries, interacting of the state system, separating of the societies which have closer ties with each other, control of the emigration, etc. (Glassner, 1993:80-84)

Holdich noted that most of the important wars have arisen over disputed boundaries, therefore authoritative diplomats like Lord Curzon emphasized the military role of the boundaries (Dikshit, 1995:68).

Generally we can categorize the functions of boundaries under:

1- Differentiation between two geographical spaces.
2- Separating line between two sovereign jurisdictions.
3- Integrating the nation.
4- The line of war and peace between two countries.
5- The line of interaction and connection between two nations.
6- The line of control of flows of goods and commodities (Hafeznia, 2000:19)

The most important function of boundary is controling interactions between two or more countries, providing them with security and also protecting their national interests.

Boundary lines influence the behaviour of the people and governments of their environs. Reciprocally, governments and people affect the behaviour and function of boundaries as well as change the function and structure of the boundaries. Similarly, behaviour and relations between two neighboring countries, to some extent, are influenced by the boundaries (Prescott, 1979: 64-80).

Boundary, an Ancient Persian Concept

While the concept of *frontier* as a vast area or a zone of contact (Kristof, 1959: 259-262) between two states is old and was well established before the modern era, many scholars treat the concept of *boundary* as if it were the product of the past few hundred years. Mirroring a tendency found in the political scientists' literature, many political geographers treat the concept of '*state*' – with its 'boundary' component—as a product of the peace treaty of Westphalia in 1648 (Glassner & de Blij, 1989: 46-59). Moreover, it is also widely accepted that the need for a precise territorial definition and segregation of states was an inevitable concomitant of modernity. This new concept is treated as the necessary outcome of imperialism's global aspirations, with its inherent global economic order and trade and communication systems (Taylor, 1989: 144-46).

The concept of 'state' and 'boundary', however, seems to be older than modern era, as 'boundary' exists only in association with a 'state' system—the legitimacy of which being tied to the normative territorial ideas (which are old): *states should be discrete territories and that the pattern of states should reflect the pattern of nations* (Alexander B. Murphy, 2003). There is little doubt that the modern concepts of *state* and *territory* were developed in modern Europe; nevertheless, it is hard to overlook the fact that they are rooted in the periods prior to the emergence of nation-states in Europe. There are indications that ancient civilizations were familiar with the notion of 'state' in connection with territorial and boundary characteristics similar to modern states. The Great Wall of China, the Hadrian Wall of Roman Britain, and Sadd-e Sekandar (Alexander's Wall) in northeast Iran (1) might indeed have been parts of wider peripheral zones of contact in the ancient world (Taylor 1989: 146). Yet, it is inevitable that even in that capacity they represented the notion of a 'line' in space designed to separate the proverbial 'us' from 'them'. In other words, they embodied the basic principle for boundary separation. Indeed, there are references in ancient Persian literature to modern-like states, territories, and boundaries. Similarly, when considering the scale of both belligerent and peaceful contacts between Roma and Iran (Persia) (2), the likelihood exists that these Persian notions could have influenced Roman civilization.

A combination of ancient Greek/Roman and Persian civilizations, however, is said to have been a major source of contribution to what culturally constitutes the "West" in our time. Taking into consideration the extent to which Greek and Roman civilizations interacted with that of ancient Persia, little doubt remains about validity of Jean Gottmann's assertion in his letter to this writer (1987) that:

> *Iran must have belonged to the 'Western' part of mankind, and I suspect that this was what Alexander the Great of Macedonia, a pupil of Aristotle, therefore, in the great Western philosophical tradition, found in Iran and that attracted him so much that he wanted to establish a harmonious, multi-national cooperation between the Iranians and Greeks within the large empire he was building (3).*

Verification of this can be sought in historical events, as when conquering Iran Alexander the Great claimed in Persepolis that he was the 'true successor to the Achaemenid Darius III'. Ferdosi (1020 AD), the famous Persian epic poet says of this in his *Shahnameh* (book of kings) (4) that: having conquered Iran, Alexander wrote to the nobles of the country apologizing for having done away with their king *Dara* (Darius III). Moreover, Alexander reassured them that: "*if Dara is no more, I am here and Iran will remain the same as it has always been since its beginning.*" He adopted the existing (Achaemenid) political organization of space, which was modified later by his successors. Alexander also proclaimed justice to be the goal, attainment of which will be his mission in Iran.

بدانید که امروز دارا منم   گر او شد نهان آشکارا منم
همان است ایران که بود از نخست   بباشید شادان دل و تندرست
جز از نیکنامی و فرهنگ و داد   ز رفتار گیتی مگیرید یاد

Bedanid ke emrooz Dara manam
    Gar'oo shod nahan ashekara manam
Haman ast Iran ke bood az nokhost
    Bebashid shadan del-o tandorost
Joz az niknamiy-o farhang-o dad
    Ze rafter guiti magirid yad

Literally meaning:

  Be informed that today I am Dara
    If he has disappeared, I am to be seen
  Iran is as it has been from the start
    Do remain healthy and happy in heart
  But of good name, culture and justice
    Learn not from the ways of the world

(Ferdosi, 1985: III, 330).

Later in the Sassanid period, the inter-linked notions of state, territory, and boundary developed substantially, coming close to their contemporary forms. However, to arrive at a better analysis of these ancient Persian notions, a brief introduction to the history of ancient Iran's political geography seems to be much consequence.

State, Territory, and Boundary in Ancient Persia

Although the Achaemenids waged wars and captured territories, in their overall political conception of space, they were more culturally oriented than concerned with the rigidity of physical space. Various satrapies were defined along the lines of cultural and ethnic divides. Indeed, eminent scholars like Will Daurant (trans.1988: 412) and Filippani-Ronconi (1978:67) maintain that the concept of 'state' is an original Persian invention, which was later adopted by the West through the Romans. Quoting from T. R. Glover's writings on Persian civilization, Nayer-Nouri, an eminent researcher of ancient Persian civilization, asserts that:

> *The Persians set new ideas before mankind, ideas for the world's good government with utmost of unity and cohesion combined with the largest possible freedom for the development of race and individual within the larger organization* (Nayer Nouri, 1971: 196).

Ancient Greek historians/geographers like Herodotus (484? - 425 BC) and Xenophon (430? - 355? BC) confirm that the Achaemenids (559 - 330 BC) founded a federal kind of state, a vast commonwealth of autonomous nations. Founder of this federation, Cyrus (*Kurosh*) the Great (559 - 529 BC), together with his successors, substantially expanded their new commonwealth and divided it into many satrapies (thirty to forty at times), each governed by a local *Satrap*, a *Khashthrapavan* or a vassal king. This was a commonwealth of global proportions, which included lands of Trans-Oxania, Sind, and Trans-Caucasus as far as what are now Moldavia, Trans-Jordan and Syria, Macedonia and Cyprus, Egypt and Libya. This was a political system of universal aspirations; ruled by a *Shahanshah* (king of kings). Thus, it could also be referred to as the '*Shahanshahi*' system. The king of kings in that system was not a lawgiver but the defender of laws and religions of all in the federation (Templeton, 1979:14). Moreover, in a state described by T. R. Glover (ibid) as *good government* that the Achaemenids created, and according to Cyrus's proclamation in Babylonia (5) that all were *equal in his realm*, ethnic or cultural groups enjoyed large measures of independence in the practice of their language, religion and economies. To uphold cultural and political independence of varying peoples of the federation and to respect their religions, the king of kings did not lay claim to any specific religion. Consequently, the peoples of conquered territories were free to keep their religions, laws and traditions. Having conquered Babylonia for instance, Cyrus the Great found thousands of Jews in captivity there. His response was to free them and send them back to their place of worship. He did not proceed to conquer Jerusalem, but his respect for captive Jews' religious freedom guaranteed their good will towards the Iranians. He became their prophet and they became the voluntary citizens of the Persian federation. Cyrus commissioned the building of their temple and their reaction was to assess his work as fulfillment of the prophecy of Isaiah (*chapter xliv*) where it says:

> *I am the lord...that saith of Cyrus, he is my shepherd, and shall perform my pleasure: even saying to Jerusalem, thou shalt be built: and to the temple, thy foundation shall be laid.* (Lockhart, 1953: 326)

Many have tried hard to determine a 'dark side' to this early example of a 'federative state' and/or 'good government'. The best that some party political considerations of our time could have contemplated - such as the former Baath Party in Iraq - has been to equate Cyrus with a warmongering king who supported the Zionists (the Jews in captivity in Babylonia). They blame Cyrus for waging wars on varying nations, implying that the vast commonwealth of the Achaemenid state has come about by the force of the arm. These criticisms are based on blatant anachronisms. Babylonia was not an Arab state but an Akkadian civilization; the Arabs first appeared in Mesopotamia when the Sassanid state created the vassal kingdom of Hirah according to Arab historian/geographers like Masudi (1977) and Maqdasi (1906) who have also indicated that Arab settlement of southern Mesopotamia increased after the advent of Islam; and finally the captive Jews in Babylonia have nothing to do with Zionism which is a 20th century phenomenon. Moreover, war has always been an inherent part of political behaviour of mankind. Even in the age of modernity when "war" is detested as an act of immorality in the domain of human behaviour, there are the moralists who defend the so-called "Just war". Babylonia was an Akkadian civilization ruled by tyranny according to biblical texts; therefore Cyrus's war against Babylonian tyranny can easily qualify as a 'just war'.

On the other hand, our knowledge of ancient Iran and its role in the ancient world is largely shrouded in obscurity and our information, all too scanty as it is, derived from foreign sources (J. H. Iliff, 1953) that were at war with Iran most of the time. It is in deed a matter of regret that we do not have historical accounts from pre-Islamic Iranians themselves that would deal with details of wars and political conflicts that involved ancient Persia or analyzing social structure and religious and gender status or differences of groups and individuals in ancient Persian societies. All we know is that the decree that Cyrus issued in Babylonia was about freedom and equality for all, including the Babylonians and the captive Jews alike, and it was for this broad-minded policy that he is so praised in the biblical literatures of the West and Islam. And that it was because of this broad-minded policy of the Achaemenid king that won allegiance of many peoples including the Greeks of Ionian cities (Templeton 1979), Cyprus and Jerusalem who joined their federation and that, other than the force of arm there must have been certain attractions in that system of government for them to join it voluntarily.

'Justice' as the Foundation-Stone of the Persian State System

Considering that 'justice' was the corner stone of ancient Iranian Political philosophy, the idea that ancient Iranian spatial arrangement have contributed to the evolution of the concept of democracy in the West cannot be too difficult to contemplate. There are those who claim that when Cyrus the Great founded the federative state of many nations in what was to become the Persian Empire (6), did not invent tolerance, righteousness, and happiness for the people out of genius of his own, but that he was following a deep-rooted age-old tradition of how an ideal king should behave. He had inherited the tradition of *good government* based on *justice*, toleration of others and respects for varying religious beliefs from the Medes whose king; Deicos (Diaxus) had collected all Iranians into one nation (Nayer-Nouri 1971: 188). Nevertheless, the earliest available evidence suggesting that *justice* formed the foundation of the good government in ancient Persian tradition of statehood as the Achaemenid king decreed freedom and equality when conquering Babylonia in 539 BC.

This tradition was observed by all those succeeded Cyrus in Iran throughout its pre-Islamic history. According to the stales left behind at *Naghsh-e Rostam* in western Iran, Darius I (*Dariush*), known as Darius the Great (521- 486 BC), organized thirty satrapies, each under an autonomous king assisted by a Satrap representing central authority of the king of kings. He appointed commanders of army and secretaries of political affairs. He fixed the tributes of each satrapy: appointed tribute-collectors and traveling inspectors called *eyes and ears* of the great king, to watch over the Satraps and army commanders. He introduced currencies of gold *darics* and silver *siglus* facilitating trade exchange in the federation (Nayer-Nouri, 1971, 221): built the 2,700 kilometers long Royal Road from Susa, northwest of Persian Gulf, to Sardis on the Aegean Sea with branches to Persepolis and other political and commercial centres (Mojtahed-Zadeh 1974: pp. 4-5 & 56-9). He ordered for the map of this road and civilized countries alongside it to be engraved on a plate of bronze (7), which was perhaps the first detailed geographic map in history. He established a postal service with relays of men and horses at short intervals, and caused a canal to be dug in Egypt to link Red Sea to the Nile (see Arbery, 1953).

In matters of state politics, while the Athenians were busy with their peculiar version of citizenship-oriented democracy, the Achaemenids, as has been elaborated, were forging a state system based on independence for cultural groups or nationalities; a federative system in which peoples of varying cultural backgrounds were given the right of governing their affairs autonomously with their religion and cultural identity respected. Thus it seems quite plausible that equality and justice were the essence of governing in that ancient tradition of statehood. The administration of *justice* however reached its zenith in the Sassanid period in the person of Anushirvan the Just, and it might be plausible to assume that these early Persian traditions of political philosophy have contributed to the development of modern concepts of democracy in the West. Some suggest (see Tavakoli 1998) that the concept of *empire* is perhaps a Roman adoption of the Persian *Shahanshahi* system. On the same premise it may not be difficult to presume that the Romans evolved their idea of *SENATE* on the basis of ancient Parthian *MEHESTAN*, the House of the Elders, or the *vice versa*.

Evolution of State and Boundary under the Sassanids

The Parthians (247BC to 224 AD) who succeeded the Macedonians in Persia created two kinds of autonomies in the federation: the internal satrapies and the peripheral dependent states-with18 of the latter enjoying greater autonomy (Vadiei, 1974:186). This system was revived by the Safavids in the 16th century Iran in the form of *ialats* and *biglarbeigis*.

Around the dawn of Christian era, the concepts of state and territory assumed greater sophistication with the advent of the notion of frontier or boundary in Iran. This was primarily the result of greater centralization of power vis-à-vis new threats from powerful adversaries such as the Roman Empire to the west and the Turans to the east. The political organization of space in the Sassanid federation (224 -651 AD) was marked by the development of such concepts as internal and external frontier-keeping states, buffer states, boundary pillars etc. There are even hints in the ancient literature of river boundary between Iran and Turan in Central Asia (8).

A look at the works of Persian literature relevant to Iran's ancient political geography such as Ferdosi's *Shahnameh* reveals that the Sassanids successfully developed the concepts of 'territory' within the framework of defined boundaries. They created an elaborated system of territorial organization of state. To begin with, the founder of the dynasty revived the Achaemenid political organization of the state, but divided it into twenty autonomous countries. He initiated a government-style cabinet by assigning ministers of state like *Bozorg-Mehr the philosopher* and then revived the ancient notion of the 'Four Corners' of the world (four quarters of the federation) by creating four separate armies for the realm. He also created an advisory board of the nobles by dividing the political structure in the form of seven classes: the ministers, the priesthood, supreme judges, and four generals commanding the four armies (Masudi, 1977: 464-5). Khosro Anushirvan the Just (531 – 579 AD) whose administration of justice is widely praised by early Islamic historian/geographers (9) lent a more practical meaning to the Achaemenid concept of the 'four corner' of the realm by placing the twenty countries of the Iranian federation in four major *Kusts* or *Pazgous*. Each of these divisions was ruled by a viceroy or regent called *Pazgousban* or *Padusban*, and an *espahbad* or general commanded the army of each Pazgous. In his epic *Shahnameh*, Ferdosi describes these *kusts* or *Pazgous* in the following fashion: 1- *Khorasan*, including *Qom* and *Isfahan*: 2- *Azarabadegan* or Azerbaijan, including *Armanestan* (Armenia) and *Ardebil*: 3- *Pars* (Persia = southern Iran) and *Ahvaz* as well as territories of *Khazar* (most likely Khuzestan): 4- *Iraq* and Roman territories (Syria and Anatolia) (Ferdosi, 1985: IV, 415).

The development of the concept of territory in the Sassanid era went hand in hand with the evolution of the concept of boundary. It is of consequence to note that the term 'boundary' existed in middle Persian. The Persian equivalents for territory and boundary, attributed to the Sassanid period by Ferdosi, appear synonymously in the form of *Marz-o Boum*, literally meaning boundary and territory. But in Ferdosi's idiosyncratic manner of using these two terms, together they assume the meaning of 'political territory' or 'country' (homeland). *Marz*, meaning boundary, however existed on its own at the time, whereas another middle Persian term for boundary was also in use in the form of *saman*—mostly in reference to a line separating houses from one another in modern Persian. Both concepts of boundary and frontier were in practical use in the Sassanid era. While appointing governors or *Padusbans* for the vassal states, they appointed mayors or *shahrigs* for the cities. They created frontier zones in the west of their federation and boundary lines to its east.

In the west of their federation, the Sassanids appear to have developed two kinds of frontier-keeping states: the internal frontier states within their four *Kusts*: and the external frontier-keeping states, the most famous of which was the state of *Hirah* or *Manazerah* in Mesopotamia (Masudi, ibid).

On the northwestern corner of the Persian Gulf, where Iranian and Roman empires' frontiers met, the vassal kingdom of *Hirah* was created in 5th century by the Sassanids on the river Tigris, not far from their Capital Ctesiphon. This frontier-keeping state, which was funded and protected by the Iranians, effectively formed a buffer state for Iran, thereby defusing pressures emanating from the Romans (Masudi, 1977:240). In a similar move, the Romans created the vassal kingdom of *Ghassan* in the region now known as Syria, (Masudi, 1977: 467). Moreover, it is notable that by virtue of its struggle against Arab rule, Iran played the role of a cultural barrier throughout the Islamic era, which guaranteed its cultural survival in the subsequent periods. The precise location of the line of this cultural barrier can be defined somewhere around western peripheries of Iranian Plateau, in Mesopotamia, which played the same role in pre-Islamic era between the Persian and Roman empires. Here David Mitrani's theory of 'Middle Zone'– defined somewhere in Central Europe, around the river Danube (Mitrani, 1950) – can be applied to the status and implications of the geographical position of Iran in that region. This geography prevented total prevalence of other cultures over the Iranian Plateau throughout the history.

To their eastern flanks the Sassanids faced the Turans. Like the Romans, the Turans also engaged in numerous wars with the Iranians. But unlike their buffer zone arrangements with the Romans in the west, at least in one instance the Iranians created precise boundaries with the Turans in the east. This must have resulted from the degree in which rivalling powers to their east and west exerted pressure on their federation. While rivalries with the Romans in the West were of geopolitical nature which evolved in a situation similar to Anglo-Russian Great Game of 19th century in Central Asia, rivalries with the Turans to the east were of intense strategic nature culminating in many wars, which in turn necessitated demarcation of boundary lines that separated the two.

It is of consequence to note that not only did the Sassanids revive the Achaemenid organisation of the state and territory, but also fashioned the term *Iranshahr* (the country of Iran), which must have arguably been for the first time that a state or a nation had assumed an identity and/or a name independent of that of its ruling dynasties (Mojtahed-Zadeh, 1999 *Iran va...*147-8). Having stated details of Bahram Gour's debate with the Roman emissary on the subject of varying Roman and Persian style of diplomacy and statesmanship, Ferdosi asserts that victorious in his campaign against eastern Turks, Bahram IV (*Gour*) (420 – 438AD) commissioned construction of boundary pillars between Iran and its Turkish adversaries. He decided that river Oxus (*Jeyhun*) would form river boundary between the two sides. In his account of this development, Ferdosi says:

بر آورد میلی ز سنگ و ز گچ   که کس را ز ایران و ترک و خلج
نبودی گذر جز به فرمان شاه   همو کرد جیحون میانجی به راه

Bar avard mili ze sang-o ze gach
                ke kass ra ze Iran-o Turk-o Khalaj
Nabudi gozar joz be farman-e Shah
                Hamoo kard Jeihun mianji be rah

Literally meaning:

(He) constructed pillars of stone and chalk (plaster); thereby ensuring that no one from Iran or Turk or other nationals would pass beyond unless permitted by the Shah who has also made Jeyhun *(river Oxus) a median in the way* (Ferdosi, 1985: III, 394).

Thus, it is Ferdosi who asserted a thousand years ago that boundary pillars were erected six hundred years earlier, and that Iranians, Eastern Turks, and third party nationals were prohibited from going beyond them unless permitted by the king himself. The king had also defined River Oxus as part of the boundary (river boundary) between the two political entities. This may be seen as a clear example of the creation of a boundary line in ancient Iran corresponding to the modern understanding of the concept. Similarly, the permission from the king for passing beyond the boundary might be considered as an early form of a passport in today's term.

In the south, the Achaemenid federation included two satrapies: Aaval, the countries now known as Bahrain, Qatar and the Hasa & Qatif provinces of Saudi Arabia, and the state (later became known as Masun) that included areas that in our time belong to Oman and the United

Arab Emirates. The *qanat* underground irrigation system – invented in Achaemenid era – was introduced to the southern coasts of the Persian Gulf at the time of Darius I (Wilkinson, 1975: 98). There are indications that the Parthians (250 BC – 224 AD) made substantial progress in seafaring, but no evidence exists suggesting how the Achaemenids and/or the Parthians treated the issue of territoriality and boundary in those areas. The Sassanids by contrast, organised territories of southern Persian Gulf into two states or satrapies. In the western section, they created the kingdom of Hagar, embracing ancient *Aaval*, whereas in the eastern half they created the vassal kingdom of *Masun* or *Mazun* to embrace modern countries of Oman and United Arab Emirates (Hawley, 1970: 38). The indigenous population of all these areas was Iranian (Dravidians, Elamites etc.) before there were any Arabs living in the coastal south. Arab immigration to these areas began in the 2nd century AD. When the *Kawadh* (*Qobads*) ruled Masun in 6th century BC, immigrant Arabs succeeded in forming a large union. Faced with this massive tribal union of migrant Arabs the Persian rulers treated the newcomers as *Shahrvandan* in Persian or *Ahlalbilad* in Arabic, literally meaning *citizens*, and accorded them a degree of autonomy under their own tribal leadership (Wilkinson, ibid.). Here the Iranian federative system is applicable even in the internal context of a vassal kingdom (see Mojtahed-Zadeh, 1999).

Conclusion

There is no doubt that the Athenians initially developed the concept of 'democracy'. However, their practice of democracy was limited to no more than the limits of the varying social strata of a city. A nationwide application of democracy had to wait until Alexander the Great of Macedonia conquered Iran and adopted the Persian way of organizing the political space – i.e. as a quasi-federal 'state' divided into discrete territories. The Achaemenids no doubt developed the original concept of state, but the idea of a vertically organized state with distinct and clearly demarcated boundaries matured under the Sassanids and began to influence Western civilizations.

When assessing the influence of Iran on the concepts of "state" and "boundary" in medieval Europe one might point to the biblical references to the Persian statehood and its tradition of respect for the rights of varying peoples (Isaiah - chapter xliv, Esther i, I, Ezra i, I etc.). According to these testimonies, despite spearheading military campaigns against the Greek cities and the Turans, the state organization created by the Achaemenid kings was essentially culturally-based and not grounded on rigid territorial conquest. This was particularly manifested in the Achaemenids' universal aspirations of statehood and good government. By developing their own version of a 'federative state' based on the notion of justice for all, the Iranians created a commonwealth of semi-independent nations or a federation of autonomous states, and arguably laid the foundation for the idea of '*state democracy*' or '*democratic state*'. This political structure of statehood was taking shape in Iran simultaneously with the advent of the Greek version of citizenship-centered democracy. In this regard it is important to note that Cyrus issued a charter in Babylonia (the text of which is now kept in British Museum) declaring *equality* and *justice* for individuals as well as freedom for religious-cultural entities in the realm. These notions formed the political fabric of the Persian State as Darius the Great also frequently refers to *justice* in the stales he bequeathed to posterity. This is to suggest that while the Athenians were concerned about the 'rights' of the individuals in society, the Persians were anxious to promote the rights of communities within their state system.

There are few other sources explaining the extent to which these ancient Persian traditions influenced the evolution of the Western concepts of "state", "boundary" and 'democracy', save for the works of scholars like Will Durant (Pers. trans., 1988). Even a philosopher as widely misrepresented as Friedrich Nietzche whose writings many philosophers found difficult to take seriously, seems to have formed his view of the civilized Western man under the influence of ancient Persian philosophy of life (Thus Spoke Zarathustra, 1892). R. Ghirshman (Iran, 1962), for instance states that:

> *Under Alexander, 'monarchy by divine right' of the Iranians became an institution of Hellenism and later was taken up by Many European states* (Nayer Nouri, 1971: 152).

R. Levy, on the other hand, identifies Arab Caliphate as an intermediate culture through which the Persian tradition of statehood influenced modern world. Quoting early Arab and Islamic records he argues that:

> *The Fakhri, an early – fourteenth century manual of politics and history, relates how the caliph, Umar, when at his wits end to know how to distribute the spoils of war which were pouring in, sought the advice of a Persian (Iranian) who had once been employed in a government office (of the Sassanid time). His suggestion was that a divan, a register or bureau, should be instituted for controlling income and this became the germ out of which grew the government machine that served the caliphate some hundreds of years.* (Levy, 1953: 61).

Of the influence of the Iranian legacy of "state" and statesmanship on the Arab Caliphate, an early Islamic historical account quotes Caliph Umar as saying: "Verily have I learnt justice from Kesra (Khosro Anushirvan the Just)" (Maqdasi, 1906: 18).

In his writings on the tradition of sacred kingship in Iran, Filippani-Ronconi, based on reliable Roman sources, states that:

> *If we want to look into the successful diffusion in the Western world of certain institutions connected with kingship, in either the religious or the lay domain, we must go back to the Roman Empire, which was the first Western state to absorb a great deal of such outside influence, especially in its political and administrative institutions regarding the status of the Emperor.*

He then proceeds to cite examples of the influence of the Iranian tradition of statehood on the Western civilization by asserting:

> *The heritage handed down by Iran to the West and still living in its ideological conceptions and cultural institutions is manifold. If its patterns are sometimes difficult to recognize and trace back to their origin, that is due to the fact that this legacy has been received through intermediate cultures and westernized models... The leading elements of what we could call the vertical organization' of the state are part of this age-old heritage. They were handed over to the modern world through the late Roman imperial structure and its medieval renaissance: through the institutions of chivalry and knighthood that, obscurely*

transmitted to European society in a Celtic-Germanic garb, were later Christianized ... (Filippani-Ronconi, 1978:67).

But just what happened to these concepts in the post-Islamic Iran might be of some interest to the scholars. The Arab Caliphate of Baghdad (Abbasid Caliphate 750 to 1258 AD) mimicked the Sassanid organization of territories almost in its entirety (Pourkamal, 1977: 7). They too created frontier-keeping states, one of which was *Khozeimeh Amirdom* of Qaenat that lasted until 1930s (see Mojtahed-Zadeh, 2004). But the prevailing notion of 'universality' in Islam would have left no scope for the evolution of the ancient idea of boundary formation in post-Islamic Iran. Consequently Iran's embrace of Shiite Islam in this period was essentially a desire to revive the country's cultural and national identity. The ancient Persian concept of *'justice'* gained new currency by transmuting into one of the five basic principles of Shi'ite Islam. More importantly the expanding anti-Caliphate protestant Shi'ism in Iran merged with other local notions of identity, thus paving the way for the revival of the concepts of territoriality and statehood.

What the Safavids revived in terms of territorial organization of space was in reality a vague adaptation of Abbasid Caliphate's interpretation of the Sassanid system and not the original version. This vagueness of the new state structure suggests that Iran had departed from its own ancient traditions of state and boundary. This was no doubt a powerful handicap that manifested itself later, especially in the face of the conceptual and physical onslaught of modern European versions of nationality and statehood.

Notes

1- This wall was built at the time of the Parthian civilization in Iran (247 BC to 224 AD) to separate that civilization from the Turans of the East.
2- The term "Iran" has constituted as the official name of the country or state known by that name in the Middle East, at least since the emergence of the Achaemenid federative state in 6th century BC. The West came to know this country as "Persia" through the Greeks of the city-states which in the 6th century BC, was not as yet familiar with the concept of state–cum–country. They named Iran as "Persia" in accordance with the on-going tradition of naming places after the name of the dynasties or ethnic groups ruling them. Hence, they named Iran as "Persia" in reference to the province of Persia in southern Iran where the Achaemenid dynasty had emerged from in mid-6th century BC. This was in accordance with the Greek tradition of political geography of the time, whereas the Iranians of the Achaemenid era were familiar with the concept of state–cum–country and the need to name countries by a term that would not exclusively refer to a particular group or ethnicity among many, but a term common to all in a federative system. It is noteworthy that the term "Iran" means the land of the Aryans and it is a name in reference to all peoples of Iranic ethnic background; peoples like the Persians, the Kurds, the Baluchis, the Guilaks, the Mazandaranis, the Khuzistanis, the Khorasanis, and the Azeris etc.
3- Professor Jean Gottmann, whose student this author was at Oxford University in late 1970s, authorized this quotation from his said letter, in a separate note dated 19th May 1992.
4- *Shahnameh* (book of kings) of Abul-Qassem Ferdosi (d. 1020 AD) is widely praised as the only reliable source in Persian literatures that studies pre-Islamic history of Iran and its association with other political entities of the antiquity, but hitherto little attention has been paid to the way it describes political relations in association with political organization of the space in the ancient world. Popularly known as an epic account of ancient Persian history, especially of the Sassanid period (224 – 651 AD), the *Shahnameh* provides a remarkable description of the development of the concept of state in ancient Iran. It carefully describes how the idea of a vertically organized state evolved in ancient Iran with clearly demarcated boundaries, which influenced such Western political conceptions as 'state', 'territory', 'boundary', and 'democracy'. Ferdosi's description of political geography of ancient world bears remarkable resemblance to the modern concepts of political geography that evolved in post-Westphalia Europe. But is it possible that he, who lived a thousand years ago, well before Westphalia treaty of 1648, had learnt these ideas from modern Europe or the fact is that what Ferdosi had described in terms of evolution of political thoughts and political geography in ancient Persia had influenced medieval Europe. This is certainly a fascinating question deserving further exploration with the help of reliable analysis of the socio-political developments of the ancient world.
5- The text of this proclamation is in cuneiform Acadian (Akkadian), inscribed on a clay cylinder now in British Museum's Persian section.
6- Some suggest that the concept of *empire* is perhaps a Roman adoption of the Persian *Shahanshahi* system (Tavakoli, 1993:828-830). However, the difference between the two is that while various nations and ethnic groups lived autonomously in the *Shahanshahi* system of Iran, peoples of different national and ethnic backgrounds enjoyed no autonomy or self-rule in the *imperial* system that the Romans developed.

7- A plate of bronze or other metals is called *jam* in Persian. Similarly a goblet of metal or crystal is jam. On the other hand, Shahnameh of Ferdosi speaks of legendary Jamshid Shah, founder of Iran, who had a *jam* showing the world. From this concept comes the mystical *crystal ball* in almost all cultures. Yet, this author is of opinion that Jamshid Shah was none other than Darius the Great who had the bronze disc '*jam*' showing the map of the civilized world. There are other reasons supporting this theory the discussion on which goes beyond the scope of this article.

8- Turan is a term used by Ferdosi (d. AD 1020) in his *Shahnameh*, the greatest work of epic literature in Persian language, in reference to peoples of Turkic origin in the eastern fringes of Iran. What constitutes 'Central Asia' now was 'Greater Khorasan' in most parts of the post-Islamic Iranian geography and its eastern most formed parts of "Turan" before that.

9- On Anushirvan's administration of justice see many early Arab and Islamic works of history and geography including:

A- Tabari, Mohammad Bin Jarir, *Tarikh-e Tabari*, Persian translation, 11 volumes, published by Bongah-e Tarjomeh va Nashr-e Ketab, Tehran 1974.

B- Maqdasi, al-Beshari, *Ahsan at-Taqasim fi Marefat al-Aqalim*, Liden 1906.

C- Biruni, Abu-Reihan, *Qanoun-e Masudi*, Published in Dakan 1955.

D- Ibn al-Faqih, Abu-Bakr Mohammad, *Moktasar-e al-Boldan*, 279 AH, Liden 1885.

E- Ibn Huqal, Mohammad, *Surat al-Ardh*, London 1938.

F- Estakhri, Ebrahim, *Al-Masalek val-Mamalek*, Liden 1889.

G- Hamavi, Abdullah Yaqut, *Mo'jam al-Boldan*, Cairo 1906.

H- Masudi, Abul-Hassan Ali Ibn Hussein, *Moravvege az-Zahab*, Pers. Trans., Bongah-e Tarjomeh va Nashr-e Ketab, Tehran 1977.

References

Arbery, A. J, 1953: *The Legacy of Persia*, Oxford Clarendon Press.

Durant, Will, *Tarikh-e Tamaddon* (History of Civilization), translated into Persian and published by *Enqelab-e Eslami* Publication 1988, Tehran.

Ferdosi, Hakim Abul-Qassem, *Shahnameh*, Original text, Javidan publication 1364 (1985), 4th print, Vol. III, Tehran.

Filippani-Ronconi, Pio, 1978: *The Tradition of Sacred Kingship in Iran,* in George Lenczowski ed., *Iran Under the Pahlavis,* Hoover Institution Press, Stanford University, USA.

Ghirshman, R., 1962: *Iran, Parthes et Sassanides*, Gallimard, Paris.

Glassner, M. I. & de Blij, H. J., 1989: *Systematic Political Geography*, John Willy and Sons, New York.

Hafeznia, M. R., 1997: *Power and Cultural Expansion in the Subcontinent*, in Daneshvar ed., (17), 17-25, Tehran.

Hawley, Donald, 1970: *The Trucial States*, George Allen & Unwin, London.

Iliff, J. H., 1953: *Persia and the Ancient World*, in A. J. Arbery ed. "*The Legacy of Persian*", Oxford Clarendon.

Kristof, L .D., *The Nature of frontiers and boundaries,* in Annals Association of American Geographers, No. 49, 1959.

Levy, R., 1953: *Persia and the Arabs*, in A. J. Arbery ed., *The Legacy of Persia*, Oxford Clarendon Press.

Lockhart, L., 1953: *Persia as seen in the West*, in A. J. Arbery ed., *The Legacy of Persia*, Oxford Clarendon Press.

Maqdasi al-Maruf be-al-Beshari, *Ahsan at-Taqasim fi Marefat al-Aqalim* (written in 375 AH), second ed. Liden 1906.

Masudi, Abul-Hassan Ali Ibn Hussein (Arab geographer/historian of 4th century AH, *Moravvege az-Zahab* (Propagator of the Way), Persian translation 1977 by Abul-Qassem Payandeh, Bongah-e Tarjomeh va Nashr-e Ketab, Tehran.

Mitrani, David, 1950: *Evolution of the Middle Zone*, Annals of American Political and Social Science, September.

Mojtahed-Zadeh, Pirouz, 1974: *New Studies on the Royal Road*, translation from Victor W. Von Hagen's article in The Geographical Magazine of June 1974, as appeared in monthly Daneshmand (Scientist) of Tehran, Vol. 11, No. 11 (Series No. 131), September.

Mojtahed-Zadeh*,* Pirouz, 1999: *Iran va Irani boudan* (Iran and to be Iranian), Ettelaat Syasi – Eqtesadi (Political – Economic Ettelaat) quarterly of Tehran, Vol. XIV, Nos. 3&4 (147-148) and 5&6 (149-150), Tehran Azar & Day and Bahman & Esfand 1378 (winter of 1999).

Mojtahed-Zadeh, Pirouz, 1999: *Security and Territoriality in the Persian Gulf*, Curzon Press, London, c.3.

Mojtahed-Zadeh, Pirouz, 2004: *Small Players of the Great Game,* Routledge/Curzon, London and New York, c. II & III.

Murphy, Alexander B., 2003: *Dominant Territorial Ideologies in the Modern State System: Implications for Unity Within and Beyond the Islamic World,* Paper presented to the 2nd International Congress of the Geographers of the Islamic World, Tehran, 16 & 17 September.

Nayer Nouri, A. H., 1971: *Iran's Contribution to the World Civilization*, Vol. II., Tehran.

Nietzsche, Friedrich (1883-85), *Thus Spoke Zarathustra*, Formally published in 1892.
Pourkamal, M., *Administration Divisions of Iran*, Tehran: Plan and Budget Organization 1977.
Tavakoli, Ahmad, 1372 (1993): *Empratouri, Shahanshah* (Empire, Shahanshahi), Ayandeh monthly, Vol. IXX, No. 7-9, Tehran.
Taylor, Peter J., 1989: *Political Geography,* 2nd edition, Longman Scientific & Technical, London.
Templeton, Peter Louis, 1979: *The Persian Prince*, Persian Prince Publication, London.
Vadiei, K. 1974: *Moghadamehi bar Joghrafiay-e Ensaniy-e Iran* (An Introduction to the Human Geography of Iran), Tehran University Press.
Wilkinson, John 1975: *The Julanda of Oman*, in the Journal of Oman, Vol. I, London.

CHAPTER I

Traditional Regions and National Frontiers of Iran: A General Overview
Keith S. McLachlan

Figure 1

Iran and neighboring states

Introduction

Iran has functioned for at least 5,000 years as a state and the centre of an empire. During this considerable period its boundaries with its neighbours have been relatively fluid (1). Nonetheless, despite the powerful influences working against the need for hard and fast borders, of which Islam is perhaps the principle one, contemporary Iran under both the Pahlavi regime and the Islamic republic has adopted very clear policies towards defining and/or protecting state territory.

The administration of Iran has historically been plagued with difficulties of exerting authority outside the main areas of population and, therefore, in fixing its national frontiers. Iran is a vast and diverse country of 1,648,000 km2, only a tenth of which is under settled forms of economic use. The rest is desert, steppe and high-mountain. In many ways Iran was until the early 20th century a set of diverse ethnic and linguistic groups unified under a single government and sharing a common literature, social ethos and culture. The largest single provincial region by population size was Azerbaijan, where there was a concentration of Azhari speakers of the Perso-Turkic group of languages. Other coherent areas with a regional consciousness could be defined, including Kurdistan in the west, the Arab zone of the Khuzistan lowlands in the southwest, the Turkmen steppe of the north and Baluch area of the southeast.

The Territorial Consolidation under Reza Shah

Reza Khan's and Sayyid Zai al-Din Tabatabai's *coup d'etat* against the Qajars in February 1921 gave Iran a short breathing space of strong central control during which the idea of a modern nation-state was imposed on the country and the national borders made generally secure. This experience was important for Iran because it enabled the government to tie its many varied provinces firmly to the centre. Beginning in 1921, Reza Khan put down regional revolts by the tribes of the Khamseh and others before beginning the process of reducing rebellion elsewhere in the west (2). Reza Khan took advantage of the Russian withdrawal from Iranian soil in September 1921 to put down the revolt of Kuchik Khan in the northern province of Gilan, marking the clear beginning of the centralization process. In the following year Reza Khan attacked rebel forces in Azerbaijan and Kurdistan and settled the northeast province of Khorasan. The process continued in 1923 in the south where the main tribes, the Bakhtiari and Qashqai, were put down and Shaikh Khazal, the regional ruler of Khuzistan, removed to Tehran.

The military consolidation of the power of the centre was developed in parallel with Reza Khan's seizure and legitimization of his own position. In 1925 Reza Shah began the political process of sealing the unity of the nation (3) by deposing the last of the Qajar dynasty, Ahmad Shah, and setting in its place the House of Pahlavi.

Reza Shah's carefully constructed state and its national frontiers were, however, far from strong. The illusion of dominance from the centre worked only in relation to the internal provinces of the country. Iran's abilities to confront the outside world were very limited despite the building of the Iranian army. The Iranian authorities also successfully engaged in legal battles with the British in the form of the Anglo-Iranian Oil Company in the south and made some gains in the 1933 oil agreement (4).

In 1941, what appeared to be a pro-German revolt by Rashid Ali in Iraq brought the Middle East region directly into the lines of conflict of the Second World War. Iran was declared neutral in this war but the Rashid Ali affair in Iraq and growing British suspicions concerning the activities of German agents in Iran put Iran's neutrality in jeopardy. The invasion of the USSR by German forces in June 1941 added to Iran's difficulties, since the Anglo-Soviet alliance exposed the country to simultaneous pressures from the north and the south. Iran increasingly became perceived by the allies as a strategic supply corridor for transferring war material to aid Russian defence (5). Iran's oil was seen as a key commodity for the use of the allies, also to be denied the axis powers (6). Iran was occupied by the British and Russians on 25 August 1941.

The Challenge of the Autonomous Republics in the 1940s

The overthrow of Reza Shah put the country's international borders into question. In the north of Iran the occupation by the Soviet Union was accompanied by the pursuit of specific territorial objectives, which could be achieved only by the seizure of parts of north Iran (7). After the end of hostilities Iran faced its first major challenge to its territorial integrity. In December 1946 an autonomous republic of Azerbaijan was declared in Tabriz under Ja'far Pishevari. The *coup* against the government in Tehran was underpinned by the presence of the armed forces of the USSR and was, it was feared in Tehran, to foreshadow the total loss of Azerbaijan to the USSR. Similar conclusions applied to the Kurdish People's Republic set up in Mahabad in west Iran in the same period. To many Western observers the establishment of the two autonomous republics was designed to move the Soviet frontier southwards in accordance with the objectives of the USSR as laid out in the Four Power Secret Pact of November 1940 between the USSR, Germany, Japan and Italy (8).

The survival of Iran's 1941 frontier in the northwest was due to a combination of Iranian political adroitness and Western pressure on the USSR (9). In January 1946 the government of the USSR refused to withdraw its armed forces from Iran, stating that its troops would remain in place until the originally agreed deadline of 2 March 1946. The Iranian government protested to the United Nations Security Council against Soviet prevarications. Help from that quarter was feeble and slow in forthcoming. It was left to the prime minister, Qavan as-Saltaneh, to fight the battle alone. He offered the USSR an oil agreement for the exploration in the five Northern provinces - Asterabad, Azerbaijan, Gilan, Khorasan and Mazandaran - occupied in 1946 by Soviet troops, providing that their forces were withdrawn and subject to ratification of the concession by the Majlis (parliament) when it was reconvened. The matter was complemented by a British military landing near Basra and the start of a major tribal rebellion in the south of Iran supported by the British (10).

In December 1946 the United States gave belated support to Qavam against the Soviet Union's attempt to rig the elections in Azerbaijan, which in effect ensured that Iranian government troops were enabled to enter Azerbaijan to supervise the elections for the Majlis on 7 December. The albeit late Soviet withdrawal and the collapse of the Pishevari republic re-established Iranian sovereignty in the northwest and permitted a return to the pre-existing international boundaries in that region.

The Revolution and the Restatement of Territorial Integrity

It is important to note that none of the peripheral regions broke away from the Iranian state during the period of unrest in 1979-80 or during the Iraqi invasions of 1980-1. This was in part a function of the internal cultural cohesion of the country and in part a result of prompt action by the central government to put down secessionist movements at their birth. At the same time, the development of Iran as a modern nation-state with a comparatively sophisticated economy in the period 1946-78 had brought about considerable rural-urban migration and trans-province movements to new work places. Together with a growth in national consciousness, these changes eroded traditional tribal and ethnic boundaries. For example, as many Azhari-origin people live outside northwest Iran as within it and the neat nature of the provinces as separate components of the state is increasingly misleading.

The only real danger for Iran from the remaining concentration of ethnic and linguistic minorities in its extreme borderlands is in Kurdistan, where an internationally sponsored Kurdish state in Iraq would be very disruptive to the present balance where the majority Iranian Kurds see themselves ethnically as Kurds but also as citizens of Iran as a distinct civilization. At present, the Iranian, Turkish and Syrian governments recently and jointly have pledged themselves to maintain the territorial integrity of Iraq. The United States, France and the United Kingdom have also reassured the United Nations Security Council that Kurdistan will not be hived off as a separate state. The prospects for an autonomous Kurdish nation seem therefore to be very small on current evidence (11).

Upheaval and Recovery, since 1979

The revolution of 1979 gave the opportunity for the ethnic groups to break away from the centre and to seek regional autonomy. In some regions there was unrest among the minorities during 1979 persisting throughout 1980. Marginal areas of the country were at times difficult of access by the government, which was unable to send its representatives, gather taxes or guarantee the security of the individual in parts of Azerbaijan, Kurdistan, Luristan, Fars, Khuzistan and the districts of the Persian Gulf. The most damaging insurrection occurred in Kurdistan, in so far as unrest was prolonged and widespread. The Kurdish rebellion persisted with isolated armed clashes between the Iranian security forces and Kurdish dissidents.

Some small-scale opposition, such as that by the Turkoman, was crushed early during 1979, though this was more a political movement of the left-wing fedayin-e khalq than an ethnic uprising. Arab separatist organizations in the oilfield province of Khuzistan were largely set up by and supported with arms supplies from Iraq. In Khuzistan, the linkage between the ethnic revolt and the problems of the oil industry was observed by one oil specialist: *"the Arab population of Khuzistan...has been active in blowing up pipelines and in sabotage at refineries"* (12). Under conditions of uncertainty in provincial areas, the British Foreign Office's off-the-record view was that *"The question of territorial fission within Iran merits serious consideration"* (13). Such judgments were not uncommon in the early 1980s in Western Europe, Japan and North America and emphasize the insecurity, even as to the territorial unity of the country, during the period from February 1979 to September 1980.

The position after the revolution was, of coarse, exceptional and would not be expected to be repeated often. Under conditions of normality, Iran's border regions and ethnic minorities do not pose problems to internal security. Indeed, the revolutionary authorities were quick to suppress lawlessness in the border regions once the initial impact of the Iraqi invasions of Iranian soil had been turned. With exception of persistent though isolated unrest in Kurdistan, the country was returned to control by the central government in 1981.

Boundary Affairs after 1988

The only shadow to arise in subsequent years was in late 1992 when proposals emanating from Baku for a united and independent Azerbaijan were published (14). Claims for a united Azerbaijan raised memories in Tehran of the attempt in 1918 to establish an Azerbaijani National Council including within it Iranian Azerbaijan, which seemed at the time to be no more than a Turkish devised-means of separating it from Iran (15). Official Iranian reactions in 1992 were also negative, as might have been expected. The notion of an integrated Azerbaijan was the first serious move from the areas of Trans-Caucasia and central Asia that suggested taking Iranian territories occupied by an ethnic or linguistic minority out of Iran. Throughout the early years of independence for the Trans-Caucasian and central Asian republics no other cross-border territorial claims were made on Iran. But the prospect for other regional movements following the course taken by the Azerbaijan Republic gave an added dimension of insecurity to the northern border, quite at odds with the conventional wisdom of the day, which presupposed that Iran sought influence and territorial gain within the new republics at the expense of others (16).

Iran as late as 1993 saw its northern neighbours as Islamic co-religionists, as cultural allies and as trading partners. There was never any expression of territorial expansionism proclaimed by the Cabinet or the Ministry of Foreign Affairs, despite the occasional private speculation in the Iranian academic community that Iran had historic claims to lands taken from it by imperial Russia in the 19th century. Iranian policies towards the Central Asia and Caucasian republics were articulated through a series of cultural and commercial linkages, both bilateral and via the Economic Co-operation Organization (ECO) (17) or Caspian group (18).

Iran's eastern borderlands gave rise to protracted negotiations between Iranian, Afghan and British interests during the 19th century (19). In the recent period the only persistent problems in this area derived from the division of waters in the Sistan Basin, although maintaining the security of the Afghan frontier has been a constant difficulty in the face of smuggling and human migration, the latter at its peak during the Afghan-Soviet war in 1979-88 (20). It has been observed that boundary problems in Sistan arise generally in years of drought such as 1946 and 1971 (21). It should be added that years of heavy rainfall had the same effect through causing rivers on the line of the international boundary to change course, as for example in 1896 and the year 1902/3 (22). By 1992 the Iran/Afghan frontier was one of great activity as Iran sought the repatriation of some 2.7 million Afghan refugees (23). Simultaneously the Iranian government also tried to end the smuggling of narcotics and other commodities into Iran and to reduce the permeability of the border region to Afghans seeking work in Iran.

Iran's western borders, inherited from the unsettled broad frontier zone of Persian-Ottoman imperial strife (24), suffered varying fortunes in the modern period. The 1932 Agreement and the 1937 Convention, which fixed the alignment of the border between Iran and Turkey, caused continuing difficulties (25). The years following the 1991 defeat of Iraq in Kuwait witnessed the Kurdish areas of Iraq falling under the protection of the United Nations and the emergence of a quasi-autonomous region governed by Kurdish people, signaled inter alia by the holding of elections in 1992.

The Iranian frontier with Turkey became subject to tensions in the modern period. The Iranian authorities were dismayed by infringements of Iranian territory by Turkish troops and aircraft in hot pursuit of Kurdish insurgents of the Kurdish Workers' Party (KKP). The Turkish government for its part appeared to believe that the KKP was using military bases in Iran as safe havens from which to launch guerrilla attacks on Turkish villages and border posts (26). The matter was resolved in November 1992 at a trilateral meeting in Ankara where Iranian, Turkish and Syrian foreign ministers agreed that the territorial integrity of Iraq would not be undermined by any of the three neighbours. Separate bilateral arrangements were also made for improved security and a cessation of Kurdish border crossings between Iran, Turkey and northern Iraq.

Iran's border with Iraq remained profoundly unstable in the modern period (27). Three great areas of dispute have been at the heart of the problem: first, the Shatt al-Arab boundary; secondly, the land frontier around Penjwin and border post 101; and, thirdly, the offshore zone at the head of the Persian Gulf. Naturally, the Shatt al-Arab international boundary dispute attracted most attention (28) since it had been both a *casus belli* and a battlefront within recent years (29). The apparent renunciation of the 1975 Accord on the Shatt al-Arab by Iraq in October 1979 indicated the fragility of the frontier zone. Grounds for continuing tensions in this area can be discerned in the failure of mediations of the United Nations Organization to get Iraq to ratify the provisions of UN Resolution 598, on which the Iran-Iraq ceasefire of 1988 was agreed. In the immediate aftermath of the war it appeared that Iraq would use its strong bargaining position visa-a-vis a military and economically weakened Iran to press for the international boundary along the Shatt al Arab to revert to that provided for under the 1937 Agreement, fixing the line on the low - water mark on the Iranian side of the river (30). Iran naturally resisted Iraqi overtures to this end and demanded that the frontier return to the *status quo ante* September 1980, which was the Iranian interpretation of the wording of UN Resolution 598.

Events took a further radical turn in 1990 following the invasion of Kuwait by Iraqi forces. Iraqi representatives offered Iran a full and absolute reversion of the border along the Shatt al-Arab to the position accepted under the 1975 Accord. Other components of the Iraqi offer to Iran were ratification of a peace agreement under the terms of Resolution 598, the return of all prisoners of war, normalization of economic and diplomatic relations and complete withdrawal of Iraqi troops behind the 1980 frontiers. In return, Iran was presumably to accept the *de facto* integration of Kuwait into Iraq. The Iranian authorities did not accede to the Iraqi proposals and continued to demand that Iraq withdraw from Kuwaiti territory as a prelude to a negotiated settlement of the issue. Iranian attempts to mediate an Iraqi withdrawal from Kuwait were rebuffed by Saddam Hussein, despite the clear desire in Tehran for a peaceful settlement, which would obviate the need for a military solution by the UN coalition led by the United States. The 1988 arrangements for a settlement of the Shatt al-Arab dispute thus came to nothing during 1990-1. In 1992 the USA and its coalition partners set up a "no-flying" zone in the south of Iraq to protect the Shi'ite community from air attack by the central government, thereby forestalling any Irano-Iraqi agreement that might have been reached. Meanwhile, Khorramshahr port was opened to river traffic in December 1992, with Iran utilizing full rights to navigation on the Shatt al-Arab (31).

Elsewhere on the Iran/Iraq borderlands, tensions were exacerbated by the inability of the Iraqi central government to enforce security. Kurdish groups were active throughout the border area and the Iranian authorities continued to support Iraq opposition groups in SAIRI (Supreme Assembly of the Islamic Revolution of Iraq), in effect making the Iran/Iraq frontier very permeable. Iranian aircraft attacked Iraqi territory in April 1992 in an attempt to bomb the headquarters of the mujahidin-i khalq organization (MKO). Both countries made recurrent protests to the UN on the matter of border violations throughout the early 1990s.

It is apparent that the Iran/Iraq border remains prone to deep problems. In part these frictions along the international frontier reflect underlying political problems between the rather different regimes in Tehran and Baghdad (32). It might be observed with justification that some of the problems affecting the frontier areas also derive from rather deep-seated difficulties arising from specifically geographical phenomena. There are, for example, the fraught questions of family, tribal and religious groups that are divided by the international border (33), together with the long-term involvement of these same peoples in smuggling, armed raiding, and drug trafficking. At the same time, the specific issues of control of navigation and sovereignty on the Shatt al-Arab remain to bedevil relations, however good general diplomatic links with the post-US occupation regimes in Iraq might or might not be (34). The geography of southern Iraq where it abuts onto the Persian Gulf in a restricted shoreline of a few tens of kilometers is out of proportion to so large and rich a hinterland. Even the most unsympathetic observer of Iraq was moved to the conclusion on Iraq's limited access to the waters of the Persian Gulf that "Iraq has never come to accept the harsh reality of its geographic predicament in relation to the Persian Gulf"(35). Limited access to the sea however, cannot constitute a right in the eyes of international law to attack other countries in order to expand territorial access for outlet in accordance with Ancel's postulate that "there are no problems of boundaries. There are only problems of nations" (36), which is applicable to the question of the conflict over the Shatt al-Arab boundary and even to confrontations over considerable lengths of the Iran/Iraq land frontier.

The Iranian frontage to the Persian Gulf, like that on the Shatt al-Arab, has remained in a state of partial flux. The majority of agreements concerning division of the continental shelf have proved to be viable - notably those with Saudi Arabia, Oman, Qatar and Bahrain. Other areas of the continental shelf have either not been subject to existing treaties or are affected by disputes over earlier agreements. An example of the former situation can be seen at the head of the Persian Gulf, where, as noted earlier, Iran, Iraq and Kuwait have failed to finalize division of the so-called "golden triangle". Acrimonious and capricious argument has characterized a number of offshore settlements, none more so than those between Iran and Britain in the past and the United Arab Emirates now. Here too powerful undercurrents are discernible, one deriving from generic insecurity and suspicion between the respective governments working within the concept laid down by Ancrel and another arising from specific local matters of sovereignty and strategic control.

The contemporary history of Abu Musa illustrates the volatility surrounding frontiers where there is chronic and latent dissatisfaction on both sides concerning the "fairness" and "legitimacy" of an existing boundary settlement. It must be emphasized, however, that there has been an episodic recurrence of difficulties that augurs badly for future stability. The nub of the local problem is one of sovereignty and the Iranian and Sharja claims to the island. The shared control since 1971 has tended to confirm the Iranian belief that it has sovereignty on an equal and shared footing with Sharjah, while the authorities in Abu Dhabi appear to view the 1971 settlement as allocating sovereignty to Sharjah but rights of military usufruct to Iran. Abu Dhabi also argues that the legal basis for the claims of the two sides in the dispute will eventually have to be examined by an impartial arbitrator or a separate political agreement reached. In the interim, Abu Dhabi has been trying hard to turn the issue of claims on the three islands of Abu Musa, and Greater and Lesser Tunb into a *cause celebre* at the Middle Eastern regional level as a symbol of Arab national resistance to the spread of Iranian influence in the Persian Gulf. This status has been a continuing theme since1971, sparking Arab consciousness of wrong done to the greater Arab nation (Qoum al-Arabiyah) as far away as Libya, where British Petroleum's assets in Concession 65 were nationalized in 1971 in protest at alleged British government complicity in the Iranian seizure of the islands.

The former regime of Iraq adopted the issue of the "Iranian military occupation" of Persian Gulf islands in setting out its case for attacking Iran in September 1980. In 1992 the same theme was raised again by the United Arab Emirates in response to the unfortunate incidents on Abu Musa, which included refusal of entry in Abu Musa of workers from Sharjah and returning school teachers in September 1992. By the end of 1992 the Abu Musa dispute had attracted some attention in the region in which the Iranian tenancy of the Persian Gulf islands was being put into question. More threatening for Iran, the dispute over Abu Musa became inextricably linked with that of sovereignty of the Tunb islands and Iran's entire strategy towards the Persian Gulf was put into question (37).

References

1- K. S. McLachlan, *Borders in the Ottoman Empire*, in Encyclopaedia Iranica, E. Yarshater (ed.), 401 (London: Routledge, 1989).
2- H. Arfa, *Under the five shahs*, 111-85 (London – John Murray, 1964).
3- D. N. Wilber, *Iran*, 126 (Princeton University Press, 1976).
4- R. Ferrier, *The history of the British Petroleum Company*, vol. 1, 632-5 (Cambridge: Cambridge University Press, 1982); J. Marlowe, *Iran: a short political guide*, 55-7, (London: Pall Mall, 1963).
5- W. E. Griffith, *Iran's foreign policy*, in *Iran under the Pahlavis*, G. Lenczowski (ed.), 370-1 (Stanford: Hover Institute, 1978).
6- Wilber, op. cit., 132.
7- Marlowe, op. cit., 71.
8- M. Sicker, *The bear and the lion*, 55 (New York, Praeger, 1988).
9- R. W. Cotton, *Nationalism in Iran*, 198 (Pittsburgh: University of Pittsburgh Press, 1964).
10- R. N. Fry, *Iran*, 87 (London: Allen & Unwin, 1954.
11- cf. M. T. O'Shea, Chapter 5 (of *Modern boundaries of Iran*, K. S. McLachlan (ed.) 1994, London: UCL Press).
12- F. Fesharaki, *Revolution and energy policy in Iran*, 25 (London: Economist Intelligence Unit, 1980).
13- Unpublished paper of the Tripartite seminar (1981), School of Oriental and African Studies, University of London, cf. paper of 14 October 1981.
14- *Tehran Times*, 27 December 1992.
15- T. Swietochowski, *Russian Azerbaijan 1905-20: the shaping of national identity in a Muslim community*, 129-30 (Cambridge: Cambridge University Press, 1985).
16- Iran seeks silken ties with Central Asian neighbours, *Financial Times*, 22 June 1992.
17- Iran's relations with the southern members of the CIS, *Background brief*, 2-3 (London: Foreign and Commonwealth Office, 1992).
18- cf. Abbas Maleki, Chapter 2 (of *Modern boundaries of Iran*, K. S. McLachlan (ed.) 1994, London: UCL Press).
19- P. Mojtahed-Zadeh, *The evolution of eastern Iranian boundaries: the role of the Khozeimeh Amirdom*, PhD thesis (Department of Geography, School of Oriental and African Studies, 1993).
20- D. Balland, *The borders of Afghanistan*, in Yarshater, op. cit., 413-14.
21- Ibid.
22- Ibid, 413; Mojtahed-zadeh, op. cit.
23- *Iran Focus* 6 (1993), 5-6.
24- McLachlan, op. cit., 401-3.
25- R. N. Schofield, *Iran's borders with Turkey*, in Yarshater, op. cit, 418.
26- *Iran Monitor* 8 (1992), 4-5.
27- S. Chubin & C. Tripp, *Iran and Iraq at war* (London: I. B. Tauris, 1988).
28- R. N. Schofield, *The evolution of the Shatt al-Arab boundary* dispute (London: Menas Press, 1986).
29- K. S. McLachlan & E. G. H. Joffe, *The Gulf war: a survey of political issues and economic consequences* (London: Economic Intelligence Unit, 1984).

30- E. G. H. Joffe & K. S. McLachlan, *Iran and Iraq: building on the stalemate*, 3-4 (London: Economic Intelligence Unit, 1988).
31- *Iran Monitor* 1 (1993), 24.
32- G. Balfour-Paul, "The prospect of peace", in *The Iran-Iraq war*, M. S. Azhary (ed.), 126-7 (London: Croom Helm, 1984).
33- Lord Kendal, "The Kurds under the Ottoman Empire", in *People without a country*; the Kurds and Kurdistan, G. Chaliand (ed.), 43 (London: Zed Books, 1978).
34- A. Cordesman, "The regional balance", in *The Gulf war*, H. Maul & O. Pick (eds), 85 (London: Pinter, 1989).
35- D. Finne, *Shifting lines in the sand: Kuwait's elusive frontiers with Iraq*, 175 (London: I. B. Tauris, 1992).
36- J. Ancel, *Les frontiers*, 196 (Paris: Galliard, 1936).
37- cf. K. S. McLachlan, Chapter 6 (of *Modern boundaries of Iran*, K. S. McLachlan (ed.) 1994, London: UCL Press).

SECTION A

IRAN'S NORTHERN BOUNDARIES

Section A1–Iran's Boundaries in the Caucasus

CHAPTER II

Stages in the Shaping of Iran's North-Western Boundaries
Mohammad Hassan Ganji

Introduction

The question of delimitation and demarcation of international boundaries that has caused many conflicts and wars in recent years is a phenomenon that is no more than two or, at the most, three centuries old, in the whole of human history. According to certain opinions, it assumed importance after the French Revolution in the late' 18th and early 19th centuries, when the Napoleonic wars in Europe and their aftermath events sharpened the national feeling of European countries that had been overrun by Napoleon and liberated after the fall of the French Empire. In France itself, the first National Assembly had ruled that the country's lands and administrative divisions be mapped, and records be kept of all surveying measurements. Other countries followed suit when defining the lines separating sovereign states from one another became a necessity that gradually evolved into one of the most critical international issues, namely, international boundaries. It was, thus, from Europe that the question found its way to other parts of the world, and Iran was no exception to the rule when, early in the 19th century, there developed a sense of frontier consciousness as result of relations just established with the European countries.

However, for Iran, settlement of international boundaries proved to be one of the greatest misfortunes that she had experienced throughout her long history, because she had to forfeit almost half of her territories to her contentious neighbours, as will be seen in the following discussion of her northwest boundary. (See fig. 2)

Historical Background

The events that have led to the formation of the present borders of Northwest Iran have their roots in the centuries past. It is, therefore, necessary to look into these events for a better understanding of the factors that have resulted in the present situations. Of particular importance are the events of the recent centuries, beginning with the time of the Safavids (1500-1722). Under this dynasty, Iran restored her full cultural identity and true political independence. This was after centuries of feudalism and appearance of several kingdoms, all over the Iranian plateau. The founder of this dynasty, Shah Esmail, established himself in the northern parts of the plateau, i.e. Ardabil district of Azarbaijan, not only by virtue of his ability as a strong military ruler that headed an army of devotee soldiers by the name of Qezellebash, but also by proclaiming twelve-imam shieism as the official religion of his kingdom, a fact that, in time, encouraged peoples of all other provinces and areas of the vast plateau to receive him heartily and to support him with utmost loyalty and fidelity. This was particularly so because of the threat that they all experienced from the frequent attacks by the Ottoman emperors, all Sunni Muslims, who pretended to be successors to the prophet. Consequently, the Safavid territory expanded rapidly to such an extent that, at the height of their power, the empire extended from Georgia in the north of Caucasian to the Persian Gulf and from Afghanistan almost to the shores of the Mediterranean.

The period of reign of Safavids in Iran coincided with the expansion of knowledge in Europe about the outside world, itself the direct result of geographical discoveries that had changed the traditional maps of the world. This, in turn, resulted in emergence of increase in international relationships which, was later realized, as the beginning of the rise of imperialism in the modern world.

During the same period the Ottoman Empire, having control over most of Eastern Europe, Southwest Asia and Northern Africa, and pursuing a policy of subduing Christian countries, was a strong force in international relationships.

Throughout the 16th Century many European countries tried to contact the Safavid kings of Iran, by means of dispatching emissaries for the purpose of establishing economic relations with them. Such attempts were motivated not only by economic reason, but also by the desire to find an ally against the Muslim Ottoman Empire that was encroaching on Christian territories of Europe.

Meanwhile in Iran, the Safavid Kings, particularly Shah Abbass the Great, were eager to accept offers from Europeans and permitted foreign merchants to establish trading centers in Iranian ports and cities under official protection of the government.

St. Petersburg Treaty and the First Russian Agression

Among many such emissaries that visited the court of Shah Abbass was a Russian prince of high standing that was commissioned by the Tsar of Russia to travel to Iran and obtain permission for Russian traders to come thereto and move about freely, doing business under protection of the crown.

Consequently, the first trading agreement between Iran and Russia was singed in 1618, as a result of which Russian business houses were created inside the country and all sorts of Russian manufactured goods found their way into Iran in exchange for raw materials and agricultural products that were admired in Russian markets. The economic relation so established prevailed for almost a century during which time changes took place in the two countries. In Russia Peter the Great, the ambitious Tsar, assumed power and proclaimed his well-known policy of securing access to warm sea waters at any cost.

In Iran, Shah Sultan Hossein was entangled in the Afghan insurgence that finally led to the downfall of the dynasty.

Meanwhile Peter dispatched a mission, headed by A.Volynskii, to strengthen the economic relations with Iran. This movement coincided with chaos caused in Iran by the Afghan insurgence, in which Shah Sultan Hossein was seriously entangled. Valenskii, who observed the state of utter confusion prevailing in the court of Safavids, reported to Tsar that there could never be a better opportunity for Russia to attack Iran and approach the warm waters of the Persian Gulf. Peter the Great, realizing the favorable conditions, led an army and took possession of Astrakhan, the strategic port of the Caspian, at the head of the great river Volga.

He then proceeded south to Darband, where he established a garrison to guard the commercial route that linked Iran to Moscow. Meanwhile, to conceal his intentions, Peter showed leniency by ordering his emissary to propose assistance and enable the Shah of Safavid to overcome the Afghan revolt. On his way to Isfahan, Peter's envoy met with Tahmaseb Mirza, heir apparent, in Qazvin and persuaded him to send a mission to Moscow and, as rightful heir, formally ask for assistance as suggested. Realizing his precarious condition, the crown prince submitted to the suggestion and ordered his close relation Isma'il Beg to proceed to Moscow and present him the crown prince's official request for help. Peter, exploiting the situation, informed the envoy that he would do so on the condition that:

1- The two cities of Darband and Badkuba (present Baku) were formally ceded to Russia.

2- The two provinces of Mazandaran and Esterabad were allocated to Russia in order to provide food and provisions for the ceded cities.

The Iranian envoy accepted the offer and signed the agreement of September 1723 (known as the St.Peterburg Treaty) which is regarded as the first official aggression of Tsarist Russian on Iranian territory.

The crown prince refused to honour the agreement and severely punished his envoy for having signed such a shameful document but alas, Russian forces had already occupied the coveted provinces on the excuse of saving them from Afghan occupation.

Russo-Ottoman Agreement of June 1724

Parallel with these developments and, worsening of the sad confusions in Isfahen, the most important rival of Safavid dynasty in the area, namely the Ottoman Empire lost no time and occupied the whole of western half of Iran, from Iravan in the north to Kermanshah in the south, including Tabriz, Maraghah etc. Furthermore, becoming aware of the St.Peterburg Treaty, this empire protested strongly to Moscow and threatened to break down all diplomatic relations with Russia. The tension thus produced between the two neighbors of Iran and, the risk of breaking out of a war in the region, made the French ambassador to intervene as a result of which, the two empires (Russia and the Ottoman) reached an agreement whereby each of the two parties became recognized possessor of the part of Iranian territory that was at the time under its occupation. According to this agreement, brought about through French intervention, all Iranian territory lying to the east of Aras-Kor junction, as far as Astrabad, was recognized as Russia's share of the booty, while all the land lying to the south of the above junction went to the Ottoman Empire. The agreement in question, concluded in June 19 1724 marks the greatest territorial revision officially recorded up to that time.

Nadir-Shah and the Treaty of Ganja

Meanwhile events in Iran nullified the above shameful agreement. The Safavid dynasty came to an end and a strong warrior, with great patriotic zeal, became Master of the scene. He was Nadir Shah Afshar who had planned to recover all the Iranian territories lost during the last years of the Safavids. After duly consolidating his forces and, being firmly determined to see that all the lands taken over by Russia and the Ottomans are returned to Iran, he arrived in Ganja from where he sent an envoy to the court of Russian Empire where Queen Anna Ivanovna had succeeded Peter the Great. Nadir showed an amicable gesture by sending presents and, at the same time, asking the queen to return, unconditionally, all the territories taken over by her predecessor, hinting that in case of failure he would take side with the Queen's enemy namely the Ottoman Empire.

The wise queen of Russia, having heard of Nadir's previous victories in reshaping his country by recovering all the lost territories and, having in mind to secure a potentially strong ally and neighbor against the Ottoman Empire, received Nadir's envoy with due respect and agreed to return all Iranian territories unconditionally. Furthermore, as a gesture of good neighborly relations, she commissioned a high-ranking Russian prince to meet Nadir in Ganja where he was eagerly awaiting the developments. Consequently, it was in that city that the Treaty of Ganja was exchanged in 1735 between the two countries.

This treaty is of utmost importance, not only because it provides the only occasion in the long relationship of the two countries, that Russia has agreed to withdraw to her previous frontier, but because, in terms of this treaty, the river Sulagh is officially recognized as the international frontier between the two countries. (See fig 2)

1783 Agreement and Seperation of Georgia

Nadir was assassinated in 1747, and Iran was again torn to pieces by his successors, local chieftains, tribal rulers and, above all, international rivalry of great European powers. Fortunately for Iran, both Russia and the Ottoman Empires, potential dangers to Iran's solidarity, were engaged in their European problems, so they could not afford to bother with the Iranian affairs. However, one event of importance accrued that is of interest to us because it involved changes in frontiers.

In 1783, the Christian Vassal of Georgia revolted against the central government of Iran, mainly on religious grounds, and sought assistance from the Empress of Russia. On this occasion, the Empress Catherine, apparently protecting Christian subjects from Islamic oppressions, accepted the vassal's plea and dispatched armies for his support. In the encounters that followed, the Iranian armies were defeated and an agreement was concluded (1783) whereby Georgia was separated from Iran and became officially part of Russian territory.

Changes of Frontiers during the Qajar Dynasty

It is recorded in Iranian histories that soon after assassination of Nadir Shah in Khorassan, his main Sardars (chief commander of forces) left the site of assassination, each heading for part of his vast empire with the intention of assuming power and establishing themselves as his successor. Thus a chaos was once again created at the court of the peacock throne that Nadir himself had brought from India after his victorious march to that country. The rivalry of power, thus brought about after Nadir, came to an end only when Agha Mohammad Khan Qajar, the founder of Qajar dynasty, himself one of the contenders proclaimed himself Shah of Iran in 1796. Like Nadir, he first consolidated his military forces by subduing all local and tribal chieftains. He then decided to regain all lost territories and, before any thing else, he aimed at chastising the vassal of Georgia that had caused separation of that province from Iran as indicated above. He personally led an army that captured and sacked Tiflis, capital of Georgia, in 1795, bringing Georgia and neighboring areas under his command. By so doing Agha Mohammad Khan pushed the frontier between his kingdom and Russia, back to its original position. However, the following year Empress Catherine of Russia recovered Georgia as a retaliatory action, and her forces proceeded south until Moghan steppes. At that point, the Empress died and Agha Mohammad Khan lost no time and once again, personally led his army into Transcaucasia. This was a fateful expedition for the Qajar monarch and a calamity for Iran, since Agha Mohammad Khan was murdered at the hands of two of his disloyal guards. (18 May 1796), Georgia thus remained under Russia and the International frontier was once again pushed south to exclude that province from Iranian domains forever.

Frontier Changes Imposed by Treaty of Golestan

The Russian aggression south from Georgia continued in later years until they had reached Iravan (capital of Armenia) during the reign of Fath'Ali Shah. In all cases their aggression was combined with utter maltreatment of the local inhabitants, particularly the Muslims, most of whom abandoned their homes and properties and migrated to other regions that were under Iranian domination.

It should be borne in mind that, at this time, Iran had become the scene of acute international rivalries among European countries particularly England, France and Russia and, of course, the Ottoman Empire.

Tehran was the scene of international intrigues when the first war with Russia broke out in1803. The Shah of Iran (Fath'Ali Shah), unaware of the nature of European politics and of what was happening in the world at large, approached the French for assistance and consequently an agreement was reached with Napoleon at Finkelstein in East Prussia (1807) and a strong body of French officers arrived in Iran to train the local forces. Napoleon's main intention was to use Iran as an ally in the war that he had in mind to start against England by invading India, with the help of Russia. However, Napoleon's plan did not materialize and relations between France and Russia became tense. The Shah of Iran, desperately engaged in war with Russia, turned to England for assistance but this new ally advised the Shah of Iran to come to terms with his northern neighbor, thus using its advisory influence in favor of Russia rather than Iran. Fath'Ali Shah reluctantly accepted the advice and came to terms with Russia. It was as a result of this reconciliation that the well-known treaty of Golestan (dated 12 October 1813) was concluded between Iran and Russia, and brought to end an expensive war that had lasted for 10 years.

The key point in this treaty was to maintain the status-quo. In other words, each of the two sides should take final possession of the territories under its control at the time of signing the treaty.

In accordance with the terms of this shameful treaty that had been imposed on Iran through the intermediary of England, Iran lost extensive territories including the fertile and economically important provinces of Georgia, Darband, Qobba, Baku, Shirvan, Shakki, Ganja, Moghan and even part of Talesh that were at the time under Russian occupation.

Actually, article 3 of the treaty of Golestan read as follows:

> *His Highness... the king of Iran considers the provinces of Qarabagh and Ganja; the khanates of Shakki, Shirvan, Qobba, Darband and Baku; all areas of the provinces of Talesh which are now occupied by Russia; all of Daghestan and Georgia; the areas of Shura-gol, Achuqbash, Karna, Monktil and Abkhaz; all of the areas and lands between the Caucasus and the present determined borders; and the lands and people of the Caucasus adjoining the Caspian Sea to be belonging and attached to the Imperial State of Russia.*

The international boundary was vaguely fixed by a straight line joining Ghizil Aghaj Bay on the Caspian to Batum on the Black Sea coast. (See fig. 2)

Second Russo-Iranian War and THE Turkmanchay Treaty

The Treaty of Golestan brought a ten year war to an end, but hostilities between the two countries did not cease, and the frontier disputes remained unsolved for years to come. Throughout those years Russia continued its encroachment on Iranian territories to the south of the provinces assigned to it in terms of the Golestan Treaty. In 1826, Russia openly claimed the district of Gokcha, a claim that was rejected by Iran. Negotiations that followed did not remedy the situations and consequently the second Russo-Iranian war began in 1825-6. Iranian armies fought brilliantly under the crown prince. Abbass Mirza, but when the well trained Russian commander, General Paskievitch, whose name is familiar to Iranian historians, arrived at the front, things changed and the Iranians were defeated. Paskevitch then took possession of Iravan and its neighborhood and advanced even to Tabriz. This time, again, Iran was persuaded by the British to come to terms with the enemy. Consequently, the Treaty of Turkamanchai was signed in February 1828 and brought the second Russo-Iranian war to an end.

Under the terms of this Treaty provinces of Iravan (present Armenia), Nakhjavan, Gharabagh and parts of Moghan steppe were separated from Iran.

The international boundary between Iran and Russia was established by article 4 of the treaty in question, more or less as it stands today.

Accordingly River Aras became the major part of the boundary all the way from Dim-Qeshlaq 43°45' East (according to Webster Geographical Dictionary) in the west to Tazakand 48° E (according the same source) in the east. Between the latter point and the mouth of the river Astara, the land boundary between the two countries shows a zigzag trend that is so shaped because of the alignment of mountain ranges and courses of rivers that it follows.

Figure 2

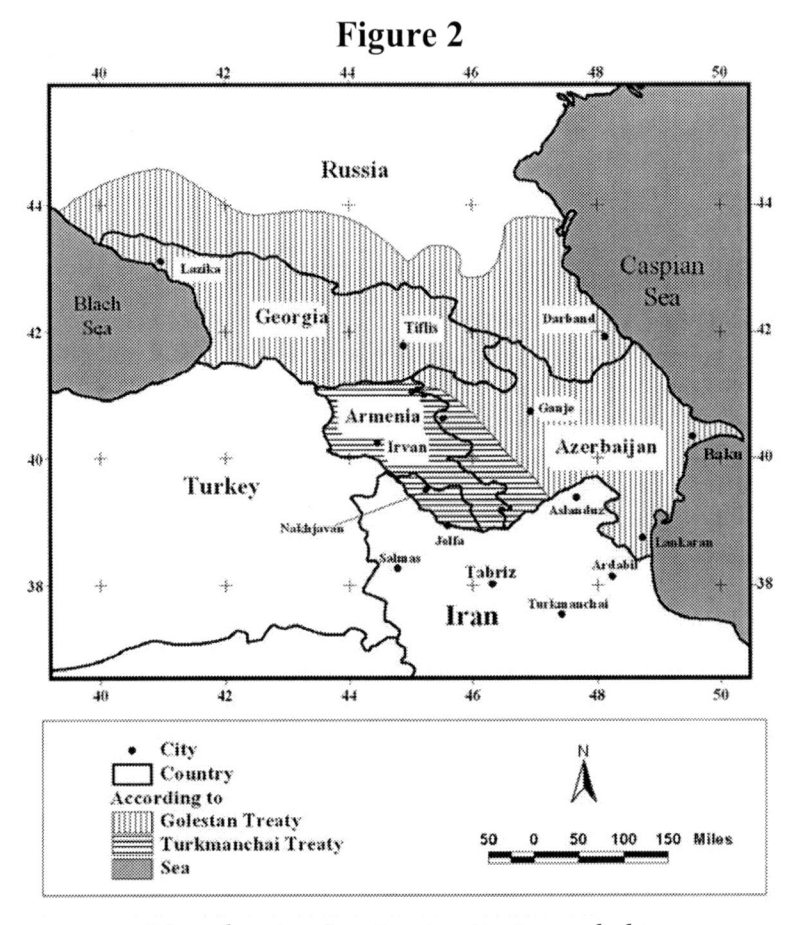

*Map showing Iranian territories ceded to
Russia in terms of Golestan and Turkmenchai treaties*

Briefly, from the mentioned points on the Aras, the boundary line cuts the Moghan steppe directly to a point on the Bala-Rud River, which is 21 Russian verses below the junction of the Adineh-Bazar and Sari-Qamish Rivers. It then follows the Bala-Rud upstream to its head waters and on to the high peak of Jegar. From this point, the boundary runs along the water divide of the ranges that separate Talesh from Arshaq and on to high peaks of Kamar-Qoueie and Kaloupooti, until it reaches the head waters of river Astara following the talweg of this river to its mouth at the Caspian Sea where the twin cities of Russian Astara and Iranian Astara lie to its north and south respectively. The land boundary thus laid down allocated a major part of the fertile Moghan steppe and the strategic port of Lankoran to Russia. (See fig 2)

The international boundary as determined by article 4 of Turkamanchai Treaty was defined very vaguely but the treaty had envisaged a joint commission to demarcate the actual boundary in due course. This commission was soon formed and hastily prepared a protocol known as "1829 protocol" that became subject of arguments for years to come. In this protocol only main habited places and salient natural points were mentioned and points of great importance for the demarcation such as villages, pastures, fields and islands, of which there were no less than 800 small and large ones, were overlooked altogether. Consequently, gradual encroachment of

Russia along the Aras continued for years and settlements and villages were occupied by the Russians one after another. Maltreatment considered by the Russians as an established policy, forced thousands of local inhabitants leave their homes and save their lives by migrating to Iran. There are at present thousands of the decendants of such refugees whose names indicate their Caucasian origin and who have played major roles in Iran's liberation and development. (See fig 2)

The Aftermath of Turkamanchai Treaty

Russian encroachment on Iranian territory went on for years after the date of the treaty. This was caused mainly by the vague and inadequate definition of the 1829 protocol and lack of much detail that could overcome misunderstandings. During the years that followed many commissions were formed but none could finalize the points of difference between the two parties.

Then came the 1907 Anglo-Russian agreement dividing Iran into two spheres of influence under which the Russians ignored all international codes of conduct and in 1910 they crossed the international boundary without any scruple and occupied the two cities of Tabriz and Mashhad where they put hundreds of innocent inhabitants to death.

The First World War and the 1921 Agreement

In 1914, after the First World War began, in spite of the fact that Iran had declared its neutrality, Russian forces occupied parts of Azerbaijan with no regard to international frontiers. Throughout the war years part of the western Iran was the land of encounters between the Allied and Central Powers. However, after the 1917 Revolution in Russia, drastic changes occurred in Russo-Iranian relationships, the main result which was the conclusion of the 1921 Agreement of friendship between the two countries. Under this treaty the newly created Soviet government waived a number of concessions that the Tsarist regime had extracted from Iran.

The question of international boundary was referred to in article 3 of this Agreement. This article clearly recorded the willingness of the two parties to settle their frontier disputes in a friendly manner.

The 1829 protocol was to be the basis of negotiation and joint commissions were to be set up to demarcate the frontier.

After conclusion of the 1921 agreement no fewer than five joint commissions were organized as follows:

Mansoor-Hakimoff, 1923
Elhami-Lazaroff in 1925
Aalam-Maevsky in 1951
Sayyah-Levrentioff in 1954
Jahanbani-Orloff in 1955

Each of the first three commissions achieved some progress in definition of vague points in the 1829 protocol but could not arrive at a definite conclusion. This was because almost in all cases of dispute, the Russian delegation openly declared and insisted that all points of dispute should be definitely ceded to them, to which the Iranian party could not agree.

The fourth commission was on the whole more successful as it arrived at signing an agreement envisaging another join commission to end up, the points of dispute. The last commission was the most effective of all those formed since 1923. It began its work in January 1955 and did not interrupt until 1957 when the job was completed.

In this joint commission the Iranian side was headed by General Amanollah Jahanbani, one of the most educated and widely experienced officers of the Iranian army. He had been trained in Russia and was quite familiar, not only with Russian language, but with the culture and customs of that country. The head of the Russian side was Paul D. Orloff, an ambassador of wide experience and good will.

The joint commission selected Astara as its headquarters, each group being settled in its respective part of the town. Ten sub commissions were created each equipped with appropriate surveying facilities and manned by expert technicians and capable interpreters.

Before starting the actual field work, the two parties had agreed that:

1- Accurate maps, to the scale of 1:10,000, were to be prepared of a 2Km strip of land all along the frontier.

2- Borderline to be defined by a line of strong wooden poles with two other lines each at 2.25 meter distance from the central line, on which concrete pillars were to be built, duly marked, numbered and painted with the respective country's colours.

3- Accurate coordinates for all points within the strip were to be calculated and carefully recorded in special books, and

4- All alterations of the past century were to be discussed on the basis of existing document until mutual consent was reached.

Demarcation began at the westernmost point of the frontier (a point at the junction of the Iranian-Turkish-Russian territories as fixed in 1925) and ended at a point specified by pillar no.144 on the Caspian coast at the mouth of river Astara, halfway between Iranian Astara and Russian Astara.

The total length of the frontier was determined to be 796.50 Km. along which, 144 main and 305 subsidiary pillars were erected. Wherever rivers were involved, median lines were demarcated. In the course of demarcation it was revealed that there were no less than 805 Islands of various sizes within the actual channel of the river Aras. Of these 427 islands belonged to Iran and the remaining 378 belong to Russia. Two of the larger islands were divided between the two countries. Of the 796.50 Km frontier between Iran and Russia some 475 Km coincide with the course of the river Aras between Dim-Ghishlagh in the west and Tazahkand in Moghan on the east. The remainder consists of the land frontier between Tazehkand and the mouth of Astara River, as indicated above.

The final protocol along with piles of maps, minutes of meetings, records of surveys, books of coordinates etc. all in Farsi and Russian were exchanged in Tehran on 11 April 1957, a date that marks the end of century old frontier disputes on the Azarbaijan borders of Iran.

Boundary Changes Since 1990

After the breakdown of the Soviet Union two nation states, namely, Republics of Azerbaijan and Armenia were created to the north of Aras River and, of the 475 kms. frontier between Iran and former USSR, some 40 kms. relate to Armenia (according to Iran's statistical yearbook 1379 p.5) and the remaining 435 kms. to Azerbaijan, divided into two sections one on each side of Armenian boundary. No dispute of importance has arisen between Iran and its neighbors to its northwest. However, it should be noted that, according to Azerbaijan sources, in connection with the disputes between the two Republics on the Qarabagh region, several districts of Azerbaijan immediately to the north of Aras River have been occupied by Armenia with the result that presently, apart from the 40 kms. Armenian boundary, about 150 kms. of the Azerbaijan boundary on the Aras River to the east of Armenia appears to be under Armenian occupation.

References

Persian Sources:
1. Jafari, Abbass, Rivers of Iran, Gita-Shenasi, Tehran,
2. Jahanbani, A. Frontiers of Iran and Sovit Russia, Tehran, Ibn-Sina, 1957
3. Iranian Ministry of Foreign Affairs, Archival materials in Persian.
4. Iranian Ministry of Energy, Energy, water resources atlas of Iran, vol. 2: Hydrology. Tehran, 1990
5. Iranian Public Statistics Department, Iran Statistical Year Book 1379, Tehran, 2000
6. Mofakham - Payan, L. Rivers and mountains of Iran, National Geographical Organization, Tehran,
7. Mokhber, M.A. Frontiers of Iran. Tehran: Keyhan. 1947
8. Kayhan, M. Political Geography of Iran, Ibn- e - Sine, Tehran, 1310

Other sources:
1. Azarbaijan Government, Aggression of the Republic of Armenia Against the Azarbaijan Republic, Baku, 1994.
2. Historical Atlas of Iran, Tehran University Institute of Geography, Tehran 1971
3. McLachlan, K., The Boundaries of Modern Iran, The SOAS / GRC Geopolitics Series 2, London 1994
4. Public Record Office. 1947. Persia, Confidential print no. 917188. Section I: Persian frontiers.E1011, 31 January 1947, 51.
5. Watson, H. S. Russian Empire, 1801-1917. Oxford University Press. 1967.
6. Webster's New Geographical Dictionary, p 65

CHAPTER III

Evolution of Russo-Iranian Boundaries in the Caucasus
Bahram Amirahmadian

After the disintegration of the Soviet Union, Iran and Russia became neighbours of no common land boundaries. The only domain that connects these two countries is the water of the Caspian Sea, which is still under the investigation of the legal regiment of the sea. Before the treaties of Golestan (1813) and Turkmenchai (1828), Iran had frontiers with Russia in the northern slopes of the Greater Caucasus mountain range in northern Caucasus (Terek River). Whereas, in the beginning of the 16th century, there used to be a frontier region that separated the two countries; it had never been limited and that frontier had always been flexible. Modern boundaries between Iran and Russia came into being as a result of the wars imposed by Russia on Iran, ending in Iran's defeat.

Iran's boundaries expanded due to her strong military power and victories in wars; they contracted because of the defeats faced. All the Iranian boundaries, including Caucasus, Mesopotamia, Afghanistan and Central Asia, are the borders that are the product of the expansionary wars and international political and economic conditions, as well as defeats in the defensive wars, which affected the boundaries shaping Iran. Therefore, Iranian culture and civilization are not only confined within the present boundaries of Iran, but still exist outside of these borders too. These boundaries, which at one time ranged from Asia Minor and Caucasus to the subcontinent of India and from the steppes of Central Asia to the fertile lands of Mesopotamia, were the signs of the vast domain of this country.

In the end of the Safavid period, when Shah Sultan Hussein, the last Safavid king in Isfahan, was overthrown, the power of the Great Safavid Empire reached its end (1). It was coincident with the time when Peter the Great came into power in Russia and the Russian Empire became strengthened. As a matter of fact, Russia and Iran have undergone two totally opposite processes. At the same time, Ottomans also faced decline due to many problems, such as domestic disorder and clashes between national forces, diversity of the nations of occupied territories and several wars in different places of Europe, Russia and Iran, and as a result, they also lost their occupied territories.

The study of borders between Iran and Russia, without considering the historical relationship of the two countries, which started from early 8th century till the fall of Russia Empire and the emerging of 1917 revolution, is impossible because the two countries started their relationship friendly, but eventually become enemies. The borders between Iran and Russia and then Iran and the Soviet Union in the Caucasus were borders of separation between nations who never wanted to become parts of Russia, neither had they any interest associated with this separation (it is said so in Iranian history writing). That is why the history of these borders is the history of the lines drawn as a result of military strength and imposed treaties to fulfill the benefits of the colonial states of that time (Britain, Russia and France), and it is the sorrowful history of the nation that become separated from itself.

The borders between Iran and the Russian Empire and modern Russia in the Caucasus Region (from west to east, including Nakhchivan autonomous republic, Armenia and Azerbaijan) similarly is the same border line which was drawn by the results of Golestan and following Turkmenchay treaties between Iran and Russia. This line begins from the confluence of the Arax and lower Qare Su Rivers and the conjunction point of Iran, Ottoman (Turkey) and Russia (Nakhchivan), following the Arax River and then the Balharud River, with continuing western slopes of Talish Mountain, reaches Astarachay river and following it from the west to the east, and ends in the coast of Caspian Sea in Astara City. The length of this line is 806 Km. (including 765Km. with Azearbaijan and Nakhchivan and 41Km. with Armenia). About the limitation of this border line, in addition to Golestan and Turkmanchay treaties, there are a few agreements and protocols, including 9 Dec. 1881, and following boundaries documents in 1881-1886, 1893-1894 during Russian Empire, and agreements on surveying, controlling and checking the borders points and border pillars in 1925, 1954, 1957, 1975, 1976, and so on during the Soviet period. There were only a few changes in boundaries during 163 years from Russian Empire to the end of the Soviet Union. Now Iran has no border with Russia. In fact Russia and Iran are borderless neighbors.

This paper is about the process of the formation of the boundaries between Iran and Russia, on the basis of historical, economic and also strategic and geopolitical considering, which are the fundamental factors of shaping the boundaries between the two countries.

The History of the Formation of Iran-Russia Boundaries

The studies of the history of the boundaries of Iran shows that Iran, in the north and northwest of its territory, was neighbored with Slavian tribes, that in the 8th and 9th centuries were united within the old Kiev Russia. Kiev Russia was developed commercial relations with eastern countries. Several trade routes passed through Kiev Russia towards many countries. The river Volga and Volga-Caspian waterways were the main connection routes for Old Russian with eastern nations. By these routes not only the commercial relation but also other relation of Russian with east implemented.

There were active commercial relations between Russia and Iranian cities and provinces such as Tabriz, Gilan, Shamakhi, Darband, Tabaristan and so on. Trade with Russia had more advantages to Iranian merchants (Dunayeva, p. 7). Still there are some families in Tabriz whose family names (Moskochi, Badkubeyi) are related with their trade with Russian cities.

In the 11th and 12th centuries, trade was developed between both sides. But in the 13th and 14th centuries, after the invasion of the Mongols in Russia, the trade relation between Russia and the east, especially with Iran, stopped for a long time.

After rescuing Russian territories from the oppressions of Tartars and unification of different regions of Russia under the flag of Moscow, the Russian political and economic relations with Islamic countries developed more.

Conquest of the Volga region and capturing Kazan and Astrakhan khanates eased the commercial exchanges. Kazan khanate had possessed the middle current of the Volga regions and Astrakhan khanate blockaded the northern part of Caspian for Russia. After conquest of Kazan khanate in 1552 and Astrakhan khanate in 1556, Russia gained access to the north coasts of the Caspian Sea. The period of Russian influences upon the Caucasus region and Caspian Sea coasts started, and from this period the formation of Iran-Russia boundaries begun.

In order for Russia to proceed southward, resistance of the people in southern territories had to be removed. Fighting with Golden Horde, Crimean khanate and Ottomans and defeating them was necessary, and Russia had to arrange these struggles which, with capturing of Kazan and then Astrakhan, made it possible to come down and having access to the Caucasus and Caspian Sea coasts (Dunayeva. p. 8).

From this time, the territories of Russia and Iran became neighbors directly. The north section of the Caspian Sea was possessed by Russia, and the eastern and southern sections belonged to Iran. The path of Volga River, which from political and economic points of view had the most importance, was located within the Russian territory.

The improved Iran-Russia relations coincided with the establishment of Safavids State in Iran [1500-1722]. The exchange of ambassadors between the two countries occurred in 1552-1553. But commercial relation was begun earlier.

In the process of drawing nearby borders, the local Caucasian rulers had significant roles. The first envoy was sent to Moscow on behalf of Kabardian nobles in 1552. In 1557, Kabarda annexed Russia voluntarily, and the relations with Daghistan strengthened. The confluence of Sunzha and Terek, which was a strategic site, served to the expansion of Russian relations. Georgia, who had connection with this strategic point via Tbilisi and Daryal passage, improved its relations with Russia. Due to this condition, Russia developed its political and economic relations with Caucasus. But, because of clashes beyond Russia, there were no more possibilities to have more presence in Caucasus and the south. Besides, with the emerging and strengthening of the Ottoman Empire and its presence in the scene of Caucasus, the region became a battlefield between Iranians and Ottomans. According to the treaty of 1555 between Iran and Ottoman, the territory of Imeretian principality, the provinces of Guria and Megrelia and western regions, and also some parts of Armenia, Shirvan, and Arran totally belonged to Iran.

In the end of 16th century, Ottomans, benefiting internal chaotic conditions in Iran, captured south Caucasus. In 1583, they occupied Baku and gained access to the western coast of the Caspian Sea and established their navigation. They also constructed stronghold in Terek banks and Daghistan.

In those difficult years, there were regular relations between Iran and Russia, and one of the first stages of the relation in boundary formation took part. Shah Khoda Bandeh of Iran [1578-1587] proposed to the Tsar of Russia military co-operation against Ottomans, in which, in return for military assistance, Iran promised to deliver the cities of Darband and Baku to Russia (which were in the hands of Ottomans at that time). In 1590, again, Shah Abbas offered the same case plus Shamakhi city.

The weakened Russian government did nothing against the Ottomans, only established a defense policy. But it didn't reject Iran's proposal either, because Ottoman control of the Caspian Sea was dangerous both for Iran and Russia and deprived them of access to the sea. Due to some reasons, military unifying of the two countries had not happened, but they continued their political and economic relations. Some disputes upon boundaries in Georgia and Daghistan were remained unsolved.

The case of Russian military strongholds in the banks of the Terek River in the 17th century was the subject of military clashes between Iran and Russia. Those strongholds were built to control the southern frontiers of Russia alongside Terek, and the southernmost of these frontiers were northern frontiers of Iran. Shah Abbas asked Russia many times to close these strongholds because they were disturbing Iranian frontiers.

Shah Abbas succeeded in securing Iranian northern frontiers and, until 1607, regained all occupied territories from the hands of Ottomans. In this period, Russia was weakened by internal conflicts, and its occupied area consisted of only small regions with Terki fortress and some small Cossack settler villages in the left bank of Terek.

Until the beginning of the 18th century, the rivalry between Iran and Ottomans to get control of Caucasus continued. Several wars happened and the new treaty of 1639 put an end to the wars. By order of this treaty, disputed areas in Caucasus were again divided. East Georgia and east Armenia, Shirvan and Daghistan (eastern section of Caucasus) were given to Iran and west Georgia; west Armenia, Abkhazia and Black Sea coast and the region of Kuban River were accorded to Ottomans. Iran was interested in obtaining west Caucasus to the Kuban region.

Several clashes between Iran and Ottomans took place in Caucasus, harassing the local population. They were looking for a powerful state to rescue them from the hard situation that they had. During this period, Russia overcame internal problems, awakened, and descended on the scene of Caucasus.

When Shah Sultan Hussain lost his throne to the Afghans (1) and Iran fell into chaos, it was the time when Peter the Great occupied Iranian coast of Caspian Sea.

Russian, and subsequently the USSR, compensated for its geo-strategic weakness with aggression on the geopolitical domain of its neighbors. Even if the testament of Peter the Great is not authentic, still the news and his publications reveal the fact that the Russian strategy was to get hold of the warm waters. And the caricature sketch, where a Russian soldier is washing his military boots in Indian Ocean waters, was a clear sign of Russia's geo-strategic wish, i.e. they had always been trying to posses the warm waters. The Russian Empire, the Soviet Union and modern-day Russia used to seek their security in those borders and revealed that, in addition to Helford Mackinder's *Heartland*, they should keep hold of the whole Central Asia. That is why, during the period of the USSR, their boundaries were widened and included Baltic States too. Therefore, Caucasus was and will always be of much importance for Tsarist Russia, the USSR, and modern Russia. At the time of disintegration, the Russian Federation was seeking its security and stability within the borders of the Soviet Union, and that is why the Commonwealth of Independent States (CIS) with the common interest was established, and regional groupings (Shanghai Pact 1997) are to strengthen their hands.

Caucasian mountain ranges were natural fortifications for the defenseless steppes of southern Russia against the southern domain of Caucasus. Chechens are situated in the center of these great mountains, and upon getting freedom, they might become a threat to the geographical defense unity, internal stability and to the sovereignty of Russia, due to the location they hold, and can undermine these sources of natural defense walls. Just because of this, Russia takes care of this region with extraordinary sensitivity, the same way Tsars used to care about this region in the last centuries. The objective of this article is the analysis of the causes of wars between Iran and Russia and the shaping of borders between them in Caucasus. By analyzing this, first we will recall the historical clues about Russia's interest in the south and towards the Caucasus. Then we will discuss how these boundaries were formed and what the objectives of Russia were concerning

---

1 It is a historical fact that Afghanistan was not at the time a separate political entity and. It was a part of the Iranian federative state (Persian Empire) and as such did not have territories independent of Iran. Hence, statements like "an Afghan attack on Iran" make little sense, whereas what really happened was an Afghan uprising against domestic chaos of the time.

occupation of this area. After that, we will analyze the factors of Iran's defeat and Russia's victory in the wars and their success in ousting Iranians and Ottomans out of the Caucasus region. The two-century supremacy of Russia over Caucasus will also be highlighted. The personalities of the outstanding political and military activities involved in Caucasus combat are also of much importance in the final shaping of these borders.

Caucasus and Its Situation at the End of 18th and Beginning of 19th centuries

Caucasus enjoyed special importance for both Iran and Ottomans, for two reasons. First, for its strategic situation, and secondly for its geographical locations, crossroads, and point of intersection for the connection between North-South and East-West directions. In addition to that, Caucasus was an Islamic domain, so it was desired by both governments. From a strategic and geographical point of view, Caucasus was a buffer region situated between the Russian Empire, Iran, and Ottoman. This was the region that worked against Russian expansion, because expansion was considered Christian aggression on Iranian and Ottoman domains. So, that is why Caucasus became an obstacle in the Russian way to the south (wars of North Caucasian Muslims against Russia in late 18th century and first half of 19th century).

The Caspian Sea was a very important region for Iran, Ottomans, and especially for Russia, because of being important trade routes of that time (Volga-Caspian). At that time, khans of the Crimea were considered to be the allies of the Ottoman Empire. With the union of khans of Crimea, Ottomans wanted the geographical connection with Muslims of Caucasus and then khan of Crimea; the only way to achieve this goal was to possess southern Caucasus and then North. Since Ottomans didn't have any territorial connection with khanat of Crimea via the coast and water ways of Black sea, Russia was the lord of the Black Sea waters and used to hinder their way and held the northern coast, not allowing Ottomans to succeed in their aims. Therefore, Ottomans looked for an alternative to access southern Caucasus from the east and hence access Daghistan, then Northern Caucasus and afterwards khanat of Crimea from the western coast of the Caspian Sea. In this way, they gained control of the Caspian Sea, could make contacts with their allies in the east of the Caspian Sea (Uzbeks and other Sunni Muslim nations), and could possess the trade routes. In this process, there were two basic obstacles in the Ottoman's way. First, two Christian principalities of Georgia and Armenia, second, khanats of the north of Arax River, which the inhabitants of it, were Shiite Muslims and were followers of Iranian religious leaders. They used to align themselves with Iran in their religious practice; and because of Shiite and Sunni differences, they had no inclination towards Ottomans. But in northern Caucasus there was Sunni Muslim, who considered themselves to be the followers of the Muftis of the Ottoman court. In addition to that, southern Caucasus was in Iranian domain, and every advancing move of Ottomans towards the east could be considered as an offence over Iranian dominion, albeit, the weakness of the central government of Iran and the corruption in the court prevented Iran's authorities in this region.

In the advancement of Ottomans towards Caucasus, Iranian borders were vulnerable, and this became the reason for a series of encounters known as the 300 years wars. The first of these wars (1514) occurred between sultan Salim of Ottoman and Shah Ismail Safavid, and ended in Iran's defeat. The last battle of this series of wars was fought between Nadir Shah and Sultan Mahmood of Ottoman in 1736, which led Iran to win the war, ending the wars between the two countries forever. Presence of Ottomans in Caucasus was an alarming sign for the Russian Empire towards the vulnerability of their southern borders, that is, why they started advancing towards South. On the other hand, Armenia and Georgia called for help from Russia to get rid of Muslims' oppression (Ottomans and Iranians) with the annexation of Georgia by Russia in 1801, which was criticized by Iranians. Russia stabilized its presence in southern Caucasus; whereas, Muslims were at war with Russia in the Northern Caucasus.

A Review of the History of Russian Presence in Caucasus

Advancement of Russia towards warm southern waters began in the middle of the 16th century, from the banks of Terek River (Benigson, Broxup and others p. 19). In 1552, Ivan the Terrible captured Kazan khanat and, in 1556, occupied khanat of Astrakhan/Hajitarkhan. At the same time, Russian borders reached the Terek River (A. Avtorkhanov, p. 127). In the 18th century the Islamic boundaries (in Russia) were situated along the Terek River in North Caucasus and Syr Darya in Turkistan (Benigson p. 99).

In 1587, Russians had reached the northern Caucasian plains, and constructed a castle in Tersky Godorok that served as their military base for their further attacks (Benigson and others, p. 34). In 1604 the Tzar, Boris Godonov started a huge raid on north Caucasus. His aim was the conquest of Daghistan so that they could receive the way to Iran. But Daghistanis, with the help of Ottomans, stood against Russians and defeated the Russian force and built their castles with the soil along the Terek plain and pushed them back to Astrakhan (Ibid. p. 35, 36). During the Iranian rule on Caucasus, in the period of Shah Abbas I in 1652, the Iranian king ordered the demolition of all Russian castles and fortifications along the rivers Ghui and Terek. Khosrokhan Beiglerbeigi of Shirvan and Surkhay Khan, the shamkhal of Daghistan along with some other leaders of Shirvan and Daghistan, in compliance with the orders of Shah Abbas II, started their military expeditions towards Caucasus and, after several encounters and clashes with Russian soldiers, they succeeded in possessing Russian castles and fortes and destroyed them all (Abbas Nameh, p. 159,160).

Twelve years after the reign of Peter the Great (1682), the fourth king of Romanov dynasty in Russia, the reign of Shah Sultan Hussain (1694) began in Iran. In the reign of Peter, Iran and Russia's previously friendly ties took a new shape. At that time, Russia generally needed Iran's help, and their ambassadors and other officials visited the Iranian court. The battle of power happened to be in Russia's favor.

After the fall of Safavids (1722) and weakening of the Iranian government, Russia expanded its southern possessions and became neighbors with Georgia; and, when Georgian kings were threatened by the Iranian court, they started seeking Russia's support (Nafisi, vol. 1. p. 66).

One of the most important aims of Peter I was to establish ties with India, through Iran, and we must say that his predecessors also had taken few steps in this regard. Famous Michael Romanov, in 1621, established relations with khan of Khiva and, after him, his successor Alexi, in 1646 and 1675, was sent to India for the initiation of trade ties with India (King Aurangzeb). But he couldn't succeed and no intimate trade ties were established. In 1759, few Russian businessmen were seen in India (Jamal-Zadeh, p. 170).

Peter's aim also included the broadening of business ties, speedy progress of Russian hold of free waters, and he had no other option but to be friendly with Iran in order to reach his goals. That is why in 1711 he sent his representative to the court of Shah Sultan Hussain. The idea was while negotiating business deals, implicitly he could gather enough information about the coastal cities of the Caspian Sea. Shah Sultan Hussein welcomed this ambassador warmly. The ambassador's good will on behalf of his government resulted in the king's issue of orders to Armenian merchants to take their products from Petersburg to Europe, instead of Izmir and Trabzon routes, specially the silk of Iran that was highly appreciated in Europe of that time.

Iranian products were exported to Europe via sea routes or via Turkey and Aleppo at that time. Peter who had the intentions of occupying southern states of Caspian Sea since long, in 1715 he sent another ambassador named Artmi Volinsky to Safavid court in Isfahan. This man was highly intelligent and wise, and Peter I had given him full authority for these business agreements. Peter I wanted to research southern Caspian states and everything related to them, from deltas to the harbors of the rivers, and also the state of Gilan. That is why Volinsky was asked to gather and bring information about geographical and military conditions, state of harbors, and to discern whether these ports had security posts or not, and the state of mountainous routes and passes, and what the barriers in military expeditions could be. Peter wanted the comprehensive information about the situation of Iran and of the strategic ways before executing his plans so as to reach his destination as soon as possible (Taj Bakhsh, 60).

In addition to that duty, Volinsky had another assignment too, that was, to request Iranian king to allow the Armenian Merchants (silk merchants) to export their product to St. Petersburg via Russian trade routes instead of Izmir and Aleppo. He had also the responsibility to inform Iranian higher authorities that their real enemies are Ottomans, not the Russians. The Russian ambassador arrived in Isfahan in March 1716. During his stay in Isfahan, and his travels along countryside, he studied carefully the socio-economic situation of the country at that time, and then presented a report to Peter I, that how they can conquer Iran easily with a lesser force. He spent his winter in Shamakhi, after his duty was over in 1718. During his travels to Isfahan, as well as on his way back to Russia, he spent some days in Shamakhi (formerly a part of the northern Iranian dominion at that time) and studied the geography of Caucasus during his stay and gathered some important information about the region. He reported to the Russian court that these Caucasian states bear a weak relationship with Iran, and Christian states, particularly Georgia, are more inclined towards Russia, and it was inevitable for Peter to take this point into account.

Peter I evaluated Volinsky's reports, and due to engaging at war with Sweden, Russian did not give up the idea of getting hold of Iran. That's why in fall 1719, Baskakov, one of the Russian military generals, was given the responsibility of the gathering information starting from delta of the river Terek to the coasts of Gilan via land and send his report to higher bodies of Russian military.

After treaty of 1720, Peter got the opportunity to reach his old goal. In spring 1720, Davud Khan of Daghistan made a conspiracy in Lezgia and Daghistan, and caused a lot of damage to the Russian inhabitants of these areas. On the other hand, due to Afghan's attack on Isfahan, Peter found an excellent opportunity to implement his war plan in Iran.

In 1722, under the pretext of the revenge of the innocent blood of the Russian prince, who was killed by an Iranian national, Peter I advanced with 30,000 soldiers and many guerrillas, under his own command, from Astrakhan intending to head towards south via the Volga River route. Before moving, he published his explanation in both Persian and Turkish languages in Shawwal month. He arrived at the Caspian Sea and, thirteen days later, he arrived in the delta of the Terek River, and after occupying Lazia and crossing the passes of Caucasus mountains, captured Darband, Center of Daghistan, the gateway to Iran (Jamal-Zadeh, p.174, 175, Azer. Sov. Ensiklopediasi, Vol. 7, p. 546). Peter, before arriving in Darband, ordered his representative in Iran named Simon Oramov, to express that his aim of military expedition in Caucasus was the destruction of rebels and if Iranian government needs any help for the internal stability against the revolts, he is ready to deploy his troops for helps.

Reducing Baku was not easy for the Russians. Because of the unavailability of food, and the onset of winter, the city could not be conquered. Peter I started heading towards Astrakhan to reach Petersburg and, in his way at the bank of Sulak river in the north, Tamir Khan Shura constructed the fortress that later became famous by the name of the sacred cross or the holy cross (Jamal Zadeh, p.147).

In 1724, Peter exploited the chaos of Iran and succeeded in capturing the attention of the Ottoman Empire by proposing joint efforts for occupation of northern and western provinces of Iran. Ottoman forces, which could never have successfully occupied Iranian territories in the Safavid period due to their sovereignty and strong military force, got an excellent opportunity to compensate for their defeats, and hence accepted the Russian offer. In 1724, an agreement was signed between the two governments, according to which, Russia would get hold of Shirvan, Daghistan, Azarbaijan, Gilan and Mazandaran where as Ottomans would hold Tabriz, Hamedan, Kermanshah and the suburbs adjacent to that (Taj Bakhsh, p. 8).

After the death of Peter in 1725, Anna Ivanova [1730-1740] got into power. She ordered the Russian Army to retreat from the borders of the Caspian Sea to prevent the forthcoming possible problems. The main reasons of pulling back her troops was the outbreak of epidemic disease among soldiers causing many casualties, for example, from 61090 soldiers only 26644 survived. Russian retreat from this fertile region never meant that they were ignoring it, but they were engaged in other important domestic affairs and tensions of the borders with their neighbors, Sweden and Ottomans.

During the reign of Shah Tahmasb II, when he was engaged in military campaign in 1732, some of the Iranian provinces previously separated by Ashraf Afghan in the east were still under Russian control.

Tahmasb Qoli Khan, who was strong enough at that time, proposed that Russia transfer occupied provinces back to Iran. The Russian government was well aware of the strength of this king and, under the agreement of 1732, transferred all of the occupied provinces back to Iran except Baku and Darband. Tahmash Qoli, who had reached the peak of his strength at that time, started his operation to rid Iran of its enemies inside the country and those who acted against her during the instability. First he purged the Russians and advanced toward Ganje where, according to the agreement signed by Russian representative at Ganje, Russia evacuated all of the occupied territory of Iran (Taj Bakhsh p. 8, 9).

The testament of Peter I, after his death, had become the focal point for all Tzars and was followed seriously in the strategies of Russian Empire (even USSR). It was indicated in the testament that India was a source of world's wealth and every obstacle should be moved in its direction and, with the decline and annihiliation of Iran, advancement towards Persian Gulf must ensue.

Russia was at war with Tatars of Crimea and Ottomans from 1735-1739, then with Sweden during 1741-1743, and again with Ottomans during 1768-1774, and again with Sweden from 1788 until 1790.

Katherine II, in her letter to Putumkin, on 22, January 1791, wrote that "It is easy to go to America or Siberia, but going to Caucasus would never be that easy" (Asadov, p. 19-20). By the orders of Putumkin, the army started its military expedition towards the Caspian Sea under the name of military training. Commandership of this Army was on the shoulders of Graf Vinovich, since this military group was on a special duty. Therefore, every military facility and equipment was considered and provided before. He had a confidential meeting with Aqa Mohammad Khan of Qajar and informed him that, in the case oft Iranian military expedition on Caucasus, Russia will not resist at all. In accordance with this decision Graf Vinovich in April 1791 formed a new alliance between Iran and Russia to encourage the revival of old relations. This was another trick of Russia on the execution of which Caucasus turned out to be a bloody battlefield.

At the time of the military expedition of Aqa Mohammad Khan of Qajar in southern Caucasus, Russia, being faithful to its promise, played the role of a spectator. They were waiting for the proper moment for their plans; this way, by the defeat of khans of the region, they could execute their plan of broadening the borders of their Empire (Ibid.).

Aqa Mohammed Khan spent the winter of 1796 in Mughan. As soon as he returned to Iran, the Russian Tzar deviated from his promise. Special military squads under the commandment of general Zubov entered southern Caucasus. He, in the context of his meeting with khans of that region, deceived and encouraged them to be disobedient with Iran and unite them with Russia. The khans of the region one after another, under the commandment of the General, became part of Russian domain. This is how Russia accelerated its occupation of the region in 19th century. Even the unity proposal of Fath'Ali Khan the ruler of Quba was rejected by the khans, and some of them for the sake of security of themselves and their families voluntarily signed the agreements and became subservient to Russia and received Russian nationality. In 1795, preparations for an attack on Iran began. Katherine II, the Empress of Russia at that time, paid special attention to this attack. Zubov had an army of 30,000 soldiers. The attack started from the church where some priests offered special prayers for security and success of the commander and his forces.

The news of this attack reached Caucasus. Christian inhabitants (Armenians and Georgians) and the Armenian priests, hurried with gifts and presents for the reception of Zubov. They arrived in Daghistan before the arrival of the commander, where they asked help from him to get themselves free from Muslims' oppression as soon as possible. Armenian priests succeeded in making the Armenians of Daghistan as their allies. On 2nd of May 1796 Darband surrendered to general Zubov without any resistance. Katherine become delighted with the news of the conquest of Darband and arranged a magnificent celebration. Russia got the key of Darband after 74 years. Zubov conquered Quba afterwards again without facing any resistance. Similarly, Shamakhi conquered without resistance, Zubov reached Caucasus without encountering any obstacles, and the conquest of one city after another surprised him. He sent messages to all of the khans to surrender one after another. Khans of Ghara Bagh, Ganjeh, Talish and Shaki sent their messengers to Zubov announced their surrender. In August, Zubov entered Baku and encamped near the city, he called upon Khan of Baku (Asadov, page, 23-25).

In 1832, after ten years of the bloody wars of Caucasus, waged by the order of Qazi Mulla against Russia, Lermantov, who was on his way to Caucasus via the Darya l passage, from the "Georgia military highway" through Tbilisi to Caucasus, named the River Terek "Death River". At the time, defense castles of the Russians along the northern bank of Terek River were attacked by Muslim warriors, especially upon Iran's borders (Lesley Blanch, p. 249).

To take control of warm waters, Russia was advancing from two directions towards the south, one from Central Asia, from khanates of Kharezm towards Afghanistan, and the other from Caucasus to Iran or Anatolia and then towards the Persian Gulf. This Russian progress towards the south was a threat to British colonies in the subcontinent. That is why the British Empire was against the war between Iran and Ottoman, was against the power imbalance in Caucasus region, wanted the Qajars to stand against Russia in that venture, and gave political and military support to Iran in this regard (training of army personnel, manufacturing and supply of arms). This was because the above mentioned Islamic domains were always the scene of military campaign and a balance of power and a buffer between the Russian and British empires. That is why Erzirum Conference and the Pact of 1847 between Iran and Ottoman brought these expeditions to an end, and the borders between Iran and Ottomans were settled for good. Although, afterwards, Iraq claimed the borders of Shat al-Arab and fought with Iran over this.

The Russians encountered two obstacles in accessing the south. First, the Muslim warriors of Caucasus posed a problem, particularly northern Caucasus (their warriors stood against Russia for 50 years, including the Imam Shamil of Daghistan and his "Imamistan" system in northern Caucasus); then, after the military expedition in southern Caucasus, Iran's defeat in its two wars, and the annexation of this land from Iran with the treaties of Golestan (12 Oct. 1813) and Tukmenchay (10 Feb. 1828), Russia stabilized its presence in northern Caucasus.

Construction of "Vaenno Gruzinskaya Doruga" (the Georgian military Highway) put Russia's southern fields in contact with the narrow valley of Terek River towards Tbilisi, so that Russia could be present in southern Caucasus.

During this time, though both Iran and Ottoman were Islamic governments, they never united and their differences resulted in the weakening of both and paved the way for colonial states of the time to benefit. Russia entered the political scenario of Caucasus and, due to the weakness of both Iranian and Ottomans, they both lost Caucasus to her.

Because of her 1002 km border with Caucasus, Russia is considered to be the biggest and at the same time the most powerful player of the region. The geographical location of Caucasus has historical importance for Russia. The expansion of the Russian Empire started in 1552, after the possession of Kazan, and continued in 1556, after the defeat of Astrakhan by Ivan the Terrible. In 1561, Ivan the Terrible, the strong emperor of Russia and the first Russian Tsar, married Maria Tamirukora, the daughter of the Kabardian prince, as his second wife. At this time, Ivan proceeded from the southern borders of Russia to Terek, where the imprisoned villagers who escaped from Russia resided in Cossacks settlements.

Russia was exploiting every single opportunity to get hold of Caucasus, but its repeated efforts went in vain, not only because of the resistance offered by Caucasus locals in the 16th to 18th centuries, but because the strategic interests of Iran and Ottoman clashed over the security of the region. Due to the two Christian dominated regions in Caucasus, one Armenia (under Iran) and the other Georgia disputed between Iran and Ottomans, the situation of the region become more complicated.

These two Christian principalities used to call help from Russia against the Muslims, and Russia, under the pretext of helping them, started advancing towards the South.

It was inevitable for Russia to pass through the northern Caucasian plains and the high mountain Range of north Caucasus, where there were nomadic tribes of northern Caucasus, who would not allow it to reach southern Caucasus. These tribes were mostly Muslims who used to consider Russians as pagans. That is why, to prevent further Russian advancement towards the south, "Sheikh Mansur" the sheikh (leader) of Chechens, declared Jihad (the holy Islamic war), and this Jihad lasted for 6 years blocking Russia from further advancement.

In addition to providing help to the Christian principalities of Caucasus, Russia had the aim of holding the natural borders of Caucasus. When they encountered the high mountain and the resistance of the locals, Russia had no more intentions of passing through the above mentioned mountains. In 1784, in the passage of Caucasus Mountains, Russian government constructed a military fortress named "Valdikavkaz" (lord of Caucasus). Also in the passage of the Terek valley, a natural gateway to Caucasus called "Daryal Passage" (Bab-al-Allan) was constructed; after that, Russia's military command took hold of the construction of the military road of Georgia itself. The road was finished in 1799, and "Paul", emperor of Russia (son of Katherine II), sent the Russian army to Tbilisi. This was the first Russian attack on the south. After that, Heraclius II, the king of Georgia, signed a treaty with Russia, according to which, Georgia was severed from Iran and annexed to Russia.

After these invasions, two periods of war took place between Iran and Russia. As a result of the first period of these wars (1803-1813), the Golestan treaty (Oct. 1813) was imposed, and according to that, the whole region situated to the north of the river Arax, comprising the provinces of Qara Bagh and Ganjeh, khanate of Shaki, Shirvan, Quba, Darband, Badkube, Talish, Daghistan regions, Georgia, Shuregul district, Guria, Mengrelia, Abzhazia and Achuq Bash, were given to Russia.

The boundary lines between Iran and Russia in Caucasus, in a northwest to southeast direction, according to the 2nd Article of Golestan treaty, were as follows:

From the beginning of Adineh Bazar: lands to the right of Mughan plain, to the passage of Yeddi Boluk of Aras (Arax) River; and from the above of Aras bank, to the confluence and junction of Kapanak Chayi; and from there, beyond [Saman] of Qarabagh, Nakhchivan and Iravan [Yerevan] provinces. Also, the bondaries of Ganjeh that connected from mentioned limits that separate the Velayats of Iravan, Ganjeh, and also the limits of Qazagh and Shamseddinlu; to the Eshak Meydan. From the watersheds of right side mountains, the routes and rivers, Hamzeh Chaman and Palang mountains, to the corner of the Mahal [district] of Shureh Goul, and from the corner of Shureh Goul, passed from the above of the mentioned snow-covered mountains, and from the frontier of the Mahal of Shureh Goul and the middle border of the Mesdareh and Artik villages, the boundary joined the Arpachay River. Because of the condition of the Khanate of Talish, which was exchanged hands to hands during the enmity, the borders of Velayat of Talish, from Ardebil and Anzali sides, after ratification of this peace pact on behalf of great kings and engineers, by using the knowledge of both sides of mountains, rivers and lakes and places, the borders should be limited.

Also, as a result of a second period of wars (1825-1828), in addition to the above mentioned domains, all areas of Nakhchivan and Yerevan were also given to Russia. According to the Turkmenchay treaty (Feb. 1828), almost all of the current borders of Iran in the northwest took their final shape.

The documents of the limitation of the border line between Iran and Russia in Caucasus, which were signed between the state commissaries in Bahram Tappeh in Mughanin, 18th, January 1829, were revised with both sides in agreement in 1954. According to the agreement between Iran and the Soviet Union on the 2nd of December 1954, which was signed in Tehran, Ghal'e Abbas Abad, the only Russian building and novelty that was an exception in the natural border line along the Aras River (which passed the width of the river and came down to the left bank), rectified, and the castle and its area was given to Iran. To replace it, the Firuze village in the north eastern border of Iran with the Soviet Union was left to Soviets. In 1954, the border lines between the two countries, with changes in a few cases, according to the Bahram Tappeh treaty, were laid on a map with the scale of 1:100,000.

Causes of Iran's Defeat and Defining Borders

From the beginning of Safavid's reign and the establishment of central and national governments in Iran in the early 16th century, and the strengthening of Iran and the Ottoman Empire in Asia endangered the interests of the western powers of Europe. That's why these powers were planning to weaken the Iran and Ottoman nations. Although the wars between Iran and Ottoman occurred in line with Shiite-Sunni clashes, it is only the one side of picture; the actual motive was geopolitical rivalries between them.

Great Britain, by colonizing the Indian subcontinent, had expanded its colonies, and the expansion of Russian and Ottoman Empires towards the south was an alarming sign for her. Therefore, it was necessary to take measures to engage these nations in regional wars, so they wouldn't be able to perform any military expeditions towards the south.

The Persian sphere of influence since the Achaemenid kings was attractive to Russian Tsars. During the reign of Shah Abbas the Great, Russia, with the help of Georgian leaders strove to increase its political and economic influence in that region. Gradually, after the death of Shah Abbas I, Russian Tsars found the time suitable to capture Georgia and come to the neighborhood of Caucasus. Russia was waiting for the successor of Shah Abbas I to show a minor weakness and slackness; then, she would exploit this opportunity and increase her influence on Georgia.

Russia's spectacular progress in Poland attracted the attention of Georgian authorities towards Russia, and stimulated better conditions and possibilities for their friendship than ever before.

Khans and rulers of Georgia used to seek help from Russia against Iran to liberate them from Islamic domination. In 1558, Levan, the governor of Kakheti, asked Ivan IV, the Tsar of Russia, for help. During the reign of Shah Abbas I, Alexander, the governor of Georgia, also asked for help from Buris Godnov, Russian Tsar, against Iran. In 1619, Tahmuris, the commander of Georgia, sent an ambassador to the court of M. Feodorovich, the founder of Romanov family, and asked him to stop Iran's influence in and interference with Georgia.

In 1780, Heraclius succeeded in his efforts to attract Russia's attention towards Georgia. He wanted to detach his country from Iran.

During the time of Agha Mohammad, Heraclius made a pact with Empress Katherine II in 1782; according to this, Georgia's foreign policy went under the control of the Russian Empress.

Agha Mohammed was afraid of the daily increasing influence of Russia in Georgia. He wrote a letter to persuade Georgia to obey Iranian law, but he received the answer, "Georgia doesn't recognize anyone else but the Russian Empress."

Heraclius's impudent answer urged Agha Mohammed to attack beyond Caucasus with fifty thousand troops in the summer of 1795. In September of the same year, he occupied Tbilisi, capital of Georgia and ruined the city. Katherine, after hearing the news of the defeat of Georgia and the escape of Heraclius, ordered Count Godovich to attack Iran. During this battle, Russians were able to capture Darband and advanced towards Badkube (Baku), occupying Lankran and the coasts of Gilan, targeting areas of Rasht and Anzali from there. After the death of Katherine II and assassination of Agha Mohammed Khan in 1796 in Shushi, the military expeditions came to their end by the orders of "Paul I", and Russians evacuated Shirvan, Sheki, and Georgia, but the following events ensued:

- Alexander I, son of Paul I declared Georgia's annexation with Russia and established government offices, employing Russian officers.
- After the accession of Fath 'Ali Shah to the Iranian throne, Georgia again attracted the attention of Shah of Iran. He began thinking how to restore Georgia's annexation to Iran.
- Georgia started its wars with the first commanders of joint forces, General Tsisisyanov, an indigenous of Georgia. After General Tsisiyanov's assassination in the hands of Hussein Qoli Khan, the ruler of Baku, Count Ivan Vasiliyevich Godovich was assigned in his place. Count Godovich faced the Iranian Viceroy Abbas Mirza, and had a tough war in Nakhchivan, where Russia faced defeat four years later. Godovich changed his direction and General Termuzov took over in Georgia.

- Because of the importance of Caucasus for Russia, most successors of Russian Tsars were assigned to run the affairs and were sent to Tbilisi. Similarly, military commanders and army officers' positions were assumed by Russian princes. Zubov, Sisiyanov, Bolgakov, Yermolov, Paskovich, Madatov, Vorentsov and tens of other politicians (like, Gribayedov) participated in deciding Georgia's fate and were responsible for imposing the treaties that exploited Russia and Iran's backwardness.
- Continuation of the dispersed wars in the borders areas.

References Relating to Iran-Russia Wars in Caucasus

Russian, European, and U.S. historiographic sources have always discussed positively the expansion of Russian domain towards south and possession of Islamic territories, such as Crimea, Volga River regions, Mesopotamia, northern and southern Caucasus. They have never considered the historical references, travel stories, and the memorandums of well reputed impartial personalities and national authorities; either they didn't deem it necessary to use them or they did not have access to such references. In fact, poor historiography and one-sided justifications about the Iranian treatment of the people of the region were the basis of assessing Russian occupation of Caucasus as the liberation of those nations from the brutalities and oppressions of the Muslims: Iranians and Ottomans.

The analysis of local references reveal that the people of this region, after Russian possession of their land, revolted against it and forced the Russians to evacuate of their land, as they wished to return to their previous status or get Iranian nationality.

Under both the Tzars and the Soviets, Caucasian references have always assessed the occupation of Caucasus as the liberalization of Caucasian nations from Muslim oppression. An interesting point is that S. Azeri, one of the modern historians of the republic of Azerbaijan, like many other Azerbaijanian historians in Soviet time and present who distort the facts, in his book "History of Azerbaijan" introduces the Safavids as an Azerbaijani government instead of as an Iranian state. He is also the first one who, after the disintegration of S.U., expressed that Russian advancement towards Caucasus was the invasion and possession of the Islamic territory, but he claimed that this invasion was the possession of Azerbaijan's territory, not of Iran's land. We should recall that, as it is clear to the political and historical circles and international organizations, these territories officially and legally belonged to Iran before 1813 and 1828, and the treaties signed by Iran and Russia – recognized by the representatives of Britain and France who witnessed the process – as well as bilateral treaties between Iran and Russia on Caucasus, including the treaties of Ganja, Rasht, Istanbul, Golestan and Turkmenchy, were all signed by Iran, not by Azerbaijan (which did not exist before 1918).

The following references can be considered as samples, in this regard.

Khanak Eshqi in his analysis about the dissatisfaction of Caucasian people writes: temporary advancement of Russia in combat against Iran and defeat of rebellions of Imereti, Quba and Ossetia and the establishment of law and order in this region was considered to be a great success for Russians so that they could succeed in strengthening beyond the regions of Caucasus exploiting their political, military and social status and utilizing the advantages of the territory was yet another success.

But there were several different factors that not only outshine all those conquests but were effective in revealing the obscurities of Iran-Russian ties equally, that become the reason of ten year wars between the two governments.

The summary of some of those factors are as follows:

1- Misbehavior of Russian commanders in Akhal-Tsikhe and dissatisfaction of inhabitants of this region with Russia.
2- Inadequate behavior of Russian Tsars toward Iran and destruction of the border regions.
3- Possession of different border regions of Iran by Russian armed forces.
4- Oppression and injustice of Russian officials in South Caucasus.
5- Disobedience of inhabitants of Caucasus of the orders of Russian officers.
6- Expansion of injustice and unhappiness of inhabitants of South Caucasus with the Iranian settlers of that region.
7- Effect of Ottoman and English policies in agitating the inhabitants and restoration of the regions occupied by Russia.

According to the varying factors indicated above, there is no doubt that the wars between Iran and Russia became definite and very near. Then in the fall 1811, a nasty war and bloody combat took place between the Iranian forces and the Russian commanders that lasted for about 10 years without break (History of Iran Russia relationship, p. 138-139).

H. Abadian indicates that the causes of Iran's defeat in these wars were affected by two external and an internal factors. From external point of view, the powerful nations of that time, such as France and Britain, signed treaties with Iran and promised many things to Iran but never observed the agreements themselves until they found Russia threatening their own interests, and were at war with her; whereas, Iran always fulfilled her side of the bargains, and if Iranian government had invested more in general volunteers, they were more likely to achieve further successes.

Long wars between Iran and the Ottoman Empire weakened and consequently depreciated the power and wealth of the two sides, resulting in their elimination from Moslem domain of Central Asia. Russia expanded its domains from north towards south and strengthened its position and, from the 19th century to the last decade of the 21st century (almost two centuries), held the fate of Muslims in that region, as a result of above mentioned wars (Iranian narration about Iran Russia wars of 1218-1228 Hijra).

References

+ **Cossacks** are Slavian tribes in south of Russia, on the lands of Stavvropol, Krasnodar and near the rivers of Don, Kuban and Terek. In Persian they are known as Kazakhs and are mistaken in other languages with the Tuskish speaking Kazakhs of Central Asia. It should be taken into account that in Persian language Cossacks (Kazakhs) of Don (stories: Kazakhs written by Tolstoy and Pacific Don by Sholokhov) and Kazaks of Central Asia (Kazakhistan) both are called Kazakhs.

1- Abadian, H .*Ravayat-e-Irani-ye Jangha-ye Iran va Rus*) The Iranian Narrative of Iran-Russia Wars), Tehran IPIS, 1380(2001 .(
2- Abdullayev, F. *Gushehayi az Tarikh-e-Iran* (Some Part of Iranian History), Translated by Gh. Matin, Tehran, 1336(1957).
3- Ahmadi, H .*Taleshan, az Dore-ye-Safaviye ta Payan-e-Jang-e-Dovom-e-Iran va Rus*) Talishs from the Period of Safavids till the End of Iran-Russia Second War) Tehran IPIS, 1380(2001.(
4- *Asnadi az Moa'hedat-e-Iran ba Mantaghe-ye-Qafqaz* (Documents of Treaties of Iran with Caucasus Region), Institute for International and Political Studies (IPIS), Tehran 1372(1993).
5- Asadov, F; Karimova, S. *Charizmi Azarbaijana Gatiranlar*) The bearer of Tsarism to Azerbaijan), Ganjlik Publisher, Baku 1993.
6- Afshar Yazdi, M. *Siyasat-e-Urupa dar Iran* (The Policy of Europe in Iran), Tehran 1358(1979).
7- *Asnad-e-Ravabet-e-Iran va Rusiye az Dorey-e-Naseraddin Shah Ta Suqut-e-Qajariye, 1267-1344 Hijri*) The Documents of Iran-Russia Relation from 1851-1925, (Tehran IPIS, 1380(2001).
8- *Asnad-e-Ravabet-e-Iran ba Sayer-e-Doval, Qesmat-e-Dovom, Shamel-e-Moa'hedat-e-Iran ba Shoravi* (The Documents of Iran-Russia Relation) (Including the Documents of Iran-Soviet Treaties), Tehran IPIS, 1380(2001).
9- Benigson, a; Broxup, M. *Mosalmanan-e-Shoravi* (Muslims of Soviet Union), Translated by K. Bayat, Tehran 1370 (1991).
10- Broxup, M. and others ,*Baruye Shomal-e-Qafqaz* (North Caucasus Barrier), Translated by Tahami, Gh, Tehran 1377(1998).
11- Eshghi, Khanak .*Siyasat-e-Nezami-ye-Rusiye dar Iran* 91790-1815 (Russian Military Policy in Iran, 1790-1815), Tehran 1353(1974).
12- Jamal Zadeh. M. A .*Tarikh-e-Ravabet-e-Iran va Rus* (The History of Iran-Russia Relations), Tehran 1372 (1993).
13- Lankarani, M. A, Akhbarnameh ,*Tarikh-e-Khanat-e-Talesh dar Zaman-e-Jangha-ye-Rusiye Aleyh-e-Iran* (Akhbar Nameh, the History of Talish Khanate During the Russian Oppressed War Against Iran), Tehran IPIS, 1380 (2001).
14- Kulagina, L. M. ; Dunayeva, E V .*Granitsa Rossii s Iranom (Istoria Formirovania)*, Rossiskaya Akademiya Nauk, Inastitut Vostokovedenia. Moskva, 1998. (Boundaries of Russia with Iran, History of Formation) Institute for Eastern Studies. Academy of Sciences of Russia, Moscow 1998.
15- Taj Bakhsh, A .*Siyasatha-ye-Rusiye-ye-Tezari ,Engelestan va Faranse dar Iran* (Colonial Policies of Russian Empire, England and France in Iran), Tehran 1362 (1983).

IRAN'S NORTHERN BOUNDARIES

Section A2 – Iran's Boundaries in the Caspian Sea

CHAPTER IV

A Review of the Oil and Gas Prospects of the Iranian Sector of the Caspian Sea and the Surrounding Areas
Mohammad Ali Ala

Iran's Ministry of Petroleum has been quoted as having stated that the *'Iranian sector of the Caspian Sea contains 20 billion barrels of proven oil reserves'*. This article reviews the meanings of the term *'reserves'* as used in the oil industry, reflects on whether the use of the term *'proven reserves'* is appropriate in the case of the Iranian Caspian sector and finally assesses the oil and gas prospects of this area in light of the available technical information.

Definition of *'Resources''*

First and foremost, it should be noted that *'reserves'* are always estimates of the quantities of oil and gas that are deemed to be ultimately recoverable from a given field or area. These estimates are based on a number of variables and assumptions and, as such, are subject to differing degrees of uncertainty. Furthermore, reserves tend to be a dynamic rather than a static quantity in the life cycle of an oil or gas field: the figures are regularly revised as new data become available during production. In the majority of cases, fields ultimately yield more petroleum than their originally estimated reserves.

Reserves are classified into several categories depending on the degree of confidence in the computed value of the estimate and these are briefly reviewed below:

In-place Reserves

This refers to the total volume of oil or gas that is present in a field before any production. It is known as the *stock tank oil initially in place* and abbreviated to **STOIIP**. This quantity is not all recoverable. The recoverable fraction is highly variable and depends on the nature of the reservoir, the production mechanism and the characteristics of the oil.

Proven Reserves

Economically, this is the most important category and refers to oil or gas in existing fields that can be produced from existing wells.

Probable Reserves

This category includes oil or gas in extensions of existing fields beyond or below the currently known limits.

Possible Reserves

This is oil or gas expected from future discoveries in areas or formations known to be productive.

Undiscovered Reserves

This category is subject to the greatest degree of uncertainty and refers to the quantity of oil and gas that could be found in an area.

Iranian Caspian Sector

Geologically, the Iranian Caspian sector falls in the South Caspian Basin (Fig 1). The sedimentary section of the South Caspian Basin reaches an estimated total thickness of 15,000 m and contains substantial oil and gas deposits in Azerbaijan and Turkmenistan (Figs 2 and 3). The key to its productivity in these countries is the delta systems built up over several million years by the Volga, Kura and Amu Darya (formerly the Uzboi) rivers. Worldwide, deltas are associated with prolific oil and gas production and examples include the Niger Delta in West Africa and the Mackenzie Delta in northern Canada.

Figure 3

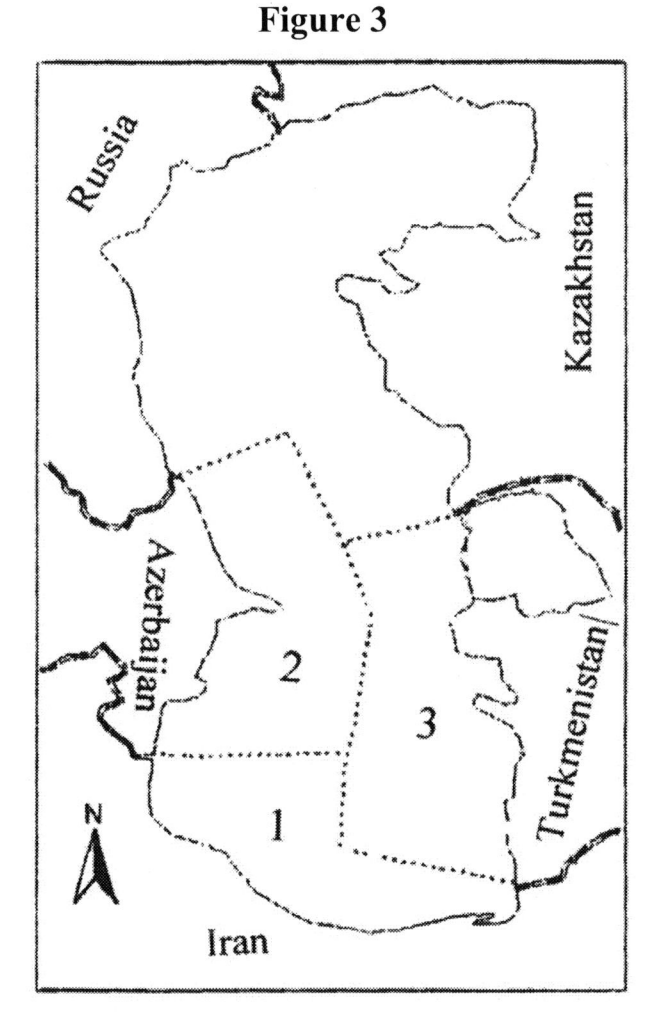

*Iran 1, Azerbaijan Republic 2, and Turkmenistan 3
sectors in the Caspian Sea*

In the Iranian sector, there is a potential delta development associated with the Sefid Rud River. However, the Iranian sector remains under-explored and the area requires a detailed and systematic study. Only three exploration wells have been drilled here by the National Iranian Oil Company (NIOC) since 1989: two in the eastern end and one in the western part of the area. The results of this drilling activity are summarised in the following table:

Well	Date	Depth reached (m)	Results
Meghdad	1995	5,964	Gas shows
Meysam	1996	5,140	
Khazar	1989	5,570	Gas shows

In December 1998 Shell and LASMO (now part of the Italian ENI/Agip Group) signed an exploration study agreement with the NIOC for the Iranian sector of the Caspian Sea, a large under-explored area. Veba (now part of Petro Canada) joined Shell and LASMO in late 1999 and the group has acquired 10,000 km of 2D seismic data in the Iranian sector. The processing and interpretation of the data have been completed, representing the first integrated evaluation of the area, and several large prospects are reported to have been identified. Under the terms of the agreement, the group is entitled to select up to 6 blocks, each about 2,000 km^2 in area, for further detailed exploration. However, progress in this regard has been slow since the prospects identified lie in relatively deep water (300-500m) in border area in dispute with Azerbaijan.

By analogy with the Azerbaijani and Turkmen parts of the basin, the Iranian Caspian sector must be considered to have significant potential. To test this potential, the NIOC has announced its intention to commence drilling in the Caspian in 2004. It is in the process of completing the construction of a semi-submersible rig capable of drilling in water depths of up to 1,000m.

Moghan Area

Situated in the north-eastern corner of Iranian Azarbaijan (Fig 3), the Moghan area contains a sedimentary section reaching a total thickness of more than 10,000 m in places and bears similarities to the petroliferous sequence of the Baku region.

There are oil and gas seeps in outcrops along the southern margin of the area and several exploration wells were drilled here by the NIOC in the late 1960s. Two discoveries of high quality oil were made at Ortadagh and Ghir Darreh with estimated in-place reserves of 2-3 billion barrels. Flow rates of up to 200 barrels per day were obtained from two of the wells. However, the poor quality of the reservoirs and the price of oil at that time (about $2 per barrel) made the development of the accumulations uneconomic.

Applications of modern recovery techniques to increase reservoir performance should be investigated. Also, the area remains under-explored and may have additional potential. It merits further exploratory drilling and its proximity to the Tabriz refinery, with a processing capacity of 112,000 barrels per day; about 170 km to the southwest is an additional favourable factor.

Conclusions

- The attribution of *'proven reserves'* to the Iranian sector of the Caspian Sea is inappropriate and inconsistent with the oil industry definition of the term.
- By analogy with the petroliferous regions of Baku to the west and Turkmenistan to the east, the Iranian Caspian sector must be considered to have significant potential.
- The Iranian sector of the Caspian Sea and its surrounding areas are under-explored and merit systematic exploration activity.

CHAPTER V

Perspectives on the Caspian Sea Dilemma: An Iranian Construct

Pirouz Mojtahed-Zadeh and
Mohammad Reza Hafeznia

Introduction

Prior to the disintegration of the Soviet Union at the end of 1991, the Caspian Sea was a closed water body bordered by the USSR and Iran. Its use, nearly solely for navigation, tended to be regulated by a series of bilateral agreements between those two countries. However, the new geopolitical climate emerging after the fall of the Soviet Union in late 1991 called into question the pre-existing legal regime, affording Iran (as well as the four newly independent countries of Russia, Azerbaijan, Kazakhstan, and Turkmenistan, which replaced the USSR around the sea) a long-awaited opportunity to assert its claim to Caspian resources as well as bolster its national interests in the region. This paper briefly outlines, from an Iranian perspective, the historical background and geopolitical environment in which efforts to develop a legal regime for the sea are being undertaken. Since Iran is a major regional power and its position and interests in the region have been discussed less widely in the ongoing Caspian debate, special emphasis is placed here on the way Iran defines its interests in relation to the Caspian issue (see also Mojtahed-Zadeh, 1998, and Hafeznia, 1999). These interests date not from the recent international focus on energy exploration, but from several centuries in which Iran has sought to assert and defend its stake in this vitally important water body.

Historical Background (1)

Iran's efforts to maintain sovereignty over what it considers its legitimate interests in the Caspian Sea date back much earlier from the present post-Soviet context, and for that matter from the period from 1917 to 1991, when it shared jurisdiction over the water body with the Soviet Union. In the 1723 Treaty of Alliance, Persia ceded the cities of Derbent and Baku, and its then-northern provinces of Mazandaran, Ghilan, and Asterabad to the Russian Empire, making the sea in effect a Russian lake.(2) From this date onward a consistent theme in Iranian diplomacy has been the country's effort to regain a measure of sovereignty and influence over the Caspian.(3) Lost provinces and cities were eventually restored to Iran, but the sea itself, reflecting Imperial Russia's foreign policy objective of blocking the Ottoman Empire's access to the sea (Sykes, 1951, p. 254), remained under Russian hegemony. An example of this control was the 1746 embargo that Russian vessels enforced on all British trade with Persia (ibid.).

Following the Russo-Persian Wars of 1804–1813 and 1826–1828, Russian commercial vessels exercised the right to navigate the entire Caspian and its shoreline, and only Russian naval vessels, to the exclusion of all other powers, were granted the right to sail throughout the Caspian (Treaty, 1828). Thus it is not surprising that Russia's navy was able to establish, over Persian protests, a naval station on an island in the south-eastern Caspian in 1840. This period was accompanied by Russian expansion, on land, into areas of present-day Turkmenistan that were claimed by Persia. The Russo-Persian land boundary east of the Caspian was finally demarcated by the 1881 Boundary Convention as beginning at Hassangholi Bay and extending eastward along the Atrek River, and was more finely delineated via two protocols in 1886.

The Bolshevik Revolution of 1917 in Russia ushered in a new stage in the legal regime governing use of the Caspian, although not immediately, as the Russian Civil War and instability in the aftermath of World War I hindered the Bolsheviks' efforts to consolidate power and secure the new borders of the Soviet Union. Gradually, Iran's rather limited rights in the Caspian Sea region were augmented by the signing of a number of legally binding instruments with the Soviet Union. Of note is the 1921 Treaty of Moscow, which restored Iran's use of the sea for navigation that had been prohibited by the 1828 Treaty of Turkmenchai (see Treaty, 1828, 1921). Also of similar significance (albeit of little practical substance) was the bilateral Iran-USSR Trade and Seafaring Agreement (Agreement, 1940). De jure, the legal use regime began to resemble more a jointly held "Soviet and Iranian sea" than a "Russian lake." Although the former Soviet Union officially recognized Iran's rights in the Caspian through these treaties and the Convention of Establishment, Commerce, and Navigation (ECN) of 1931 and 1935, (4) *de facto* it never fully respected Iranian claims to Caspian resources and navigation rights. During the Cold War, despite some cooperation between the Soviet Union and Iran in natural gas trade and arms transfers (Saivetz, 1989), Iran was not allowed to maintain a naval presence in the Caspian: Moscow even frustrated Iran's attempt in the 1950s at onshore petroleum exploration in its northern coastal province of Mazandaran. More interestingly, even Britain, the wartime ally of Soviet Union, appreared to support Moscow's dictatorial behaviour towards Iran's rights in South Caspian shores and interfering in her domestic affairs. Disregarding the fact that the Soviets had created a confusion by mixing the US oil companies' prospecting for oil in Iran's Caspian shores with other activities of US representatives in Iran, a confidential report to the British Foreign Office, Britain's diplomatic mission in the Soviet Union states:

> *As regard the Soviet Government's note to the Persian Government of 31st January, 1948 in which the Persian Government's attention was drawn to the fact that the activities of military and other US representatives in Persia were translating the territory of Iran into a military-strategic base of the USA, this series of facts, despite the statements contained in the Persian Government's note of 18th May, 1949, shows the complete validity of the Soviet Governmental statement"* (5).

Observation of the Geopolitical Setting

One dimension of the geopolitical environment surrounding efforts to arrive at a legal regime for the Caspian is Iran's strategic location between that water body and the oil-rich Persian Gulf. In fact the country occupies a pivotal position among the states of the Caspian region, all of which, except for Iran, are either landlocked or have limited access to open seas. The importance of this Caspian-Central Asian region, and Iran's position within it, has been noted by a number of Western observers (e.g. Kemp, 1997, pp.14-16; Kullberg, 2000, p.1; Bonine 2003, p.1) clearly Iran offers an attractive, the shortest, and arguably the most economical route for the export of the region's hydrocarbon resources to outside markets (e.g., see Bonine, 2003, p.27), and already possesses infrastructure (ports, refineries, pipelines) that could be utilized as part of a framework to support such export activities. (6) Nonetheless, largely for political reasons and more specifically the fact that the United States views of Iran as a major source of insecurity in the region (an exporter of Islamic revolution and supporter of terrorism), the focus has been on the search for and development of alternative routes to bypass Iran, such as Baku-Tbilisi-Ceyhan and Caspian Pipeline consortium route through southern Russia to Novorossiysk on the Black Sea.

Compounding the particularly unfriendly relationship with the United States, which included Iran in its post-September 11 "axis of evil" states supporting terrorism, Iran has had strained relations with most of its neighbours over the past several decades (e.g. see Bonine 2003, p.22). This highly unfavourable political climate, as well as the Iranian Foreign Ministry's inconsistent proposals regarding demarcation (either that the entire sea be declared a condominium or that 20 percent of the sea be allocated to each of the five littoral states) has limited Iran's opportunities to seek a multilateral, negotiated solution to the Caspian Sea legal regime. Iran has sought to counter efforts to isolate it geopolitically by actively participating and in some cases sponsoring organizations promoting regional economic cooperation. The Economic Cooperation Organization (ECO), for example, includes the Muslim republics of Azerbaijan, Kazakhstan, Turkmenistan, Uzbekistan, Tajikistan, Kyrgyzstan, Afghanistan and the old members of Regional Cooperation for Development (RCD), namely Iran, Turkey, and Pakistan.(7) Internal rifts and rivalries have made attainment of an effective alliance among the member states difficult.(8) Another problem hampering the ECO regional grouping relates to the fact that its Caspian–Central Asian members are also part of the Commonwealth of Independent States (CIS). The latter organization was established in 1991 to assume some of the functions of the former Soviet Union, but Russia's dominant role keeps it from being an organization of equals.

In an effort to overcome these difficulties complicating efforts to develop a widely accepted legal regime for the Caspian Sea, Iran in 1992 formed the Council of Caspian Sea Countries (CCSC), an organization intended to include the five littoral states. Although this council has been slow to define its specific role in the region, it nevertheless has the potential to provide a more workable forum for dealing with the immediate affairs of the region than either the ECO or the CIS.

Many Iranians, based on their historical experience, view contemporary maneuvering among U.S., Russian, Iranian, Turkish, and other interests in and around the Caspian as disturbingly similar to the Great Game of geopolitics played out by British and Russian powers in 19th century Central Asia, a game resulting in extensive territorial losses by Persia/Iran (e.g., Koolaee, 1998). From this perspective, concerns have arisen in Iran that a regime carving up the Caspian into national sectors could produce a similar outcome—loss of territorial and economic rights legitimately accruing to Iran.

These concerns have been heightened by the post–September 11, 2001 American military activity and presence in Afghanistan and Iraq. Similarly unsettling is the maintenance of military bases in Central Asia, and most recently (in August 2003) joint naval exercises involving Azerbaijani ships and sailors and U.S. Navy officers (see *Russkiy kur'yer*, August 16, 2003, p. 6).(9) Also worrisome to Teheran is the more active Russian naval presence in the Caspian, as evidenced by naval exercises accompanying Russian President Vladimir Putin's visit to Baku in January 2001 (Golotyuk, 2001), and later by maneuvers conducted by Russia's Caspian Flotilla in August 2002. Russia continues to project itself as the main power in the Caspian region, and has sufficient leverage to claim a dominant role and the right to promote a predominantly

Russocentric geopolitical vision for the region. These developments raise doubts about Russia's stated desire that the region remain an independent geostrategic entity, and have complicated Russia's geostrategic cooperation with Iran. Furthermore, they give credence to Iranian fears that Iran's regional interests are being threatened by an American-led coalition to militarize the entire region.

Post-Soviet Approaches to Demarcation

In its Caspian policies, Iran has arguably placed itself in a difficult position by modifying its position on the legal settlement of the Caspian Sea issue at different times. However, other littoral states, most notably Russia, also have articulated differing positions in the post-Soviet period as well. In debates over demarcation of the Caspian in the early 1990s, Iran articulated a position sometimes identifiable with Russia's initial approach—that the Caspian Sea should be a condominium or an "area of common use" for the littoral states. Similar to Moscow's position prior to late 1996, Tehran argued that the Soviet-Iranian treaties of 1921 and 1940 should determine the legal status of the Caspian Sea as a condominium.

However, in late 1996, Russia's position changed (10) to one that favoured exploring the possibility of dividing the seabed within a 45-mile coastal zone into national sectors, with the interior portion of the sea continuing to be administered as a condominium. This general, multilateral concept was followed in early 1998 by an agreement in principle between Russia and Kazakhstan to demarcate their adjacent sectors (Blum, 1998a, p. 149; Sciolino, 1998, p. WK16).

By this time, a growing number of parties, including some in Iran (e.g., The Legal Regime, 1998) came to see as impractical the establishment of a condominium legal regime for the entire length and breadth of the Caspian as well. The Iranian government, apparently also arriving at this conclusion, now seems more open to the concept of some form of maritime division. A joint communiqué issued in Tehran by the deputy foreign ministers of Iran and Russia as early as July 1998, proclaimed that, as far as the two states were concerned, a "con-dominium" legal regime would remain effective until a new regime, acceptable to all parties involved, could be elaborated for the Caspian (see What Is Happening, 2003). In the interim, Iran has endeavoured to involve its state-owned companies in oil and gas development, as well as to try to initiate export projects with Azerbaijan, Kazakhstan, and Turkmenistan. (11) Some analysts of the region consider these to signal a growing willingness on the part of Tehran to proceed with the development of Caspian resources without waiting for the realization of a comprehensive settlement delimiting offshore areas (see Horton and Mamedov, 2000).

Officials of the Iranian Foreign Ministry have in recent times, such as the 2002 summit meeting of leaders of the Caspian countries in Ashgabat, (12) advanced a different concept: that, if some division of the seabed into economic zones is *fait accompli*, then the division should be into five equal parts (20 percent) among the littoral states. In April 2002, in the wake of the summit, which generated no accord, Russian President Putin stated that if agreement on Caspian issues could not be accomplished multilaterally, Russia would seek to "settle individual issues bilaterally with its neighbours" (Shiryayev, 2002, p. 2). Shortly thereafter, in May and September 2002, Russia signed protocols demarcating its relevant maritime areas of the Caspian with Kazakhstan and Azerbaijan, respectively (see *Daily Iran* [Teheran, in Persian], May 23, 2002, p. 3; Ignatova and Grigoryeva, 2002; Reutov, 2002). These actions were seen in Tehran as formulas designed to put pressure on other Caspian states, particularly Iran, to come to terms with Moscow's new approach to a Caspian legal regime.

Figure 4

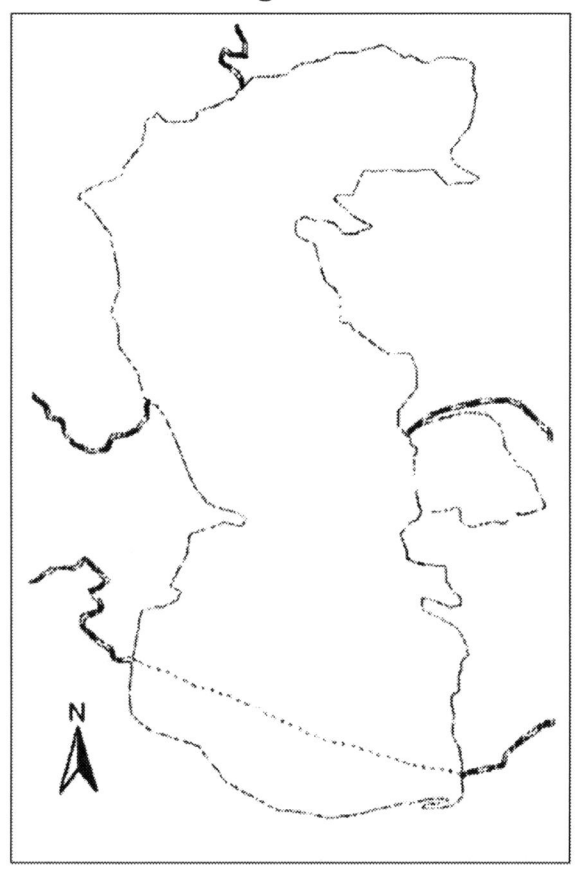

Imaginary Astara-Hassangholi line, claimed by Azerbaijan and Kazakhstan as having been imposed by the Soviet Union as the northern limit of Iran's claim to the Caspian Sea. The authors' examination of relevant archival material in Iran revealed no evidence that such a line has any historical or legal basis.

Is a Viable Solution Possible?

A definitional conundrum resides at the heart of the current dispute over the Caspian. Although the Caspian Sea hydrologically is a "lake" and not an open sea, and therefore is not subject to the logic of international conventions for open seas (e.g., the 1982 Convention on the Law of the Sea), its size and international significance defy this traditional definition.(13) It is a unique case, and given its singularity and strategic significance, a legal regime specific to the Caspian is in order; continued development of energy resources in the absence of a clearly defined legal regime could lead to serious conflicts.

As described above, from the collapse of the Soviet regime to the present, the debates over a legal regime for the Caspian Sea have featured two main positions: 1) "common use" (condominium); and 2) the division of the sea bed into exclusive economic zones among its littoral states in an approach resembling international regulations pertaining to open seas.

Figure 5

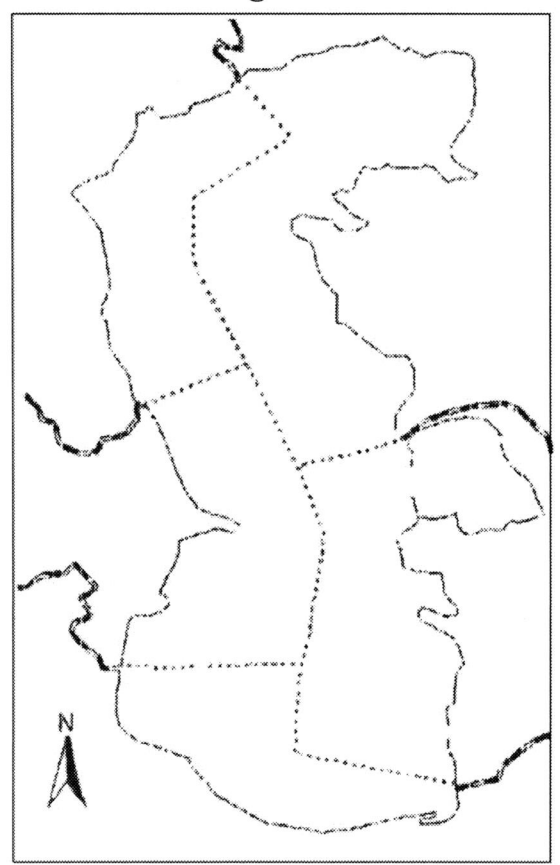

Boundaries in the Caspian based upon an equal division of the sea surface, seabed, and subsoil.

Currently, there appears to be movement in the latter direction, toward an agreement in which the territorial rights of each state would be delimited clearly. Such an agreement would clear the way to development of Caspian resources, but differences among the littoral states remain complicated and serious. In the search for a solution, the interests of each of the five Caspian littoral states should be taken into account. Iran's position is that it is an independent state whose relations with the states emerging in the wake of the Soviet Union's collapse are dictated by international relations. In such a situation, it is clear that the domestic decisions of one state with respect to maritime arrangements cannot be binding on others unless such arrangements are officially accepted and signed by all interested parties.

If the Caspian littoral states were to accept the terms of the 1982 UN Convention on the Law of the Sea as a starting point for effecting the demarcation of economic zones, maritime boundary lines could only be defined by extending out to sea land boundaries at the angle at which they intersect the shoreline. Such a boundary could not be broken suddenly at the shoreline and made to extend out to sea in a diagonal fashion, as traced by the so-called Astara-Hassangholi line (Fig. 1) (14). Under such delineation, Iran's coastal sector would be so small that it would be virtually impossible to maintain a navy or to conduct offshore exploration for oil and natural gas. In keeping with international practice, if the Caspian legal regime were to be decided on the basis of generally accepted principles for dividing seas, the Iranian-Azeri and Iranian-Turkmenistan boundary lines would be drawn in a horizontal direction out to the middle of the sea (Fig. 2). These boundary lines would be drawn in a similar fashion should the Caspian legal regime be based on defining a 40-to-45 mile exclusive economic zone for each of the littoral states.

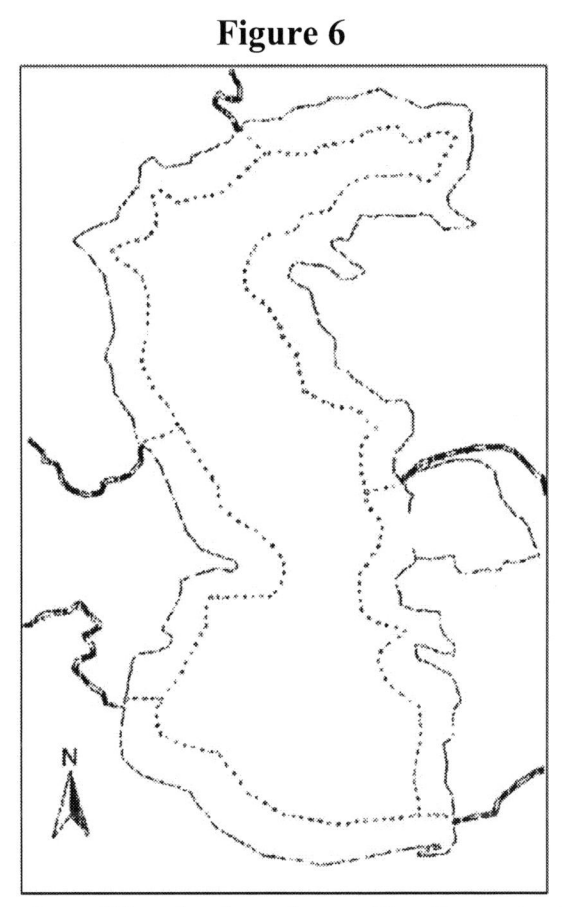

Figure 6

Formula for delineation of Caspian based on a 12-mile territorial zone (dark grey pattern) or 45-mile exclusive economic zone (light grey pattern) in coastal areas, with a central area designated as an area of common use (condominium regime)

One solution that might accommodate the varying positions on the issue would divide the sea among the littoral countries but leave a sizable condominium area in the middle for the common use of all five states (Fig. 3). The initial actions taken by some Caspian states, such as the bilateral agreements between Russia and Kazakhstan and Russia and Azerbaijan, suggest the potential for a sophisticated formula that would allow for: 1)- delimitation of a strip of coastal waters (40–45 miles wide) around the sea to be divided among the five littoral states as their exclusive economic zones(15); 2)- declaration of the remaining body of water and surface of the sea as the Caspian Condominium for the "common use" of the littoral states (16); and 3)- division of the seabed and subsoil areas of the condominium, including its subsoil resources, among the littoral states on the basis of the same principles as in point (1) above(17).

Thus, the recent bilateral offshore arrangements between Russia, Kazakhstan, and Azerbaijan need not undermine the ultimate goal of a commonly accepted legal regime by the five countries. Rather, these attempts may encourage the two remaining states (Iran and Turkmenistan) to seek and enforce their own legal regimes in relevant areas. Iran's effort in the summer of 2001 to stop exploration by British Petroleum vessels working for the Republic of Azerbaijan in areas claimed by Iran must be seen in this context (see Frantz, 2001). The action was justified as an attempt to stall initiatives by other littoral states to unilaterally or bilaterally enforce their own interpretations of the disputed legal regime. Thus Iran's action arguably signals the country's willingness to work toward a mutually acceptable agreement for dividing the Caspian Sea that comports with the norms of international maritime law. The challenge is to build on that willingness so that a legal regime for the Caspian can be forged that recognizes the sea's unique character and the mutual interests of its surrounding states.

Notes

1- In addition to the specific citations in the text, general information concerning the historical background can be found in Avery et al. (1991), Fisher (1968), and Sykes (1951).

2- Whether Iran ceded the entire Caspian to the Russians via this treaty is debated by historians. For background, see Parry (1969, pp. 425-428), Sicker (1988, p. 10), and Avery et al. (1991, pp. 318-319).

3- Iran's historic interest in the Caspian and its littoral regions runs deeper than issues of sovereignty, navigation, and mineral resources. The coastal region, encompassed by the two present-day provinces of Mazandaran and Guilan, where humid air must rise to pass over the high Elborz Mountains to the south, receives ample to abundant rainfall in an otherwise arid country. This makes Caspian frontage of crucial importance agriculturally; the two provinces account for only 4 percent of Iran's total land area, but provide for roughly 40 percent of its agricultural output (Khajehpour-Khouei, 2000, p. 75; Bonine, 2003, pp. 2). (The authors are of the opinion that considering rapid urban development in the two provinces in recent years, these statistics may not apply exactly at present.) Furthermore, Iran's Caspian fisheries traditionally have accounted for a substantial share of export revenues. After Russia, Iran has been the world's second-ranking exporter of caviar, a $50 million business annually until its recent decline from overfishing and pollution in the Caspian.

4- RCD was established in the 1960s, originally with the blessing of the United States, and expanded its membership in February 1992 to include the Caspian–Central Asian states that formerly were member states of the Soviet Union.

5- Iranian Oil Company: Fresh Soviet Note to Persia, document attached to report of 22 June 1950, E P1081/2, FO 371/82332A.

6- The accord emphasized equality of access to the sea and equality in its use (e.g., Colombos, 1961, p. 164; Kemp, 1997, p. 28; Bonine, 2003, p. 27), recognizing a 10-mile exclusive fishing zone for each littoral states (Agreement, 1940), and leaving the rest of the sea as a common shipping condominium. This arrangement set a legal precedent for dividing the offshore areas between the coastal states and setting aside the rest as a condominium or area of common use. Furthermore, articles 11 and 12 of the 1921 treaty contained an implied recognition of Iran's right to operate naval vessels on the Caspian, and the two ECNs specified that each party accorded to the vessels flying the flag of the other the right to engage in cabotage of passengers and cargo in the Caspian Sea (Treaty, 1921).

7- Iran's advantage as an exporter of Caspian oil is suggested by its unique geographic position relative to the Caucasus, Central Asia, the Persian Gulf, Gulf of Oman, Turkey, Iraq, Afghanistan, and Pakistan. The northern part of Iran had a total oil refining capacity of ca. 650,000 barrels per day in the late 1990s, which could be adopted for oil swaps with Azerbaijan, Kazakhstan, and Turkmenistan. Furthermore, Iran has a number of pipelines, with a combined capacity of one million barrels per day that are no more than 50-150 km distant from its Caspian ports. It also has extensive export facilities on the Persian Gulf, capable of handling over 2.5 million barrels per day above its export capacity in the year 2000 (Ghorban, 2000, p. 149).

8- Turkey's desire for European Union membership, for instance, arguably overshadows its commitment to membership in a decidedly Asian structure such as the ECO. Similarly, the bulk of Pakistan's geopolitical attention is focused on territorial and strategic rivalries with India. These circumstances, together with existing rivalries between Iran and Afghanistan, have thus far posed obstacles to more complete regional cooperation within ECO.

9- The exercises, known as GOPLAT (Gas and Oil Platform), ostensibly were designed to train Azerbaijan's naval forces in defending offshore drilling platforms, but are worrisome to Iran in that they may presage deeper forms of cooperation in the future (Useinov, 2003).

10- This may reflect a range of factors, including pressure from Western oil companies, fear that its own oil and gas companies would be left out of potentially lucrative offshore projects, discovery of significant offshore petroleum resources in the zone that would become Russia's national sector under such a demarcation (Sciolino, 1998), and a political victory in Russia of a pragmatic policy coalition (consisting of Russia's oil and gas lobby and financial oligarchs) over a "geopolitical coalition" (consisting of officials in Russia's Foreign Ministry, the fishing industry, environmental groups, and the scientific community) (see Blum, 1988a).

11- 11-In December 1997, Iran completed construction of a pipeline from Turkmenistan's Korpeye gas field to Kuy north-eastern Iran, the only natural gas export pipeline from Central Asia thus far to bypass Russia. Negotiations are under way for another 1500 km pipeline extending from Turkmenistan across Iran to Turkey (see Bonine, 2003, pp. 27-28). In addition, since 1995, Iranian companies have engaged in collaborative oil prospecting efforts with Azeri and Russian companies (Joint Exploration, 1995). The joint Iranian-Azeri exploration effort is a trust-building measure, designed to thwart either party from extracting an unfair portion of the resource from oil fields in the Caspian Sea that extend across areas of the sea claimed by both Iranians and Azeris (Mojtahed-Zadeh, 2000).

12- For background, see Akhundova (2002).

13- International legal scholars have noted that the legal status of an international lake (inland sea) does not automatically determine its regime of use (Blum, 1998b), as there is no well-defined, comprehensive body of inter-national law concerning such water bodies. The littoral states may elect virtually whatever regime they wish, as long as such action does not prejudice other states.

14- The line connects the coastal terminus of Iran's north-eastern boundary line at Hassangholi Bay (the mouth of the Atrek River) to the coastal terminus of Iran's northwestern boundary line at Astara.

15- Any designated national territorial waters or continental shelf areas would be limited to this strip.

16- Each of the littoral states would have equal right of access to the Sea for commercial, navigational, and other maritime activities.

17- Delegates at the recently concluded International Seminar on the Caspian Sea (October 19–20, 2003, University of Mazandaran, Babolsar, Iran), with representatives from each of the Caspian littoral states (as well as Georgia and Armenia), issued a declaration (Babolsar Declaration, 2003) that included support for a formula considering parts of the coastal waters as an exclusive economic zone for each country, with the middle part being declared as an area of common use ("condominium") for all the littoral states.

References

1- Agreement, "Gharardad-e Bazargani va Bahrpeymaeiy-e bein-e Dolat-e Shahanshahiy-e Iran va Etehad-e Jamahir-e Shoraviy-e Socialisti (Trade and Seafaring Agreement between the Imperial Government of Iran and the Union of Soviet Socialist Republics)," signed in Teheran and dated 5 Farvardin 1319 (March 25, 1940).
2- Akhundova, Elmira, "Enigmas of Caspian Arithmetic," *Obshchaya gazeta*, April 25–May 1, 2002, 2 (translated in *Current Digest of the Post-Soviet Press*, May 22, 2002, 1).
3- Avery, Peter, Gavin Hambly, and Charles Melville, eds., *Cambridge History of Iran*, Vol. 7. Cambridge, UK: Cambridge University Press, 1991.
4- "Babolsar Declaration on the Caspian Sea Problems," adopted by delegates of the International Seminar on the Caspian Sea, Mazandaran University, Babolsar, Iran, October 19–20, 2003.
5- Blum, Douglas, "Domestic Politics and Russia's Caspian Policy," *Post-Soviet Affairs*, 14, 2:137-164, April–June 1998a.
6- Blum, Douglas, *Sustainable Development and the New Oil Boom: Cooperative and Competitive Out-comes in the Caspian Sea*. Cambridge, MA: Davis Center, Harvard University, PONARS Working Paper Series, No. 4, May 1998b.
7- Bonine, Michael E., Iran: The Pivotal State of Southwest Asia," *Eurasian Geography and Economics*, 44, 1:1-39, January–February 2003.
8- Colombos, John C., *International Law of the Sea*. London, UK: Longmans, 1961.
9- Fisher, W. B., ed., *Cambridge History of Iran. Vol. 1: The Land*. Cambridge, UK: Cambridge University Press, 1968.
10- Frantz, Douglas, "Iran and Azerbaijan Argue Over Caspian's Riches," *New York Times*, August 30, 2001, A4.
11- Ghorban, Narsi, "By Way of Iran: Caspian's Oil and Gas Outlet," in Hooshang Amirahmadi, ed., *The Caspian Region at a Crossroad*. New York, NY: St. Martin's Press, 2000.
12- Golotyuk, Yuriy, "Russia's Caspian Flotilla: Gunboat Diplomacy with Cruise Missiles," *Vremya novostey*, January 10, 2001, 1 (translated in *Current Digest of the Post-Soviet Press*, February 7, 2001, 15).
13- Hafeznia, M. R., "Differences and Disputes in the Caspian Geopolitical Region," *Central Asia and Caucasus Quarterly* (Tehran), 18, 27, 1999 (in Persian).
14- Horton, Scott and Natik Mamedov, "Legal Status of the Caspian Sea," in Hooshang Amirahmadi, ed., *The Caspian Region at a Crossroad*. New York, NY: St. Martin's Press, 2000.
15- Ignatova, Maria and Yekaterina Grigoryeva, "Five Divided by Two—Russia and Kazakhstan Come to Terms on Developing Caspian Resources," *Izvestiya*, May 14, 2002, 5 (translated in *Current Digest of the Post-Soviet Press*, June 12, 2002, 19).
16- "Joint Exploration Activities to Start Soon in the Caspian Sea," *Ettelaat International* (London), 344:10, September 12, 1995.
17- Kemp, Geoffrey, *Energy Superbowl: Strategic Politics and the Persian Gulf and Caspian Basin*. Washington, DC: Nixon Center for Peace and Freedom, 1997.
18- Khajehpour-Khouei, Bijan, "Survey of Iran's Economic Interests in the Caspian," in Hooshang Amirahmadi, ed., *The Caspian Sea Region at a Crossroad*. New York, NY: St. Martin's Press, 2000, 75-86.

19- Koolaee, Elaheh, "Geopolitical Impact of Exploration of Oil Resources," *Rahbord Quarterly*, 13:19-36, Spring 1998.
20- Kullberg, Anssi K., "The Return of Heartland," *The Eurasian Politician*, 1, May 21, 2000 [http://www.teh-politician.com/issue1/art.htm].
21- Mojtahed-Zadeh, Pirouz, "Iranian Perspectives on the Caspian Sea and Central Asia," in Iwao Kobori and Michael H. Glantz, eds., *Central Eurasian Water Crisis*. Tokyo, Japan/New York, NY/Paris, France: United Nations University Press, 1998, 105-124.
22- Mojtahed-Zadeh, Pirouz, "The Geo-politics of the Caspian Region," in Hooshang Amirahmadi, ed., *The Caspian Region at a Crossroad*. New York, NY: St. Martin's Press, 2000, 175-186.
23- Parry, Clive, ed., *Consolidated Treaty Series*, 31. Dobbs Ferry, NY: Oceana Publications, Inc., 1968.
24- Reutov, Aleksandr, "Russia Conclusively Defines Its Borders on the Caspian," *Kommersant*, September 24, 2002, 2 (translated in *Current Digest of the Post-Soviet Press*, October 23, 2002, 17-18).
25- Saivetz, Carol, *The Soviet Union and the Gulf in the 1980s*. Boulder, CO: Westview Press, 1989.
26- Sciolino, Elaine, "It's a Sea! It's a Lake! No. It's a Pool of Oil," *New York Times*, June 21, 1998, WK16.
27- Shiryayev, Vyacheslav, "Zigzag of Failure—Over Three Days Vladimir Putin Changed Russia's Approach to Solving Caspian Problems," *Novyye izvestiya*, April 27, 2002, 2 (translated in *Cur-rent Digest of the Post-Soviet Press,* May 22, 2002, 3).
28- Sicker, Martin, *The Bear and the Lion*. New York, NY: Praeger, 1988.
29- Sykes, Percy, *A History of Persia*, Vol. 2. London, UK: Macmillan and Co., 1951, third ed. "The Legal Regime of the Caspian Sea: Interview with Dr. Pirouz Mojtahed-Zadeh," *Ettelaat* daily (Teheran), June 1, 1998, 12 (in Persian).
30- Treaty, "Moahedeh Mabein Iran va Russ dar Turkmanchai Betarikh-e 22/10 Fevriyeh 1828, Motabegh-e 5 Shaban 1243 Monaghed Shodeh (Treaty Concluded between Iran and Russia at Turkmenchai on February 22/10 1828 Corresponding to 5 Shaban 1243)," 1828.
31- Treaty, "Ahdnameh-e Mavadat Mabein Iran va Russieh (Treaty of Friendship between Iran and Russia)," signed in Moscow and dated 8 Hut 1299 AH (February 26, 1921).
32- Useinov, Arif, "Iran Angry Over Appearance of American Military in Caspian," *Nezavisimaya gazeta*, August 19, 2003, 5 (translated in *Current Digest of the Post-Soviet Press*, September 17, 2003, 15-16).
33- Also; Pirouz Mojtahed-Zadeh, *"What Is Happening in the Caspian Sea and What Should We Do?"*, *Ettelaat Siasi-Eqtesadi* (Teheran), VII, 185-186:4-16, January–February 2003 (in Persian).

CHAPTER VI

Iran's Caspian Oil and Gas Dilemma
Hossein Askari and Roshanak Taghavi*

Introduction

The Caspian Sea is the world's largest inland body of water and was deemed a Soviet and Iranian Sea before the break up of the Soviet Union in 1991. With the breakdown of the Soviet regime, Azerbaijan, Kazakhstan, and Turkmenistan joined Iran and Russia as the Caspian's littoral states. The eventual division of the Caspian, which could harbor 5% to 10% of the world's oil reserves, and the exploitation of its potential oil and natural gas reserves, have increased tension in the Caspian Basin as Iran and Russia, vying to strengthen and maintain influence in the region, have been hampered by the increasing influence of the United States over the three new coastal states. Outside interference by the United States, the European Union, and Turkey has slowed down the establishment of transport routes for the Caspian's hydrocarbons as well. Iran, which harbors up to 15 billion barrels [BBL] and 11 trillion cubic feet [Tcf] in potential oil and natural gas reserves, also serves as the optimal location for the shortest and most cost- efficient transport routes in the region. Construction of the US- backed Baku-Tbilisi-Ceyhan [BTC] pipeline, which completely bypasses both Iran and Russia at a cost of over $200 million dollars in subsidies paid by the US, is progressing despite mounting concern over Azerbaijan's financing and the availability of Iran as a cheap and efficient alternative.

This paper has been divided into seven sections. In the first section, the authors give an overview of the different methods currently being considered for the Sea's division and present the stance of each littoral state. Percentages of the Sea received by each country with each method of division are also provided by the authors, who for the first time have established that Iran would receive almost 3% less of the Sea with the Turkmen- preferred technique than it would with the modified median line method (1). Agreements and disputes between the coastal states are then covered, followed by an explanation of the size and importance of the Caspian's proven and potential oil and natural gas reserves. Maps depicting the location of the Caspian's oil and natural gas assertions. Charts showing the value of proven and potential offshore oil and natural gas reserves received by each littoral state with each method of division are also included.

In section three, the authors explain the geopolitical reasons for the creation of the US- sponsored Baku-Tbilisi-Ceyhan pipeline and describe the threats posed to the pipeline by the on-going conflict in Nagorno-Karabakh and Georgia's internal instability. The authors then examine the advantages of increasing oil swaps in Iran and provide an overview of the financial costs and benefits of constructing a trans-Iranian pipeline for the shipment of Caspian oil and/ or forming a new pipeline to connect to Iran's existing network. Oil pipelines that could involve Iran, US-backed natural gas pipelines that would avoid Iran, and natural gas pipelines that would include

Iran are also discussed. In section five, it is established that Iran could in fact benefit more financially by increasing oil swaps and establishing a pipeline route running through Iranian territory even if she receives less than 20% of the Sea. The authors then highlight the financial impact on both the US and Iran as a result of sanctions imposed on Iran by the US, and explain how a slight relaxation on the US' approach towards sanctions could benefit the US financially and curb the expansion of Russian influence in the region. Finally, the authors propose that the optimal way for the littoral states to maximize revenues received from the sale and shipment of Caspian hydrocarbons is to establish a Caspian Oil and Gas Company to be owned by all five littoral states. Such a venture would allow for the Caspian's oil and natural gas to get to markets as quickly and efficiently as possible and would enable Iran to demonstrate her capacity to act as a partner rather than a pariah.

1- How to Divide the Caspian

Iran maintains that the regional treaties between Persia and the Russian Soviet Federated Socialist Republic in 1921, and between Iran and the USSR in 1935 and 1940, which call for joint sharing of the Caspian's resources between the two countries, are still valid and should be the basis for the decision dividing the Sea (2). The last two treaties classified the Caspian as a Soviet and Iranian Sea, but did not institute any nautical limits for the two states (3). The Almati conference of December 1991 affirmed that the international obligations of the former USSR were international obligations of the replacing four [states] (4). Hence, Iran's first and preferred proposal with regard to the division of the Caspian is referred to as the "Condominium" method, where all five littoral states jointly own any exploration within the Caspian Sea. This method of "joint-rule,"(5) which was initially introduced by Russia in the early 1990s, would require consensus between all littoral states on any energy development decisions made, thereby allowing each state to reject any particular decision. With the Condominium method, Iran would profit from transportation privileges and would gain direct access to markets and Russian territory (6). The institution of a common regime would also be advantageous to Iran, who must carry out considerable economic reforms to join the World Trade Organization (WTO) and reserves, as well as the various methods of the Sea's division, supplement our would undoubtedly begin to undergo such reform under the auspices of a common regime.

Russia, Azerbaijan, and Kazakhstan would like for the Caspian to be divided into national zones that adhere to the length of each littoral state's coastline. This method of division abides by the modified median line principle, whereby a line equidistant from the closest mainland points of each of the two countries is drawn (7). A modified median line takes de facto boundaries into consideration and is adjusted to ensure that no two countries have to split a single oil field in which one country has already invested (8). Using this method, Kazakhstan, Russia, and Azerbaijan would each receive 28.4%, 19%, and 21%, respectively. Turkmenistan would receive 18% of the Sea, and Iran would end up with a 13.6% share of the Caspian. In the past, Russia has also proposed the joint development of all deposits and structures falling on the median line. Any deposits and structures that fall along the median line would be divided equally among both countries, even if there are more on one side of the line than on the other. Iran, sharing resources with Azerbaijan and Turkmenistan, would receive a 17% share of the Caspian with such a proposal.

Iran would also like for all of the littoral states to put off all offshore oil developments until the official status of the Caspian Sea has been determined. Iran claims that all unilateral and bilateral agreements on the use of the sea are unacceptable, and contends that the Caspian should either be used in common, or its floor and water basin should be divided equally among the five littoral states. Iran's alternative to the Condominium method is to divide the Caspian as equally as possible between the five littoral states, thereby giving each state approximately 20% of the sea territory, regardless of how each state actually borders the sea. This proposition involves using the Mirza Kuchik Khan point to divide the sea into five sections, and would lower the share of Kazakhstan and Azerbaijan and increase those of Iran, Russia, and Turkmenistan (9). Iranian Oil Minister, Bijan Namdar Zanganeh, stated in March 2002 that in the absence of an acceptable solution, Iran would soon begin developing its 20% of the Sea and would not allow others to explore and produce in Iran's sector. As of January 2003, Azerbaijan has reconsidered its stance on the Caspian's division (10) and is close to reaching an agreement with Iran to divide the Sea into five equal parts (11).

2- Agreements and Disputes

In 1997, Kazakhstan and Azerbaijan agreed to adhere to the borders of the sectors along the median line until an agreement on the legal status of the Caspian is made (12). Kazakhstan and Turkmenistan also signed a communiqué pledging to divide their respective sections of the Caspian along median lines, as defined during the Soviet era, until all littoral states succeeded in achieving an agreement on the new status of the Caspian. In July 1998, Russia and Kazakhstan made a bilateral agreement dividing the Northern Caspian seabed along median lines between the two states, with the waters (including shipping, fishing, and environment) staying under dual ownership. The two countries agreed to develop deposits on the median line jointly. This agreement was finalized on May 13, 2002 at the Eurasian Economic Summit, with the signing of a bilateral agreement by Kazakh president Nursultan Nazarbayev and Russian president Vladmir Putin (13). In January 2001, there was a communiqué between Russia and Azerbaijan in which the two states agreed to divide the seabed while allowing free navigation of the water surface (i.e. common water, divided sea floor) (14). On September 24, 2002, the two nations made a final agreement to divide the Caspian seabed, leaving the waters for common use. In November 2001, at the Commonwealth of Independent States Summit (CIS), Kazakhstan and Azerbaijan signed a bilateral agreement defining their sectors of the Caspian, in line with the modified median line method.

Each country is motivated by a number of sometimes-divergent considerations. Kazakhstan is dependant on Russian military aid, has a 35% Russian minority in the north that controls the flow of grain, and has 55% of its imports coming from Russia. Kazakhstan, therefore, in complete accordance with Russia, holds that the modified median line method of division, which gives Iran 13.6% of the sea, is an appropriate one. Azerbaijan originally held that Iran's section of the Caspian must be defined via the Astara-Hoseingholi line (15), which connects Iran's northeastern boundary line at the Hoseingholi Bay to the end of her northeastern boundary line at Astara, giving Iran only 11% of the Caspian's waters (16). American endorsement and fear of Russia prompted Azerbaijan to agree with Russia and Kazakhstan on the use of the modified median line method for the division of the Sea. Russia also proposed the common use of the water surface for transportation, environmental issues, and fishery (17). This method of division not only allows the Russian navy to have free use of the Caspian, but also allows Russia to remain influential in the Caucasus and Central Asia, two extremely important geo-political regions. Russia has also proposed a method of division whereby the Caspian would be divided into northern and southern sectors. Russia and Kazakhstan would receive 49% of the Sea to the North, and Iran, Turkmenistan, and Azerbaijan would divide the remaining 51% of the Sea to the South equally, each receiving 17% of the Sea. Azerbaijan would lose 4% from this method of division and has therefore rejected it.

Turkmenistan, harboring no Russian minority and sharing a border with Iran, has a much closer relationship with Iran than with Russia (18). Turkmenistan supports the use of median lines for the division of the sea, but has recommended that each sector have a width of approximately 45 miles for which each littoral state would have exclusive rights. The rest of the water would be used for the common employment of all five littoral states. With this method of division, Kazakhstan, Azerbaijan, and Turkmenistan would each respectively receive approximately 26.8%, 12.7%, and 12% of the Sea. Russia would end up with roughly 12.9% of the Sea, leaving an Iranian share of 10.1%. The area of common use would comprise a little over 25.5% of the Sea (19). In September 2001, Khoshgeldy Babaev, the chairman of Turkmenistan's State Caspian Sea Enterprise, stated that Turkmenistan would like for the median line to be situated via a method of equidistant points calculated by the width of the offshore area between the two countries. Such a method entails establishing points on directly opposite shores of both countries and then dividing the space in half using a median line. The same method would also be used for the demarcation of the Azeri sector and would not permit Azerbaijan to place its point of departure for measuring the width of the sea on the Abshuron Peninsular, which juts out sharply east into the Caspian (20). Azerbaijan would not receive a larger share of the Sea with this method. Turkmenistan has not been able to arrive at an agreement with Azerbaijan over the actual execution of the division, however, as both countries claim to own the Kapaz (Sardar) oilfield.

Azerbaijan, Kazakhstan, and Turkmenistan have begun to rely on American support in an effort to maintain their political and economic independence from Russia. Because of the significant Russian presence in each country, the threat of an increase in Iranian influence, and Turkey's desire to boost its ailing economy, these three countries have become considerably dependant on the US (21). At the same time, the US is looking to completely block any and all Iranian participation in the Caspian and adamantly opposes the construction of any pipelines in Iran. Former US President Clinton's Executive Orders banned any significant investment by American companies in Iran's energy industry. The Iran- Libya Sanctions Act of 1996 further supported this through sanctions on non-US companies that do so. More importantly, the US has used its vast global political influence to deter both the construction of a pipeline through Iran and oil swaps involving Iran. Russia, meanwhile, continues to maintain an extensive network of connections with the former Soviet republics and will persistently oppose all attempts to increase the political or military influence of third countries in the states adjoining Russia (22).

3- Size of Reserves

The Caspian Sea contains six separate hydrocarbon basins. As of June 2002, forty oil and gas deposits have been discovered in the Sea, in addition to more than 400 promising structures (23). Proven oil reserves for the Caspian are placed at about 10 billion barrels, while potential reserves are estimated at about 233 billion barrels of oil (24). Total proven oil reserves in the Caspian therefore comprise approximately 1% of the world's total proven oil reserves, while total potential oil reserves make up roughly 5% to 10% of the world's potential reserves (See Maps I through IV and Tables I and II) (25). The proven natural gas reserves for the Caspian region are estimated to be 170.4 Tcf, comprising 2.8% of the world's proven natural gas reserves. Potential gas reserves could produce an additional 293 Tcf, roughly 4% of the world's potential gas reserves (See Maps I through IV and Tables III and IV) (26).

Iran has about 90 billion barrels of proven oil reserves, which is equivalent to approximately 9% of the world's proven reserves; Caspian oil reserves would further enhance Iran's reserve base (27). Most of Iran's crude oil reserves are located in onshore fields in the Southwestern Khuzestan region. Iran's current sustainable crude oil production capacity is equal to approximately 3.85 million bbl/day. Iran relies very heavily on oil export revenues, which comprise approximately 80% of Iran's total export earnings, 10-20% of GDP, and 40-50% of the government's budget (28). Under the assumption of the modified median line method, Iran's sector of the Caspian holds only 0.1 billion barrels of proven oil reserves, and up to 15 billion barrels of potential oil reserves, which is equivalent to approximately 6.4% of the Caspian Sea's potential oil reserves (29). Preliminary seismic surveys carried out by Lasmo and Shell have indicated reserves of 2.5 billion barrels of oil (30).

Iran also holds the second largest proven gas reserves in the world after Russia, with approximately 18% of the world's natural gas reserves, and is looking to have its natural gas production capacity, which is currently at 300 mm cm, doubled by 2005 (31). Iran's areas near the Caspian Sea currently have no proven natural gas reserves, but hold 11 Tcf in potential natural gas reserves.

4- Pipeline Routes

The only non-Russian and non-Iranian pipeline routes that connect Asia to the Black Sea must pass through the Caucasian states of Azerbaijan, Georgia, and Armenia (32). These routes, Baku-Supsa and Baku-Ceyhan ["Main Export Pipeline"], are the two routes favored by the United States, whose main goal is to limit Iran and Russia's involvement in the Caspian. The route most sought after by the US is the Baku-Tbilisi-Ceyhan route through Turkey, which would avoid Iran, Russia, and the problem of heavy traffic in the Bosphorous. Kazakh and Turkmen oil would be shipped via Trans- Caspian pipelines, which would connect to other pipelines from the Caspian region, such as the proposed Main Export Pipeline (33). Current export routes for Azeri, Kazakh, and Turkmen oil involve Russia because of the Chechen bypass and the Caspian Pipeline Consortium (CPC) pipeline. By supporting East- West pipeline routes from Azerbaijan, Kazakhstan, and Turkmenistan to serve as alternatives, the US fulfills its goal of having pipeline routes avoid Iran while reducing Russian dominion over the transit of oil and gas. A route running through Ceyhan is also favored by the West because Turkey understands western market principles and is in good proximity to the burgeoning markets in southern and Western Europe. Avoiding Russian influence is nearly impossible, however, as Nagorno-Karabakh is vital to the Baku-Ceyhan route. Russia will continue to arm Armenia and the Karabakhis, making the transport of Azeri oil in a war-torn area extremely difficult (if not impossible), and Armenia will be extremely upset at being left out as the wealth of two of its enemies—Georgia and Azerbaijan—significantly increases (34).

Nagorno-Karabakh is vital to the Baku-Supsa route as well, as the pipeline goes around the region as well as other Armenian-occupied territory as it leaves Azerbaijan and goes into Georgia. Armenians, particularly radicals in the Javakheti region in south-central Georgia, have spoken about interfering with the flow of Azeri oil (35). In addition, Georgia is dependant on Russian peacekeeping forces to contain its problems in southern Abkhazia. Russia will continue to fuel the conflict by arming the Abkhazis, ensuring that not only does Georgia remain completely dependant upon Russia, but also that Azeri oil will not be able to bypass Russian territory. The United States and the West must therefore keep in mind that Russia has a significant influence over Georgia's internal affairs and could brutally disrupt Georgia's internal stability, as well as any pipelines going through the region, if she is not satisfied with any future trade agreements (36).

Iran and all major oil companies have consistently held the view that routes to the Persian Gulf through Iran are the shortest and least expensive means of exporting oil from the Caspian Sea. The demand for oil in Asia is forecasted to increase very quickly and eventually command a price that would be higher than that of the Mediterranean markets that the majority of the competing pipelines would serve (37). Oil would be shipped either via pipelines that pass though an Iranian route to the Persian Gulf, or—to avoid restrictions imposed upon Iran—via oil swaps where Azeri, Kazakh, and Turkmen oil would be sent to oil refineries in northern Iran. The same amount of Iranian oil would then be exported via Persian Gulf terminals (Kharg Island). Iran would charge a swap fee for services performed, and the high regional demand for oil in Iran would be satisfied without significant spending on Iran's part (38). Were a major pipeline to run through Iran, Iran would gain a large amount of influence over the other Caspian states and the already large amount of world oil that is shipped through the Persian Gulf would increase. Swapping natural resources would alleviate the heavy use of Iran's natural resources that have to be transported from the South to the North. An Iranian route would therefore not only be more cost-effective for Turkmenistan and Kazakhstan, but would also provide Iran with the oil and gas that it uses so heavily in its northern regions.

As the only littoral state with warm water access, Iran's strategy should be to use the Caspian for diplomatic advancement and to gain economically from the construction of the pipeline, its maintenance, and from the transit fees that would be charged. The two options for an Iranian route would be to build a new trans-Iranian pipeline dedicated to Caspian oil and a new pipeline to hook up with Iran's existing network. The first choice would cost approximately $2 billion for a one million barrel per day (b/d) pipeline, with roughly thirty percent of this in local Iranian content. For the second option, if the two-phase pipeline program proposed by Iran were to be implemented, the first phase would hypothetically produce 300,000 b/d and have a construction cost of $450 million (fifty percent local Iranian content). The second phase would increase production by one million b/d at the cost of $1.2 billion (thirty percent local content). If one were to assume a $2 billion cost for a one million b/d pipeline through Iran, which is at least $1.2 billion less than the cost of the Baku-Ceyhan route, then $600 million of this cost (over a two year period) would be for Iranian contracts (39). Maintenance of the pipeline would cost approximately $50 million per year, and transit fees would come out to approximately $0.80 per barrel, or $300 to $450 million per year (if the volume ordered would be about 1-1.5 million barrels per day) (40).

If Iran were to swap oil from Caspian sources for its northern refineries for Iranian crude on the Persian Gulf, Iran would gain approximately $0.50/ barrel or roughly $90 million per year; benefits are likely to increase significantly within the next two years. As of 2001, Iran has been able to conservatively use 500,000 b/d of Caspian crude for its northern refineries and this could be conservatively expanded to 750,000 b/d by the end of 2003 (41).

In June 2001, Tehran's ambassador to Baku, Ahad Qazaie, stated that the transport of oil and gas via Iranian territory would be the most secure and cost-efficiet decision (42). Since the beginning of 2001, the cost to transfer one ton (7.3 barrels) of Turkmen crude had decreased from $21 to $16, and that of Kazakh crude had fallen to $13 (43). With Amirabad, Iran's Caspian port, and the port's connection to the state railway system, Iran hopes to be the focal point of a vast system of gas distribution, giving the other littoral states' the option of not only exploiting their natural gas in an economical manner, but of having access to Iran's energy swap facilities as well (44). At present, there is no Iranian oil or natural gas production in the Caspian region. In March

2001, however, the National Iranian Oil Company (NIOC) signed a $226 million agreement with Sweden's GVA Consultants and Iran's Sadra to construct an oilrig in the Caspian Sea off Mazandaran Province. There are other pipeline projects and energy swaps that could involve Iran.

5- Oil Pipelines

Kazakhstan- Turkmenistan- Iran Pipeline

This pipeline would transport oil via Turkmenistan to central Iran, where it would connect to an existing pipeline system and carry oil south to Iran's ports on the Persian Gulf. This $1.2 billion dollar pipeline would be 900 miles long and would be able to transport up to 1-million bbl/day. The most recent version of this pipeline would involve an oil pipeline from Omsk in Russia that runs through Kazakhstan and Turkmenistan (45). Nursultan Nazarbayev and Mohammad Khatami have both described the Iranian option as the most cost-effective means of transporting Kazakhstan's oil (46). Iran has also proposed that Azeri oil be shipped to Turkmenbashi via this pipeline, where it would connect with the [proposed] Kazakhstan- Iran pipeline.

Iran- Azerbaijan Pipeline

Iran has also proposed the creation of a 190- mile pipeline through which oil from Tabriz (Northwest Iran) would be transported to Baku. In Tabriz, the pipeline would connect with existing Iranian pipelines and refineries. Total Fina Elf has already suggested a 200,000- 400,000 bbl/day pipeline be built for this purpose, and in May 2001, Iran's oil ministry approved the construction of a refinery near Iran's Caspian Sea border with Azerbaijan. Iran, Russia, and Azerbaijan's 1995 goal to create mutual exploration companies would be fulfilled with the realization of such a venture (47). Azerbaijan has stated, however, that problems with Iran regarding the Caspian's division must be resolved and Iran's relations with the West must improve before the two countries can proceed with this project (48).

South Pipeline (Central Asia Oil Pipeline)

This pipeline would begin in Kazakhstan and run through Turkmenistan to Gwadar, Pakistan and other world markets via either Iran or Afghanistan. This 1040- mile pipeline would cost $2.5 billion and would have the capacity to ship one million bbl/day. Funding for the pipeline would be provided by Unocal, whose plans to construct the pipeline have re-emerged since the removal of the Taliban government by the US in December 2001. The US has expressed a willingness to support private companies proposing the construction of commercially feasible pipelines running through Afghanistan. It is highly unlikely that conflicts between ethnic Afghan factions, which could disrupt the flow of oil to Pakistan, will be resolved anytime soon, however. Without regional stability in Afghanistan, Iran should become the optimal route of choice (49).

In July 2002, Iran also suggested changing the former Iran- USSR gas pipeline into an oil pipeline. Iran hopes that reviving the pipeline, which has not been active for ten years, will enable their refinery in Tabriz to receive oil from the Caspian region (50).

6- Natural Gas Pipelines

At present, there are two potential routes for the transit of gas that would involve Iran. The first pipeline was proposed in February 2002, when Armenia, Greece, and Iran discussed the possibility of building a 141 km Iran- Armenia pipeline. Greece would contribute significantly to the $120 million cost and would act as the main distributor of gas (51).

The Korphezhe- Kurt-Kui pipeline, which opened in December 1997, is the first "export pipeline" that avoids Russia, connecting Iranian regions in the north to Turkmenistan's natural gas fields. Turkmenistan, looking for an alternative to the Russian pipelines that were previously the only means of transport for Turkmen gas, sought to transport its gas to Turkey via Iran. Iran would be able to purchase Turkmen gas, which she could either use domestically or re-export via an anticipated pipeline to Turkey (52). As of September 2001, Khoshgeldy Babaev, the Chairman of Turkmenistan's State Caspian Enterprise, stated that Iran is one of the most important routes necessary for the transport of Turkmen gas to Turkey and ultimately to Europe (53). Turkmenistan initially intended to have annual deliveries of Turkmen gas Iran increase to 8 billion cubic meters. Plans have recently come to a halt however, as Turkmenistan has decided to sell its gas directly to Turkey in order to charge a higher price.

Gas Pipelines That Do Not Involve Iran
Baku- Tbilisi- Erzurum

In March 2001, Azerbaijan contracted to deliver 3.1 Tcf of natural gas from Baku to Erzurum via Tbilisi. This 540- mile pipeline, which bypasses both Iran and Russia, will transport gas to Turkey from 2004- 2018 and will cost approximately $1 billion. Iran's Naftiran Intertrade Company (NIOC) has managed to get a 10% stake in the project (54). Russia, however, would prefer to buy and re-transport Caspian region gas via her Blue Stream Pipeline, which passes under the Black Sea from Tuapse to Samsun (55). The potential effect of the completion of this pipeline on Georgia's internal stability must therefore be considered, as Russia may decide to rekindle the Abkhazi dilemma if she is not happy with the pipeline's route.

Kazakhstan- Turkmenistan- Azerbaijan

A pipeline for the shipment of liquefied natural gas (LNG) would transport gas from Kazakhstan and Turkmenistan to Baku, where the gas would be shipped to Turkey and other markets via the Georgian port of Batumi (56).

Trans- Caspian Gas Pipeline (TCGP)

The 1020-mile TCGP would cost $2 billion to $3 billion and would transport gas to Turkey via Turkmenistan, Azerbaijan and Georgia (57). Before the construction of the TCGP can begin, however, a framework stipulating the division of the Sea must be created and Azerbaijan and Turkmenistan must reach an agreement on pipeline volumes.

7- Iran's Financial Stake in the Caspian and the Future

In Table V, we have calculated Iran's benefits from the development of the Caspian. We have found that instead of holding out for 20% of the Caspian, possibly getting no oil for transshipment to the Persian Gulf and no oil for swaps, it may in fact be more beneficial for Iran to accept a smaller share of the Sea and get a smaller—but still significant—share of the entire development (oil production, transit fees, oil swaps).

8- Conclusion and the Road Ahead

Kazakhstan, Russia, and Azerbaijan prefer the modified median line method of division because these three nations will receive the largest share of the Caspian; with 28.4% and 21% of the Sea, respectively, Kazakhstan and Azerbaijan may not stand for the loss of wealth that would result from an equal division of the Sea. Russia, despite ending up with 19% of the Sea, would actually gain more with the modified median line method of division, as the country would share resources that fall on the median line with Azerbaijan and Kazakhstan, and its navy would also have free access to the Azeri and Kazakh sectors of the Caspian waters. Receiving only an 18% sector of the Sea with the median line method, Turkmenistan would definitely benefit from the roughly 2% gain that an equal division would give. However, by agreeing to a modified median line approach with the 45-mile width exception, Turkmenistan would still stand to benefit, as the area of joint use would inevitably increase Turkmenistan's share in the Caspian's wealth and would help mollify disputes over the rightful ownership of the Kapaz (Sardar) oil field.

Another factor that encourages finding an alternative to the equal division method is that no littoral state would necessarily be guaranteed an exact 20% share of the Caspian. In 2002, it was found that the geographical shape of the Caspian Sea and the varying length of each state's coastal line in fact do not allow for an *exactly* equal partition of the Sea (58). Additionally, an equal division of the Sea would entail having Iranian waters in front of the Azerbaijani coast and having Azerbaijani waters in front of the Russian border of the Caspian, which is not practical (59).

With the modified median line method of division, Iran would be the only littoral state to suffer a significant loss. The other littoral states must therefore recognize that it is unrealistic to expect Iran to accept a share of the Caspian Sea that is significantly less than 20% and have all transportation routes bypass her. Before the break up of the Soviet Union, the Caspian was considered to be a *Soviet-Iranian* Sea, a stance reaffirmed by the Almati conference in 1991. Iran has not requested to receive, nor does Iran expect to receive, half of the Caspian Sea. Iran cannot be expected, however, to receive the smallest sector of the Sea with the least amount of oil reserves and to have no role in the transportation of the Caspian's oil and gas to world markets. Concessions must be made by all five states for the optimum legal regime.

In order for all five littoral states to come to an acceptable agreement, Iran will have to recognize her financial stake in the transport of the Sea's rich hydrocarbon reserves. Iran should explore alternatives to the equal division method because the notable losses that would be incurred by the other littoral states with this method will produce a stalemate that will take years to overcome, promoting the construction of pipelines that do not go through Iran.

The cheapest routes for the shipment of Kazakh and Turkmen oil and gas must respectively run through Russian or Iranian territory and would avoid the considerable environmental damage that would be produced by the US sanctioned Baku-Ceyhan and Trans-Caspian Gas Pipelines. The damage that would be caused by the creation of these pipelines, which would connect to pipelines running underneath the Caspian seabed, would be irreparable. In addition, were the TCGP pipeline to crack, highly dangerous hydrogen-sulfite gas would be released to the detriment of coastal life (60). Not only would the extensive exploration necessary for these alternative routes cause severe damage to the Caspian seabed and waters, but the life of the already endangered Sturgeon, which Iranian caviar exports also depend on, would be threatened as well. In determining what routes will be used and how they will be put into operation, the littoral states must recall the tragic demise of the Aral Sea, which is now deemed a "disaster area" after having undergone years of careless and abusive practices (61).

If the United States would like to improve US- Iranian relations, she should encourage Iran's economic cooperation with her neighbors, giving Iran added incentive to integrate further into the world community. In striving to limit the Iranian share of the Caspian while at the same time aiming to prevent Iran's inclusion in the transport of the Caspian's riches, the United States is furthering Iran's isolation and appearing as vindictive to every segment of Iranian society. US opposition to Iran's participation in Caspian oil/ gas and its transportation through Iran will only fuel future regional conflicts and instability throughout the Caspian Basin.

Another incentive for the United States to relax its stance on foreign investment in Iran's oil and gas sector would be the considerable economic gain that would result for US companies. In his statement before a subcommittee of the US House of Representatives in May 2001, William Reinsch, President of the National Foreign Trade Council, pleaded for an end to US sanctions against Iran and Libya, emphasizing the significant loss that American farmers and business owners have had to suffer as a result of cutting off relations with Iran. Not only has the US lost the Iranian market for motor vehicles, airplanes, and agriculture to Europe, but great investment opportunities in Iran's large oil and gas sector have been given up as well. He claimed that not only have "unilateral sanctions failed to achieve their stated purposes, but…cannot achieve them." He went on to state that American attempts at Iranian isolation have served only to generate distortions in the development of the Caspian region's substantial petroleum resources and appear to be nothing but counterproductive for US interests there (62).

One would estimate the loss that US companies have had to undergo as a result of severing contact with Iran to be approximately $600-$720 million; assuming that the US could have won about sixty percent of new business ventures and that the extra return (compared to opportunities in the US) would have been ten percent on the investment. US companies will continue to suffer losses even after sanctions are lifted, as they would have significantly less information on and familiarity with Iranian oil and gas fields and would be less competitive in winning related and new projects in Iran (63). In addition, as of 2000, it has been calculated that the Baku-Ceyhan pipeline will require $200 million per year in American subsidies (64).

To isolate Iran now would ultimately go against the US' additional goal of avoiding an increase in Russian influence in the Caspian region. Iran could have served to offset growing Russian dominion in the Caspian region, but because of consistent US efforts to hamper Iranian growth, Iran must follow the path of the other Caspian littoral states and turn to Russia for support in its Caspian endeavors. Iran is now working with Russia to increase oil drilling in Iran. Russia has also pledged to help Iran build pipelines for the transport of Iranian oil, including one that would run from Iran to India (65).

One must also take note of Vice-President Dick Cheney's statement at the Collateral Damage Conference held at the Cato Institute in June 1998 that "*unilateral* economic sanctions imposed by the United States," particularly "in the Caspian Sea area," rarely work (66). He went on to make the point, which William Reinsch reiterated in 2001, that "the most striking result of the government's use of unilateral sanctions in the [Iranian] region is that only American companies are prohibited from operating there." He claimed that American firms have lost and will continue to forego opportunities that develop with respect to Iran, and also with respect to opportunities to obtain access to Caspian resources (67). Finally, one must ask the question as to why Azerbaijan, deemed by Transparency International as one of the most corrupt countries in the world (68), had sanctions against it removed by the Bush administration as a reward for its assistance to American forces during military operations in Afghanistan, while Iran, who also provided support to the US, was not at all recognized (69).

Active participation in oil swaps, along with the creation of new pipelines across Iran, could make up for much—if not all—of the loss Iran would undergo by accepting a smaller percentage of the Sea, (See Table V). Moreover, while the size of oil reserves is important, it also matters when the oil is brought to market; the earlier the oil is brought to market, the better it is for all littoral states, including Iran. The size of the Iranian share of the Caspian Sea will inevitably be linked to its level of participation in transporting the Caspian's hydrocarbon reserves. The impact of the decisions that will finally be made with regard to the legal regime of the Caspian and the pipeline routes and destinations that will be used will have permanent effects on not just the littoral states, but on the relations between those states and third parties that are participating in negotiations. It is counterproductive to leave Iran, who has every right to benefit from the wealth of a Sea it partially owns, resentful. Additionally, US coercion of potential investors into refraining from investing in Iran's energy sector plainly goes against Alan Larson's statement before the House of Representatives' Committee on International Relations in July 1997 that a common, multilateral approach on Iran is essential for US diplomacy (70).

Oil swaps with Iran would not only allow Iran's northern requirement for oil and gas to be fulfilled, but would give the Caspian states a cheap and efficient way of getting their hydrocarbons to outside markets via the Persian Gulf. Pipelines enabling Caspian oil and gas to run through Iran would avoid extraneous costs and would involve less complicated and less dangerous routes than those promoted by the US. Iran would depend less on Russian backing, would avoid unnecessary spending and excessive utilization of its own resources, and could work on improving its economy. If the US appeared to be a little less antagonistic towards Iran, Iranian conservative claims against US policies would inevitably be weakened, giving reformists much more latitude in the determination of governmental policies.

Iran should not wait and let the US determine the future of Caspian oil and gas and Iran's relations with its northern neighbors. By announcing the relocation of its military base in Encerlik, Turkey to the Azeri island of Abshuron, the United States is vying to militarize the region (71) in the hopes that a significant American military presence will eventually outweigh the Russian one. Not only has the US agreed to provide Azerbaijan with significant military aid during 2002, (72) but it is also arranging for military consultants to be sent to both Georgia and Kazakhstan. The main goal of these efforts, besides increasing the significance of the American presence in the Caspian region, is to protect the creation of the Baku- Ceyhan pipeline, which began in September 2002.

Iran should go on the policy offensive. A bold option open to Iran is to propose a Caspian oil and gas company to: (i) develop all Caspian oil and gas, (ii) ship the fuels through the most economic route, (iii) conduct swaps and all other transactions, and (iv) divide the total revenues (oil, gas, transit fees) in an "equitable" manner. Such a venture could be readily financed on international capital markets, as all participants would benefit from its implementation. By reaching an amicable agreement, future conflicts would be less likely. Risks associated with the overall development of the Caspian would be significantly reduced, giving investors the appetite to finance all projects associated with the Caspian at competitive rates. Joint development would also result in large economies of scale. Despite joint exploration and exploitation of the Caspian's resources, each littoral state would be able to maintain political and navigational control over a national sector of the waters. Nevertheless, decisions regarding the exploration of the Sea and the exploitation of its resources would be made together.

The undertaking of such a proposal would reward all littoral states sooner as opposed to later. Using any reasonable social discount rate, countries would compromise in order to get the fuels to markets sooner and thus maximize their discounted revenues. Besides ensuring significant Iranian participation in the transport of the Caspian's hydrocarbons to world markets, this venture would fulfill Iran's 1992 objective of forming a "Council of Caspian Sea Countries" (73).

Iran would also be exposed to more moderate ideas and would adhere to more liberal rules and regulations if financing for such a venture was partly provided by western nations and if western companies were also involved in the development of such a company. Recognition by the Bush administration to such a course of action would be in line with the tenets set forth by

President Bush in the United States' National Security Strategy. American endorsement of such a venture would indisputably promote free trade, discourage regional conflicts, allow the United States to strengthen its relationship with Russia—a former enemy— and promote Iranian economic and ideological development.

References

1- With the method proposed by Turkmenistan, the median line method of division is used, with one exception. Each sector has a width of 45 miles, leaving an area to be used in common by all littoral states.
2- Robert M. Cutler, "Russia Reactivates its Caspian Policy with New Demarcation Approach," Central Asia/ Caucasus Analyst, June 21, 2000.
3- "Developments in the evolving Caspian legal regime: Part 1 of 2," NewsBase, August 24, 2000.
4- Pirouz Mojtahed-Zadeh, "A Look at Iran's Geopolitical Perspective of Caspian Region," SAWA IV, Seminar on West Asian Security, March 2002, p.7.
5- Robert M. Cutler, "Russia Reactivates its Caspian Policy with New Demarcation Approach," Central Asia/ Caucasus Analyst, June 21, 2000, p.1.
6- Abbas Maleki, "Caspian Sea and Foreign Policy of Islamic Republic of Iran," Jomhuri Eslami, October 23, 2001, Vol. 23, No.6474.
7- Robert M. Cutler, "Russia Reactivates its Caspian Policy with New Demarcation Approach," Central Asia/ Caucasus Analyst, June 21, 2000, p.1.
8- Ibid., p.2.
9- Abbas Maleki, "The Legal Status of the Caspian Sea: Discussions on Different Iranian Views," International Institute for Caspian Studies, April 2001, p. 3.
10- "Iran," Energy Information Administration, May 2002, p.7.
11- "Iran and Azerbaijan Nearing Agreement on the Caspian Sea, Caspian News Agency, 17 January 2003.
12- "Caspian Sea Region," Energy Information Administration, February 2002, p.2.
13- "Iran denies Caspian allegations," www.newsbase.com, May 24, 2002.
14- "Caspian Sea Region," Energy Information Administration, February 2002, p.2.
15- The authors have chosen to refer to the latter location as "Hoseingholi," although this location is also referred to as Hassangholi, Esenguly, and Gasan Koli.
16- Pirouz Mojtahed-Zadeh, "A Look at Iran's Geopolitical Perspective of Caspian Region," SAWA IV, Seminar on West Asian Security, March 2002, p.4.
17- Abbas Maleki, "Caspian Sea and Foreign Policy of Islamic Republic of Iran," Jomhuri Eslami, October 23, 2001.
18- "Turkmenistan," www.princeton.edu, 1998.
19- The authors calculated these values using data received from Iain Brown of Wood Mackenzie Ltd in an email dated 11 October 2002.
20- "Interview with the Chairman of Turkmenistan's State Caspian Sea Enterprise, Khoshgeldy Babaev," www.platts.com, 24 September 2001.
21- "US's interests," www.princeton.edu, 1998.
22- See "Andranik Migranyan's article in Nezavisimaya Gazeta, Moscow, 1994." Source: Oleg Stolyar, "Geopolitics in the Caspian: Can Russia Keep Control in Its Own Backyard?" 1998.
23- "Promising yields found in Caspian Sea," www.newsbase.com, June 8, 2002.
24- 24-"Caspian Sea Region: Reserves and Pipelines Tables," Energy Information Administration, July 2002.
25- 25-Percentage calculated by authors using world total potential oil reserves as reported by USGS in March 2000; USGS estimates the "total amount of future technically recoverable oil,

outside the US, to be about 2120 bbl." The authors calculated this value using the EIA finding that the Caspian harbors up to 233 bbl in potential oil reserves, although others have found potential oil reserves in the Caspian to be as low as 40 bbl as well. Others report high figures for global potential reserves; this is in part due to definitional problems.

26- Percentage calculated by authors using world total potential gas reserves as reported by USGS in March 2000.
27- "Iran," Energy Information Administration, May 2002, p.3.
28- Ibid.
29- "Caspian Sea Region: Reserves and Pipelines Tables," Energy Information Administration, July 2002.
30- "Iran," Energy Information Administration, May 2002, p.6.
31- "Iran aims to more than double gas output by 2005," www.gasandoil.com, 18 June 2001.
32- Oleg Stolyar, "Geopolitics in the Caspian: Can Russia Keep Control in Its Own Backyard?," 1998, p.2.
33- "Caspian Sea Region: Oil Export Options," Energy Information Administration, February 2002, p.7.
34- "Nagorno- Karabakh," www.princeton.edu, 1998.
35- Ibid.
36- "Georgia," www.princeton.edu, 1998.
37- "Caspian Sea Region: Oil Export Options," Energy Information Administration, July 2002.
38- "Iranian Oil Routes," www.princeton.edu, 1998.
39- Hossein Askari, John Forrer, Hildy Teegen, Jiawen Yang, "U.S. Economic sanctions: Lessons from the Iranian Experience," Business Economics, July 2001, Vol. 36, Issue 3, p.15.
40- Ibid.
41- Ibid., p.16.
42- "Iran ready to co-operate with Caspian neighbors," Alexander's Gas and Oil Connections, July 17, 2001, Vol. 6, issue #13.
43- Ibid.
44- Ibid.
45- Abbas Maleki, "The Iranian Foreign Policy Decision Making: the Case of the Caspian," August 2002.
46- "Iran Pipe Route Preferred," www.caspiancenter.org, 5 March 2002.
47- Pirouz Mojtahed-Zadeh, "A Look At Iran's Geopolitical Perspective of the Caspian Region," SAWA IV, Seminar on West Asian Security, March 2002.
48- "Caspian Sea Region: Oil Export Options," Energy Information Administration, February 2002.
49- Ibid.
50- "Iran Proposes to Azerbaijan to Supply Oil through Idle Gas Pipeline," www.caspiancenter.org, 15 July 2002.
51- "Greece Interested in Iran- Armenia gas pipeline construction," Alexander's Gas and Oil Connections, 13 February 2002.
52- "Caspian Sea Region: Natural Gas Export Options." Energy Information Administration, February 2002.
53- "Interview with the Chairman of Turkmenistan's State Caspian Sea Enterprise, Khoshgeldy Babaev," www.platts.com, 24 September 2001.

54- "Construction of Baku- Tbilisi- Erzurum Pipeline Delayed," www.newsbase.com, 4 September 2002.
55- "Caspian Sea Region: Natural Gas Export Options," Energy Information Administration, February 2002.
56- "Caspian Sea Region: Natural Gas Export Options," Energy Information Administration, February 2002.
57- Ibid.
58- Pirouz Mojtahed-Zadeh, email to authors, 5 August 2002.
59- Farshid Farzin, email to authors, 27 August 2002.
60- Alec Rasizade, "The Mythology of the Munificent Caspian Bonanza and Its Concomitant Pipeline Geopolitics," Comparative Studies of South Asia, Africa, and the Middle East, Vol. XX, Nos. 1&2 , 2000.
61- "MSF Calls for Action on Behalf of People around the Aral Sea," www.msf.org, March 2000.
62- 62-William A. Reinsch, "Statement of William A. Reinsch…Before the Subcommittee On the Middle East and South Asia Committee on International Relations, U.S. House of Representatives," www.usaengage.org, 9 May 2001.
63- Hossein Askari, John Forrer, Hildy Teegen, Jiawen Yang, "U.S. Economic sanctions: Lessons from the Iranian Experience," Business Economics, July 2001, Vol. 36, Issue 3, p.15.
64- Alec Rasizade, "The Mythology of the Munificent Caspian Bonanza and Its Concomitant Pipeline Geopolitics," Comparative Studies of South Asia, Africa, and the Middle East, Vol. XX, Nos. 1&2 , 2000.
65- 'Russia plans cooperation with Iran despite US opposition', Alexander's Gas & Oil Connections, Vol.7, Issue #16 (23 August 2002).
66- Richard B. Cheney, 'Defending Liberty in a Global Economy', speech delivered at the Collateral Damage Conference, Cato Institute (23 June 1998).
67- Richard B. Cheney, 'Defending Liberty in a Global Economy', speech delivered at the Collateral Damage Conference, Cato Institute (23 June 1998).
68- 'Transparency International Corruption Perceptions Index 2002', www. transparency.org (28 August 2002).
69- 'US concern for Caspian security grows', www.newsbase.com (4 May 2002).
70- 'Iran-Libya Sanctions Act- One Year Later', Hearing before the Committee on International Relations, House of Representatives (23 July 1997), pp.5.
71- Pirouz Mojtahed-Zadeh, "A Look at Iran's Geopolitical Perspective of the Caspian Region," SAWA IV, Seminar on West Asian Security, March 2002.
72- 'US concern for Caspian security grows', www.newsbase.com (4 May 2002).
73- Pirouz Mojtahed-Zadeh, "A Look at Iran's Geopolitical Perspective of the Caspian Region," SAWA IV, Seminar on West Asian Security, March 2002.

IRAN'S NORTHERN BOUNDARIES

Section A3- Iran's North-Eastern Boundaries

CHAPTER VII

Emergence and Evolution of Iran's North-Eastern Boundaries
Pirouz Mojtahed-Zadeh

Preface: Turan = Turkistan = Turkmenistan

Turan is an ancient Persian term for areas to the east of Central Asia known throughout history as Turkistan. The western peripheries of these areas have since time immemorial been known as Khorasan. The expanse in question geographically stretched from the Caspian Sea to the western provinces of China. It included both desert and highlands and the fertile Farghanah valley at its centre. This stretch of land has been occupied by peoples of nomadic traditions speaking in Persian or Turkish dialects. Among its historic centers are Bokhara, Samarqand, Balkh, Marve and Tashkent, most on the ancient caravan trail known as the Silk Road. The western half came under Iranian control as from 6th century BC, Moslem dynasties of Turko-Iranian origin controlled the area – by then known as Khorasan - from 7th century AD. Iranian control of western half was restored in 16th century AD and Russian control of the area began in the 18th century. The eastern half was contested between the Chinese empires and various nomadic peoples, such as the Mongols and the Khojahs.

During the 19th century, Russian, Chinese and Afghanistan began to impose centralized governments on the region. In 1884 East Turkistan became the Chinese province of Sinkiang – now known as the Xinjiang Uygur Autonomous Region. Under Russian control, after the Civil War in 1921 West Turkistan was divided into five Soviet republics of Kazakhstan, Turkmenistan, Uzbekistan, Tajikistan and Kyrgyzstan. All five republics declared independent in 1991 in the wake of the collapse of the Soviet Union.

Introduction

The Perso-Turan boundary lines of early Christian era are undoubtedly the first examples of "boundary", in the modern meaning of the term, in the history of mankind.

While the concept of 'frontier', as a vast area, or a zone of contact (1) between two states, is old and has existed for centuries, custodians of modern political geography tell us that "boundary" is new and evolved in the post-industrial revolution Europe. They believe that the need for defining precise lines of separation and points of contacts between states emerged with the emergence of 'world economy' in the nineteenth century. This new phenomenon – one of the earliest examples of which was created in the eastern flanks of Iran - was the inevitable outcome of the expansion of imperialism of global aspirations in the earlier periods, and its inherent global economic order and new trade and communication systems (2). No doubt the assumption in this analysis is correct that 'frontier' is old concept and 'boundary' is new. But should Western political geographers study some of the eastern literatures of historical geography, they might conclude that both concepts have existed long before the emergence of global imperialism. A look at the works of Iran's historical geography would demonstrate that Iranians of the Sassanid era (AD 224- 651) successfully developed both concepts, by creating frontier zones in the west of their empire and boundary line in its east. In the west, the Sassanids appear to have developed the concept of 'frontier zone' in clear terms. They created two kinds of frontier-keeping states: the internal frontier states within their four *Kusts*: and the external frontier-keeping states, the most famous of the latter being the state of Hirah or Manazerah in Mesopotamia.

On the northwestern corner of the Persian Gulf, where Iranian and Roman empires' frontiers met, the vassal kingdom of Hirah was created by the Sassanids in the 6th century AD on the river Tigris, not far from their Capital Ctesiphon. This frontier-keeping state, paid annually and defended by the Iranians, played the role of a buffer state for Iran, defusing pressure from the Romans (3). In a similar move, the Romans created the vassal kingdom of Ghassan in the region now known as Syria, to play the same role vis-à-vis Iran for the Romans (4).

In their eastern flank the Sassanids faced the Turans. Like the Romans, the Turans also fought many wars with the Iranians. But unlike their political geography arrangements with the Romans in the west, the Iranians created precise boundaries with the Turans in the east, which evolved throughout the ages, and the study of that constitutes the main aim of this article.

Turan is a term used by Ferdosi (d AD 1020) in his Shanameh, the greatest work of epic literature in Persian language in reference to peoples of Turkic origin in the eastern fringes of old Khorasan. What constitutes 'Central Asia' now was 'Greater Khorasan' in most parts of the past twenty centuries or so.

Khorasan has always been considered as the birthplace of Iran. Prophet Zoroaster, (about 1000 BC) whose teachings form the essence of what was to become Iran, propagated his religion originally in the lands of Khorasan. Traditionally Zoroaster is believed to have converted legendary king Goshtasb of Shahnameh's Iran, at Balkh in Central Asia in 588 BC, but some scholars locate the event earlier and elsewhere, perhaps around 1000 BC and at Herat or in Khwarezm. Both these localities are in Central Asia, the ancient Khorasan (5).

The Turanis were tribally organized and were nomadic powers in territorial contests for centuries with the Iranians to their west. They were lucked in a geopolitical game of pushing and throwing territories and boundaries with Iran, which eventually settled the political geography of Central Asia and Iran in its present form.

Emergence and Evolution of Iran-Turan Boundaries

Although the Achaemenid Cyrus the Great (BC 559 – 529), founder of Iran, was killed during his Eastern campaign, it was under his leadership that all lands to the west of Oxus were incorporated into the Iranian (Persian) Commonwealth of semi-independent nations that the Achaemenids had created. Cyrus the Great's campaign in the East did not, however, settle the north - eastern borders of his commonwealth. The Parthians have been in contests with the Kushan Empire – also of Iranian descent - to their east for a long period of time. Legends have it that raids and wars between Iran and the Turanic tribes of north - east reached such an intolerable level at the time of the Parthian feudal empire (247 BC to 224 AD) that they constructed the wall that is generally known as *Sadd-e Sekandar* (Alexander's dam). This wall was separate Iran from Turan in order to defuse pressure from the latter.

Some political geographers argue that ancient walls, such as the Great Wall of China, the Hadrian Wall of Roman Britain were not 'boundary' lines. They were parts of much wider frontier zones, constructed solely for the purpose of separating civilizations from primitive powers.

When the Sassnid state was at its highest in Iran, new tribal movements in Central Asia caused widespread disruption in the geopolitical world of late 4th and early 5th centuries. Shapur II (AD 309 – 379), who was crowned as the 'king of kings' of the Sassanid federative system while still in his mother's womb, had defeated the Chionites and had even persuaded them to help him in his Roman wars. His death encouraged the Hepthalite Huns of the east, who called themselves *Kushans,* to ravage northern fringes of his empire (6).

The Chionites, the Kidarites, the Huns and Hepthalite Huns were peoples of Indo-European origin. Arrival in Central Asia of tribes of Turkic origin in early 6th century led to a kind of mixture that the native populations became completely absorbed by the new comers. It is this mixture that Ferdosi refers to as the "Turans". Ferdosi, however, dates the origin of the "Turaninans" to the beginning of the mankind. In his legend of geographical dispersion of mankind, comparable to that of biblical stories of dispersion of mankind by Prophet Noah, Ferdosi asserts that Afreidun, the founding father of Iran, had three sons: Salm Tur and Iraj. He gave the West (Rome) to Salm, the East (Turkistan) to Tur, and bestowed Iran to Iraj (7).

If Ferdosi's epic work of literature, partly based on legends and in part on history, is to be taken as evidence, then there is no doubt that 'boundary' was first invented by the Iranians. The Shahnameh of Ferdosi speaks of precise land and river boundary lines between Iran and Turan at the time of Sassanid Varahram V (Bahram-e Goor = reigning from AD 421 to 439). Ferdosi reveals that at the end of Varahram's wars with the Turanis the two sides agreed to erect boundary pillars to mark their land borderlines. He does not, however, give the precise location of the boundary line. But when it came to the river boundaries, Ferdosi states that the two sides agreed to put their boundary on river Oxus (Amu-Darya = Jeihun) (8).

Historical records although verify that Varahram's eastern campaign was thoroughly successful, but his sun Pirouz (459 – 84) was defeated by the Hepthalites and killed in the war. Iran was forced to pay annual tribute to the Turans until 557 AD when Khosro Anushirvan the Just (Anushah-Ravan = the imortal sol) (531 – 79) felt strong enough repudiate the agreement to pay the tribute. He allied himself with the Turks, who had recently arrived in Trans-Oxania.

> *Together they utterly defeated the Hepthalite forces and divided the kingdom between themselves: the Turks took the territories north of the Oxus, while Khusrau ruled over much of Afghanistan (9).*

The Post-Islamic Developments

The Sassanid tradition of royal patronage of science, arts, and literature was perhaps the most important factor in the expansion of Iranian culture and traditions in the lands of Turan. One of the lasting impacts of this tradition was the successful Persianisation of most parts of Central Asia and the survival of Persian language itself in Iran and Central Asia in the post-Islamic era. Quoting Ebn Bibi, Philippani-Ronconi gives an example of the impact of Iranian culture in the lands of Turan, stating;

> *... the historian Ibn Bibi, describing the Seljuq ruler's accession to the throne, gives an account of a number of Iranian and even Indo-Iranian traditions followed on that occasion, such as the release of Captives (10). These attest to the overwhelming influence of Persian patterns that preserved the traits of an Indo-European protohistorical tradition (11).*

In the post-Islamic era the lands known as Turan were in the control of the eastern Turks: the Seljuqs, the Ilak Khans, the Atabaks, and the Teimurids. These dynasties succeeded in thoroughly Turanising the north - eastern fringes of the Iranian plateau, from what is now Kyrgyzstan in the east, to Turkmenistan in the west. This Turanising of northern fringes of the Iranian plateau continued as far west as living its marks on the peoples and territories to the west of the Caspian Sea, namely the people of Azerbaijan who adopted a highly Persianised Turkish dialect without actually being Turks or Turanis by origin.

It was at the height of Iran's struggle for self-preservation in the face of expanding Arabisation of eastern Caliphate in fifth century AH that a new wave of Iranian identity seeking emerged in the shape of Shiite dynasties of Iranian stock with some Ismailite tendencies. These were dynasties like the Samanids, Saffarids, and Deilamids. But this wave was soon challenged by a new political storm from the eastern parts of the Iranian Plateau. A number of new dynasties of Sunni persuasion and Turkish background began to expand their control over Turan and eastern parts of Iran. The Qaznavids were the first of these who were descendants of Alp Takin, a Turkish slave of the Samanid king. Though like their Seljuqid successors, the Qaznavids were different from the Iranians in their ethnic and cultural origin and somewhat alien to the Iranian civilisation, they built and expanded their empire in Central Asia and Khorasan almost exclusively on the basis of Iranian culture and civilisation. Their success in this regard was so immense that without physically or politically being revived, Iran became the heart of Islam. The more fascinating aspect of this was that unlike their Qaznavid overlords the Iranians themselves were increasingly embracing the Shiite sect of Islam at the time and fighting for the revival of their non-Arab identity at the heart of Islam. When Sultan Mahmud Qaznavid died in 1030, his kingdom stretched from Samarqand in Central Asia to Gujerat in India, from Kashmir in Pamir to Mesopotamia:

> *Although narrow-minded, bigoted, and strictly Sunni, his plans did not include founding any civilisations that were not to be both Iranian and Islamic, and with this aim he enriched his court in Ghazna (the present Afghanistan) with literary men, scientists, and philosophers virtually kidnapped from every corner of his empire. The great philosopher and physician Ibn Sina (Avicenna), the scientist and historian al-Biruni, the philosopher Abu Sahl al-Masihi ("the Christian"), and the so-called pleiad consisting of such Persian poets as 'Unsuri, Farrokhi, Asadi* (12), *and Ferdowsi were sometimes his enforced guests* (13).

However fanatical Sunni and unsympathetic to the Shiites of Iran were the Qaznavida and Seljuqids of Turan, their rule in practice encouraged rise of the spirit of Iranianism, which in turn, fenced off domination of Iranian Plateau by Arab or Turanic identities. Their patronage of Iranian science, arts and literature sew the seeds of revival of Iran as a 'nation' and a 'country'. It was this cultural controversy that introduced the ruling Turanis to the dual life in Iranian Plateau: on the one hand they remained alien to the spirit and civilisation of Iran, and on the other, they found themselves obligated to propagate these phenomenon. It was at the time of these dynasties that Iranian culture and civilisation were promoted far and wide, from Trans-Oxania and India to Mesopotamia. It was at the time of these dynasties that Persian language became the second language of the World of Islam, only because the Holy Quran was in Arabic, and Persian could not, therefore, become the first language of Islam. It was in their time that Iranian science, literature, arts, philosophy and Gnosticism enriched the Islamic civilisation. It somehow seems as if Persianisation of the World of Islam by Turanic dynasties became a tradition that survived for many centuries. Even as late as 16th century the Safavid dynasty of Iranian origin but of Azeri dialect (a Turkic language), took upon themselves to revive political Iran, and in the 18th and 19th centuries the Qajarid Shahs of Turanic origin constantly endeavoured to present themselves as more Iranian than others.

It is true in the mean time that that the rule of Turanic dynasties helped expansion of Iranian spirit and civilisation, the impact of centuries of their political rule Turanised the northern fringes of the Iranian Plateau – Tokharestan and Fargheneh of ancient Turan. Local clans like the Ilek Khan and Ghozz started this process, which was later reinforced by the Mongolian onslought of 1217 AD, followed by settlement in those fringes of Turkic tribes coming from east of old Turan (14). Even in their case, the rulers however, whether Timurid, Mongolian, or Sheibanid, continued to assert their spiritual adherence to Iranian civilisation. But as far as the political side is concerned no doubt that the Seljuq Empire represented the peak of Iranian influence on the lands of old Turan. It is sufficient to recall two names from that period: one, Nezam al-Molk, the grand vazir of Malek Shah (d. 1092), one of the greatest statesmen of the Moslem world: and the other, Imam Mohamad Ghazali (d. 1111), who settled once and for all the reciprocal relations between faith, mysticism, and philosophy in Islam (15).

The Mongolian invasion and its devastating consequences, especially in the eastern parts of Iranian Plateau resulted in the downfall of the Abbasid Caliphate in Iran in 1257 AD and brought the Ismaili movements of Iran to an end. The ascent of Amir Teimur Gurkani and the extensive empire that he created in the Iranian Plateau did not help revival of Iranian civilisation. Nevertheless, a number of his successors, like Shahrokh, Ologh Beig, Baisonqor, and Abu Saeed, made some efforts in promoting the culture and civilisation of Iran in the lands of old Turan. Amir Teimur's grandson Baber, founder of great Mongolian Empire of India (rule from 1483 to 1530) promoted Persian culture and Iranian civilisation in the Indian sub-continent.

The Revival of Iran, and Iran-Turan Boundary Arrangements

At the time of the revival of Iranian political geography, the Safavids managed to restore the country's territorial expanses of the pre-Islamic Sassanian period. Before Russia obtained a footing on the eastern shores of the Caspian Sea, there were no fixed boundaries between the great Iranian province of Khorasan and what was left of the Turan to the north. Shah Abbas the Great initiated the practice of settling and maintaining colonies of Kurdish and other warlike tribesmen in the mountainous country in the north of Khorasan in order to keep at bay the predatory Turkmans. Nader Shah not only followed this policy actively, but also over-ran the whole Turkmen country, up to and including Marv, Khiveh in modern Turkmenistan, as well as subduing Bokhara and Samarqand in modern Uzbekistan. This extension of Iranian authority to the north and north - east was purely ephemeral. On Nader Shah's assassination in June 1747, the northern slopes of the mountains Kopet Dagh, Kuran Dagh, Kuh-e Hezar Masjed and other ranges to the south-east of these mountains, once again came to constitute the northern frontiers of Iran and what was left of the ancient Turan.

When Peter the Great began extending Russian authority to south-east corner of the Caspian Sea, the southward shifting of Pers-o Turan boundaries began. Iran's humbling defeat by the Russians in two major wars resulted in the conclusion of the treaty of Golestan in 1813 and the disastrous treaty of Turkmanchai of 21 February 1828. Not only did Iran loose extensive and valuable territories in the Caucasus under these treaties, Russia was granted the right of Capitulation in Iran, which was later granted to the British and other powers. This territorial disintegration of Iran was coupled with the political decline of the country as a consequence and put Iran at the mercy of the Great Game of imperialistic geopolitics played by the Russians and the British in its east and north-eastern flanks (16). As these two treaties debarred Iran from maintaining warships flying her flag on the Caspian Sea, she was unable to cope with the piratical activities of the Turkmans on the south-east coasts of the Caspian. Their raids became so extensive that in 1834 Tehran requested assistance from Moscow to restore order in Turkistan. This request gave Russia the opportunity of pushing its military activities within Iranian territories. They established a force on Ashuradeh Island, which was maintained for a long period of time, ostensibly for preventing Turkman raids, despite repeated protests from Iran.

The rebellion of Prince Kameran, the vassal king of Iran's dependent province of Herat in early 1830s, coincided with the lawlessness in federal Iran's other dependencies in Turkistan. Rebellion in Marv, Bokhara, Khiveh, and other countries of the Turkman and Uzbek peoples intensified, and they "then continued depredation in Asterabad (17) and the neighbouring districts" (18). The Iranian Government of Haj Mirza Aghasi prepared two expeditions in 1836: one against Herat and the other against Marv, Khiveh and Bokhara, which was to proceed to the north - east after Herat was subdued. The expedition against Herat agitated Sir John McNeil, British Minister in Tehran, who suspended Anglo-Iranian relations and left Iran in protest. British military undertaking against Iran in 1837 frustrated Iran's military expeditions in the east and north - east, and reassured the Russians of Iran's complete political decline. This development encouraged the Russians to push their frontiers southward to include all of Turkistan and Central Asia.

In 1869, when Russia seized Qezel-Su (which she renamed Krasnovodsk, the Russian equivalent of the Turkish name) and Balkhan Bay, Iran protested against their seizure of that locality and asked them what was the purpose of constructing a fort at Krasnovodsk. Tehran also asked Moscow of an assurance that Russia would not interfere with the Yamut Turkmans who inhabited the country round the mouth of the Atrak and Gorgan rivers. In reply, Russia acknowledged Iran's authority as far north as the mouth of the Atrak (19). The Iranian Government acquiesced, as they were under the impression that the Russian claim to the territory north of the Atrak applied only to a coastal strip extending inland no more than 30 or 40 miles.

Evolution of Russo-Iranian Boundaries in Turan Country

It did not take the Russians a long time to bring into open their expansionist drive eastwards and south - eastwards from Krasnovodsk. In 1873 Russia took Qezel Arvat and conquered the principality of Khiveh from Iran. Soon afterwards the Russians claimed from Iran the northern half of the whole basin of the Atrak. Similarly they erected a fort at Chikishliar, a place on the Caspian coast 9 miles north - west of the Gulf of Hassan-Qoli. In 1880-81 Russian forces, commanded by General Skobelev, attacked and completely crushed the Akhal Tekke Turkman. This military adventure extended Russia's occupation of Turkistan territories as far south as the northern foothills of the Kopet Dagh and south - eastward as far as Ashkhabad (this name is a Turkish corruption of Persian Eshgh-Abad) and beyond. Having established themselves well inside Turkistan territories of Iran the Russians imposed on 21 December 1881 a frontier convention in Tehran, which defined new border between the two states from the mouth of Atrak River to the small town of Lotfabad, 60 miles east – north - east of Quchan. At the time, Atrak flowed into the sea on the southern side of the Gulf of Hassan-Qoli (20).

Atrak River itself formed the boundary line between Iran and Russia as far as the junction of Sumbar at Chat, 75 miles east – north - east of the Gulf of Hassan-Qoli. From this point eastward the boundary was rather poorly defined. From Chat however, this boundary line ran first north -

east and then east, along the ridges of the Songu Dagh and Sagirim Mountain range for 55 miles. It then swung to the north, crossed the Chandir - a territory of the Atrak, just the west of the ruined fort of Yangi Qal'eh - and bore east again until it reached the Copet Dagh mountain. The boundary then followed the ridge of this and the subsequent mountains in a predominantly south - easterly direction as far as Lotfabad. This boundary line left the village and district of Firouzeh – on the road from Guk Tappeh to Shirvan – on the Iranian side. This convention also provided for the demarcation of the boundary line as far as Lotfabad.

A year later (1882) the Russo-Iranian delimitation and demarcation commission began its work, which lasted three years. The commission recognised the Lotfabad village as belonging to Iran, but the exact frontier eastwards from this point to Sarakhs on the Tajan River was not ascertainable at the turn of the twentieth century. Lord George Curzon believes that most of the ambiguous points were clarified in a secret treaty signed in 1883 between Russia and Iran (21). However, demarcation of the boundary was not easier than its delimitation. The nomadic Yamut Turkman tribes who had occupied both sides of Atrak were in the habit of crossing the river at certain seasons of the year. Although the treaty of 1881 had given them the right to do so, complications arose in respect of tax collection. This situation led to the Russian officials frequently crossing the border-river in their attempt to collect tax from the Iranian Yamut Turkmans on the Gorgan River. This infringement of frontier arrangement led to a dispute, which was eventually settled by shifting the boundary to the south of the river in the 1893 treaty. Moreover, It was subsequently discovered that the Iranian commissioners had, either because of lack of adequate geographical knowledge of the frontier areas or through bribery, accepted an artificial irrigation canal of Atrak as the main body of that river and as the extreme western portion of the boundary. This canal had been constructed several miles south of Atrak inside Iran. Acceptance of the said canal had left thousands of acres of fertile agricultural lands to the Russians. A further complication arose when river Atrak changed its course in its lower reaches, and took a more northerly route to the Sea. Correlated to these was a two fold Russian object in seeking to extend their frontiers further to the south. In the first place, the arable lands in the southerly parts of the lower Atrak basin was of better quality than the land in the north; secondly, by establishing themselves further to the south, they were able to secure control over practically the whole of the Yamut Turkmans. To achieve these objectives, the Russians imposed another border convention on the Iranians on 8th June 1893 whereby the Iranians ceded the village and district of Firuzeh to Russia, and received in return the following districts; the small area on the south bank of the Aras opposite Abbasabad in the Caucasus; the village and district of Hasar situated a short distance to the south – east of Lotfabad.

This convention defined the boundary south – eastwards from Lotfabad to Zolfaqar Pass, where it meets General McLeen's 1891 Boundary line between Iran and Afghanistan (22), and completes the definition of the whole of Russo-Iranian boundaries on the eastern side of the Caspian Sea. This convention also provided for the demarcation of the boundaries south – eastwards from Lotfabad.

Russia's Southward Expansionism Continues

The nomadic lifestyle of the Turkman tribes of Greater Khorasan (Central Asia) served as an excuse for the Russian intervention and ultimate absorption of those regions. Similarly, in the case of Iran, the incursion by the Turkman tribes of cross- border areas provided the Russians with a good excuse to continue her campaign of encroachments on the northern frontiers of Iran. Worse still was the uncertainty and confusion still looming over Russo-Iranian boundaries in Turkistan.

In 1834 Britain's famous Arrowsmith published a map to illustrate Captain Burnes' travel in Iran in which he placed the Iranian boundary to the north of the Atrak River. Another map was published in Britain in 1848 by C. Zimmermann, in which the Iranian boundary was placed some distance above the Atrak. This was in harmony with Sanson's Atlas of 1700, which also placed the said boundary on the north of Atrak River. In 1863 Murray published a map to describe Vamber's travels in Persia. In this map the Rivers Atrak and Gorgan were given to Turkman and the Qara Su was described as forming the northern boundary of Iran near the Caspian Sea. When in 1869 the Shah of Iran questioned Russia's intention with regard to areas around Atrak River, the Russians replied in an assuring manner that can be considered as a new understanding between the two sides. The Shah had sought explanation from M. Beger, the Russian Minister in Tehran, as to the purpose of a fort being built by the Russians at Krasnovodsk and an assurance that they should undertake to build no more forts at the confluence of the Atrak and Gorgan rivers. The Shah had also sought an undertaking from the Russians not to interfere with the affairs of the Turkman and Khorasan territories of Iran. After communicating with his government, Beger informed the Iranian Court in December 1869 that the Tsar *"recognises the authority and sovereignty of Persia up to the banks of the Atrak river"* (23). The Russian Government further explained that their occupation of Ashuradeh Island was meant to protect the caravans from attacks by Turkman tribesmen. The Iranian Government accordingly informed the Governor of Astarabad (later Gorgan) that the Russians were not to cross the Atrak which belonged to Iran, while on the other side of the river the Russians would be at liberty to build whatever they liked (24).

Three years later (1873) articles appeared in the British press, specially the one in the *Morning Post,* suggesting that a secret treaty had been signed on behalf of the Shah and the Tsar whereby Iran cede to Russia the valley of River Atrak (25). These reports were, however, denied officially by the officials of foreign ministries of both governments. What was true at that time, however, was that the Iranians began to suspect Russian movements along the course of the Atrak.

Russia was deeply involved in rivalries with Britain at the time, and the so-called Great game of geopolitics between the two giants of the nineteenth century involved occupation of Iranian and Afghan territories by one or the other. Intelligence in Britain of Russian intention of occupying frontier areas of Qezel-Arvat, Barani and Baorma, caused the Iranian Minister in London to express his Government's anxiety on the subject, and to enquire whether the time had not yet come for recognising the integrity of Iran as well as Afghanistan. British Foreign Office informed Iranian Minister in London that an understanding between England and Russia of 1834 existed upon the subject of independence of Iran, and that it had been confirmed by Lord Palmerston in 1838.

It is worth noting that Iran was at that time greatly apprehensive of the might and power of her two giant neighbours: Russia and British India. The government of Iran could not seriously and openly remonstrate against Russian activities and thus expose itself to the full burst of Russian anger. Indeed, its fears were at times concealed by hopes that Russia would become its protector in the face of British interference in the Iranian affairs. The British, at the same time, were wary of Iran's 'collusion' with Russia against territories controlled by them in Afghanistan and beyond. It was because of these suspicions that Britain decided to support separatist drive of the principality of Herat from Iran and the creation of the state of Afghanistan to play the role of a buffer state between herself and the suspected Russo-Iranian axis (26). Against these British suspicions, the reality was that Russia was busy by one excuse or another in their scheme of encroaching on the Iranian territories. On 10th March 1873 a detachment of the Russian troops crossed the Atrak and attacked the Yamut Turkmans within eight miles of Astarabad. In reply to the question by the Iranian Government, the Russians explained that the action in question was one of necessity and could not be avoided as it had left the Iranian frontier unguarded and the Russian authorities felt it their duty to punish the Turkmans. It was stated, however, that the act was not one of agression, and Russia renewed her assurances that she fully recognised Atrak as the northern boundary of Iran (27).

Having gradually assumed the right of punishing the Yamut Turkmans, the Russian Government took a bolder step in 1874 when General Lamakin landed with a number of soldiers at a place called Shah Qadam, eight stages from Astarabad. There he issued a circular to the Yamut Turkmans telling them that from Gorgan River – three miles from Astarabad – as far as Khiveh belonged to Russia. The circular in which the General styled himself as the commander over the Turkmans, meant to call upon the Turkmans to adopt peacefull habits and to refrain from molesting Russian Trade (28). The political significance of this step could have been the assumption by Russia of authority over the Turkmans and over the Atrak and Gorgan rivers. Once again the Iranians seemed to have been easily satisfied with the explanation from the Russians about this incident. In spite of their satisfaction of the explanation, General Lamakin went to occupy Qara-Qal'eh on the Atrak with 600 men and two guns. Compared with the silence of the Iranian authorities, the British felt some anxiety at this movement of the Russian troops as they considered the occupation of any strategic points on Atrak as a first step towards the occupation of Marv, and the beginning of constant intrigues in Afghanistan. On 12th December 1874 Thomson of British Legation at Tehran suggested in a telegraph from Tehran that the British should give Iran moral support in their protest against the Russian movements. Convinced of Iran's lack of real courage in standing before the Russians together with realising the confused state of the frontiers between her and Russia, British Foreign Office informed Thomson that it would be better for the British to stay out of the incident (29).

At the same time, the Russians adopted a conciliatory policy towards the Turkmans to secure their confidence and pave the way for their complete subjugation. This policy bore favourable results and in some cases not only did the Turkmans show submission but showed inclination to assist the Russian troops. On 11th August 1875 the Russians landed building material at Qezel-Su apparently for the purpose of constructing a new fort at Bezat-Haji on the Atrak, about 90 miles east of Hassan Qoli. Earlier on, General Lamakin started from Krosnovodsk on the so-called scientific exploration of the ancient bed of the Oxus and on 21st July he passed Qezel-Arvat to attack the Tekke Turkmans. Moreover, in September 1875, the *Journal de St. Petersburgh* announced that the Akhal Tekke tribe submitted to the Russian rule (30).

The Iranian Ministry of Foreign Affairs sent a note to the Russian Minister at Tehran on 26th December 1874 enquiring about the boundary line on the river Atrak and Iran's authority therein. The Russian Minster repudiated, on the strength of the terms of the 1869 arrangement, the Iranian claim exercising authority over the tribes. The Iranian Foreign Minister, in reply, reminded the Russian Minister that:

> *The arrangement of 1869 was sudden and telegraphic, the heads of the matters were stated, but details were not entered into. It does not follow that because all the old established rights of Persia were not inserted therein they should be made a subject for doubt and refutation* (31).

In his reply to this letter, the Russian rejected the repeated complaints of the Iranian Government on 5th March 1875, and stated that the arrangement of 1869, though telegraphic, was nevertheless an arrangement concluded after long discussions. He added that both governments considered it as perfectly clear and sufficient (32).

In his subsequent letter to the Russian Minister, the Iranian Minister of Foreign Affairs stated on 7th March 1875 that action such as Lamakin's addressed to the Turkman tribes was done in direct opposition to the very arrangement of 1869. *"Furthermore"*, stated the Iranian Foreign Minister, *"if the Russian Minister referred to his own letter No. 82, of 21st Ramezan 1286 (3rd December 1869)* which after the telegraphic reply from the Imperial Minister for Foreign Affairs, he addressed to the Persian Foreign Department, he would perceive *"that the essential and high object of the Persian Government has been and is still, the maintenance of their ancient sovereign rights over the Turkman tribes"* (33).

New Adjustments in Soviet-Iranian Boundary Arrangements

Russian southward expansionism stopped with the signing in Tehran of the 1893 convention while the Iranians remained unhappy about having to cede to Russia some of their undisputed territories in the frontier areas concerned. The rise into power of new regime of Soviet Union after the October revolution of 1917 marked a turning point in Russia's territorial attitude towards Iran. On 26th February 1921 the Soviet Government concluded a treaty of friendship with the new regime in Iran. Article III of this treaty states the two powers agree:

> *...to accept and respect the Russo-Iranian frontiers as drawn by the Frontier Commission (sic) in 1881. At the same time, in view of the repugnance, which the Russian Federal Government feels to enjoying the fruit of the policy of usurpation of the Tsarist Government, it renounces all claim to the Achuradeh (Ashuradeh) islands and to the other on the Astarabad Litoral, and restores to Persia (Iran) the village of Firouzeh and adjacent lands ceded to Russia in virtue of the convention of 28th May (equivalent to 8th June, new style), 1893. The Persian Government agrees for its part that the Russian Sarakhs or 'old' Sarakhs and the land adjacent to the Sarakhs River, shall be retained by Russia.*
>
> *"The two High Contracting Parties shall have equal rights of usage over the Atrak River and the other frontier rivers and waterways. In order finally to solve the question of the waterways and all disputes concerning any territories, a Commission composed of Russian and Persian representatives shall be appointed* (34).

Article XI of this treaty of friendship states that as the treaty of Turkmanchai was abrogated (35), Iran was no longer precluded by article VIII of that treaty from maintaining a fleet (36) on the Caspian Sea, and that both powers should, from the moment of signature of the present treaty, *"enjoy reciprocally the right of navigation on the Caspian Sea under their own flag (37).* It is noteworthy that, in spite of this display of magnanimity, the Soviet Union did not return to Iran, either at the time or at any time thereafter, any of the vast territories that Tsarist Russia had acquired from Iran by virtue of the treaties of Golestan and Turkmanchai.

It is curious that the 1921 treaty of friendship limited itself to recognition of the boundaries between the two countries only as laid down by the treaty of 1881. It makes no reference at all to the remaining portion of the borderline as defined by the convention of the 8th June 1893.

Developments subsequent to the conclusion of the 1921 treaty are, to some extend, shrouded in obscurity. While, on the one hand, the former bed of the lower Atrak seems to have been accepted by the Soviet Union as the extreme western portion of the boundaries, available evidence shows that until 1939, the village of Firouzeh was regarded in the Soviet Union as belonging to that country. Bolshaya Sovietskaya Entsiklopedia of (article on Firouzeh in 1936) and Bolshoy Sovietskiy Atlas Mira of 1939, for instance, show Firouzeh on the Soviet side of the border.

Attempts were made however, by the Russo-Iranian boundary commission in 1922 and in subsequent years to delimit the Western point of the frontier, but little or nothing could be accomplished. This was because of the evasiveness of Soviet officials, as an official document of British Foreign Office describes (38). As the lack of a definite borderline later gave rise to problems, it was agreed in March 1936 that a new Russo-Iranian commission should demarcate the boundary as defined by the 1881 treaty. Once again there was no reference to the frontier as defined by the convention of 8th June 1893 whereby some border areas were given to Iran in return for the village of Firouzeh being ceded to Russia.

It was reported in July 1926 that the Soviet Union was to return to Iran 185 square versts (39) of territory in the neighbourhood of Pol-e Khatun, on the left bank of the Hari-Rud river just south of the point where it is joined by the Kashaf-Rud. The Russians had taken this land from Naser ad-Din Shah of Iran in the latter part of the nineteenth century (40). Since all the land on the west side of the Hari-Rud and Tajan (41) in this region was already in Iran, the area in question must have been on the east bank of that river to the south of old Sarakhs.

Even as late as 1945, when Professor Lockhart's questions on the state of Soviet-Iranian-boundaries were put to the Iranian Ministry of Foreign Affiars, the ministry stated in reply that the entire frontier between Iran and Soviet Union, including that between lotfabad and Dahaneh Zolfaqar has been delimited. Some differences exist only (42).

Iran-Soviet Hydropolitics of Border Rivers

Representatives of Iran and Soviet Union met in February 1926 in a convention to determine necessary arrangement for the use of water of the border rivers between the two countries. Water in the relatively dry countries of Khorasan and Turkmanistan is of much significance in local agricultural and animal husbandry. British observers testify the local Soviet authorities had for long looked with a jealous eye upon all land that could be irrigated in those regions, together with sources of water. In his despatch of March 1926, Sir R. Hodgson, for instance, stated that:

> *The Russians from time immemorial had not only insisted that all water of the frontier rivers should be devoted to irrigating the cotton fields of Turkmanestan, but had gone so far as to compel the Persian inhabiting the frontier regions to root up all their trees so that no part of the water should be absorbed in Persian territory. As a consequence, considerable districts formerly fertile had been reduced to an arid state (43).*

The river convention of the two countries of February 1926 however resulted in signing a treaty, which puts the two countries' river boundary on the middle of the border rivers and divides the water between the two sides on equal basis. Article XVI of which concerns division of water in Atrak River. This article provides that:

> *All the water of the Atrak River, which is co-extensive with the frontier between the contracting parties, shall be divided into two equal parts; one part from Persia and the other for U.S.S.R.*
>
> *The measurement of the water of the Atrak River shall be conducted by technicians of the contracting parties, for a distance of 14 versts from the frontier up stream on the territory of Persia. All of the water obtained as result of the said measurements is subject to division into two equal parts.*
>
> *In case Persia should decide, after the signing of the present Convention, to erect hydrotechnical installations along the Atrak River, on its territory, for the purpose of damming the water, the Government of Persia shall undertake to let pass, during the irrigation period, to the frontier between Persia and U.S.S.R., where the division of the water of the Atrak River begins, the same quantity of water that would have been available in accordance with meteorological conditions and in the absence of such installations. Persia shall forewarn U.S.S.R of its decision to establish such installations* (44).

Curiously enough the convention had not sough the same undertaking by the Soviet Union in its use of extra water by using hydrotechnical installations along the Atrak River on its territory for the purpose of damming the water. Nevertheless, the convention has successfully prevented serious disputes erupting between the two countries on water uses of the river.

Thanks to the water from Atrak River, Dasht-e Gorgan or Gorgan Plain, in the south of that river's basin has been developed both through mechanised cerial cultivation and through more intensive grazing. A plan was drawn up in August 1957 by a joint Soviet-Iranian venture for building a number of irrigation reservoirs on the Atrak River.

Unlike the equal division of the river Atrak's water between Iran and the Soviet Union, the 1926 Water Convention gave Iran less than a third of the water of river Hari-Rud (Tajan). Article XV of the convention reads:

> *All the water of the Geri-Roud (Tajan) River, down stream from the Pul-I-Khatun Bridge and co-extensive with the frontier between the contracting parties, shall be divided into ten equal parts; three parts shall be utilized by Persia and seven parts by U.S.S.R.*
>
> *The measurement of the water of the Geri-Roud (Tajan) River shall be conducted by technicians of the Contracting Parties at the village of Doulat-Abad and on all the canals diverting from the Geri-Roud River into the territory of Persia, as well as conducted on the territory of U.S.S.R. along the entire distance of the Geri-Roud River from the village of Doulat-Abad up to the Pul-I-Khatun Bridge. All the water obtained as a result of the said measurements shall be subject to division into ten equal parts.*
>
> *For the purpose of accurately dividing the water of the Geri-Roud River at Doulat-Abad, technicians of the Contracting Parties will erect a permanent water gauge. The expense for the erection of this gauge will be borne by the Contracting Parties, in accordance with a mutual agreement concerning this project and proportionately to the quotas received by them at that point* (45).

The convention however contains no explanation as to why and on what basis only three-tenth of the water of Hari-Rud or river Tajan was allocated to Iran and seven-tenth to Soviet Union. Similarly, the Iranians do not appear to have questioned, then or at any time thereafter, this obvious infringement of Iran's right to the water of Hari-Rud Tajan River.

The Soviets, however, continued interference with Iran's right to the water of the border rivers. An incident in 1950 provoked a note of complaint to the Soviet Union on 18th May that year. Soviet press carried Moscow's reply to the Iranian Government on22 June 1950 (46), which was, in essence, dismissive of the complaint of the Iranian Government. A few days early, in an interview with the British diplomats, Iran's Deputy Foreign Minister explained that: *a dispute had arisen over the distribution of the water in the Hari Rud...* and that *the local inhabitants had moved across from the Soviet to the Iranian side in order to demolish the channel through which the Iranians drew off their water.* The British Embassy despatch continues that the incident had been terminated by the river drying up and that the Ministry of Foreign Affairs tried without success to get the Soviets to agree to a proper demarcation of the frontier (47).

This was the post-war era when Soviet reluctance in withdrawing its forces from the Iranian Azerbaijan signalled the beginning of the Cold War between the East and the West for the rest of the twentieth century. Not only was not Soviet Union prepared to stop infringement of Iran's rights to the border rivers' water, but prevented Iran from exploiting its oil resources on its own territories south of the Caspian See, requesting concession from Iran to exploit these resources for herself, which was turned down (48).

Figure 7

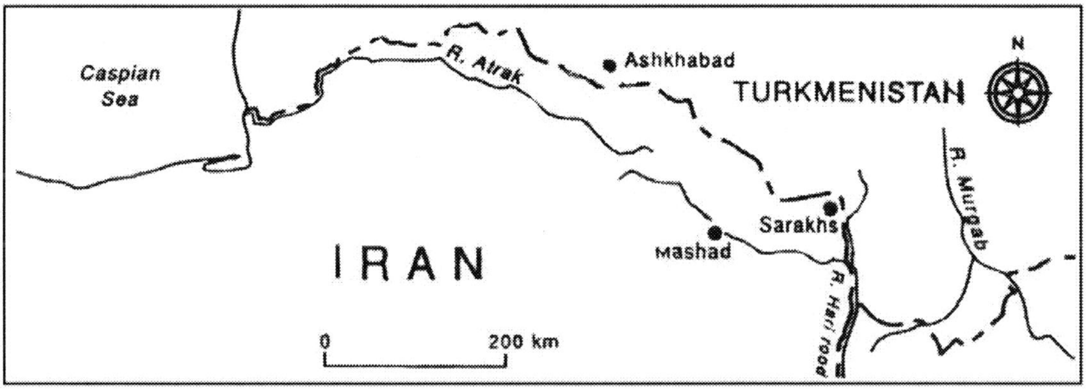

The North-Eastern Boundaries of Iran:
Boundaries of Iran and Turkmenistan

Conclusion
The Iran-Turkmenistan Frontiers of Friendship and Cooperation

Relations improved with the Soviet Union in mid 1960s after Iranian and Soviet leads met in Moscow in June 1965 and settled border differences. A new line of boundary demarcation on both sides of the Caspian Sea put an end to the border differences between the two countries. Under the new and improved relations an economic cooperation agreement made it possible for the Iranian natural gas too be piped to the Soviet Union in return for the construction in Iran of a still mill at Isfahan by the Soviets. Soviet Prime Minister recalls:

We invited the Shah to negotiate with us. We made considerable concessions to Iran on the disputed border. Some of their claims we compromised on, and others we satisfied completely. We signed a protocol establishing a mutually acceptable line of demarcation on the map. We were pleased to have liquidated one of the major obstacles, which had stood in the way of good Soviet-Iranian relations (49).

Subsequently, a number of joint-venture investments on utilisation of water from border rivers took place between the two countries. Relations improved further in the wake of the Islamic Revolution of Iran, which put an end to Soviet Union's anxieties over Iran's close cooperations with the United States. An agreement signed between the Islamic Republic of Iran and waning Soviet Union in 1991 permitted freedom of cross-border travel by ethnic Azeri and Turkman populations up to 45 miles on either sides of the two countries' boundaries (50). Earlier on a Memorandum of Understanding was concluded (15 February 1990) between the two countries whereby 11 transit points were selected on the borderlines, four of which were in the north – eastern border areas (51).

Emergence of the Republic of Turkmenistan, in Central Asia, in the wake of the collapse of the Soviet Union in 1991, marked a new chapter and a new turning point in Iran's relations with the country on her north – eastern flank. The new country that emerged to represent the ancient Turan and medieval Turkistan in the twenty first century began its relations with Iran on the basis of appreciation of cross-border cooperation. Many agreements of friendship and economic cooperation have been signed between Iran and the new republic that has replaced ancient Turan and modern Soviet Union to the north – east. In June 1995 Turkmenistan signed a tripartite agreement with Iran and Armenia to expand overland trade among the three (52). March that year witnessed inauguration of the linking of Turkmenistan and Central Asian railway networks to those of Iran. These railway networks were hooked up in March 1996 (53). Expansion of cross-border cooperation led to the inauguration in December 1997 by the presidents of Iran and Turkmenistan of a new gas pipeline between the two countries (54).

No matter what was done to Iran's north – eastern territories and frontiers by the Russians in the beginning and by the Soviets subsequently, border areas and the boundaries inherited from them by the Republic of Turkmenistan with Iran, have proved to be stable and reliable. These frontiers have proved to be the frontiers of friendship and cooperation between the two nations.

Notes and References

1- L. D. Kristof, *The Nature of frontiers and boundaries,* in Annals Association of American Geographers, No. 49, 1959, PP. 269-82.
2- Peter J. Taylor, *Political Geography,* second edition, Longman Scientific & Technical, London 1989, PP. 144-46.
3- Abul-Hassan Ali Ebn-e Hussein Masudi, (Arab geographer/historian of fourth century AH), *Moravvege az-Zahab* (Propagator of the Way), Persian translation by Abul-Qassem Payandeh, Bongah-e Tarjomeh va Nashr-e Ketab, Theran 1977, PP. 464-5.
4- Ibid. P. 467.
5- Peter Louis Templeton, *The Persian Prince,* Persian Prince Publications, London 1979, P. 11.
6- Georgina Herrmann, *The Iranian Revival,* of The Making of the Past series, Planned and Projected by Elsevier International Projects Ltd., Oxford 1977, P. 120.
7- For more on the subject see: Pirouz Mojtahed-Zadeh, *Joghrafiay-e Tarikhi-e Khalij-e Fars (Historical Geography of the Persian Gulf),* Tehran University Press No. 1492, Tehran 1975, PP. 10-11.
8- Hakim Abul-Qasem Ferdosi, *The Shahnameh,* English Translation by Arthur G.Warner and Edward Warner, London 1925, Vol. VIII, PP. 92, 160, 161 and 164.
9- Georgina Herrmann, op. cit., P. 122.
10- F. Pareja, *Islamologia 1,* 111-13.
11- Pio Fillipani-Ronconi, *The Tradition of Sacred Kingship in Iran,* in George Lenczowski's *Iran Under the Pahlavis,* Hoover Institutuion Press, Stanford University, USA 1978, P. 67.
12- Most probably 'Asjodi' or 'Asjadi' is meant by this name.
13- Pio Fillipani-Ronconi, op. cit., P. 77.
14- For more details, see: Pirouz Mojtahed-Zadeh, *Iran va Irani Budan (Iran and to be Iranian),* a two part article in Ettelaat Siasi – Eqtesadi (Ettelaat Political-Economic), Nos. 147-148 & 149-150, Azar – Dey & Bahman – Esfand 1378 (Winter of 1999-2000), PP. 21-2 of the first part.
15- P. Fillipani-Ronconi, op. cit., P. 78.
16- For more on this see: Pirouz Mojtahed-Zadeh, *The Amirs of Borderlands and Eastern Iranian Borders,* Urosevic Foundation Publication, London 1995, Chapter IV; The Partitioning of Khorasan, PP. 263-310.
17- Modern city of Gorgan.
18- Captain G. H. Hunt, *The Persian Campaign,* Otram & Havelock's, London 1858, P. 92.
19- *Persian Frontiers,* an official document of British Foreign Office, Confidential 17188, FO 371/45507, P. 7.
20- Ibid.
21- George N. Curzon, *Persia and the Persian Question,* Longmans, Green and Co. London 1892, PP. 135-6.
22- For more on this, see: Pirouz Mojtahed-Zadeh, *The Amirs of the Borderlands and Eastern Iranian Borders,* op. cit., PP. 315-321.
23- FO 65/991, enclosure in Thomson's No. 10, dated 29th January 1873.
24- Ibid, Thomson's No. 21, dated 7th February 1870.
25- Munnawwar Khan, *Anglo-Afghan Relations, The Great Game in Central Asia,* Published in Peshawar (Pakistan) 1964, P. 249.

26- For more on this subject, see: Pirouz Mojtahed-Zadeh, *The Amirs of the…, op. cit., the Conclusion,* PP. 465-82.
27- FO 65/991, Loftus's No. 147, dated 5th April 1873; No. 150, 16th April 1873; No. 157, 23rd April 1873. Also, Thomson's No. 30, dated 16th March 1873. See also the letter of the Russian Minister at Tehran to the Persian Minister of Foreign Affairs, dated 13th April 1875, FO 65/878.
28- FO 65/904, Confidential from Lord Derby to Lotus, dated 6th November 1874.
29- FO 65/991, Confidential from Derby to Thomson, dated January 1875.
30- FO 65/991, Confidential from Loftus to Derby, dated 2nd September 1875.
31- FO 65/927, Despatch from Thomson, dated 7th March 1875.
32- Ibid.
33- Ibid.
34- FO 371/45507, dated January 31, 1947, P. 8.
35- In article I of this treaty the Government of Soviet Union declared *"the whole body of treaties and conventions concluded with Persia by the Tsarist Government, which crushed the right of the Persian people, to be null and void".*
36- The word *fleet* is given here, as it is the equivalent of the word "Flot" which was used in the original Russian text of the treaty. The Iranian delegate to the League of Nations communicated to that body a French translation of the treaty in which "Flot" was erroneously rendered as *bateauz* (see League of Nations, Treaty Series, Volume IX, Page 406). The English version of the treaty in the British State papers was translated from this French text, and consequently gave *vessels* as the equivalent of *bateauz* (see Volume CXIV, Page 904). The matter is rendered perfectly plain by a reference to article VIII of the treaty of Turkmanchai. The first paragraph of that article states that Iranian merchant ships were to enjoy the same rights of navigation on the Caspian Sea as Russian merchant ships, while the second paragraph contained the prohibition in regard to the maintenance of Iranian warships on that sea.
37- This part of the treaty of Friendship of 1921 was never practised by Iran as the Soviet Union, for as long as it lived, did not allow Iran to maintain a naval fleet in the Caspian Sea or to assume a military role therein.
38- FO 371/45507, Confidential on Persian Frontiers, 31 January 1947, P. 9.
39- Russian measure of length, about 1.1 kilo metres (0.66 mile) from Russian versta.
40- E 4067/100/34, Meshed despatch No T/24, dated 20th May 1926. Repeated in FO 371/45507, P. 9.
41- Hari-Rud is known as *Tajan* below its junction with Kashaf-Rud
42- E8126, No. 676/6/45, From British Embassy, Tehran to the Foreign Office, London, dated 27 October 1945.
43- E2211/100/34 Persia, despatch No. 229, from Sir R. Hodgson to the Foreign Office, dated 19th March 1926. Repeated in FO 371/45507.
44- Leonard Shapiro, *Soviet Treaty Series, 1917-1928,* Vol. 1, Georgetown University Press, Washington DC 1950, P. 315.
45- Ibid. P. 314.
46- FO 371/82332A, Confidential No. 514, dated 22 June 1950.
47- FO 371/82332A, Confidential from British Embassy in Tehran to Foreign Office in London, dated 12th June 1950.
48- Ettelaat daily of Tehran, dated 15 November 1976.

49- N. Khrushchev, *Khrushchev Remembers (The Last Testament),* Translated into English and Edited by Strobe Talbot, London 1974, P. 298.
50- The Echo of Iran, *New Republics – Problems of Recognition,* Vol. XXXVI, No. 12 (47), December 1991, P. 6.
51- Abbas Maleki, *Iran's northeastern borders, from Sarakhs to Khazar (the Caspian Sea),* in K. S. McLachlan ed. *The boundaries of modern Iran,* The SOAS/GRC Geopolitics Series 2, UCL Press, London 1994. P. 19.
52- Ettelaat International, *Iran signs trilateral Agreement with Turkmenistan and*
53- *Armenia,* No. 246, London, Tuesday June 6, 1995, P. 10.
54- Ibid.
55- Pirouz Mojtahed-Zadeh, *Geopolitics and Reform under Khatami,* in Global Dialogue, Vol. 3, Nos. 2-3, Nicosia/Cyprus Spring/Summer 2001, PP. 53-62.

SECTION B

Emergence and Evolution of Western Boundaries of Iran

A General Introduction
Western Boundaries of Iran
Pirouz Mojtahed-Zadeh

Iran's western boundaries with Turkey and Iraq are of a unique type in the Middle East: Geographically, the area along the boundary consists of a highly complicated morphology; it passes through mountains and valleys, deserts and along the entire length of Mesopotamian lowlands. Historically, considering that the Zohab Treaty of 1639 between Iran and the Ottoman Empire makes references to "Perso-Ottoman frontiers", one might conclude that no other boundary processes longer evolutionary history then those in the Western peripheries of Iran. This boundary has long displayed the classic characteristics of a *political frontier* zone (1), defined and redefined from that date until 1990. The 1639 treaty of Zohab and the subsequent treaties of Hamadan (1727), Kerend (1746), and Erzeroom (1823) (Erz-e Rome) (2) were little more than momentary truces in a long religious dispute with some references to the frontiers of the two empires. But the second treaty of Erzeroom 1847 for the first time properly deals with the issue of boundary between the two.

In the western section, the boundaries of Iran with her two neighbours constituted as one for about three centuries; it was Iran's boundaries with the Ottoman Empire down to 1921 when the modern states of Iraq and Turkey emerged in place of the Ottoman Empire. Hence the pre-1921 assessment of the boundary affairs constitutes for the history of Iran's boundaries with Turkey, and as a historical background to Iran's boundaries with Iraq.

Having gone through the preliminary stages of references to the western boundaries of Iran in the aforementioned treaties, the boundaries of Iran and Turkey were settled with the signing of the second treaty of Erzeroom in 1847 and the protocol of 1913.

The 1874 treaty of Erzeroom and its explanatory notes were the result of intense and continued negotiations between the two contacting parties as well as Britain and Russia. The two countries' land boundaries were delimited in this treaty, but curiously river boundaries were put on the eastern banks of the Shatt al-Arab. Masses of documents pertaining to this treaty do not make it clear on what right and/on what legal premise the river boundaries were put on eastern banks instead of the middle of river in accordance with international regulations being formulated it the same period. This obscurity was so universal that even Lord Palmerston, Britain's Secretary for Foreign Affairs, wrote in 1851 that the Iran-Turkey boundaries will never be settled fully and finally unless through the Anglo-Russian arbitration (3).

These disputes, however, continued and repeated protests led to further negotiation and the inking of a protocol of Tehran in 1911 whereby the two countries agreed to set up new boundary commission to study the demands of the two countries on the basis of the 1847. 18 meetings of this commission led to no agreement and pressure for Russia and Britain prevented the case from being referred to the International Court of Justice at the Hague. Finally in 1913 the Ottomans agreed to the enforcement of a new boundary line which in effect was the same as defined in the 1847 treaty, but with some adjustments regarding parts of Shat al-Arab in the 1914 boundary demarcation.

Iran's western borders, inherited from the unsettled broad frontier zone of Persian-Ottoman imperial strife (4), suffered varying fortunes in the modern period. The 1932 Agreement and the 1937 Convention, which fixed the alignment of the border between Iran and Turkey, caused continuing difficulties.(5) The years following the 1991 defeat of Iraq in Kuwait witnessed the Kurdish areas of Iraq falling under the protection of the United Nations and the emergence of a quasi-autonomous region governed by Kurdish people, signaled inter alia by the holding of elections in 1992 (6).

In 1921 the Ottoman Empire disintegrated and the boundary disputes with Iran were divided into two sections: the upper section with Turkey, and the lower section with Iraq. These boundaries are studied in more details in the following three chapters of this section of the book by Dr. Masud Moradi, Dr. Farzad Sharifi-Yazdi, and by the author.

References

1- J. Prescott, *Boundaries and Frontiers*, London, Croom Helm 1978.
2- Erzerome (name of a town in Turkey) literally means the territory of Rome in reference to former Eastern Roman Empire.
3- For details see: Pirouz Mojtahed-Zadeh, *Khalij-e Fars; Keshvar-ha va Marz-ha = The Persian Gulf; Countries and Boundaries*, Ataei publication, Tehran (1379) 2000, pp. 548-9.
4- K. S. McLachlan, *Borders in the Ottoman Empire*, in *Encyclopaedia Iranica*, E Yarshater (ed), London: Routledge 1989, p. 401-3.
5- R. N. Schofield, Iran's borders with Turkey, in *Encyclopaedia Iranica*, E Yarshater (ed), London: Routledge 1989, p. 418.
6- K. S. McLachlan ed., *The boundaries of modern Iran*, SOAS/GRC series 2, UCL Press, London 1994, p.6.

CHAPTER VIII

The Borders of the Persian and the Ottoman Empires: An Analysis of Persian Sovereignty over the District of Qotur

Masud Moradi

Introduction

The definition of the peripheral limits of Iran began centuries before the advent of Islam (in the seventh century) and the European concept of a boundary. Following the spread of Islam into the empire, the Safavids created a stable state in Iran and re-established the country's borders in accordance to roughly the same geographical dimensions that had been established in the Sassanid era.

Therefore, Iran's modern day western boundary began to take shape under the rule of the Safavids in the 17th century and as a result of successive conflict and power struggles that ensued between them and the neighboring Ottoman Empire. Only through many years of conflict, negotiation, mediation and arbitration between Iran, the Ottomans, Britain and Russia, did this border area (Iran-Turkey) begin to take the permanent and stable form (following World War I) that is the same today.

The dispute between Iran and the Ottomans over sovereignty of Qotur district, now part of North West Iran, played a definitive role in shaping Ottoman-Persian relations and the establishment of their common boundary.

This paper attempts to overview Persian Ottoman relations, with specific focus on the dispute over the sovereignty of Qotur and the role that this dispute played in shaping the actual Border between the two states.

Persian-Ottoman Relations-Historical Background

Following the 1821-1823 war between Safavid Iran and the Ottoman Empire and despite Iran's relative military inferiority, Ottoman statesmen considered Iran as a potential military threat, particularly in the event of a Russian invasion of Anatolia.

In 1639, a boundary separating the Persian and Ottoman empires was established much as it appears today between the Aras River and the Persian Gulf. However, little effort was made to implement it over the next two centuries. It was only under the pressure of the British and Russians, both of whom had interests in the region that Persia and the Ottomans agreed to stabilize boundary conditions in the uplands between the two countries.

In 1847 a mixed commission including Britain and Russia helped form the Treaty of Erzerum, which vaguely outlined the limits of the two empires. A second commission consisting of the same four countries was then appointed to begin the accurate delimitation The Persian-Ottoman boundary remained in an indefinite state until 1911, when an agreement was signed providing for a mixed commission to establish a definitive line based on the 1847 Treaty. This commission conducted a number of meetings in which approximately three-quarters of the Ottoman-Persian Boundary was redefined. The settlement of the remaining quarter was left to be determined on the ground.

The Constantinople Protocol of November 1913 embodied the work of the commission. This protocol established a bi-national group which, by October 1914, had demarcated the entire boundary except for the 40 miles of the Qotur district.

The work on the boundary was interrupted by World War One. Furthermore, the creation of the British Mandate in Iraq in 1920 meant that the Persian–Ottoman border was considerably shortened. Four years later, the Ankara Frontier Convention was concluded between Turkey and Iran, reviewing their common boundary and providing for the resolution of disputed areas.

By the Tehran Convention of 1932 three exchanges of territory were agreed upon. One in the region of Mt. Ararat in favor of Turkey, a second near Bajirge, north west of Rezaiyeh (Orumiyeh) in Iran's favor and a third in the district of Qotur, in Iran's favor.

With the underlying criteria of preventing Russian domination of the Balkans, the Berlin Conference was held by the German Chancery in June-July of 1878 (9). Iran's representative in this conference was Mirza Malkom Khan, who advocated the return of Qotur to Iran.

In accordance to clause 60 of the agreement of this Congress, this was finally implemented and Turkey was instructed to cede to Persia the border area of Qotur (10).

However, this agreement would not be implemented for many years following the refusal of Sultan Abd Al-Hamid 2nd to accept any conditions of this agreement.

The Iranian Foreign Ministry has published a number of documents related to the Ottoman claim to Qotur. Two of these are particularly relevant. One is a letter from the Ottoman embassy to Iran's Foreign Ministry and the other, is a letter written by Sir Henry Lython Belver (England's Ambassador to Iran) on 20th November 1861.

The Ottoman embassy in their later stated that the Iranians had unlawfully raided the Qotur region and thus requested actions be taken to prevent such violations (7). Sir Henry Lython Belver's letter, (whilst stressing England's neutrality between the Persians and Ottomans), referred to this matter and stated that existing documents justified Ottoman ownership of Qotur (8).

It is important to note that during the various power struggles between the Persians and Ottomans in the 16th, 17th and 18th centuries over Eastern Anatolia and the Caucasus and Iraq, the Ottoman's focus of interest lay in Azerbaijan and the Caucasus region, whilst Persia held greater interests in Iraq (containing some of Shiite Islam's holiest sites).

The first military clash between Iran and the Ottomans took place during the reign of Ottoman king Salim I and Safavid Shah Ismail I of Iran. The reason that triggered the clash was the role of the Sufis of Anatolia. As Salim felt danger from them, began to remove them. In august 1514AD, he defeated Shah Ismail in Chaldoran and seized Tabriz (1) the capital city of all Azerbaijan.

As such, the region of Qotur, covering an area of 150 Km^2 held particular strategic importance to the Ottomans, as a hallway to Azerbaijan and the Caucasus region and thus as a means of exerting domination over the Van Lake (2).

In 1849 AD the Ottomans, having sent 1200 soldiers to the region, occupied Qotur under the leadership of Dervish Pasha (3). Iran meanwhile looked to the Britain and Russia, (both of which held strategic reasons for curbing Ottoman growth and influence in the region) to force the Ottomans out. Indeed, whilst Russia saw Iran as an important pawn against its struggles with the

Ottoman's, Britain saw Iran and specifically its ownership of Qotur as a means of reducing Russian advances further south (4).

By the time of the meeting and drafting of the second Treaty of Erzerum (1852), Moshiroddoleh refused to attend talks in Baghdad, stating that he would only be prepared to attend the meeting provided the Ottomans left Qotur immediately (5). Britain and Russia promised Iran that they would force the Ottoman's to leave (6). It would take many years for this promise to materialize.

Between 1842 and 1852, the commission carried out surveys of the border area but its work was interrupted by the Crimean War (1853-1856).

For 13 years following the war, the representatives worked to prepare maps of the boundary, resulting in the "Carte indentique" of 1869, a highly inaccurate map which showed a border zone 25 miles in width, within which the boundary lay.

Figure 8

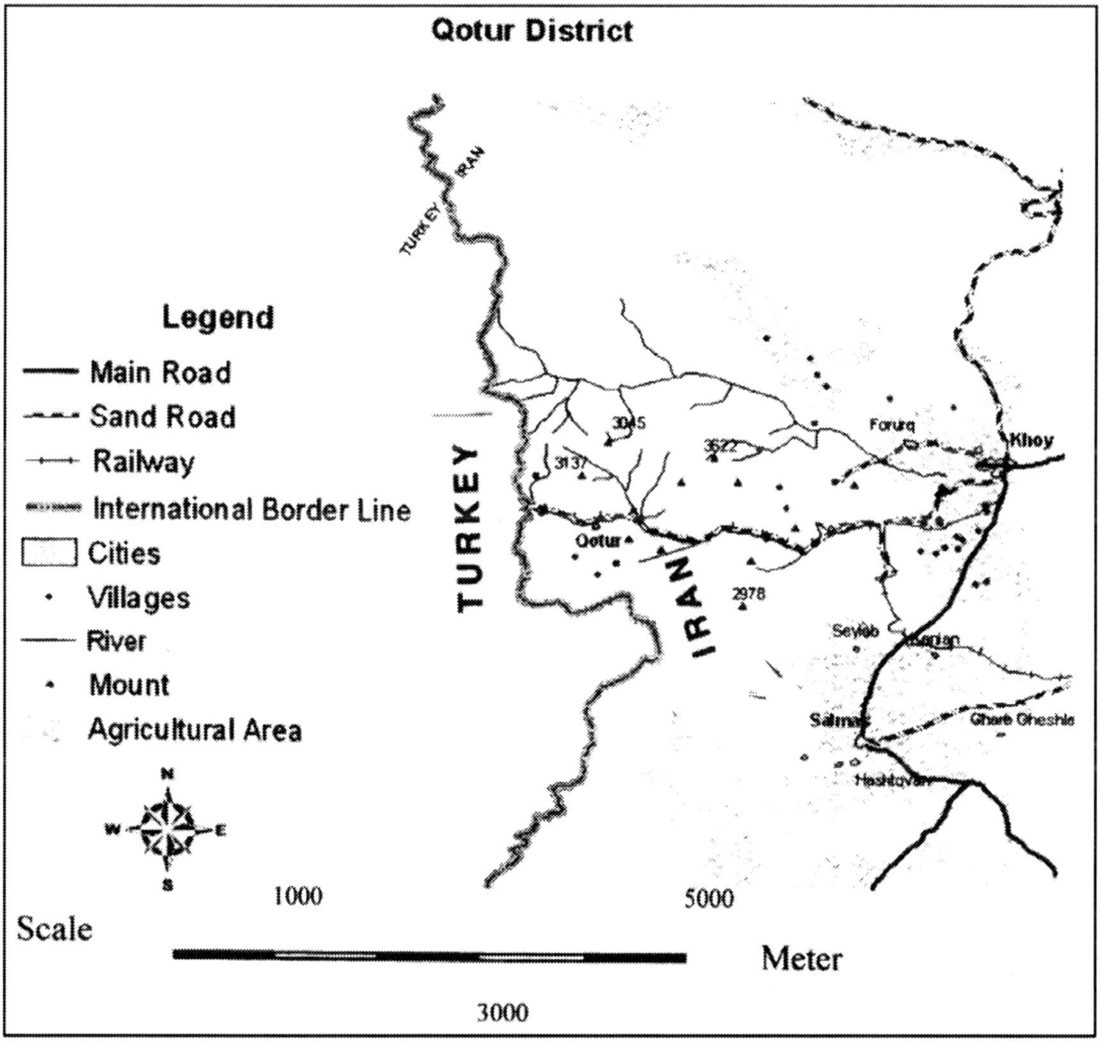

A topographic profile of Qotur district

Qotur District and Ottoman Border Violations

It is important to note that during the various power struggles between the Iranians and Ottomans in the 16th, 17th and 18th centuries over Eastern Anatolia and the Caucasus and Iraq, the Ottoman's focus of interest lay in Azerbaijan and the Caucasus region, whilst Iran held greater interests in Iraq (containing some of Shiite Islam's holiest sites).

The first military clash between Iran and the Ottomans took place during the reign of Ottoman king Salim I and Safavid Shah Ismail I of Iran. The reason that triggered the clash was the role of the Sufis of Anatolia. As Salim felt danger from them, began to remove them. In august 1514AD, he defeated Shah Ismail in Chaldoran and seized Tabriz (1) the capital city of all Azerbaijan.

As such, the region of Qotur, covering an area of 150 Km² held particular strategic importance to the Ottomans, as a hallway to Azerbaijan and the Caucasus region and thus as a means of exerting domination over the Van Lake (2).

In 1849 AD the Ottomans having sent 1200 soldiers to the region, occupied Qotur under the leadership of Dervish Pasha (3). Iran meanwhile looked to the Britain and Russia, (both of which held strategic reasons for curbing Ottoman growth and influence in the region) to force the Ottomans out. Indeed, whilst Russia saw Iran as an important pawn against its struggles with the Ottoman's, Britain saw Iran and specifically its ownership of Qotur as a means of reducing Russian advances further south (4).

By the time of the meeting and drafting of the second Treaty of Erzerum (1852), Moshiroddoleh refused to attend talks in Baghdad, stating that he would only be prepared to attend the meeting provided the Ottomans left Qotur immediately (5). Britain and Russia promised Iran that they would force the Ottoman's to leave (6). It would take many years for this promise to materialize.

Iranian-Ottoman Claims to Qotur

The Iranian Foreign Ministry has published a number of documents related to the Ottoman claim to Qotur. Two of these are particularly relevant. One is a letter from the Ottoman embassy to Iran's Foreign Ministry and the other, is a letter written by Sir Henry Lython Belver (England's Ambassador to Iran) on 20th November 1861.

The Ottoman embassy in their later stated that the Iranians had unlawfully raided the Qotur region and thus requested actions be taken to prevent such violations (7). Sir Henry Lython Belver's letter, (whilst stressing England's neutrality between the Persians and Ottomans), referred to this matter and stated that existing documents justified Ottoman ownership of Qotur (8).

Berlin Congress-1878

With the underlying criteria of preventing Russian domination of the Balkans, the Berlin Conference was held by the German Chancery in June-July of 1878 (9). Iran's representative in this conference was Mirza Malkom Khan, who advocated the return of Qotur to Iran.

In accordance to clause 60 of the agreement of this Congress, this was finally implemented and Turkey was instructed to cede to Persia the border area of Qotur (10). However, this agreement would not be implemented for many years following the refusal of Sultan Abd Al-Hamid 2nd to accept any conditions of this agreement.

Finalizing the Qotur Issue and Persian-Ottoman (Iran-Turkey) Boundary

The Persian-Ottoman boundary remained in an indefinite state until 1911, when an agreement was signed providing for a mixed commission to establish a definitive line based on the 1847 Treaty. This commission conducted a number of meetings in which approximately three-quarters of the Ottoman-Persian Boundary was redefined. The settlement of the remaining quarter was left to be determined on the ground.

The Constantinople Protocol of November 1913 embodied the work of the commission. This protocol established a bi-national group which, by October 1914, had demarcated the entire boundary except for the 40 miles of the Qotur district.

The work on the boundary was interrupted by World War One. Furthermore, the creation of the British Mandate in Iraq in 1920 meant that the Persian–Ottoman border was considerably shortened. Four years later, the Ankara Frontier Convention was concluded between Turkey and Iran, reviewing their common boundary and providing for the resolution of disputed areas.

By the Tehran Convention of 1932 three exchanges of territory were agreed upon. One in the region of Mt. Ararat in favor of Turkey, a second near Bajirge, north west of Rezaiyeh (Orumiyeh) in Iran's favor and a third in the district of Qotur, in Iran's favor.

References

1- Mohammad Farid Almahami, *History of Islamic government*, Ehsan Haghi, Beirut, Darolnafaies, 1408 (1988), p.191.
2- *A selection of Iran and Ottoman documents*, Vol. I, published by the Institute of Political and International Studies, Ministry of Foreign Affairs, Tehran 1369 (1990), p. 570.
3- Ibid.
4- Ibid., p. 578.
5- Ali Asghar Shamim, *Iran in Qajar period*, Tehran, Elmi publisher, volume 2, 1370 (1991), p.206-211.
6- A selection of......, op. cit., Vol. 2, p.16.
7- Ibid., Vol. 2, p.98.
8- Ibid., Vol. 2, p. 106.
9- Cité par Jacques Aancel, *La question d'Orient*, Paris: Centre de Documentation Universitaire, Tournier & Constans, Ancel, p. 153; Documents diplomatique français, 1ère série, tome 2, p. 258-261; confidentielle de Saint-Vallier à Waddington du 24 février 18787.And also see: Masoud Moradi. Les Origines des crises balkaniques.Tehran. Aftab-mahtab.2004, p.110-115.
10- Document diplomatique Français, *traite de Berlin*, 13 juillet 1878, ministre des affaires estrangers, Paris 1930, p.218-221.

CHAPTER IX

Evolution of Iran's Western Boundaries
Farzad Cyrus Sharifi-Yazdi

Introduction

Of the long stretch of territorial boundaries that shape and define Iran's distinctive landmass, none have attracted as prolific a degree of academic attention and analysis as that which bounds its west with Turkey and Iraq. It can be argued that historically and strategically this *political frontier* (1) or *border march* (2) region may have been Iran's most important; acting as it has, as the focus of long established rivalries, disputes and regional power struggles, firstly between Iran and the Ottoman Empire and later Iran and Iraq.

Embroidering these prominent rivalries have been a series of critical internal and external factors of influence, ranging from conflicting religious beliefs (Ottoman Sunnism and Iranian Shiism), Britain and Russia's strategic (imperialist) interests in the region, the plight of the Kurds, Arab claims to the Iranian province of Khuzestan (3) and of course the politics of oil and strategic access to the Persian Gulf (4). Indeed, explanations of the evolution of Iran's western boundaries can be found deeply embedded in the dynamics of these factors and regional rivalries and, the many successive disputes and battles that have arisen out of them; from the first major Perso-Ottoman war in 1508 which saw Baghdad temporarily fall to the Persian Safavids, right up to the most recent conflict of 1980-1988 between Iran and Iraq.

Usually, it follows in international relations that where there have been many disputes and wars between two or more states, there have also been many flawed, indecisive and violated agreements between them. The frontier region of interest has been no exception to this general pattern; subject to and largely shaped by a whole host of successive truces and agreements (Fig 1), from the very first in 1555 (Treaty of Amasya), right up to the most recent (Algiers Accord) in 1975. This chapter provides an analysis of the evolution of Iran's western boundaries through an overview of a number of these agreements and developments in the regional political milieu that necessitated them.

Agreements Relating to and Affecting the Western Boundaries of Iran

Date	Name of Agreement	Key element of Agreement
1555	Treaty of Amasya	Confirmed large loss of territory for Iran and laid down border as broad zone
1639	Treaty of Zohab	General Peace Settlement and vague boundary delimitation
1727	Treaty of Hamadan	Persian territory ceded to Ottomans north of Aras river
1746	Treaty Kurdan	Reaffirmed Treaty of Zohab
1823	1st Treaty of Erzerum	Reaffirmed Treaty of Kurdan
1847	2nd Treaty of Erzerum,	Iran granted free navigation of Shatt al-Arab
1878	Treaty of Berlin	Iran Gained Qotur
1907	Anglo-Russian Convention	Division of Influence in Iran
1911	Tehran Protocol	New Boundary Negotiations
1913	Constantinople Protocol	Delimitation Commission
1926	Anglo-Turco-Iraqi Boundary Treaty	Persian boundary with Turkey considerably shortened
1914	Boundary demarcation	Boundary Commission report
1929	British Judicial Agreement with Iraq Abolished	League of Nations: Unratified
1932	Accord realtif a la Fixation de la Ligne Frontiere entre Perse et al Turquie'	Small changes to the 1914 line in Turkeys favour.
1937	Turco-Persian boundary negotiations	Ratification and finalisation of Turco-Iranian boundary
1937	Irano-Iraqi Boundary Treaty	Confirmed Constantinople Protocol
1937	Treaty of Friendship	Treaty of Amity Between Iran and Iraq

Date	Name of Agreement	Key element of Agreement
1975	Algiers Accords	Iran Thalweg claims on Shatt al-Arab accepted
1988	UN Resolution 598	Status Quo Ante Bellum: Unratified

Source: Adaptation of table by Keith Mclachlan (5) Ottoman-Safavid rivalry and the development of a broad frontier zone: 1501-1639

It is widely recognised that the modern state of Iran took shape under the rule of the Safavid dynasty (1501-1736). More specifically, the story of Iran's present day western boundaries begins in earnest with the ascendancy to power of the Safavids in 1501.This ascendancy, came upon the crest of a strong Shiite movement that had its origins in the northwest region of the country, close to the Ottoman border.

The growth of Safavid Persia under Ismail Shah and the adoption of Shiite Islam as the states official religion in 1501, acted as significant threat (6) and challenge to the eastward expansion of the powerful and fermenting empire of the Sunni Ottomans; an expansion that had to this point been based on the belief system that Ottoman caliphs had the birthright of ruling all the Muslim world (7).

Specifically, there existed the threat that the Shiite propaganda being instigated by the Safavids would appeal to the heterodox and semi-nomadic inhabitants of eastern Anatolia (Asia Minor). Ismail Shah was also known to harbour the desire to gain a hold of central and southern Iraq-with its holy Shiite sites at Najaf and Karbala and Baghdad's symbolic value as the seat of the old Abbasid Empire (8). For the Ottomans, control over Iraq would no doubt have been essential to keep it as a Sunni-controlled buffer state that would reduce the threat of Shiism spreading to Anatolia.

In 1508, the Safavids, led by Ismail Shah conquered Baghdad, initiating a long series of protracted wars with the Ottomans along what was essentially an undefined border. One of the most significant of these wars was the Battle of Cahlidiran in 1514, where under the leadership Sultan Selim, the Ottomans attacked and defeated the Safavids taking from them the Caucasus, Northern Iraq and even the Safavid capital of Tabriz (9).

During the reign of Ismail's successor Shah Tahmasb (1524-1576), the Persians lost control of further territory including Kurdistan and Mesopotamia to the Ottomans (10), who also re-took Baghdad in 1535. By 1555 the two rivals had signed the Treaty of Amasya, which brought a temporary end to their fighting and vaguely set out their shared frontier as a broad zone (rather than defined line) running through Georgia, Armenia, and the western Zagros mountains a far as the Basra (11). This arrangement was largely confirmed in the Treaty of Constantinople in 1590 (12).

Under the Strong leadership of Shah Abbas in 1623 (1587-1629), the Safavids pushed the Ottomans west of Tabriz and re-took Baghdad. They were however expelled for the last time by Sultan Murad IV's army in 1638 and (13) by 1639, the Treaty of Zohab had officially established Ottoman dominance over Iraq (14), putting virtually all of the Arab Middle East under their rule-a integration that would last for nearly 400 years.

From the 1639 Treaty of Zohab to the 1823 Treaty of Erzerum

The 'Treaty of Peace and Demarcation of Frontiers, better known as the Treaty of Zohab, laid down in 1639 between Sultan Murad IV of the Ottoman Empire and Shah Safi of Persia remains, in name at least, the earliest explicitly territorial agreement signed between two states in the Middle East (15). In it, the frontier was defined in approximate terms though without actual demarcation, to run from the head of the Persian Gulf at the Shatt al Arab to the Aras River near the Ararat mountains (in present day Eastern Turkey) into the Caucasus (16).

Whilst it incorporated Iraq into the Ottoman Empire, and contained a pledge from each (Ottomans and Persians) not to interfere in one another's domestic affairs, it created "*a border so vague as to resemble a broad zone generally about a hundred miles wide where neither exercised much jurisdiction*" (17). In 1724, the Ottomans invaded Iran and by 1727, had signed a treaty (Hamadan) with Ashraf-the Afghan ruler of Persia (1725-30) – that ceded Persian territory north of the Aras River to the Ottomans.

Hostilities between the two empires resumed in 1743 and by 1746, in a further treaty (Kurdan) signed between the two sides, the territorial status quo of the Zohab agreement was retained (18). This was again reaffirmed in the 1823 Treaty of Erzerum, following yet another Perso-Ottoman war. Though the 1823 treaty ensured that each side once again agreed to the principle of non-interference (19), it failed, as in the agreements that had preceded it, to provide more detailed delimitation of the boundary in question.

Indeed, it is worth noting that the agreements signed between 1639 and 1823 had served as little more than temporary truces in sporadic 'low intensity conflicts' (20) between the Ottomans and Persians, engaged in their frictional efforts to impose their respective dichotomous interpretations of Islam upon the Zagros-Mesopotamia region.

As far as territorial allocation was concerned, these agreements only identified a wide strip of land where Ottoman and Persian authority and the allegiance of numerous nomadic tribes (21), remained indefinite, weak and disputed (22). Indeed, it should also be noted that relations between the political centre of both the Ottoman and Persian Empires and their outer dependencies and principalities along the given border region was very weak (23). As a result, local dynamics were often more important than imperial policies, for establishing spheres of Persian or Ottoman control and influence along their border region (24).

Imperial Intervention and the Final Treaty of Erzerum (1847)

Despite the numerous non-interference clauses in the agreements that had been established, little over a year passed after the signing of the first treaty of Erzerum before the Persians backed a Kurdish rebellion in the north-eastern Iraq region. Fourteen years on, the two states were again on the verge of war-with the Ottomans having attacked the Persian port city of Muhammara (Khorramshahr) located on the Shatt al Arab (25). Both this act and the Persian support of Kurds constituted violations of the Treaty of Erzerum and thus served to emphasise the weakness of this and preceding treaties that had been designed to defuse the tensions between the Ottomans and Persians across their vague and indefinite border.

Another all-out Perso-Ottoman war was only averted this time with the intervention of Britain and Russia. Russian conquests in the Caucasus and British domination over India now gave the two powers direct interest in Ottoman-Persian affairs. Russia was keen to maintain tranquillity in its newly acquired provinces of Armenia and Georgia from where it planned to build a road to Baghdad. It therefore also saw it in its interest to see the development of a clearly defined boundary between the Ottomans and Persians to fortify negotiations for such a project (26).

Britain on the other hand, was doubtless aware that further Ottoman-Persian clashes could leave both sides vulnerable to its expansionist rival, Russia. Furthermore, it would almost certainly have been aware of the threat of further conflict to its burgeoning commercial interests in Mesopotamia (27). In particular, it was interested in developing a shorter imperial route to India via a mixed communications link running overland from the eastern Mediterranean to Baghdad and then by steamship to the Persian Gulf along the Tigris and the Shatt al Arab (28).

As such, Britain and Russia offered their mediation of the Muhammara question and other existing territorial disputes between the Ottomans and Persians. Both sides accepted and a subsequent quadripartite Turco-Persian Boundary Commission was formed in the spring of 1843, comprising representatives from both local and European powers. Many sessions of this commission were held between May 1843 and 1846 mostly at Erzerum, an Ottoman Armenian town in eastern Anatolia (29).

By November 1846, the mediating commissioners had drawn up a nine-article treaty dealing predominantly with international limits to territory at the head of the Persian Gulf. This draft treaty survived with no modifications to comprise the Second Treaty of Erzerum, eventually signed on 31st May 1847 by the Ottomans, Persians, Russia and Britain at Erzerum (30).

The treaty allocated the Ottoman-Persian land boundary for its entire length while further south a territorial limit was rather vaguely defined along the east bank of the Shatt al Arab River. More specifically, it declared that the southern part of the Shatt al Arab would be the starting point for the boundary between the two states and in doing so, the eastern bank of the Shatt al Arab was to be Persian, while the Ottomans were given full sovereignty over the areas lying on the west bank (31).

One key provision was that Persian vessels were granted free navigation of the Shatt al Arab waterway, thereby implying complete Ottoman control over it (32). This implication was affirmed in an explanatory note (though not to the Persians) issued by the Russian and British governments on April 14th 1847 (33). Also in the treaty, Iran abandoned all claims to the town of Sulaymaniyah and ceded the lowlands of the province of Zohab to Turkey. In return, Turkey ceded the mountainous area of the province and the Kirind valley to Iran (34).

A number of factors nonetheless remained the source of protracted dispute between the Persians and Ottomans and prevented this treaty fulfilling its aim of comprehensively settling the boundary issues that had for so long laced the relations of these two neighbours and rivals (35). For example, individual nomadic tribes spread across the border, particularly around the Shatt al Arab River, were a constant source of friction between the two states for purposes such as military conscription.

In the north, efforts to survey the boundary were also being marked by a *"spirit if chicane, and encroachment"* (36). Indeed, the complete reluctance for compromise by the Ottoman's and Persians with regards such issues led the British Foreign Secretary, Lord Palmerston, to comment in 1851 that *"the boundary between Turkey and Persia can never be finally settled except by a arbitrary decision on part of Great Britain and Russia"* (37).

From the 1869 Carte Identique to the 1913 Constantinople Protocol

Between 1848 and 1852, the mediating commissioners carried out surveys of the border area between the Ottomans and Persians, only to have their work interrupted by the Crimean War (1853-1856). For 13 years after the war, the British and Russian surveyors met at St. Petersburg working to prepare maps of the boundary.

By 1869 a joint map was produced that came to be known as the 'Carte Identique', a well presented yet largely inaccurate map showing the border zone (between present day Iran and Turkey) to be 25 miles in width, within which the boundary [somewhere] lay (38). The mediating powers then advised the Ottomans and Persians that they should seek to establish the precise boundary line themselves, somewhere within the limits identified by the maps (39).

Nine years later, by the Treaty of Berlin (1878), Turkey agreed to cede to Persia the border area of Qotur (Khotur), the territorial status of which had long been an open sore in Perso-Ottoman relations (40). This agreement however, was not immediately implemented and thus the issue of Qotur was to fester for some years to come.

From 1905 onwards a number of Ottoman encroachments upon disputed or recognised Persian territory in the northern stretch of the frontier from Bayazid south to Vazne began to take place (41). These developments and the minor skirmishes and disputes that followed during the first decade of the twentieth century ultimately resulted in the signing of the Tehran Protocol on December 21st 1911. This Perso-Ottoman agreement provided for a technical commission to demarcate the boundary based on the 1847 Erzerum Treaty and the submission of any points on which the commissioners disagreed within six months, to the International Court of Arbitration (42).

This development was again encouraged by the British and Russians, who having effectively divided Iran into separate zones of influence and control four years earlier, were now keen to stabilise Iran's territorial integrity and thus its boundary with the Ottoman Empire (43). It is perhaps important in this respect to also note that in 1908 the British had discovered oil in Iran-predominantly in the southern regions close to the Persian Gulf. As such, greater strain was being put on Muhammara (Khorramshahr), Iran's conduit for oil going out and heavy machinery coming in. Resultantly, Ottoman intervention in Iran's growing involvement in world trade was for the first time now, unacceptable to Britain (44).

The work of the 1911 commission laid the groundwork for the Constantinople Protocol of November 17th 1913, which delimited the entire Ottoman-Persian boundary in detail and again provided for a commission to demarcate it on land. In 1914 the entire land boundary was demarcated with pillars from the Persian Gulf to Mount Ararat, except for about 40 miles in the neighbourhood of Qotur, by a commission consisting members from Iran, Turkey, Russia and Great Britain.

The river boundary along the Shatt al-Arab as determined by the commission followed the low water mark on the left (Iranian) bank with the exception of the Muhammara area. There, the line followed the *midline* from the Karun River to the point that the boundary departs the river (45).

Following the signature of the Mudros Armistice in October 1918, Turkey ceased to have any responsibility for Mesopotamia, which held the status of occupied territory until the establishment of the Hashemite Kingdom of Iraq after the Cairo Conference of March 1921. After this territorial change was ratified and embodied in the Anglo-Turco-Iraqi boundary treaty of June 5th 1926, the length of Persia's frontier with Turkey was notably reduced (46).

Whilst the international peace conferences convened in Europe following World War I to decide, *inter alia*, the fate of former Ottoman provinces, Persia forwarded territorial claims which would have considerably expanded its western frontier. These claims to Turkish Kurdistan, Mosul and Diyarbakir were however rejected at the 1919 Paris peaces conferences.

Figure 9

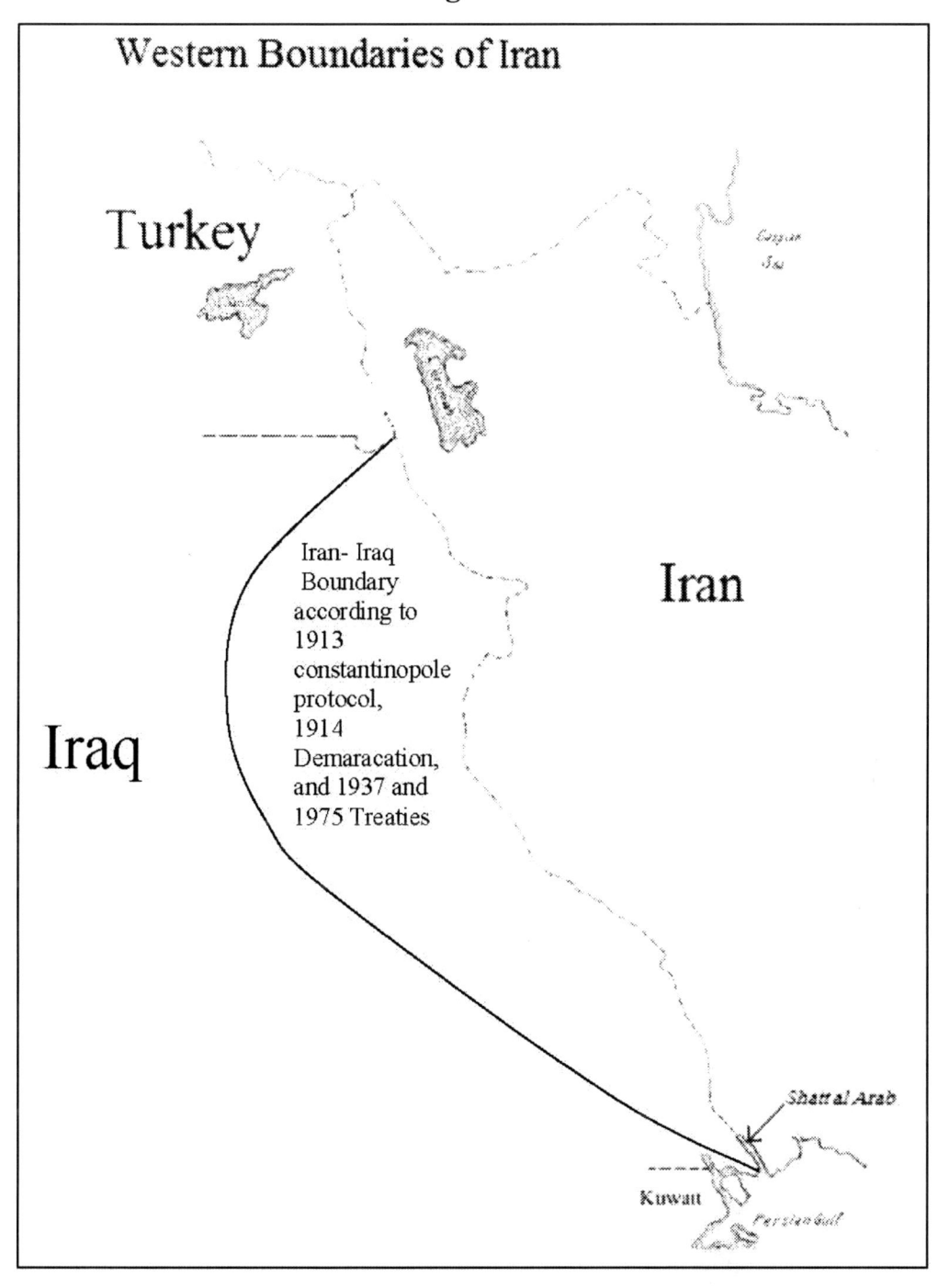

Western Boundaries of Iran

Turkey

Iraq

Iran- Iraq Boundary according to 1913 constantinopole protocol, 1914 Demaracation, and 1937 and 1975 Treaties

Iran

Shatt al Arab

Kuwait

The break up of the Ottoman Empire and final developments in the evolution of Western Iranian boundary

By 1925 a Kurdish uprisings against the Turkish government, though quashed by Turkish forces, had led to renewed interest in the Persian-Turkish boundary. Indeed, efforts to stabilise conditions in the area by demarcating a boundary line had impinged upon the seasonal migrations of the nomadic Kurds that straddled the border zone (47). Following escalating border incidents in the late 1920's the Turkish and Persians signed two frontier agreements on April 9th 1929.

Most notably the alignment of the 1914 line was confirmed by this agreement, but it was stipulated that a mixed boundary commission further survey the areas of Bulak Bashi, Qotur and two small villages in the southern border zone, Siro and Sartaq, before coming to any decisions regarding the precise delimitation of the boundary in these regions (48).

On January 23rd 1932, the foreign ministers of Persia and Turkey convening in Tehran signed the '*Accord realtif a la Fixation de la Ligne Frontiere entre Perse et al Turquie*', which embodied small yet significant changes to the 1914 line, predominantly in Turkeys favour. Most notably, the line was pushed eastwards in the north to give Turkey total control over the Lesser Ararat and Ari Mountains and also in the middle stretch between the Armenian village of Guirberan and Kuch Dagh, so as to leave Turkey with an additional ninety square miles in the neighbourhood of Qotur (49).

Persia was, by way of compensation, awarded a small strip of land in the northern extreme of the border region close to Lake Borolan (as named in the agreement). Finally, the 1914 line was projected westwards in the south to give Persia complete control over an additional eighty square miles between Bajirge and Kuner Kota Dagh.

The boundary was again demarcated and a final agreement in May1937, which provided for minor ratifications some 25 miles above the southern terminus of the boundary, was signed. Since 1937 and following World War Two, Persian-Turkish relations have been relatively sound and there has been little diplomatic activity between the two nations concerning a boundary that in part had been a focus of over three centuries of dispute.

The present day Iran-Turkey boundary (See Fig 2) as finalised in the 1937 agreement between the two nations runs a total of 310 miles in length beginning from its north junction at the Aras River, to its southern junction at the tripoint Iran-Turkey-Iraq boundary point.

Final Stages in the Evolution of the Iran-Iraq Boundary

It would perhaps be fair to argue that throughout the three to four centuries of rivalry and dispute between the Persians and Ottomans over their border region, the most salient and dubious issue or area of interest had almost always been the division of the Shatt al Arab River. This thorny and enduring source of contention was inherited by Iraq when it became a newly mandated state in 1921.

Since then, though particularly following the nationalistic Iraqi revolution of 1958, the Shatt al Arab dispute between Iran and Iraq has served as a source and symbolic manifestation of a deep rooted and politicised [Arab-Persian] rivalry between the two states. Indeed, it can also be accounted for as the original, although by no means only or most important, source of the damaging eight-year (1980-1988) war between the two nations (50).

Given such consideration, it is not surprising to find that the annals of international relations and geopolitical studies literature pertaining to Iran and Iraq's boundary has predominantly been occupied by work on the Shatt al Arab. The relative dearth of studies on Iran and Iraq's land boundary was however, somewhat filled following the eight year war between the two states, which saw numerous territorial encroachments and usurpations from both sides (51).

Though it is not in the scope of this paper to examine the details of the territorial dynamics of the war, it is relevant to note that by the time it had conclusively ended following the announcement of United Nations resolution 598, the Iran-Iraq land boundary and indeed the status of the Shatt al Arab waterway returned to that which existed prior to the war-and has stayed that way since.

As for Iraqi claims to Khuzestan, (chiefly a rhetorical response to Iran's support to Kurdish minorities in northern Iraq) (52) this issue can be argued to have essentially been de-valuated or indeed nullified during the course of the 1980-1988 war. Case in hand that the population of Khuzestan remained loyal to their Iranian nationality throughout the war, despite Saddam Hussein's call on them (and offer of assistance) to rise up against Iranian forces (53) and end what the lexicon of Arab nationalists had long labelled 'the Iranian occupation' of the region (54).

So how does the present day land boundary between Iran and Iraq stand? Interestingly, and somewhat remarkably, it remains more or less consistent with the demarcation of the Ottoman-Persian frontier in 1914, when Iraq still formed part of the Ottoman Empire (55). This boundary, stretching between the tri-point area with Turkey and the terminal point of the Shatt al Arab, extends 906 miles in length.

Whilst details of the dispute over the Shatt al Arab since the 1913 Constantinople protocol and Iraq's formation in 1921 forms the focus of subsequent chapters??, it suffices to say that subject to the conditions of the 1975 Algiers Accord, the waterway has since the end of the 1980-1988 war, gone back to being governed (de facto) by the *thalweg* principle of river delimitation. However, given that this understanding has yet to be ratified, the Shatt al Arab dispute still stands as the last un-finalised chapter in the story of Iran's western boundaries. What remains to be seen, is whether and how long this will continue to be so in the politically uncertain and volatile era of post Saddam Hussein Iraq.

Notes and References

1- J.R.V. Prescott, *Boundaries and Frontiers*, (London: Croom Helm, 1978): pp. 39-48.
2- R. Schofield. '*Interpreting a Vague River Boundary Delimitation. The 1847 Erzerum Treaty and the Shatt al-Arab before 1913*,' in K. S. McLachlan (ed.), The Boundaries of Modern Iran (London: UCL Press Ltd, 1994), pp.72-92: p75.
3- A predominantly Arab speaking province of south-western Iran rhetorically claimed by the Iraqi Baath party following their [Iraq's] nationalistic revolution in 1958. For more details on the subject see S.Chubin & S.Zabih, *Foreign Relations of Iran* (London: University of California Press, 1974): pp.181-183 see also B.Ingham 'Ethno-linguistic links between southern Iraq and Khuzestan' in K.Mclachlan (ed.), The Boundaries of Modern Iran (London: UCL Press Ltd, 1994):pp.93-100
4- The Shatt-al Arab waterway in providing Ottoman Empire/Iraq's sole practical outlet to the Persian Gulf has for long been a highly important and contested area of the Iran-Iraq/Ottoman boundary. See views of P. Mojtahed-Zadeh on Iraq's invasion of Kuwait on *After Midnight* (London: Channel 4 T.V production, 1990) See also R. Schofield, Boundaries, Territorial Disputes and the GCC states, in David E. Long and Christian Koch [edis] 1997, *Gulf Security in the Twenty First century*, ELSR, pp: 133-168 p138
5- K.S. McLachlan 'The Iran-Iraq Boundary Question' in *The Iranian Journal of International Affairs*, Vol. 5,Nos.3&4 (fall/winter 1993/1994).pp584-603: p.589
6- A. Goldschmidt Jr, *A Concise History of The Middle East*: Sixth Edition (Boulder, Colorado: Westview Press, 1999): pp.128-129
7- Pirouz Mojtahed-Zadeh, *The Amirs of the Borderlands and Eastern Iranian Borders* (London: Urosevic Foundation Publication No.2. 1995): p.32 See also: P. Mojtahed-Zadeh *Political Geography and Geographical Politics* (Tehran: SAMT, 2002): pp.335-337.
8- R. Mathee '*The Safavid-Ottoman Frontier: Iraq-I Arab As Seen By The Safavids*' in? pp. 1-2
9- B. Lewis, *The Middle East, 2000 Years Of History from The Rise Of Christianity To The Present Day* (London: Phoenix Press.2001): p.114 See also: K.S. McLachlan, '*Iranian Boundaries with the Ottoman Empire*' in E. Yarshater (ed.), *Encyclopaedia Iranica*, vol. 4, (New York: Routledge, 1989): pp401-403: p.401 and P. Mojtahed-Zadeh, *The Amirs of the Borderlands and Eastern Iranian Borders* (London: Urosevic Foundation Publication No.2. 1995): p.32.
10- K.S. McLachlan, '*Iranian Boundaries with the Ottoman Empire*' in E. Yarshater (ed.), *Encyclopaedia Iranica*, vol. 4, (New York: Routledge, 1989): pp401-403: p.401.
11- *Ibid.*,p.401.
12- *Ibid.*,p.401.
13- R. Mathee 'The *Safavid-Ottoman Frontier: Iraq-I Arab As Seen By The Safavids*' in? p.1-2.
14- G.S.Cruz '*Iran and Iraq, Perspectives in Conflict*' www.globalsecurity. org/ military/library/report/1998/GGS.htm, p.8.
15- R. N. Schofield. '*Interpreting a Vague River Boundary Delimitation. The 1847 Erzerum Treaty and the Shatt al-Arab before 1913*,' in K. S. McLachlan (ed.), *The Boundaries of Modern Iran* (London: UCL Press Ltd, 1994),pp.72-92: p75.
16- Foreign Office, *Extracts from foreign Office correspondence relative to Persian Frontiers*.FO371/40219.
17- Schofield (1994), *Op. cit.*, p. 75.

18- Foreign Office, *Extracts from foreign Office correspondence relative to Persian Frontiers*. FO371/40219.
19- *Ibid.*
20- G.S. Cruz '*Iran and Iraq, Perspectives in Conflict*' in http:/www.globalsecurity.org/military/library/report/1998/GGS.htm, pp1-78: p.8.
21- I.e. Bani-Ka'b Arabs of the southern-Shatt al Arab region and the Kurds of the northern region. For further details of the former and their role in this boundary issue see R. N. Schofield. '*Interpreting a Vague River Boundary Delimitation. The 1847 Erzerum Treaty and the Shatt al-Arab before 1913*,' in K. S. McLachlan (ed.), *The Boundaries of Modern Iran* (London: UCL Press Ltd, 1994), pp.72-92: p.75.
22- *Ibid.*, p. 75.
23- Pirouz Mojtahed-Zadeh, *The Amirs of the Borderlands and Eastern Iranian Borders*, (London: Urosevic Foundation Publication No.2. 1995): p. 33.
24- K.S. McLachlan, '*Iranian Boundaries with the Ottoman Empire*' in E. Yarshater (ed.), *Encyclopaedia Iranica*, vol. 4, (New York: Routledge, 1989): pp401-403: p.401.
25- J.J. Cusimano '*An Analysis of Iran-Iraq Bilateral Border* Treaties' in Western Reserve Journal of International Law, Vol.24 Issue 1, (winter 1992). pp. 1-23: p.2, taken from http://macam.ac.il/~aron/Int-ME/extra/AN%20ANALYIS%200F%20 IRAN. H P2c.
26- G.S. Cruz '*Iran and Iraq, Perspectives in Conflict*' in http:/www.globalsecurity.org/military/library/report/1998/GGS.htm, pp1-78: p. 9.
27- R. N. Schofield. '*Interpreting a Vague River Boundary Delimitation. The 1847 Erzerum Treaty and the Shatt al-Arab before 1913*,' in K. S. McLachlan (ed.), *The Boundaries of Modern Iran* (London: UCL Press Ltd, 1994), pp.72-92: p.76.
28- A. Melamid, '*The Shatt al Arab boundary dispute*', The Middle East Journal 22 (1968), pp. 351-7 see also *Ibid.*, p.76.
29- Schofield (2994), *Opt .cit.*, pp.76.
30- D. Gillard (ed), *British Documents On Foreign Affairs*: Reports and Papers From the Foreign Office Confidential Print, Series B, Vol. 10, Persia 1856-1885, pp.322-339, p.322.
31- J.J. Cusimano, '*An Analysis of Iran-Iraq Bilateral Border Treaties* in Western Reserve Journal of International Law, Vol.24 Issue 1, (Winter 1992). pp. 1-23:p.2 Taken from http://macam.ac.il/~aron/Int-ME/extra/AN%20ANALYIS%200F%20 IRAN.H P2c.
32- G.S. Cruz '*Iran and Iraq, Perspectives in Conflict*' in http:/www.globalsecurity.org/military/library/report/1998/GGS.htm, pp 1-78: p.9.
33- Foreign Office, "*Translation d'une Note officiale [sic] remise par son Excellence Rechid Pacha a Sir Stratford Canning*", I June 1847. FO 881/10041.
34- D. Gillard (ed), *British Documents On Foreign Affairs*: Reports and Papers From the Foreign Office Confidential Print, Series B, Vol 10, Persia 1856-1885.pp.322-339.
35- *Ibid.*, pp. 322-339.
36- C.J. Edmonds, *Kurds, Turks, and Arabs* (London, Oxford University Press, 1957): p. 132.
37- Foreign Office, *Lord Palmerston to Sir G. H.Seymour*, dated 11 October 1851. FO 78/2716.
38- R. K. Ramazani, *The Foreign Policy of Iran*, (Charlotsville: Va, 1996): p. 55, See also C.H.D. Ryder, '*The Demarcation of the Turco-Persian boundary in 1913-14*", in Geographical Journal no.66 (1925), p.228
39- Ramazani, *Ibid.*, p.56.
40- R. N. Schofield '*Iran's borders with Turkey*', in E. Yarshater (ed.), *Encyclopaedia Iranica*, Vol. 4, (New York: Routledge.1989): pp. 415-417: p. 417.

41- R.N. Schofield, *The Iran Iraq Border, 1840-1958*, Vol. II, XV (Farnham Common: Archive Editions, 1989): p. xxi.
42- *Ibid.*
43- Foreign Office, *Extracts from foreign Office correspondence relative to Persian Frontiers.* FO371/40219.
44- G.S. Cruz '*Iran and Iraq, Perspectives in Conflict*' in http:/www.globalsecurity.org/military/library/report/1998/GGS.htm, pp1-78: p.9.
45- P. Mojtahed-Zadeh, in N. Bescharner, St. J.B. Gould and K. S. McLachlan (eds.), *GRC* (London: SOAS Publication, 1990): pp. 66-68: p. 66.
46- R. N. Schofield '*Iran's borders with Turkey*' in E. Yarshater (ed.), *Encyclopaedia Iranica*, Vol. 4 (New York: Routledge.1989): pp.415-417: p.417.
47- *Ibid.*, p. 417.
48- *Ibid.*, p. 417.
49- *Ibid.*, p. 417.
50- M. Anderson, *Frontiers, Territory and State Formation in the Modern World*, (Cambridge: Polity Press.1997) :pp. 97-99.
51- For example see explanations of transferred territories between 1980-1988 in K. S. McLachlan '*The Iran-Iraq Boundary Question*' in The Iranian Journal of International Affairs, Vol. 5, Nos.3&4 (fall/winter 1993/1994). Pp. 593-603.
52- S. Chubin & S. Zabih, *Foreign Relations of Iran* (London: University of California Press, 1974): pp.182-183.
53- J. Tagavi '*The Iran-Iraq war :The First Three Years*' in B. M. Rosen (ed.), *Iran Since The Revolution: Internal Dynamics, Regional Conflicts & The Superpowers* (New York: Colombia University Press.1985): p.67.
54- S. Chubin & S. Zabih, *Opt. cit.*, p.183.
55- The work of the 1913-1914 Border Commission has however been subject to constant yet minor changes since its work finished-these changes were very much finalised by the end of the Iran-Iraq war in 1988 see K. S. McLachlan '*The Iran-Iraq Boundary Question*' in The Iranian Journal of International Affairs, Vol. 5, Nos. 3&4 (fall/winter 1993/1994). Pp. 593-603; see also Foreign Office, *Extracts from foreign Office correspondence relative to Persian Frontiers.* FO371/45507.

References

1- *After Midnight* (London: Channel 4 T.V. Production, 1990)
2- Goldschmidt Jr, *A Concise History of The Middle East*: Sixth Edition (Boulder, Colorado: Westview Press, 1999).
3- Lewis, *The Middle East, 2000 Years Of History from The Rise Of Christianity To The Present Day* (London: Phoenix Press.2001)
4- B.M. Rosen (ed.), *Iran Since The Revolution: Internal Dynamics, Regional Conflicts & The Superpowers* (New York: Colombia University Press.1985)
5- C.J. Edmonds, *Kurds, Turks, and Arabs* (London, Oxford University Press, 1957)
6- David E. Long and Christian Koch [edis] 1997, *Gulf Security in the Twenty First century*, ELSR.
7- D. Gillard (ed.) British Documents On Foreign Affairs: Reports and Papers From The Foreign Office Confidential Print, Series B, Vol. 10, Persia 1856-1885.pp.322-339.
8- *Encyclopaedia Iranica*, vol. 4, (New York: Routledge, 1989): pp401-417.
9- Foreign Office, FO371/40219, FO371/45507, 1851.FO 78/2716.
10- *Geographical Journal* no.66 (1925), p.228.
11- J.R.V. Prescott, *Boundaries and Frontiers*, (London: Croom Helm, 1978): pp. 39-48.
12- K. S. Mclachlan (ed.), The Boundaries of Modern Iran (London: UCL Press Ltd, 1994).
13- M. Anderson, *Frontiers, Territory and State Formation in the Modern World* (Cambridge: Polity Press.1997).
14- N. Bescharner, St.J.B. Gould and K. S. McLachlan (eds.) *GRC* (London: SOAS Publication, 1990): pp.66-68.
15- P. Mojtahed-Zadeh *Political Geography and Geographical Politics* (Tehran: SAMT, 2002): pp.335-337.
16- P. Mojtahed-Zadeh, *The Amirs of the Borderlands and Eastern Iranian Borders* (London: Urosevic Foundation Publication No.2. 1995).
17- R. Mathee 'The Safavid-Ottoman Frontier: Iraq-I Arab As Seen By The Safavids'
18- R. K. Ramazani, *The Foreign Policy of Iran* (Charlotsville: Va, 1996).
19- R. Schofield, *The Iran Iraq Border, 1840-1958*, vol. II, XV (Farnham Common: Archive Editions, 1989).
20- S. Chubin & S. Zabih, *Foreign Relations of Iran* (London: University of California Press, 1974).
21- *The Iranian Journal of International Affairs*, Vol. 5, No's.3&4 (fall/winter 1993 /1994).pp. 584-603.
22- *The Middle East Journal* 22 (1968), pp.351-7.
23- *Western Reserve Journal of International Law*,) Vol.24 Issue 1, (winter 1992):pp.1-23.
24- www.globalsecurity.org/military/library/report/1998/GGS.htm
25- www.law.fsu.edu/library/collection/LimitsinSeas/IBS028.pdf
26- www.law.fsu.edu/library/collection/LimitsinSeas/IBS164.pdf

CHAPTER X

Evolution of the Shatt al-Arab Dispute after the 1913 Protocol
Pirouz Mojtahed-Zadeh

Introduction

After the signing of the Protocol of 4th November 1913 by the Ottoman, Persian, British and Russian representatives at Constantinople, a commission was appointed to carry out the demarcation of the boundaries specified in that document. A substantial part of the boundary was demarcated without too much difficulty, but during the following year fundamental disagreements arose mainly over the status of Shatt al-'Arab which, according to the 1913 Protocol, was left under Ottoman sovereignty. The section of the protocol which defined the boundary along the Shatt reads as follows:

> *...From the mouth of the Nahr-i Hazaibeh the frontier shall follow the course of the Shatt as far as the sea, leaving under Ottoman sovereignty, the river and all the islands therein subject to the following conditions and exceptions"* ...(1)

> *...The modern port and anchorage of Mohammara above and below the junction of the river Karun with the Shatt al-'Arab, shall remain within Persian jurisdiction in conformity with the Treaty of Erzurum; the Ottoman right of usage of this part of the river shall not, however, be affected hereby, nor shall Persian jurisdiction extend to the parts of the river outside the anchorage"...* (2)

The 1914 Protocol

The Iranian government refused to accept the terms of such provisions, insisting on placing the boundaries of the two sides in the middle of the river bed on the thalweg line. The Iranian government's demand that the boundaries should be shifted was mainly related to the development of the modern port of Muhammara, later re-named Khorramshahr, which was seriously hindered by the prevalence of Ottoman jurisdiction under the terms of the 1913 Protocol. Finally, by the end of 1914 the two sides agreed on a settlement of the issue by placing the boundary in the middle of the river from a point one mile below the mouth of the Karun to a point about four miles above it.

By the end of World War 1 the port of Abadan had begun to play an important role in the region, with the development of the oil industry in Iran. The volume of oil exports started to increase, with a commensurate increase in the number of oil tankers using the waterway and the port of Abadan. More oil tankers began to anchor outside Iranian waters. In 1921 the state of Iraq was created in the former Ottoman Pashaliks of Baghdad, Basra, and Mussel; it inherited the boundary disputes with Iran from the Ottoman Empire.

The 1937 Agreement

In 1934 the Iranian government requested a shift in the portion of the Shatt al-'Arab boundary near Abadan, similar to the shift of boundaries near Khorramshahr in 1914. British interests once again coincided with those of the Iraqis. The British considered the Shatt to be a major waterway in the line of communication between Europe (the Mediterranean) and India.

> ...the particular British interest in the Shatt al-'Arab other than (a) the fulfillment of British obligations under the Alliance, which is primarily an Iraqi interest, and (b) the Anglo-Persian oil company and other commercial shipping, which could in the last resort use Bandar Shahpur, is presumably the existence of RAF units in Iraq so long as the Euphrates corridor is requested as a link of air communication between the Mediterranean and India, the Shatt al-'Arab is a vital waterway for the supply, reinforcement and naval support of these units (3).

The British therefore suggested the formation of a joint Anglo-Persian-Iraqi Conservancy Board for navigation and control of the Shatt al-'Arab waterway (4), but the Iranian government refused to accept such a proposal.

As a result of the constant friction between Iraq and Iran, Iraq took the matter to the League of Nations in December 1934. (5) After lengthy debate at the League, Iraq decided to refer the matter to the International Court of Justice at The Hague. The offer was declined by Iran. In the mean time, Britain renewed her earlier proposal to form a conservancy board. The Iranian government refused for the second time, suspecting that British participation might work in favour of Iraq. The two parties did, however, agree to negotiate for a peaceful settlement of the dispute.

Finally, on 4th July 1937 when Iraq's nationalist Prime Minister Nouri as-Saeed established friendly relations with Iran of Reza Shah Pahlavi and the two states joined Turkey and Afghanistan in the Sadabaad Pact, the two governments reached an agreement which consisted of six articles. Article I defined the boundary line as the one agreed upon in the Constantinople Protocol and subsequently by the 1914 demarcation commission. Article II defined the thalweg anchorage to be ceded to Iran off Abadan. This treaty also recognized Iranian sovereignty over the island of Mohalla and the rights of Iran and Iraq to use the whole course of the river.

Relations between the two countries remained friendly from the time of Iraq's creation in 1921 until 1958 when the first military coup d' etat brought down the monarchy and Nouri as-Saeed's government in Iraq. It was in this period that Iraq's young king Faisal II asked for the Shah of Iran for the hand of his daughter in marriage. Though this marriage never took place, relations remained cordial mainly owing to Nouri as-Saeed's superior interest in Iraqi nationalism and cooperation with the neighbours in comparison with the policies of Arab nationalism and confrontation with non-Arab neighbours (6).

Events Leading to the Conclusion of 1975 Accord

The importance of the ports of Khorramshahr and Abadan for the Iranian economy increased considerably after World War II. The question of the Shatt al-'Arab was raised again in December

1959 when the Iraqi military leader 'Abd al-Karim Qassem denounced the 1937 agreement and claimed Iraq's sovereignty over the whole of the Shatt. He declared that Iraq signed the 1937 agreement under duress (7). Conflict appeared imminent. Both Iraq and Iran were sensitive to the Shatt al-'Arab's strategic position and as a result they began to reorganize their navigational operations in the Shatt al-'Arab. Iran, for its part, sought alternatives to Abadan as centres for trade and communications in other ports along the coasts of the Persian Gulf in a project known as "project CHAM" (Persian: Chahar Mantagheh meaning "four regions"). Moreover it was soon realized that the Shatt was unsuitable for oil exports as newly-developed supertankers could not use its relatively shallow draft. Thus, the ports of Bandar Shahpur (now Bandar Khomeini), Bandar Mahshahr, Bandar Bushehr and Kharg Island were expanded with petrochemical, heavy and electronics industries. Iraq too developed its port of Fao, near the Shatt estuary, in the 1950s. The 1960s witnessed the completion of the Khor al-Ummariya oil terminal south of Fao, which was later complemented by the construction of port Mina al-Bakr in 1970.

In February 1968 an Iranian delegation visited Iraq still ruled by the Arif brothers; the subjects of boundary disputes between the two countries in general and the Shatt al-Arab question in particular were discussed and, as discussions ran into difficulties in spite of friendly pasture of the Arif regime towards Iran, the Iranian delegation put its views into writing in the form of a draft treaty. The note stated that the thalweg line should constitute the official border between the two countries along the whole course of the Shatt al-'Arab. The Iraqi authorities refused to discuss this matter and the Iranian delegation returned empty-handed (8).

Before leaving Baghdad, the Iranian delegation handed a note to the head of the Iraqi delegation informing the Iraqi government:

> *...whereas the 1937 treaty has been constantly violated by Iraq ever since it was signed; whereas the treaty is contrary to all international practices and the principles of International Law relating to frontier waterways; therefore, the aforesaid facts have rendered the treaty null and void* (9).

On 15th April 1969, under the new coup d; etat regime of Baath Party of Hassan al-Bakr and Saddam Hussein, the Iraqi Deputy Foreign Minister summoned the Iranian Ambassador in Baghdad and told him that ships flying Iranian colours should lower their flags, otherwise all ships bound for Iranian ports would be intercepted and any Iranian Navy personnel on board such ships would be forcibly removed by the Iraqi authorities (10).

The Iranian Senate called upon the Foreign Ministry to explain the situation and inform the Senate of the measures which had been taken to safeguard Iranian interests in the Shatt al-'Arab. The Iranian Deputy Foreign Minister, Mr. Amir-Khosro Afshar, made a statement before the Senate in which he enumerated instances of violation of the main provisions of the 1937 treaty by Iraq and declared that, because of these violations, the treaty had been rendered null and void (11).

Iran subsequently sailed ships in the Shatt al-'Arab under the protection of her armed forces and thus unilaterally enforced the thalweg as the Shatt al-'Arab boundary. The dispute was aggravated by political and ideological differences between Tehran and Baghdad and relations deteriorated. Return to Iran of the islands of Abu Musa, Greater and Lesser Tunb near the Strait of Hormuz on 30th November 1971 led to the break-off of diplomatic relations altogether.

The Algiers Accord of 1975

Finally, on 6th March 1975, the leaders of the two countries met during the Algiers OPEC summit as a result of months of mediation works of President Bu Medien of Algeria between the Shah of Iran and Saddam Hussein, the strong man of Iraq. Relations improved rapidly. The Accord signed on that date provided that:

    a) Iran and Iraq would define their frontiers on the basis of the Constantinople Protocol of 1913 and the verbal agreement of 1914;

    b) They would define their river frontiers according to the thalweg line, the middle of the deepest shipping channel;

    c) They would re-establish security along their common frontier an undertake strict and effective controls to end infiltrations by "subversive characters" on either side and;

    d) The parties would regard these provisions as indivisible elements of a comprehensive settlement and, in consequence, any breach of one of them constituted a violation of the spirit of the Algiers agreement (12).

Following this declaration, representatives of Iran and Iraq and committees of delimitation and demarcation consisting of panels of experts from both countries, met from time to time in their respective capitals to draft a comprehensive treaty which was ratified by the parliaments of both countries. Relations improved over the next five years and Saddam Hussein visited Iran and invited the Shah to visit Iraq.

Figure 10

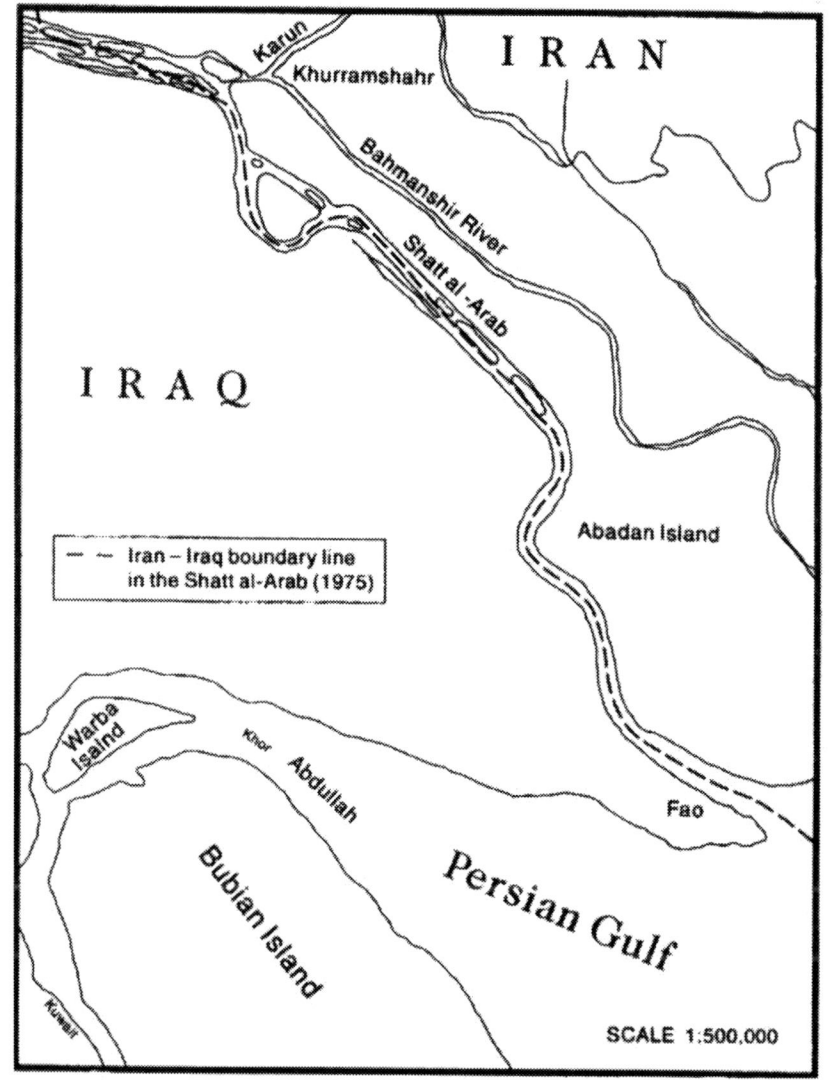

Iran's Thalweg boundary with Iraq in Shatt al-Arab

Subsequently, Iraq's relations improved with her Arab neighbours. In a short period after the declaration of the Algiers accord of March 1975, Iraq signed border agreement with Saudi Arabia and divided the Neutral Zone between the two countries. The signing of a new agreement for cooperation with Jordan improved Baghdad's strained relations with Amman. In another agreement with Kuwait, Iraq received such concessions as use of the Kuwaiti port of Shoaibah and diplomatic relations were established with the Sultanate of Oman after years of Baghdad's support for the communist separatists of Dhufar in southern Oman.

The Wars and Iraq's Return to Algiers Accord

But the Baath regime's departure from the policy of aggression and mal treatment of the neighbours lasted only for a short while. With the fall of the Shah's regime in Iran and when Iran was still in revolutionary turmoil Saddam Hussein appeared on the Iraqi national television and tore off the Algiers Accord, unilaterally declaring the 1975 boundary agreement between the two countries null and void because *'the accord was imposed on Iraq under duress'* he insinuated. Iraq subsequently invaded Iran in September 1980 and imposed a war of attrition on her which lasted for eight years and resulted in no other achievements but great devastation of the two countries and more than a million dead or maimed. This was Baath Party's final act as the war was followed by a series of events which ended the life of the Baath regime in Iraq and its menace for the region.

These events began with Saddam Hussein's claim of victory in war with Iran. In spite of failing to attain its declared war aims, the Baath regime celebrated the "victory" in its war against Iran and asked the Arab World to reward Saddam Hussein by giving the state of Kuwait to him.

This demand for rewards of unbelievable kind met no response from the Arab World and encouraged Saddam Hussein to invade Kuwait in 1990, only two years after cease fire was declared in war with Iran, and occupied that country. The occupation of Kuwait triggered an unprecedented military alliance in the West and in coalition with Arab World against the Baath of Iraq. Rapid military build up on Iraqi borders in the south forced Baghdad to prepare for a massive strategic defence. To do this, Baghdad needed to relocate its forces from the Iranian border areas to the southern borders.

During his official correspondence with the President of the Islamic Republic of Iran in 1990s for securing Iran's agreement to his proposal for the demilitarization of the border areas of the two countries, Saddam Hussein wrote on 14 August 1990 to President Rafsanjani of the Islamic Republic of Iran, officially agreeing Iraq's return to the terms of the 1975 Algiers Accord. In that letter (see appendix), Saddam Hussein declared that Iraq was ready to demarcate the two countries' boundary line in Shatt al-Arab along the thalweg of the river in accordance with the Algiers Accord of 1975 (13). Certainly by declaring to the President of the Islamic Republic of Iran in the said letter that: *"With this decision of ours everything has been clarified and thus, whatever you had desired and emphasized will be attained"* (14), Saddam Hussein and the Baath Party and those replacing them any one else in Iraq or elsewhere for that matter, cannot claim once again that the 1975 Algiers Accord had been imposed on either parties under duress. Meanwhile, port Khorramshahr was opened to river traffic in December 1992, with Iran utilizing full rights to navigation on the Shatt al-Arab on the basis of understanding of 14 August 1990 with Iraq (15).

12 years of military siege and severe political and economic sanctions and a major war by the United States and their British allies in 2003 brought down the Baath regime of Saddam Hussein in Iraq paving the way for a genuine democracy in that country which would inevitably bring about good relations with the neighbours in Iraq's foreign policy approaches.

References

1- League of Nations Official Journal, February 1935, p. 201.
2- League of Nations Official Journal, February 1935, pp. 201-2.
3- L. Bagally to Sir Archibald Clark Kerr, Ambassador to Baghdad, December 1935, FO 371/18977.
4- S. H. Lonrigg, *Iraq: 1900-1950*, Oxford University Press 1953, p. 267
5- League of Nations, Official Journal, February 1935, pp. 196-208.
6- Pirouz Mojtahed-Zadeh, *Khalij-e Fars: Keshvarha va Marzha = The Persian Gulf, Countries and Boundaries*, Ataei Publications, Tehran 1379 (2000), p. 550.
7- Times, 17th and 19th December 1959.
8- Foreign Ministry of Iran, *Facts about Shatt al-Arab Disputes*, May 1969, p. 7.
9- Ibid.
10- Ibid.
11- Ibid.
12- *Keesing's* Contemporary Archives, April 1975, P. 2705.
13- Iran Focus, Vol. 3, No. 6, London June 1990.
14- Pirouz Mojtahed-Zadeh, Khalij-e Fars…, op cit., pp 554-558.
15- Iran Monitor, Vol. 1, 1993, p. 24.

APPENDIX TO CHAPTER X

English Texts of Saddam Hussein's Letter of 14 August 1990 to the President of the IRI and the IRI Response

Text of the Iraqi President's letter dated 23 Moharram 1411 H.Q.[23 Mordad 1369 H. S., 14 August 1990]

In the Name of God, the Compassionate, the Merciful

His Excellency Mr. Ali Akbar Hashemi Rafsanjani
Honorable president of the Islamic republic of Iran

Trusting the Almighty and Exalted God and in order to remove obstacles in the path of brotherly relations with all Muslims, and those Muslims in the neighboring country of Iran who choose brotherhood and are in the path of creating space for deep bonds with all the pious so as to confront the evil and malevolent forces opposing Muslims and the Arab *umma;* and with the motivation to keep away Iran and Iraq from the blackmail and deceit of evil-seeking international forces and their cronies in the region and in harmony with our innovative spirit which, with the object of attaining a comprehensive and lasting peace in the region, was announced on 12/8/1990; and, in order to take away anti-bonding excuses from those wavering and suspicious seekers of excuses and so that none of Iraq's capabilities is left unutilized in the big battle and in order to mobilize all these capabilities for the pursuit of objectives that all the honorable Muslims and Arabs concur in their rightfulness, and for the prevention of the conflict of positions* and removing doubts and suspicions so that the benevolent can find their way for establishing normal relations between Iraq and Iran; and as a result of discussions between us which lasted in a direct manner from our first letter dated 21/4/90 to your last letter dated 8/8/90; and since final and clear solution will not leave any excuses for those seeking excuses, we have taken the following decisions:

    1- We are in agreement with your proposal presented in your letter of 8 August 1990 which our representative in Geneva, Mr. Barzan Takriti received from your representative, Mr. Cyrus Nasseri and which observes the necessity of recognizing the 1975 Treaty as the basis due to its being related to the principle mentioned in our letter dated 30 July 1990,

---

* If this phrase is translated literally it will read: "… and for the prevention of the permeating trenches..."

especially those concerning the exchange of prisoners and paragraphs 6 and 7 of Security Council Resolution 598.

2- On the basis of this letter and the contents of the letter dated 30 July 1990, we are prepared to dispatch a delegation to Tehran or to receive a delegation from your side in Baghdad so that while preparing the relevant agreements, we can provide the groundwork for the signing of the agreements on the level that will be acceptable to both sides.

3- In order to demonstrate our good will, we shall begin our withdrawal from Friday, the 17th of August 1990, and except for retaining a symbolic force along with our border officers and police which remain only for the sake daily duties under ordinary conditions, we shall recall our forces all along the border from regions where they confront your forces.

4- The immediate and comprehensive exchange of all prisoners of war, captive in whatever numbers in Iran and Iraq to be undertaken from (land) borders, the Khanegein-Qare-Shirin road, or other mutually agreed upon roads. We shall be the initiator of this action and shall begin the exchange strating from 17/8/1990.

Brother Ali Akbar Hashemi Rafsanjani, the president…..With this decision of ours everything has been clarified and thus, whatever you had desired and emphasized will be attained, and no other action other than the exchange of document will remain, so that together from the position of responsibility we can be a witness to a new life filled with cooperation under the auspices of the principles of Islam, to respect one another's rights; and thus, in this way we can hold back from our shores those who try to fish in troubled waters, and even cooperate in certain areas, so that we can, as a result, convert the (Persian) Gulf into a waterway of peace and security without the presence of foreign warships and forces who are lying in wait for us. Furthermore, this kind of cooperation may come to include other aspects of life. God is great and praise be to him.

Saddam Hussein
President of Iraq
23 Moharram 1411 H.Q.
14 August 1990

Text of reply of the President of the Islamic republic of Iran Dated 27 Moharram 1411 H.Q.[27 Mordad 1369 H. S., 18 August 1990] to Iraqi President's letter dated 23 Moharram 1411 H.Q.[23 Mordad 1369 H. S., 14 August 1990]

In the Name of God, the Compassionate, the Merciful

"Praise be to God for His grace, and thanks be to Him for His inspiration"

The Honorable President of Iraq
His Excellency Mr. Saddam Hussein

Your Excellency's letter dated 23/5/69 (August 14, 1990) has been received. The announcement of the re-acceptance of the 1975 Treaty from your side has paved the way towards the implementation of the resolution 598, and can convert the existing ceasefire into a permanent and lasting peace.

We consider the commencement of the withdrawal of your forces from the occupied territories of Iran as reason of your sincerity and seriousness on the path of peace with the Islamic Republic of Iran; fortunately, at the specified time the release of prisoners [of war] has also begun; and we hope that the withdrawal of your military, according to the announced timetable and the release of the prisoners [of war] of both sides, will continue and be completed with more deliberation and speed.

Just as we informed you through our representative in Geneva, we are now ready to receive your representatives in Tehran and hope that with the continuation of the positive environment and existing good will, we can, by protecting all the legitimate rights and limits of the two peoples and the two Islamic countries, attain a comprehensive and lasting peace.

Va Ssalam Aleikom (Peace be upon you).

Akbar Hashemi Rafsanjani
President of the Islamic Republic of Iran
27/5/1369 [18 August 1990]

SECTION C

Emergence and Evolution of Eastern Iranian Boundaries

CHAPTER XI

The Partitioning of Eastern Provinces of Iran
Pirouz Mojtahed-Zadeh

Introduction

Since this work is aimed at the study of the role of the Khozeimeh Amirdom in the Anglo-Russian Great Game of geopolitics of 19th and 20th centuries and the study of the evolution of political geography of lands on which this game had been played on , and as the partitioning of Sistan and Baluchistan in early 1870s was justified on the merits of political developments of the post-Nader Shah events in Khorasan, no positive assessment of the evolution of the said political geography can escape an adequate study of the those developments. In other words, since the partitioning of lands forming the chess-board on which the Great Game was played out was, in reality, but an aftermath of the partitioning of Khorasan and Creation of Afghanistan in the preceding two decades, or so, a better understanding of the circumstances leading to the major development needs to be examined somewhat closely.

It seems only appropriate to open this section with a quotation from Lord George N. Curzon whose works on Iran works on Iran and Afghanistan are regarded as authoritative in late nineteenth century. He asserts:

> *Persia cannot forget that what is now Western Afghanistan has through the greatest part of history been Eastern Khorasan, that Herat has been habitually ruled by Persian sovereigns, viceroys, governors, or vassals, that is inhabited by people of Persian rather than Afghan traditions and sympathy, and that it is severed by no physical or ethnographical barrier from Meshed...* (1)

The term 'Khorasan' is an ancient Persian term, derived from the word 'Khor' which means 'sun' and 'Asan' or 'Ayan' which means 'the place where it comes from', together they mean 'the place where the sun come from'. Alternatively, the composition implies that the country of such a name is the ultimate 'Khavar' or east. 10th century famous Persian poet, Rudaki Samarqandi, said; Khorasan is the place where the sun comes from.

Historically, Khorasan included the entire Afghanistan, Sistan, Trans-Oxania, most of Central Asia as well as the north-eastern parts of present day Iran. In the time of Arab Caliphate of the Abbasids, Iran was divided into three distinct political zones; a middle zone – from ray (near Tehran) to Bandar Abbas, separated the two eastern and western zones. This middle zone was generally known as 'Eraq-e Ajam' or the 'non-Arab Iraq'. Areas to the west of this zone were known as 'Eraq-e Arab' or the 'Arabic Iraq', and areas to the east were generally known as 'Khorasan'. Many of the famous names in Persian literature, born and bred in that vast province describe themselves as the children of Khorasan. The aforementioned Rudaki, for instance, says;

It is time now that the entire world wrote his words
It is time now for the world to know he is a poet of Khorasan

The eastern and north-eastern parts of Khorasan were partitioned in the second half of the nineteenth century, and were included in the countries of Afghanistan and Russia respectively. What is now known as Khorasan, used to be the largest province in Iran until 2002. This province is now divided into three (subdivision) provinces.

While some Iranian historians consider Afghanistan as a problematic appendix of Iran, Afghan historians have, in the past century or so, endeavoured to present a picture in which Iran and Afghanistan emerge as two different entities, busy colonizing each other since the dawn of man's history (2). How wrong are they both? The fact that remains is that Iran and most of Afghanistan, Pakistan, Iraq, Turkey and countries of the Caucasus, Central Asia, and lower Persian Gulf were one in the Old Persian Empire of over 2000 years. As from the second half of the 18th century, when British Indian power began to consolidate its influence in the largest parts of south and Central Asia, other European powers, mainly France and Russia, extending the sphere of their geopolitical aspirations eastward and continued their rivalries with the British all over Asia. Iranian power was on the decline following the assassination of Nader Shah Afshar in June 1747, and the chaos that it caused. By contrast, British India's power and influence were on the rise. To counter the influence of the rival powers on its western flank, British India Empire began the policy of creating a buffer zone between itself and Iran and Russia, the former suspected by India, throughout most of Qajar period (1779 – 1924) of being influenced by the French and specially Russia. Hence, eastern Iranian frontiers became the subject of a series of changes and modification, shifting from the easternmost parts of Greater Khorasan, Greater Sistan and Greater Baluchistan, to the central parts of these extensive provinces of old Persia, resulting in the creation of Afghanistan, British Baluchistan (later Pakistan), and countries of Central Asia.

Break-up of Greater Khorasan and Creation of Afghanistan

Having almost completed his long and arduous campaign of unifying Iran, Nader Shah Afshar was assassinated in the middle of the night on June 19th 1747 after a brief struggle with his assassins. The next morning the whole camp was in chaos, some leaders took their contingents and headed towards their own districts. The Afghan and Uzbek contingents held together, under the command of Nour Mohammad, seconded by Ahmad Khan Abdali. Both these two men, loyal to the memory of the late sovereign, took up arms and prevented the pillage of the royal tents. This act of loyalty would not, in any way, suggest that the Afghans were, by then, considering themselves as being people of a different country. In his first and most important decree issued, as the new sovereign, on 16 Shavval 1167 (1753) Ahmad Khan Abdali does not even mention the name "Afghanistan". Instead he speaks of hopes that he would *"God willing…bring under control the whole of Iran…"* (3).

Having found themselves outnumbered by the rest of the Naderi forces, however, the Afghan commanders led their troops in their fateful march towards east. On their arrival in Qandehar, leaders of the Afghan tribes decided to go their own way by choosing their own king and creating their own kingdom. They selected Ahmad Khan Abdali of the Dorrani tribe for the post, giving him the title 'Shah' of Afghanistan.

G. P. Tate, an authority on Afghanistan history describes this development in the following terms: "Sabir Shah who had followed Ahmad to the camp, rejoined him on the way eastwards. This person was one of those wandering and semi-insane fakirs (very common even in the present day), whose incoherent utterances and irresponsible actions are regarded still with awe by superstitious persons, as inspired by the Almighty...

The leaders of the tribes, such as Haji Jamal Khan, the Barakzai, Muhabat Khan Popalzai, Musa Dungi the famous Eshakzai chief, Nur Mohammad, Alizai, Naser-Ullah Khan, the Nurzai Sardar and others, met in solemn conclave at the shrine of Surkh Sher Baba. They were quite unanimous that it was very expedient that they should have a king to manage their affairs, for the times were troublous and there were persons on all sides asserting their claims to independence (in all Persia). The question to be decided was who should be king. Not one of these powerful chiefs would acknowledge the superiority of the claims of his peers. Ahmad Khan by virtue of his rank and family was present at the debates, and sabir Shah's calling also made him welcome. He cut short the discussion by producing a tiny sheaf of wheat, and placing it in Ahmad Khan's turban, declared that no one in that assembly was so fit for the kingship as Ahmad Khan, the flower of the Duranis. The words and act of the eccentric fakir were regarded by all as a happy solution of the difficulty. Probably, also, they were regarded as a manifestation of the Divine will revealed through the holy man to the assembled chiefs. The scene was the shrine of a well known saint, who might be regarded therefore as being interested in the debate" (4).

This was how the first kingdom of Afghanistan came into being under the rule of its first monarch, Ahmad Khan Abdali, then titled as 'Ahmad Shah Dorrani' (5).

The name 'Afghanistan' was, according to some historians, invented in the 16th century by the Moghul Empire of India, as a convenient term referring to the districts and dependencies of Kabul. The term had existed in the old chronicles, first used in the Ghaznavid writings of the 13th century, when the term was applied to the mountain and cultivable tracts which were of the Afridis and Vaziris. Sir Percy Sykes asserts that General Houtrum Schindler believed that the Afghans were termed "Aghvans" in the Safavid times (6).

The kingdom of Afghanistan which emerged in mid-18th century was largely the home of three distinct races or national identities:
1- The Hazarahs located mostly to the west of the road from Qandehar to Kabul, who are Shiite and (Dari) Persian speaking, mostly of Mongolian origin.
2- Tajiks and Uzbeks, who include most of the settled population. They are agriculturalists with (Dari) Persian as their native language. They are the descendants of the ancient race, who had migrated from Central Asia to Iran. Tate describes the Tajiks as: one people and in all probability they represent the original Iranian or Aryan race, among whom Zoroaster published his doctrine; among whom the Greek colonists of Alexander settled... (7)
3- Three) The Pashtuns who are nomadic by origin and consider themselves as warriors. They are said to be Pathans, the name of the people mentioned by writers of antiquity. Pashtun or Afghan is applied to the tribes collectively, and also to the pastoral nomads among them. They are strict Sunni Muslims and speak Pashtun, and almost all of them can also speak (Dari) Persian.

The history of Afghanistan is practically the story of two great confederacies led by the Dorranis and Ghelzais, both of whom have ruled the territories of Afghanistan from time to time.

Abdali – Khozeimeh Rivalries and Partitioning of Khorasan

Nader Shah Afshar's assassination in 1747 marked the beginning of territorial disintegration of the Persian Empire. The unity of Greater Khorasan had similarly remained intact until that date. It included the cities and districts of Mashhad, Nishabour, Herat, Quchan, Bokhara, Samarqand,

Marv, Farah, Qandehar, Qohestan etc. located in today's Iran, Afghanistan, Turkmenistan, Uzbekistan and Tajikistan.

Among Nader Shah's successors, nobles and generals, Ahmad Khan Abdali and Amir Alam Khan Khozeimeh were concerned that Khorasan should remain undivided in the wake of their sovereign's assassination, each one of them for a different reason. Ahmad Khan Abdali – by then "Ahmad Shah Dorrani' – the first ruler of Afghanistan, wanted the entire Khorasan to be affiliated to his new kingdom, probably to be extended later to include the rest of Iran, thus, reviving Nader Shah's empire. Whereas, Amir Alam Khan Khozeimeh wanted to maintain the entire Khorasan as a part of Iran, preferably under his own rule, probably without necessarily including Kabul.

It was for the attainment of this goal that Amir Alam Khan attacked Mashhad soon after Nader Shah's assassination and subdued Shahrokh Mirza, Nader Shah's grandson, who was installed on the Naderi throne by some of the generals. The Amir dispatched, hurriedly, a troop to Herat, where his brother, Amir Masum Khan Khozeimeh succeeded in capturing the city and its dependencies, albeit this victory was very short lived. This event led to Amir Khan and Bahlul Khan, Shahrokh Mirza's men in Herat, writing to Ahmad Shah at Qandehar, informing him of the state of confusion in Herat. This news was received by Ahmad Shah with delight. He marched his troops of twenty thousand men on Herat in the spring of 1749, where he met Herati citizens' resistance. The city was finally opened had he marched on Mashhad where he restored Shahrokh Mirza on the throne, who, in turn, acknowledged the Afghan suzerainty (8). In the eyes of Nader Shah's generals rivaling Ahmad Shah Dorrani, by so doing, Shahrokh Mirza lost the legitimacy inherent in the tradition of the Iranian monarchy. In the eyes of the contestants for the leadership of Iran (i.e. Amir Alam Khan Khozeimeh, Mohammad Hassan Khan Qajar, and Karim Khan Zand), Shahrokh Mirza was no longer fit to rule as he had acknowledged suzerainty of Ahmad Shah Dorrani, by then a foreign sovereign. In other word, Shahrokh himself had paved the way for his adversaries, the Khozeimeh Amir and the Qajar Khan, to dethrone him and dispose of his rule in Khorasan.

Following these developments, Ahmad Shah Dorrani captured considerable parts of the Iranian Khorasan. Amir Alam Khan I marched on Mashhad, dethroned Shahrokh Mirza for the second time, captured territories to the north of Mashhad as far as Quchan, and marched on Nishabur. His capture of Nishabur was yet to be completed when news of Ahmad Shah's forces' arrival in Mashhad reached him. He had prepared to meet Ahmad Shah's challenge and defeated some of the advance parties of the Afghan troops, when the Khorasani Kurdish contingency of his forces deserted him and by so doing, instigated a mass desertion. Amir Alam Khan was left alone and was subsequently killed.

Ahmad Shah's expedition in Khorasan was not to last long either. Events in the east, especially in relation to India, drew his attention away from Khorasan. The blind Shahrokh Mirza, reinstated by Ahmad Shah, was left in charge of the province where his rule continued for approximately half a century. Meanwhile, Agha Mohammad Khan Qajar had taken over from his father, Mohammad Hassan Khan, the task of contesting for the leadership of Iran. He arrived in Khorasan in 1795 and overthrew Shahrokh Mirza, thus, putting a final end to the weak and corrupt rule of the grandson of Nader Shah. The rest of Iran was, at this period in time, ruled by Karim Khan Zand (1747 – 1799) except the northern parts of the country which were under the control of the Qajar family. Shahrokh Mirza still possessed many of the priceless jewels that nadir Shah had brought from India. Some of his collection, including the renowned Kuh-e Nour diamond had been taken from him by Ahmad Shah Dorrani, and the rest, including the Darya-e Nour diamond, were seized by Agha Mohammad Khan Qajar who left them as the property of the Iranian Crown, and have remained so to this date (9). Agha Mohammad Khan had turned to Khorasan after achieving paramouncy over the rest of Iran by defeating the heroic Lotf Ali Khan Zand and after subduing the rebels in Gorjestan (Georgia).

Ahmad Shah Dorrani died in 1773 and with his death was gone Shahrokh Mirza's adherence to the Dorrani suzerainty, though this was long exhausted. On his arrival in Khorasan, Agha Mohammad Khan was greeted by the local chiefs and vassal rulers, including Amir Ali Khan Khozeimeh of Qaenat who submitted to the Qajar Shah. Nader Mirza, son of Shahrokh Mirza Afshar sent his brothers to Herat and himself followed them shortly, leaving his old, blind and feeble father behind to make his own submission to the founder of the Qajar dynasty in Iran. Having completed the task of returning western parts of Greater Khorasan to Iranian sovereignty, Agha Mohammad Khan returned to Tehran (10) taking with him Shahrokh Mirza Afshar who died on the way in 1796 (11).

In his book *The Kingdom of Afghanistan* G. P. Tate claims that at the time of Agha Mohammad Khan Qajar, which coincided with the demise of Ahmad Shah Dorrani's new kingdom of Afghanistan, "Iran recognized the state of Afghanistan" (12). The reason given in support of this bizarre claim is Agha Mohammad Khan's decision in sending Hassan Khan Qaraguzlu to the Court of Shah-Zaman, the ruler of Kabul in 1796. What Tate has overlooked is the fact that Ahmad Shah Doran's former realms were divided into three principalities of Herat, Qandehar and Kabul all three going back to their traditional status as dependencies of Iran.

Though the true nature of the dependency of these three principalities to Iran had always been a matter of various degrees of ambiguity, officials going back and forth between the Central Government of Iran and the courts of these principalities had never amounted to the recognition of their independence. Whereas sending emissaries back and forth between Tehran and Kabul, Herat, Qandehar and/or Central Asian dependencies had been an on-going practice since the time of the Safavid Empire. Moreover, Iran's so-called recognition of Kabul as the 'state of Afghanistan' without the Afghan principalities of Herat and Qandehar being part of it, sounds more like wishful thinking on the part of Tate, who must have been more concerned about historical justification for later events regarding the partitioning of Khorasan and creation of Afghanistan for the second time, than anything else.

In Khorasan, however, Nader Mirza, son of Shahrokh Mirza and great-grandson of Nader Shah Afshar, hearing of Agha Mohammad Khan's assassination in July 1979, left Kabul, and having put together some troops, returned to Mashhad and took possession of the city declaring himself as the rightful heir to the Naderi throne of Persia. In Tehran, Fath-Ali Shah Qajar had succeeded his uncle Agha Mohammad Khan Qajar on 28th July 1979. He warned Nader Mirza of the consequence of his actions which was heeded by the latter. Some Afghan historians view Nader Mirza's claim in Mashhad of being the rightful heir to the throne of Nader Shah, as yet another manifestation of Afghanistan's resumption of sovereignty over Khorasan (13). These writers do not, of course, see it as their responsibility to specify as to how the rebellion in Khorasan of the great-grandson of former Iranian sovereign Nader Shah against a new Iranian sovereign would amount to the resumption of sovereignty of the non-existent state of Afghanistan (at the time) over the Iranian province of Khorasan?

Fath-Ali Shah, however, marched on Mashhad and recovered all towns and cities of the province. Nadir Mirza was seized by the inhabitants of Mashhad after he had desecrated the holy shrine of Imam Reza and had slain with his own hand an ayatollah. He was subsequently put to death (14).

The British Interest – A New Dimension

A new dimension was added to this general state of affairs in the region in the form of a westward expansion and geo-strategic interest of the British Indian Empire. Britain began, as from early 19th century, to view the principalities of Afghanistan and to some extent, Iran itself, as vulnerable gateway through which attacks could take place by either France or Russia or possibly the two together with Iran, against its possession in India. Both France and Russia had realized that although it was difficult, if not impossible, to challenge British supremacy at sea, it would be easily possible by land through Afghanistan. An additional source of anxiety for the British was the active efforts of French diplomacy in Iran (15) as well as all over Asia. A French mission, led by Monsieur Olivier arrived in Tehran in 1795 seeking friendship and alliance. Britain found the activities of Napoleon's representatives in the east, especially in Iran, for the purpose of contracting alliance, hostile to its position in India. At the same time, the British came to the conclusion that Shah-Zaman, ruler of Kabul, was posing serious threats to the stability of India and the position of the British India Company (16). This whole situation provoked a wide-range of British reaction which manifested itself in two different ways:

1. To counter the weight of the French in Iran by endeavouring to seal treaties of friendship and alliance with the Iranians.
2. To expand their influence throughout the Afghan territories and to bring all three Afghan principalities under an effective political control.

In the first instance, Mirza Mehdi-Ali Khan, as officer of the East India Company at Bushehr, was sent to Tehran in 1799 to prepare the ground for the launch of British diplomacy in Iran. The following year, Captain John Malcolm, envoy of the Viceroy of India arrived in Tehran. He gave Fath-Ali Shah two diamonds each worth 50,000 rupees, and succeeded in signing two treaties with Haji Ebrahim Khan, the Prime Minister, in January 1801; one on trade and the other political. The political treaty was signed in five articles which, not only ended the activities of the French in Iran, but also guaranteed an Iranian punishment of Afghan principalities if they threatened India (17). This treaty realized the ostensible object of Malcolm's mission which was to instigate Fath-Ali Shah to move an army upon Herat so as to divert Shah-Zaman from his threatened invasion of India. The Iranian move, which was motivated by the domestic situations in Herat and by the question of its loyalty to Iran, had already been made before John Malcolm appeared in Tehran (18). In addition, when Fath-Ali Shah sought British assistance in 1804 in the war with the Russians, the British declined, arguing that the war had been started by Prince Abbas Mirza, the Crown Prince of Iran. Fath-Ali Shah wrote to Napoleon asking him to renew the old friendship. Napoleon's personal secretary, Monsieur Joubert was sent to Tehran in 1805 where he prepared a new treaty which was signed at Finken Stain in the spring of 1807 (19) by Mirza Mohammad Khan Qazvini on the part of Iran and Bernard Maret on behalf of France.

This treaty provided for General Gardan, Napoleon's adjudant to arrive in Tehran as French Ambassador, with a group of officers and engineers who started their task of training and equipping Iranian troops. General Gardan was also assigned to conclude a defence treaty with the Iranian Government. However, as Napoleon disregarded the question of the war between Iran and Russia in his meeting of Tilsit with the Tzar in 1808 when the two European powers agreed on cooperation against Britain (20), Fath-Ali Shah lost hope and confidence with the French.

The Franco-Russian agreement of Tilsit, on the other hand, raised anxieties in London and Bombay of a new and more powerful threat to their Indian possessions. These anxieties led the British to attempt once again to secure the friendship of Iran and preclude her from joining the dangerous combination that had emerged, in the wake of peace between Iran and Russia. Sir

Harlford Jones was sent to Tehran in 1809 for the purpose, who signed later that year a provisional treaty with the Court of the Shah, according to which the Franco-Iranian treaty of Finken Stain was declared null and void. A loan of 200,000 tumans was extended to the Iranian Government by the British India Government which also undertook to prepare and train Iranian troops for the defense of the Iranian realms (21). The British Government ratified this treaty in 1810 and assigned Sir Gore Ousely as London's Ambassador to Tehran who prepared a new treaty to be signed between London and Tehran. Meanwhile, the British India Government, anxious about the situation arising from the possibility of a combined Franco-Russian threat to India, and probably uncertain that the direct diplomacy of London in Tehran would pay enough attention to this situation, sent Sir John Malcolm back to Tehran to secure Iran's cooperation in that regard. Fath-Ali Shah refused to see him and his rivalries with Sir Gore Ousely resulted in his return from Iran in the summer of 1810 (22). Sir Gore Ousely signed the 1812 treaty of friendship with Iran and mediated between Tehran and Moscow which resulted in the conclusion of the treaty of Golestan in 1813, whereby Iran lost many of her northwestern provinces to Russia (23).

The second British reaction to this situation concerned her relations with the Afghan principalities. These principalities had gone through a long period of chaos in the wake of Shah-Zaman's deposition in 1803. Two years earlier, Shah-Mahmud, brother of Shah-Zaman revolted against the latter, when Zaman was still threatening India. Mahmud declared himself as vassal 'Shah'. The city of Herat and its dependencies were, at this time, tributaries of Iran. The per annum taxes paid to the treasury of Tehran was one million rupees and fifty thousand ass-load (kharvar) of grain (24). When Agha Mohammad Khan, founder of the Qajar dynasty, marched troops to Khorasan to put an end to Shahrokh Mirza's obedience to Ahmad Shah Dorrani, the Governor of Herat declared his allegiance to the Qajar Government of Iran. He made the official speech at the public prayer (khotbeh) in the name of the Shahanshah of Iran (the king of all kings of Persian Empire) and reinstated payment of annual taxes to the treasury in Tehran.

Shah-Mahmud, in the meantime, succeeded in dethroning his brother Shah-Zaman in 1803 after the countenance offered to him by the Shahanshah (Fath-Ali Shah). Mahmud appointed Prince Firouz ad-Din as Governor of Herat, who in turn, appointed Shah-Mahmud's son, Prince Kameran, as Governor of Farah, a dependency of Herat. Shah-Mahmud was dethroned in 1804, by Shah-Shoja, and escaped to Iran a year later (25). At the same time, Firouz ad-Din sent troops to capture Ghurian in accordance with a pre-arrangement with the Deputy Governor of the district who surrendered the town in the event. Not only was this move viewed in Tehran as a violation of Iran's sovereignty in the eastern provinces, but also signified Firouz ad-Din's rebellion against Herat's traditional dependency to Iran. Iranian troops defeated Firouz ad-Din's forces in Ghurian and Mohammad Vali Khan, Governor-General of Khorasan, marched on Herat to punish Firouz ad-Din for his breach of faith and to collect the tribute which had been in arrears for two years. The city of Herat was invested in 1810. Firouz ad-Din apologized for his conduct and sent his son Malek Hussein Mirza to stay in Tehran or Mashhad as a guarantee of his good faith in future. He also sent to the treasury in Tehran the tributes in arrears with promise of discharging the taxes punctually in future. Six years later, he revolted again and invaded the district of Ghurian (1816). This time Prince Hassan-Ali Mirza Shoja as-Saltaneh, new Governor-General of Khorasan, recovered Herat and not only did he collect from Firouz ad-Din the tributes in arrears, but also extracted from him an extra 50,000 tumans as punishment. He was obliged to guarantee punctual payments of the annual tribute, to read the Khotbeh in the name of Shahanshah, and to make the coinage in his name (26).

In Kabul, unlike his brother Shah-Mahmud who was faithful to Iran and whom he had dethroned in 1804, Shah-Shoja was wholly reliant on the British from whom he received many valuable gifts. The British envoy, Mount Stewart Elphinson, had signed a treaty with him on June 17, 1809 whereby Shah-Shoja undertook 'on behalf of all Afghans' to prevent any attack on India from northwest of that country (27). This agreement did not survive for long as Shah-Shoja was dethroned in the same year. Shah-Mahmud's struggle against Shah-Shoja brought much chaos to the Afghan dependencies of Iran. Shah-Mahmud eventually succeeded in settling in Herat with his son Prince Kameran with the consent of Tehran. Chaos in Kabul and Qandehar deepened as Shah-Shoja was recalled in 1917 by Sardar Mohammad Azim Khan to become 'Shah of Afghanistan' in Kabul. This chaotic state of affairs worsened as Sardar Mohammad Azim Khan fought Shah-Shoja, the so-called monarch he himself selected for all Afghanistan. Shah-Shoja was defeated and forced out of Qandehar, and the Sardar lost Kabul to Dust Mohammad Khan. The new-comer and his brother, Kohandel Khan, divided the principalities of Kabul and Qandehar among themselves respectively (28).

In Herat, Shah-Mahmud and his son Kameran, the last of the Abdalis, fell out and fought a number of times against one another (1820 – 1821) until the people of Herat mediated between them and arranged for Mahmud to remain Shah, and Kameran as his Prime Minister in charge of the affairs (29). Firouz ad-Din had already escaped to Mashhad when Shah-Mahmud arrived in Herat in 1818. He had taken refuge with the Governor-General of Khorasan.

British direct diplomacy in Afghanistan, by this time, succeeded in establishing a considerable degree of influence, especially in the principality of Kabul. In Iran, a series of events further provoked geopolitical apprehension of the British concerning the situation in Central Asia. Iran fought another war with Russia which resulted in the conclusion of the disastrous treaty of Turkmanchai in 1828 with the mediation of Sir John MacDonald Kinner, British envoy in Tehran (30). This treaty was signed on February 21, 1828, granted the Russians the right of capitulation, excluding Russian subjects from prosecution under Iranian laws (31). Although the British and other foreign subjects were later granted the same right, the sudden expansion of Russian influence in Iran in the wake of this treaty gave rise to the British anxieties of Russian threat via Iran to their possessions in India, bringing the strategic importance of Herat to their attention more than ever before. The followings are examples of the views expressed confidentially to the British Government by British diplomats in Iran:

> *The key of all Afghanistan towards north is Herat.*
> *The country between the frontiers of Persia and India is far more productive than I had imagined it to be; and I can assure...that there is no impediment, either from the physical features of the country or from the deficiency of supplies, to the march of a large army from the frontiers of Georgia to Kandahar, or, as I believe, to the Indus.*
> *There is therefore...no security for India in the nature of the country through which an army would have to pass to invade it from this side.*
> *On the contrary, the whole line is peculiarly favourable for such an enterprise.* (32)

The anxiety over a Russian design on Herat and eventually, India, become an obsession among the British, especially after arrival in Herat of Count Simonich, the Russian envoy in

Tehran, with the Iranian troops in 1838. Suspicious of this move, British Minister in Tehran told his government:

> *It is currently reported and believed here, though I cannot say on what grounds, that there is a secret arrangement between Persia and Russia to exchange Herat for some of the districts beyond the Arras which formerly belonged to Persia. This report was first mentioned to me at Tehran in March last; but I then paid no attention to it, because I could not see how Russia was to get at Herat, and I still am inclined to regard it as probably unfounded, though Count Simonich certainly threatened Mahommed Ameen, a servant of Yar Mahommed Khan (who was sent with a message from his master to the Persian camp) that if Herat did not surrender to the Shah, he would march a Russian army against it.* (33)

In a letter to Sir John McNeil, British Minister Plenipotentiary at Tehran, the Secretary to the Government of India states:

> *The political interests of Great B retain and of British India are even more concerned that their commercial interests in the exemption of the countries between India and Persia from foreign aggression from the westward. There is too much reason to apprehend that Persia, under its present sovereign, has evinced an unprecedented degree of subserviency to Russian counsels... The pertinacity with which Persian Government has persisted in this design...* (34) *is of itself a sufficient ground for apprehending the existence of some ulterior and unfriendly design towards our interests.* (35)

Russo-phobia became widespread in India, and the theory of a Russian threat to British possessions in India via Iran and Afghanistan had become so realistic in the eyes of the British that fortification of the countries of Afghanistan against this threat, not only became the cornerstone of the foreign policy concerns of British India in Asia, but it became a kind of universal obsession among British politicians, diplomats, and military officers alike. This apprehension of a Russo-Iranian design on India was further aggravated by an approach made by Iran, top Sardar Kohandel Khan of Qandehar, who had renewed his predecessor's loyalty to the Iranian Government. A treaty was signed in 1838 between Mohammad Shah Qajar and Kohandel Khan whereby, the Governor of Qandehar engaged his principality to renew its historical dependence to Iran in return for Iranian protection. The Shah also, according to article I of the treaty, was to bestow the principality of Herat onto the ruler of Qandehar *"as a reward for their faithful services performed to him since his accession to the throne of Persia"* (36). This treaty is said to have been signed by Count Simonich as the guarantor on his own behalf as representative of Russia in Iran. The British found this whole affair as yet another proof of a Russo-Iranian design on countries on the way to India. This suspicion provoked great alarm among the British and paved the ground for Sir John McNeil's great design of creating a buffer state between India and Russia, thus, signally the beginning of the Great Game. He wrote in August 1838:

> *If the treaty has really been guaranteed by Russia, and not by Count Simonich personally, Russia becomes by it indisputable mistress of the destinies, political and commercial, of all Central Asia; for Great Britain, having been forced back*

to the Indus, Khiva and Bokhara must submit if they are attacked; while Persia and Afghanistan will already be entirely at her disposal. (37)

Observing these developments with dismay as they could no longer rely upon the ability of the Afghan chiefs to play the role of a barrier, separating India from the potential threats coming from the west and northwest, the British decided to apply the policy of direct intervention if Afghanistan.

Meanwhile, Prince Kameran, Tehran's appointed Governor of Heart, styled himself in 1829 as 'Shah" of that principality (38) and began a series of raids and incursions against other Iranian territories, especially in Sistan. These acts of rebellion angered the Central Government in Tehran, already agitated by the rebellion and lawlessness taking place in Marv, Khiveh, and Bokhara in Central Asia, the countries of Turkmans and Uzbeks who "*had then continued depredations in Asterabad and the neighbouring districts*" (39).

The Government in Tehran prepared two expeditions in 1836, one against Herat and the other against marv, Khiveh and Bokhara, which was to proceed to the north-east after Herat was subdued. The expedition against Herat began its march in 1937. Prince Kameran, seeing no hope of assistance from any quarter, turned to Sir John McNeil, British Minister at Tehran. McNeil protested against the action of the Iranian Government knowing full well that Tehran's action against the rebellion of one its own appointed governors of dependant principalities was provoked by the governor himself. In a dispatch, dated Tehran, February 24, 1837, McNeil says that even if we were to ignore Herat's traditional dependence on Iran and assume it and Iran as two independent states: I am inclined to believe that the Government of Herat will be found to have been the aggressor. He, further, adds:

> *Under these circumstances, there cannot, I think, be a doubt that the Shah is fully justified in making war on Prince Kameran: and though the capture of Herat by Persia would certainly be an evil of great magnitude, we could not wonder if the Shah were to disregard our remonstrances and to assert his right to make war on an enemy who has given him the greatest provocation, and whom he may regard himself as bound in duty to his subjects to punish, or even to put down. I therefore doubt whether the measures proposed by the Government of India would have the desired effect.* (40)

Whilst Iranian expedition against Herat was in progress, Herati envoy, Fateh-Mohammad Khan arrived in Tehran on the intervention of Prince Asef ad-Doleh, commander of Iran's expeditionary force and Governor-General of Khorasan. Tehran demanded that Herat should submit and send a personality of some significance to remain in the capital assuring guarantee of their submission. In reply, Yar-Mohammad Khan, Vazir (administrator) of Herat, wrote to Tehran submitting to the demands for submission and sent an agent to stay in Tehran as guarantee of their submission. Yar-Mohammad Khan's proposals were as follows:
1- There is to be a cessation of war and of marauding; the capture and sale of prisoners are to be utterly abolished.
2- Should the Shahanshah intend to undertake military expedition against Turkistan, and should he require troops from Shah Kameran, the latter is to supply troops to the extent of his ability, and they shall accompany the Governor of Khorasan on any expedition against

Turkistan. Should troops be required on the frontiers of Azerbaijan, Shah Kameran shall furnish them in such manner as may at the time be practical, and shall not withhold them.
3- A sum of money shall be paid annually as tribute at the festive of Nowrouz.
4- Merchants from every quarter, who arrive in Herat and its dependencies, are to receive full protection, and suffer no injury in person or property.
5- One person, who shall be a descendant of Shah Kameran, and some other persons who shall be relations of Vazir Yar-Mohammad Khan, and of Shir-Mohammad Khan, shall reside for two years at Mashhad as guarantors. When the period of two years has elapsed, if the Minister of Herat has performed the foregoing engagements, and has committed no infraction, the above guarantors shall be dispatched to Herat, and shall not be detained more than two years. Should any infraction of the above engagements have been committed, the guarantors are to be retained until the time of their fulfillment.
6- A Vakil or Agent from Shah Kameran shall always reside at the Court of the Shahanshah (41).

Notwithstanding the fact that Yar-Mohammad Khan's dispatch to Tehran indicated clearly Herat's agreement to the revival of its dependence and loyalty to the Central Government of Iran by accepting to pay its annual taxes, its terms and conditions did not satisfy Tehran, especially in that it failed short of other customary undertakings for submission such as coining the money in the name of Shahanshah, and having the prayer (Khotbeh) read in his name. Thus, Prime Minister Haji Mirza Aghasi wrote in reply the terms and conditions that were, from his point view, appropriate for Herat's submission. The first two points of his memorandum dated 14th Rabi al-Aval 1253 (July 1837) reads:

1- War, marauding, and the capture of prisoners shall cease, as all these things are opposed to obedience, it is evident that they will, as a matter of course cease, when Prince Kameran acknowledges subjection to Tehran. He who is obedient must be obedient under every circumstance.

2- As Herat with its dependencies is one of the provinces of Persia, whenever the exigencies of the State require troops to be dispatched in any direction, Herat, like other provinces of the kingdom, must furnish troops and provisions (42).

Although Prince Kameran was referred to in Yar-Mohammad Khan's letter as 'Shah Kameran' and true that in his reply to Herat's propositions, Haji Mirza Aghasi demanded the title 'Shah' be abandoned by Prince Kameran, the fact is that use of such titles by vassal kings in the Iranian tradition of state organization did not contradict the dependence of the vassal kingdoms to the Shahanshah of Iran. In a letter addressed to Mohammad Shah Qajar in March 1840 by "Shah' Kameran, for instance, he declared himself to be the 'faithful servant of the Shahanshah' (43).

While this debate was going on between Tehran and Herat, however, the expedition against Herat was in progress and Herat was put under siege by the forces from Tehran. Prince Kameran turned to Sir John McNeil, British Minister at Tehran since 1836, for help. McNeil protested against the expedition and left Tehran in the spring of 1838, suspending Anglo-Iranian relations because, in spite of acknowledging Iran's right to end Kameran Mirza's rebellion in Herat, he believed Iran's repossession of Herat was an evil against British interests in the region (44).

In a dispatch to Lord Palmerston, British Prime Minister, McNeil strongly advised British Government to intervene in this affair in support of rebellious Prince Kameran, because British envoy in Kabul was engaged in separate arrangement between India and Herat in direct rivalries with the Russian envoy there. He writes:

> *Captain Vicovich continues to remain at Kabul, and I learn from Captain Burnes's communications that the success of his negotiations there will in a great measure depend on the failure of the Shah's enterprise against Herat. At kandahar our position is even more precarious; and I have the honour to enclose a translation of a draft of a treaty between the Shah and the Chief of Kandahar, which it is proposed to conclude by the mediation and under the guarantee of Russia, and which has for its object to unite Herat and Kandahar under a chief, who shall be nominally subject to Persia, but actually under the protection of Russia. I am unable to inform Your Lordship what progress has been made towards the conclusion of this treaty, or what view the Shah may have taken of the position, in respect to these countries, in which, by this arrangement, he would be placed; but the treaty is said to have been signed by Kohundil Khan, and I am not without any serious apprehensions that, even before the fall of Herat, Kohundil Khan may be induced to co-operate with the Shah; while in the event of Herat's being reduced, I cannot doubt that the Chief of Kandahar will consider it to be for his advantage to connect himself with Persia and Russia rather than with England.*
>
> *I therefore continue to be of opinion that the fall of Herat would destroy our position in Afghanistan, and place all, or nearly all, that country under the influence or authority of Russia and Persia.*
>
> *I need not repeat to Your Lordship my opinion as to the effect which such a state of things would necessarily have on the internal tranquility and security of British India; and I cannot conceive that any treaty can bind as to permit the prosecution of schemes which threaten the stability of the British empire in the East.* (45)

Thus, convinced that Iran's undertaking against rebellion in Herat would seriously jeopardize vital British interests, Lord Palmerston and the Governor-General of India, Lord Auckland (46), informed the British public that it was imperative to defend Herat against Iran. Meanwhile a young British officer, named Eldred Pottinger, who had lived among Heratis for sometime, supposedly on his own initiative as a Muslim Darvish, was encouraging the Heratis against Iran.

The siege of Herat, however, began on November 23, 1837 and lasted between 3 to 10 months according to different reports. Most of the Afghan dignitaries were in favour of Iran's action in Herat: Dust Mohammad Khan of Kabul had practically encouraged the Shah to invest Herat. Omar Khan, son of Kohandel khan of Qandehar, joined the military action against Herat. Shams ed-Din Khan, an associate of Prince kameran saw to the food requirements of the troops. Even Jalal ad-Din, son of Prince Kameran, fought on the side of the Central Government (47).

The British observers of the time, viewed the historical dependency of the Afghan chiefs on the Iranian government in a different light, interpreting it variably to suit various arguments. Captain Hunt, for instance blames these chiefs' dependence on Iran, on the inadequacy of British policies (48). This argument ignores or negates the fact of history that the Afghan chiefs had traditionally been parts of the periphery dependents of the central authority of the Persian Empire. As an example of this political arrangement, it suffice to mention a letter by Dust Mohammad Khan, Amir or Chief of Kabul to the central authority of the Shahanshah at the time of Captain Hunt, in which he testifies that:

In the past years and in the olden times, the chiefs of [his] *dynasty considered their country and governments dependents of the mighty Government of late Shahanshah and from their heart, not in the form of lip service, joined the Government of universal proportions.* (49)

As dependants of Iran, these chiefs would naturally align themselves with Tehran in the situation of uncertainties, unless planned for secession which was the case with Prince Kameran of Herat at the time.

With the direct and indirect assistance provided by the British, which was an obvious interference in Iran's internal affairs, Herat withstood the siege for several months. The British government in India dispatched from Bombay a naval task force which attacked Iran's southern provinces on the Persian Gulf. Sir John McNeil sent in July 1818 written message to Mohammad Shah informing him of the British action in the Persian Gulf and warned him of the consequences of his Government's undertaking against Herat. Apart from all else, McNeil argued in this message that the Iranian enterprise in Herat was being 'totally incompatible with the spirit and intention of the alliance which (had) been established between Great Britain and Persia' (50). McNeil's reference in this regard is not clear as to which treaty or engagement would support his claim. There was no instance in any of the treaties signed prior to these developments between Iran and Great Britain that would support McNeil's argument. Articles 2 and 3 of the Political treaty of January 1801 speaks of the Iranian Government discouraging the Afghan King (Shah-Shoja) from his possible designs against India, while article 4 speaks of British military support for the Iranian Government in the event of an attack against Iran by the Afghan ruler (51) which was the case with Prince Kameran, whose action was considered by Mr. McNeil, in his dispatch of February 24, 1837 (52), as an aggression that gives the Central Government of Iran every right to punish him. Moreover, article IX of the Anglo-Iranian treaty of November 25, 1814, in fact prevented the British from interfering in any incident between Iran and the Afghan chiefs unless asked by both sides to do so (53).

The forces dispatched from Bombay, under the command of Colonel Shariff, landed on Iran's Khark Island in the Persian Gulf. This measure proved to be effective as Prime Minister Haji Mirza Aghasi was evidently aware of the greater importance of Iranian possessions in the Persian Gulf compared with the Afghan dependencies. The British had already begun spreading their influence around the Persian Gulf. A series of treaties had already been signed, as from 1820, with the chiefs of the tribes of the lower Gulf, the traditional Iranian sphere of influence (54). Though Haji Mirza Aghasi later in mid-1840s declared all these treaties as 'unacceptable', the position in the Persian Gulf was viewed in Tehran as more vulnerable than that in the Eastern borderlands, thus, the Iranian Government decided to abandon its undertaking in Herat by complying with the terms of McNeil's message. Mirza Taghi Khan Amir-Nezam (Amir Kabir) was assigned to meet McNeil, to induce him not to leave Iran (55).

The Iranian Government, thus, decided to lift the siege and to withdraw its forces from Herat without punishing its rebellious chief. Subsequently, the Iranians had to make some considerable concessions in order to satisfy the British. These concessions included relinquishing Iran's rights to the district of Ghurian, south of Herat and north of Sistan. Article 2 of Haji Mirza Aghasi's letter to Viscount Palmerston states that Asef ad-Doleh, Governor-General of Khorasan had orders to give up Ghurian and deliver it to the Afghan chiefs after the return to Iran of the British ambassador (56). Enclosure No. 2 of this dispatch was the English text of an 'imperative' decree from Mohammad Shah to the Governor-General of Khorasan, dated 15th September 1839, ordering him to give up the fort (of Ghurian) and deliver it to the Afghans (57).

Britain's Direct Diplomacy in Afghanistan

The whole episode of the siege of Herat, however, increased urgency for the British to expand their influence in the principalities of Afghanistan. Still wary of the possibility of some Russian designs on the Afghan principalities, Lord Auckland, Governor-General of India, sent a mission for the expansion of commerce to Afghanistan. This mission contacted the Amir of Kabul. When the mission reached Pishavar, a letter from W.H. MacNaghton, secretary to the Indian Government, to the mission, turned it into a purely political mission (58).

Dust Mohammad Khan, Amir of Kabul, received the mission with the kind of enthusiasm which did not last long. His brothers, the rulers of Qandehar, had already revived their alignment with the Iranians, and their treaty with Iran greatly troubled the British, especially that article 2 of the treaty put the Sardars of Qandehar in possession of Herat. This undertaking on the part of the Iranian Government to the Sardars of Qandehar remained as a source of discomfort to the British who considered that *"no state of affairs in Central Asia more favourable to the interest of British India, than the (then) division of power among the several rulers of Afghanistan"* (59). Moreover, the British resolved to bring all Afghan principalities under their influence. They reached understanding with Shah-Shoja (al-Molk) Abdali and the Governor of Sekuheh, both of whom facilitated the British invasion of Afghanistan in 1839 with a force of 45,000 strong (60), and established their influence as far north as the southern slopes of Hindukush. In the west, Vazir Yar-Mohammad Khan, by then Governor of Herat, soon forced Lieutenant Pottinger out of Herat and made overture to the Iranian Government in March 1839 and to the chiefs of Qandehar, to cooperate with him against Shah-Shoja and his British backers.

The rapid progress of the British in the principalities of Afghanistan and the inactivity of the Iranians, however, prevented realization of Yar-Mohammad Khan's dream of cooperation against them. Qandehar was occupied shortly and Yar-Mohammad Khan was among the first to congratulate Shah-Shoja on the occasion (61).

The British finally managed to conclude a series of treaties with the chiefs of Qandehar and Herat in 1839, thus recognizing these Iranian dependencies as independent Afghan principalities (62).

Success of British military expedition together with the treaties they signed with the chiefs of Herat and Qandehar placed British India within Iran's eastern dependencies. It was from the beginning of the 1840s that the powers began to push the frontier areas between them back and forth, a political process which eventually resulted in the formation of the Iran-Afghanistan boundaries.

Though Herat's traditional (historical and cultural) ties with Iran was too strong to be severed by these acts of rebellion, encouraged and supported by Britain, early in January 1840 the British Government demanded restoration of Ghurian to Herat. In reply, the Iranian Prime Minister informed Lieutenant Colonel J. Sheil, British Charge d' Affairs at Erzerum that Prince Kameran, former sovereign of Herat, so recognized by British India, had declared himself to be the faithful servant of the Shahanshah, that, *"he merely tolerated the presence of the English envoy for expediency, although he was by no means niggardly in the expenditure of money, jewels, &c and that his hopes were in the asylum of Islam"* (63). Upon receiving the news of this letter and overtures made to Iran by Vazir Yar-Mohammad Khan the new ruler of Herat, the British began to strengthen their position in Herat and other principalities close to the Iranian frontier areas. Within a short period of time between 1839 and 1840, the British reoccupied Kalat, negotiated and brought under their control the principality of Khiveh, while Dust Mohammad Khan, Amir of Kabul, had also surrendered his principality to the British without any resistance (64). Accompanied by 150 members of his family and relations and servants, Dust Mohammad Khan went to live in India. On their way back from Afghanistan, the British forces annexed the district of Sind and Punjab (65). This new territorial gains established the British Indians all along eastern Iranian borderlands.

The British Government sent Sir John McNeil back to Iran in 1841 to restore political relations with the Court of Qajar. The Afghan principalities were in turmoil and the British had strengthened their position in the strategic points near the Iranian frontier areas, including Girishk and Hirmand districts. During the British occupation of Afghan lands, maintenance of Girishk was always considered an important object, as it not only defended the high road, and offered security to travelers, but presented a good military point against Herat. When the Afghan unrest broke out in November 1841, the Governor of Herat was unfriendly with the British. Hence, it was particularly important to the British to maintain Girishk, and with this view Major Rawlinson, then political agent at Qandehar, was anxious not only to retain on the Hirmand the regiment to whose care the fortress was entrusted, but to strengthen the position with reinforcements from the Qandehar garrison (66).

Events Leading to Iran's Occupation of Herat

In Herat, Yar-Mohammad Khan revolted against Prince Kameran in 1839 and took his place as the ruler of the principality. He informed Tehran of his loyalty and thereupon ventured on capturing Ghurian (1840), and forced Meimanah and Hazarah to become tributaries of Herat. It was in 1841 when Yar-Mohammad Khan expelled British officer in residence, Major Todd from Herat, and returned the principality to the traditionally exclusive dependence on Iran.

In 1847 when Hassan Khan Salar and Jafar Khan revolted in Mashhad and Sarakhs against Hamzeh Mirza Asef ad-Doleh, Young Naser ad-Din Shah's uncle and Governor-General of Khorasan, the latter asked for Yar-Mohammad Khan's assistance. He dispatched troops to Mashhad where the Heratis succeeded in freeing Hamzeh Mirza and took him to Herat. The Governor-General remained in Heart for about three months, during which time, Prince Morad Mirza, another uncle of the young Shah, put down the revolt. Yar-Mohammad Khan was rewarded by the Shah for his services by investing upon him the title 'Zahir ad-Doleh', literally meaning 'supporter of the state'. This title came to Yar-Mohammad Khan in the form of a *farman* (decree) accompanied with four cannon as present from the Shah (67). Having received the farman, Yar-Mohammad Khan officially restored Herat's traditional position as a dependant principality of Iran, by coining the money in the name of the Shah of Persia, and by considering Herat as a portion of the Persian dominions (68).

In 1850, the Sardars (chiefs) of Qandehar, later allies of Iran according to the treaty of 1856 (69), revolted against Yar-Mohammad Khan, Sardar Shir-Ali Khan, son of Mehr-Del Khan, advanced as far as Lash which was then a dependency of Herat. Mohammad-Sadeq Khan, son of Kohandel Khan, occupied Chokhansur, and later entered Girishk. Yar-Mohammad Khan's forces pushed Shir-Ali Khan out of Lash, and defeated Ahmad Khan Eshaqzai, another Sardar of the district. He invited the defeated Sardars to unite with him, but before making any progress in this venture he died (1850). Yar Mohammad Khan's son Said-Mohammad Khan, Governor of Lash and Jovein, succeeded him, and immediately declared loyalty to the Central Government of Iran by writing to the Shah. Having been named by the Shah as Governor of Herat in his father's place, and having received his official dress of honour, he continued to serve loyally like his father (70).

Shortly after this development, Mohammad-Sadeq Khan of Qandehar entered Herat to take Said-Mohammad Khan's place, on the pretension that the people of Herat wanted him to do so. Said-Mohammad Khan asked for help from Tehran. Iranian troops, led by Abbas-Qoli Khan entered Herat and occupied the citadel of the city in April 1852 leaving some of the troops at Ghurian, later reinforced by Sam Khan Ilkhani of Daregaz. Sam Khan was recalled in January 1853, but Abbas-Qoli Khan remained in Herat as Vazir to Said-Mohammad Khan. The Qandehari Sardars had also left Herat, on the understanding that as a different principality of Iran, they had no business in Herat whilst Iranian forces were there to continue their protection of that principality.

Apprehensive of the deepening dependence of Herat and Qandehar on Iran, British Minister at Tehran, Colonel Sheil, did all he could to mobilize his government to put an end to this process. In a letter to the Sadr-e Azam (Prime Minister) Mirza Agha Khan Nouri (71), Sheil warned him of the consequences of 'Iran's interference' in Herat. An Iranian document states:

> *every day he had something for the Iranian Ministers to do. Finding that his object could not be attained by these means, he wrote something plausible to his Government, and the British Ministers suspended all interactions with Shafie Khan, Iran's Charge d' Affaires in London, and distinctly informed that until the Iranian Ministers settled the affairs of Herat with Colonel Sheil, relations would not be resumed with him.* (72)

Eventually the Iranians gave up and hoping to exclude the British from interfering in Herati affairs, Sadr-e Azam Nouri concluded an agreement with them on January 25, 1853, which restricted both governments from interfering in Herat. The agreement, however, was signed in a way that clearly acknowledges Herat's traditional dependence on Iran. Paragraph 2 of the section on the engagement prohibits Iran from interfering in the internal affairs of Herat, except the same amount which took place at the time of late Zahir ad-Doleh, Yar-Mohammad Khan (73). More interesting was the undertaking of the British which included that:

> *If any foreign power, such as the Afghans, or others, should wish to interfere, and take possession of Herat territory, or its dependencies, and the Persian Ministers should request the British Ministers to prevent them by friendly means, and by advice from doing so, they will not object to do so.* (74)

Meanwhile, said-Mohammad Khan, Governor of Herat, was overthrown in 1855 by his deputy, Nayeb Isa Khan, whose secret dealings with the British were suspected from the beginning. He claimed to have represented the will of the people of Herat for Said-Mohammad Khan's removal from the office. The latter was by then tainted with insanity.

Nayeb Isa Khan sent for Prince Yusof Abdali, grandson of Prince Firouz ad-Din in Mashhad, to come and claim the seat of authority in Herat. He entered the city on 15th September 1855 as the new ruler. Said-Mohammad Khan was subsequently murdered and some of his and his father's wealth was extracted by the Nayeb and the Prince (75). All these events took place under the watchful eyes of the Iranians who were neither consulted in advance nor were extended a message of loyalty by the new rulers, a right for Iran which had been recognized by the British in all their engagements with Iran on Herat and other Afghan principalities. Herat's seat of authority was, thus, usurped by the Nayeb and the Prince who had also murdered the overthrown ruler and confiscated the private properties of the murdered ruler's family. This lawlessness, together with the general chaos that they brought to the principality, forced Prime Minister Nouri to amass troops under the command of the Shah's uncle, Hessam as-Saltaneh Morad Mirza, Governor-General of Khorasan.

Capture of Herat and Conclusion of Paris Treaty of 1857

Iranian troops' mission was to reduce Herat, avenge the murder of its ruler, and to bring order back to the principality. Nayeb Isa sought assistance from Dust Mohammad Khan, Amir of Kabul, who had, with the help of the British, made a come back on the scene of Afghan politics. The Amir of Kabul shunned any assistance and, like his Qandehari brothers, cousins and nephews, refused to meddle with Iran's 'internal affairs'. The Nayeb was, thus, left with no alternative but to send Prince Yusof to Prince Morad Mirza as guarantee of loyalty, promising to make up for his conduct. The Prince was taken to Tehran where he was tried and executed for having murdered Said-Mohammad Khan. The siege of Herat which began in April 1856 continued. Ch. A. Murray, British Minister had departed from Tehran on December 5th 1855, as a result of misunderstandings with the Iranian officials. Mirza Shafie Khan (76), Iran's Charge d' Affairs in London was informed that relations between the two governments were suspended (77). Iranian forces however, succeeded in capturing Herat on 25th Safar 1273 (1856). An Iranian poet (Mirza Shafa) marked the date in the following words:

As seventy three was added to a thousand and two,
it marked the date of the capture of Herat

The British, on the other hand, had assisted the return of Amir Dust Mohammad Khan to Kabul and helped his dominion to expand almost all over Afghanistan. He had taken possession of Qandehar from his nephews in August 1855 (78), and Herat was the only Afghan principality that was left outside his newly expanded kingdom. As Iranian forces entered Herat, the Khans and tribal chiefs of the entire region went to Prince Morad Mirza Hessam as-Saltaneh declaring their allegiance to the Government of Iran. These whole events apparently disturbed the British and Dust Mohammad Khan, the latter being assisted by the former to revive Ahmad Shah Dorrani's kingdom of Afghanistan.

British Foreign Office confidential documents contain messages to the British from a certain 'Essan Khan' asking them to intervene in Herat. This name does not appear in the local documents and is unfamiliar within local history. The only likelihood that this author can see is that the messages came from Nayeb Isa Khan. He, according to these documents, sent a petition (79) to Mr. Murray pledging himself, the principality and the people of Herat to the British, asking them to take over his principality. His double dealings must have become known to the Iranians, and probably this is why he was killed on his way back from the Iranian camp outside the city of Herat. The Iranians appointed Soltan Ahmad Khan, son of Mohammad Azim Khan, who had turned against Dust Mohammad Khan, his own father-in-law, as the new Governor of Herat. He immediately assumed the title 'Shah' of Herat as was customary of Herati leadership within Iranian Shahanshahi at the time. He made coinage and Khotbeh in the name of Naser ad-Din Shah Qajar, 'Shahanshah' of Iran (80).

The Iranians, on the other hand, suspected that Dust Mohammad Khan must have taken Qandehar with the help of the British and at their instigation, and that he intended to take Heart as well (81). In their correspondence with the Iranians and the intermediatories, the British Indians denied having anything to do either with Dust Mohammad khan's annexation of Qandehar, or with his designs on Herat. Nevertheless, the correspondence between British diplomats and military officials and the British government personnel that have survived suggest otherwise. In a dispatch to London, Sir John Sheil expresses delight that Dust Mohammad Khan had occupied Qandehar. He asserts: *"Candehar has escaped from the control of Persia, and should be preserved from again falling under it"* (82). Furthermore, when Mohammad-Sadeq Khan, son of Dust Mohammad Khan took Farah, a dependence of Herat (83), not only did not the British protest against the move, but were thinking of paving the way for the success of Dust Mohammad Khan's designs on Herat. In a dispatch to the Chief Commissioner for Punjab, Lieut. Colonel Edwards had suggested that Nayeb Isa Khan in Herat should keep that principality as a dependence of the Amir of Kabul (84) in the same way that it was a dependent of Iran.

All these contradicted the obligations suggested in the British Government's contracted engagements with Iran, relative to Herat in a number of agreements, specially that of January 1853, whereby they accepted to 'prevent, by friendly means, foreign powers, such as the Afghans, or others' from 'interfere, and take possession of the Herat territory, or its dependencies' (85). Interestingly, clause 3 of the testimonies of the envoys of Essan Khan (Nayeb Isa Khan), so cherished by the British, points out 'Afghanistan', alongside Iran, Khiveh and Bokhara, as the enemy of Herat (86).

Seemingly encouraged by testimonies of the envoys of Nayeb Isa Khan, Britain declared war on Iran on November 1st 1856 (87). British forces, commanded by General Outram, occupied a number of Iranian ports and islands in the Persian Gulf and informed the Iranians of their conditions for peace. Their conditions contained mainly withdrawal, on the part of Iran, not only of all military forces from Herat and dependencies, but also of all claims to Herat and what was then termed as the 'countries of Afghanistan'. The Russians, suspected of mobilizing to support Iran, were pacified. In a letter to Lord Woodehouse, the Earl of Clarendon expresses satisfaction that Britain's principal conditions were considered reasonable by the Russian Government (88).

Though the Russians proved in practice that they had no desire to team up with Iran and use Iranian territories to attack India, Russo-phobia intensified among the British in India and drove them to create the buffer state of Afghanistan by dismembering the eastern dependencies of the Iranian federal system. They began openly disregarding Iran's legal position and her legitimate interests in Herat by claiming that the action in Herat was a display of an intention of threat against Qandehar and other areas occupied by Amir Dust Mohammad Khan of Kabul. Not only did not the British raise objections to Dust Mohammad Khan's occupation of Qandehar and Farah, as was promised in the 1853 engagements, but East India Company signed an agreement with him on 6th January 1857 whereby the British allied themselves with him and undertook to pay him monthly as long as the latter kept the Iranians busy in war (89).

Amir Dust Mohammad Khan signed this agreement with the British against Iran, in direct contravention of the fact attested by himself in a letter to the Shah of Iran (90) that, not only Herat and Qandehar, but also his own principality of Kabul had been dependencies of Iran (91). British forces, however, occupied the Iranian island of Khark in the Persian Gulf on December 4th, 1856; British Indian troops disembarked at Bandar Abbas on December 9th; the Iranians were dislodged from Bushehr on January 27th, 1857; General Outram landed at Bandar Abbas on February 8th, 1857; Iranian forces were defeated at Borazjan on March 26; and Khorramshahr (then

Mohammareh) was occupied by the British forces (92). This military expedition, once again made Iranian Government give up Herat, as Sadr-e Azam Nouri seems to have been aware of the superior importance of Iran's position in the Persian Gulf, compared with the dependencies in Afghan countries. At the same time, London seems to have *'looked on the Indian Government's expedition of the entire Iranian coasts and islands of the Persian Gulf with discomfort'* (93). This seems to have been the reason for the British to make overtures to Napoleon III of France who had also been approached by the Iranians. French mediation, however, resulted in the conclusion of a treaty of 15 articles in Paris on March 4, 1857, whereby the Iranians once again submitted to the conditions laid down by the British. This treaty was signed by Farrokh Khan Amin al-Molk, Iran's Ambassador extraordinary to Paris and R. H. H.R.C. Baron Cowley, British Ambassador extraordinary to Paris. From Paris, Amin al-Molk proceeded to London where he was received by Queen Victoria.

Article 5 of the Paris treaty of 1857 dealt with the withdrawal of Iranian forces from Herat and the adjacent districts (94). Article 6 compels Iran to relinquish all her rights and claims in connection with Herat and the 'countries of Afghanistan'. Furthermore, the Iranian Government undertook other concessions, including recognition of Herat's independence and never to attack or interfere with independence of the state of Herat and other principalities of Afghanistan. This treaty was ratified at Baghdad on May 2, 1857.

As eastern Iranian frontiers shifted, therefore, to the territories west of Herat, Ghurian, and Farah, and as boundary delimitation was next on the agenda of British India's political designs, article 6 of the 1857 peace treaty of Paris provided also for the British to be party to such boundary arrangements between Iran and Afghanistan. Paragraph 3 of article 6 of this treaty makes it clear that;

> *In case of differences arising between the Government of Persia and the countries of Herat and Afghanistan, the Persian Government engages to refer them for adjustment to the friendly offices of the British Government and not to take up arms unless those friendly offices fail of effect.* (95)

A similar treaty with Dust Mohammad Khan of Kabul in the same year gave the British the same right of mediation in Afghan boundary disputes with Iran. In Herat, despite the developments leading to it's separation from Iran, Sardar Soltan Ahmad Shah, appointed by Iran as Governor a year earlier (96), not only continued in this capacity until 1863, but also remained loyal to Iran in spite of the clear terms of first paragraph of article 6 of Paris treaty of 1857 which engaged Iran not to "*demand from the Chief of Herat, or of the countries of Afghanistan, any marks of obedience, such as the coinage of 'Khootbeh', or tribute*" (97).

There is no evidence suggesting that Iran asked Herat to remain loyal to the Central Government at Tehran or to pay annual tribute. Sardar Soltan Ahmad Shah of Herat (father-in-law of Amir Shokat al-Molk I Khozeimeh) on his own initiative continued loyalty to Iran after the signing of 1857 peace treaty of Paris which effectively declared Herat independent of both Iran and Afghanistan. This was not what Amir Dust Mohammad Khan of Kabul desired and the British found it difficult to understand how a vassal state, severed from the Persian federation, opts to return to the tradition of being a member of that federation.

Having established himself firmly in Qandehar and having seized Herat's southern dependency of Farah, Dust Mohammad Khan ordered Sardar Mohammad Sharif, his Governor of Farah, to march his troops northwards. Herat's dependencies of Ghurian and Sagher were seized in 1860. Sardar Soltan Ahmad Shah, for his part, moved troops southward and recaptured Farah in 1861. This move gave Dust Mohammad Khan the much needed excuse for taking action against Herat itself. On 28 June 1862, intelligence received in Tehran that Amir Dust Mohammad Khan had reached Qandehar, with the aim of marching on Herat. The Iranian Government informed British Minister in Tehran that Sardar Amin Khan and Sardar Sharif Khan had invested Farah on Behalf of Dust Mohammad Khan, and asked for British intervention. This was in accordance with the last paragraph of the 1857 Paris treaty of peace which engages British Government:

> *When appealed to by the Persian Government, in the event of difficulties arising* [with the state of Afghanistan], *will use their best endeavours to compose such difference in a manner just and honourable to Persia.* (98)

The British, nevertheless, remained inactive and Farah fell on 28th July that year. Dust Mohammad Khan marched on Herat. He took Sabzevar (now in Afghanistan) on 22nd July (99), and put Herat under siege immediately, which lasted for several months (100).

During the siege of Herat, Soltan Ahmad Shah's wife, Amir Dust Mohammad Khan's daughter, died (January 1863). Shortly after her death, the two sides had to stop hostility as Soltan Ahmad Shah himself passed away (April 1863). The defence of the city was continued by Soltan Ahmad Shah's son, Sardar Shahnavaz Khan, also Dust Mohammad Khan's grandson. The grandson's resistance against the grandfather's tightening siege proved ineffective, and Dust Mohammad Khan entered Herat shortly afterwards.

Iranian Government appealed to the British Government to assist Sardar Shahnavaz Khan by lifting the siege of Herat. Mr. Eastwick was assigned by the British Legation at Tehran to see to the matter. He was made Her Majesty's Charge d' Affairs at Herat, but returned to Tehran empty handed. Thus, Dust Mohammad Khan occupied Herat and fulfilled the British design of creating the Kingdom of Afghanistan. His joy was but short-lived, and he died on 19th June 1863 (101), a few months after the death of his daughter and son-in-law and only a week or two after capturing Herat.

In conclusion, it must be said that the political and military paralysis of the Iranian Government, resulting from the terms of the 1857 peace treaty, allowed finalization of the partitioning of Khorasan, and paved the way for the creation of Afghanistan. Ahmad Shah Dorrani (102) had in the second half of the eighteenth century created the Kingdom of Afghanistan, but it collapsed with his death in 1772, for it did not have the necessary geographical, historical, and cultural substances that is necessary for nation building and would hold Herat and Qandehar together with Kabul in a lasting union. Herat, for instance was more of a Khorasani environment than anything else and as Lord Curzon has asserted, it was geographical, historical, and cultural extension of Mashhad rather than being Afghan.

Dust Mohammad Khan succeeded in the second half of the nineteenth century in reviving the Afghan Kingdom with direct and indirect assistance of the British in India whenever this assistance was needed. These assistances were given because it served British geo-strategic designs of wanting to create a buffer state between India and Russia. It had nothing to do with British excuses that Iran had territorial designs against the countries of Afghanistan. Afghanistan was thus created to suit geo-strategic needs of British India, that is to say; the clamours that had intensified throughout British empire in the 1830s through to 1850s of a possible joint Russo-Iranian design against India was only to serve the enthusiastic geopolitical and geo-strategic assumptions of Sir John McNeil, Sir Justin Sheil and other political strategists of British India.

Sir John McNeil's fantastic assessments of geo-strategic position of Herat was adopted by the British whereas London appears to have remained somewhat uneasy on the question of depriving Iran completely of her rights in Herat as a British Foreign Office document states: *"Persia's claims to Herat were of long standing. It had been the capital of Eastern Khorasan and geographically was not separated by any natural barrier from Mashhad."* (103)

This is an echo of the statement made earlier by Lord Curzon on the fact that Herat had been a historical part of Iran's Eastern Khorasan (104). Yet, convinced of the vitality of Sir John McNeil's geo-strategic assessments, Lord Curzon, like most other officers and diplomats serving in India, was critical of the London Government's repeated proposals on returning Herat to Iran. He stated that *"Lord Beconsfield after the war of 1878 committed the inexplicable error of proposing once again to hand over Herat...'Key of India' to Persia to the tender mercies of the Czar"* (105).

Notes and References

1. George N. Curzon, *Persia and the Persian Question*, Vol. II, P. 586.
2. See for example; Mir G. Mohammad Ghobar, *Afghanistan dar Masir-e Tarikh*, Published in Kabul 1965.
3. Ahmad Shah Dorrani's *farman* of 16 Shavval 1167 (1753), as appeared in "*Farhang-e Iran Zamin*", Persian publication, Tehran 1958, PP. 161-63.
4. G. P. Tate, MRAS, FRGS, *The Kingdom of Afghanistan*, reprinted in Delhi 1973, PP. 68-9.
5. The first revolt of the Abdalis of Afghanistan against the Persian Governor of their district took place at the time of Shah Abbas the Great (Safavid) in late 17th century. The Government at Isfahan commissioned Gorgin Khan, Governor of Gorjestan (Georgia) as governor of Qandehar (1692) who brought the unrest under control by expelling the Abdali leaders.
6. Sir Percy Sykes, *Ten Thousand Miles in Persia*, John Murray, London 1902, *footnote to page 364*.
7. Tate, op. cit., P. 4.
8. Sir Percy M. Sykes, *History of Persia*, London 1915, Vol. II, PP. 370-371-372.
9. The famous piece of diamond known as Kuh-e Nour eventually found its way from Afghanistan to Great Britain and is now part of the British Crown Jewels.
10. Tehran was, at this time, chosen by Agha Mohammad Khan Qajar to be the new capital of Iran.
11. Robert Grant Watson, *History of Persia*, London 1866, P. 96.
12. Tate, op. cit., P. 6.
13. See for example; Ghobar, op. cit.
14. Dr. Mahmud Afshar Yazdi, *Afghan Nameh*, Tehran 1980, Vol. II, P. 26. This source indicates that when Fath-Ali Shah finished off Nader Mirza's rebellion by putting him to death, exclaimed that a parallel vengeance had taken place. What he meant was that his great grandfather, Fath-Ali Khan had been killed by Nader Mirza's great grandfather, Nader Shah Afshar, and now Nader Shah's great grandson is killed by Fath-Ali Shah.
15. Iranian Foreign Ministry Collection of Documents = *Ahdnameh-hay-e Tarikhi*, hereafter referred to as the '*Green Book*', Tehran 1971, P. 91.
16. Tate, op. cit., P. 105.
17. Political Treaty with England, *Green Book*, op. cit., P. 91.
18. Asghar H. Bilgrami, *Afghanistan and British India*, New Delhi 1972, P. 19.
19. The *Green Book*, op. cit., P. 70.
20. Ibid, P. 71.
21. Ibid, P. 73.
22. Ibid, P. 73-4.
23. Ibid, P. 73.
24. Ghobar, op. cit., P. 395.
25. Ibid.
26. Mohandes Mohammad Ali Mokhber, Marzhay-e Iran, Tehran 1945, P. 24.
27. Ghobar, op. cit., P. 396.
28. Ibid., PP. 397-8.
29. Ibid., P. 403.
30. Under article 3 of Golestan Treaty of 1813, Iran lost to Russia the cities and dependencies of Karabakh (Gharabagh), Ganjeh, Shakki, Shirvan, Qobbeh, Darband, Baku (Republic of

Azerbaijan), Shureh-Gel, Achuqbash, Kurieh, Mankerbel etc. – Article 3, Treaty of Golestan, *Green Book*, op. cit., P. 128. Under article 3 of the Treaty of Turkmenchai of 1828, Iran lost to Russia the principalities of Armenia and Nakhjevan. – Article 3, the Treaty of Turkmenchai, the *Green Book*, op. cit., P. 131.

31- Capitulation continued in Iran until it was abolished by Reza Shah Pahlavi in 1929.
32- Extract of a letter from Sir John McNeil to Viscount Palmerston, dated Mashhad, June 25, 1838, *Blue Book*, PP. 131-2, FO 539/1-10 (microfilm), PP. 131-3.
33- Ibid.
34- Referring to the siege of Herat by the Iranian forces in 1837.
35- Extract of a letter from Mr. Macnoughten to Mr. McNeil, dated Fort William, November 21, 1838, "Correspondence relating to the Affairs of Persia and Afghanistan" section B., P. 2, FO 539/1-10 (microfilm).
36- The only copy of this treaty this author has come across was cited in General Ferrier's book. The treaty has no date and shows the signature of Major H. C. Rawlinson as the translator of the document. – General J. P. Ferrier, Caravan Journeys and Wandering in Persia, Afghanistan, Turkmanistan, Baloochistan, London 1857, PP. 508-9.
37- From Mr. McNeil to Viscount Palmerston, dated Camp near Tehran, August 1, 1838, No. 39, Vol. 10, Part 1, section A, P. 1, FO 539/1-10 (microfilm).
38- Ghobar, op. cit., 404.
39- Captain G. H. Hunt, *The Persian Campaign*, Outram & Havelock's, London 1858, P. 92.
40- Extracts from Mr. McNeil's dispatch to Viscount Palmerston, dated Tehran, February 24, 1837, No. 13, P. 3, FO 539/1-10 (microfilm).
41- Extracts from enclosure 1 in No. 3 of dispatch by Mr. McNeil to the British Government, dated Camp Tehran, July 1838, FO 539/1-10 (microfilm).
42- Extracts from the translation of a memorandum by Haji Mirza Aghasi in reply to Yar Mohammad Khan's proposals, enclosure 3 in No. 3, of Mr. McNeil's dispatch to Viscount Palmerston, dated July 1837, PP. 11-12, FO 539/1-10 (microfilm).
43- Ferrier, op. cit., P. 160.
44- The *Green Book*, op. cit., P. 74.
45- Extract of letter from Mr. McNeil to Viscount Palmerston, dated Camp before Herat, April 11th, 1838, P. 85, FO 539/1-10 (microfilm).
46- Lord Auckland had replaced Lord William Bentinch in March 1837 as Governor-General of India.
47- Ghobar, op. cit., PP. 404-5.
48- Captain Hunt, op cit., P. 138.
49- Extracts of letter from Dust Mohammad Khan to Mohammad Shah, FO 248/162. This letter has no date, but it is a reply to Mohammad Shah's letter dated Rabi al-Avval 1270 (1854).
50- Extracts of written message delivered by Lieut. Colonel Stoddart to the Shah, enclosure 1 in No. 32, July 1838, FO 539/1-10 (microfilm).
51- Political treaty with England, *Green Book*, op. cit., P. 91.
52- Ibid.
53- Persian text of the treaty as appears in the *Green Book*, op. cit., PP. 91-126. This treaty was signed by Henry Allis, British Minister at Tehran. John McNeil was, at the time, secretary to the British Legation and replaced Allis as Minister in 1836.
54- See: Pirouz Mojtahed-Zadeh, *Emirates of the Persian Gulf*, Persian text, Ataei Press, Tehran 1970.

55- From McNeil to Viscount Palmerston, No. 49, dated Sept. 11, 1838, FO 539/1-10 (microfilm).
56- Extracts of the letter of 15th September 1839, from Haji Mirza Aghasi to Viscount Palmerston, FO 539/1-10 (microfilm).
57- Enclosure 2 of the above document.
58- From Macnoughten to Burnes, dated 11 September 1837, FO 539/1-10 (microfilm).
59- Extracts of a letter from Mr. Macnoughten to Captain Burnes, dated November 1837, FO 539/1-10 (microfilm).
60- Ghobar, op. cit., P. 446.
61- Ferrier, op. cit., P. 526.
62- Ghobar, op. cit., P. 448.
63- Ferrier, op. cit., Appendix F, P. 528.
64- Ghobar, op. cit., P. 448.
65- Sir F. Goldsmid, *Eastern Persia*, London 1876, Vol. I, PP. IX-X introduction.
66- Ferrier, op. cit., P. 311, footnote.
67- Ghobar, op. cit., P. 409.
68- Extracts of clause 9 of the translation of paper drawn by the Iranian Ministers for publication in Europe, doc. 2, enclosure 1 of Mr. Murray's dispatch to Earl of Clarendon, dated Tabrees, January 22, 1856, P. 3, *British Documents of Foreign Affairs: Reports and Papers from the Foreign Office Confidential Print*, part 1, from the mid-nineteenth century to the First World War, section B, the Near and Middle East, 1856-1914, edited by David Gillard, Vol. 10, Persia, 1856-1885, University Publication of America 1984, hereafter referred to as "*F.O. Book of Documents on Persia*", The actual Foreign Office reference number for these documents at P.R.O are from FO 60/207 to FO 60/227.
69- For text see: the *Green Book*, op. cit., PP. 180-1.
70- *FO Book of Documents on Persia*, op. cit.
71- Mirza Agha Khan Etemad ad-Doleh Sadr Azam Nouri was Prime Minister from 1851 to 1857.
72- Extracts of clause 10, doc. 2, enclosure 1, *FO Book of Documents on Persia*, op. cit., January 22, 1856.
73- Extracts of Anglo-Iranian Agreement of 1853, *FO Book of Documents on Persia*, op. cit, doc. 210, enclosure in doc. 209, PP. 161-2.
74- Ibid.
75- Tate, op. cit., P. 158.
76- A great grandfather of this author.
77- The *Green Book*, op. cit., P. 75.
78- Tate, op. cit., P. 158.
79- Extracts of statements made by Essan Khan's messengers to the British authorities in India, dated August 12, 1856, FO *Book of Documents on Persia*, op. cit., doc. 155, enclosure in doc. 154, PP. 126-7.
80- Extracts of paper drawn by Persian Ministers, *FO Book of Documents on Persia*, op. cit., P. 3.
81- Ibid.
82- Extracts of Sir Justin Sheil's dispatch to M. Hamond, dated Dec. 18, 1856, doc. 209, *FO Book of Documents on Persia*, op. cit., P. 160.
83- From Lord Stratford de Redcliffe to the Earl of Clarendon, dated Jan. 18, 1857, *FO Book of Documents on Persia*, op. cit., doc. 234, P. 181.

84- Clause 14 of dispatch of Lieut. Colonel Edwards to the Secretary to the Chief Commissioner for the Punjab, dated Huzara, September 18, 1856, *FO Book of Documents on Persia*, op. cit., doc. 189, P. 147.
85- Extracts of Engagement Contracted by the Persian Government, relative to Herat, dated January 25, 1853, *FO Book of Documents on Persia*, op. cit., doc. 210, P. 162.
86- See: Essan Khan's message to the British authorities, dated 12th August 1856, *FO Book of Documents on Persia*, op. cit., doc. 155, enclosure in doc. 154, PP. 126-7.
87- Tate, op. cit., P. 212.
88- Extracts of letter from the Earl of Clarendon to Lord Wodehouse, dated F.O. December 25, 1856, doc. 217, *FO Book of Documents on Persia*, op. cit., P. 165.
89- Tate, op. cit., P. 212.
90- Original Persian text of this agreement and a number of relevant letters do not have any detectable date. The enclosure to the dispatch to James Murray by Secretary to the Gov. of India, dated Feb. 25, 1856, FO 248/16.
91- Ibid.
92- Tate, op. cit., P. 212.
93- Ibid.
94- Treaty of Peace between Her Majesty the Queen of the United Kingdom of Great Britain and Ireland, and His Majesty the Shah of Persia, FO 60/403, P. 2.
95- Extracts of third paragraph of article 6 of 1857 Peace Treaty of Paris, op. cit.
96- See previous pages.
97- First paragraph of the 1957 Peace Treaty of Paris.
98- Engagements of British Government under article 6 of 1857 Peace Treaty of Paris, FO 60/403, P. 8.
99- Ghobar, op. cit., P. 587.
100- G. P. Tate asserts that the City of Herat was invested by Amir Dust Mohammad Khan on 27th July 1862, which cannot be correct as Dust Mohammad Khan died on 19th June 1863, only a week or so after the capture of Herat.
101- Ghobar, op. cit., P. 589.
102- Ahmad Shah Dorrani was born in 1722, and died in 1772.
103- *Persian Frontiers*, Section on boundaries with Afghanistan, RRX/7/I, FO 371/40219, P. 2.
104- See introduction and relevant references.
105- Curzon, op. cit., P. 586.

CHAPTER XII

Emergence of Khorasan and Baluchistan Boundaries
Pirouz Mojtahed-Zadeh

Introduction

Herat's occupation in 1863 by Amir Dust Mohammad Khan of Kabul, which finalised the partitioning of Greater Khorasan, was discussed in the previous chapter. Afghan encroachment into Iranian territories did not, however, stop at Herat's occupation by Dust Mohammad Khan with the help of the British. These encroachments continued in various forms of direct military operations and tribal raids. Amir Dust Mohammad Khan was succeeded in 1863 by his son, Amir Shir-Ali Khan who almost immediately after acceding to power, resumed expansionist activities in the territories well beyond the western districts of Herat and Qandehar, particularly in Sistan district.

Meanwhile, returning from their Afghan expedition British forces captured Sind and Punjab in the two battles of Mianeh (1843) and Gujerat (1848). Annexation of these two countries pushed British India's frontiers westward to a line reaching from Pishavar on the north and Karachi on the south. A considerable segment of the state of Baluchistan thus came under the sovereignty of British India. By late 1860s British India began to implement a project of telegraph lines between India and Great Britain which was to pass through Iran's southern Baluchistan (Makran) and the Persian Gulf. These two developments necessitated the establishment of clearly defined boundaries of European nature between Iran and India in Baluchistan area, and between Iran and Afghanistan in Khorasan and Sistan provinces.

Of these three sections, delimitation of Sistan boundaries (the middle section) consumed the longest time involving great complications, as they involved the issue of Hirmand River. Hence, the study of the emergence of the middle section of these boundaries will be the subject of the following chapter.

This chapter, however, will deal with the emergence of Khorasan and Baluchistan boundaries, which can assist a better understanding of the way territorial games were conducted in the region by the big and small players of the Great Game. This chapter will, therefore, fall into two distinct parts: first section examines evolution of the northern (Khorasan) section: and the second deals with the emergence of the southern (Baluchistan) section.

Khorasan Boundaries

Herat's legal secession from Iran in 1857 and its actual occupation in 1863 by Dust Mohammad Khan of Kabul finalised the British colonial strategy of partitioning of Khorasan. The frontier between what were left of Khorasan and the newly established Kingdom of Afghanistan was put on Ghurian and Farah to the west of Herat. This line of boundary is 337 miles in length, in addition to the length of Hari-rud, which forms the northern most of the borderline between Iran and Afghanistan.

Though Herat was captured by the founder of the Barakzaei dynasty of the newly formed Kingdom of Afghanistan, the frontiers between Herat (Afghani Khorasan) and Iranian Khorasan remained undefined. It was only natural that complications resulting from the partitioning of Greater Khorasan would cause much disputes and affrays between the two countries and among local holders of title to lands therein. These disputes intensified to the extent that defining a clear boundary line in the central areas of Greater Khorasan became a necessity.

Not only did not Shir-Ali Khan do anything to alleviate Iran's suspicions of his designs against Iranian territories, but also initiated military operations in the vicinity of Sistan, which aggravated Iran's anxieties of his intentions. The Iranian Government informed British Minister at Tehran in December 1878 that the Amir of Afghanistan had assembled 20 regiments of foot soldier and cavalry with 50 guns at Herat with the intention of attacking Sistan (1). Moreover, the Iranian Government enquired whether British intervention under clause 6 of 1857 Paris treaty of peace could be counted on. While referring this enquiry to the Government in London, the Governor General of India claimed that Calcutta was not aware of any ill intention against Iranian territories on the part of the Afghan Amir (2). In spite of British Indian officials' apparent lack of interest in Iran's anxieties and grievance of the conduct of the Amir Shir-Ali Khan, political affray and local raids intensified in the border areas of Qaenat and Hashtadan districts and became so serious the necessitated boundary delimitation between the two countries.

Hashtadan Arbitration and MacLean's Line

The Hashtadan Plain forms the eastern and greater portion of a tract, the northwestern point of which forms part of the Iranian district of Bakharz. Karat, Farzaneh, Raona, and Garna were, at the time of 1880s arbitration, included in the sub-division known as '*Parin Velayat*' or Lower Bakharz (3). The Hashtadan valley, according to General MacLean's memorandum of July 1891 (4), was bounded on the north by the Senjedi hills which the Afghans call *Kuh-e Darband*; on the south by *Kuh-e Gedayaneh*; on the east by Sang-e Dokhtar and Yal-e Khar ranges, and on the west by the watershed between Hashtadan qanats and the streams flowing into Iranian territory.

The valley is about 24 miles in length, and its greatest breadth from the Dahaneh-e Shurab to the crest of the Kuh-e Gedayaneh, is about 16 miles. The valley consists of three distinct regions (5):

- The Shurab basin, around the head of which lie the traces of former habitation and cultivation.
- A belt of level steppes which surrounds the Shurab basin on three sides, and has no visible signs of surface drainage.
- An outer slope at the foot of the hills and drainage of which is, for the most part, lost in the steppe, and does not appear to reach the Shurab except that from the Sanjideh and perhaps some from the Sang-e Dokhtar during heavy rain.

The Shurab has six principal tributaries, which unite before leaving the valley by the Dahaneh-e Shurab. Thence it takes the name Qaleh Kala, which to the point of junction with Hari-rud near Tuman Agha, forms what was then the acknowledged border between Iran and Afghanistan. There are ruins of several villages in Hashtadan Plain, which had been deserted for generations. There were also the remains of 39 qanats, at the time of arbitration, in the valley, all of which were out of repair and dry. The number of Hashtadan's qanats in the older times was said to have been eighty (*hashtad*) and this is where the name *Hashtadan* comes from. The Governor

General of Khorasan undertook in April 1885 to clear out and repair some of these qanats. The work was interrupted by the Afghans who destroyed the plants and tools of the Iranian labourers (6). This incident brought the two governments in direct dispute over the district. Both Iran and Afghanistan approached the Government of British India requesting their invitation.

The Government of British India decided in 1886 to depute Brigadier General C. S, MacLean, the Consul General at Mashhad, to arbitrate between Iran and Afghanistan in the Hashtadan disputed. The investigation work was delayed for various reasons. By late April 1888 General MacLean began his works in Hashtadan district. Iran was represented in the arbitration commission by Mirza Moheb-Ali Khan Nezam al-Molk, the Kargozar of Khorasan, and his team included his son Mirza Jahangir Khan, and General Mirza Mohammad-Ali Khan as professional advisers (7). Afghanistan was represented by General Qotb ad-Din accompanied by a number of lawyers and tribal chiefs from Herat; one member of the group was Mirza Mohammad-Omar, designated by the Amir of Afghanistan to keep a check on the Afghan commissioner (8).

Before leaving for Hashtadan, MacLean asked both representatives of both countries to submit to him their written claims. In their initial claims the Afghans wished to restrict the investigation to lands of Kolukh, Pardeh and Hashtadan (9). But as the arbitration commission met on 30th of April 1888, and the Iranian representative claimed the whole of Hashtadan valley and lands up to Sang-e Dokhtar, the Afghans changed their mind instantly and claimed Farzaneh, Garmab, and places situated well within Iran's undisputed territory (10). Apart from these conducts, the greatest handicap for the investigation was that Hashtadan was virtually uninhabited at the time of arbitration. The testimonies of the inhabitants of a disputed territory normally are the best indication of ownership. The Hashtadan population, according to MacLean's first memorandum, had left the plain more than a century before the arbitration investigation began probably because of an epidemic throat disease (11).

In the absence of local testimonial, the arbitrator had to consider, for the most part, on determining the history of the former population's allegiance to either of the two governments. The arbitration also had to rely on the evidence provided by the two sides. Representatives of Iran and Afghanistan supplied MacLean with their written claims supported by eleven and ten documents of proof respectively. In his memorandum of 14th December 1889, MacLean provides a list of the summary of Iran's eleven documents, at the end of each one which, he registered his evaluation of the documents, rejecting almost all of them. When it came to the ten documents supplied by the Afghan Side, he enclosed all of them in their original form without registering an opinion of his own on their validity (12).

As both parties were not forthcoming in a compromise for the settlement of the dispute, the Viceroy of India wrote to the Amir of Afghanistan asking him to advise his representative to give up unjustifiable claims on places within Iranian possession and to accept limits defined by MacLean (13). As for the Iranians, General MacLean found an opportunity to meet Naser ad-Din Shah (1848 – 1896) during the latter's visit July 1889 to the United Kingdom. It was in this meeting that MacLean must have concluded that the Imperial Court in Tehran was too ignorant of the lands in dispute to be aware of its importance for Iran. At the conclusion of this meeting, the Shah decided though *'the Afghans were nothing'* he would give them the whole of Hashtadan with all its qanats, other water resources, agricultural lands and whatever of the population therein, only *'because the feeling of friendship'* (he) *'entertained towards the English Government* (14). As a result of this incomprehensible generosity the whole of Hashtadan was given to the Afghans save for the baron hills of the same name situated on the western extreme of Hashtadan Plain. Furthermore, in order to keep his own nation oblivious of this generosity, the Qajar Shah requested that the new maps should have the word '*Hashtadan*' marked on the Iranian side of the borderline. Informing the viceroy of India of this turn of event, British Minister at Tehran asserted that MacLean deserved 'very great credit' for this achievement (15).

This development, however, enabled MacLean to delimit 103 miles of Khorasan boundaries between Iran and Afghanistan. He surveyed and delineated the boundaries from Hashtadan Plain, some 60 miles to the west of the city of Herat, to Zolfaghar Pass where Iran-Pakistan-Afghanistan frontiers meet. The MacLean line consists of 39 turning points, which leaves the entire plain on the Afghan side, with the Hashtadan hills on the Iranian side. In his memorandum of 6th July 1891 MacLean describes this line of boundary as follows:

> *The line commences at the northern point of the Kuh-I-Kadanna passes round the heads of the southern group of Kanat immediately north of the Hashtadan mound. It then passes round the Hashtadan mound, leaving the mound on the Persian side of the line. Thence across to the foot of the Hill, and thence due north to the crest of the Sanjitti range. The line then follows the crest of the range eastward to the crest of the Hills on the northern side of the Dahana-I-Shorab, and thence in a straight line to a point on the left bank of the Kali-I-Kala 300 yards below the place where the old canal takes off towards Kafir Kala. The line then follows the Kali-I-Kala up to the Hari-rud.* (16)

The proposed settlement of the Hashtadan boundary dispute was reported to the governments of Iran and Afghanistan through the Viceroyalty of India in 1890. In his letter of 29 September 1890 to the Afghan Amir, the Viceroy urged to accept the proposed settlement. A favourable response to this resulted in General MacLean's immediate assignment for carrying out the demarcation of the Hashtadan boundaries. He concluded this task by July 1891 and submitted a copy of the synopsis together with its map of the line to the Indian Government. The Viceroyalty submitted a copy of MacLean's report to the Amir of Afghanistan who accepted it with much delight.

International reaction to Naser ad-Din Shah's incomprehensible generosity in giving the Hashtadan Plain to Afghanistan out of his friendly feelings towards the British Government were no less than a disgrace to the political leadership of Iran. The Russians, for instance, claimed as Iranian territories were effectively up for the grab, Hashtadan should be given to them. In a message to Amin as-Sultan, the Iranian Prime Minister, the Russian Charge d' affairs stated that in view of the circumstances, Hashtadan was virtually given to the British. Similarly, the French demanded that the Iranian Island of Khark be given to them (17).

What had happened in Hashtadan was indeed no less than simply giving up Iranian territories in favour of the Afghans. Not only were the Russians and the French aware of this scandalous undertaking by Naser ad-Din Shah in connection with the British, but also in his own memorandum of 14th December 1889, General MacLean states openly:

> *It will be noticed that the Afghans bring forward no proof of their having actually occupied Hashtadan either before or after Ahmad Shah's time. The leaves of the Herat revenue record they allude to have no date, and, therefore, even if genuine, give no indication of the period during which Kulukh, Pardai paid revenue to Heart.* (18)

Figure 11

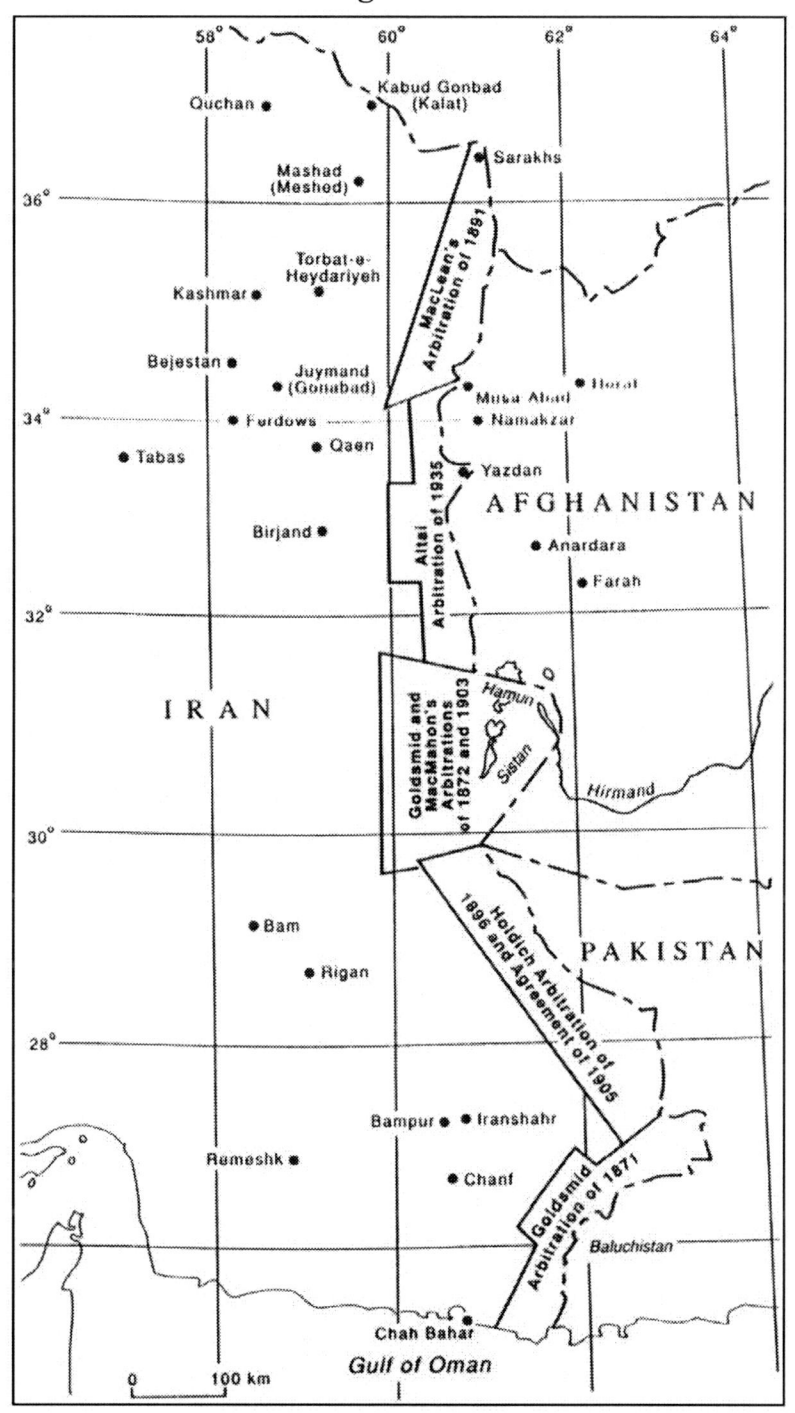

*Hashtadan and Hari-rud boundaries of northern Khorasan
(General MacLean's arbitration of 1891)*

Qaenat Arbitration and Altay's Line

General MacLean's arbitration of 103 miles of Khorasan boundaries left the remaining 234 miles of Iran-Afghanistan boundaries in Qaenat district of Khorasan undefined. This length of border areas began from Musa-Abad hamlet, south-east of MacLean's pillar No. 39, running through the salt lake '*namakzar*', to east of Qaenat, ending in the start of McMahon's line of 1905 at Kuh-e Malek Siah, which is the beginning of Sistan boundary. A number of areas in this stretch of frontier were in dispute between Iran and Afghanistan. Moreover, the long lasting raids on Iranian settlements by Afghan elements increased noticeably. Writing in 1857, General Ferrier asserts:

> *It is only five or six years since Kerim-dad Khan (Chief of Hazarah tribes) followed the (noble) profession of pillage: he plundered caravans, and extended his forays to the south of Iran in the district of Qaen, where he sacked the villages and carried off the people to sell them to the Uzbeks. His depredations were so frequent, and gave rise to so many complaints, that Assef Doulet sent to Yar Mohammad Khan and informed him that, as he seemed unable to keep his own vassal in order, he should chastise himself as the head of an army.* (19)

Reports and confidential diaries of British consulates at Mashhad, Birjand, and Sistan contain a large number of instances where Afghan raids on the towns and villages of Khorasan, Qaenat and Sistan, which increased in their frequency from the beginning of the twentieth century (20). These cross border raids came to a head in late 1934 when Afghan tribesmen who had previously entered Iran and decided to return to Afghanistan causing considerable damage to lives and properties in the border area of Zurabad, apparently on the instigation of local Afghan officials. Reuters reporting from Tehran described the incident as follows:

> *Tehran, 16th December 1934; a party of Afghans consisting of prominent persons and military officers entered Persian territory via Zorabad, plundered 25 villages, murdered 3 road guard and took away 2,000 Persians as prisoners with a large quantity of arms. The loss following on this incident is estimated at #50,000 sterling. Because of this incident the Persian press is bitterly attacking the Afghan Government.* (21)

This report, though proved to be exaggerated in the case of 2000 people being taken prisoner and was thought to have been the number of tribesmen crossing the border, caused uproar in Iran. Iranian authorities formally protested to the Afghans who, in return, invited Iranian representatives to jointly inspect the site of the incident (22) in order to establish validity of the report. The press in Afghanistan, in the meantime, denied the whole thing and the Afghan Ambassador in Tehran carried out a campaign of smear among foreign diplomats against Iran as a nation (23). This joint commission eventually concluded that the Zurabad incident took place without the knowledge of the Afghan Government, but had been provoked by Afghan tribal leaders and other Afghan subjects. The Afghan Government subsequently undertook to punish the offenders and compensate for the losses occurred and to return the stolen goods (24). Notwithstanding the terms of this joint communiqué which implies that neither the Afghan Government nor any Afghan Government official had been directly or indirectly involved in this incident. Yet, British observers in the region were aware that:

For a long time it has been the policy of the Naib Salar of Herat to locate the toughest elements in the province on the frontier. These consist of well-armed tribes of nomads who with their flocks and camels are not confined to any one area and at the same time are in a position to raid with impunity in any direction having no immovable which can be threatened. (25)

Apart from these cross-border incidents the Afghans began a series of claims against Iran's territorial possessions as from 1931, and began interfering with the existing border arrangements. In a telegram to the Government of India, for instance, the British Consul General at Mashhad indicates: "*a boundary pillar on Bakharz frontier, recently removed by Afghans, has been replaced by Persian troops. Both sides have increased the frontier posts and relations are strained*" (26).

In addition to these activities, the Afghan authorities claimed the village of Musa Abad, southwest of pillar 39 of General MacLean's line, arguing that Musa Abad had been given to Afghanistan by MacLean boundary award of 1891. In 1903 a party of Afghan soldiers visited Musa Abad (27), in direct contravention of MacLean's award. That award had invited both Iran and Afghanistan to observe a status quo in the tract to the south of pillar 39 of Hashtadan boundary. This act violated the fact that Musa Abad was the property of Mohammad Sadeq, an Iranian subject who was at the time deputy governor of the Iranian district of Bakharz.

A report prepared for the Government of India in May 1904 by Captain C. B. Winter, H. B. Majesty's Consul at Torbat Heydariyeh, identifies many instances of Afghan encroachments at Musa Abad (28). Forwarding this report to the Government of India, the British Consul General in Khorasan concluded that:

According to paragraph 12 of General MacLean's report and boundary pillar No. 39 Musa Abad would certainly appear to belong to Persia (29). The Iranian Kargozar of Torbat Heydariyeh reported to Tehran in 1904, for instance, that *an Afghan official has visited Khushabeh from Ghurian, and has told the people that Khushabeh belonged to the Afghans.* The report ads *that an Afghan official from Ghurian visited Musa Abad, Khushabeh and Kuh-e Sang-e Dokhtar twice a week; and if he sow Iranian flocks grazing there, prevented them from grazing.* (30)

In his despatch of 28th September 1904 to the British Government reporting on his meeting with Iranian Prime Minister Moshir ad-Doleh, the British Minister at Tehran indicated that he informed the latter of British India's representation at Kabul. He also added that the Iranian Premier had told him that the Afghans encroached not merely at Musa Abad, but also at a place in its vicinity named Ayubi (31).

In September 1932 the Afghan Government asked the British at Kabul whether the Government of India could give the Afghan Government any information and documentary evidence (32) proving that Musa Abad was given to Afghanistan by MacLean's Hashtadan awards. The two neighbours had, by this time, started talks on these boundaries and related issues. The Afghan Government had asked once again if the British Government "*could supply them with documentary evidence supporting their claims, whilst they had in their possession copies of General MacLean's award in which the demarcated boundaries are described as starting from the northern points of the Koh-I Kadana (Kuh-e Gedayaneh), passes round the heads of the southern group of kanats…"* (33). This description of the southern end of MacLean's Line, clearly leaving out Musa Abad to the southwest of Kuh-e Gedayaneh and pillar 39 which is the last pillar of MacLean's Line, south of Hashtadan plain. Furthermore, the Afghan Government put the above request to the Government of British India knowing that they had in 1897 asked the Viceroyalty of India the same question. In his letter to the British the Afghan Amir even insinuated that the British and Iranians had, one way or another considered Musa Abad as an Afghan possession (34). In his reply to this, the Viceroy of India denied that MacLean's awards had given the Musa Abad to the Afghans and asked him to prevent his officers from taking any steps which might lead the Persians to press their claims and perhaps disturb the peace of the frontier (35).

A second question in September 1932 of the same nature had a similar reply from the British India authorities. This time the Government of India referred to another similar question put to the British by the Afghans in 1903. On that occasion, Lord Curzon had made it clear to the Afghans that Musa Abad did not belong to them (36). The Afghan nevertheless continued claiming not only Musa Abad, but also the district of Yazdan, further south to Musa Abad, the Namakzar (salt lake) and Chekab, all located within Iranian possession.

Arbitration Process

As dispute intensified, both governments agreed on 8th March 1934, under article 10 of Iran-Afghanistan treaty of 1921, to go to arbitration. This time the Turks were asked to arbitrate. The Turkish Government agreed in the same month to arbitrate and assigned General Fakhr ed-Din Altay to lead the arbitration team. It was arranged for the two sides to submit their written claims to the arbitration commission through the Turkish Government before October that year. The commission was given an audience by Reza Shah Pahlavi at Amol of Mazandaran in October 1934, then it visited the area in dispute for preliminary survey. From there it proceeded to Kabul in November. The commission returned to the frontier, for further investigations on 22nd November that year (37).

Among General Altay's arbitration team was one Colonel Zia Bey whom, the British diplomats at Kabul recognised as an old friend of Senior Afghan officers (38).

The Iranians, in the meantime, began noticeable military movements in the eastern areas of the country dispatching troops to the frontier in the neighbourhood of Torbat-e Jam and Khaf (39). These movements of troops though were not directly attributed to the border considerations, but presented clear indications of Iran's determination that unlike the past experiences, this time the matter of boundary disputes would be treated seriously (40).

Tehran however, appointed Mr. (later Senator) Mehdi Farrokh (Mo'tasam as-Saltaneh) as Iran's commissioner, aided by a group of twenty experts (41) and Kabul assigned the Governor of Herat, Abd ar-Rahim Khan Nayeb Salar to lead the Afghan delegation to the Boundary arbitration commission.

The Commission spent three weeks at Mashhad and returned to Ghurian on 29th December 1934 for further local investigation, only to meet again with the representatives of Iran and Afghanistan on 18th January 1935 for the final study and exchange of documents related to the two sides' claims. From Ghurian, the arbitration commission proceeded to inspect the frontier from the Afghan side, because it was impossible to do so – for reasons not stated – from the Iranian side. This arrangement was hailed with delight by the Afghan delegation.

The commission inspected the disputed border areas as far south as Siah Kuh and on January 17th returned to Herat. The Iranian delegation who had not been with the commission during the proceedings also arrived in Herat on the same day. The next day General Altay addressed both delegations at a joint sitting and a brief deliberation followed (42). Disturbances ensued around Namakzar area a few days after Turkish arbitrator left for his country. Apprehensive of another border arbitration going against them, Tehran asked Amir Masum Khan Hesam ad-Doleh III of Qaenat to compile documentary evidence in support of the Iranian claims (43), but the renewed conflicts caused delay in deliberation of boundary arbitration by the Turks. A British diplomat, reporting to his government from Turkey, stated that the Turkish Government:

Decided to withdraw their mission unless Persian and Afghan governments both express simultaneously in advance and abide by an award which Turkish mission would make without further discussion (44).

These assurances were given to the Turks by both sides and Turkish Government finally delivered on 15th May 1935 to the Iranian and Afghan Ambassadors at Ankara Altay's arbitral awards (45), which was written in Turkish. On 6th October 1935 the Iranian Majlis passed the bill prepared on the basis of this award (46), and a joint Iranian-Afghan demarcation commission was formed immediately to erect the boundary posts.

The award included the following major points (47):

1- Musa Abad was a hamlet at the time of arbitration and a spring of fresh water. The afghan guards had occupied the largest of the three houses there and another Afghan occupied the other two. The qanat from which Musa Abad received its water had been constructed by Khozeimeh Amir Mohammad Reza Khan Samsam ad-Doleh on behalf of the Khozeimeh family (48). General Altay began his line by sharply turning to the west so that he could give half of Musa Abad district to the Afghans. This was done in contravention of the fact that Musa Abad was the personal property of an Iranian subject and that it is situated tens of miles to the west of MacLean's border mark 39 (see section 1 of figure MI 16).

2- From Musa Abad to the north of Namakzar, General Altay put his border marks 40 to 51. From this point the boundary line follows Rud-e Sargardan riverbed for about 10 kilometers until it reaches the point where the new channel of the river branches out from the old channel. Border mark 52 was put there. From this point the borderline follows the old channel of the Rud for a further 10 kilometers (northwest to southwest), leaving the Afghan Siah Kuh to the Afghans and the Iranian Siah Kuh to Iran. This line continues to the northern costs of Namakzar where border mark 53 is put (49). General Altay continued his line southward, dividing the Namakzar into two. He gave the eastern half of the lake to Afghanistan and its western half to Iran (see section 2 of figure MI 16) solely because a document that was produced, expressed an individual Iranian's consent to the use of the salt of the lake by the Afghans.

3- Yazdan, at the time of arbitration, was a small village of a few inhabitants with an agricultural field, a gendarmerie and a custom office, all belonging to Iran (50). The village and lands also belonged to the Khozeimeh Amir Mohammad Reza Khan and Amir Hussein Khan. Twelve kilometers to the south of Yazdan is situated the small village of Kabudeh with a few inhabitants with agricultural lands and qanats, all of which were owned by Amir Hussein Khan Khozeime Alam. The Khozeimeh Amir had also constructed a new qanat, which he had named Taher Abad, after his daughter Tahereh.

Between Yazdan and Kabudeh was situated the Nazar Khan Field which belonged to an Afghan subject (51). The arbitration decided to put his decision on the basis of existing possessions. He/thus decided to give Iran the villages of Yazdan and Kabudeh, and to give Afghanistan the Nazar Khan Field (see section 3 in figure MI 16).

4- Chekab, the borderline from Kabudeh follows as far as Kuh-e Rigu where border mark 72 was placed. Thence the line turns and follows a gentle northwest- southeasterly direction as far as Kuh-e Kharmagah where border mark 80 was placed. In his award Altay named this mountain after himself and refers to it as Kuh-e Altay. To the south of this point Altay did not take into consideration Amir Mohammad Ebrahim Khan Khozeimeh Shokat al-Molk II Alam's ownership of a hamlet (52). He referred to this locality as of unknown ownership and/ thus gave it to the Afghans so that the straight line of the boundary would not have to be changed (53) (see section 4 in figure MI 16).

Altay even does not name this locality in his award. The place was in fact a hamlet with few inhabitants and a number of agricultural lands named Chekab. Interviewed by this author on 5th January 1992, Amir Hussein Khan Khozeime Alam stated:

> *Chekab was owned by my father's uncle and my father-in-law Amir Ebrahim Khan Shokat al-Molk, Amir of Qaenat and Sistan at the time. Though his ownership of the hamlet and its field and springs were established, the arbitration decided to give them to Afghanistan solely on the basis of the testimony given by Amir Shokat al-Molk's former Mobasher (local representative) who was an Afghan and hoped to own them if given to Afghanistan. But Amir Shokat al-Molk continued ownership of the locality for some years afterwards.*

Monsef is the only source that deals with this matter in more details. In his book he asserts that Amir Shokat al-Molk's continued enforcement of cross-border ownership of Chekab eventually led to protest from the Afghan Government…. Reza Shah summoned the Amir as a result and after a lengthy discussion ordered him…to give up Chekab if the Afghans purchased his interests (54)

From Asperan the borderline continued in a north to south direction as far as Siah Kuh, which is the beginning of McMahon's line of the Sistan boundary. Altay's final border mark (No. 87) is placed at the highest peak of this mountain (55).

Though ratified by their Majlis, the Iranians remained unhappy about the outcome of the arbitration process. They have enumerated a number of theories for Altay's awards favouring Afghanistan. One such theory concerns the fact that Altay inspected the frontier areas only from the Afghan side without the presence of the Iranian delegation, which could have been instrumental in his better appreciation of Afghan argument and claims. Another theory is that Colonel Zia Bey, Altay's assistant's friendship and constant contacts with the Afghan military officers led the arbitration to favour Afghan interests. In his letter of 20th November 1989 to this author, Abdol-Hussein Meftah, a former Locum Foreign Minister, who has since passed away, touches on a different theory. He wrote:

> *Once in Ankara I met Feiz-Mohammad Khan, Afghan Ambassador, who was Afghanistan's Foreign Minister at the time of Altay arbitration of 1935. He told me privately: I know that the arbitration was received in Iran with a stern face (both Reza Shah and Forooghi were angry), but whose fault was it? It was the fault of the Iranian Government for sending a mentally unbalanced person as*

head of their Commission. These words shocked me, and I kept staring at him in surprise. He continued: Mr. Meftah, don't be surprised; I will just tell you a little about his behaviour and leave it to your judgement. This man used to get up at each meeting, and while keeping his hands behind his back, walked up and down like a teacher in a classroom, spelled out French words and expressions, suffering from a superiority complex, in a manner that both General Altay and I, were totally nervous. When you send such an impolite and unbalanced person to such an important job, what do you expect?

Figure 12

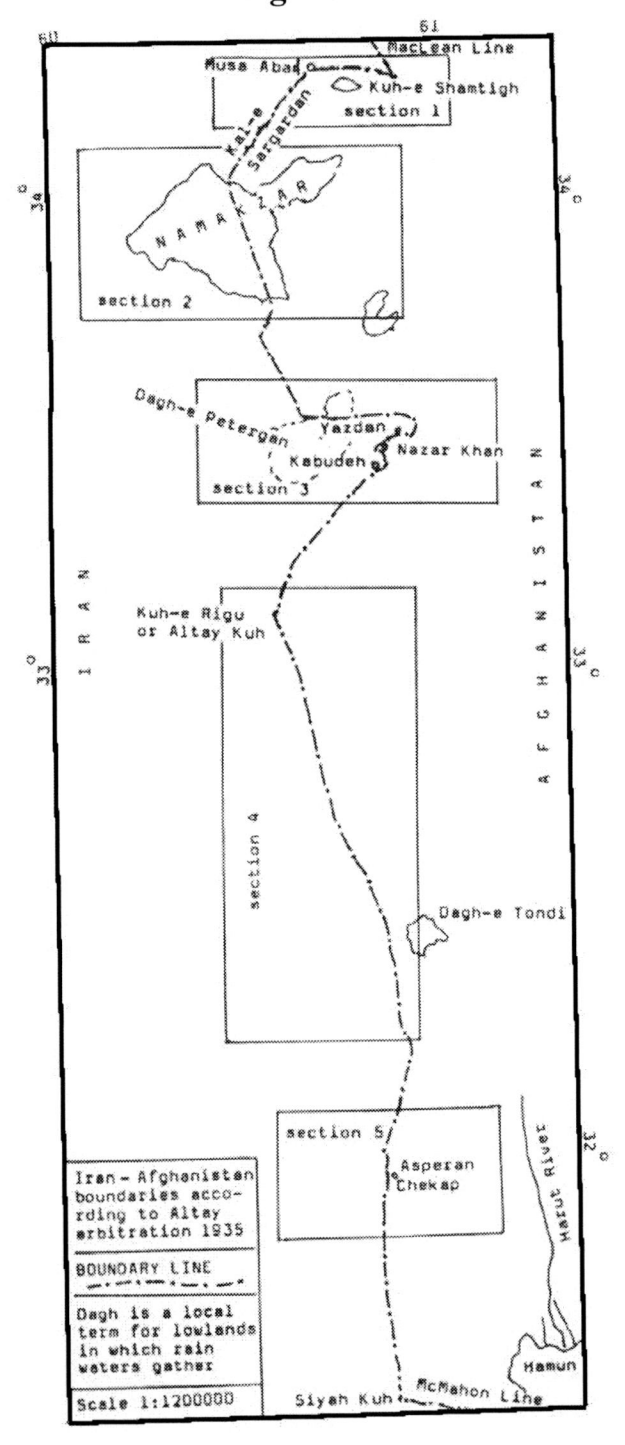

The Musa-Abad, Namakzar, and Qaenat boundaries (the Altay Line)

This theory is quite popular among the older generation of Iranian diplomats, but others who served in the Iranian Government and are more familiar with the overall view of Iran's relations with Afghanistan dismiss it. Dr. Ali-Naghi Alikhani, a former Minister in the Iranian Government told this author on 18th March 1991:

> *Though there is no doubt about Farrokh's irrational behaviour, it is not easy to believe that a boundary arbitrator would base his decision of creating permanent frontiers between two countries on such petty considerations as disliking the behaviour of a colleague. If Altay's arbitration favoured Afghanistan, the reason must be sought elsewhere.*

Late Mr. Meftah's letter, nevertheless, indicates that top Afghan officials admitted privately that Altay's arbitration award favoured Afghanistan at the expense of loss of territories to Iran.

The joint Iran-Afghanistan demarcation commission was however, set up immediately after the official announcement of Altay's award in may 1935. This commission completed the demarcation works along the whole of the 234 miles of the Altay Line by early 1936.

Partitioning of Baluchistan and Frontiers with British India

Historical Background

The Safavid Empire of Iran (1501-1731) succeeded in reviewing the traditional political union of Iran approximately within the frontiers of the pre-Islamic Persian empires. Baluchistan district – from river Hirmand to the coasts of the Indian Ocean, and from Indus to Kerman – was under Iranian sovereignty throughout the Safavid era. The rise to power of Nader Shah Afshar in the 1730s put an end to about ten years of confusion that had occurred resulting from the Abdali rebellion of 1722 and guaranteed Baluchistan's return to Iranian sovereignty after a brief period of turmoil. When in 1730 (1143 H.) Nader Shah (then Nader Qoli) was busy subduing a revolt in Herat at the outset of his career, sent Mohammad Momen Beik Marvi to Abdullah Khan, leader of Brahuei Baluch and Governor of Baluchistan, for assistance. Abdullah Khan was preparing for this task when war broke out between him and the Governor of Sind, during which he was killed. His sons, Amir Mohabbat and Amir Eltiaz, wrote to Nader informing him of the incident. Nader Shah bestowed the Governorship of Baluchistan upon Amir Mohabbat, the elder son of Abdullah Khan (1736). Having completed his Indian expedition, Nader Shah ordered the southwestern sections of the province of Sind to be included in the Governorship of Baluchistan (56).

During the period when Iran was leaderless following Nader Shah's assassination in 1747 Abdullah Khan's younger son, Nasser Khan seized power in Kalat, and accepted the suzerainty of Amir Alam Khan I, the Khozeimeh Amir of Qaenat and Sistan who had by then expanded his dominion to include Baluchistan. Immediately after the murder of Amir Alam Khan I, which took place shortly after Nader Shah's murder, Nasser Khan allied himself with Ahmad Shah Durrani who had just founded the kingdom of Afghanistan. On Ahmad Shah's demise in 1772, Nasser Khan claimed independence and began expanding his dominion within Iran (57).

Iran was, at this time, in a state of confusion, suffering from armed conflicts between the houses of Zand and Qajar led by Lotf-Ali Khan and Agha Mohammad Khan respectively. Nasser Khan died in 1795 and on his death the Gitchkis took advantage of the confusion at Kalat to shake off the Kalat yoke. They were reduced again in 1831 by Mehrab Khan (58).

By the turn of the 19th century the Qajars had established themselves firmly in control of Iran. Claims of sovereignty to the whole of Baluchistan were revived by Mohammad Shah Qajar (1834-47), and Bampur was taken from the rebellious chiefs in 1834 (59). The newly appointed governor of Kerman, Ebrahim Khan subsequently recovered Geh, Qasreqand, Dizzak, Bahu and Sarbaz. Esfandak and Chahbahar were recovered in 1872. Chahbahar had hitherto been held by the Arabs of Muscat for a brief period of time (60). The Qajar, nevertheless failed not only in recovering all of Iran's lost possessions in Baluchistan, but also in defining a clear framework within which relationships with the autonomous chiefs of the peripheral districts of the country would be governed. They also failed in defining any comprehensible frontier limitation around the country.

The Qajars even failed to place troops in charge of the localities they recovered from the rebellious chiefs in Baluchistan. Thus, at the time of boundary delimitation in the district of Baluchistan in 1870s it had become clear that the eastern half of Makran and Baluchistan had fallen to the autonomous Khan of Kalat who had accepted British protection and suzerainty, and the western half had returned to Iran.

British influence in Baluchistan and Sistan began as from the turn of the nineteenth century. Realising the importance of Bulan Pass to the security of India, the British during their expedition to Afghanistan, sent troops to Kalat to punish Mehrab Khan who had caused them much trouble. Kalat was reduced and the Khan killed in the war. Two years later, the Baluchis revolted against British interference and fought against them, which resulted in their submission to the rule of Nasser Khan II (61).

Having annexed Sind in 1843 and Panjab in 1848, the British increased their influence in Baluchistan. In 1854 they signed an agreement with Nasser Khan whereby the British undertook to pay him annually in return for his acceptance of becoming a British protectorate (62). Nasser Khan II died in 1857 and was succeeded by his brother Mir Khodadad who adhered to the said agreement with the British in return for the annual payment to be doubled. These developments brought Iran and Britain face to face in Baluchistan and cause frictions between them. Expressions of the desire by the British to extend their telegraph line westward from Gwader to the Straits of Hormuz at Jask deepened these frictions and necessitated a well defined boundary between the two powers. Coinciding with these developments was friction between Iran and the newly revived state of Afghanistan over the province of Sistan. The Afghan Amir Shir-Ali Khan had asked the British to intervene on behalf of his government (63) by offering arbitration between the two countries, which was accepted.

Goldsmid Line of Perso-Kalat Boundaries

In 1870 it was agreed that the disputed frontiers of Iran and Afghanistan should be settled through British arbitration, but the Afghans informed the British that the arbitration should be postponed for a year or so owing to the internal problems of that country (64). The Iranian Government appointed as Commissioner, Mirza Masum Khan Ansari, an officer of Foreign Ministry, apparently related to Mirza Saeed Khan (Ansari), Naser ad-Din Shah's Foreign Minster for 28 years. The Government of India had already assigned, on the persistence of the Afghan Amir, Colonel (later General) Frederick Goldsmid, director of British Telegraph Wire Construction in southern Baluchistan as the arbitrator (65).

The Afghan Amir's request in 1870 for British intervention in his border disputes with Iran provided the British with the opportunity of defining a borderline in Baluchistan. It was a year earlier that India Office had urged the Foreign Office to invite the Iranians to agree to adjustment of their eastern frontier (66).

As delimitation of Iran-Afghanistan boundaries in Sistan was delayed, however, Goldsmid was instructed to proceed with the delimitation of Baluchistan boundaries. Goldsmid – by this time promoted to the rank of Major General – proposed in a letter to the Governor of Bombay to proceed from Bampur to the most north-easterly point practicable on the Baluchistan frontier, proceeding thence southward to the sea (67). The Government of India, who had actually advised Goldsmid as to where precisely the Baluchistan boundary should be defined, agreed to this proposal. In clauses 3 and 4 of his letter to General Goldsmid, Secretary to the Foreign Office of the Government of India actually names all the places that the latter should take into consideration as belonging to Iran or Kalat (68). The unfavourable disposition British India towards Iran's rights of sovereignty even in its own section of Baluchistan was further demonstrated in clause 8 of the same letter. There the authorities at Bombay suggest involving the Muscat Arabs in the proceedings of Baluchistan boundary arbitration, because they once had leased Gwater and Chahbahar from the Iranian Government.

The first dispute between the two commissioners, however, occurred before the actual commencement of the surveying of the frontiers. The initial dispute was on the introduction of Faqir Mohammad Khan a well-known British protégé, as Commissioner representing the Khan of Kalat. The Iranian commissioner argued that the boundary commission was there only to survey and draw up a map of the frontier areas for the diplomats of Iran and Britain to negotiate in Tehran for settlement, not to carry out boundary adjudication that would necessitate participation of Kalat representative. His argument was based on the contents of the letter in which the Iranian foreign Minister informed the British of Iran's conditions for agreeing to their proposals of boundary delimitation. In that letter he stated:

> *The said commission will be at liberty to ...draw a map of Persia's possessions in Baloochistan...and bring the same with themselves to Tehran. That question will be then justly decided with the knowledge of the British Government... (69)*

The problem was solved however, as a result British use influence in Tehran which secured an instruction from the Iranian Foreign Ministry to Mirza Masum Khan to "*accept Kalat Commissioner if all right*" (70).

Before settlement of this problem was effected another problem of greater magnitude threatened the mission. This time Tehran brought to the attention of the British Minister on the 5th of March that: according to some reports from the Iranian Commissioner, General Goldsmid had undertaken a series of proceedings deemed to be damaging to the rights of Iran around the disputed areas and were provocative.

> *According to the reports from the Persian Commissioner, General Goldsmid had openly declared places avowedly Persian to belong to Kalat, and had unsettled men's mind by enquiring about the right of Persia to other places already in her possession, and indisputably belonging to her. Another subject of complaint was that of the tumultuous demonstrations on the part of the Kalat authorities, and the expedition of troops with drums, trumpets, & c., from Gwadur into the Kaj territory at the instigation of the British authorities. His Majesty, the Minister observed, was so offended at these proceedings, that he would consider himself justified in recalling his commissioner. His sole object with regard to the disputed Perso-Kalat frontier was that the Commissioners should conduct an*

inquiry into the matter in an orderly and quite way, draw up a map of that frontier line, and bring it to Tehran, where the subject would be settled between the Persian and British Governments. (71)

On his part, in the despatch No. 67 to the Secretary of State for India, dated 18th March 1871, General Goldsmid accused Mirza Masum Khan of similar undertakings and suggested that:

The whole action of the Persian Commissioner leads me to the thankless conclusion that an enquiry such as contemplated by Her Majesty's Government cannot now be carried out on the Perso-Baluch frontier unless under diplomatic influence at Tehran. (72)

The differences between the Iranian Commissioner, supported by Sardar Ebrahim Khan Governor of Bampur, and British Commissioner, supported by the Khan of Kalat, stemmed principally from Mirza Masum khan's distrust of the true intentions of the British arbitrator. In a despatch to the Ministry of Foreign Affairs, he indicated that since all intentions of Goldsmid could be seen in his notes, he would send to the Foreign Ministry the collection of notes of his conversation with the "English officer". He added:

This officer had no intention other than supporting and strengthening the Khan of Kalat and making up documentary evidence to prove that Kaj, Tump, and...belonged to the (said) *Khan, and that* (Goldsmid) *was very annoyed with him because of lack of cooperation in furthering the intentions of the said officer.* (73)

As these differences intensified between the two commissioners, both governments advised their respective commissioners to cooperate with each other. Nevertheless, the two commissioners continued the task of surveying frontier areas without tension between them subsiding. When Goldsmid assigned Captain Lovett of his commission to survey and draw up the map of border areas, it was discovered Iran's claims on certain localities was not acceptable to the Kalatis. He wrote to Mirza Masum Khan about this, stating:

...as the claim made by Persia to Kuhak and Isfandak have not been accepted by the other side and as they have several witnesses on their side ready, I think it advisable that this matter should be at once enquired into...(74)

Mirza Masum Khan protested against this suggestion and asserted in reply:

First, Kuhak and Isfandak are dependencies of Dizzak, and have nothing to do with the enquiry you are appointed for. Secondly, the Kalat Commissioners have been specially appointed to discuss the question of the frontier of kaj and its dependencies. What right have they to make a claim on Dizzak and its dependencies that they should waste your time and delay us in these useless matters? (75)

Having disputed Goldsmid's method of determining opposing Iran-Kalat sovereignties in the disputed areas, Mirza Masum Khan kept aloof. Nevertheless Goldsmid continued with his work without Mirza Masum Khan's cooperation. He thus completed his task and telegraphed the British Minister at Tehran on April 19th, suggesting that his findings and maps be put forward for discussion in Tehran (76). This happened the way it was suggested and the Iranian Government accepted on 23rd August that boundary awards should be made on the basis of Goldsmid's findings and his map. This was done by the Iranian authorities in spite of writing to the British Minister at Tehran a week earlier expressing regrets for the way General Goldsmid had, on his own, conducted the survey of the border areas (77).

Not only did the Iranian Government accept Goldsmid's one-sided report and map as the basis for discussion, but also limited the so-called discussion to one meeting between its Foreign Minister and the British Minister at Tehran accompanied by General Goldsmid. Mirza Masum Khan's absence in that "meeting" was blamed on having "fallen ill" (78). Goldsmid's suggested boundary line was then referred to the Shah who modified it partly by including in the Iranian side of the border line such localities as Kuhak in the north, and lands comprising the Nahang and Dasht rivers – from Mond to the sea, abandoning Gwadur Bay and Kaj (79). Finding the Iranians so serious on the question of Kuhak, General Goldsmid advised the Government in India that Kuhak should be given to Iran (80). His advice was not taken on board in India, and British Minister at Tehran officially informed the Iranian Foreign Ministry in a memorandum on 1st September 1871 of the boundaries delineated in Baluchistan, from Guater as far north as Jalq in accordance with Goldsmid's map and his findings. The memorandum outlines in part:

> *To summarise: Punjgur and Parun and other dependencies with Kuhak; Boleida, including Zamiran and other dependencies; Mond, including Tump, Nasser Abad, Kaj, and all districts, dehs and dependencies to the eastward; Dasht with its dependencies as far as the sea; these names exhibit the line of actual possession of Kalat, that is to say, all tracts to the east of the frontier of actual Persian possession, which frontier comprises Dizzak and Bampusht, Sarbaz and Peshin, Bahu and Dustyari. (81)*

Replying to this memorandum, the Iranian Minister of Foreign Affairs stated his government's acceptance of the delimitation in spite of Iran's clear right over most of Baluchistan (82). Notwithstanding the strange way in which Iran accepted Goldsmid's Line in Baluchistan, Iranian officials unofficially informed British Minister at Tehran that Kuhak and parts of Mashkil Valley should go to Iran. These demands soon proved that a final agreement of these boundaries was impossible and the question of Kuhak and Mashkil Valley remained to be settled later. It was shortly after the completion of the delineation tasks and Goldsmid's departure from Iran that Sardar Ebrahim Khan, Governor of Bampur, captured Kuhak and other parts of the Mashkil Valley.

Holdich Line of Perso-Kharan Boundary

Whilst the Goldsmid's line defined the limits of Iran's possessions in Baluchistan, Kuhak and Esfandak remained out in the cold. The Iranian Government though accepting in principle the Goldsmid Line, did not agree with his decision on the northern section of that line. Apart from Kuhak, Esfandak and Mashkil Valley, the remaining stretch of frontier areas included a long space as far north as River Hirmand in Sistan. That stretch of land included in all, 300 miles of undefined and unmapped frontier (83).

The decision to leave areas to the north of Jalq undefined by Goldsmid's Commission was due to the fact that Azad Khan, chief of Kharan, considered himself and his dominion to be independent of that of the Khan of Kalat. In 1884 however, under Sir Robert Sanderson's auspices, Azad Khan obtained recognition with the Khan of Kalat as one of his Sardars (84). Without any historical and legal dependency of Kharan to the Afghans, he wrote to the Amir of Afghanistan to ask if there was any objection in Kabul to his submitting to the British Government (the British had by then bought Kalat from its Khan). Seeing his own survival and that of a united Afghanistan largely dependent on British good will and on the geostrategic consideration of the British Government in Central and South-West Asia, the Afghan Amir gave his consent (85) to Kharan submission to Kalat. This was, in effect, giving consent to Kharan's submission to the British Indian Government, which was, by this time, in direct control of the whole of eastern Baluchistan including Kuhak. The Iranians, at this time, reasserted their control of Kuhak, which motivated the British authorities to seek delimitation of boundaries in these frontier areas. There were a number of reasons for the British to enforce boundary lines in the tracts to the north of Jalq and Mashkil river as outlined by Captain Macdonald in a memorandum on the subject (86).

By December 1895 however, the two sides decided to demarcate the tracts between Kalat and Sistan territory. An agreement signed in Tehran by the Iranian Prime Minister and British Legation allowed the demarcation of these boundaries to proceed (87). The British had, by this time, resolved that more than twenty years of Iranian possession of Kuhak and Esfandak was too long a period of time to be easily ignored (88). Kuhak and Esfandak were, thus, returned to Iran.

The actual delimitation of these boundaries was agreed by the two parties in Tehran on the basis of Colonel Holdich's final report on the proceedings of the Irano-British Baluchistan Frontier Delimitation Commission. The details of this delimitation appear in the Tehran agreement of 27th December 1895, which allowed the two sides' representatives to carry out demarcation of the boundary.

Figure 13

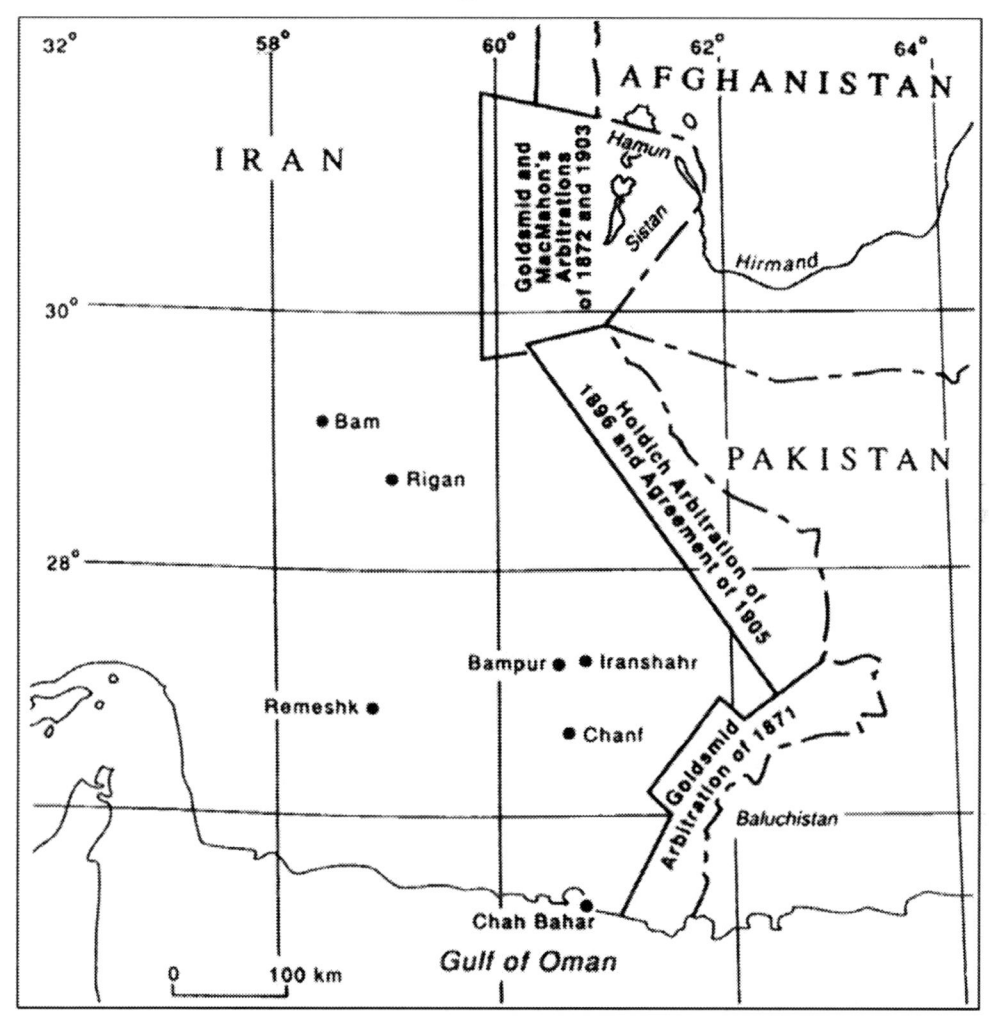

The Iran-Pakistan boundaries of 1871, 1872, 1903 and 1905

Colonel T. Hangerford Holdich and his Iranian counterpart completed the demarcation task by late March and signed on 24th March 1896 an agreement on the completion of demarcation which was submitted to their respective governments in early April 1896, finalising the boundary settlement of northern Baluchistan (89). This boundary has recognised Kuhak, Esfandak and areas west of Mashkil River as Iran's possessions. It, nevertheless, deprived Iran of most of the Mashkil district and more importantly, the Mirjaveh town and district and its strategic points. British authorities were aware of Iran's losses in this settlement as British boundary expert, Captain Durand stated in his letter of January 20th 1896 to the Marquis of Salisbury.

> *Your Lordship will see that the convention secures for Kelat considerably better terms than the Government of India was willing to accept. I thought it desirable to keep something in hand for future exchange or concession. Our Commissioners will now be in good position for they can make considerable*

concessions to Persia if they should wish to do so, while still reserving to Kelat all that the Government of India thinks necessary…(90)

It is also noteworthy that in 1900 the Government of India bought the interests of the Khan of Kalat in the Nushki district (91) in order to safeguard their protectorate's interests in that district.

The 1905 Settlement

When settling the boundary to the north of Jalq Colonel Holdich based his information on a map that the British claimed to have proved by subsequent investigations, to be wrong. Realising this the British discovered that if they were to demarcate the boundary on the basis of this map, the result would very likely bring their Padaha post well within Iranian territory. They, therefore, assigned Captain Webb Ware to survey the areas concerned and prepare a report on the actuality of the boundary line. This he did in 1902 and the map he prepared put Mirjaveh within Indian territories. This action disturbed the Iranians and friction occurred between the two countries. In his lengthy memorandum of 5th November 1904, Colonel McMahon, British Arbitrator of Sistan boundaries, proposed a new line to be imposed upon the Iranians, which he alluded to as *the red line* as opposed to that of Holdich's *blue line*. This proposal was to take more of Iranian territories so that an Iranian objection would lead to a compromise satisfactory to India (92). The Government of India rejected his proposed *red line* on the advice of British Minister at Tehran who believed that they could not ever induce the Iranian Government to accept it (93). He suggested that if the Iranians 'behaved themselves' in Sistan and instructed Amir Heshmat al-Molk Khozeimeh from interfering in the India trade, "we would leave them Mirjaveh" (94).

The case of Heshmat al-Molk referred to in this document was that Amir Ali-Akbar Khan Heshmat al-Molk II, the Khozeimeh Amir of Sistan, allegedly supported by the Russians, had enforced an order prohibiting exports of supplies to the British Indian frontiers. In a despatch to the Indian Government in February 1902, the British Vice-Consul for Sistan and Qaen reported that in his meeting with Amir Heshmat al-Molk he was told that:

> *Mr. Miller (Russian Consul) had also been to visit him to impress on him the existence of this order and to warn him that it was his duty to punish Katkhodas of villages who disobeyed it. The Amir added that Mr. Miller had also reminded, 'if you cannot look after your frontier yourself, you know that some one else will have to do it for you'. The Amir regarded this as an indication of Mr. Miller's future designs with regard to our border. On the subject of supplies the Amir said that an order prohibiting their export did exist; but that an exception had always been made in the case of our thanas on the trade route, as the provisions were required not for purposes of trade but as a means of sustenance for the garrison.* (95)

A year later Amir Heshmat al-Molk's position as Governor of Sistan was threatened, not only by his younger brother, Amir Ebrahim Khan Shokat al-Molk II Amir of Qaenat, but also by Moazez al-Molk who was then acting as Governor of Qaenat. In the face of these threats to his position, Amir Heshmat al-Molk decided to throw in his lot with the British (96). He protected British lives and property in July 1903. This undertaking resulted in the Russian Consul for Sistan deciding *"to get the Amir Heshmat-ul-Mulk dismissed for his action in protecting British property and interest"* (97). Finding the dismissal of the Amir in that circumstance a grave injury to their prestige vis-à-vis Russia in eastern Iran (98), the British instructed their Minister at Tehran (Sir A. Hardinge) to accept in an agreement the Iranian demands in the frontier to the north of Holdich Line's pillar No. 11. In return they asked for Amir Heshmat al-Molk to remain in his position as Governor of Sistan. The agreement, signed on the 13th March 1905 (99) though secured the post at Qaleh Sefid for the British, left Holdich's blue line delimited on the Talab water course which left both Old and New Mirjaveh to Iran together with the stretch of 300 miles of disputed frontier areas. The two governments agreed to the survey and delimitation of the section of the boundary from the neighbourhood of Mirjaveh to Kuh-e Malek Siah. This undertaking produced no other results but mapping of the frontier areas in question (100). In 1938-9, similar agreements were reached between the two governments, which proved fruitless also. In 1948 British Baluchistan lost its identity simultaneously with the disappearance of British India Empire, and was reincorporated in the newly created state of Pakistan.

The British Government supplied the Government of Pakistan in 1950 with all documents relevant to this portion of frontier area (101). On August 13th 1950 the daily Ettelaat of Tehran reported that the governments of Iran and Pakistan had agreed to demarcate the Mirjaveh-Malek Siah Kuh boundary (102). This stretch of boundary was demarcated during this author's visit to Mirjaveh in May 2002, with barbed wires in place at Mirjaveh area.

Notes and References

1- Extract of Telegraph to the British Government from Governor General of India, dated January 24, 1878, FO 60/217.
2- Ibid.
3- General MacLean's memorandum of 14th December 1889, FO 60/538, P. 10 of 279.
4- Memorandum of General MacLean, dated Mashad, 6th July 1891, FO 60/538, PP. 310-405.
5- Ibid.
6- The Persian written claims, enclosed in MacLean's memorandum of 14th December 1889, FO 60/538, P. 11 of 280.
7- Mohammad-Ali Mokhber, *Marzhay-e Iran* (The boundaries of Iran), Tehran 1945, P. 29.
8- From Brigadier General MacLean to Secretary to the Government of India Foreign Department, dated Camp Hashtadan 29th April 1888, FO 60/538, P. 120.
9- From the Viceroy and Governor General of India to the Amir of Afghanistan, dated Simla 7th September 1888, FO 60/538.
10- Ibid.
11- Extract of General MacLean's Memorandum of 14th December 1889, op. cit., P. 11 of 280.
12- Ibid., PP. 279-295.
13- Extract of letter from H.E. the Viceroy and Governor General of India to H.H. Amir of Afghanistan, dated Simla 7th September 1888, FO 60/538, P. 123.
14- Text of General MacLean's notes on his interview with Naser ad-Din Shah of Iran, FO 60/538, PP. 1-2 of 158.
15- Telegram dated the 7th December 1889, from Sir H. Drumond Wolff, H.B. Majesty's Minister at Tehran to Viceroy, Calcutta, FO 60/538, P. 275.
16- Extract of Memorandum of 6th July 1891, FO Press – No. 575 – 29 – 3 – 90 – 44, FO 60/538, P. 2 of 310.
17- From Sir H. Drummond Wolff, H.B. Majesty's Minister at Tehran, to the Viceroy, Calcutta, dated 9th December 1889, FO 60/538, P. 1 of 275.
18- Extract of Memorandum dated 14th December 1889, FO 60/538, P. 14 of 281.
19- General Joseph Pierre Ferrier, *Caravan Journey and Wandering in Persia, Afghanistan, Turkistan and Baloochistan*, William Clawes & Sons, London 1857, PP. 191-2. Yar Mohammad Khan was at the time in control of Herat.
20- For more detail on these instances see: Pirouz Mojtahed-Zadeh, *The Amirs of Borderlands and Eastern Iranian Borders*, Urosevic Foundation Publication, London 1996, PP. 322-3.
21- Enclosure No. 1, to Kabul despatch No. 147, dated the 27th December 1934, FO 371/1940, P. 192.
22- Enclosure No. 2, to Kabul despatch No. 149, op. cit., P. 195.
23- British Legation, Tehran despatch No. 114, dated 9th March 1935, FO 371/19408, P. 248.
24- Text of agreement between the two officials of the two sides, dated 24th January 1935, enclosure to Kabul despatch No. 35, dated the 20th March 1935, FO 371/19408, PP. 1 & 2 of 255.
25- Clause 2 of Confidential report of H. B. Majesty's Consul General at Mashhad, dated 9th December 1934, FO 371/19408, P. 222.
26- Telegram from Government of India to Deputy Secretary of State, dated 19th July 1932, FO 371/16279.

27- From British Legation at Kabul to Deputy Secretary to the Government of India, No. 348 (E), dated 23rd September 1932, FO 371/16279.
28- Extract of Captain Winter's report on Afghan encroachments at Musa Abad, enclosed in Colonel Minchin's confidential despatch No. 20, to Secretary to the Government of India, dated Meshed 21st May 1904, FO 60/711, PP. 1-2.
29- Clause 4 of Colonel Minchin's Confidential despatch to the Secretary to the Government of India, in the Foreign Department, No. 20, dated Meshed 21st May 1904, FO 60/711, P. 1.
30- Enclosure in despatch No. 168 of British Legation at Tehran to Foreign Office, dated 8th September 1904, FO 60/711, P. 22.
31- From A. H. Hardinge of British Legation at Tehran to the Marquis of Lansdowne, No. 168, dated 8th September 1904, FO 60/711, PP. 22-3.
32- From British Legation at Kabul to Deputy Secretary to the Government of India, No. 348 (E), dated 23rd September 1932, FO 371/16279.
33- See Memorandum of 6th July 1891 of General MacLean, No. 575 – 29 – 3 – 90 – 44, FO 60/538, P. 2 of 310.
34- Extract of letter from H. E. Viceroy and Governor General of India to H. H. the Amir of Afghanistan quoting passages of a letter from the latter, dated Simla, July 1897, FO 371/19408, PP. 230-1.
35- Ibid.
36- From the Indian Government to H. Majesty's Envoy and Minister at the Court of Afghanistan, No. D. 4777-F/32, dated New Delhi the 21st November 1932, FO 371/16279, PP. 377-8.
37- Afghanistan annual confidential report for the year 1934, No. 1358/-1358/97, Kabul February 22, 1935, FO 371/1942, P. 41.
38- Clause 4 of Despatch from His Majesty's Minister, Kabul, to His Majesty's Secretary of State for Foreign Affairs, London No. 141, dated the 13th (received 18th) December 1934, FO 371/19408, P. 173.
39- Confidential report of British Consulate General, dated Mashed, 9th December 1934, FO 371/19408, PP. 222-3-4.
40- From R.R. Maconachie, British Legation at Kabul to V. A. L. Mallet, British Legation at Tehran, dated 11th December 1934, FO 371/19408, PP. 182-3.1.
41- Mokhber, op. cit., P. 32.
42- From British Legation Kabul to British Legation Tehran, dated 11th December 1934, FO 371/19408, PP. 182-3.
43- Clause 2 of H. B. Majesty's Consulate General of Khorasan and Sistan Confidential Diary for January 1935, FO 371/19421, P. 3 0f 142.
44- Mr. Morgan's despatch No. 457, dated Angora, 1st January 1935, FO 371/19408, P. 179.
45- From British Embassy at Ankara to the Foreign Office, dated Angora May 22, 1935, FO 371/19408, P. 261.
46- British Legation at Tehran, despatch No. 447, dated Tehran 18th October 1935, FO 371/19408, P. 271.
47- Altay's Award, the Persian version of which this author has found in Mohammad Ali Mokhber's, *Marzhay-e Iran*, Published in Tehran 1945, PP. 31-35.
48- Altay's award, Mokhber, op. cit., P. 41.
49- Altay's award, Mokhber, op. cit., P. 43.
50- Altay's award, Mokhber, op. cit., P. 44.
51- Ibid.

52- In his Consular report Captain Hunter of Her Britannic Majesty's Sistan Consulate makes references to Shokat al-Molk's ownership of this locality, Consular Report dated 19th August 1912, FO 248/921, P. 15.
53- Altay's award, Mokhber, op. cit., P. 48.
54- Mohammad-Ali Monsef, *Amir Shokat al-Molk Alam*, Tehran 1972, PP. 193-4.
55- Altay's award, Mokhber, op. cit., P. 49.
56- Afghanistan Confidential Annual Report 1935, from Lieutenant Colonel Fraser-Tayler to Mr. Eden, No. 31, dated Kabul March 7, 1936, FO 371/19423, P. 48.
57- For more details on this see: a document on "the history of Baluchistan", which exists in the British Public Record Office under FO 60/385, P. 61 of 60.
58- Ibid, op. cit., P. 62.
59- The dates given here are disputable. A letter from Acting Secretary to the Government of India suggests that the capture of Bampur by the Iranians took place about 1845 and the subsequent invasion of Geh and Qasreqand about 1849. See: letter of the Acting Secretary to Government, Bombay, No. 9 of 3rd June 1861, FO 60/385, P. 25 of 42.
60- G. P. Reverand Badger to the Government of Bombay, No. 10, dated June 5th 1861, FO 60/385.
61- Mokhber, op. cit., P. 54.
62- Ibid.
63- From Colonel F. R. Pollock to the Secretary to the Indian Government, dated Peshawar 17th June 1870, FO 60/386, P. 206.
64- From H. H. Amir of Afghanistan to the Governor General of India, dated 8th October 1870, FO 60/386, P. 462.
65- Extract of telegram from the Viceroy to the Secretary of State, dated 14th May 1870, No. 784p, FO 60/386, P. 249, section 182.
66- FO 60/387, P. 14 of 60.
67- Confidential letter from C. U. Aitchison, Secretary to the Government of India, to Major General Goldsmid, dated Fort William 24th January 1871, No. 169P, FO 60/387, P. 158.
68- Clauses 3 and 4 of Aichison's letter to Goldsmid, dated Fort William 24th January 1871, FO 60/387, P. 158.I.
69- Extract of translation of memorandum from Mirza Saeed Khan, Iran's Foreign Minister, dated Tehran 24th July 1870, FO 60/386, P. 431.
70- Telegram from the Iranian Foreign Minister to the Iranian Commissioner, as repeated in Mr. Alison's telegram to Goldsmid, dated Tehran the 2nd of March 1871, FO 60/390 – 169256, P.4.
71- Extract of letter from C. Alison, H. B. Majesty's Minister at Tehran to Right Hon'ble the Earl Granville, dated Tehran 9th March 1871, No. 22, FO 60/390, P. 57.
72- Extract of clause 12 of despatch No. 67, from Major General Goldsmid to His Grace the Duke of Argyll, dated Camp Gwadur 18th March 1871, FO 60/388, P. 5.
73- From Mirza Masum Khan to Mirza Saeed Khan, dated 29 Safar 1288 (19th May 1871), document 93 of *'Yeksad Sanad-e Tarikhi'*, by Ebrahim Safaei, Tehran March 1974.
74- From General Goldsmid to Mirza Masum Khan as contained in Mr. Alison's telegram to Goldsmid, dated 3rd March 1871, FO 60/388, PP. 11-2.
75- From Mirza Masum Khan to General Goldsmid, dated Bampoor 8th February 1871, FO 60/388, P. 23.
76- From General Goldsmid to Mr. Alison, dated 17th April 1871, FO 60/390.

77- Memorandum from Mirza Saeed Khan to C. Alison, H. B. Majesty's Minister at Tehran, dated 17th August 1871, FO 60/391, P. 33.
78- From Alison, Tehran, to Viceroy, Simla, dated 18th July 1871, FO 60/390, P. 101.
79- From Goldsmid to Foreign Secretary, Simla, dated Tehran 14th August 1871, FO 60/390.
80- Ibid.
81- See text of Memorandum from C. Alison to the Persian Minister of Foreign Affairs, dated Gulhak the 1st September 1871, FO 60/391, PP. 1-2 of 37.
82- From Mirza Saeed Khan, Iranian Minister of Foreign Affairs to Mr. Alison, dated 14th September 1871, FO 60/391, P. 2 of 37.
83- Boundary between Persia and Northwest Baluchistan, Confidential Foreign Office Document, dated 19th September 1893, FO 60/627, P. 1.
84- From Foreign Secretary to General Goldsmid, dated 26th May 1871, enclosure 12 to Government of India Secret letter No. 61, dated 26th September 1871, quoted in Boundary between Persia and Northwest Baluchistan, op. cit., dated 19th September 1893, FO 60/627.
85- Boundary between Persia and Northwest Baluchistan, a Foreign Office document dated 19th September 1893, FO 60/627, P. 4.
86- See Memorandum of Captain F. W. P. Macdonald of Indian Staff, dated London 15th August 1893, FO 60/627, P. 17.
87- See text of agreement, dated Tehran December 27, 1895, FO 60/627 in 3 pages.
88- From the Viceroy to her majesty's Government, dated 16th December 1895, FO 60/627.
89- From Colonel T.H. Holdich, H. B. Majesty's Commissioner for the delimitation of Perso-Baluch Frontier, to the Secretary of the Government of India Foreign Department, dated Camp Panjgur the 5th April 1896, No. 34, FO 60/627.
90- From Durand to marquis of Salisbury, dated Tehran January 20th 1896, No. 5, FO 60/62.
91- Major Percy Sykes, *The Thousand Miles in Persia*, London 1902, P. 358.
92- Clause 14 of McMahon's memorandum No 2540, dated Camp Kohak the 5th November 1904, FO 60/712, P. 3.
93- From Sir A. Hardinge, H. B. Majesty's Minister at Tehran, to Foreign Secretary, Telegram No. 5, dated 9th January 1905, FO 60/712.
94- Ibid.
95- Clause 4 of despatch No. 331, from Major R.A.E. Benn, H. B. Majesty's Vice-Consul for Sistan and Kain, to the Secretary to the Government of India, Foreign Department, dated Sistan 23rd February 1902, FO 60/712, P. 2.
96- Notes by Major Benn, dated 21st May 1903, FO 248/789.
97- H. Dobbs, Consul for Sistan, to the Indian Government, 7th July 1903, Confidential, FO 248/790.
98- Ibid.
99- From Mr. Cook to the Foreign Office, 1st Sept. 1950, FO 371/82332A, No. 4170/1, P. 2.
100- Ibid.
101- From L. Barnett of Foreign Office to C. E. Diggines of Commonwealth Relations Office, dated 11th August 1950, FO 371/82332A (EP1081/3).
102- Daily Ettelaat, Tehran 13th August 1950.

CHAPTER XIII

Emergence and Evolution of Sistan Boundaries
Pirouz Mojtahed-Zadeh

Introduction

The province now known as Sistan had throughout the history been named variably: Sakestan, Nimrouz, Zarang, Zabolestan, etc., and it formed the 14th satrapy in the Achaemenian Commonwealth system (559-330 BC), and formed part of the Kust of Khorasan under the Sassanid federation (AD 224-651). In the post-Islamic era Sistan became a major centre of struggle for the revival of Iranianism, many movements began in Sistan and engulfed the entire Iranian Plateau. The Saffarids of Sistan were the first dynasty to throw off the yoke of the Abbasid Caliphate. The subsequent dynasties have always made a point of including Khorasan and Sistan within the countries of Iran. Throughout the Safavid Federation of Iran (1501-1722) Sistan formed the eastern province of Iran and Nader Shah Afshar (1730-1747) included Sistan in his empire almost at the outset of his career after a negligible period of approximately eight years of confusion in Iran resulting from the Abdali uprising.

Following Nader Shah's assassination in 1747, Iran fell into chaos again and Ahmad Khan Abdali (Durrani), who founded the Saduzaei Kingdom of Afghanistan. He used the opportunity Iran's chaos and 1749 occupied the larger part of this province after defeating Amir Alam Khan I, the Khozeimeh Amir of Qaenat who had in 1747 included in his dominion the whole of Khorasan, Sistan, and Baluchistan. From that time the eastern parts of Sistan remained under the control of Ahmad Shah Durrani until he died in 1772, a mere 23 years in all.

The Saduzaei kingdom in Afghanistan fell into chaos in the wake of Ahmad Shah's demise while chaos in Iran was still prevailing as a result of continued armed struggle between the houses of Zand and Qajar. This situation was further aggravated by a number of other rebellions by various chiefs around the country, who began a life of autonomy. This was mainly because there was not a one outright leader in whose favour the traditional custom of allegiance could be practiced. The principalities of Herat, Qandehar, and Kabul quietly returned to their traditional status as autonomous dependencies of Iran, and Sistan was under the Amirdom of the Keyani family who claimed to be the descendants of legendary Keyanian of ancient Iran. It was during their term of amirdom that the Baluchi chiefs expanded their domination of Sistan.

From time immemorial Sistan had been associated with Khorasan, even frequently referred to as the 'bread basket of Khorasan'. In the period of the Keyani amirdom however, the province became so thoroughly Baluchized that no longer it could be identified with Khorasan in any way. This change of character made the reassertion of the Khozeimeh amirdom in Sistan very difficult. Even Khozeimeh Amir Alam Khan's establishment of family ties, through strategic marriage with many Baluchi tribes did not completely do away with the Sistani sense of rejection of the Khorasani (Birjandi) domination of Sistan in 19th and 20th century. Even in early 20th century political organisation of space in Iran, Sistan was merged with Baluchistan in the separate province of 'Sistan and Baluchistan. This change of character has left an almost incomprehensibly long-lasting sentiment among the population that even now one needs to be somewhat careful in referring to Sistan association with 'the Birjandis' of Khorasan or the 'Sardars' of Baluchistan.

The Keyanis however, accepted in a bizarre manner the nominal suzerainty of Ahmad Shah Durrani's successor Teimur, who used force against them. There was no definite leader in Iran at the time to protect them against Afghan pressure. It was under Fath-Ali Shah Qajar that the whole of Sistan, Baluchistan and Khorasan was recovered between 1810 and 1840. Since then, the governments in Iran never allowed an interval to elapse without immediately reasserting sovereignty over this province.

By the time of the Anglo-Iranian war which was concluded by the signing of the 1857 treaty of Paris, both Herat and Qandehar laid claims on sections of Sistan. Sardar Ali Khan Sarbandi of Sekuheh, the hereditary chief of Sistan who had officially declared in 1853 allegiance to Iran (1), felt threatened by the claims from Herat and Qandehar and personally went to Tehran to be officially appointed as Governor of the province. To further strengthen his position, he married a cousin of Naser ad-Din Shah. This move caused apprehension among some officers of British India that Iran (of feeble Qajar government) could, in conjunction with Russia, pose threats to the security of the British India Empire if Sistan was to remain in its entirety as a province of Iran. At the same time, when Herat authority were planning encroachment in Sistan, Colonel Taylor, British Commissioner in Herat, was trying to convince his government to deprive Iran of her rights of sovereignty over Sistan. He wrote:

> *should Persia be permitted to continue the exercise of her influence in Sistan, she may have it in her power to propagate falsehood to the prejudice of India and, being so near the frontier of the latter, they could be freely circulated. On the other hand, if Sistan were the instrument of a friendly power, she might when occasion required, be made to inflict very serious injury to the commerce of Persia by distributing her southeastern frontier and plundering all caravans.*
> (2)

It was rumoured at the time however, that Ali Khan Sarbandi was to return to Sistan with two regiments of regular infantry and a few field guns, together with able men from Sistan. Before even the Afghan chiefs heard of this rumour, James Murrey, British Minister at Tehran addressed the Iranian Prime Minster on the 5th May 1858 saying that he hoped the rumour of that intention was incorrect '*as the occupation of Sistan*', he added, "*which is part of Afghanistan, by Persian troops would be a direct violation of the treaty of Paris*" (3). Replying to this strange claim, the Iranian Premier wrote on 13th May stating:

> *The Persian ministers have always considered, and do now consider, that Sistan ab antiqua, has formed an integral part of the Persian territory, and it is at the present time in the possession of the Persian Government, on whose part it is therefore not necessary that troops or soldiers should be sent, or a new occupation of the place effected.* (4)

This statement naturally did not satisfy British authorities of India, who wished to strengthen the western flanks of the buffer state of Afghanistan. Thus, replying to the Iranian Premier on

15rth May 1858, James Murrey informed him that the British would not admit the correctness of his view, and claimed that not only by the virtue of political history, but also because of its geographical position, *which is represented in every existing map*, Sistan is a part of Afghanistan (5). This letter was brought to an end by presenting the following threats on behalf of the British Government.

> *It is my duty to inform your highness that, if the Persian Government were to send troops into Seistan, a province which is much nearer to Candahar, the centre of Afghanistan, and to the British Frontier, than Herat itself, Her Majesty's Government would consider such a step as a direct violation of the treaty of Paris.* (6)

Sardar Ali Khan, however, returned to Sistan with an escort of 300 cavalry men and two field guns, and was murdered in October 1858 by his own nephew, Taj Mohammad Khan, an ex-chief in the Sistan province. Taj Mohammad Khan too declared his allegiance to the Iranian Government after a while, and declared himself as being an Iranian subject (7). Before his declaration of allegiance to Iran, the Iranian Government had decided to send military forces to Sistan to punish those involved in the murder of Sardar Ali Khan. The new British Minister at Tehran, Mr. Doria asked in a letter to the Iranian Prime Minister what was the purpose of wanting to send troops to Sistan. In his letter of reply, the Iranian Prime Minister stated that the Shah intended to issue orders to the governors of Qaenat and Kerman to hold in readiness a number of troops to march on Sistan for the punishment of Taj Mohammad Khan and all concerned in the assassination of Sardar Ali Khan. But this was in the event of the people of Sistan refusing to deliver over to the government the perpetrator of the murder (8). He was once again reminded that the British Government considered Sistan as belonging to Afghanistan, a country that was not in existence at the time. In spite of British insistence that Sistan was a part of Afghanistan, Taj Mohammad Khan declared his own loyalty and that of Sistan Governorship to Iran. In a letter to the Government of India, British Minister at Tehran, Mr. Doria informed them of the process and ceremonies of Sistan's declaration of allegiance to Iran. He wrote in a cynical manner:

> *Two persons were introduced by the deputy master of ceremonies bearing a tray, upon which, were some gold coins. A long letter was then red aloud, pretended to have been written by the ruler of Seistan, making protestations of fidelity and obedience as subjects to the king. The coins on the tray were Shahee Ashrefees struck in His Majesty's name in Seistan.* (9)

Eventually, being convinced of the Iranian Government of determination with regard to the prosecution of their ancient rights to sovereignty of Sistan, the British in India found it wise to drop baseless claims to Sistan for Afghanistan and to acknowledge Iran's rights to that province. In his brief *History of Sistan and Lash-Jowain*, prepared for the British Foreign Office in 1870, H. L. Wynne reminds us of the fact that Lord Stanley endorsed Mr. Eastwick's memorandum on 18th December 1862 with these remarks:

> *The general conclusion the fact noted on the preceding memorandum appear to be that Seistan has been for ages, and from a period even antecedent to the dawn*

of history down to the death of Nadir Shah in 1747, an integral portion of the Persian Empire.

He further noted:

It...appears that Seistan can be in no sense included in Afghanistan, being inhabited by different people, who are, for the most, Sheahs like the Persians, and not Sunnis like the Afghans, who speak a different language from the Afghans, and who have never yielded more than a nominal obedience to the Afghan rulers, except to Ahmad Shah, and that only for a period so short as would not invalidate the claim of sovereignty on the part of Persia, - a claim based on the two titles recognised by international law, viz., first occupancy and uninterrupted possession. (10)

Events Leading to the Partitioning of Sistan

Dust Mohammad Khan, Amir of Kabul, marched in July 1861 a sizeable army on the semi-independent principality of Qandehar, which was traditionally but vaguely a dependency of Iran save for the duration of Afghanistan's consolidated monarchy of Ahmad Shah Durrani (1749-1772). This development disturbed the Iranians who were convinced that Dust Mohammad Khan's plan was to take Farah, Herat, and Sistan eventually, as Farah was captured shortly afterward. In a letter to his Government in May 1861 British Minister at Tehran wrote that the Court of Qajar in Tehran was disturbed by the news that Mohammad Sharif Khan, son of Dust Mohammad and Governor of Farah, had been contemplating an attack on Sistan under the pretext of punishing certain Baluchis who had plundered Qandehar territory. He added that the British Government could not, in justice, expect Iran to submit quietly to the invasion of Sistan (11).

British Government must have been aware of Dust Mohammad and his son's plan to capture Sistan as Kabul Diary of the British Legation of 28th April 1861 indicates that Sharif Khan was contemplating this step. A servant of Taj Mohammad Khan of Sistan brought the news to Mashhad, and said that Sharif Khan had first of all taken Rudbar that belonged to Baluchis, and had then advanced on Jahan-Abad in Sistan, capturing it also. Governor General of Khorasan wrote to the governors in Sistan telling them to be firm in maintaining their position until news came from Tehran (12).

With the experience of losing Herat in the same way, the Iranian authorities appeared to have resolved to go about solving the problem of Sistan in accordance with treaties and documents exchanged between Iran and Britain, specially the treaty of 1857. This was in order to avoid any situation that could lead to the British declaring another war on Iran in support of another Afghan attempt to seize territories from Iran.

In spite of repeated appeals by the Iranian authorities, including the Shah himself, to the British in accordance with article 6 of Paris treaty of 1857, to prevent Dust Mohammad Khan and his lot from invading Iranian territories, the British preferred to remain inactive in that event. Dust Mohammad Khan captured Farah as well as Qandehar and put Herat under siege in July 1862. With the capture of Qandehar and Farah, Dust Mohammad Khan effectively captured important places in Sistan, such as Chokhansur, Qaleh Fath, and Qaleh Nad-e Ali, which in previous times adhered to Qandehar under the authority of Kohandel Khan and his sons who had reaffirmed their dependency on Iran. Dust Mohammad Barakzaei's son's capture of Jahan-Abad in the Hirmand delta effectively partitioned the province of Sistan. After some enquiries made by way of correspondence with Dust Mohammad Khan, the British government concluded that the Barakzaei Amir of Kabul had no intention of crossing Iranians frontier and to pursue his war inside Iran (13). This view was stated at the time when Dust Mohammad Khan's son had occupied Jahan-Abad, an undisputed Iranian town in Sistan. To justify this conclusion, the British in India decided to change their stance by denying once again that Sistan belonged to Iran. This changed attitude would make it possible for the British not to consider Dust Mohammad Khan's encroachment in Sistan as '*crossing Iranian frontiers and taking his war into Iran*' (14). When the Iranian envoy to the Ottoman Court explained to British Foreign Secretary that Great Britain was bound under the treaty of 1857 "*to remove all causes of dispute between Iran and Afghanistan,*" Lord Russell replied that "*all that Britain was obligated under that treaty was to endeavour to compose such differences.*" Further discussion revealed to the Iranian envoy that as far as Britain was concerned Dust Mohammad Khan was entitled to capture Herat but not to invade Iran proper. Lord Russell told the envoy:

> *If Dost Mahommed should get possession of Herat and assume an attitude threatening to Persia, then certainly Persia, subject to the provisions of the treaty, might take arms to defend herself.* (15)

By July 1863, less than a month after Dust Mohammad Khan's death, his son and successor, Shir Ali Khan despatched his younger brother, Mohammad Amin Khan, at the head of an Afghan force against Sistan. The long serving Iranian Foreign Minister, Mirza Saeed Khan, met Mr. Thomson, British Minister at Tehran, and informed him that: "*the expedition had been ordered by Dust Mohammad Khan, but that it had been subsequently relinquished in consequence of that Chief's death.*" Mirza Saeed Khan added that the Afghans were certain, sooner or later, to renew this project and to attempt the occupation of Sistan. But, the Iranian Government considered Sistan to belong to the Iran, forming an integral part of it, and that they would not hesitate for a moment, should Afghan troops enter Sistan, but would at once despatch a force to resist any such aggressive movement. Replying to the remarks of British Minister that the sovereignty of Iran over Sistan had never been recognised by the British Government, Mirza Saeed Khan stated that this was because there being no mention of Sistan in the treaty with England. Iran would not forego her claims in the matter, but would maintain her right to that province even should hostilities with the Afghan ensue (16).

The Iranian Government subsequently pleaded that since the Afghan occupation of Chokhansur, Qaleh Fath, Nad-e Ali, and Jahan-Abad had in practice partitioned Sistan and there was no reason to believe that their push into Sistan would not go further, if the British did not act to stop them, should, at least, acknowledge Iran's rights of self-defence in accordance with the provisions of article 7 of the treaty of 1857. Article 7 of the treaty of 1857 referred to by the Iranians asserted:

> *In case of any violation of the Persian frontier by the states referred to above (Kabul, Herat, and Qandehar) the Persian Government shall have the right, if due satisfaction is not given, to undertake military operation for the repression and punishment of the aggressor; but it is distinctly understood and agreed to, that any military force of the Shah which may cross the frontier for the above mentioned purpose, shall retire within its own territory as soon as its object is accomplished, and that the exercise of the above mentioned right is not to be*

made a pretext for the permanent occupation by Persia, or for the annexation to the Persian dominions of any town or portion of the said states. (17)

This provision of Paris Treaty of 1857 made it abundantly clear that Iran had the right of self-defence in the face of Afghan aggression in Sistan and was determined to repel the aggression. It made it further clear that the Iranian military operation in the Afghan occupied areas of Sistan would not amount to crossing any frontier into any country in pursuit of the aggressors in order to inflict punishment on them and then withdraw from that country's territory. Iran's frequent representations to the British Government eventually resulted in the British Foreign Secretary, Lord John Russell, writing on the 5th of November 1863 the important despatch, agreeing with Iran to assert her right in Sistan by force of arms. Lord Russell's letter stated:

I have the honour to acquaint your excellency, in reply, that Her Majesty's Government, being informed that the title to the territory of Seistan is disputed between Persia and Afghanistan, must decline to interfere in the matter, and must leave it to both parties to make good their possession by force of arms. (18)

Though this despatch was in keeping with article 7 of 1857 Anglo-Iranian treaty of peace, the Iranians did not take it as a 'permission' for immediate action. The Iranian Foreign Ministry, in fact, informed Mr. Eastwick of the British Legation at Tehran that 'the Iranian Government had decided upon sending Mohammad Kord-Bacheh to Sistan, where he had formerly been employed, but Iranian troops would not enter that province unless an aggressive movement were directed against it by the Afghans' (19). This aggressive movement came in October 1865, but in a different form. Ahmad Khan, Governor of Lash-Jowain of Sistan, who had been for years a self declared subject of Iran and in receipt of salary from the Iranian Government, was persuaded by the Afghan Amir Shir Ali Khan to join him. Ahmad Khan married the daughter of Shir Ali and arranged submission to him, not only of himself but also of the dominion under his governorship. A similar intrigue resulted in Ebrahim Khan, another chief of Sistan to act similarly and to take his quarter of Sistan over to Shir Ali Khan (20).

Loss of vast portions of Sistan in this manner forced the Iranian Government to resort to military operations in order to enforce the above named chiefs' dismissal and to recover territories transferred by them to the Afghans. This military operation, the Iranians argued was sanctioned by the British Foreign Secretary's despatch of 5th November 1863 in accordance with article 7 of 1857 treaty of peace. Amir Alam Khan III Heshmat al-Molk, the Khozeimeh Amir of Qaenat was empowered to advance on Sistan at the head of a cavalry and infantry regiment with two guns, where he was joined by four more regiments and four guns from Sistan (21). Amir Alam Khan was put in charge of all forces in Sistan in June 1866 and was given the governorship of Sistan in addition to his own hereditary amirdom of Qaenat. His first task was to deal with Ahmad Khan the Governor of Lash-Jowain who had sold out himself and the dominion he was entrusted to the Afghan Amir. Ahmad Khan and others of lesser note were arrested and deported to Tehran (22) where he remained for some years before his return to Sistan. Amir Alam Khan had also attacked Ebrahim Khan, another chief in Sistan who had also sold out to the Afghans. The Amir of Qaenat and Sistan recovered Jahan-Abad, Jalal-Abad, and Fort Nade Ali. Ebrahim Khan appealed to the Afghan authorities for assistance, but his application was turned down. Amir Alam Khan put some of his men in charge of Fort Nade Ali and returned to his headquarters at Naser-Abad (now Zabol) on the western side of the Hirmand River. He received from Naser ad-Din Shah the titles 'Heshmat al-Molk' and 'Amir Tuman', which signified the Shah's pleasure with his success in repelling aggression against Sistan.

Frustrated by the Afghan Chief's lack of enthusiasm in defending him, Ebrahim Khan turned to the British for assistance, but to no avail.

Goldsmid's Arbitration of Sistan Boundaries

The Afghan Amir Shir Ali Khan formally asked the British in 1870 to intervene on behalf of his Government in Sistan (23). British authorities in India contacted the Iranian Government offering arbitration between the two neighbours in accordance with article 6 of the Paris treaty of Peace of 1857 (24). The Iranians accepted the offer on the condition that a British commissioner should go to Tehran and proceed from there to Sistan in company of the Iranian Commissioner. They were to inspect current Iranian possessions in Sistan and to bring the maps conjointly to Tehran, which after being laid before the Shah, would be communicated to the British Government. The British would then in friendship and according to the first basis entered upon between the Iranian Foreign Ministry and British Legation in Tehran, in conformity with Earl Russell's letter and the memorandum sent to the Legation, amongst which was the one dated the 19th April, define the boundaries of Iranian possessions in Sistan, and also of that portion which the Iranian Government had not yet endeavoured to obtain possession of according to its natural sense of justice (25).

These conditions were received and acknowledged by the British in India (26). The arbitration Commission, led by Major General (later Sir) Frederick Goldsmid, was formed on 9th August 1870 on the instruction of the British principal Secretary of State for India (27). Goldsmid was joined by Mirza Masum Khan Ansari as Commissioner for Iran, and Seyyed Nour-Mohammad-Shah Khan Foshenji as Commissioner for Afghanistan. Shortly afterward the Afghan Amir requested a delay of approximately one-year for the boundary arbitration work to start in Sistan owing to the disturbances occurring in his country. As was described in the previous chapter, the arbitration Commission proceeded with the delimitation of Baluchistan boundary between Iran and Britain in the Makran and Kalat districts. This task was completed in September 1871, while General Goldsmid had been re-assigned in May to lead Sistan boundary arbitration commission (28). From the Iranian side, Mirza Masum Khan Ansari was also re-assigned as the Iranian Commissioner. Mirza Masum Khan and General Goldsmid were re-appointed to this task in spite of great difficulties had developed in their relationship during the Baluchistan boundary delimitation, which prevented cooperation between them.

Before any problem occurred between the two commissioners in their new assignment, a difficulty emerged resulting from the advance of an Afghan force towards Iranian territory in Sistan, seemingly to start war on Iran because the latter would not accept British arbitration. The British Minister at Tehran, being informed of the matter, wrote to the Viceroy of India asking him to induce the Afghan ruler to abstain from hostility (29). This was done satisfactorily (30). The reason for the Iranian Government's reluctance was that the British had proposed a few conditions in order to increase Goldsmid's authority in deciding where to go in Sistan, what to do, whom to see, and when to return. The Shah eventually acceded to these conditions in October 1871, and the British Minister at Tehran communicated the news to the Government of India (31). The arbitration commission, thus, assumed full legal status and was furnished with masses of literature on relevant correspondence and historical account of Sistan disputes, including H. L. Wynne's 75 pages of *History of Sistan and Lash Jowain,* which was prepared on July 6, 1870 for the Government of British India. These literatures bluntly favoured the Afghan claims on Sistan.

The British in India in the mean time pacified the Amir of Afghanistan in his military threats against Sistan and assigned Colonel (later General) F. R. Pollock to supervise the Afghan Commissioner during the arbitration proceedings. The Iranians questioned the purpose and the nature of this appointment as will be examined later. Moreover, the Iranian Commissioner began his suspicions of General Goldsmid's misguided approach towards Iran's rights to the sovereignty of Sistan began from the beginning of Baluchistan boundary arbitration a year earlier. A fierce correspondence started between the two commissioners as soon as the arbitration proceedings began in Sistan. The Iranian Commissioner, for instance, wrote to the British Commissioner on the 9th of February 1872 warning that the passage in arbitration agreement, which allows the arbitrator to visit any place he may deem expedient, does not mean that current Iranian possessions in Sistan should be again submitted to enquiry (32). To this, Goldsmid replied that regrettably he could not change the opinion he had already communicated to the Iranian Commissioner (33).

Not satisfied with this reply, Mirza Masum Khan raised the issue of Colonel Pollock's role in the arbitration task and wrote to Goldsmid stating:

> *I have again to request that you will be kind enough to inform me in what capacity and with what object Colonel Pollock accompanies the Afghan Commissioner?* (34). In an evasive reply Goldsmid wrote back stating: *the above mentioned gentleman, will on arrival, give me such assistance in the work of the mission as I may require from him.* (35)

General Goldsmid's description of Colonel Pollock's role in the arbitration process was not completely honest, especially when where he claimed that Pollock's mission was to aid him, whereas official documents had it that he was specifically assigned to supervise Afghan Commissioner. Despatch No. 1614 of the Government of India, for instance, specifies Pollock's mission as:

> *Carefully advise the Afghan Commissioner as to his proceedings, and without assuming a position of partiality, should see generally that the views of the Cabul Government, whom the Commissioner represents, are fully and fairly explained.* (36)

Colonel Pollock, accompanied by the Afghan Commissioner and a large escort, arrived in Sistan in early March 1872. The Iranian Commissioner protested against the presence of such a large number of local chiefs from Afghanistan accompanying Colonel Pollock and Afghan Commissioner on the Iranian soil. In a letter to Goldsmid, Mirza Masum Khan stated:

> *I have thought it necessary to ask you the reason for the presence of Sardar Ahmad Khan and Mardan Khan, and Dust Mohammad Khan and others, with such a following; and why they accompanied the Afghan Commissioner into Iranian territory, give me, please, speedy information on this matter.* (37)

Most of these individuals and the armed men were, as a result of this protest, returned to Afghanistan and though Amir Alam Khan III, the Khozeimeh Amir of Qaenat and Sistan received Colonel Pollock with due honour and respect, he refused to receive the Afghan Commissioner.

A further complication occurred regarding the arbitration team's flying of the Union Jack in front of their tents which gave rise to unpleasant rumour among local people and headaches for the Amir of Qaenat and Sistan. After a long argument the Iranian Commissioner found a solution in flying the flag above the tent to be suggested in a letter of explanation from Goldsmid to the Amir who could use it in explaining the position to his subjects. This letter was sent and the problem was solved.

The arbitration commission decided to visit not only the frontier areas, but also places within Iran's undisputed possessions. This decision caused more friction between Goldsmid and Mirza Masum who protested against Goldsmid's examination of areas in actual Iranian possession. Mirza Masum thus suspended his own mission in Sistan and returned to Tehran in the vain hope that the Iranian authorities would act on his protests against Goldsmid's proceedings in Sistan. In the absence of Mirza Masum the arbitration commission visited the Hirmand delta and other places in and around the province and interviewed many people. It arrived at the conclusion that the both the ancient and recent rights of the two sides must be taken into consideration, based on examining the actual possessions and documentary evidence produced by the two governments. The Afghan Commissioner handed over to Goldsmid a lengthy written statement of documentary evidence. Evidently, it did not matter to the arbitration commission that no such written statement was provided by the Iranian side as Mirza Masum had departed from Sistan.

Other determining factors taken into consideration were testimonials of the local chiefs and khans as to whom their loyalty would go to as their sovereign government. In order to determine the nature of claims of sovereignty over Sistan, the arbitrator concluded that Sistan was:

> *A province on the Eastern Frontier of Persia, which had become comprehended in Afghanistan on its first conversion into a consolidated monarchy by Ahmad Shah Durrani, but which, by a common process of intrigue and encroachment, had lapsed almost imperceptibly to her stronger neighbour on the west... Persia, on the other hand, laid claim to Sistan by virtue of a more ancient sovereignty than that of Ahmad Shah: and justified recent conquest and annexation, within its limits, as the mere assertion of dormant rights.* (38)

This conclusion is another example of attempt by British officers in India trying to establish a historical precedence for territorial claims of the newly established state or country of Afghanistan. If the interests of British India favouring Afghan claims were not known, it would not be easy to understand how the arbitrator could ignore at least three centuries of Iran's uninterrupted sovereignty of Sistan before it was occupied and annexed by the one-man kingdom of Ahmad Shah Durrani (1749-1772). Indeed it would have been difficult to understand as to how could he justify this annexation as culminating any right of sovereignty of Sistan for Afghanistan.

Ahmad Shah Durrani, as has been explained hitherto, occupied Sistan as well as Herat, Qandehar, and Baluchistan in the wake of Nader Shah's assassination in 1747 when Iran was leaderless. Moreover, the arbitrator ignored the fact that both Herat and Qandehar revived their traditional dependency on the Iranian Federation as autonomous principalities shortly after Ahmad Shah's death and the chiefs of Sistan and Baluchistan declared their allegiance to Iran at the same time. Should the arbitrator acknowledge these facts, he would not consider *"revival of Iran's traditional sovereignty in Sistan and Baluchistan"* as *"intrigue and encroachment"* in Sistan on the part of Iran. Strangely when defining the boundaries in Baluchistan a year earlier, the same arbitrator did not consider any right for Afghanistan in Baluchistan in spite of the fact that, like Sistan, parts of Baluchistan had also been conquered and annexed by Ahmad Shah Durrani in the wake of Nader Shah's assassination. When considering these historical facts Amir Alam Khan Khozeimeh's undertaking in recovering lands in Sistan transferred to Afghanistan by Sardars Ahmad Khan and Ebrahim Khan as a result of intrigues by Amir Shir Ali Khan of that country, could hardly amount to '*intrigue and encroachment*' on the part of Iran. Amir Alam Khan III entered Sistan on the order of the Shah of Iran, punished the two rebellious chiefs and recovered Iran's lost territories in Sistan. This whole process was in keeping with article 7 of the 1857 Anglo-Iranian peace treaty of Paris, and was sanctioned by British Government in the form of Lord Russell's despatch in this context.

The arbitrator, nevertheless, decided to examine the two countries' historical rights in Sistan on the basis of events of one hundred years preceding the arbitration date, which conveniently included the closing years of Ahmad Shah Durrani's career. This peculiar and arbitrary choice of historical background for determination of sovereignty rights in Sistan conveniently excluded at least twenty centuries of Iran's sovereignty in Sistan prior to Ahmad Shah's temporary kingdom of Afghanistan, including two centuries of Safavid's undisputed sovereignty. To fill the historical gap between Ahmad Shah's death in 1772, and Dust Mohammad Khan's conquest and annexation of Herat and Qandehar in 1861 and 1863, the arbitrator decided to consider the above named principalities as having been parts of "Afghanistan". By doing do, the arbitrator ignored the fact that Afghanistan did not exist between 1772 and 1863, and that the interim years the principalities of Herat and Qandehar had returned to their traditional status as dependencies of Iran. It is, thus, inconceivable as to how Sistan's dependence on either Herat or Qandehar in that interim period could culminate in '*historical rights of sovereignty*' for Afghanistan. Yet, the arbitrator evidently was not concerned. He conveniently assumed that if Sistani chiefs adhered, from time to time, to Herat and Qandehar principalities of Iran would culminate 'right of sovereignty', not for Iran, but for a country (Afghanistan) that did not exist in that interim period. He also conveniently assumed that recovering Sistan's breakaway territories did not amount to anything because no fighting was involved (39).

By so assuming, the arbitrator dismissed the recovery by military means of territories that had been taken into Afghan dominion by Ahmad Khan and Ebrahim Khan as constituting any right for Iran, arguing that it was done at a time when Afghanistan was leaderless. Here, once again the arbitrator shows that he was predisposed in favour of Afghanistan. Easily he ignored the fact that Amir Shir Ali Khan was the leader of Afghanistan. Albeit temporarily losing Kabul to his rebellious son, Shir Ali Khan was in so firm a position in Qandehar that he successfully intrigued with Sardars Ahmad Khan and Ebrahim Khan of Sistan to join him, an act which precipitated Iran's military action for the recovery of territories lost there. Furthermore, the arbitrator considered Ahmad Shah Durrani's temporary occupation of Sistan together with Herat and Qandehar (1749), when Iran was truly leaderless after Nader Shah's assassination, as culminating sovereign rights for Afghanistan, but Iran's recovery of its occupied territories in Sistan did not have the same effect in his eyes. The arbitrator eventually rejected Iran's historical rights altogether (40). He even rejected personal testimonies of allegiance to Iran by the local chiefs as representing the desire of the general public of Sistan (41).

The initial suspicion that Goldsmid intended to give all of Sistan to Afghanistan was proved to be true during the proceedings. Reporting to the Government of India, Goldsmid asserted:

> *Ameer of Kain has great power. Persian Commissioner plays his game and talks of Lord Russell's despatch, arguing that no present possession is to be discussed. Writes politely, but acts mischievously and in hostile spirit. Meanwhile much*

information obstructed and survey far advanced. I hurry completion to be prepared for contingencies. (42)

Based on this information, the Government of India decided that all of Sistan could not be given to Afghanistan and it should be partitioned. In a letter to Colonel Pollock adviser to the Afghan Commissioner, they asked:

Government gathers from papers received that the position is this – Persia holds chief parts of Sistan so firmly that arbitration opinion must be in favour of Persia, but that a boundary on Helmund (Afghan pronunciation of the term Hirmand) from Ameer of Kain's bund (43) upwards, might be secured and also a line of river onwards to lake. Can you confirm this as being the position? If so, would such boundary, though not giving all that is desired, satisfy sufficiently Afghan interests?…and would Ameer of Afghanistan probably be convinced that it is the best obtainable…(44)

The arbitrator thus decided to carve up the province into two sections, referred to them as 'Sistan proper' and 'outer Sistan'. He gave Afghanistan the larger portion and gave Iran the smaller part, and defined the main channel of river Hirmand on the easternmost part of the delta as the boundary between the two. This decision allocated much of Iran's actual possession such as Nad-e Ali, Qaleh Fath and much of the territories occupied by the Afghans in the preceding years, to the Afghan claimants. This was contradictory to the circumstances described by Goldsmid as leading him to believe that documents produced in support of Afghan claims did not convince him of any sovereignty rights for Afghanistan in Sistan (45).

Commenting on Goldsmid's arbitration awards in Sistan, Sir Percy Sykes believed that the arbitrator tried to work out an absolute justice that is to give little importance to historical evidence and to put more emphasis on the actual possessions. He asserts: *"the arbitrator had to decided, not so much as to claims – both of Afghans and Persians having laid the district under tribute at various periods – but as to the actual status quo"* (46). Yet, when considering the actual status quo, the arbitrator decided to ignore a number of actual Iranian possessions. Amir Alam Khan III Khozeimeh's actual possessions at Nad Ali and Qaleh Fath and their dependencies on the left bank of Hirmand River, for instance, were ignored. Similarly a number of actual possession of the Sanjarani and Nahruei Baluchi tribes of Iran on the left bank of Hirmand were ignored (47). Not only did Goldsmid's award fail to satisfy the local chiefs whose lands were given to a foreign government, but also proved to be unpopular with the local inhabitants as well as the injustice that the Iranian Government considered to have occurred to her rights in Sistan. By putting the boundary on the main branch of Hirmand River in the delta region, Goldsmid put 'Sistan proper' at the mercy of the Afghans who could easily deprive the more fertile part of the province of its water supplies from that river. This proved to be the case in the subsequent periods.

The Iranian commissioner, Mirza Masum Khan, evidently endeavoured to prevent the partitioning of Sistan by creating as much inconvenience for the arbitration process as was possible. In his book *'Eastern Persia'* General Goldsmid complains extensively of Mirza Masum Khan's behaviour towards the British arbitration commission. Sir Percy Sykes goes further in accusing the Iranian Commissioner of being *"only anxious to make money, he saw that by fostering this mistaken idea he could advance his private interests"* (48).

It is noteworthy that not only was not Mirza Masum Khan accused of such intentions in any other documents that this author has examined, but there are indications that the opposite might have been true. Letters from Amir Alam Khan III, Heshmat al-Molk's sons Amir Ali-Akbar Khan and Amir Esmail Khan Khozeimeh to the Shah in 1903 indicate that British Arbitration Commission attempted to buy their father's consent by offers of bribes (49).

Sir Percy Sykes did not stop at accusing Mirza Masum Khan of trying to make money by confronting British arbitrator in his conduct of arbitration proceedings, but also accused Amir Alam Khan III of 'ignorance' and 'jealousy' because of lack of cooperation that the arbitrator expected from him. Even Goldsmid did not accuse the Amir of ignorance and jealousy in that proceeding. In fact his account of the role of Amir Alam Khan III, Khozeimeh Amir of Qaenat and Sistan was much more realistic than that of Sir Percy Sykes. Describing a governor's endeavour in preventing eastern half of his dominion from being given to a neighbouring country, as resulting from his 'ignorance' and 'jealousy' can hardly constitute for a fair and impartial observation of events. Not only did the Amir's efforts fail to prevent eastern Sistan from falling to the Afghans, but also many of his personal lands and villages on the left bank of Hirmand were given to them. This was done despite the fact that the arbitrator had confirmed that *"Outer Sistan, on the other hand...is in possession of Baluchi chiefs who profess to acknowledge Persian sovereignty, or disclaim allegiance to any sovereignty power but Afghanistan"* (50).

General Goldsmid's arbitral award of 19th August 1872 was, however, submitted to the two governments of Iran and Afghanistan. This award delimited the Sistan boundary in the following manner:

From Siah Kuh, near Bandan, which is the beginning of the Qaenat district a line to be drawn to the southern limit of the Neizar towards Lash-Jowein. Thence the line continues to a point named Shahi, which is the end of Hirmand's main waterbed.

1- From Shahi the boundary takes a more northwest to southeast direction to Korki.
2- From Korki the boundary follows Hirmand River's main channel upstream as ar as Kuhak.
3- From Kuhak the boundary takes a north-east to south-west direction in a straight line across desert as far as Kuh-e Malek Siah, the highest peak of which is the beginning of Baluchistan and the dividing point of Iran- (Pakistan)-Afghanistan boundaries.

The map prepared by the engineers of the Arbitration Commission showed inaccuracy in tracing the boundary line, especially in areas northeast of Mian Kangi and southeast of Lash-Jowein. This inaccurate map caused many disputes later and was used by the Afghans to justify their encroachments in the Iranian side of the river.

General Goldsmid, however, entered Tehran on 4th June 1872. For reasons unknown, once again Mirza Masum Khan, The Iranian Commissioner, was absent in Tehran. Having left Sistan in protest of Goldsmid's arbitration proceedings, he disappeared from the scene. In Tehran, famous Iranian diplomat Mirza Malkam Khan Nezam ad-Doleh replaced him as Iranian Commissioner. He and Goldsmid met twice in Tehran in the presence of the Afghan Commissioner, discussing the terms of the award (51). Commissioners for Iran and Afghanistan raised a number of objections to various aspects of the award, the most significant which came from the Iranian Commissioner concerning the two neighbours' rights to the Hirmand water in delta region.

In their appeal against this award, the Iranian Government contended, inter alia, that the Iranian Sistan could not live without adequate control of Hirmand, up to Rudbar. This was a statement of fact, which has been attested to by the passage of more than 130 years. The tripartite meeting of the commissioners in Tehran however, was mostly dominated by questions and answers on the Iranian Commissioner's reassertion of Iran's claims to the whole of Sistan.

As the parties concerned could not agree, the arbitration opinion was referred to Lord Granville, British Secretary of State for Foreign Affairs for adjudication. He over-ruled all objections raised by the two sides and confirmed Goldsmid's arbitration in its entirety on 7th March 1873, which was communicated to both governments of Iran and Afghanistan who subsequently ratified it.

The Afghans did not raise any objection to Goldsmid's water award, but took issue with British interpretation of clause 4 of the award. They were satisfied by the British Foreign Secretary's decision in allowing them to minimize supply of water to Sistan, and permitted the Afghans to repair the old canals as well as constructing new ones. The Foreign Secretary made his decision permanent.

The way this award was compiled and the manner in which it was accepted by the Iranian Government was in complete contradiction of the condition laid down by the same Government when agreeing to the Afghan-British request for delimitation of the Sistan boundary and Goldsmid's boundary arbitration.

Hirmand's Hydropolitics and McMahon's Water Award

Rising in the Baba mountains of northwest of Kabul, Hirmand river flows through the length of Afghanistan for most of its course, but before emptying into the Lake Hamun it forms the boundary between Iran and Afghanistan for about 40 to 50 miles (52).

The name of the river is an ancient Persian adjective: a combination of the two words '*hir*' meaning 'water' in pre-Islamic Persian, and the common suffix '*mand*' which implies abounding in. The combination, thus, means '*the river of abundant water*'. Similar descriptive adjectives exist in modern Persian such as '*honarmand*' which means a person of abundant artistic talent. The name 'Hirmand' appears in this form in all Persian and Arabic works of geography and history of the post-Islamic centuries. Referring to the city of Bost in Afghanistan, Maqdasi (53) states that the city and fortress, surrounding by great suburbs, stood one league above the junction of the river Khardaryu (54) (modern Arghandab) with the Hirmand (55). It is for unknown reason, however, that the British travellers and recorders of local geography in the 19th century adopted the term 'Helmand' or 'Helmund', a corruption of the actual name, used locally in Afghanistan.

Flowing for about 650 miles in a northeast to south-westerly direction, Hirmand enters the Iranian border area at Kuhak. Its drainage system includes most of the central and southern Afghanistan. It carries a great deal more water in its upper section and its width at Zamin Davar (end of mountain areas and beginning of Afghanistan's central plain) is little less than one kilometer in the spring and summer months, and is about 300 meters in the winter months (56). Little is known of the cycle of years of drought and high flood. Thus, Hirmand remains one of the most unpredictable rivers of the world (57).

The highest watermark left by the flood which can be traced around the lake Hamun is five feet above the level in 1903, the year of McMahon's Sistan water award. When the lake establishment this record the discharge of the Hirmand must have been not less than 200,000 cubic feet a second (58). In all probability the year that saw such an expansion of the lake area was 1885. This flood prepared the ground for the change of Hirmand's course in the delta region from the old channel to Rud-e Parian, which was completed by another high flood in 1895/6 (59).

The latest reported flood of some consequence took place in April 1991 after many years of law water and droughts, which caused extensive damage in Sistan. This cycle of high flood was followed by a new cycle of drought which is going on at present (2002) and Hirmand has not brought any water to Sistan since the year 2000.

The question of allocation of utilization of Hirmand water in the delta has always been the most important aspect of border disputes between Iran and Afghanistan in Sistan. Though the actual location of the boundary has long been accepted by both states, disputes concerning allocation and other reparian rights have not as yet been resolved. This is in spite of several attempts in the past 130 years to settle these disputes. The original problem was that the Amir of Afghanistan considered the Hirmand as an internal river of his country, reserving for Afghanistan the right to utilize its water in whatever way she wished. McMahon's Memorandum of 25 September 1904 asserts that: the Afghan Government do not admit that there is any water question in dispute, as their geographical position makes them sole owners of the whole of Hirmand above the Band-e Sistan (60).

By harbouring such consideration, the Afghan Amir, not only ignored the rights of the people of downstream Hirmand whose life depended solely on the water supplies from that river, but also ignored international trends towards recognizing status of rivers passing through more than one country as 'international rivers'. This trend began with rights on the river Elbe (61) and evolved through a number of treaties and agreements concluded between two or more reparian nations (62), embodying, by late 19th century, the internationally accepted description of international rivers which can be summarized as follows:

1- crossing the territories of two or more countries;
2- dividing two or more countries' territories,
3- being of economic consequence to two or more nation (63).

River Hirmand 'crossing Afghan territory into Iranian Sistan, and separating Iran from Afghanistan in Sistan, and being of vital economic consequence to both Iran and Afghanistan', is undoubtedly an international river in the downstream sections where neither Iran nor Afghanistan should claim exclusive rights. In fact the arbitral award of 1905 and subsequent agreements recognize the status of the international river for Hirmand downstream effectively from band-e Kamal Khan in southwest Afghanistan.

McMahon's Sistan Boundaries & Hirmand Water Award

Not only did not Goldsmid's Sistan boundary award of 1872 settle border disputes between Iran and Afghanistan, but also added the causes of frictions. Goldsmid's boundary award was followed by further disputes between the two neighbours on the Sistan section of their mutual boundaries. Recurrence of disputes was caused as a result of changes in the course of Hirmand River in delta region, which began by an unusually large flood in 1896. While both Iran and Afghanistan were unhappy about Goldsmid's arbitral award of their mutual boundary of 1872, the new alteration in the course of the river added new dimensions to the old disputes.

In 1896 the Hirmand burst into a new main channel which was subsequently named Rud-e Parian. Afghanistan claimed that boundary line should also follow the changed main course of the river, thus leaving the district of Mian Kangi to the Afghan side of the frontiers. Iran rejected the suggestion and maintained that the boundary should be left where they were defined, that is along the old channel (Nade Ali channel) of the river and changes in geographical description of the locality should change the course of boundary lines. Ignoring Iran's argument, the Afghans occupied Mian Kangi, the fertile and valuable stretch of lands to the east of the new channel of Parian and to the west of the old channel. Furthermore, they constructed new dams and canals diverting much of the water from Hirmand to their side of Sistan. The Iranians complained to the British Minister at Tehran in July 1902 against Afghan encroachments in Sistan and requested their intervention to stop the Afghan territorial encroachment (64). The Indian Government undertook to remind the Iranians not to resort to force in the disputed frontier and proposed to remind the Iranians 'of their obligation under article (6 of 1857 Anglo-Persian peace treaty of Paris) to refer the dispute to the British Government (65).

The viceroy wrote to the Amir of Afghanistan asking him also to refer the dispute to the British Government in India for arbitration (66). In another letter in September 1902 to the British Foreign Secretary in London, the Government of India proposed that Major Henry McMahon should be appointed as the arbitrator of the 'disputed Sistan frontiers' (67). Both Iran and Afghanistan expressed to the British their lack of willingness in referring their frontier disputes to the arbitration of British Officers, which was ignored and McMahon's arbitration went ahead.

The Russian Dimension

The Iranians intimated to the British Minister at Tehran that the attitude of Russia was the real reason for Iran's lack of desire for British arbitration. Writing to the British Foreign Secretary, the Marquess of Lansdowne, British Minister at Tehran informed him what the Iranian Prime Minister had told him about Russian Minister asking the Shah to allow a Russian delegation to accompany the Iranian Commissioner and the Shah had not objected to the proposal. This the British could not accept (68) and their Minister at Tehran told the Iranian Prime Minister to remind the Russians of Iran's treaty obligations (69).

The idea of a Russian involvement in Sistan boundary arbitration was so irritating to the British that they went as far as threatening the Iranians that if they did not submit to McMahon's arbitration the Afghans would be allowed to interfere with water supply in Sistan. This development signified intensification in Anglo-Russian rivalries in the Great Game of geopolitics in the east at the turn of the 20th century. The British were convinced that the Russians viewed Sistan as the real key to India and/thus, attached great strategic significance to the position of Sistan vis-à-vis India. Their Consul for Sistan, Mr. Miller, the British thought, had become accordingly highly active in the region. An article appearing in the Russian paper 'Novoe Vremya' on January 2, 1903 fueled British suspicions of Russian objectives in Sistan. The article reads:

> *Sistan, by its geographical position and intrinsic nature, deserves, rather than Herat, the name of the 'key to India'. Sistan, that flank positions on the road to India, which it is impossible to turn. Were it in our hands the advance to India would be made far easier. In English hands, all our operations are rendered considerably more difficult. Lord Curzon had a keen appreciation of the extreme importance of Sistan, and he is therefore striving to place it as quickly as possible under British influence. The railway from Quetta to Nushgki, i.e. towards Sistan, is already under construction. But the Indian Viceroy is not satisfied with this somewhat slow progress towards the object in view. He wishes to accelerate matters.*
>
> *What would Lord Curzon say if we despatched a mission, with a becoming escort to Qandehar? We have as much right to be disquieted by disputes between the Afghans and neighbouring tribes on the East of Afghanistan, as the English have by such disputes on the West of that country. (70)*

The author of this article felt so badly about British arbitration in Sistan without a Russian involvement that he proposed active undertakings to remedy the situation. The article stated:

> *What role will Major McMahon's mission play in Sistan, that of the representative of Afghan interests, or of a Court of arbitration? In any case we cannot sit as indifferent spectators of such a mission in Sistan. If the English are protecting Afghan interests, we must protect those of Persia. If the English desire to pose as mediators we ask, who requested their mediation? The disinterestedness of England in all affairs that concern her interests is sufficiently well-known. They will so delimitate the Perso-Afghan possessions, in dividing the waters of the Hirmand between the disputants, that in the end the whole of the southern course of the river will be in their own hands. (71)*

The Russian Minister at Tehran, in the meantime, informed the Iranian Prime Minister on 2nd January 1903 that the Russian delegate should be involved in the arbitration and Russia should be party to any settlement in Sistan (72). In a conversation with the British representative, the Prime Minister complained:

> *no political step could be taken by him without exposing himself to suspicious inquiries and interference on the part of either Russia or England. And that these two great powers, instead of discussing their rivalries with each other, always made Iran the victim of their mutual jealousies. (73)*

The size and strength of the armed escort accompanying Major McMahon was also a major cause of friction. The Kargozar of Sistan had informed the Iranian Government that, on the authority of the Indian press, Major McMahon was bringing with him to Sistan frontier areas an armed force of 800 men and artillery. The Iranian Foreign Minister wrote to the British Minister at Tehran in December 1902 protesting that McMahon's mission did not necessitate the presence of so large an armed body and gun (74). To this letter, the British Minister replied:

> *Major McMahon's escort consists of a single company of foot soldier and a troop of Sawars, which, as he has to move through a wild part of Afghanistan, can scarcely be deemed an excessive guard for the protection of an important diplomatic mission. (75)*

This reply did not convince Iranians Foreign Minister who wrote back expressing the desire for the abandonment of the proposed arbitration altogether (76). Clearly such a change of heart on the part of the Iranians came as a disappointment to the British who were adamant on going ahead with the boundary arbitration in Sistan and keeping the Russians out of it. Hence, in response to the Iranian foreign minister, the British minister at Tehran informed him on 7th January 1903 that the arbitration had to go ahead because his government preferred to adhere to the procedure prescribed by the treaty of 1857 rather than trust to chance that the rise of the river might prevent, once and for all, a recurrence of the difficulties (77). He further notified the Iranian Government that the British Government would not accede to the proposal of Russia being represented in the boundary arbitration (78). The British Government went a stage further by instructing McMahon to proceed with arbitration work whether the Iranians agree or not (79).

The Russian Ambassador, in the meantime, held a lengthy discussion with the British Foreign Office authorities during which he seems to have acknowledged satisfaction with the assurance given by the British authorities with regard to the strength of Colonel McMahon's escort. The Russians had apparently argued that the matter concerned Russia because they had agreements with the British on the maintenance of Iran's integrity and independence and that it was maintenance of Iran's integrity that concerned Russia in this matter. This argument was replied to by the British Foreign Office in a note that stated:

> *the British and Russian governments have, it is true, on more than one occasion agreed to respect the integrity of Persia, but it can, however, scarcely be contended that an arbitration for the purpose of settling a local dispute as to water rights can be regarded as affecting the general principle of the integrity of Persia.* (80)

The Russian Ambassador further declared that there was a considerable Afghan force concentrated near the Iranian frontier and that the Russian Government would not agree to any change in the boundary line laid down by British arbitration in 1872 (81). The explanations and assurances given to the Russians by the British authorities in London and by the Iranians in Tehran appear to have convinced the Russians to let the arbitration go ahead. The Iranian Prime Minister, in the meantime, informed the British Minister at Tehran in February 1903 that the Russians had abandoned the idea of their participation in the arbitration proceedings and decided to send an officer of their own, to watch proceedings independently (82).

The Arbitration Proceedings

These developments coincided with heavy rainfall in Sistan and the rise of Hirmand River, which increased tensions between the two sides. British Consul's confidential diary of Sistan for the period 1st to 15th December 1902 states:

> *Hirmand had risen considerably. Half the Sistan Band at Kohak had been carried away, and the Afghan Band at Shahgol, which had been one of the main causes of water difficulty, had also been demolished. A band constructed by the Sistanis just above the Poozeh Jang Jah channel was also carried away.*

The same diary reports that Akhund-Zadeh, Afghan Commissioner in McMahon's arbitration commission, had completed the long canal he had been engaged in digging from Kushk above the Sistan Band to Jaroki (83).

McMahon's arbitration commission was well established in Sistan by June 1903. He was assigned, in the meantime, to extend a telegraph line from India to Sistan and thence to Mashhad. The Russians decided to station their own military signalers at principal points of the telegraph line between Sistan and Mashhad. This decision made Colonel McMahon postpone work on extending the line (84).

Meanwhile the friction between the Iranians and the Afghans continued. The Afghans dug a canal in 1902 carrying off all the water of the Sikh-Sar channel of Hirmand River (northern continuation of Nad-e Ali or old main bed of the river) to cultivate the lands between Deh-e Yar Mohammad and Deh-e Hassan Kharut. Abdul-Hamid Khan Ghaffari Yamin Nezam, the Iranian Commissioner, contended that the dry channel of Sikh-Sar northwards into the Neizar, marks the main bed of the Hirmand laid down as boundary between Iran and Afghanistan by Goldsmid (85). The Afghan Commissioner Musa Khan (later replaced by Faqir Mohammad Akhund-Zadeh) contended that the old main bed of the river followed the dry channel then known as the Shileh Shamshiri and that therefore all land to the east of that is Afghan territory (86).

McMahon asserts in his report of 16th June 1903 that: undoubtedly the main bed of the Hirmand in past time did run in the Shileh Shamshiri (87). Having said this, he immediately asserted that there was reason to believe that at the time of Goldsmid's award the main bed followed the Sikh Sar channel. Deh Dust Mohammad and other important villages in the tract between Shileh Shamshiri and Sikh Sar channels were all of recent date within the previous 25 years or so, and were all Iranian. The Afghan villages on the east of the Sikh Sar were also, with the exception of Qaleh-e Kang, of recent date. Among the local people, Iranian and Afghan alike, the Sikh Sar appeared to have long been recognised as the boundary line (88).

Colonel McMahon's survey of the disputed lands made it clear that if Goldsmid's line was in the Sikh Sar channel, the Afghans were in occupation of Iran's cultivable lands between Deh-e Yar Mohammad and the Neizar. But if Goldsmid's line continued northwards to follow the edge of the Neizar, the Iranians were in occupation of Afghan lands in Neizar beyond its edge. To define a line between these lands McMahon found it admissible to search for neighbouring permanent landmarks instead of demarcation in a low-level tract liable to inundation. He, therefore, concluded that the boundary line should follow a line of prominent mounds 'tappeh' in a series of straight lines from Tappeh-e Kurki and then to the point Salgumi just north of Tappeh-e Shahi (89). The land around all these tappehs is sour salt soil of no value.

McMahon's above proposed line differed from that of Goldsmid's in areas between Deh-e Yar Mohammad, and Takht-e Shahi was to the disadvantage of Iran. Yet, having declared the proposed line as being more to Iran's advantage than Afghanistan (90), McMahon accused Yamin Nezam, the Iranian Commissioner, of being responsible for the anxieties of the Shah and the Iranian Government because of reporting to Tehran the incorrect assumption of sinister intentions on McMahon's part. As regards the Afghan attitude on this point, Colonel McMahon believed that protest would be made from Kabul against inclusion of Takht-e Shahi in Iranian territory. However, he thought that it would not be a strenuous protest because of Takht-e Shahi being an Iranian possession for a long period of time (91).

Meanwhile, conflict broke out between the Iranian Sistanis and Afghan subjects in the Neizar, which resulted in three Afghans being wounded and an Afghan horse being killed. The boundary arbitrator, being informed by the Afghans of the incident, wrote to the Iranian Commissioner proposing a line temporarily separating the actual possessions of the antagonists (92). This proposal was received by the Khozeimeh Amir of Sistan, Amir Ali-Akbar Khan Heshmat al-Molk II, with much suspicion. British Consul for Sistan suspected the Russian Consul of being behind it all. In his Consular diary of 9th July 1903 he states:

> (Amir Heshmat-al-Molk) *received the order very suspiciously, and informed me that Mr. Miller (the Russian Consul) had told him that the Viceroy had bargained with the Amir of Afghanistan that the British were to receive all lands south of the Hirmand from Afghanistan, and to give in exchange to Afghanistan a large slice of Sistan land. I disabused his mind of this notion by all the arguments at my command, but I fear he does not yet quite believe in our good faith. Another matter, which makes the Hashmat-al-Molk suspicious of, the English is that the Mostofi of Mashad informed him that they were backing up his enemy, Saeed Khan Nahrui.* (93) & (94)

The Sistanis in the mean time gathered in large number at the Band-e Sistan to restore it after being damaged by flooding in the spring of 1903. In his diary of 24th August 1903, Colonel McMahon remarks that there seemed to be a difference of opinion on the subject of between the Khozeimeh Amir and the Iranian Commissioner:

> *The latter do not want the band made while the mission is here…The Governor says, very wisely, that he and his people are not going to lose a season's water for anything the Mamur* [officer] *may think.* (95)

McMahon's proposed line of boundary differed noticeably from that of Goldsmid line at the northern continuation of Sikh Sar channel. The new line necessitated exchange of a few patches of land between the two sides in order to settle the differences resulting from the implementation of the new line. After some deliberation however, the Iranians accepted Colonel McMahon's proposed line.

Yamin Nezam, the Iranian Commissioner, who had been implicitly described by McMahon as being under the instruction of the Russian Consul (96), showed him confidential telegrams of the Iranian Foreign Ministry's report on the acceptance of the proposed line (97). Moreover, Yamin Nezam assured McMahon that his letter strongly advocated the new line, and attributed the indecision in Tehran to the Russian interference. He informed McMahon on the same day that he would carry out Tehran's instruction and could say to the Iranian Government that the proposed exchange will be advantageous to Iran.

Yamin Nezam's above recommendation was in clear contradiction of McMahon's own description of the lands to be exchanged. In the report of his proposed boundary line of 16th June 1903, McMahon described that lands occupied by Afghans and proposed for exchange, as being "*small tract of poor worthless land*" (98). He described the lands occupied by the Iranians and proposed for exchange, as being "*patches of poor cultivation in the Neizar*" (99). This was not true as the lands that Iran was to give up to the Afghans included some villages as well. Even British officials sensed that Yamin Nezam was suspected by the Iranian authorities of being bribed to support the proposed settlement. In his despatch of 24th October 1903 to the Foreign Office, British Minister at Theran states:

> *the attitude of the Iranian Government on this question is very foolish, and can only be explained by the supposition that their inveterate suspiciousness of our intentions in Sistan has led them to conjecture that Col. McMahon's proposal conceals some trap and that the Yamin's support of it is due to his having been bribed or talked over.* (100)

These were soon to be proved wrong by new revelations. An accountant at the Imperial (British) Bank branch in Sistan gave out information in March 1904 that 'Yamin Nezam had deposited 10,000 qarans with the bank, which he received from the boundary arbitration' (101). A further proof of falsehood of recommendation by Yamin Nezam to the Iranian Government that exchange of villages in question was in favour of Iran, came later in a letter to the Amir of Afghanistan by the Viceroy of India who pointed out ' from the Band-e Kohak to the Neizar the frontier follows practically the old bed of the Hirmand or Sikh Sar, but runs a little to the west of this in one place to include villages now in Afghan possession. These substantial advantages to the interests of Your Highness are qualified only by a slight concession which Col. McMahon has felt called upon to make in the direction of Takht I Siah to the Iranians' (102). In his letter of 24th October 1903 British Minister at Tehran informed British Foreign Office that the Iranian Government had made their acceptance of propose line and exchange on the condition that the Afghans engage not to construct any dam upon the upper Hirmand from Band-e Sistan to Rudbar (103). In his telegram of 12th September to Hardinge, McMahon rejected outright doing anything about preventing the Afghans from constructing bands on the Hirmand above Band-e Sistan. He argued that the question raised about Afghan bands above Sistan lies outside the jurisdiction of his arbitration tribunal, and he had strictly avoided any reference whatever to it in discussions with the Iranians (104). The table eventually was turned against Iran and Hardinge indeed succeeded in preventing the Iranians from continuing with these conditions. In a meeting with Iranian Foreign Minister, Moshir ad-Doleh, the British Minister at Tehran was told that following an interview that the latter had with the Shah, the Iranian Government withdrew these conditions. Instead, they only asked that the Afghans undertake not to destroy the existing Band-e Sistan without Iran's prior consent (105).

To secure the Afghans' agreement to his proposed line, Colonel McMahon decided to tell them bluntly but indirectly how wrong they were in relying confidently on the vague definition of Goldsmid's boundary line. In a despatch to Hardinge in Tehran, which was referred to the Foreign Office, McMahon noted success in doing so as well as stating that he discovered the Afghans did not possess copies of Goldsmid's award (106). This tactic seems to have secured Afghan Government's acceptance of his proposed line. The Iranian Government's unconditional acceptance of the particulars of McMahon's boundary line was telegraphed to him by the British Charge d' Affairs at Tehran on 1st November 1903. The Shah had, on 8th October asked the British through his Foreign Minister that he would like McMahon, after the delimitated line was agreed upon with Yamin Nezam north of Hirmand, to mark out the Irano-Afghan frontier line between Hirmand and Kuh-e Malek Siah so that doors should be closed to a recurrence of the controversies (107).

McMahon concluded his boundary arbitration award and communicated to the two countries' commissioners in November 1903 (108). This award stated:

> *The boundary line in Seistan between Afghanistan on the east and Persia on the west should run as follows, i.e., from the Malik Siah Koh in a straight line to the Band-I-Kohak and thence along the bed of the Helmand river to the junction of its two branches, the Rod-I-Pariun and Nad Ali channel. From here it should follow the bed of the Nad Ali channel into Sikhsar and along the bed of the Sikhsar to the point near Deh Yar Mohammad where the Sikhsar has been diverted towards the west in the water channel shown in the map which joins the Shela-i-Shamshiri near to Deh Hassan Kharat. The boundary line should follow the left bank of this water channel to the Shela-I-Shamshiri leaving Deh Hassan Kharot on the east. It should then run in a straight line separating the hamlets of Deh Ali Mardan on the west from Deh Ali Jangi on the east of Tappa-i-Tilai; thence in a straight line to the most western of the mounds of Tappa-I-Shaharak; then in a straight line to the most western of the mound of Tappa-I-Kurki; thence in straight line to Salgumi and thence in a straight line to Siah Koh, Bandan. (109)*

In separate letters to the Iranian and Afghan Commissioners, McMahon gave more details of various aspects of his boundary award.

In spite of being deprived of much of their possessions in the areas to the north of Sikh Sar channel and in the Neizar, the Iranian Government accepted McMahon's boundary award, but the Afghans complained and argued against it for nearly a year. The Amir of Afghanistan declared his acceptance of the award and stated his agreement to demarcation of this boundary in October 1904.

Colonel McMahon's boundary award was accompanied by a water award, which was issued on 25th September 1904 (110). In that he determined that Iran and Afghanistan should receive from Hirmand, below Band-e Kamal Khan, half the water each (111) regardless of the requisite consumption of the two sides, which have been naturally developed throughout the ages and regardless of the fact that Iranian Sistan was repeatedly acknowledged as being more extensively cultivated and in need of more water compared with the Afghan side of Sistan which was acknowledged by General Goldsmid to be generally barren. Moreover, for reasons unknown McMahon changed this decision later in his formal award by giving one third of Hirmand water to Iran and two third of it, from below Band-e Kamal Khan, to Afghanistan.

Colonel McMahon, however, completed his demarcation of the Sistan boundary in a few months time (112), and communicated to the Government of India on the 21st of February 1905, his report on the final settlement and demarcation of the boundary between Iran and Afghanistan in Sistan. Clauses 1 to 19 of this report deal with the historical background of the dispute and Goldsmid's arbitration. And clauses 20 to 43 explain the way he determined the Sistan boundary. McMahon had on the 1st of February 1905 communicated to the Iranian and Afghan Commissioners his report on the demarcation of this boundary.

McMahon's water award came as a great disappointment to the Iranian Government while his boundary award dismayed the Sistanis. In a letter to the editor of 'Trans-Caspian Review' of Russia, appearing on 19th March 1905, an unnamed Sistani remarked:

> *We beg to request you to have the following particulars printed in your esteemed journal, so that all of the lovers of their native country may know that we have complained, and do complain, about the question of the Sistan boundary delimitation, by which a large and valuable portion of the sacred Persian territory has been added to Afghan territory. But it is a matter of great regret that the high officials of the Government do not listen to our representations and complaints.*
>
> *Now, it is three years since that this English Arbitration Mission have come to Sistan, where they have pitched their camp on the banks of the Hirmand in Persian territory. When they arrived, they said that they would finish their work of arbitration, and that, please God, they would depart in two or three months. But now three years have passed, and yet they say the same, i.e., that they would depart in two or three months. At present they have replaced their tents by building regular houses and apartments. God knows when they will go!*
>
> *The thing to be wondered at is that this mission was appointed to arbitrate about the waters of the Hirmand. Gradually they began to say that the limits should be duly recognised and fixed. And before the poor people were aware of the matter, the British Mission suddenly fixed a boundary between Sistan and Afghanistan, and built up high and round pillars on the line, in such a way that cattle-owners, flock-owners and cultivators saw that all their pastures and 'Neizar', which specially belonged to the cattle-owners of Sistan, and cultivated*

and other lands, were transferred to Afghanistan. The wonder is that the high officials of the Persian Government had appointed a Commissioner for the frontier to look after it. But when this delimitation was effected, where was he, why did he not prevent them, or at least report actual facts and all the particulars to the high officials of the Government?

The mission from the beginning, up to the present, have been saying that no new changes would be made, but that the boundary line laid down about 32 years ago by General Goldsmid, between Iran and Afghanistan, would be renewed, as in most places it had become obliterated and was not clear.

The correspondent then gives some particulars of the boundary laid down by General Goldsmid, and states, "*Some of the lands, which by that delimitation belonged to Sistan, have now by this fresh boundary line passed to Afghanistan*" (113).

The author of this letter continued accusing the British of planning to take Sistan for themselves. An accusation much in the same fashion advocated by the Russians at the outset of McMahon's Sistan mission. These suspicions were encouraged by such extremist recommendations as that of Major Percy Sykes, British Consul for Kerman, who asserted:

As regards the Province of Kain, such is, I understand, not the case, but yet, my Lord, I am convinced that its possession by Russia would constitute a permanent menace to the Indian Empire. The buffer State of Afghanistan is apparently doomed to succumb, and as our minimum share of it would include the watershed, I would submit that we must not leave the flank of Western Afghanistan unprotected. (114)

Nearly a century had to go by to prove the idea that Russia intended to take possession of Qaenat to be unfounded, but the resultant McMahon water award proved to be a real menace to Iran and a devastating blow to the inhabitants of Sistan.

Hirmand Water Disputes in the 20th Century

Colonel McMahon concluded his mission by the 1st of July 1905, on which date he sent his report to the Government of India and received from them a congratulatory letter dated 15th July 1905 (115), whereas Sistan's population continued voicing their disappointment with the outcome of his arbitration.

The Times of London featured a long report on McMahon's arbitration proceeding, praising him for the work (116). Not only were the Times of London wrong in stating that the water award had been decided on existing rights and practices, but it was wrong in stating that the award had been decided in May 1905. This author has not come across any evidence, among Persian and English documents, suggesting Iran's final acceptance of McMahon's waters award.

Disputes on the water distribution from Hirmand continued however. By 1930s Reza Shah Pahlavi had established a strong central authority in Iran, and he began fresh attempts to settle the Sistan water dispute through direct negotiations with Mohammad Nader Shah's consolidated monarchy in Afghanistan. The first attempt to enter in negotiations with the Afghans took place in 1930. The two countries decided to send their negotiating teams to Sistan where negotiations could be conducted on the site of the dispute. Iran's mission was led by Amir Mohammad Ebrahim Khan Shokat al-Molk II, the Khozeimeh Amir of Qaenat and Sistan who had by then assumed the surname 'Alam'. His appointment was obviously prompted by his vast knowledge of the problem and his deep interest in the matter. The Afghan mission was led by Abd al-Ahad Khan, Speaker of Afghan Majlis (117).

The two delegations met at Deh-e Mohammad in Sistan and continued the discussions for two months. When the Afghan mission referred to the arbitration of Goldsmid and McMahon, the Amir said we are not prepared to base our talks on foreign arbitration, which had never been officially endorsed. Moreover, those missions were not for the settlement of differences, but to create more cause for disputes between two brothers in religion. Thus, it is not to the interest of either side to negotiate on that arbitral mission (118). The Amir, therefore, succeeded in opening up fresh possibilities in the Iran-Afghanistan negotiations on Hirmand water distribution. He demanded for the water supplies in the delta region to be distributed between the two countries on the equal basis, each side receiving half of the water flowing down from Band-e Kamal Khan downstream. The Afghans apparently accepted the principal of equal division of Hirmand water in the delta region, but they proposed for the division to take place from Nahr-e Shahi on the border between the two countries. Hence the two delegations failed to come to a final agreement on the issue of water division in Sistan.

Failure of this mission was immediately followed by eruption of new disputes between the two sides as Foreign and Diplomatic Department of the Government of India reported in November 1931 to the Foreign Office in London, outlining these newly erupted disputes (119).

An incident occurred in Sistan in 1938 involving nationals of the two countries, which brought the urgency of a settlement to the Hirmand water dispute to the attention of the Governments. Mohammad Nader Shah's friendly attitude towards Iran at this time made it possible for an amicable settlement to the disputes. An agreement of friendship was signed between the two countries in 1921. A second agreement signed on 31st October 1927 provided for the direct diplomatic settlement of disputes between the two states. A protocol attached to this agreement stated:

> *Taking into consideration Article six of treaty of friendship between the Governments of Iran and Afghanistan, the two contracting parties have agreed to the method of appealing for arbitration that, in the event of differences occurring between the two parties, if settlement was not achieved through political means, each side will select an important personality of their country with full authority, and if agreement was not achieved by them, they will jointly select an important personality from a third country and the opinion of the third party arbitrator will be final and binding.* Dated sixth of Azar of 1306 (31 October 1927). (120)

It was on the strength of this treaty that Turkish arbitration was requested by the two countries to settle their disputed land boundaries in areas of Musa Abad, Yazdan, Namakzar and Qaenat regions in 1935 (see previous chapter).

As for Hirmand water disputes, what affected a new treaty was the commencement of a new diplomatic movement in the region involving all neighbours of Iran except Russia (Soviet Union) and Britain (British India). Both these two supper-powers made their disapproval of Reza Shah's new diplomatic initiative known to all, and later (during World War II) send him into exile. Reza Shah's new diplomatic move included the signing of a regional pact between Iran, Afghanistan, Turkey and Iraq at Sad-Abad Palace of Tehran in 1937 which gave implicit recognition to the existing border arrangements among the participating states. It was on the strength of the new friendship and alliance that Iran and Afghanistan decided on a fresh attempt for settlement of Hirmand water dispute.

Mr. Baqer Kazemi, Iran's Ambassador to Afghanistan, was instructed to enter negotiations with the Government of Afghanistan. Negotiations between Kazemi and Afghan Foreign Minister, Mr. Ali Mohammad Khan, resulted in the conclusion of a new treaty between the two countries, which was signed on 26th January 1939, articles I and II of which recommended that:

- A- The Governments of Iran and Afghanistan agree to divide in equal shares all waters of the Hirmand River, which flows to band-e Kamal Khan (30 miles inside Afghan territory), between Iran and Afghanistan.
- B- In order not to use more water then what is taken now between Deh-e Chahar Borjak and Band-e Kamal Khan, the Government of Afghanistan engages not to construct any other stream in the said distance and even not to repair any of the existing ones (121).

This agreement, though a significant improvement on McMahon's incomprehensible water award, at least from the Iranian point of view, also failed to put an end to the disputes. Notwithstanding the fact that the 1939 treaty was in line with the accepted international standards concerning international rivers, it failed in effect not because of geographical reasons but because of political sensitivities. The Hirmand has not changed its course in the delta region since 1939, but the prevailing atmosphere of distrust and lack of goodwill have prevented genuine efforts for solving the disputes. This agreement was not enforced because the Afghans declined to ratify it, arguing that the Iranian Government should undertake, in a separate official communiqué, ratified by Iranian Majlis, to make no objection to Afghanistan's complete freedom of interference in the Hirmand water above Band-e Kamal Khan (122).

Within eight years, between 1949 and 1957, and with the help of the Americans, the Abgardan Boghra dam was built at Girishk, the Boghra Canal was constructed in 70 kilometers with a capacity of 2800 cubic feet per second, and the Kajaki reservoir dam was constructed with a capacity of 1.5 million cubic feet. Furthermore, the Arghandab dam was built on the Arghandab branch. Also the Hoghian Kamaraq, Akhtechi, Gohargan, Juy-e No, Archi Sarvi, and a number of other canals were constructed with disastrous consequence for Sistan (123). Iran's expression of dissatisfaction with these attempts for diverting Hirmand water before reaching Sistan made little difference to the situation. Prior to these developments, as Afghanistan continuously failed to reply to Iran's suggestions for settlement of the problem, the Iranian Government instructed their permanent representative at the United Nations in 1947 to refer the case of the UN Security Council. Before Iranian representation was made to the Council, the US Government intervened and their Ambassador in Tehran, George Allen was instructed to persuade the Iranians to continue negotiations with the Afghans in Washington. The Government of Iran agreed to this course of action and all parties decided to allow an impartial commission to study the amount of water, the size of cultivable lands on both sides of the border river and the water needs of each side, before serious negotiations took place. As a result of this decision a commission was formed of three international water experts from impartial countries, all from the American continent. These were:

1- Mr. F. F. Domingez, a water expert and a university professor from Chile;
2- Mr. Robert L. Lowry, a water expert from the United States and;
3- Mr. Chritopher E. Webb, a water expert from Canada (124).

Having completed their investigation in Afghanistan, the commission continued investigation of the relevant water and agricultural situations in the Iranian Sistan in 1948. Iran's then Deputy Minister of Agriculture, Amir Hussein Khan Khozeime Alam hosted and guided the Commission inside Iranian. He told this author on 10 April 1991 that the Commission inspected relevant district on either side of the river and came up with the incomprehensible recommendation that Iranian Sistan should receive at least 22 cubic meters per second of the Hirmand water.

Though this amount per second of Hirmand was less than the amount determined by McMahon in 1905, the Afghans decline to accept it. The Iranian Government eventually succeeded in obtaining Afghanistan's consent to a new round of talks on the question of Sistan water on the basis recommendations of this Commission. The two Governments, therefore, decided on conducting their own direct negotiations in the United States. Amir Hussein Khan Khozeime Alam headed the Iranian delegation, which included also Mr. Ghodratollah Tashakkori and Mr. Soleimanpour as water engineers, Mr. Abd al-Ahad Dara, Mr. Mohammad Sarvari, and Dr. Mohammad Hassan Ganji. In Washington the delegation was joined by Dr. Ali Amini, Iranian Ambassador to the US who later served as Prime Minister in Iran. He acted as Iran's chief negotiator. The Afghan delegation was led by Mr. Ludin, Afghan Ambassador in Washington, and included Abd al-Majid Khan Zabuli, Dr. Tabibi and Mr. Reza as water engineers.

The summary of 'confidential' notes of the mission sent to this author by Professor Ganji indicates that the negotiations were doomed to fail from the beginning mainly because of the fact that the Afghans were not prepared to consider any quota of water for the Iranian Sistan above 22 meters per second (125). On 19th and 20th March 1959 direct negotiations were resumed between an Iranian delegation in Kabul and the Afghan Prime Minister Sardar Mohammad Davood Khan, who later staged a *coup d etat* against Afghan Monarchy and became Afghanistan's first President of republic. The Iranians put forward a series of proposals to the Afghans during these talks, none of which was accepted.

The Governments of Iran and Afghanistan eventually signed in Kabul on March 13 1973 a new agreement with two protocols about water division of Hirmand River. This treaty though ratified by the two Majlis with much difficulties, did not enter into effect because of the Afghan *coup d' etat* of that year.

Mr. Mahmud Foroughi Iran's Ambassador at Kabul between the latter years of 1960s and early years of 1970s (126), who was involved in the preparation for this treaty, provided this author with a report based on his personal notes of the process leading to the signing of the 1973 agreement. After explaining the result of his investigations in Afghanistan in this report, Mr. Foroughi added that *"negotiations with the Afghan Prime Minister in late 1966 resulted in his agreement to the proposed investment on joint projects to be implemented in the Afghan territory."*

The Iranian Government instructed Mr. Foroughi to proceed with the negotiation with the aim of settling the differences on the basis of acceptance by Iran of the 28 cubic meters quota with joint projects and investments for increasing Iran's share of the water in mind. These contacts continued for several years until Foroughi's duration of diplomatic mission in Afghanistan came to an end in 1971. He was sent back to Kabul by the order of the Shah less than a year later. He indicated in his confidential notes:

> *I was sent to Kabul at the head of a delegation for a temporary mission in Shahrivar of 1351 (August-September 1972). I resumed negotiations there. This time the basis of negotiations was the quota of 26 cubic meters per second. But according to a table prepared by the Ministry of water and power of Iran, additional quota of water would be purchased annually in a separate agreement to be signed with the Afghans.*
>
> *Agreements between United States and Canada, between United States and*

> *Mexico and agreements between some states of the United States on the rivers flowing from one county to another and ways of purchasing water were studied... The final draft on the measurements of the water was prepared.* (127)

Foroughi's advice to the Iranian Government was that if Iran wanted to sign a treaty with Afghanistan on the basis of 26 cubic meters quota per second, it would only be worthwhile if it allowed joint ventures along the river for water management. On the joint project and investments, he pointed out:

> *The experts of the two countries had concluded that 'the Musa Qaleh branch of Hirmand was the most suitable site for the construction of the intended dam. In an amateurish sketch that I have attached, the approximate positions of the rivers joining Hirmand are shown* (see sketch MI 19).

In an earlier correspondence Mr. Foroughi wrote to this author:

> *After a few months His majesty instructed me to go back to Kabul accompanied by a delegation to resume efforts aimed at settlement of Hirmand problem. There eventually we agreed that the new agreement should be first ratified by the Afghan Majlis and signed by the King, then the treaty of water purchase should be signed and the whole package to be presented to the Iranian Houses of the Majlis and the Senate for ratification, to be signed finally by the Shah.*
>
> *The remaining task still to be sorted out was the method of measuring Hirmand water. A few days (after Mr. Foroughi's return to Iran), Prime Minister Amir Abbas Hoveida informed me that Mr. (Safi) Asfia, Deputy Premier was to go to Kabul accompanied by a delegation. I apologized for not being able to go too...but learnt that treaties were signed and ratified by the Iranian Parliament with no news of water purchasing agreement.*

The treaty of 1973 was a complex text, which included 22 cubic meters per second as Iran's share of Hirmand water, plus 2 meters per second of water purchased from the Afghans by Iran, and another 2 cubic meter per second that Mohammad Zaher Shah of Afghanistan presented to Mohammad Reza Shah of Iran as his gift to Iran. Ratification of the 1973 treaty met stiff opposition in both countries' parliaments. One of the vociferous opponents of this treaty was the then Senator Amir Hussein Khan Khozeime Alam who told this author in an interview on Wednesday 10th April 1991:

> *My opposition was motivated by two aspects of the treaty; firstly the treaty on the whole denied Iran of her ancient rights to half of the Hirmand water reaching Iranian borders, and: secondly, it recognised all dams and bands and canals that the Afghans had constructed above and below Band-e Kamal Khan contrary to the terms of 1939 treaty and contrary to the previous arbitral opinions concerning the same.*

Notes and References

1- *Persian Frontiers*, a document prepared for the Government of British India, No. RRX/7/I, FO 371/40219, P. 10.
2- From Colonel Taylor to Lord Conning, dated 2nd February 1858, repeated in H. L. Wynne's account of *History of Sistan and Lash Jowain*, FO 60/386, P. 18.
3- H. Leopoer Wynne's account of the *History of Sistan and Lash-Jowain*, prepared for the British Indian Government, dated July 6, 1870, FO 60/386, P. 20.
4- Ibid.
5- Ibid.
6- Ibid., P. 21.
7- *Persian Frontiers*, op. cit., P. 10.
8- H. L. Wynne, op. cit., P. 22.
9- H. L. Wynne, op. cit., P. 231.
10- Ibid., P. 22.
11- From Mr. Alison, Her Britannic Majesty's Minister at Tehran to Lord Clarendon, dated May 20th 1861, repeated in Wynne's report on Sistan, FO 60/386, P. 25 of 227.
12- Confidential Diary of Kabul, repeated in the *History of Sistan and Lash Jowein*, dated 28th April 1861, FO 60/386, P. 25 of 227.
13- From India to the Foreign Office, dated 11th August 1862, repeated in the *History of Sistan and Lash Jowein*, op. cit., P. 36-7.
14- From India Office to the Foreign Office, op. cit., P. 37.
15- H. L. Wynne, *History of Sistan and Lash-Jowain*, op. cit., PP. 37-8.
16- From Mr. Thomson to the Government of India, dated 8th July 1863, repeated in Wynne's *History of Sistan…*, op. cit., P. 33 of 231.
17- Article 7 of the Anglo-Iranian peace treaty of 1857, op. cit., PP. 8-9.
18- Despatch from Lord Russell to Mirza Saeed Khan, dated London 5th November 1863, repeated in Wynne's *History of Sistan…*, op. cit., P. 39.
19- Extract of letter from Mr. Eastwick to the Indian Government, dated Tehran 28th January 1864, repeated in Wynne's *History of Sistan…*, op. cit., P. 41.
20- From Mashhad Agent to the British Legation at Tehran, dated 28th October 1865, repeated in Wynne's *History of Sistan…*, op cit., P. 43.
21- From Mr. Alison to lord Clarendon, dated 10th January 1866, repeated in Wynne's *History of Sistan…*, op. cit., P. 43.
22- From Sir H. Green to the Government of India, dated 13th November 1867, as repeated in Wynne's *History of Sistan…*, op. cit., P. 46.
23- From Colonel F. R. Pollock to the Secretary to the Indian Government, dated Peshawar 17th June 1870, FO 60/386, P. 206.
24- From Secretary to the Government of India to Secretary to the Government of Punjab, dated Simla 8th September 1870, No. 1613, FO 60/386, P. 382.
25- Extract of Mirza Saeed Khan's memorandum of 24th July 1870, enclosure in Mr. Alison's despatch to the Earl of Granville, No. 38, dated 25th July 1870, FO 60/386, P. 431.
26- Telegram No. 1963p from the Viceroy to Alison, dated Simla the 16th September 1871, FO 60/390, P. 188, enclosure No. 24.
27- F. J. Goldsmid, *Eastern Persia*, Vol. I, London 1876, P. xiv.

28- From Indian Government to Goldsmid, dated 16th May 1871, No. 905p, FO 60/388, P. 2.
29- Telegram from Mr. Alison to the Viceroy of India, dated 12th October 1871, FO 60/390, enclosure No. 30.
30- From the Viceroy to Mr. Alison, dated Simla the 15th October 1871, No. 2217p, enclosure 31, FO 60/390, P. 6.
31- From Mr. Alison to the Viceroy of India, dated Tehran 23rd October 1871, FO 60/390-169256, enclosure 35, P. 7.
32- From the Persian Commissioner, Nasirabad, 9th February = 28th Zulkhadeh, enclosure No. 22, FO 60/392, PP. 26-7.
33- From General Goldsmid, Nasirabad, 9th February = 28th Zulkhadeh, enclosure No. 22, FO 60/392, PP. 26-71.
34- From the Persian Commissioner, Nasirabad, 9th February = 28th Zulkhadeh, enclosure 23, FO 60/392, P. 27.
35- From General Goldsmid, Nasirabad, 10th February = 29the Zulkhadeh, enclosure 25, FO 60/392, P. 27 of 73.
36- Extract of clause 5 of despatch No. 1614 of Aitchison to the Secretary to the Indian Government of Punjab, dated Simla, 8. 9. 1870, FO 60/392, P. 383.
37- Extract of Mirza Masum Khan's letter in C. U. Aitchison, Secretary to the Indian Government to the Secretary of the Government of Punjab, dated Simla 8th September 1870, No. 1614, FO 60/386, P. 383.
38- General Sir Frederick Goldsmid, *Eastern Persia*, London 1876, P. xiii.
39- Goldsmid, op. cit., PP. 411-12.
40- Goldsmid, op. cit., P. 407.
41- Ibid.
42- Telegram from General Goldsmid through Henjam to Foreign Secretary, Calcutta, dated 12th April 1872, FO 60/392.
43- Referring to Band-e Sistan dam.
44- Telegram from the Foreign Secretary of India Government to General Pollock, dated 27th April 1872, No. 1042p, FO 60/392.
45- Goldsmid, *Eastern Persia*, op. cit., P. 405.
46- Sir Percy Sykes, *Ten Thousand Miles in Persia*, London 1902, P. 368.
47- Goldsmid, *Eastern Persia*, P. 409.
48- Sykes, op cit., P. 368.
49- See letter by Amir Ali-Akbar Khan Khozeimeh to his agent in Tehran, dated 26th Zihajeh (26th March 1903), and letter by Amir Esmail Khan Khozeimeh to his agent, dated 18th Moharram 1321 (17th April 1903), enclosed in despatch No. 56, from A. Hardinge to the Marquis of Lansdowne, dated 30th April 1903, FO 60/711. Both letters were addressed and delivered to the Shah.
50- Goldsmid, *Eastern Persia*, op. cit., P. 267-8.
51- *Ketabcheh-e Tahdid-e Sistan = The notebook of Sistan boundary delimitation*, as appeared in monthly 'Farhang-e Iran Zamin', Vol. 28, Tehran 1990, PP. 301-315.
52- Donald N. Wilber ed., *Afghanistan*, Human Relations Area File, 1956, P. 24.
53- Maqdasi, Maruf be al-Beshari, is a fourth century A.H. Arab Geographer.
54- Khardarya is the correct version of the name.
55- Guy Le-Strange, *The Lands of Eastern Caliphate*, London 1966, P. 345.
56- Mohammad Ali Mokhber, *Marzhay-e Iran = The Boundaries of Iran*, Tehran 1945, P. 101.

57- For more details on particulars of Hirmand water regime, see: Pirouz Mojtahed-Zadeh, *The Amirs of Borderlands and Eastern Iranian Borders*, Urosevic Foundation publication, London 1996, Chapter VIII.
58- G. P. Tate, *Travel on the Borders of Persia and Afghanistan*, London 1909, Part III, P. 245.
59- Ibid., P. 246.
60- Paragraph 3 of clause 69 of McMahon's Memorandum of 25th September 1904 on *Sistan Water Question*, FO 60/727, P. 11.
61- Whittermore Bogg, *International Boundaries, a Study of Boundary Function and Problems*, New York, Columbia University Press, 1940, P. 117.
62- See above/and also: L. E. L. Oppenheim, International Law & Treaties, in H. Lauterpacht's 8th edition, New York, Longman, 1955.
63- See above and other materials on international rivers.
64- From H. B. Majesty's Charge d' Affairs at Tehran to Foreign Secretary of India, No. 25, dated 1st August 1902, FO 60/463.
65- Telegram from Government of India to Lord George Hamilton, Secretary of State for India, dated July 21, 1902, FO 60/463, P. 118.
66- From His Excellency the Viceroy of India to His Highness Amir Sir Habibollah Khan of Afghanistan, dated Simla 31st July 1902, FO 60/659.
67- From Government of India to Lord G. Hamilton, No. 1, dated September 30, 1902, of Persia and Arabia Confidential, FO 60/659.
68- From Lord G. Hamilton to Government of India communicated by India Office, dated December 31, 1902, FO 60/711.
69- Extract of Telegram No. 83, from Sir A. Hardinge to the Marquess of Lansdowne, dated Tehran, December 29, 1902, FO 60/711.
70- Extract of the translation of an article that appeared in the Russian paper 'Novoe Vremya', dated January 2, 1903, enclosure of despatch No. 3 of British Embassy at St. Petersburg to the Marquess of Lansdowne, same date, FO 60/711, P. 4.
71- Extract of translation of article..., op. cit., PP. 3-4.
72- Confidential despatch of Sir Arthur Hardinge, British Minister at Tehran, to the Marquess of Lansdowne, No. 5, section 9, Persia and Arabia, dated January 26, 1903, FO 60/711.
73- Ibid. P. 1.
74- From Moshir ad-Doleh to Sir A. Hardinge, dated 27th December 1902, repeated in Sir A. Hardinge's letter to Moshir ad-Doleh, dated 6th January 1903, enclosure 1, in No. 1, FO 60/711, P. 2.
75- Ibid.
76- Ibid., PP. 2-3.
77- From Sir A. Hardinge to Moshir ad-Doleh, dated January 7th, 1903, inclosure 3 in No.1, FO 60/711, P. 3.
78- Ibid.
79- Telegram from Foreign Office to Viceroy of India, dated 13th January 1903, FO 60/711.
80- Extract of despatch from Foreign Office to India Office, repeated to British Minister at Tehran, dated February 21, 1903, No. 39, FO 60/711.
81- Ibid.
82- From Sir A. Hardinge to the Marquess of Lansdowne, dated Tehran, February 9, 1903, No. 9, FO 60/711.

83- Clause 3 and 4 of Confidential Diary No. 18 of H. B. Majesty's Consul for Sistan and Kain, for period 1st to 15th December 1902, repeated in FO 60/711, P. 127.
84- Telegram No. 1892F, from His Excellency the Viceroy, to His Majesty's Secretary of State for India, dated Simla 3rd July 1903, enclosure No. 44, FO 60/725, P. 20.
85- From Colonel A. H. McMahon to Secretary to the Government of India in Foreign Department, No. 824, dated Camp Kohak 16th June 1903, enclosure No. 45, FO 60/725, P. 21.
86- Ibid.
87- Ibid.
88- Ibid.
89- Clauses 9 and 10 of McMahon's despatch dated 16th June 1903, op. cit., PP. 21-2.
90- Clauses 12 and 13 of McMahon's despatch of 16th June 1903, op. cit., P. 22.
91- Extract of Clause 15 of McMahon's despatch of 16th June 1903, op. cit., P. 22.
92- Letter from Colonel McMahon to Yamin Nezam, dated Camp Kohak 14th June 1903, FO 60/725, PP. 23-4.
93- Sardar Saeed Khan Nahruei was Amir Heshmat al-Molk's brother-in-law.
94- Clause 2 of Diary No. 12 of Mr. H. Dobbs, H. B. Majesty's Consul for Sistan and Kain, for the period 16th June to 9th July 1903, FO 60/726, P. 4.
95- Extract from the Diary of Colonel A. H. McMahon for period ending the 24th August 1903, FO 60/725, P. 14.
96- Ibid.
97- Colonel McMahon's telegram No. 422 to Sir Arthur Hardinge, dated Seistan 12th September 1903, enclosure 21, FO 60/725, PP. 14-15.
98- Clause 8 of despatch No. 824, from McMahon to the Iranian Government, dated Camp Kohak 16th June 1903, enclosure No. 45 of FO 60/725, P. 21.
99- Ibid.
100- Extract from despatch of Sir A. Hardinge to the Marquess of Lansdowne, dated Tehran 24th October 1903, FO 60/725, P. 2.
101- Extract from confidential Diary No. 7 of Captain A. D. MacPherson H. B. Majesty's Consul for Sistan and Kain, for the period 16th to 21st March 1904, FO 60/726, P. 1.
102- Extract from letter from His Excellency the Viceroy of India to His Highness the Amir of Afghanistan, No. 8, dated 22nd November 1903, FO 60/711, PP. 2-3.
103- From A. H. Hardinge to the Marquess of Lansdowne, dated Tehran 24th October 1903, FO 60/725.
104- Ibid.
105- Telegram No. 422 from Colonel McMahon to Sir A. Hardinge, dated 12th September 1903, enclosure 21, FO 60/725, P. 15.
106- From Hardinge to Marquess of Lansdowne, dated Tehran 24th October 1903, FO 60/725.
107- Telegram from A. Hardinge to the Marquess of Lansdowne, No. 129, dated Tehran 8th October 1903, FO 60/711.
108- From McMahon to Secretary to the Indian Government in the Foreign Department, No 1258, dated Camp Kohak, the 14th November 1903, enclosure 66 of FO 60/725, P. 41.
109- From Yamin Nezam to Colonel McMahon as appeared in McMahon's Diary of 8th June 1904, dated 2nd June 1904, FO 60/727.
110- From Col. McMahon to the Government of India, No. 2407, dated the 25th September 1904, FO 60/727, PP. 1 to 20.
111- Ibid.

112- From McMahon to the Government of India, dated 21st February 1905, FO 60/728.
113- Extracts from translation of a letter from Sistan as appeared in the *Trans-Caspian Review*, dated the 12th Moharram 1323 H. (19th March 1905), enclosure No. 14 of FO 60/728. P. 7.
114- Extract from Major Percy Molesworth Sykes's (later Sir Percy Sykes) despatch to the Marquess of Salisbury, dated Kerman June 29, 1900, No. 4, FO 60/621.
115- From the Secretary to the Government of India in the Foreign Department to Colonel A. H. McMahon, No. 2575F, dated Simla the 15th of July 1905, FO 60/729.
116- The Times (of London), Friday September 29, 1905, FO 60/729, P. 20.
117- Mohammad Ali Monsef, *Amir Shokat al-Molk Alam*, Tehran 1975, PP. 184-189.
118- Monsef, op. cit., P. 187, quoting notes from the first round of talks.
119- Telegram N0o. 2799S, from Government of India to the Foreign Office in London, dated 17th November 1931, FO 371/15550, P. 8.
120- Translated by the author from original Persian text of the protocol sent to the author by Document Centre of the IPIS, Iranian Ministry of Foreign Affairs on 17 Mordad 1369 (8th August 1990).
121- Articles I and II of the treaty of Hirmand Division, signed between the Imperial Government of Iran and the Royal Government of Afghanistan, on sixth of Bahman of 1317 (26th January 1939), text in Persian, from the archive of the Ministry of Foreign Affairs of the Islamic Republic of Iran, sent to this author by the Document Centre of the IPIS on 8th August 1990, Ref. 94.
122- Afghanistan's proposals as attached to the letter of 11 Sharivar 1319 (1st February 1941) from Deputy Foreign Minister to the Prime Minister, Iranian Documents of the Office of Prime Minister, Series No. 102010.
123- Pirouz Mojtahed-Zadeh, *Eastern Iranian Boundaries*, paper presented to the Seminar on the Iranian boundaries, at the Geopolitics and International Boundaries Research Centre, SOAS, University of London, on December 9th 1991. Information contained in this section were compiled from various Afghan sources.
124- Iranian Documents of the Office of Prime Minister, series No. 102010.
125- A summary of the notes of negotiation of Iranian delegation in Washington with the Afghan delegation on Hirmand water division, prepared in Persian and sent to this author by Professor Mohammad Hassan Ganji, dated 9th March 1991, translated into English by the author.
126- For a fuller content of Mr. Foroughi's confidential notes to this author, see Chapter VIII of: Pirouz Mojtahed-Zadeh, The Amirs of the Borderlands and Eastern Iranian Borders, Urosevic Foundation publication, London 1996.

CHAPTER XIV

HYDROPOLITICS OF HIRMAND AND HAMUN
Pirouz Mojtahed-Zadeh

Introduction

A substantial environmental disaster has been in progress in the eastern parts of Iran in the past ninety years or so. The Hamun,[1] apparently a much larger lake in the past than it can ever be in a high-water-level year of our time, has gradually diminished and with it almost the whole of the Neyzar (reed forest) and its related economic life, with disastrous environmental consequences for the Sistan province of Iran. Hamun, the only fresh-water lake in Asia, is not only the main source of irrigation in Sistan, but other than river Hirmand, it also provides many water-associated economic activities - hunting in the Neyzar, ferrying goods and passengers across the lake, fishing and reed-associated handicrafts - and has a pivotal role in the living of the population of this southern edge of Central Asia. With the diminishing body of the lake and the Neyzar, all these economic activities are diminishing, while the damage to the agricultural life of the province has forced thousands of the local population to migrate from Sistan to Gorgan and other areas near the borders with Turkmanistan.

The Geographical Setting

The district of Sistan constitutes the middle section of the eastern Iranian borderlands. It is 36,000 sq.km. in land area with a population of 274,611 and this density of 33.8 per sq.km. makes Sistan the most populated region in the entire eastern Iranian borderlands.[2]

Sistan is predominantly a flat land, and is mostly made up of sediments from Hirmand.[3] The lowest point of the district is Hamun-e Hirmand which drains all water in the region. The surrounding lands have an almost negligible slope towards the lake. The only mountainous part of Sistan is its north-western corner where the Bandan range ends and its western flanks where the Kuh-e Plangan range represents the highest peak in the region.

Although Sistan geographically is located in the Iranian plateau of Central Asia, most of it falls politically under Afghanistan, with a small portion in Pakistan. Almost the entire area of the Iranian part of Sistan is formed of sediments from river Hirmand, creating one of the most fertile lands in Iran. But utilisation of its fertility cannot be maximised because of water shortage and precipitation. A major climatical feature of the province is a high-velocity northerly wind blowing from the mountains of Afghanistan in the spring and early summer months with a speed of 70 to 100 miles per hour, bringing in hot and dry air mixed with sand. This continues for 110 to 120 days and this wind is locally known as "the wind of 120 days". This wind, together with a high temperature causes intense evaporation of the sheets of water in Sistan.

Having frequently been referred to in the historical documents as the "bread basket" of Khorasan (old Khorasan, now known as Central Asia), Sistan's traditional economic fortune has diminished as a result of the diminishing water supplies from River Hirmand into Lake Hamun. River Hirmand and Lake Hamun are the main geographical features in Sistan.

Lake Hamun

Due to its geographical location, perennial character and its fresh water, Lake Hamun, historically known as "Sea of Zereh", is the most important lake of eastern parts of the Iranian plateau. As a major basin, Hamun collects water from a considerable area - of which about three-quarters comes from Afghanistan - and flood waters from the mountains of its immediate vicinity. This factor together with the lake's shallowness - no more than 10 metres deep at the most[4] - and with the minimum slope of the shore-lands and because of the inconstant regimes of the various tributaries, are responsible for the considerable variations in the surface occupied by the lake in the course of the year, as well as from one year to another. The sheet of water at the end of the high-water period (May) of each year can reach an area of about 3,200 sq.km. While in the dry season the surface area of the lake reduces to a mere 1,200 sq.km.[5]

During the low-water season the lake is divided into, at least, four separate sheets of water locally known as Hamun-e Saberi to the North which is the deepest, Hamun-e Puzak to the north-east and in Afghan territory, Hamun-e Shapour to the South and a central pool known as Hamun-e Hirmand. These separate sheets of Hamun water become one at flood times when the level of the lake rises. The surplus water flows out, at the southern end of the lake, through the channel of Shileh Shallaq into the depression of God-e Zereh inside Afghanistan.[6] This annual mechanism has not, however, functioned for several years owing to the diminishing water level of the lake. The rise in the water level of the lake in the very recent years does not represent a change of hydropolitical decision; it is because of lack of control in the war-torn Afghanistan.

Hamun Lake, according to historical documents, covered a much larger area than it may cover in a very high-water year in our time. G.P. Tate described the lake, at the turn of the twentieth century as something like 150,000 square miles.[7] The highest water mark which can be traced around Lake Hamun is five feet above the level recorded in 1903 by Colonel McMahon's Arbitration Commission, when the lake established this record.

Hirmand River

There are a number of streams emptying into Lake Hamun of which Hirmand is the only perennial and far more important than all other tributaries put together. Hirmand's delta region is measured as being 150,000 sq.km. The course of the river upstream of the delta, lies entirely in Afghanistan.

Rising in the mountains of north-west of Kabul, Hirmand flows towards Iranian Sistan, after meandering for about 1050 km in Afghan mountains and plains. Throughout its course in Afghanistan, Hirmand receives from a number of significant tributaries, of which two are most important; Musa Qaleh and Arghandab.[8] Having received Arghandab near Bost (or Bist) at the edge of mountain zone, Hirmand crosses the deserts for about 400 km before reaching Chahar-Borjak which is the beginning of Greater Sistan, 70 km. upstream of the Iranian border, where there is a measuring station. Of the water that Hirmand drains and brings in to its delta annually, more than one billion cubic metres. are used for agricultural irrigation in the Sistan of Iran. The utilisation of the accumulated waters, if limited to the middle basin of the river, would have a strong repercussion on the delta region.

In the delta which begins at Kuhak, Hirmand divides into two main branches of Rud-e Sistan and Rud-e Parian, each subdividing into many branches and canals. Data available from Colonel McMahon's Arbitration Commission's measurements of Hirmand water at the turn of the twentieth century indicate annual flows (from October to September) of three years - 1902 to 1905 - respectively of 7.7, 5.4 and 3.6 billion cubic metres; minimum monthly flows of 45-50 million cubic metres; and a maximum of about 2000 million cubic metres.[9] Against these figures, data gathered in the period between October 1946 and September 1950 by the Hirmand Delta Mission, shows that the flows were 2.2, 4.5, 6.6 and 6.5 billion cubic metres respectively, with minimum monthly flows in the months of September and October (excluding the exceptionally low September 1947) of 30 x 10 cubic metres. (equal to a capacity of about 11-12 cubic metres. per second) and with a maximum of 1.8 - 2.6 x 10 cubic metres. in the months of April and May (700 - 1000 cm. per second).[10]

The above two sets of data show a drop in the average amount of water flowing in Hirmand downstream in the first half of the twentieth century during which there was no diversion dam nor a canal constructed in Afghanistan. Hirmand river's average annual debit in the 1990s is estimated at 2 to 3 billion cubic metres. This debit was 6000 cubic metres per second in 1990, and 3000 cubic metres per second in 1993. This figure further reduced to a mere 45 cubic metres. per second in 1994, of which only 15 cubic metres per second entered Iranian Sistan.[11]

The latest reported flood of major consequence took place in April 1991 after many years of low water and droughts, causing extensive damage in Sistan. This flood was the outcome of a combination of high level snow melting and lack of control in Afghanistan, both administratively and technically, owing to the prevailing political situation in that country.

Evolution of the Water Disputes

Although the actual location of the boundary between Iran and Afghanistan in Sistan has since long been accepted by both sides as being in the middle of Hirmand's main delta branch, disputes concerning allocation and other riparian rights have not as yet been resolved. This in spite of several attempts in the past 120 years to settle these disputes. The original problem was that rulers of the British protectorate of Afghanistan at the turn of the twentieth century considered river Hirmand as an internal river of that country, reserving for Afghanistan the right to utilise its water in whatever way it wished. McMahon's Memorandum of 25 September 1904 asserts:

> *The Afghan Government does not admit that there is any water question in dispute, as their geographical position makes them sole owner of the whole Helmand above the Band-i-Sistan.*[12]

By thinking so, not only did the Afghan rulers ignore the rights of the people of downstream Hirmand whose life depended so exclusively on the water supplies from that river, but it also ignored international trends towards recognising the status of rivers passing through more than one country as "international rivers". Prior to this, when the local rulers of Khozeimeh dynasty were in control of affairs and defence of Sistan and eastern Iranian borderlands, regional interests were served effectively and the local inhabitants benefited. But as local advice began to be ignored by the national government, especially from the early years of the twentieth century when administration of affairs of all regions of Iran was put under the control of a centralised authority, national interests of Iran in Sistan were not served well.

The actual problem began when British boundary arbitration officer, General F. Goldsmid decided in 1872 to put the Iran-Afghanistan boundary in Sistan on the main branch of the Hirmand in the delta region without making any arrangement or recommendation for water division between the two sides.[13] The only mentioning of Hirmand water made in Goldsmid's boundary award was that:

> *It is, moreover, to be well understood that no works are to be carried out on either side calculated to interfere with the requisite supply of water for irrigation on both banks of Hirmand.* [14]

Further disputes occurred between the two countries, mainly because the river changed its course in the border area in 1896. British arbitration was sought once again and Colonel Henry McMahon was assigned in 1903 to delimit and demarcate new boundaries. McMahon's new boundary was, in practice, the same as previously defined by General Goldsmid, except for the fact that McMahon had made a water award in 1905,[15] which created more problems than it was supposed to settle.

Having decided to divide the Hirmand water at the border area, equally between the two sides in 1903-4,[16] Colonel McMahon changed his decision in 1905 for reasons unknown and allocated two-third of Hirmand water in the delta to Afghanistan and one-third to Iranian Sistan,[17] which is much more fertile and a great deal more populous than the corresponding Afghan border district of Nimrouz. The injustice done to the Iranian Sistan in this water award can be measured by reading McMahon's own comments on the unfairness to Iran of his first award (1903-4) which divided the Hirmand water equally between the two neighbours. On the equal division of Hirmand water Colonel McMahon stated:

> *Even an Afghan, however, must acknowledge, when it is brought home to him, as it should be, that any settlement which restricts Persian rights to water to certain limits is in the present case a distinct gain for Afghanistan who has hitherto taken off, only 16/100ths of the whole river from Rudbar downwards, while the Persians have taken 62/100ths. Any deferred settlement of the question might have to recognise the Persian right to what custom may have entitled them to....*[18]

Having acknowledged the above facts about Iran's rights to the Hirmand water, McMahon allocated two-third of that water to Afghanistan in 1905. The Iranians, however, found McMahon's 1905 water award of one-third to Iran, two-third to Afghanistan unacceptable and refused to ratify it. Local peasantry was so offended by this award that they decided to actively defy its terms. The Afghans, by contrast, were pleased with this water award.[19]

As the summer months of 1905 drew closer and Hirmand water began to become scarce in Sistan, local Sistanis opened two new canals from the main stream of Hirmand where both sides were debarred by McMahon's water award from cutting off from the river. Since his award had not been accepted by either side at the time, McMahon could not do much about it. The action, however, renewed the disputes between the two sides. Letters of complaint from the Sistan population scorning McMahon and the British for their "conspiracy" against their water rights appeared in the opposition Iranian newspapers abroad and in the Russian newspapers. The

Russians wrote letters to the Iranian Crown Prince expressing their displeasure of what the British arbitration did to the water rights of the people of Sistan.[20] Local Sistanis attacked and burnt down British arbitration headquarters[21] and the Iranian government requested fresh arbitration which never materialised.

The dispute, however, continued for years. In his confidential diary of December 1929, the British Consul of Sistan indicated, for instance, that there had been some affrays between Iranian and Afghan subjects in Sistan as a result of continued disputes in connection with Hirmand water distribution.[22]

As friendly relations developed in the 1930s between the new and centralised government of Reza Shah Pahlavi in Iran and the independent government of Mohammad Nader Shah in Afghanistan, fresh attempts for the settlement of Hirmand water disputes resulted in the conclusion of the 1939 treaty. Article I of this treaty recognised that "the governments of Iran and Afghanistan agree to divide in equal shares all waters of the Hirmand river which flows to Band-e Kamal Khan (30 miles inside Afghan territory) between Iran and Afghanistan," and Article II provided that in order to use more water than that is taken now between Deh-e Chahr-Borjak and Band-e Kamal Khan, the government of Afghanistan would not construct any other stream in the said district and not even repair any of the existing ones.[23]

This treaty, though in line with the accepted international standards and a significant improvement of McMahon's water award, from the Iranian point of view, also failed to put an end to the disputes, mainly because the Afghans failed to agree on it amongst themselves and because of the changed political circumstances in Iran during World War II when the British and the Russians exiled Reza Shah in 1941. The Afghans refused to ratify the treaty and the disputes were revived, especially after the Americans began the construction of diversion dams and canals on the river as a result of contracts they concluded with the Afghans in 1945. The Sistan population was convinced that the consequence of these dams and canals was going to be immediate. The political diary of the British Consul General of Mashahd records a long spell of drought in Sistan in the summer of 1947. It remarks:

> *From Zabol a report has been received that no water from the Helmand has reached the town for a month and that outlying villages have been without it for some three months. The drought-stricken population will not believe that failure of last winter's snow is the reason and they have expressed their intent of crossing into Afghanistan and forcibly release the water on which they depend and which they are convinced the Afghans are illegally stealing or diverting by their new American engineered irrigation scheme in the neighbourhood of Girishk.* [24]

Having inspected the new diversion canal in Afghanistan in 1947, the Iranian Ambassador reported to his government that the canal was 65 miles. The depth of water all along the canal was 2 metres and its breadth 30 metres reducing progressively until 12 metres at the end. It carried between 15 to 20 thousand square feet of water which was meant to go to Sistan.[25]

The construction of two major dams, Kajaki reservoir and Boghra diversion in Afghanistan in 1949 caused great uproar among Iranians. The two countries eventually sent representatives to Washington in 1959 for negotiation through American mediation. These negotiations failed to achieve any result[26] and the disputes continued until 1973 when the two countries prepared a draft agreement regulating their respective water share of the delta region, which failed to be ratified.

According to the abortive 1973 treaty, Iran was to receive a 22 cubic metres per second of Hirmand water in the delta region as its share, and was to purchase an additional four cubic metres per second from the Afghans, summing up to 26 cubic metres per second.

The quota of 22 cubic metres per second became the basis of the Afghans' argument since it was determined by a so-called impartial commission which was set up by the Americans in 1948 to determine the water needs of the two sides in the delta region.[27] Although this amount per second of Hirmand water for Sistan was even less than the amount of one-third determined by Colonel McMahon's arbitration award of 1905, the Afghans had declined to accept it. The quota, nevertheless, became the cornerstone of their argument at any negotiation thereafter. The Afghan Coup d'etat of 1973, however, prevented ratification of that year's treaty. The Iranian monarchy was, too, overthrown by the Islamic Revolution of February 1979. Subsequently, Afghanistan was occupied by the former Soviet Union, and their puppet government of Dr. Najibollah collapsed in 1992. This development resulted in a civil war in Afghanistan which is still prevailing. These events prevented the two neighbours from making fresh efforts for the settlement of Hirmand water disputes between them. Paradoxically, it must be said that, the prevailing political chaos in Afghanistan has resulted in lack of administrative and technical control of Hirmand water and the free flow of water in the delta region has restored Lake Hamun, albeit temporarily. The Iran-Afghanistan disputes on the Hirmand water rights, however, have played a major role in the two countries' relationships, preventing cooperation between the two with an increasingly disastrous environmental impact on the Sistan province and its population.

The geographical catastrophe taking place regarding Sistan and Lake Hamun is almost an exact, but more slow, repetition of the catastrophe which diminished Lake Aral in another corner of Central Asia where the Soviets diverted a large body of river Amudarya (Oxus) thus creating an environmental disaster of major proportion.

Settlement of Hirmand disputes is long overdue and I make the following recommendations in the hope of paving the way for a morally and technically acceptable solution to the problem:[28]

1. Complete depolitisation of the Hirmand issue both in Afghanistan and Sistan. Hirmand has never been a national issue in Iran since McMahon's water and boundary awards of 1905.

2. Both nations of Iran and Afghanistan should become fully and consciously aware of the fact that the Hirmand river, below the confluence of Arghandab, particularly below Band-e Kamal Khan, is not the exclusive right of either one of them, and that both Sistan of Iran and Nimrouz of Afghanistan have rights to the river in accordance with their agricultural prospects and water needs.

3. Carrying out thorough surveys of agricultural lands and irrigation possibilities in Sistan and Nimrouz provinces and determining the scale of the annual water needs of each.

4. Distributing the Hirmand water to Sistan and Nimrouz provinces in accordance with the determined annual water needs of each.

5. Undertaking joint venture for investment on construction of regulatory and reservoir dams in suitable places below the confluence of Arghandab.

6. Embankment and regulation of the course of branches and channels on both sides to prevent wastage.

7. Embankment of Hamun and rehabilitation of the Shileh Shallaq.

8. Establishing at Kuhak (where the two countries' boundary starts) on the Parian-e Moshtarak a permanent dam with sluice gates to regulate subdivision of waters between Iran and Afghanistan in that section.

9. Implementation of a rational canalization to ensure an equitable distribution of the irrigable waters, eliminating wastage and unlawful uses of water.

10. Construction of reservoir dams wherever possible to conserve flood waters in the two provinces of Sistan and Nimrouz, which will be of noticeable benefit to the irrigation needs of the region.

Notes and References

1- Hamun is an ancient Persian word meaning "Lake".
2- Official Statistics in 1986, Census Taking Centre of Iran, The Census of 1986, Vol. 142-3, p.1
3- Hirmand is also an ancient Persian word meaning "abundant in water".
4- See geography of Lake Hamun in Pirouz Mojtahed-Zadeh's "Evolution of Eastern Iranian Boundaries", Ph.D. thesis, University of London 1993, pp.89-99.
5- Italconsult, "Socio-Economic Development Plan for the South-Eastern Region", Rome 1959, p.48.
6- Pirouz Mojtahed-Zadeh, op. cit., p.96.
7- G.P. Tate, "The Frontier of Baloochistan = Travel on the Border of Persia, and Afghanistan", London 1909, p.237.
8- Pirouz Mojtahed-Zadeh, op. cit., p.100.
9- As quoted in Italconsult's "Socio-economic..." op. cit., p.52.
10- Ibid.
11- Omur-e Ab-e Sistan, a report by the Governorate of Zabul, dated Feb./March 1995, p.6 - courtesy of Mr. Mohtadi of the Centre for Middle East Scientific Research and Strategic Studies - Tehran.
12- Paragraph 3 of clause 69 of McMahon's Memorandum of 25th September 1904 on Sistan Water Question, FO 60/727.
13- Pirouz Mojtahed-Zadeh, op. cit., pp.578-81.
14- Extract of Goldsmid's Sistan Boundary Award regarding Hirmand river, last paragraph, as appeared in General Goldsmid's book "Eastern Persia", London 1876, p.414.
15- Pirouz Mojtahed-Zadeh, "Eastern Boundaries of Iran" in The International Boundaries of Modern Iran, ed. K.S. McLachlan, UCL Press, London 1994, p.135.
16- McMahon's Memorandum, op. cit.
17- McMahon's Final Draft of Water Award, Award "B", No.29 of FO 60/728, pp.34-6.
18- Paragraph 82 of McMahon's Memorandum, op. cit.
19- Colonel McMahon's Telegram No. 947 to the Foreign Secretary of British India, 12th April 1905, enclosure No. 6, FO 60/728, p.8.
20- Copy of the report of the Russian Legation at Tehran to H.I.H. The Vali-ahd (Crown Prince), July 20, 1905, FO 60/729, p.48.
21- From British India Office to Foreign Office, 23 November, 1905, FO 60/729 p.280
22- Paragraph 97 of Confidential Diary of H.B.M. Consul for Sistan for 15 Nov. to 31 Dec. 1929, FO 371/14526, p.3 of 211.
23- Articles I and II of the Iran-Afghanistan Treaty of Hirmand Water Division, dated 6 Bahman 1317 (26 January 1939), text in Persian. Document in the Document Centre of the Islamic Republic of Iran's Ministry of Foreign Affairs.

24- Extract from Secret Political Diary of British Consulate General Meshed, No.8 of 1947, dated 5 August 1947, FO 371/62024.
25- Extract from telegram No.252, from the Iranian Ambassador in Kabul to the Foreign Ministry of H.I.M. Government of Iran, 1947, but no details of the date, Iranian Documents of the Office of Prime Minister, Series No. 102010.
26- Private notes of Prof. M.H. Ganji, Secretary of Iranian Mission to the Washington negotiations, sent to this author on March 9, 1991.
27- Private information provided to this author by Amir Hussein Khan Khozeime-Alam, Iran's Deputy Minister of Agriculture in 1948 who was personally involved in the work of the so-called Impartial Commission in that year. He was interviewed on April 10, 1991.

CHAPTER XV

Behavioral Analysis of Iran-Afghanistan Boundary
Mohammad Reza Hafeznia

Introduction

Iran and Afghanistan in their historical perspective are the twins among the peoples living on the Iranian plateau. Therefore they are homogeneous in terms of history and culture. The history of their separate political lives dates back to the mid-18th century only. In the advent of the assassination of Nader Shah Afshar, the last emperor of the veining Persian Empire in 1747, Ahmad Khan Abdali, an eminent commander of Nader Shah, established the independent State in Qandahar, then the centre of Pashtun tribes, and crowned himself as Ahmad Shah Durrani of Afghanistan. But officially Afghanistan was separated from Iran after the Paris Treaty in 1857 and success of Dust Mohammad Khan's capture of Herat in 1863 (Aliabadi, 1996:124). Though officially separated from Iran, Afghanistan had to endear British geo-strategic designs for years until it succeeded in achieving its real independence in 1919 under King Amanollah (Centre for Afghanistan Studies, 1991:160).

It was after achieving national independence that specification of boundary with neighbouring countries came under consideration. Afghanistan's boundaries with Iran were delimited in the second half of the nineteenth century by three arbitrations:

1- The line between Zulfaqar pass to Hashtadan plain, totaling 103 miles, including thalweg of Harirud River, which was delimited by British Consul General at Mashhad, General MacLean in 1891 (Mojtahed-Zadeh, 1995:315-320).

2- The line between Musa Abad to Siah kuh (Pillars No.39-95), which was defined by Turkish General Altai's arbitration in 1935 (McLachlan & Mojtahed-Zadeh, 1994:129).

3- The line between Siah kuh to Kul-e-Maleksiah (Sistan). This section of the boundary was defined on two occasions and by two arbitrations. First, in 1872, when Sistan was divided into two sections by Goldsmid, one half was given to Iran and the rest to Afghanistan, with a boundary line separating the two. This arbitration determined the main branch of Hirmand as the common boundary between the two countries in Sistan proper. Then when in 1903 this arrangement was disturbed by the exceptionally high flooding of the river Colonel McMahon redefined the same line of boundaries with new adjustments especially in respect of water use of the border river, giving two -third of Hirmand water to Afghanistan and one-third to Iran (Mojtahed-Zadeh, 1999:35).

The above mentioned arbitrations established the common boundaries of the two countries, which remained in force since then without any adjustment until 1936 when the disagreement on water use of the border river started to dominate the two countries relations (Mojtahed-Zadeh, 2000:423). Since then the dispute has caused 12 diplomatic crisis and 27 bilateral negotiations between Iran and Afghanistan (Karimipour, 2000:138).

A Brief Geography of Iran-Afghanistan Boundary

In the most recent event of this nature the heads of the two states (President Khatami of Iran and President Karzai of Afghanistan) met and signed a Memorandum of Understanding in Tehran on 26 February 2002, paragraph 13 of which emphasizes on Hirmand water division in accordance with the 1972 agreement (Text of document, 2002:4). This agreement allocates only 26 cubic meters of Hirmand water in the delta region to Iran.

Also there is a territorial dispute on a small space in the region of Islam- Qalah, that has reminded unsettled in spite of the 1975 negotiations (Fuller, 1994:258).

The length of the present common boundary of Iran and Afghanistan from Zulfaqar Pass to Kuh-e-Maleksiah is 945 km in total. This figure represents an amalgam of the following details: the Harirud – Zulfaqar Pass, 157 km: Hirmand and Sikhsar 55 km: Hamun lake 24 km: the southern section in the desert area 709 km (Jaafari, 1995:2).

The boundary in the northern area and central section (Qaenat) is mountainous, but there are vast and dry plains in between such as the Sistan Plain, Nehbandan, Patergan, Amrani, Hashtadan, Jam, and Taybad plains.

From the point of view of human geography the settlers of areas on both sides of the boundary lines have strong cultural, economic, social and religious ties, which allow for interactions among them to continue. These varying aspects of physical and human geography of the Iran-Afghanistan borderlands present a complicated feature, which renders great difficulties in controlling boundary areas. This is why that in comparison with Iran's other boundaries, this boundary has been the most mysteriously treated during the past century with very little information on its interactions with the world beyond it, and that has made Iran most vulnerable from its eastern flank. It was this vulnerability that the United States began to exploit in 1990s with the help of Pakistan when the two assisted the emergence of Taliban terrorist group with the hope that it could form Afghanistan's new governing body.

Factors Affecting the Function of These Boundaries

Functionally the Iran-Afghanistan boundaries are affected by the following factors:
- a- Political systems of both countries and the pattern of relation between them.
- b- Relation patterns of each state with other states in the regional and at global level.
- c- Existence or the lack of it in foreign relations of the state systems that have taken over in Afghanistan throughout the past two centuries.
- d- Land-locked situation of Afghanistan and its need to access to easy and reliable international transit facilities via Iran.
- e- Location of Iran in the route of narcotics trafficking from Afghanistan to the west.
- f- Structure of physical geography of the borderlands (topography, dry climate, deserts, etc.)
- g- General poverty and under development of the regions and spaces located throughout the border areas.
- h- Human structure in the borderlands and cultural, religious, economic, social and spiritual ties and relations between peoples settled ob the two sides of boundary.
- i- Eastern Iran's (Sistan's) vital dependence on the Hirmand water.

j- The religious regards of the Sunni population of Iran's eastern border areas for Sunni Afghanistan and the religious and cultural-linguistic regards of the Shiite and Tajik, Uzbek and Hazarah population of Afghanistan for Shi'ite and Persian speaking Iran.

Boundary and Boundary Behaviours

The year 1979 may be considered as a turning point in the functions of Iran-Afghanistan boundaries. Prior to this date due to the existence of a global geopolitical balance of power, and because of a seemingly static situation in the by-polar geopolitical system, and also because of the existence of integrated State in both countries, a condition of normalcy dominated relationships between Iran and Afghanistan with direct effect on their boundary issues. The 1978 Nour Mohammad Taraqi *coup d' etat* and the Soviet military occupation of Afghanistan, which was concurrent with the 1979 Islamic revolution in Iran, caused great upheavals in the region and tremendously influenced the functions of Iran-Afghanistan boundaries and boundary behaviour of the countries.

Afghan Behaviour

The existence of Marxist regimes and the presence of Soviet Union in Afghanistan turned that country into a new centre for pressure and push against the common boundary with the neighbours.

The Afghan Moslems groups began their armed resistance against the Marxist regimes as well as Soviets' military occupation of their country. Emigration, homelessness and a great movement of refugees towards Iran and Pakistan were the expected results of that situation.

Moreover, common boundaries with these two states were not ready for such an influx and control became difficult. The result was the injection of huge waves of refugees into Iran, who settled mostly in the border areas. Furthermore, for political, religious, and ideological reasons the Islamic government in Iran positioned itself against the presence of the Soviet Union in Afghanistan, and welcomed Afghan refugees in mass.

The prevailing forms of Afghan settlements in Iran were to be seen under the following categories:

- a- In the form of individuals, the majority, who scattered throughout the country and settled both in rural and urban areas.
- b- In the form of living in various camping places under the supervision of UNHCR (seven camps in total existed in the country).
- c- In the form of small group, living in small colonies in Iran's border areas such as Torbat-e Jam, Taybad, Khaf, Zirkuh-e Qaenat, Darmian, Gazik, Nehbandan, Sistan, etc. In the year 1987 about 25 such colonies existed in the townships of Torbat-e Jam, Taybad and Khaf (Hafeznia, 1987:337).

Unfortunately there has never been precise and accurate statistics existed about the number of Afghan emigrants or refugees, but according to the statistics from official sources, at its climax there were about 2.3 million Afghan refugees in Iran. According to a UNHCR voluntary repatriation plan about 214587 refugees should have returned to Afghanistan up to April 2003 (Ettelaat, 28 August 2002:3).

Influx of Afghan refugees into Iran took place from all means of passages. These can be categorized into two kinds:

a- Roads and formal passages including: Zarang to Zabul, Farah to Doruh, Shindand to Yazdan, and Herat to Taybad roads.
   b- Informal passages which are about 15.

In addition to these, there are the clandestine roots and/or secret passages, which are used by smugglers.

Meanwhile there are two formal passages for the repatriation of the refugees:
1- Dugharoon in Khorasan, on the road from Taybad to Herat.
2- Milak in Sistan. This passage was officially opened in accordance with paragraph 8 of the Memorandum of Understanding of February 26, 2002 signed by the heads of the two countries.

Other Issues Pertaining to the Afghan Behaviour

1- The presence of Afghan refugees in Iran were said to have caused the kind of problems that the Iranians categorize under the following form:
   a- Changing the human landscape of the border areas by forming non-native societies on the Iranian territories.
   b- Demolition of pastures in the borderlands due to overgrazing by the refugee animals and their other activities.
   c- Population mixture through inter-marriage with Iranians and changing the demographic nature of the border province.
   d- Proliferation of contagious diseases (human and animal).
   e- Smuggling Iranian goods and money into Afghanistan.
   f- Smuggling narcotics and weapons into Iran from Afghanistan.
   g- Spread of insecurity in the urban and rural areas especially in the form of hostage takings.
   h- Development of social disorder such as forgery, robbery, murder, etc.
   i- Spying for Kabul regimes, especially in the decade between 1980-90.
   j- Providing cheap labour especially in areas of low-paid jobs.
   k- Acquisition of property especially in the border areas, and creation of ethnic ghettos (karimipour, 2000:154).

2- Another important kind of behavioural problem generating from within the Afghan territories and affecting the border areas is the smuggling of narcotics. Due to its location on the route of narcotic trafficking from Afghanistan to the west, Iran is highly affected (www.adccp.org.Iran/country). A 1999 report by the United Nations Drug control programme (UNDCP) shows that production of opium in Afghanistan amounted to 4600 tons in that year, which twice the amount produced in 1998. (L' Mond, 1999:35)

Other UN reports show that during the period 1996 to 2000 a total of 5024 clashes took place with smugglers in which 720 of Iranian military officers were killed. Clearly the trends of statistics during these years have been upward (www.undcp.org/report-2000).

The Number of (opium) addicted people in Iran was estimated at one million for the year 1981, but it increased dramatically to about 2.5 million in the year 2000 (karimipour, 2000:151).

In addition to this, smuggling of the other goods such as fuel, food- stuff, etc. have increased and continue to increase in the same manner (Haqpanah, 1998:156).

3- The third kind of behaviour is development of Afghan state-sponsored insecurity in Iran, especially during 1997-2000 when the Taliban enmity against Iran's Shi'ite state (Islamic Republic of Iran) reached its peak. Insecurity appeared in the form of cross-border raids and hostage taking inside Iran's eastern provinces and explosion of bombs in various Iranian cities, which were deemed to be of political nature.

The increased incidents of hostage taking in Iran's urban and rural areas in the last years of the Taliban rule in Afghanistan provoked much anxiety among people and officials in Iran, which in turn, resulted in various forms of action. The number of hostages taken only in Khorasan province during 1997- mid 2000 reached 1243 cases (Karimipour 2000:151).

The above three mentioned models show that Afghanistan's pattern of behaviour towards boundaries with Iran in the period under review was pro-active or offensive in nature. As a centre generating refugees, narcotics and insecurity, Afghanistan acted as the generator of pressure against Iran, pushing crisis into Iran via common boundaries.

Iranian Behaviour

In the beginning of the Afghan upheavals Iran welcomed and assisted Islamic resistance to foreign occupation of that country on the basis of both Islamic and humanitarian sympathies as well as allowing entrance of Afghan emigrants into Iran. But as the effect of the influx of refugees began to be felt in terms of economy and security, a gradual changing in Iran's approach began to show. In their reaction towards the influx of Afghan refugees, the IRI politicians decided to expand the policy control over the border areas, and take contract ional policy for more control of the boundary. Therefore, Iran's pattern of behaviour towards common boundaries during the period in review was reactional, that was to prevent Afghan push and penetration. It was in that direction that Iran adopted the following measures in reaction to the boundary problems with Afghanistan:

1- Evacuation of the villages situated within 5 Km of the boundary, and in some cases those situated within 20 Km from the boundary line.
2- Construction of new posts and small watchtowers.
3- Reinforcement of the existing posts and improving on their equipments.
4- Construction of boundary communication network for better access.
5- Construction of canals and embankment especially on the caravan routes of narcotics.
6- Erection of fences and barbed wires and other obstacles in the vulnerable places.
7- Re-organization of frontier control forces.
8- Establishment of electronic control project in some parts of boundary line.
9- Increasing cooperation among border-guards and village-dwellers on matters of border security, especially in latter years.
10- Emplacement in 1988 of an especial force at the border areas to fight against narcotic traffickers.
11- Implementation of projects aimed at familiarizing the Afghan refugees and emigrants with life inside Iran, and starting efforts for encouraging voluntary repatriation in collaboration with UNHCR, which started as from 9th April 2002.
12- Increasing penalties against smugglers of narcotic, goods, weapons as well as human.
13- Increasing diplomatic activities to attract the international attention to the problem in the hope of benefiting from increased cooperation by the United Nation and other countries in settling the problems of refugees, narcotics smuggling, etc.
14- Signing a Memorandum of Understanding with the new Afghan leaders in 26 February 2002 for efforts in replacing poppy cultivation, fighting against terrorism and insecurity. The cooperation is agreed upon on the basis of non-interference in each other's internal affairs and promotion of peace and security in the region. The MOU also included such

issues as development of transportation network in roads (Dugharoon to Herat, and Zeranj to Delaram), and railway (Sangan to Herat).

The politics and actions mentioned hitherto have to some extent been effective and have reduced illegal interactions in terms of security in large measures. But human and narcotic trafficking, smuggling of goods, etc. have continued especially in the mountainous areas where effecting control is a great deal more difficult compared with other areas.

Also, according to some unofficial news Russia had proposed to assist Iran in bringing its eastern border areas under greater control. This was because Russia claimed that drug smuggling from Afghanistan was affecting its domains via Iran and a Russian effort on the Iranian side of the boundaries would compliment the undertakings by the United States of America to establish control on the Afghan side of the same boundaries. The Iranians however, felt this could revive the old East-West geopolitics of Great Game and would again work against Iran's interests and independence as it did last time round.

Conclusion

Following political transformation both in Afghanistan and Iran, which began in 1979, the function of Iran-Afghanistan common boundary changed. Then Afghanistan came as the centre of crisis toward the boundary.

Afghanistan's behaviour towards the boundaries with Iran included such matters as movements of refugees, narcotic trafficking, and pushing insecurity inside Iran. These patterns suggest that Afghanistan's behaviour has been actional. Whereas Iranian behaviour towards the boundary has been reactional aimed at more effective control and reduction of crisis.

The collapse of State in Afghanistan generated all the problems, especially after the collapse of Soviet Union. Also lack of responsible national government in Afghanistan caused the intensification of the boundary crisis.

Establishment of Taliban control over the greatest part of the Afghan territories, especially their control of Kabul and borderlands, increased the militarization of the boundary and intensified the danger of war between the two neighbours, especially in 1999.

As a result of changes in circumstances that have occurred since the 1979 political changes in Iran and Afghanistan, the two countries mutual boundaries became the most crises redden boundary for Iran. These problems and changed nature of the boundaries made considerable impacts on the Iranian society; the influx of about 2.5 million refugees and the increase of drug addiction in Iran to the astonishing level of 2.5 million addicts might explain some of these negative impacts.

In spite of much effort by the Iranians the boundaries with Afghanistan on the whole have never came under complete control. Iran has done as much as it could do in this direction, but events have proved that the rest will be accomplished and a satisfactory control of boundaries can come about only with the establishment in Afghanistan of a stable national government which could settle such problems in that country as economic underdevelopment, narcotic production, common poverty, deprivation and underdevelopment of the borderlands.

References

1. A group of researchers (1997), *Afghanistan*, Tehran: Bonyad-e-Daeratolmaaref-e Eslami.
2. Aliabadi, A. (1996) *Afghanistan*, Tehran; Published by the Ministry of Foreign Affairs.
3. Centre for Afghanistan Studies (1991), *Proceedings about Afghanistan*. Tehran: Representative of the Leadership on the affairs of Afghanistan.
4. Dikshit, R. (1995), *Political Geography*, New Delhi: Tata Mc Graw-Hill.
5. Ettelaat daily newspaper. No.22567. Tehran, date 28 August 2002.
6. Fuller, G. (1991), The centre of universe - The Geopolitics of Iran, West view press U.S.A.
7. Glassner, M.(1993), *Political Geography*, New York: John wiley & Sons.
8. Hafeznia, M. (2000), *The principals of socio political studies*. Qom: The organization of Islamic schools aboard, Vol. 1.
9. Hafeznia, M. (1987), *Military Geography of Khorasan*, Tehran: Tarbiat
10. Modarres University.
11. Haqpanah, J. (1998), *Narcotics smuggling and its effect on Iran*. Strategic Studies Quarterly, Vol. 2.
12. Jaafari, A. (1995), *Physical Geography of Iran*, Tehran: Gitashenasi.
13. Karimipour, Y. (2000), *Iran and her Neighbours*, Tehran: Teacher Training University.
14. L' Mond Diplomatic, 2 Novemebr 1999.
15. Mc Lachlan, K. S. & Mojtahedzadeh, P. (1994), *The boundaries of Modern Iran*, London: SOAS, UCL Press.
16. Mojtahedzadeh, P. (1995), *The Amirs of the Borderlands and Eastern Iranian Borders,* London: Urosevic foundations.
17. Mojtahedzadeh, P. (1998), *Eastern boundaries of Iran*, Gofto-go quarterly, Tehran, No.21
18. Mojtahedzadeh, P. (2000), *Geopolitical Ideas and Iranian Realities*, Tehran: Nashr-e-Nai.
19. Prescott, J. (1979), *Political Geography*, Translated to Persian by Dorreh Mirhaidar, Tehran: University of Tehran
20. Text of the Document (2002), *Memorandum of Understanding*, Signed by the presidents of Iran and Afghanistan on 26 February 2002.
21. WWW.odccp.org/Iran/country
22. WWW.undcp.org/report-2000

SECTION D

Iran's Southern Boundaries

CHAPTER XVI

Maritime Boundaries in the Persian Gulf
Pirouz Mojtahed-Zadeh

Introduction

As the Government of Great Britain announced in January 1968 the decision of withdrawing Pax-Britannica from the Gulf, the states in the region developed a sense of urgency for closer cooperation that would enable them to fill the gap potentially emerging in the wake of the British withdrawal. To this end, settlement of outstanding territorial and boundary differences became a necessity, especially in the off-shore areas of the Gulf where exploration and exploitation of new oilfields were expanding rapidly (1).

This expansion in off-shore oil exploitation underlined the urgency of defining various states' boundaries before the matter developed into issues of conflict (2). Iran had in 1965 started negotiations with the British for off-shore boundaries settlement in the Gulf, but successful negotiations had to wait until late 1960 and 1970s.

The Anglo-Iranian negotiations, however, established the median line of the Persian Gulf as a principle upon which the continental shelf between Iran and her Arab neighbours was to be divided in that sea. It was on the basis of this principle that the subsequent continental shelf delimitation agreements in the Persian Gulf were achieved (3).

On 11 February 1966 Mr Mohammad Reza Amir Teimur of the Iranian Ministry of Foreign Affairs and Sir Roger Allen of British Foreign Office initialled an agreed minute in which Iran on the one side, and Great Britain on behalf of its protectorate Arab states on the Persian Gulf, on the other, reaffirmed the principle of median line of the Persian Gulf as the basis for dividing the continental shelf of that sea, and divided the Iran-Qatar continental shelf (4).

With an area of 155,000 square kilometres and an average depth of about 50 metres, the whole of the Gulf is an extended continental shelf, and its geographical shape - a curved rectangle - puts Iranian territories on the one hand, and territories of most Arab states of the lower Gulf on the other, on opposite sides of each other. Such a geographical situation necessitates the consideration of a median line down the Gulf. But the problem was that different states claimed different base lines. The location of different islands - claimed by some government to be the base line - added further complication to the matter. Solving these whole areas of disagreements needed real cooperation and understanding which was, at the time, elevated by the announcement of the said British decision.

Iran had announced on 15 July 1934 her territorial waters in the Persian Gulf, Strait of Hormuz and Gulf of Oman to be six miles from the low-water marks of her coastline. On March 19, 1949 Iran announced her rights of continental shelf oil exploration. Thereafter the littoral Arab states of the lower Gulf followed the example and each issued a similar declaration; Saudi Arabia on May 29, 1949; Qatar on June 8, 1949; Abu Dhabi on June 10, 1949; Kuwait on June 12,

1949; Dubai on June 14, 1949; Sharjah on June 16, 1949; and Umm al-Quwain and Ajman on June 20, 1949 (5).

On May 18, 1955 Iran claimed the seabed resources of her continental shelf in the Persian Gulf, Strait of Hormuz and the Gulf of Oman. On April 22, 1959 Iran changed the limits of her territorial sea from six to 12 nautical miles in the Persian Gulf and the Gulf of Oman (6) and later claimed an area adjacent to her territorial sea, as her contiguous zone, the outer limit of which is 24 nautical miles from the baseline.

Iran and the Arab states of the region have claimed exclusive fisheries zones of their own and continental shelf claims extended to continental shelf boundaries to be established at the equidistant lines. In the Gulf of Oman Iran has claimed an exclusive fisheries zone extending to the equidistant line with the United Arab Emirates and Oman.

Anticipating future discovery of oil or gas structures across boundaries in the maritime areas of the Persian Gulf, Iran decided to enforce a provision in her continental shelf agreements with the states on the opposite side to prevent inappropriate exploitation of such structures.

According to this provision, appearing in all Iran's continental shelf boundary agreements in the region, if a petroleum structure extends across the boundary and could be exploited from the other side of the boundary, then (i) there shall be no sub-surface well completion within 125 metres of the boundary (500 metres in the case of maritime boundary with Saudi Arabia) without the mutual agreement of the two parties; and (ii) the two parties shall attempt to agree on coordination or unitisation of operations with respect to such structures.

In the Persian Gulf, like elsewhere in the world, the laws of maritime areas of littoral states have developed gradually. Among others in this region the Government of Iran compiled all her laws of maritime areas of the Persian Gulf and Oman Sea in one single comprehensive text in 1993. This single act was protested to by the Government of the United States in January 1994 and the US protest was replied to by the government of the Islamic Republic of Iran in the same year. Both texts and the act itself contain many important legal aspects of maritime delimitations, which go beyond the scope of the main discussion of this book on maritime political geography. These texts are, therefore, reproduced at the end of this chapter in the form of an "appendix to the chapter" as an example of the legal aspects of maritime delimitations of the world in general, and of the Persian Gulf in particular (7).

However, Oman and the Yemen had in 1960 granted fishing concessions to Japan, the Soviet Union and South Korea in their "Exclusive Fishing Zone" in the Gulf of Oman and the Arab Sea. To clarify the inherent obscurity of this undertaking, Oman declared in 1981, an Exclusive Economic Zone in its adjacent waters. The limits of these zones were still uncertain until the United Nations declared in 1982 that all coastal states are entitled to a 200 nautical mile of Exclusive Economic Zone. This UN law of sea convention not only standardised the 200 nautical miles of the body of sea as the EEZ entitlement of the coastal states, but also standardised the territorial waters of the coastal states to 12 nautical miles off-shore (8). Nevertheless, for reasons of their on-going territorial disputes with Bahrain and Iran, the governments of Qatar and the United Arab Emirates officially declared their belts of territorial waters at 12 miles as late as 1992 and 1993 respectively.

The eight states littoral to the Persian Gulf need, at least, sixteen continental shelf boundaries among them (for the purpose of this study, internal United Arab Emirates' boundaries are not considered). Of these 16 continental shelf boundaries, seven have been negotiated of which the following six have entered into force:

Bahrain-Saudi Arabia

Iran-Saudi Arabia
Iran-Bahrain
Qatar-Iran
Qatar-United Arab Emirates (Abu Dhabi)
Iran-Oman

There are at least ten other continental shelf boundaries to be settled in the region. These are:
1 - Iran-United Arab Emirates
2 - Oman-United Arab Emirates (one undefined boundary in the Persian Gulf and two boundary lines in the Gulf of Oman and Arab sea)
3 - Qatar-Saudi Arabia (the case of Dohat al-Salwa)
4 - Saudi Arabia-Qatar (the case of Khor al-Adid)
5 - Saudi Arabia-Abu Dhabi (the case of Khor al-Adid
6 - Kuwait-Iran (the case of Golden Triangle) which has been negotiated
7 - Kuwait-Iraq (the case of Golden Triangle)
8 - Kuwait-Saudi Arabia
9 - Iran-Iraq (the case of Golden Triangle)
10 - Bahrain-Qatar (the case of Hawar Islands)

Of these:
A - The Iran - United Arab Emirates continental shelf boundaries appear to be the most complicated of the kind in the Gulf, not only because there are seven emirates of the UAE each claiming its own continental shelf limits, but also because of the joint Iranian - Sharjah sovereignty exercised in Abu Musa island.
B - Oman - United Arab Emirates continental shelf boundaries are not defined owing to the age-old inland boundary disputes in the Musandam Peninsula between Oman and the emirates of Sharjah in the Gulf of Oman and Ras al-Kheimah in the Persian Gulf.
C - Saudi Arabia - Qatar and UAE continental shelf are not divided mainly owing to the Qatar - Bahrain disputes over Hawar Archipelago in the al-Salwa Bay on the one side of Qatar Peninsula, and the complication that the 1974 Saudi Arabia - Abu Dhabi Boundary agreement has caused in the Khor al-Adid Bay on the other. It was announced in October 1996 that Saudi Arabia and Qatar jointly commissioned a French company to demarcate their mutual inland boundaries.
D - Iraq - Kuwait maritime boundaries are not negotiated because of the two states' inland territorial and boundary disputes, which automatically include the offshore areas of the two countries.
E - Kuwait, on the other hand, has not been able to define her continental shelf limits with Saudi Arabia owing to their disagreements on the question of sovereignty over the islands of Kubbor, Qaruh and Umm al-Maradim.
F - Defining the Iran - Iraq continental shelf boundaries in the so-called Golden Triangle will depend, on the one hand, on the settlement of Iraq - Kuwait territorial and boundary disputes, and on the other, it will depend on the final settlement of Iran - Iraq boundary dispute in the Shatt al-Arab.
G - Official delimitation of the continental shelf boundaries between Iran and Kuwait is similarly prevented by territorial and boundary disputes between Iraq and Kuwait albeit the two signed a draft agreement in 1962 governing their mutual maritime areas. Here

also Iran believes that its baseline must start from Khark Island as it did in the case of maritime boundary delimitation with Saudi Arabia. Kuwait, in response, claims that its baseline must start from its Failakah Island which is situated in the middle of the sea and that is not acceptable to Iran.

H - Bahrain and Qatar have not been able to negotiate delimitation of their continental shelf boundaries owing to their conflicting claims of sovereignty over the Hawar Archipelago which will be discussed in the second section of this book.

Iran's four continental shelf boundaries, defined and delimited with the Arab neighbours in the Persian Gulf, are as follows:

Iran-Saudi Arabia

The continental shelf boundary agreement between Iran and Saudi Arabia was signed in 1968. Continental shelf legal experts consider this boundary agreement as a unique example of new maritime boundary settlement in the world (9).

That part of the Persian Gulf where this boundary line is defined is 138.7 nautical miles wide. Nevertheless, coastlines considered in the negotiations for this agreement are between 95 to 135 nautical miles with the deepest point being 75 metres.

For years the two countries had experienced a complex dispute in the areas of their mutual off-shore boundaries. The dispute included the question of ownership of the two Farsi and Arab islands and the over-lapping oilfields of their claims. Both Iran and Saudi Arabia had granted concessions to different oil companies. When the overlapping areas of the two concessions were realised, the two countries decided to settle the problem on the basis of the international principle of median line. The problem which slowed down the progress of negotiations was that Iran insisted on the low-water-mark of the Khark Island be considered as the base line. But Saudi Arabia insisted on a shore-to-shore median line with no regard to Khark or any other island.

Interviewed by this author on Thursday 4 April 1996, Dr. Parviz Mina, Iran's chief technical negotiator in the continental shelf delimitation negotiations of 1968 with Saudi Arabia, disclosed that:

> *Initially, the uncompromising Saudi posture led to the continental shelf delimitation between Iran and Saudi Arabia to be negotiated on the basis of no effect for Khark Island. Such an arrangement would naturally shift the boundary line closer to the Iranian coasts in an area of the sea with substantial oil deposits and highly valuable seabed resources.*
>
> *Learning of the particulars of this method of maritime settlement, the Shah was not accommodating; he asked us to find ways of giving full effect to the geographical situation of Khark Island in the delimitation calculations. Fortunately King Faisal had enough goodwill to accept a proposal for solution based on giving half effect to Khark Island.*
>
> *Not only did this adjustment shift the boundary line to the proper median line of the Persian Gulf, but gave Iran her rightful share of the huge oil resources of the border area.*

Negotiations continued however, until October 24, 1968 when Iran and Saudi Arabia successfully delimited their mutual continental shelf boundary on the basis of (10):

1 - recognising Iran's sovereignty of the Farsi Island and Saudi Arabian ownership of the Arabi Island;

2 - territorial waters of 12 miles from the low-water-mark of the two islands of Farsi and Arab to be respected for both islands, but where they overlap, the median line would run half-way between them (see figure III);

3 - recognition of Khark Island's low-water-mark as part of Iran's mainland coast line, and delimitation of the median line on that basis;

4 - a 500 metre oil exploration restriction area to be applied to either side of the entire length of the median line which would prevent the two parties from drilling diagonally for oil from the other side (11). This agreement was signed on October 24, 1968 and enacted on January 29, 1969.

Article 1 of the agreement recognises Saudi Arabian sovereignty over the island of Al-Arabiyah and Iranian sovereignty over the island of Farsi. Article 3 cites the coordinates of the turning and terminal points:

(a) Except in the vicinity of Al-Arabiyah and Farsi, the boundary line is determined by straight lines between the following points whose latitude and longitude are as specified below:

Point	*North Latitude*	*East Longitude*
1	27 10.0'	50 54.0'
2	27 18.5'	50 45.5'
3	27 26.5'	50 37.0'
4	27 56.5'	50 17.5'
5	28 08.5'	50 06.5'
6	28 17.6'	49 56.2'
7	28 21.0'	49 50.9'
8	28 24.7'	49 47.8'
9	28 24.4'	49 47.4'
10	28 27.9'	49 42.0'
11	28 34.8'	49 39.7'
12	28 37.2'	49 36.2'
13	28 40.9'	49 33.5'
14	28 41.3'	49 34.3'

(b) In the vicinity of Al-Arabiyah and Farsi, a line laid down as follows:

At the point where the line described in paragraph (a) intersects the limit of the belt of Farsi, the boundary shall follow the limit of the belt on the side facing Saudi Arabia until it meets the boundary line set forth in Article I which divides the territorial seas of Farsi and Al-Arabiyah; thence it shall follow that line easterly until it meets the limit of the belt of territorial sea around Al-Arabiyah; thence it shall follow the limit of that belt on the side facing Iran until it intersects again the line described in paragraph (a). (12)

The boundary is 138.7 nautical miles in length and has 16 turning and Terminal points of above description. In the south this boundary joins the Iran-Bahrain continental shelf boundary. Small Saudi Arabian islands have not been given effect in the calculation of the equidistant line.

For the northern 25 percent of the boundary, the Iranian island of Khark has been given "half-effect" on the determination of the equidistant line. Khark is situated approximately 17 nautical miles from the Iranian mainland and has an area of about 12 square nautical miles. In principle, this segment of the boundary generally has been determined by calculating equidistant lines giving full weight to Khark base points and then disregarding completely the effect of the island and then splitting the arial difference. From the agreement it is not known for certain if this was the exact method-utilised (13).

Figure 14

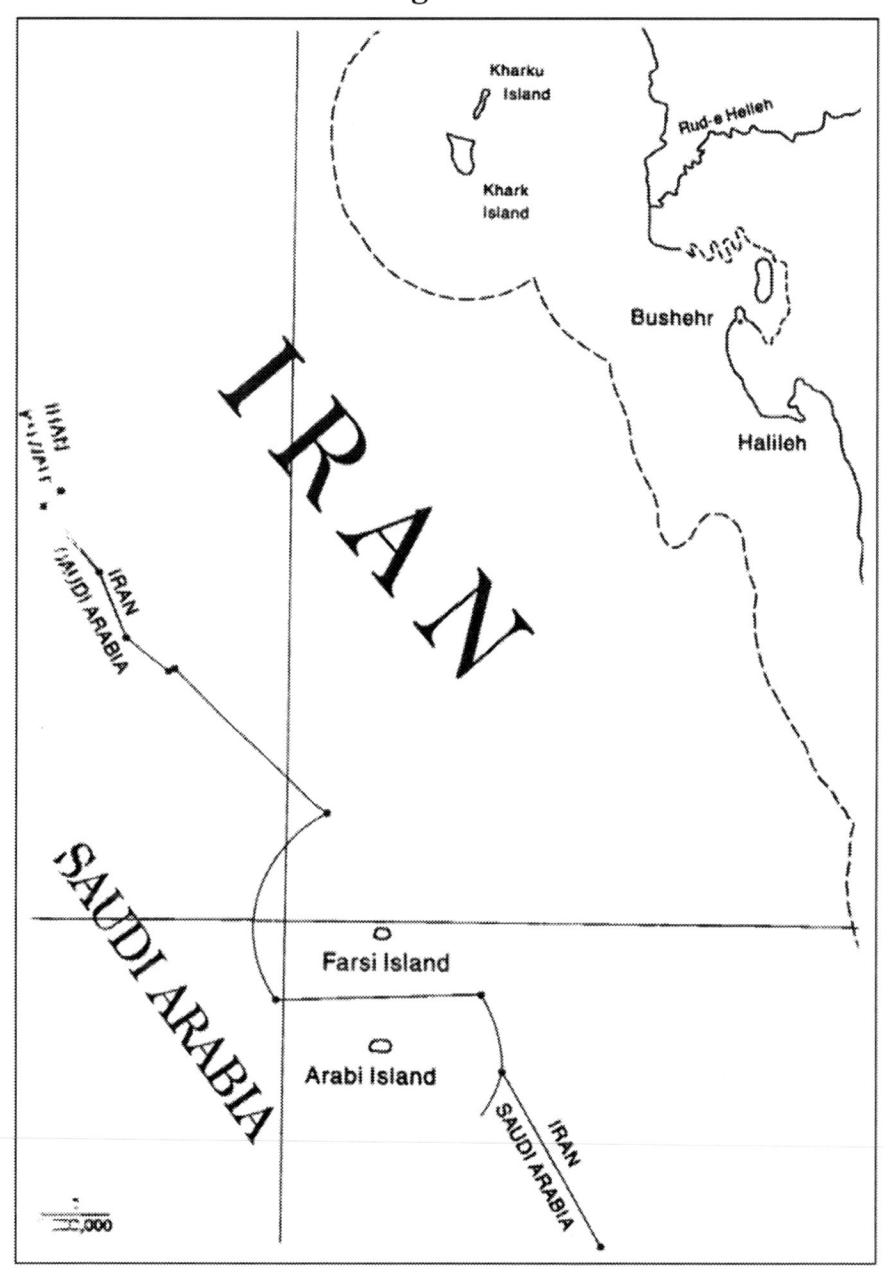

Iran - Saudi Arabian Continental Shelf Boundaries
Source: Limits in the Sea, No. 94

Considering enormous complications caused by various claims from both Iran and Saudi Arabia, it is not impossible to imagine that this boundary would not have been settled in an ordinary circumstance in the region for many years. Settlement of these boundaries with all their complications needed expediency, goodwill and indulgence from both governments. These were exercised owing to the political urgency that had emerged as a result of the announcement in January 1968 by the British Government of withdrawing their presence from the Gulf by December 1971. There were a number of coincidences in Iranian and Saudi Arabian political considerations at the time which assisted a speedy settlement of this boundary dispute; both governments had special relations with the United States which encouraged cooperation between the two for the preservation of status quo and stability in the region in the wake of British withdrawal from the Gulf; both governments were determined to keep Soviet Union's geopolitical ambitions in the Persian Gulf at bay; and both governments were determined to counter strategic threats posed by the Baathist regime of Iraq in the region. These coincidence of political considerations, further strengthened by the British announcement, created the political urgency, which encouraged the two governments to employ their top experts to settle their mutual boundary complications.

Qatar-Iran

Following its continental shelf boundary agreement with Saudi Arabia in 1968, Iran moved to delimit similar boundaries with other states on the opposite side of the Persian Gulf. Qatar was, at the time, the only Arab state of the region, other than Saudi Arabia, ready and able to enter such agreements with her neighbours.

Iran and Qatar are situated as opposite states on the Persian Gulf. Their continental shelf boundary, which was delimited on the equidistance, is approximately 131 nautical miles in length and involves six turning and terminal points. It runs in a northwesterly - southeasterly direction in the central part of the Persian Gulf (see figure IV). The precise location of the terminal point in the northwest will not be known until a Bahrain-Qatar boundary is calculated. In the southeast, the terminal point coincides with the northern terminal point of the Qatar-Abu Dhabi maritime boundary. Here, Qatar had in the same year (1969) delimited a continental shelf boundary with Abu Dhabi. The northward terminus of this boundary was defined in the two states' agreement by specific geographic coordinates. Iran and Qatar used this same point, which is approximately equidistant from Iran, Qatar and Abu Dhabi, as the southern terminus of their boundary. The course of the boundary is described in Article 1 of the treaty as:

> *The demarcation line separating the territory of Iran on the one hand and that of Qatar on the other merges with the geodesic line linking following points:*
> ***Point (1)*** *is the one located at the extreme western part of the most western zone of the demarcation line north of the continental shelf belonging to Qatar and which is linked to **point (2)** below at an angle of 27.8, 14', 27" by a geodesic demarcation line.*

	Latitude			*Longitude*		
Point (2)	27	0'	35"	51	23'	00"
" (3)	26	56'	20"	51	44'	50"
" (4)	26	33'	25"	52	12'	10"
" (5)	26	06'	20"	52	42'	30"
" (6)	25	31'	50"	53	02'	05" (14)

These boundaries were negotiated on the basis of the two mainland' actual coastlines according to the negotiations and agreements of Iran and Britain in 1966. This meant that Iran had ignored pertinence of geographical situation of its islands of Kish, Lavan and Hendorabi in this agreement. This was done on the understanding that Iran's undisputed sovereignty over these islands was acknowledged (15).

Since Iran was still claiming sovereignty over Bahrain at the time of negotiations with Qatar, together with the fact that Qatar and Bahrain had no continental shelf boundary between them for reasons of their own territorial disputes, locating a northwestern terminus of the Iran-Qatar boundary became a major difficulty. This made the Iranians decide particularly on specifying the northwestern point of the start of their continental shelf boundary with Qatar. In a report to the Minister of Foreign Affairs, the Legal Department of that ministry stated in 1968 that:

It has been commented in that context that Bahrain islands, situated on the west of Qatar peninsula, are indivisible parts of Iran - In any event they have separate continental shelf and the spot where borders of Iran's mainland's continental shelf and these islands and Qatar peninsula come together can be accepted as the western point of the start of Iran-Qatar continental shelf boundaries. (16)

The northwestern terminal point on the Iran-Qatar boundary was, thus, described as lying on a specified azimuth.

Economic considerations motivated the parties to delimit the boundary but did not affect its location. Qatar had issued offshore concessions to Continental Oil Company, Shell Company of Qatar Petroleum Company Limited, and Iran had granted offshore concessions to Iranian Offshore Petroleum Company and Lavan Petroleum Company.

Anticipating the existence of a trans-boundary petroleum structure, which later materialised in the form of a huge natural gas field, the agreement contains a provision that would appear in all Iran's subsequent continental shelf boundary agreements, providing that, a petroleum structure extends across the boundary and could be exploited by directional drilling from the other side of the boundary, then:
- (i) there shall be no sub-surface well completion within 125 metres of the boundary without the mutual agreement of the parties; and
- (ii) the parties shall attempt to agree on coordination or unitisation of operations with respect to such structures.

Environmental considerations were not taken into account in the delimitation. From the point of view of legal regime, the agreement deals exclusively with continental shelf jurisdiction. It expressly states that it does not affect the status of the superjacent waters or airspace.

Geographically, the opposite relationship of the parties' coasts was the predominant factor affecting the location of the boundary, which was delimited by use of the equidistance method, whereas geology and geomorphology did not affect the delimitation. The seabed in the vicinity of the boundary averages only 30-80 metres in depth and contains no significant relief features.

Figure 15

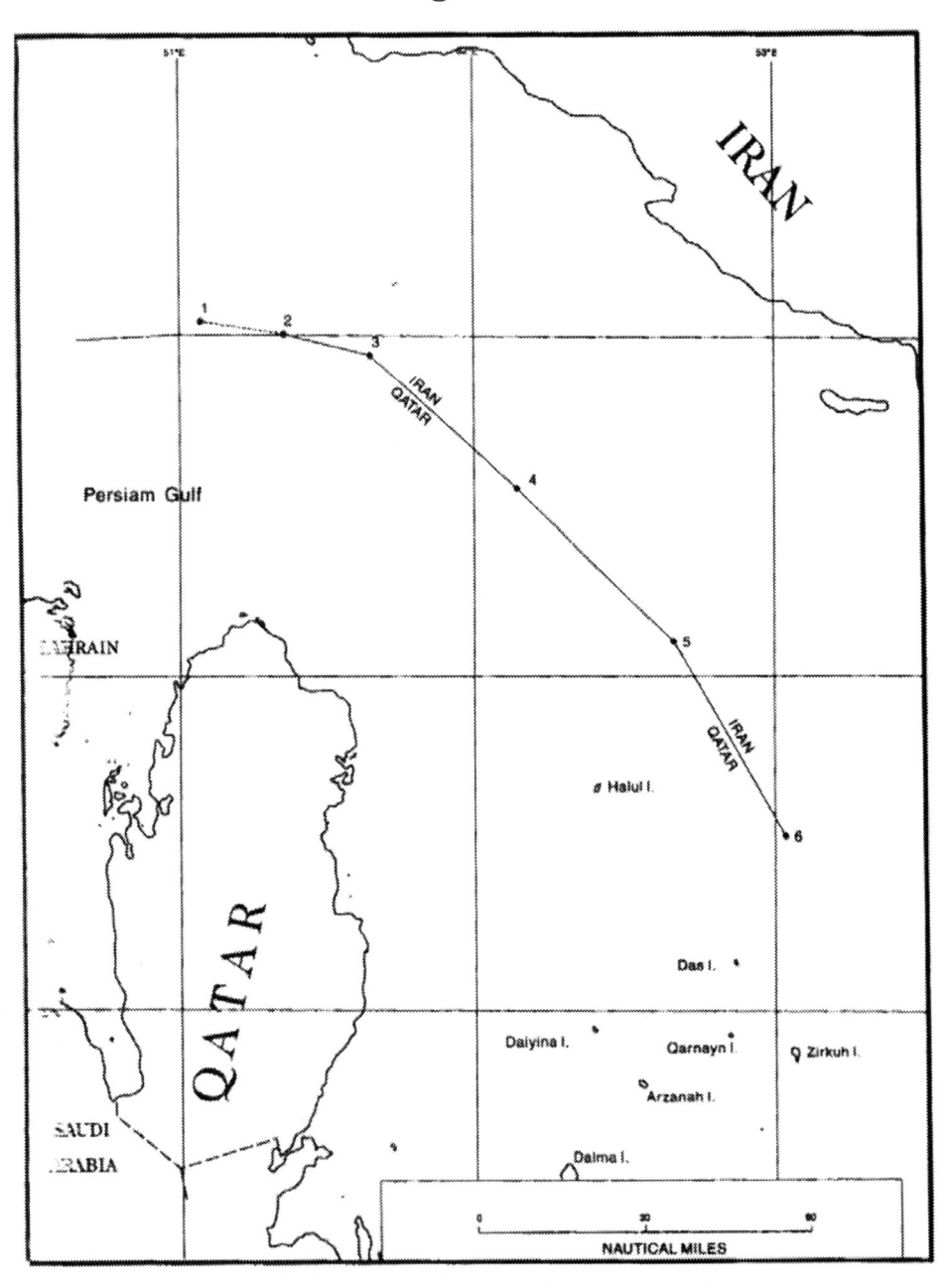

Iran - Qatar Continental Shelf Boundary
Source: Limits in the Sea No. 94

The delimitation was part of an effort by Iran to establish her continental shelf boundaries in the Persian Gulf for economic reasons and reason of political geography. Iran had declared a system of straight baselines at the time of the agreement. This claim did not affect the delimitation, however. The boundary was delimited using the equidistance method, disregarding islands, rocks, reefs and low-tide elevations. The boundary was delimited so as to be equidistant from the nearest points on the coasts of the opposite's mainland territories. It consists of geodetic lines connecting the turning and terminal points, illustrated on British Admiralty Chart No. 2837, copies of which were signed by representatives of both governments (17). This agreement was executed in Persian, Arabic and English languages, all text being equally authoritative.

This maritime boundary agreement was signed on 20 September 1969, and entered into force upon the exchange of instrument of ratification on 10 May 1970 (18).

Iran-Bahrain

In 1971, shortly after Iran's claims of sovereignty to Bahrain Archipelago were withdrawn, the two states entered negotiations aimed at defining their mutual boundaries.

The actual task of delimitation of the Iran-Bahrain continental shelf areas was not complicated at all. But, Bahrain's dispute with Qatar over the Hawar archipelago, which has prevented delimitation of continental shelf boundaries between them, was a matter of some concern. Nevertheless, since the northern tip of the two states' continental shelf boundary could not differ much from whichever way the Bahrain-Qatar continental shelf boundaries went, conclusion of the Iran-Bahrain treaty of June 17, 1971 met little difficulty (19).

Article I of the treaty specifies the course of the boundary line as follows:

The line dividing the continental shelf lying between the territory of Iran on the one side and the territory of Bahrain on the other side shall consist of geodetic lines between the following points in the sequence hereinafter set out:

Point (1) *is the Eastern-most point on the Eastern-most part of the Northern boundary line of the continental shelf appertaining to Bahrain as formed by the intersection of a line starting from the point having the latitude of 27 degrees, 00 minutes, 35 seconds North and longitude 51 degree, 23 minutes, 00 seconds East, and having a geodetic azimuth of 278 degrees, 14 minutes, 27 seconds, with a boundary line dividing the continental shelf appertaining to Bahrain and Qatar, thence:*

Lat. North		**Long. East**
Point (2)	27 02' 46"	51 05' 54"
Point (3)	27 06' 30"	50 57' 00"
Point (4)	27 10' 00"	50 54' 00" (20)

The Iran-Bahrain agreement delimits the continental shelf boundary of the maritime area of the two countries in the central part of the Persian Gulf.

This boundary extends for a distance of 28.28 nautical miles, and connects four points by straight lines. The terminal points of the agreed boundary were determined by Iran's existing boundary with Qatar and Saudi Arabia. Point 1 of the boundary is undermined and is to coincide with point 2 of the Iran-Qatar boundary of 1969, and point 4 coincides with point 1 of the Iran-Saudi Arabian boundary of 1968.

These points are not equidistant from the nearest points on the two countries' land territories. Terminal point 1 (eastern) of this boundary is approximately ten nautical miles closer to the Iranian coasts than those of Bahrain, and terminal point 4 (western) is approximately five nautical miles closer to Iran than to Bahrain. This occurred probably because of Bahrain's location in the sea which makes the Iran-Bahrain median line at point 4 of this boundary to fall about five nautical miles south of the general Arab-Iranian median line in the Persian Gulf. The Iranians must have agreed on bringing the two countries' median line at point 4 to the said general median line in the Persian Gulf. These two terminal points, nevertheless, appear to have been established by use of the equidistance method. This can be attributed to the scale of the particular hydrographic chart used to plot these points.

The agreement which was signed on 17 June 1971, entered into force upon the exchange of instruments of ratification on 14 May 1972 (21).

Geographically, equidistance method was used to establish the turning and terminal points on this boundary reflecting the opposite relationship of the two countries' coasts, while neither geology nor geomorphology played a role in the delimitation of this boundary. The waters in the vicinity of this boundary are quite shallow, but on the deep scale of the Persian Gulf average, ranging from approximately 60 to 75 metres. The seabed is relatively flat and devoid of any distinguishing geomorphologic features.

Delimitation of this boundary was primarily motivated by economic considerations. Both Iran and Bahrain had granted offshore concessions prior to the delimitation to various companies.

The preamble to the agreement states that the parties are "desirous of establishing in a just, equitable and precise manner", the boundary between their respective continental shelves. The boundary line has been illustrated on the British Admiralty Chart No. 2847 (scale 1 750,000) and consists of geodetic lines joining the coordinated points.

Although Iran has claimed a straight baseline system, this claim did not affect the location of the two equidistant turning points on the boundary. The Iranian islands of Nakhilu and Jabarin were, nevertheless, given full effect in the location of the two equidistant turning points because the islands were within Iran's straight baselines. These islands are situated slightly more than three miles off the Iranian mainland.

The Bahraini island of Al-Moharraq (which is that island-country's second most important island and is connected to Bahrain's main island "Manamah" by a causeway) was considered a part of the Bahrain's mainland for delimitation purposes.

With respect to trans-boundary deposits, the agreement provides that if a petroleum structure extends across the boundary and could be exploited by directional drilling from the other side of the boundary then:
  (i) there shall be no sub-surface well completion within 125 metres of the boundary without the mutual consent of the parties; and
  (ii) the parties shall attempt to agree on coordination or unitisation of operations with respect to such structures.

As for the legal regime considerations, the agreement delimits the boundary "between the respective areas of the continental shelf over which [the two countries] have sovereign rights in accordance with international law...." It provides further that "nothing in this Agreement shall affect the status of the superjacent waters on air-space above any part of the continental shelf". Iran subsequently claimed exclusive fisheries jurisdiction in the Persian Gulf coextensive with its continental shelf jurisdiction.

This treaty provides for a 125 metres of restricted zone on either sides of the line, within which the two governments are prohibited from drilling for oil (22). The agreement was reached on the basis of the British Admiralty map No. 28447 (23).

The Iran-Qatar Agreement, which was signed some 21 months earlier than the Bahrain-Iran Agreement, appears to reflect an assumption that the Bahrain-Qatar boundary, when eventually determined, would intersect the common geodesic to the west of the eastern extreme point (as otherwise no point would exist which would satisfy the description of Point 1 in the Iran-Qatar Agreement) (24). The Iran-Qatar Agreement does not, however, impose a westward limit on the location of the intersection point. The point at 27°02'46" N 51°05'54" E (the *western extreme point*), which is Point 2 of the Bahrain-Iran Agreement, is not referred to in the Iran-Qatar Agreement. The Iran-Qatar Agreement does not, therefore, *per se* prevent Qatar from claiming a boundary, which will intersect the common geodesic at or west of the Western extreme point.

Figure 16

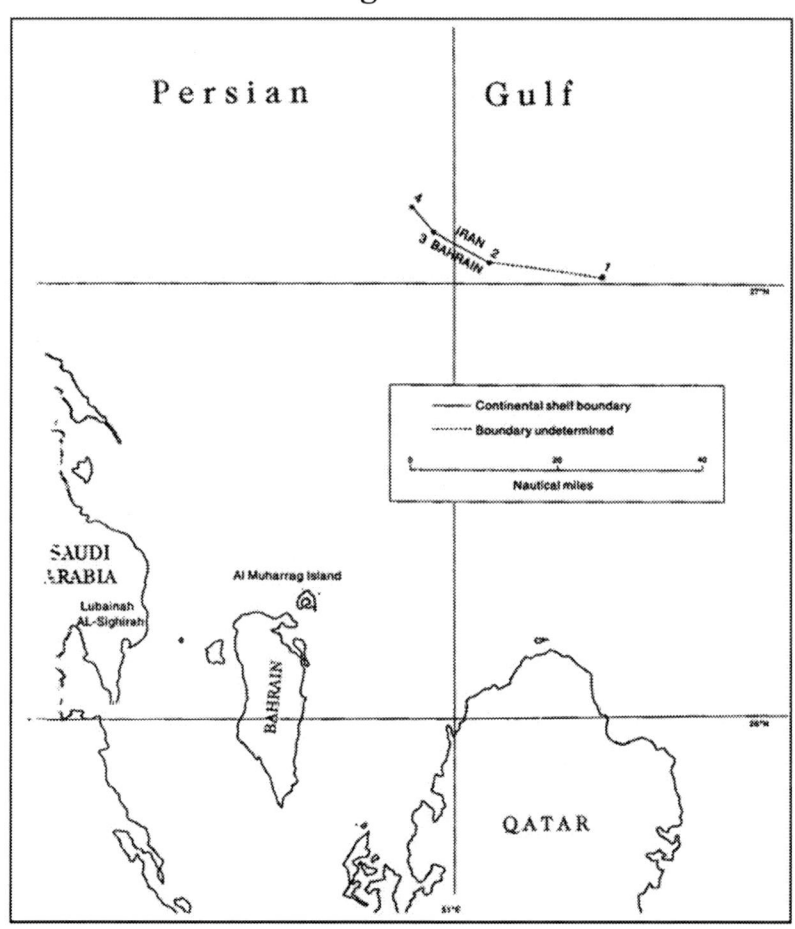

Iran - Bahrain Continental Shelf Boundary
Scale: in the map appearing in Limits in the Sea No. 94 (1981)

The Bahrain-Iran Agreement, for its part, appears to reflect an assumption that the Bahrain-Qatar boundary, when eventually determined, would intersect the common geodesic to the east of the western point (as otherwise no point would exist which would satisfy the description of Point 1 in the Bahrain-Iran Agreement) (25). The Bahrain-Iran Agreement also appears to assume that this intersection would be located to the west of the eastern extreme point. Qatar may argue on the basis of this assumption that Bahrain, having signed the Bahrain-Iran Agreement, may not today claim a boundary, which will intersect the common geodesic at or east of the eastern extreme point.

It seems difficult to believe that Iran would have signed agreements with Qatar and Bahrain respectively which might give rise to conflicts between the two countries' respective claims, without protecting itself against the possibility of such conflicts. One is therefore tempted to speculate that Qatar may have assured Iran that it would not subsequently claim a boundary with Bahrain which would intersect the common geodesic at or west of the western extreme point, and that such an assurance may have been transmitted to Bahrain in the course of negotiating the Bahrain-Iran Agreement.

The mere fact that Qatar or Bahrain may, during negotiations, have made a prediction as to the other state's probable negotiating posture, or a statement concerning its intentions *vis-à-vis* the other state, will naturally not bind the other state.

Iran-Oman

Iran and the Sultanate of Oman defined and delimited their mutual Continental Shelf boundaries in the Strait of Hormuz. This agreement - signed on July 15, 1974 and entered into effect in January 1975 - also provides for a 125 metres oil exploration restriction on either side of the line (26). The twelve miles territorial waters of the two countries at the Strait of Hormuz overlap in a stretch of 15 miles where the median line puts both territorial water limits and continental shelf boundaries on the same line.

The Iran-Oman boundary treaty of July 1974 defined the two countries' continental shelf boundaries on the basis of British Admiralty map No. 2888 of 1962. It coincided with another agreement between the two governments, which allows both countries to patrol in each other's respective territorial seas for the maintenance of security in the Strait of Hormuz (27).

Iran and Oman have opposing coasts in the Strait of Hormuz area. The northern Oman coast of Musandam, that part which constitutes the elbow of the Strait, consists largely of offshore islands. Iran's coastline is also fringed with islands.

The boundary agreement of 1974 does not specify any method of delimitation except that the boundary line is clearly calculated on equidistance between the coastlines of the two countries' islands. Article I of the agreement defines the turning and terminal points (22 in all) in the following manner:

> *The line dividing the continental shelf lying between the territory of Iran on the one side and the territory of Oman on the other shall consist of geodetic lines between the following points in the sequence hereinafter set out:*
>
> *Point (1) is the most western point which is the intersection of the geodetic line drawn between point (0) having the coordinates of 55° 42' 15"E, 26° 14' 45"N and point (2) having the coordinates of 55° 47' 45"E, 26° 16' 35"N with the lateral offshore boundary line between Oman and Ras al-Kheimah.*

	Long. E.	*Lat. N.*
Point (2)	55 47 45	26 16 35
Point (3)	55 52 15	26 28 50
Point (4)	56 06 45	26 28 40
Point (5)	56 08 35	26 31 05
Point (6)	56 10 25	26 32 50
Point (7)	56 14 30	26 35 25
Point (8)	56 18 30	26 35 35
Point (9)	56 19 40	26 37 00 W. Intersect of Larak 12m.
Point (10)	56 33 00	26 42 15 E. Intersect of Larak 12m
Point (11)	56 41 00	26 44 15
Point (12)	56 44 00	26 41 35
Point (13)	56 45 15	26 39 40
Point (14)	56 47 45	26 35 15
Point (15)	56 47 30	26 25 15
Point (16)	56 48 05	26 22 00
Point (17)	56 47 50	26 16 30
Point (18)	56 48 00	26 11 35
Point (19)	56 50 15	26 03 05
Point (20)	56 49 50	25 58 05
Point (21)	56 51 30	25 45 20

Point (22) is the most southern point located at the intersection of the geodetic demarcation line drawn from point (21) (specified above) at an azimuth angle of 190° 00 00' and of the lateral offshore boundary line between Oman and Sharjah. (28)

Figure 17

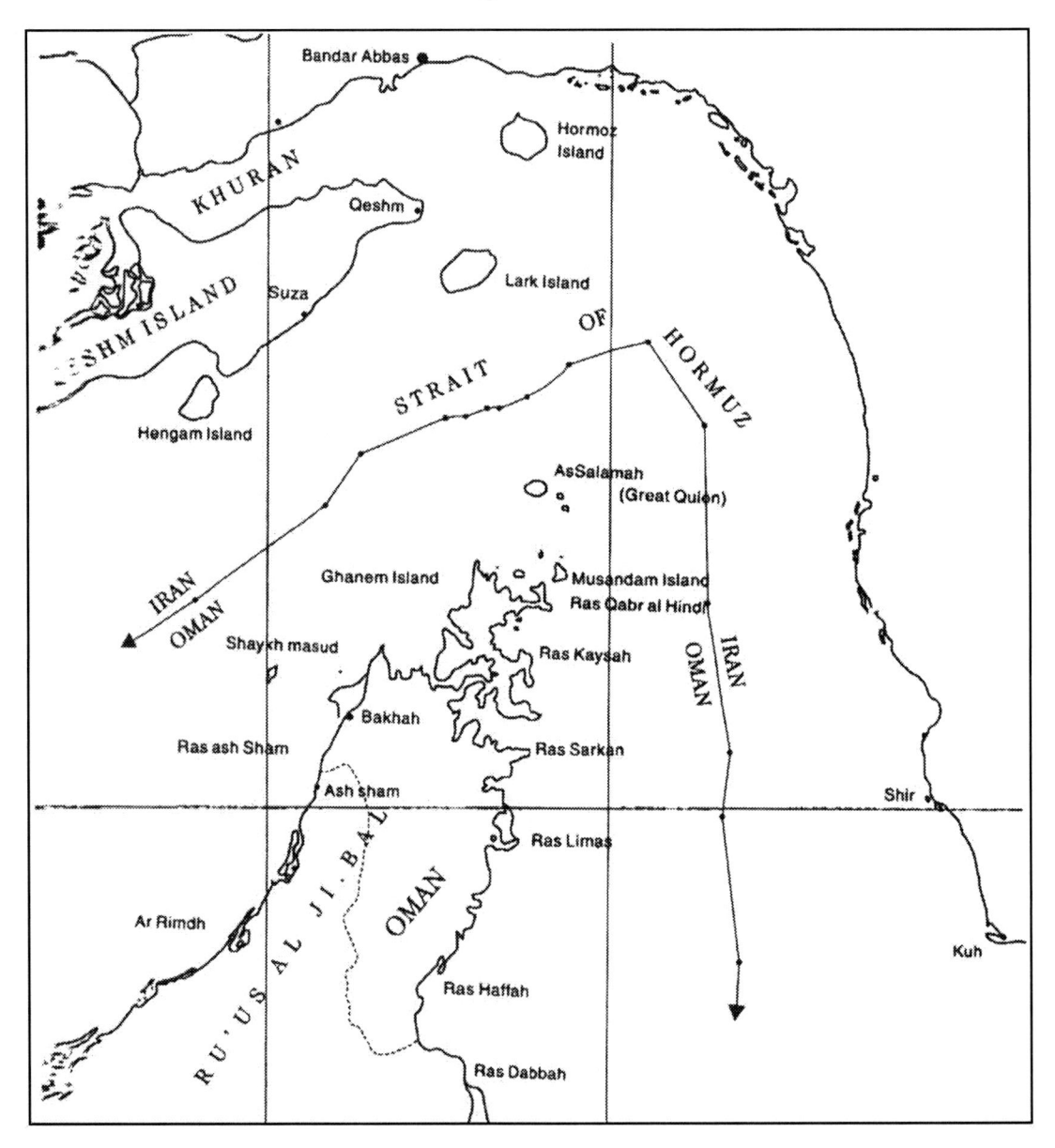

*Iran-Oman Continental Shelf Boundaries and shipping lanes
in the Strait of Hormuz
Source: Pirouz Mojtahed-Zadeh, Security and Territoriality in the
Persian Gulf, London 1999, p. 95*

This boundary runs for approximately 124.8 nautical miles and has 20 turning points. The terminal points, both in the Persian Gulf and in the Gulf of Oman, are not defined pending Oman's negotiations with the United Arab Emirates on their mutual continental shelf boundaries on both sides. This boundary in the Strait of

Hormuz is essentially an equidistant line except for one area in which the boundary line follows the 12 nautical mile arcs drawn from the Iranian Island of Larak.

Other Agreements

In the other parts of the Gulf, though no official offshore agreements exist between Iran and the other states, median line, is in practice, the principle of their mutual boundaries. Such understandings exist between Iran and some Arab countries like Kuwait (29) and between Iran and some emirates of the UAE. With Sharjah, the 1971 memorandum of understanding on Abu Musa Island provides for the enforcement of the Iranian regulation of 12 miles territorial waters, from the island's low-water mark base line. Sharjah had granted a concession to the Butes Oil and Gas Company, prior to the 1971 agreement with Iran, for the exploration and exploitation of oil from Abu Musa's offshore oilfield of Meidan Mobarak. The 1971 agreement with Iran permitted the BOGC to continue oil exploration in that oilfield, but the profit from it was agreed to be equally shared by Iran and Sharjah. Abu Musa's 12 miles territorial waters, on the other hand, overlapped that of Umm al-Quwain, where Occidental Oil Company was given exploration concession. The problem was subsequently settled by an informal agreement, which granted Umm al-Quwain 15% share of the oil revenues from the area (30).

An agreement was signed on August 31, 1974 between Iran and Dubai defining continental shelf boundaries between the two sides (see figure VIII) (31). Iran ratified the agreement on March 15, 1975, but the United Arab Emirates has not. The boundary needs to be continued to the east and to the west. An eastward extension will be complicated by the uncertainty resulting from claims of full sovereignty over the whole of Abu Musa Island by both Iran and UAE.

The 1974 agreement established a boundary, 39, 2 nautical miles in length that appears to be equidistant from the respective mainland and ignores the influence of islands. One section of the boundary follows the 12-nautical mile territorial sea drawn for the Iranian Island of Sirri. Using all territories the boundary is situated nearer to either the Island of Abu Musa or Sharjah's Island of Sir Bu Noair than to any other Dubai territory (32).

A draft agreement also exists between Iran and Abu Dhabi defining the two sides' continental shelf boundaries in the Gulf. Ratification of this boundary agreement is prevented by the boundary complications, which exist between Abu Dhabi and Saudi Arabia on the one hand, and Iran and the United Arab Emirates on the other.

Finally, in Tehran, foreign ministers of Iran and Pakistan signed a maritime boundary division agreement on 16 June 1997. The agreement, which defines the two countries' continental shelf boundaries, in the Gulf of Oman as far northeastward as Gwatar Bay, is described as a means of maritime cooperation between the two countries. The draft of this agreement was prepared in 1992 by the political and marine experts of Iran and Pakistan on the basis of international laws governing the division of seabed and sub-soil resources (33).

Figure 18

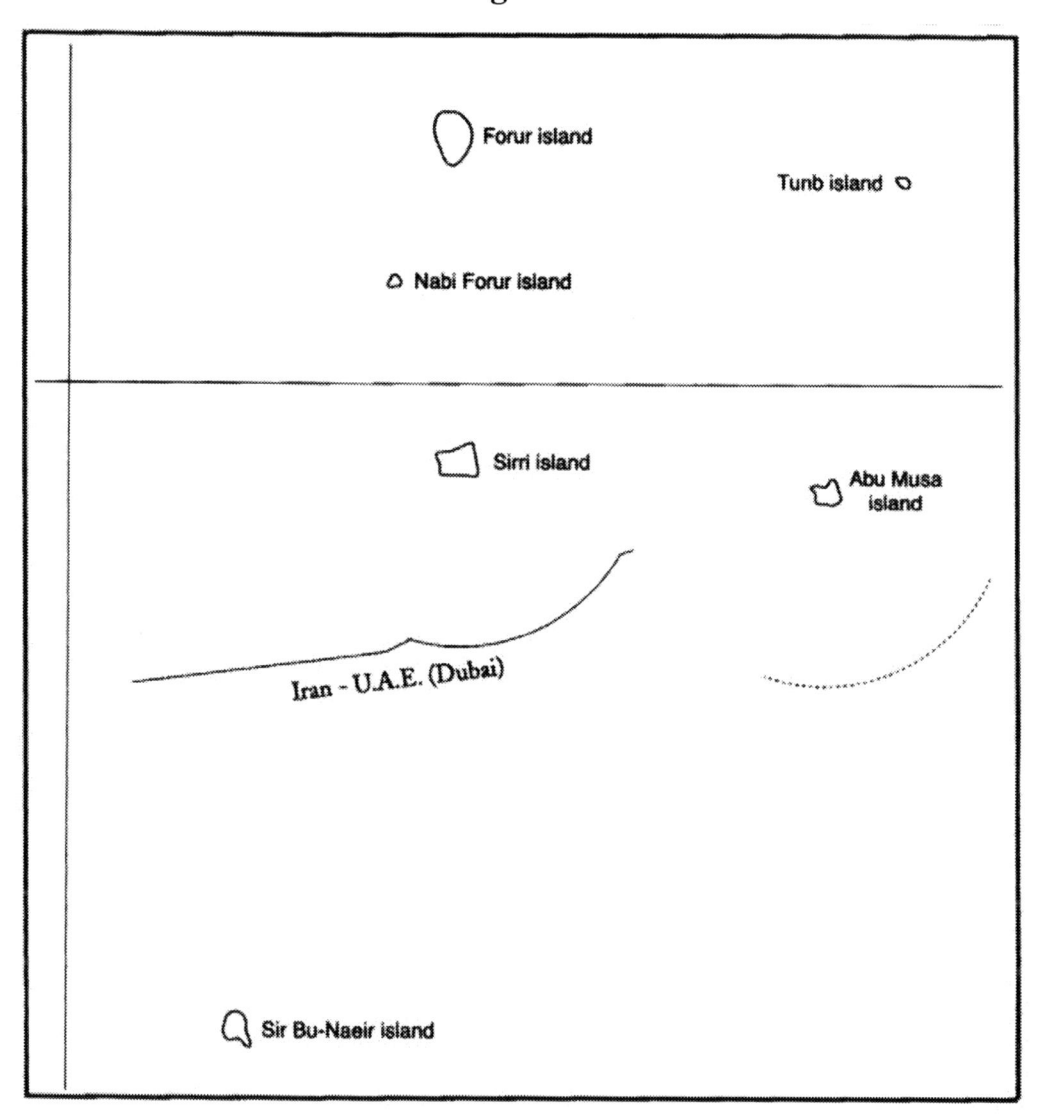

*Iran-Dubai Continental Shelf Boundaries in the Persian Gulf
Based on the map appearing in Limits in the Sea No. 94 (1981)*

References

1- Pirouz Mojtahed-Zadeh, "Political Geography of the Strait of Hormuz" Geography Department Publication, London University, January 1991, p.59.
2- Confidential from National Iranian Oil Company to the Ministry of Foreign Affairs, dated 21.7.1344 (13 October 1995). 1539/84, in Persian.
3- Confidential, from British Embassy in Tehran to Imperial Iranian Government dated 4 May 1966.
4- Pirouz Mojtahed-Zadeh, "Sheikh Neshinhay-e Khalij-e Fars = The Sheikhdoms of the Persian Gulf", Ataei Publications, Tehran 1970, p.22.
5- Iranian Foreign Ministry Book of Documents, IFM Ninth Political Bureau, Tehran 1976, pp.97, 100, 102, 104.
6- See appendix to the chapter for the documents.
7- G.H. Blake and R.N. Schofield, "Boundaries and State Territory in the Middle East and North Africa", MENAS Press Ltd., 1987 London, p.123.
8- Extract from letter of 13.12.1336 (12.3.1958), No. 2682, from Moshfeq Kazemi, Ambassador of the Imperia Government of Iran in India, to the Ministry of Foreign Affairs, "Gozideh-e Asnad-e Khalij-e Fars = A Selection of Persian Gulf Documents", IPIS publication, Vol. III, Tehran 1994, p. 187.
9- Richard Young (1970), "Equitable Solutions for Offshore Boundaries", The American Journal of International Law, Vol. 64 pp.125 to 157.
10- Pirouz Mojtahed-Zadeh, "Political Geography of the Strait of Hormuz", op. cit., pp.58-9.
11- Archive of Iran's binding treaties with other states, in Persian, Iranian Ministry of Foreign Affairs, Tehran 1976, p.33.
12- Limits in the Sea, 1981, op. cit., p.7.
13- Limits in the Sea 1981, op. cit., p.8.
14- Article II and III of Iran-Qatar continental shelf boundary agreement of 1969, Iranian Foreign Ministry, "Relations with UAE, Oman, Qatar", Tehran 1976, pp.109-111.
15- Confidential from National Iranian Oil Company to the Ministry of Foreign Affairs, dated 21.7.1344 (13 October 1965): No. 7539/84, p.1.
16- Report (in Persian) from the Legal Department of the Ministry of Foreign Affairs to the Locum Minister of that Ministry, dated Tehran 3.12.1347 (21.11.1968), No. 7193/18, page 2, paragraph 4, Iranian Foreign Ministry documents, File 34, No. 4-12, titled "The Iran-Qatar Petroleum".
17- Ibid.
18- National Legislative Series, UN Document No. ST/LEG/SER. B/16, p. 416 (1974)
19- Pirouz Mojtahed-Zadeh, "Political Geography of the Strait of Hormuz", op. cit., p.60.
20- Limits in the Sea, op. cit., pp.2 - 3.
21- National Legislative Series, UN Document No. ST/LEG/SER. B/16, p. 428 (1974).
22- Iranian Foreign Ministry, Documents & Treaties, op. cit., p.110.
23- Ibid.
24- National Iranian Oil Company, internal memorandum to the President of the Board of Directors, dated 28.9.1349 (19 December 1970), No. 90504/4922/Sh.W.
25- Ibid.
26- Iranian Foreign Ministry, Documents and Treaties, op. cit., p.116.
27- Pirouz Mojtahed-Zadeh, "Political Geography of the Strait of Hormuz", op. cit., p.61.

28- Article I of the treaty of Iran-Oman Continental Shelf Boundary, Iranian Foreign Ministry's Documents and Treaties, op. cit., p.177.
29- A draft agreement signed in 1962 governs unofficial Iran-Kuwait maritime boundary arrangements.
30- Pirouz Mojtahed-Zadeh, "Political Geography of the Strait of Hormuz", op. cit., p.60.
31- From Ministry of Foreign Affairs to National Iranian Oil Company, No. 119/18 dated 9/1/1352 (30/3/1973), selection of Persian Gulf Documents, Vol. 4, Document No. 331 34, IPIS, Tehran, 1995, pp. 93-6.
32- Limits in the Sea, No. 94, op. cit., p.3.
33- Ettelaat International, London, 18 June 1997, p.10.

APPENDIX TO CHAPTER XVI

Act on the Marine Areas of the Islamic Republic of Iran in the Persian Gulf and the Oman Sea, 1993

PART I
Territorial sea
Article 1
Sovereignty

The sovereignty of the Islamic Republic of Iran extends, beyond its land territory, internal waters and its islands in the Persian Gulf, the Strait of Hormuz and the Oman Sea, to a belt of sea, adjacent to the baseline, described as the territorial sea.

This sovereignty extends to the airspace over the territorial sea as well as to its bed and subsoil.

Article 2
Outer limit

The breadth of the territorial sea is 12 nautical miles, measured from the baseline. Each nautical mile is equal to 1,352 metres.

The islands belonging to the Islamic Republic of Iran, whether situated within or outside its territorial sea, have, in accordance with this Act, their own territorial sea.

Article 3
Baseline

In the Persian Gulf and the Oman Sea the baseline from which the breadth of the territorial sea is measured is that one determined in Decree No. 2/250-67 dated 31 Tir 1352 (22 July 1973) of the Council of Ministers (annexed to this Act) (*); in other areas and islands, the low-water line along the coast constitutes the baseline.

Waters on the landward side of the baseline of the territorial sea, and waters between islands belonging to the Islamic Republic of Iran, where the distance of such islands does not exceed 24 nautical miles, form part of the internal waters and are under the sovereignty of the Islamic Republic of Iran.

Article 4
Delimitation

Wherever the territorial sea of the Islamic Republic of Iran overlaps the territorial seas of the states with opposite or adjacent coasts, the dividing line between the territorial seas of the Islamic Republic of Iran and those States shall be, unless otherwise agreed between the two parties, the median line every point of which is equidistant from the nearest point on the baseline of both States.

Article 5
Innocent passage

The passage of foreign vessels, except as provided for in article 9, is subject to the principle of innocent passage so long as it is not prejudicial to the good order, peace and security of the Islamic Republic of Iran.

Passage, except as in cases of *forcemajeure*, shall be continuous and expeditious.

Article 6
Requirements of innocent passage

Passage of foreign vessels, in cases when they are engaged in any of the following activities, shall not be considered innocent and shall be subject to relevant civil and criminal laws and regulations:

(a) Any threat or use of force against the sovereignty, territorial integrity or political independence of the Islamic Republic of Iran, or in any other manner in violation of the principles of international law;

(b) Any exercise or practice with weapons of any kind;

Any act aimed at collecting information prejudicial to the national security, defence or economic interests of the Islamic Republic of Iran;

(d) Any act of propaganda aimed at affecting the national security, defence or economic interests of the Islamic Republic of Iran;

(e) The launching, landing or transferring on board of any aircraft or helicopter, or any military devices or personnel to another vessel or to the coast;

(f) The loading or unloading of any commodity, currency or person contrary to the laws and regulations of the Islamic Republic of Iran;

(g) Any act of pollution of the marine environment contrary to the rules and regulations of the Islamic Republic of Iran;

(h) Any act of fishing or exploitation of the marine resources;

(i) The carrying out of any specific research and cartographic and seismic surveys or sampling activities;

(j) Interfering with any systems of communication or any other facilities or installations of the Islamic Republic of Iran;

(k) Any other activity not having a direct bearing on passage.

Article 7
Supplementary laws and regulations

The Government of the Islamic Republic of Iran shall adopt such other regulations as are necessary for the protection of its national interests and the proper conduct of innocent passage.

Article 8
Suspension of innocent passage

The Government of the Islamic Republic of Iran, inspired by its high national interests and to defend its security, may suspend the innocent passage in parts of its territorial sea.

Article 9
Exceptions to innocent passage

Passage of warships, submarines, nuclear-powered ships and vessels or any other floating objects or vessels carrying nuclear or other dangerous or noxious substances harmful to the environment, through the territorial sea is subject to the prior authorization of the relevant authorities of the Islamic Republic of Iran. Submarines are required to navigate on the surface and to show their flag.

Article 10
Criminal jurisdiction

In the following cases, the investigation, prosecution and punishment in connection with any crimes committed on board the ships passing through the territorial sea is within the jurisdiction of the judicial authorities of the Islamic Republic of Iran:

(a) If the consequences of the crime extend to the Islamic Republic of Iran;

(b) If the crime is of a kind to disturb the peace and order of the country or the public order of the territorial sea;

If the master of the ship or a diplomatic agent or consular officer of the flag State asks for the assistance and investigation;

(d) If such investigation and prosecution is essential for the suppression of illicit traffic in narcotic drugs or psychotropic substances.

Article 11
Civil jurisdiction

The competent authorities of the Islamic Republic of Iran may stop, divert or detain a ship and its crew for the enforcement of attachment orders or court judgements if:

(a) The ship is passing through the territorial sea after leaving the internal waters of Iran;

(b) The ship is lying in the territorial sea of the Islamic Republic of Iran;

The ship is passing through the territorial sea, provided that the origin of the attachment order or court judgement rests in the obligations or requirements arising from the civil liability of the ship itself.

PART II
Contiguous zone
Article 12
Definition

The contiguous zone is an area adjacent to the territorial sea the outer limit of which is 24 nautical miles from the baseline.

Article 13
Civil and criminal jurisdiction

The Government of the Islamic Republic of Iran may adopt measures necessary to prevent the infringement of laws and regulations in the contiguous zone, including security, customs, maritime, fiscal, immigration, sanitary and environmental laws and regulations and investigation and punishment of offenders.

PART III
Exclusive economic zone and continental shelf
Article 14
Sovereign rights and jurisdiction in the exclusive economic zone

Beyond its territorial sea, which is called the exclusive economic zone, the Islamic Republic of Iran exercises its sovereign rights and jurisdiction with regard to:

(a) Exploration, exploitation, conservation and management of all natural resources, whether living or non-living, of the seabed and subsoil thereof and its superjacent waters, and with regard to other economic activities for the production of energy from water, currents and winds. These rights are exclusive.

(b) Adoption and enforcement of appropriate laws and regulations, especially for the following activities:

(i) The establishment and use of artificial islands and other installations and structures, laying of submarine cables and pipelines and the establishment of relevant security and safety zones;

(ii) Any kind of research;

(iii) The protection and preservation of the marine environment;

(c) Such sovereign rights as granted by regional or international treaties.

Article 15
Sovereign rights and jurisdiction in the continental shelf

The provisions of article 14 shall apply *mutatis mutandis* to the sovereign rights and jurisdiction of the Islamic Republic of Iran in its continental shelf, which comprises the seabed and subsoil of the marine areas that extend beyond the territorial sea throughout the natural prolongation of the land territory.

Article 16
Prohibited activities

Foreign military activities and practices, collection of information and any other activity inconsistent with the rights and interests of the Islamic Republic of Iran in the exclusive economic zone and the continental shelf are prohibited.

Article 17
Scientific activities, exploration and research

Any activity to recover drowned objects and scientific research and exploration in the exclusive economic zone and the continental shelf is subject to the permission of the relevant authorities of the Islamic Republic of Iran.

Article 18
Preservation of the environment and natural resources

The Government of the Islamic Republic of Iran shall take appropriate measures for the protection and preservation of the marine environment and proper exploitation of living and other resources of the exclusive economic zone and the continental shelf.

Article 19
Delimitation

The limits of the exclusive economic zone and the continental shelf of the Islamic Republic of Iran, unless otherwise determined in accordance with bilateral agreements, shall be a line every point of which is equidistant from the nearest point on the baseline of two States.

Article 20
Civil and criminal jurisdiction

The Islamic Republic of Iran shall exercise its criminal and civil jurisdiction against offenders of the laws and regulations in the exclusive economic zone and continental shelf and shall, as appropriate, investigate or detain them.

Article 21
Right of hot pursuit

The Government of the Islamic Republic of Iran reserves its right of hot pursuit against offenders of laws and regulations relating to its internal waters, territorial sea, contiguous zone, exclusive economic zone and the continental shelf, in such areas and the high seas.

PART IV
Final provisions
Article 22
Executive regulations

The Council of Ministers shall specify the mandates and responsibilities [powers and duties] of different ministries and organizations charged with the enforcement of this Act.

The said ministries and organizations shall, within one year after the approval of this Act, prepare the necessary regulations and have them approved by the Council of Ministers.

Pending the adoption of new executive regulations, the existing rules and regulations shall remain in force.

Article 23

All laws and regulations contrary to the present Act, upon its ratification, are hereby abrogated.

The above Act, comprising 23 articles, was ratified at the plenary meeting of Tuesday, the thirty-first day of Farvrdin, one thousand three hundred and seventy-two (20 April 1993), of the Islamic Consultative Assembly and was approved by the Council of Guardians on Ordibehesht 12, 1372 (2 May 1993).

II. PROTESTS FROM STATES AND COMMUNICATION
1. Protests from the United States of America, 11 January 1994

The Permanent Mission of the United States of America to the United Nations presents its compliments to the United Nations and has the honour to advise that the Government of the United States of America has studied carefully the legislative acts of the Islamic Republic of Iran setting forth the Islamic Republic of Iran's maritime claims, including the Act on the Marine Areas of the Islamic Republic of Iran in the Persian Gulf and the Oman Sea of 2 May 1993, and Decree-Law No. 2/250-67, 31 Tir 1352 [22 July 1973] of the Council of Ministers, taking into account the relevant provisions of international law as reflected in the 1982 United Nations Convention on the Law of the Sea, which will enter into force on 16 November 1994.

The United States is of the view that certain provisions of these acts are inconsistent with international law, and the United States reserves its rights and the rights of its nationals in that regard.

The United States wishes to recall that, as recognized in customary international law and as reflected in the 1982 United Nations Convention on the Law of the Sea, except where otherwise provided in the Convention, the normal baseline for measuring the breadth of the territorial sea is the low-water line along the coast as marked on large-scale charts officially recognized by the coastal State. Only in localities where the coastline is deeply indented and cut into, or if there is a fringe of islands along the coast in its immediate vicinity, may the coastal State elect to use the method of straight baselines joining appropriate points in drawing the baseline from which the breadth of the territorial sea is measured.

The United States notes that, notwithstanding the fact that the Iranian coastline is rarely deeply indented or fringed by islands, the Islamic Republic of Iran has employed straight baselines along most of its coastline and that, in the vicinity of most segments, the Iranian coastline is quite smooth. Consequently, the appropriate baseline for virtually all of the Iranian coast in the Persian Gulf and the Gulf of Oman is the normal baseline, the low-water line.

While the Convention does not set a maximum length for baseline segments, many of the segments set out in Iranian law are excessively long. In fact, 11 of the 21 segments are between 30 and 120 miles long. The United States believes that the maximum length of an approximately drawn straight baseline segment normally should not exceed 24 nautical miles.

The United States also wishes to recall that islands may not be used to define internal waters, except for situations where the islands are part of a valid straight baseline system, or of a closing line for a juridical bay. Article 3 of the 1993 Marine Areas Act of the Islamic Republic of Iran asserts that waters between islands belonging to the Islamic Republic of Iran where the distance of such islands does not exceed 24 nautical miles form part of the internal waters of the Islamic Republic of Iran. This claim has no basis in international law. The United States notes that article

19 (2) (h) of the 1982 Law of the Sea Convention provides that "any act of wilful and serious pollution contrary to this Convention" may be considered prejudicial to the peace, good order or security of the coastal State. In specifying activities in its territorial sea that the Islamic Republic of Iran does not consider to be innocent, article 6 (g) of the 1993 Marine Areas Act includes "any act of pollution of the marine environment contrary to the rules and regulations of the Islamic Republic of Iran". The United States assumes that the relevant Iranian rules and regulations will conform to the accepted rule of international law set out in article 19 (2) (h) of the 1982 Law of the Sea Convention.

The United States recalls that, under articles 21 and 24 of the 1982 Law of the Sea Convention, a coastal State may adopt laws and regulations relating to innocent passage relating to the design, construction, manning or equipment of foreign ships only if they are giving effect to generally accepted international rules or standards, and may not adopt requirements that have the practical effect of denying or impairing the right of innocent passage or of discriminating in form or in fact against the ships of any State or against ships carrying cargoes to, from or on behalf of any State.

The United States notes that the Islamic Republic of Iran's claim in article 7 of the right to adopt "such other regulations as are necessary for the protection of its national interests and the proper conduct of innocent passage" cannot confer upon it any greater rights than those authorized under international law.

The United States also notes that international law permits a coastal State to suspend temporarily in specified areas of its territorial sea the innocent passage of foreign ships if such suspension is essential for the protection of its security, and that such suspension may take effect only after having been duly published.

Article 8 of the Islamic Republic of Iran's 1993 Marine Areas Act cannot be accepted as removing the requirements that any suspension of innocent passage through parts of its territorial sea be temporary and that it take effect only after being duly published.

Article 9 of the 1993 Marine Areas Act impermissibly seeks to require foreign warships, and vessels carrying dangerous or noxious substances harmful to the environment, to obtain prior authorization from the Islamic Republic of Iran to pass through the Islamic Republic of Iran's territorial sea.

Such a requirement has no foundation in the provisions of the 1982 Law of the Sea Convention, and the United States will continue to reject, as contrary to international law, any attempt to impose such a requirement on the exercise of the right of innocent passage of all ships.

The United States assumes that the Islamic Republic of Iran will not seek to exercise criminal jurisdiction, pursuant to article 10 of the 1993 Marine Areas Act, on board ships other than merchant ships and government ships operated for commercial purposes, or to exercise civil jurisdiction, pursuant to article 11 of this Act, in situations not contemplated by article 28 of the 1982 Law of the Sea Convention.

The United States further recalls that the scope of a coastal State's authority in its contiguous zone, a maritime zone contiguous to and seaward of the territorial sea in which freedoms of navigation and overflight may be exercised, is limited to the exercise of the control necessary to prevent and punish infringement of its customs, fiscal, immigration and sanitary laws and regulations committed within its territory or territorial sea, and that the authority of the coastal State to enforce its environmental laws seaward of its territorial sea is as prescribed in article 220 of the Convention.

The claim in article 13 of the 1993 Act to adopt measures in the Islamic Republic of Iran's contiguous zone necessary to prevent infringement of its security, maritime and environmental laws exceeds that permitted by international law.

Although a coastal State may establish, in accordance with article 60, paragraphs 4 and 5, of the 1982 Law of the Sea Convention, safety zones of a radius not exceeding 500 metres around artificial islands and other installations and structures located within its exclusive economic zone, international law does not authorize a coastal State to establish so-called security zones in such areas. Article 14 (b) (1) of the 1993 Marine Areas Act impermissibly asserts the right to do so. That provision also appears to claim more authority to control the laying of submarine cables and pipelines on the Islamic Republic of Iran's continental shelf than is permitted by international law as reflected in article 79 of the 1982 Law of the Sea Convention.

Further, international law permits a coastal State to regulate only marine scientific research in its exclusive economic zone, not "any kind of research" as claimed in article 14 (b) (2) of the 1993 Marine Areas Act. In particular, hydrographic surveys conducted seaward of the territorial sea are not marine scientific research and are not subject to coastal State jurisdiction.

The United States notes that, to the extent article 16 of the 1993 Marine Areas Act seeks to prohibit in the Iranian exclusive economic zone the exercise by foreign warships and military aircraft of their freedoms of navigation and overflight, it contravenes international law. The United States has previously protested the Islamic Republic of Iran's claim in this regard, and will continue to operate its ships and aircraft consistent with its rights under international law.

The Government of the United States wishes to assure the Government of the Islamic Republic of Iran that its objections to these claims should not be viewed as singling out the Islamic Republic of Iran for criticism, but is part of its worldwide effort to preserve the internationally recognized rights and freedoms of the international community in navigation and overflight and other related high seas uses, and thereby maintain the balance of interests reflected in the Convention.

This is only one of a number of United States protests of those claims by coastal States, which are not consistent with international law as reflected in the 1982 United Nations Convention on the Law of the Sea.

The Government of the United States requests that this Note be circulated by the United Nations as part of the next Law of the Sea Bulletin.

2. Comments from the Islamic Republic of Iran concerning the viewpoints of the Government of the United States of America regarding the Act of Marine Areas in the Persian Gulf and the Oman Sea

The Government of the Islamic Republic of Iran took careful note of the viewpoints of the Government of the United States of America regarding the Act on the Marine of the Islamic Republic of Iran in the Persian Gulf and the Oman Sea as expressed in the latter's note of 11 January 1994, and would like to make, in this respect, the following comments:

In the note of the United States, reference was repeatedly made to customary rules and regulations of international law as embodied in the United Nations Convention on the Law of the Sea of 10 December 1982; and it appears that the United States believes that the provisions of the Convention are of a customary nature, the observance of which being obligatory to all States whether or not they are parties to the Convention; and on this basis some provisions of the Marine Areas Act have been considered as inconsistent with the rules of international law.

In this regard, it is necessary to explain that the Islamic Republic of Iran, unlike the United States, does not consider all provisions of the Convention as customary law and believes that many of them which are the result of years of negotiations in the framework of the Third United Nations Conference on the Law of the Sea and preparation of regulations in the form of a package deal, are of contractual nature the binding force of which depends on the entry into force of the Convention on the Law of the Sea for the States Parties. The Islamic Republic of Iran had already declared, at the time of signing the Convention on 10 December 1982, that:

> *Notwithstanding the intended character of the Convention being one of general application and of law-making nature, certain provisions are merely [the] product of quid pro quo which do not necessarily purport to codify the existing customs or established usage (practice) regarded as having an obligatory character. Therefore, it seems natural and in harmony with article 34 of the 1969 Vienna Convention on the Law of Treaties, that only States parties to the Law of the sea Convention shall be entitled to benefit from the contractual rights created therein.*

It is also to be noted that the United States, in its note, referred to 16 November 1994 as the date of the entry into force of the Convention, a reference which will be necessary if the provisions of the Convention were of a customary nature.

It is quite clear that making a distinction between customary and conventional rules of international law is a complicated task and as long as a general belief on the binding force of a particular conduct is not definitely realized, one may not speak of it as a custom. From the viewpoint of the Islamic Republic of Iran, the adoption of different laws by States on their rights and jurisdiction in seas, which are in many cases inconsistent with the 1982 Convention, is an indication of the fact that as yet no definite custom has been formed.

The method of decision-making on some of the provisions of the Convention in the proceedings of the Third United Nations Conference on the Law of the Sea also demonstrates the uncertainty of their customary nature. For instance, reference can be made to the issue of the right of coastal States to enforce regulations for their security in the territorial sea which was emphasized in the course of the Conference by the Group of 27 (including the Islamic Republic of Iran) and a proposal was submitted for amendment of article 21 of the preliminary draft Convention. Although, on the request of the Chairman of the Conference, the Group agreed not to insist on voting for the proposal, in his statement of 26 April 1982, the Chairman stated that:

> *The sponsors of the amendment have persisted that this decision would not in any way damage the right of littoral States in taking necessary measures for the safeguard of their security interests according to articles 19 and 25 of the suggested text of the Convention.*

Until the enactment of the recent Act in the Islamic Republic of Iran, there existed several laws and regulations, each one of them covering a part of issues relating to the law of the sea matters, while in some cases developments in such rules concerning the expansion of States' jurisdiction were not provided for. The Marine Areas Act was therefore prepared and approved with the aim of compiling all relevant regulations in a single comprehensive text so as to replace previous laws and at the same time to include the most recent developments of the law of the sea. A list of the relevant laws and regulations is attached to the present note.

Decree No. 2/250-67, dated 31 Tir, 1352 (22 July 1973) is amongst such regulations approved and put into force nearly 20 years ago. Usage of the straight baselines is in one way considered as an unusual measure, as other States, too, use the same method under similar circumstances. The reason for further emphasis on the Decree of 1973 was that since its enforcement and in spite of its international circulation in the collections circulated by the United Nations Secretariat, so far no objections have been received thereto. The Islamic Republic of Iran, therefore, considers this as a recognition of its content by the international community.

As mentioned in the United States' note, there is no criterion in international law to determine the maximum length of parts of the straight baselines; thus the reference made by the United States to 24 nautical miles lacks legal foundation. Instead, in drawing the line, effort has been made to employ those criteria, which have been internationally important and were later mentioned in the Convention. Among them is the drawing of straight baselines in a way that they do not depart in any appreciable extent from the general direction of the coast (article 7, para. 3), and it has also been taken into account that in determining the straight baselines, the coastal States may consider the economic interests peculiar to the region concerned, the reality and importance of which are clearly evidenced by long usage.

As for the declaration of waters between islands whose distance is less than 24 nautical miles as internal waters it is noteworthy to recall the Act on Territorial Waters and the Contiguous Zone of Iran dated Tir 24, 1313 (July 1934), and its amendment of 22 Farvardin 1338 (11 April 1959), according to which similar rules have been provided in connection with islands belonging to the Islamic Republic of Iran, and in the recent Act the criterion for the distance between islands has been changed in conformity with the extension of the breadth of territorial sea. Moreover, in recent years, the context of some of its provisions, such as the authority of the Government of the Islamic Republic of Iran in the field of marine scientific research in areas beyond the territorial sea, while being consistent with the recognized rules of international law, has been observed by other States, and for example marine scientific research in the areas under the jurisdiction of the Islamic Republic of Iran has been carried out after a prior consent has been granted. In this connection, the Islamic Republic of Iran assumes that any kind of scientific research in the exclusive economic zone, because of its effects on the exploration and exploitation of living and mineral resources and economic interests, is directly linked to the rights of the coastal State (in this case Islamic Republic of Iran) and should be conducted with prior authorization. In accordance with the Law of the Sea Convention, even in cases where the scientific research is conducted exclusively for peaceful purposes and in order to increase scientific knowledge of the marine environment for the benefit of all mankind, the matter has not been excluded from the jurisdiction of the coastal state and under normal circumstances such a State is merely requested to grant its consent without reasonable delay (article 246 (3) of the Convention). Therefore, hydrographic research, even though it falls under this category, would require the authorization of the coastal State.

In drafting the Act, the ecological and environmental conditions of the Persian Gulf are another main issue, which was taken into consideration, to which fundamental importance should be attached. From an environmental point of view, the Persian Gulf as a semi-enclosed sea is very vulnerable and that is why it has been recognised as a special area in some international treaties relating to the marine environment. The limited width of the Persian Gulf (as the share of each opposite State in the widest parts is less than 100 miles), its shallowness, the volume of economic activities, particularly in the field of fishing and the oil industry, and the scope of navigation traffic have created a situation where the smallest incident inflicts severe enduring pollution of the marine environment. The sinking of a Russian cargo ship, "Kapitan Sakharov", a few months ago, which brought about hazards and damage, particularly in fishing and navigation, could be set as a good example for the importance of the issue. With regard to this matter, the littoral States of the Persian Gulf have taken coordinated measures, in the framework of the Kuwait Convention (1978) and its protocols, to protect the marine environment, which, in comparison, have been more comprehensive than the measures taken in other regions.

Some of the objections raised by the United States to the Marine Areas act of the Islamic Republic of Iran are also in connection with the regulations drawn up with due consideration to this very particularity of the Persian Gulf region, such as not regarding as innocent the passage of ships which, against the laws and regulations of the Islamic Republic of Iran, cause any sort of marine pollution in the territorial sea.

The requirement of obtaining a prior authorization for the passage of some categories of foreign vessels, especially for ships carrying hazardous substances, was also put in to have more supervision of the traffic of such vessels and with the aim of protecting the marine environment of the region. The same argument applies to the environmental regulations to be enforced in the contiguous zone.

As for the question of a 500 metre zone around oil platforms and installations, it is necessary to emphasize that, due to the high number of exploitation platforms and the volume of shipping traffic, the establishing of such a zone is completely necessary for the security of installations as well as international navigation. As for the competence of the coastal State in laying submarine cable sand pipelines, it is also to be noted that the Government of the Islamic Republic of Iran, having due regard to the same considerations, deems a prior permission a necessary requirement: to give an example, it clearly emphasized this point in its reservations, at the time of signing the 1958 Geneva Conventions on High Seas and on the Continental Shelf.

As for article 16 of the Act, attention is to be given to the fact that, due to the multiplicity of economic activities in the region, it is possible that such activities, for which the coastal State enjoys sovereign rights, could be harmed by military practices and manoeuvres; accordingly, those practices which effect the economic activities in the exclusive economic zone and the continental shelf are thus prohibited.

---

*The text of Decree No. 2/250-67 dated 31 Tir 1352 (22 July 1973) is not annexed to this Act; it has already been reproduced in: United Nations Legislative Series, National Legislation and Treaties relating to the Law of the Sea (ST/LEG/SER.B/19), p. 55.

CHAPTER XVII

The Unfinished Case of Iran - Kuwait Maritime Boundary Delimitation
Sohrab Asghari

Introduction

Iran's presence in the Persian Gulf is a fact of long history. However, the contemporary history of the Persian Gulf is significantly characterized by events that relate to extra-regional powers, which, since the discovery of oil in the region, have held rival economic and strategic interests in the region. Such interests and more importantly the discovery of oil has played a key role in highlighting the need and accelerating the push towards the delimitation of maritime boundaries in the Persian Gulf over the last half-century or so.

Many instances of boundary delimitation have since been negotiated, signed and enforced in accordance with international law. However, several remain undecided and pose the potential for further dispute in the future. This paper concentrates on Iran-Kuwait maritime boundary, its historical background, current complications, and the prospects for its future settlement.

Iran's first effort to delimitate its maritime boundaries in the Persian Gulf dates back to 1965, when Iran and Britain (as protectorate of the Arab Emirates) discussed the question of maritime boundaries in the Persian Gulf. Based on these negotiations the adoption of an equitable line was accepted as a principle for Persian Gulf continental shelf delimitation between Iran and its Arab neighbors.

Iran - Saudi Arabia.

Iran delimited its first maritime boundary Saudi Arabia in 1968. This delimitation remains the longest maritime boundary in the Persian Gulf and arguably the most complicated because of the presence of many energy fields around the line and the question over the sovereignty of Farsi and Al-Arabi islands. However, an agreement was reached whereby Iran's sovereignty over the Farsi Island and Saudi Arabia's sovereignty over the Al-Arabi Island was finalized, with a 12 nautical mile territorial sea determined for the two islands.

In an attempt to avoid an unsatisfactory situation for either side with regards the Kharg Island, the parties agreed to give half effect to Kharg by dividing in half the disputed zone located between the median lines drawn by Iran. Based on this compromise, on October 24th 1968 the parties singed the final agreement that came into force on January 29th 1969.

Undefined Maritime Boundaries

Iran has yet to delimit its maritime boundaries with Kuwait, Iraq and United Arab Emirates.

Iran and Kuwait Maritime Boundary Negotiations (1965-1970)

The difficulties between Iran and Kuwait arose in 1963, when the National Iranian Oil Company (NIOC) declared its announcement regarding offshore explorations in a gas field area (al-Dorra) not yet delimited and thus, claimed by both countries.

In June 1955 the Iranian Parliament had approved "The law concerning natural resources discovery and exploitation in the continental shelf of Iran in the Persian Gulf". Subsequent to that ratification, in August 1957, there was another approval that was named "the law of oil". Based on this law the National Iranian oil Company (NIOC) was allowed to perform any operations necessary in order to accelerate the refinery, transportation and selling of exploited oil. The NIOC therefore divided the northern Persian Gulf into several sections and put them to international tender.

In June 1963, Kuwait protested against Iran's action on the grounds that it violated Kuwait's territorial sovereignty and continental shelf. This was the main factor that henceforth motivated the two countries to try and reach an agreement.

On June 9th 1965 (19th Khordad 1344) a schedule on primary continental shelf delimitation was signed by Iran's charged' affairs in Kuwait and that country's Foreign Minister. This was, in effect, a preface to later talks.

During bilateral talks on October 18th 1965, the Kuwaiti delegation presented a memorandum containing a preliminary scheme by which the Kuwaitis wanted to use all of the islands as a part of baseline for both sides. Nevertheless, they proclaimed that if Iran wanted to ignore all of the islands and accept the main land as a base line, then they would do too. But they said that it would have to be on the condition that such base lines are to be considered in a wider area and that Saudi Arabia, which protested Kuwaiti-Iranian exploitations in the area, be invited to attend the negotiations as well.

On October 19th 1965, spurred by their inability to reach an agreement over overlapping oil concessions with Kuwait, the Iranian delegation offered a scheme to the Kuwaitis, which sought to answer two main questions. These were: 1- which limits and 2- which factors must be considered in the continental shelf delimitation? After examining all dimensions of the difficulty, Iran worked out and suggested three possible solutions, which were:

1- The Kuwaiti delegation must determine the limitation in such a way that Saudi Arabia would not protest against it.
2- The talks include not only Kuwait's main land but also the neutral zone's continental shelf, so that Iran and Kuwait would not have any problems in the future.
3- An invitation to be extended to Saudi Arabia to attend in trilateral talks, so that an ultimate solution is reached in the neutral zone as well.

Kuwait rejected Iran's scheme and announced that it was not responsible for a third country's (Saudi Arabia) claim. It added that negotiations at that time were about Kuwait-Iranian continental shelf delimitation and Saudi Arabia would not accept the results of talks about neutral zone. This highlighted two important factors:

That the definition of Kuwaiti continental shelf limitation will be based on Shell Oil Company's definition of exploitation limits.

At present Kuwait will only consider for negotiations only the common coastline pertaining to Iran and Kuwait line, not that that of the neutral zone's. At this time Kuwait thought it appropriate to approach bilateral maritime boundary delimitation talks rather than trilateral negations i.e. neutral zone with Saudi Arabia.

In another meeting between the two parties on October 21st 1965, Iran's delegation described in detail, historical and contemporary factors, which would effect any continental shelf delimitation:
1- The principle of fact, which includes geographical details of the area concerned, and it is necessary in this context to consider the historical and residential basis of these areas.
2- Enforcement of the principal of law; in this context application of the international conventions and national laws is intended.
3- Enforcement of the principal of equity.
4- Considering the economic conditions of the two countries, as well as their population size, per capita income, economic development conditions and, domestic oil consumption.
5- The existing situation pertaining to guaranteeing the two parties' rights and interests.

Having signed a protocol, both sides wanted negotiations to continue until a final agreement is reached. In October 1965, Sheikh Abdullah Salem as-Sabah, Ruler of Kuwait addressing the Kuwaiti parliament said:

> *Recently my government has signed an agreement with the friendly government of Iran according to which a technical committee will be formed to negotiate the two countries' continental shelf boundaries. My government will confirm any steps that extend relationships between Arab States and Islamic countries and wishes success for them.* (5)

Two further rounds of joint negotiations were held in Tehran in December 1967, in which the concession agreements with IPAC, SIRRIP and Shell were also discussed. On these matters the Iranian delegation declared that Iran's continental shelf limitations had been determined by the agreements with Pan American (presumably this is the same as IPAC) and SIRRIPP, which had been verified both by the Iranian government and parliament. This delegation added that the criteria applied to determine the outer edge of IPAC is consideration of the full effect of Kharg Island on the opposite side of Kuwait's main coastline. The Kuwaitis in response declared that Failakah group of islands such as Owhah and Ras al-Yahi as that country's baseline like Kharg Island.

On the effect of the Kharg Island, the Iranian delegation stated that in consideration of their previous position on the issue of coast-to-coast median line as well as considering the full effect of Kharg Island, they are prepared to accept Failakah as an exception like Kharg Island. The Kuwaiti delegation's response to this was that if hypothetically they were to accept these terms, then what would Iran's situation be if Saudi Arabia didn't accept it in respect of the coats of the Neutral Zone?

To this, Iran responded by noting that reaching a comprehensive agreement regarding Kuwait's main land continental shelf would be based on an agreement on a neutral zone continental shelf. At this meeting, Iran also protested against Shell Oil Company's exploitation area. Subsequently, negotiations ended with out any agreement.

A report sent by the National Iranian Oil Company on April 14th 1975 to the Iranian Foreign minister specified the followings. 'The agreed principles of negotiations during the December

1967 meeting accepted the full effect of Kharg Island and the Fasht al-Mava tidal raising on the Iranian side, and the full effect of Failakah Island and the tidal raising of Rasalyahe on the Kuwaiti side. This report was repeated in the letter of 28 January 1969, from the Iranian Foreign Minister to his Kuwaiti counterpart.

The report adds that negotiations continued again in December1968, where the Kuwaiti delegation withheld acceptance of the principles of negotiations of December 1967, and only agreed to the full effect of the Kharg Island and the Kuwaiti exclusive zone. Iran suggested that by means of avoiding a deadlock in negotiations, the two countries should base their agreement on the principle of dividing the energy field in the disputed areas in accordance with Saudi-Iranian agreement. Kuwait did not accept this suggestion.

On July 8[th,] 1970 Ardeshir Zahedi, Iranian Foreign Minister visited Kuwait at the end which a joint statement was issued. One of the matters this statement addressed was the delimitation of the two country's maritime boundaries. It was also indicated in this statement that "the two sides discussed the issue of the two countries' continental shelf and have agreed that the tasks of the technical committees should be complete as soon as possible so that the final agreement can be concluded (6).

Though it was expected that Iran-Kuwait maritime boundaries be determined and delimited, but this was not to happen as the Kuwaitis changed their original position.

In the Meantime, a report prepared by the Undersecretary of state for Iranian Petroleum Ministry for International Affairs on January 13th 1998 entitled: 'Continental shelf delimitation between Iran with the countries of the Persian Gulf countries and Caspian Sea. This report specified that eventually a draft agreement had been prepared in 1970 but was not concluded. It was specified in the draft agreement that on the subject of continental shelf delimitation, Iran and Kuwait accepted the full effect of the Kharg Island and that of the shoals of Fasht al-Moa on the Iranian side and full effect of Failakah islands and shoals of Ras al-Yasi on the Kuwaiti side (7). This draft agreement was not finalized and the issue of maritime boundaries of the two states remained unresolved.

The 1970-1990 Negotiations

During 1970s, 1980s and 1990s there were no continental shelf delimitation negotiations between Iran and Kuwait until diplomatic and economic incentives prompted Kuwait and Saudi Arabia to delimit their mutual continental shelf for the Neutral Zone; an important precursor to any Iran-Kuwait agreement.

With the commencement of Saudi Arabian-Kuwait negotiations for the delimitation of the continental shelf areas of former Neutral Zone, the Iranian-Kuwaiti diplomacy was also mobilized. In January 1996, the former Iranian Petroleum Minister visited Kuwait, where after negotiating with Kuwaiti authorities he announced that Iran and Kuwait were to postpone signing a continental shelf delimitation so as to allow Kuwait and Saudi Arabia to delimit their maritime boundary. He added that in light of this development he predicted that the Iran and Kuwait continental shelf delimitation would be finalized in the near future.

Geographical Limits of Iran –
Kuwait Maritime Boundary and Resource Dispute

As has been illustrated, a number of reasons have stood in the way of the settlement of the Iran and Kuwait maritime boundary. If the two countries (Iran and Kuwait) were to accept each other's base line, then the starting point of the boundary would be between point's three and four on the Saudi Arabia and Kuwait continental shelf line. The end of boundary would be at the apex of a triangle, which comprises Iraq's continental shelf – a three-point boundary area between Iran, Iraq and Kuwait.

Indeed a factor that complicates the finalization of this boundary is its three-point dimension, which thus requires agreements between all three countries, before Iran and Kuwait can realistically approach their delimitation.

Subsequently, a tri-point agreement has yet to be reached between Iran, Kuwait and Saudi Arabia. For this to be done and therefore to pave the way for an ultimate Iran-Kuwait delimitation, a remaining problem with the Kuwait-Saudi Arabia neutral zone continental shelf delimitation, signed in July 2000 requires adjustment. This agreement contains a preface and ten articles. Article number regards four points, which form the boundary line. A part of this article describes the fourth point: 'from point 4 the line dividing the submerged zone adjacent to the divided zone continues in an easterly direction'.

This point has violated Iranian and British consent mentioned earlier and has entered Iranian territorial waters. Iran's Foreign Ministry has presented its protests to Kuwait and Saudi Arabia's position; however, the issue has yet to be publicized, most likely in an attempt to avoid the interference of sub-regional powers into the matter.

In May 2000 Iran began to quietly perform exploitation and drilling operations in Arash (Al-Dora) gas field, which straddled the area claimed by Kuwait. Not surprisingly, Kuwait and Saudi Arabia protested against Iran's operation on May 13th 2000. Saudi Arabia's protest was based on the annexation context of the July 2000 agreement between Kuwait and Saudi Arabia which indicates the two country's consent to the partition of any energy fields straddling the boundary line of a neutral zone.

According to an 'involved authority's' statements from the Iranian Foreign Ministry, the motive of Iran's clandestine operation in the Arash (Al-Dora) field was to prompt the Kuwaiti government to consider (which to this point it had not shown any clear indication of wishing to despite the repeated requests of the Iranian foreign ministry) talks with Iran. Indeed, following well publicized Kuwaiti protest, Shell Oil Company halted operations until ownership of this field could be distinguished.

The Arash (Al-Dora) energy field was discovered in 1967 by Kuwait. It is a large gas field holding estimated reserves of 368 tcf (trillion cubic feet). The field remains to be exploited because of the un-settled legal and technical factors that have prevented an Iranian-Kuwaiti maritime delimitation-which leaves both Iran and Kuwait placing claims to the field.

According to a recent statement made by Iran's current Oil Minister Bijan Namdar Zanganeh, 'the Kuwaitis believe this field as a common field'. Furthermore, the two authorities of both countries have since stated that there are no differences between Iran and Kuwait regarding the Arash (Al-Dorra) energy field. This matter was published when Kuwait's Oil Minister Sheikh Saud Nasser as-Sabah visited Iran on July 27th 2000, where the two parties played down the existence of any differences regarding their positions on the continental shelf delimitation.

Fresh bilateral negotiations between the two states were resumed in December 2000, with both countries deciding not to publish anything about the matter until talks reached a comprehensive agreement. On February 27th 2002 'Kuwait Times,' a popular Kuwaiti newspaper wrote that Kuwait and Iran might reach an agreement on the issue of marine borders between the two countries in the near future. The sources cited that a consensus might be reached soon, although Iran had suggested that the negotiations should be conducted with Kuwait and Saudi Arabia separately.

Conclusions – Reasons Iran and Kuwait Have Yet to Reach an Agreement.

During the past 4 decades various difficulties have affected Iran and Kuwait's relationship with one another. Some of them have been systematically significant in dictating the path of progress whilst others, created by dynamic regional conditions have played an important role for only a short time. Therefore, it is possible to classify the problems faced by Iran and Kuwait in their negations with one another as having been either interim or permanent.

Permanent Obstacles

Although talks began in a friendly atmosphere in the early 1960s, problems began to appear immediately. The first and seemingly permanent issue relates to the base line of the two countries. Iran in April 1959 modified the law of delimiting the territorial sea and contiguous zone, changing the breadth of its territorial sea to 12 nautical miles.

Meanwhile, according to the 1899 pact between Britain and Sheikh Mobarak, ruler of Kuwait at the time, all of its foreign affaires had been left for the British Empire to handle. Therefore, based on British law, the width of Kuwait's territorial sea was 3 nautical miles.

Another thus far ongoing and permanent problem affecting negotiations has been Iraqi opposition to any Iranian-Kuwaiti maritime delimitation settlement. This issue stems from Iraq's historical claims to Kuwait as belonging to Iraq, and thus its resistance to genuinely accepting Kuwaiti sovereignty. (Only after the 1994 Gulf War did a UN imposed agreement/resolution signed between Iraq and Kuwait officially outline Iraq's recognition of Kuwait's sovereignty.)

Indeed, following Iranian-Kuwaiti negotiations in December 1967, The Iraqi Foreign Ministry issued a declaration claiming Iraq's sovereignty over Kuwait's territorial sea, continental shelf and its bed. This declaration emphasized that any installations constructed in this area would belong to the Republic of Iraq.

Interim Obstacles

One must also note the importance of regional political changes during the 1970's and early eighties, which affected the political structures within, and relations between, countries of the Persian Gulf region. In 1971 Britain in adhering to its former announcement of 1968, withdrew its military and administrative presence from the Persian Gulf region after almost 80 years of rule and domination.

Iran's Islamic revolution in 1979 drastically affected the geopolitical order in the Middle East region with a substantial affect on Kuwaiti society, as hundreds of Shiites and Iranians residing in Kuwait announced their support for the Islamic revolution. This matter worried the rulers of Kuwait who saw their own authority threatened by the potential feverous spread of Iran's revolutionary ideology beyond Iranian borders. They therefore imposed restrictions on Shiites and Iranian residing in Kuwait, which led to an immediate deterioration of relations between the two states.

Furthermore, though Kuwait had initially announced its impartiality in the Iran-Iraq conflict following Saddam invasion of Iran in 1980 it was one of the Arab States, which later provided Political, military, and economic support to Iraq during imposed war against Iran.

Sheikh Sabah al-Ahmad al-Jaber as-Sabah Kuwait Foreign Minister and Prime Minister's deputy, on July 10th 1984 in an interview with B.B.C Radio 4 remarked:

"We cannot accept occupation of an Arabic country. It is our duty to support it. More to do with Iran's export of revolution and the fear the monarchies had of their own existence being threatened by similar religious uprisings".

Besides allocating "Shoaibeya" port to send ammunitions and armaments to Iraq, Kuwait granted a portion of its army's equipment. In the middle of November 1984, during an official visit to Baghdad, Sheikh Sabah, the Kuwaiti Prime Minister, accepted Iraqi request for their Iraqi forces to use Kuwait's three islands Warbah, Bubiyan and Failakah to attack Iran.

Indeed, Kuwait's financial support to Iraq was more than other Arab States and as such did further to damage Iranian-Kuwaiti relations and further make the prospect of future maritime boundary delimitations between the two states highly problematic.

A little needs to be said here about the negative impact on progress of maritime delimitation that the gulf war and us military build up in the region, had and maybe as way of finishing off-a little about the current possibilities and consequences of war in the region (new Iraqi regime??) on a eventual settlement- i.e. with the Saudi-Kuwait agreement finalized the onus is now on Iran to approach the issue- as such it would be very likely Iran's next move to be underlined by a strong tactical and political agenda in light of further us build up in the region- indeed it appears Iran has been strengthening relations with Arab nations of late-particularly Kuwait.

References

1. National Iranian Oil Company's secret letter to foreign ministry, dated 21 Mehr, 1344 (13 October, 1965) in Persian language.
2. DR. Mojtahed-Zadeh, Pirouz, security and territoriality in the Persian Gulf, translated to Persian by Amir Masoud Ejtehadi, political and international studies office, Tehran, 2001 (1380), p: 99.
3. Tajbakhsh, Gholam-Reza, *"Falate Qarreh-e Iran dar Khalije Fars"* Continental Shelf of Iran in the Persian Gulf seminar on Persian Gulf, 30 Mehr 1341 (22 October 1962) Tehran.
4. Razavi, Ahmad, Continental Shelf Delimitation And Related Maritime Issues In The Persian Gulf, Martinus Nijhoff publication. London, 1997, p: 219.
5. Extracted from: Foreign Ministry report to Petroleum Ministry, titled: *"Barresy-e savabegh mozakerate tahdid hodode falate gharreh Iran va Kuwait dar daheh-e 40"*. Review of Iran and Kuwait continental shelf negotiations during 1960s (in Persian).
6. Jafari Valdani, Asghar, *"Kanonha-ye bohran dar Khalij Fars"*. Centers of crisis in the Persian Gulf, Kayhan publications 1371 (1992) p: 318.
7. "Akhbar va Asnad" (Az Farvardin ta Shahrivar 1349) News and Documents, from March to September 1970. Iran Foreign ministry magazine p: 25.
8. *"Tahdid hodud falat qareh-e Iran va keshvarha-ye hashieh-e Khalij Fars va Darya-ye Khazar"* continental shelf delimitation between Iran and Persian Gulf countries and Iran and Caspian sea countries, Petroleum Ministry's international affairs deputy, 13 January 1998 (23 Day 1376).
9. Salam daily paper, 4 Bahman 1374 (24 January 1996).
10. Agreement between Saudi Arabia and the State of Kuwait concerning the submerged zone adjacent to the divided zone, Kuwait 2 July 2002.
11. Baquer-pour, Boundary Legal Department of the Iranian Ministry of Foreign Affairs, Farvardin 1381 (February 2002).
12. IRNA, Islamic Republic's News Agency. 13 Tir 1379 (4 July 2000)
13. Ibid, 2 Tir 1379, (23 June 2000)
14. Ibid, 5 Mordad 1379 (27 July 2000)
15. Kuwait times, 27 February 2002
16. Razavi, op. cit, p: 28
17. Jafari Valdani, Asghar, *"Barrasy-e Tarikh-e Ekhtelafat-e marzi-ye Iran va Araq"* Historical review of Iran and Iraq boundary disputes, Political and International Studies Office, 1370 (1991) p: 315
18. Ibid, p: 416
19. Crystal, Jail, oil and politics in the Persian Gulf, translated to Persian by Nahid Jourkesh. Contemporary Historical Studies Institute. 1999 (1378), p: 157.
20. Islami, Masoud, *"Rishe-yabye mavaze va amalkard-e Kuwait dar jang-e tahmili-ye Araq Aleih-e Iran"* An analysis of Kuwait's position and functions during Iraq's imposed war on Iran, Hamrah Publication. 1990 (1369), pp: 258-261
21. Ibid, p: 302
22. Dr. Mojtahed-Zadeh, Pirouz, *"Khalij-e Fars: keshvarha va marzha"* The Persian Gulf, countries and boundaries, Tehran, Ataee Publications, 2000 (1379), p: 594.

23- Yergin, Daniel, the prize, translated to Persian as *"Tarikh-e jahani-ye naft"* The global history of oil. Gholam-Hussein Salehyar, Ettelaat publications, 1998(1378), volume II, p: 1301.

CHAPTER XVIII

Disputes over Tunbs and Abu Musa
Pirouz Mojtahed-Zadeh

Geography of Islands in Dispute
Greater Tunb
17 miles south-west of Qeshm, the island of Tunb is situated on the north of the Gulf's median line. This island's distance from the Iranian port of Bandar Lengeh is 30 miles, and it is situated at more than 46 miles from the Emirate of Ras al-Kheimah. The term Tunb is Tangestani dialect (southern Persian) which means "hill". In his book of journey through Iran and the Persian Gulf, famous British diplomat James Morier, states: *"On the 20th February we were close to the two islands called the Greater and Little Tomb, which bear Persian names of the Persian side, an arid piece of land..."* (1).

Since Tunb is located relatively far from the entrance of the Persian Gulf, its strategic value, individually, is far from being significant. However, in the perceived Iranian strategic view point, Tunb is highly valuable as it forms part of the Iranian defence line against the entrance of the Strait of Hormuz.

Lesser Tunb
Eight miles south-west of Greater Tunb is situated the 35 metre high rock island of Lesser Tunb. It is an uninhabitable island with some significance as a connecting point secondary to the Greater Tunb in Iran's perceived defence line at the entrance of the Persian Gulf.

Abu-Musa
Abu Musa is situated at the westernmost point of the six islands, forming the last point of the perceived Iranian strategic curved line against the opening of the strait of Hormuz. It is located between longitude 55.01'E. to 55.04' and latitude 25.51'N. to 25.54'N. It is situated at 31 miles east of Sirri island of Iran and 42 miles south of Bandar Lengeh, and its distance from the port of Sharjah is about 40 miles.

Abu Musa is larger than two Tunbs, almost rectangular in shape, and about 3 miles diagonally between opposite corners. This island is relatively low land consisting of sandy plains, particularly towards the south and centre, with dry grass which is grazed by domestic animals. The surface is uneven, with hills rising high northwards, eventually ending in a volcanic shape peak known as Mount Halva. This mountain peak is about 360 feet (110 metres) high.

Figure 19

Geographical position of the Islands of Tunb and Abu Musa near the Strait of Hormuz
Based on: TPC H-7D

There is fresh water from a number of wells on the island, and plantation of date-palms is a familiar sight. Abu Musa is particularly known for its deposits of red oxide of iron. The first concession for its exploitation was given to a native of Bandar Lengeh, in the late nineteenth century, by the Qasemi Sheikh of Lengeh in return for an annual royalty of £250. This concession was given to Haj Moin Bushehri, a famous Iranian industrialist of the turn of the twentieth century, after the Qasemi autonomy of Bandar Lengeh was abolished in 1887. Lorimer estimated the number of people (Iranians) working on these mines, around the turn of the twentieth century at 100, adding that "the amount of oxide removed annually is said to average 40,000 bags" (2).

There are about 2000 inhabitants working on the Iranian side of the island, under Iranian sovereignty, most of whom are employed by the Governorate of Bandar Abbas. These are in addition to the military personnel stationed in the island. Several development projects have been implemented mostly in connection with services for the island including creation of two small but modern settlements; one for the local fishermen and the other for the government employees. These two settlements have the necessary facilities including electricity, a 16 miles road and a primitive air-strip. The Northern Fisheries Company of Iran has begun a fishery industry project in the island. Two small farms of fruit and vegetable have been created which are still in their early stages. A desalination plant provides fresh and drinkable water for the inhabitants (3).

On the Sharjah side of the island also some development projects have been implemented for the native settlers of 700 or so. Population of this section increases during the times of the year when the weather is more suitable, thus, the village of Abu Musa is gradually becoming a holiday camp for visitors from the emirates. New buildings have been constructed to accommodate newcomers and visitors. The settlement has electricity and a water distillation plant.

Contact between the two Iranian and Sharjah populations of the island is rare, but in the event of emergencies such as disfunctioning of distillation plants, they assist each other. A small boat "Khater" ferries between the Arab section of the island and Sharjah twice weekly, whereas the Iranian inhabitants are connected to Bandar Abbas by air as well as by regular boat services.

Concession for exploitation of Abu Musa's iron mines was given to the German company "Woenckhaus" in the modern times. This concession was later (1912) given to the British company "Golden Valley Colour Limited", and the Japanese joined in at a later stage. All these concessions were granted by the Sheikh of Sharjah endorsed by Iran following the Iran-Sharjah Memorandum of Understanding of November 1971.

Abu Musa's oil is produced from the nearby Meidan-e Mobarak, which is of the best quality produced in the Persian Gulf. Oil is produced from the three wells of the field by Butes Oil and Gas Company, the concession for which was granted by Sharjah and the latest was endorsed by Iran in December 1971 on the understanding that the profit from the exploitation should be equally divided between Iran and Sharjah.

Following the November 1971 Iran Sharjah settlement, and following restoration of Iran's sovereignty rights to the island, Iran's 12 mile territorial water limit was applied to Abu Musa. Application of this territorial water limit overlapped that of the emirate of Umm al-Quiwain, where exploration concession was given to the Oxidental Oil Company in 1969. A solution was found to the problem by Iran, which was reportedly based on the allocation to Umm al-Quiwain of 15% of Sharjah's income from Abu Musa's oil output.

Abu Musa's oil is produced from the nearby Meidan-e Mobarak, which is of the best quality produced in the Persian Gulf. Oil is produced from the three wells of the field by Butes Oil and Gas Company, the concession for which was granted by Sharjah and the latest was endorsed by

Iran in December 1971 on the understanding that the profit from the exploitation should be equally divided between Iran and Sharjah.

Following the November 1971 Iran Sharjah settlement, and following restoration of Iran's sovereignty rights to the island, Iran's 12-mile territorial water limit was applied to Abu Musa. Application of this territorial water limit overlapped that of the emirate of Umm al-Quwain, where exploration concession was given to the Occidental Oil Company in 1969. A solution was found to the problem by Iran, which was reportedly based on the allocation to Umm al-Quwain of 15% of Sharjah's income from Abu Musa's oil output.

Emergence of State in Iran

The term 'state' assumed a meaning similar to the modern sense of the word in the Persian Gulf when the Achaemenids consolidated their empire in the mid-sixth century BC. The empire included most of the civilised world of the time, stretching from India in the east to Egypt and Libya in the west. When the Sassanids (AD 224-685) assumed power in Iran, territorial contentions between the Persian and Roman empires settled Iran's western flanks in Mesopotamia where the Sassanids created their frontier-keeping vassal kingdom of Hirah.

Arab raids on Iranian possessions in the Persian Gulf began in the early Christian era, and by the time the Sassanids consolidated their power, these raids became frequent.

Shapur I made a naval reprisal in the Persian Gulf, which was completely successful. The raids, nevertheless, continued until Shapur II became of age. His reprisals were so effective that an end was put to the problem once and for all. Quoting early Islamic historians and geographers in his highly acclaimed book *The Persian Gulf*, Sir Arnold Wilson notes:

> *The reign of Shapur II (AD 309-37) was marked by frequent raids upon the Persian coasts by the Arabs of Hajar, which then included Hasa, Qatif, and Bahrain.*
>
> *Almost for the first time since the expedition of Sennacherib, we read of a naval expedition against these raiders in the Persian Gulf, commanded by the king himself, which was completely successful.* (4)

Almost all Arab and Islamic historians/geographers of the early Islamic era, such as Tabari, Masudi, Yaqubi etc., confirm that all areas of the Persian Gulf belonged to Iran in the pre-Islamic periods.

The first dynasty of the post-Islamic era to revive the dominion of Iran was that of the Buyids, albeit the Iranians began moving towards a revival of their identity and independence almost from the beginning of the emergence of the Arab Caliphate. The Samanids and Saffarids, however, revived the state in Iran in the third Islamic century (AH 204 and 253 respectively).

Ahmad Moez ad-Doleh (AH 334-356) and his powerful nephew Azad ad-Doleh (AH 356-367) of the Buyids not only added Mesopotamia to their dominions, but restored Iran's control of the southern Gulf. This dominion remained more or less the same throughout the years of the Seljuqs, Ghaznavids, Mongoloids, and Atabaks down to the Safavid period (AD 1051-1722).

Nader Shah Afshar (AD 1736-1747) brought under control the chaos that followed the downfall of the Safavid Empire, and restored stability throughout Iran and in the southern coasts of the Persian Gulf by sending a task force to those coasts.

Emergence of the Emirates

The tribes of the Musandam Peninsula and other coasts of the lower Gulf, living peacefully for fear of Nader Shah (5) used the opportunity arising from his assassination in 1747 and resumed their activities outside the peninsula. This chaotic situation continued until Karim Khan of Zand's rise into prominence in central and southern provinces of Iran in 1757. Unlike Nader Shah, the Khan of Zand preferred the friendship and cooperation of the Arabs on both shores in his struggle for power in Iran. His leniency towards Arab tribes proved most helpful for the Qasemis on their way to paramountcy in the subsequent period. They began their organised interference in the maritime trade and commerce in an effective manner. Their sea power had, by the turn of the nineteenth century, grown substantially. The British who had, by then, established themselves as the masters of the eastern waters, deliberated that their control of the Persian Gulf and Strait of Hormuz was essential for the security of India. This policy led the British to move their forces into the Gulf on the pretext of eradicating acts of alleged piracy by the tribes of the lower Gulf. British naval units, commanded by General Sir William Grant Keir, attacked Jolfar and defeated Qasemi forces in 1819.

A peace treaty was signed in February 1820 by the British and five tribal leaders of Musandam peninsula whereby, these tribes were brought under the control of the British. Articles 3, 6 and 10 of this treaty provided some hints of recognition by the British of these tribal units, for the first time, as political entities independent of each other and of neighbouring states. Article 3 for instance, allowed the tribal chiefs signatory of the treaty to *"carry by land and sea a red flag, with or without letters in it"* (6). This was to become the independent tribes' flag of identity while their progress into territorial states had to wait for nearly one century and a half. In fact, when in 1864 authorities of the Indo-European telegraph line suggested determination of territorial dimension with defined boundaries for the Trucial tribes which would ensure security of the said telegraph line, Colonel Lewis Pelly, British Political Resident in the Persian Gulf, opposed the idea on the grounds that implementation of these European concepts in Eastern Arabia at the time was "inexpedient" (7) and would result in great complications. The well-informed and shrewd politician that Pelly was knew very well that the issue of sovereignty in the Musandam Peninsula did not extend to territory. He knew well what J. B. Kelly described a century later. Kelly asserted in 1964:

> *The concept of territorial sovereignty in the Western sense did not exist in Eastern Arabia. A ruler exercised jurisdiction over a territory by virtue of his jurisdiction over the tribes inhabiting it. They, in turn, owed loyalty to him.... his (the tribesmen's) loyalty is personal to his tribe, his Sheikh, or a leader of greater consequence, and not to any abstract image of state.* (8)

These words were echoes of what Sir Rupert Hay, a former British Political Resident in the Persian Gulf, had stated a decade earlier:

> *Before the advent of oil the desert was in many ways similar to the high seas. Nomads and their camels roamed across it at will and, though there were vague tribal limits, there were few signs of the authority of any established government outside the ports and oases.* (9)

With this background to the political geography of Musandam Peninsula in mind it is not too difficult to understand how a tribe exercised independence and loyalty to another authority at the same time, or exercised loyalty to two different claimants of sovereignty seasonally. Writing on the political status of the tribes of northern Musandam, Lorimer asserts:

> *From local enquiries.... it seemed certain that Kumzar and Khasab on the western coast, together with the villages between them, actually acknowledged the sovereignty of the Sultanate of Oman; but some doubts remain as to the status of the inhabitants of Film, Shabus and Shisah on the eastern side of the promontory, whom were said to be virtually independent while at home and to become subjects of the Sheikh of Sharjah in the date season...* (10)

The Qasemis of what was later to become Sharjah, like other tribes of Musandam Peninsula continued their traditionally vague connection with the rulers of Muscat in the first half of the nineteenth century, whereas the rulers of Muscat themselves had some similar vague arrangement with the Iranians.

While the Sultans of Muscat administered territories around Bandar Abbas and Chah-Bahar of Iran's southern coasts in the form of lease arrangement with the Iranian government, (11) their forces attacked and occupied places in the lower Gulf including Bahrain islands on behalf of the Iranian government.

The Qasemi Sheikhs signed in 1864 a separate treaty with the British whereby their sheikhdom became a British protectorate and their foreign relations were restricted to those with the British only. This treaty accepted Sharjah's political status as an emirate independent of all others in the region, and the name "Sharjah" was fashioned from then on. This political status still did not recognise territorial extension of the Qasemi dominion, which had to go through a long process of disintegration and reunification beginning in 1866.

Sheikh Sultan bin Saqar who had ruled since 1803, died in 1866. Before dying, he appointed his sons and brothers as representatives in the towns of Ras al-Kheimah, Diba, Kalbah, and Khor Fakkan, urging them to obey his elder son Sheikh Saqar in the event of his death (12).

Ras al-Kheimah was separated from Sharjah a year later (1867) and was reincorporated into Sharjah in 1900. Twenty-one years later (1921) Ras al-Kheimah was separated from Sharjah for the second time and has remained so ever since. Fujairah also claimed separation from Sharjah in 1901, but was forced to continue payment of tribute to Sharjah until 1952 when its separation from Sharjah was officially recognised by the British. The eastern district of Kalbah had also claimed independence from Sharjah but was reincorporated into that emirate in 1951. These territorial upheavals encouraged the British to bring stability to the region by introducing European concepts of territorial sovereignty and political boundaries into the region. Exploration of oil resources was an added factor, which necessitated territorial and boundary divisions in southeastern Arabia.

In 1954, J.F. Walker, a British arbitrator, was assigned to carry out territorial divisions and boundary delimitation enquiries, and began his work by defining the realm of each emirate and designing boundary lines among them. His work continued until 1961 and his territorial and boundary awards became official in 1962, whereby the emirates assumed territorial status for the first time. This territorial arrangement among the emirates was still an alien phenomenon to the tribal rulers until their collective statehood emerged in 1971. Dr. John Wilkinson of Oxford University described this situation in 1977 in the following terms:

"This ludicrous partitioning of territory is of recent origin and stems in large measure from the imposing of European notion of territorialism on a society to which they were foreign. The ad hoc process by which this happened started a century and a half ago when Britain initiated a series of treaties with the Sultan of Muscat and the coastal Sheikhs of northern Oman, with the purpose of limiting their maritime activities and foreign relationships. Subsequently, as Britain sought to develop an exclusive influence in the Gulf and, later still, to favour the claims of particular companies to act as concessionaries for oil exploration, she was forced first into defending the protégé coastal rulers from attack from the hinterland and then of proclaiming their authority over the population and resources of "Greater Oman", by dividing it into a number of territories subject to them. This is not to say that the embryonic states she helped create were entirely artificial. Rather it is to imply that from the start the terms of reference by which they came into existence more or less disregarded important aspects of traditional organization within the region..." (13)

The seven emirates of northern Oman were, however, merged into a federation created in the wake of British announcement of 1968 of withdrawing Pax-Britannica from the Persian Gulf. This federation came into official existence on the first day of December 1971 with Abu Dhabi as its capital. The new entity was named "The United Arab Emirates" and became a member of the United Nations on December 9th, 1971.

Qasemi (Jawasim) Autonomy in Bandar Lengeh

No study of the historical background to Iran-UAE differences over Tunbs and Abu Musa can escape a brief look at the role of the Qasemi autonomy in Bandar Lengeh. One of the local chiefs in the Persian Gulf who used the opportunity of Nader Shah's death to set up their independence was an Iranian admiral, Mulla 'Ali Shah, who managed to establish himself as autonomous governor of Hormuz. Mulla 'Ali refused payment of tribute to the central government as early as 1747 and sought alliance, by marriage, with the powerful Qasemi Sheikhs of Jolfar on the Musandam coast. In 1751 the Qasemi Sheikh sent a fleet to the northern shores of the Strait of Hormuz, seemingly to pay a courtesy call on Mulla 'Ali upon the marriage of his daughter, but in reality to expand his influence to the districts of the northern Gulf (14). When robbers attacked the British Political Agent's residence in Bandar Abbas in 1759, the East India Company sought redress from Karim Khan Zand. Sheikh Naser Khan, Governor of Lar, was assigned to sort out the chaos at Bandar Abbas and Hormuz. Inevitably war broke out between his forces and those of Mulla 'Ali Shah. An army of 1000 fighters, commanded by the Qasemi Sheikh of Jolfar himself, landed at Bandar Abbas in support of Mulla Ali.

As the war dragged on, a branch of the Qasemis managed to establish themselves at Lengeh, Laft, Shenas and Qeshm Island. Karim Khan Zand (1757-1779) was tolerant towards the autonomous Arab tribes on the northern coasts, actually seeking their assistance in his struggle for power. His leaning towards these Arab tribes, meanwhile, helped the Qasemis of both shores to achieve prominence in the late eighteenth and early nineteenth centuries. In his time, the headmanship *(zabeti)* of Bandar Lengeh was given to Sheikh Saleh, the Qasemi chief of that locality (15), and was inherited by Sheikh Saleh's sons and grandsons in accordance with Iran's old federative tradition and without in any way contravening Iran's sovereignty over Lengeh and its dependant ports and islands. Kish, Tunb, Abu Musa, Sirri and 26 other islands had always been dependencies of the governorship of Lengeh. Therefore, the Qasemi authority at Lengeh, like all those before them, included these islands as well as the coastal ports of Charak, Mogham and Chiru. A number of French and British official maps confirm this including the French Foreign Ministry's *Carte du Golphe Persique* of 1764, the British *A Map of the Empire of Persia* made by D'Anville in 1770, and *A Map of the Empire of Persia*, similarly compiled by D'Anville in 1794.

On the basis of the agreement of 12 August 1798 between the East India Company and the Sultan of Muscat concerning Bandar 'Abbas and Qeshm, the British General, Sir William Grant Keir moved over 1000 troops to Basaidu on Qeshm island after defeating the Qasemi tribesmen at Jolfar in 1819. Soon after, they established a military depot on Qeshm in spite of clear indications of opposition from the Iranian government. In 1822, having established their control over the Musandam coast, the British decided to send an expeditionary force to Lengeh to subjugate the Qasemis of the Iranian coast. Iranian authorities opposed the idea on the grounds that the Qasemi Sheikhs of Lengeh were Iranian subjects. To prevent any misunderstanding on the part of the Persian government of the object of the British expedition - particularly operations against the Sheikhs of Lingeh and Charak - a special emissary, Dr Dukes, was despatched in advance with reassuring letters from the governor of Bombay for the governor-general of Fars and the Persian governor of Bushire. Another letter was sent to the British chargé d'affaires in Tehran, to enable him to inform the Shah. The Shah, however, was not appeased and the Prince of Shiraz wrote to Keir requesting him to refrain from interference at any of his ports, especially Lingeh. Keir therefore thought it inadvisable to land any troops on the Persian soil (16) & (17).

Although the British could have been in no doubt that Lengeh and its dependencies were integral parts of Iran and that the Qasemis of Bandar Lengeh were Iranian subjects and officials of the government of Iran, Grant Keir's forces attacked Bandar Lengeh and destroyed many of the vessels at anchor there. When faced with mounting Iranian criticism and protestations, the British sought an agreement with the Iranian government. This agreement was signed by Mirza Zaki Khan Nuri (18) on behalf of Iran and Sir William Bruce on behalf of the British East India Company. Article 3 reads: 'The representative of British Government must compensate in kind for the damages incurred as a result of the destruction of sailing and non-sailing boats of the people of ports of Lengeh and Charak' (19).

That the British were in no doubt about Iran's undisputed sovereignty over Bandar Lengeh and its dependent ports and islands at the time when the Qasemi Sheikhs were still in control of the Lengeh governorship was also demonstrated in the form of a map produced in 1835 by the acting British Political Resident in the Persian Gulf, Captain S. Hennell. In order to prevent conflicts among the Arab tribes of the southern coasts of the Persian Gulf during the pearl-fishing period of that year. Captain Hennell suggested a maritime truce, which was signed on 21 August 1835. He drew a line on the map of the Gulf separating possessions of the Arab tribes from those of Iran. His map specified the ports of Lengeh, Laft, Charak, as well as the islands of Qeshm, Tunb and Abu Musa as possessions of Iran (20).

A similar map was produced later by Major Morrison, who introduced a new line of territorial specification in the region, from Ras az-Zur near Kuwait to the Sharjah island of Sir-Bu-Na'ir, continuing to Ash-Shams near Ras Musandam. This line too showed the three islands of Tunb and Abu Musa and the Qasemi governorate of Lengeh as within Iran's jurisdiction. On a British Admiralty map of 1881 the islands of Tunb and Abu Musa are the same colour as Lengeh and the rest of the Iranian mainland.

Meanwhile the Qasemis of Lengeh, throughout their time there, demonstrated their loyalty to Iran, assisting various Iranian expeditions against the rebellious Arab tribes of southwestern Iran or against British interference in Iran's dependent territories such as Bahrain in the 1860s.

The Iranian government decided in 1885 that the old Safavid administrative organisation of the country was no longer viable in the modern world. They introduced a new organisation dividing the country into 27 provinces *(ayalat)*, of which the 26th was the Province of the Ports of the Persian Gulf (21). The same year, Sheikh Yusuf Qasemi, who had ruled in Lengeh since 1878, was murdered by his relative, Sheikh Qadhib bin Rashid, an event, which decided the Iranian government to put an end to Qasemi autonomy in Lengeh and its dependencies and to include this *velayat* in the 26th province. Tehran's first step was to increase its direct involvement in the affairs of Lengeh. This policy seems to have been adopted by the former Governor-General of the 26th province Amin as-Soltan, who was Prime Minster of Iran in 1887. 'The years 1887 and 1888 were signalised....by a spasmodic attempt on the part of the Persian Government to assert themselves in the politics of the Persian Gulf' (22).

In 1886, Prince Mohammad Mirza was appointed Governor-General of Fars, when Sa'd al-Molk was Governor of Bandar 'Abbas and Lengeh. The Prince Governor of Fars demoted Sheikh Qadhib Al-Qasemi's position in Bandar Lengeh from 'autonomous governor' to 'deputy governor'. The next year, when Amin as-Soltan was Prime Minister, Prince Mohammad Mirza added Bushehr and its dependencies to the province of Persian Gulf Ports and Islands under the governorship of Qavam al-Molk, and Brigadier Hajji Ahmad Khan was appointed as the new Darya-Begi (Maritime Frontier-keeper) in the Gulf. He Visited Abu Dhabi and Dubai in the newly purchased Iranian naval vessel *Persepolis*, and continued correspondence with the Sheikh of Abu Dhabi.

On instructions from Amin as-Sultan, in 1887 Sheikh Qadhib al-Qasemi was arrested for the murder of Sheikh Yusuf; he was subsequently taken in chains to Tehran where he died. The Qasemi autonomy of Lengeh was thus brought to its end, and Lengeh was entrusted to a new Governor, appointed by Amin as-Soltan. Then in 1898, Sheikh Muhammad, son of Sheikh Khalifah bin Sa'id, a former Qasemi Governor of Lengeh, seized Lengeh and retained it until he was expelled the following year by the Iranian authorities. Sheikh Muhammad was later reported to be in the vicinity of the Trucial Oman trying to muster a force to return him to Lengeh.

The Iranian government asked the British government to prevent any act of aggression from the southern side of the Gulf against Iranian territories at Lengeh or at any other part of the Iranian coasts. The British government accordingly issued warnings to the Sheikhs of the Trucial Oman not to interfere in the affairs of Iran by assisting Sheikh Muhammad. As has been noted, in 1900 Darya-Begi Hajji Ahmad Khan established cordial correspondence with Sheikh Zayid bin Khalifah of Abu Dhabi, with the aim of isolating him from the other rules of the Trucial Oman and preventing him from joining any attack on Lengeh.

The Sheikh of Abu Dhabi was also concerned, in the relationship, to secure favourable Iranian consideration of claims made by some of his subjects to properties in Iran. The Sheikhs of Sharjah and Dubai, apparently still unhappy about events in Lengeh, reported the matter to Khan Bahador Abdol-Latif, British Political Agent in the Persian Gulf, connecting this relationship with a perceived Russian effort to gain a foothold in the Trucial Oman. They argued that Sheikh Zed's friendly correspondence with the Iranian official was in breach of the bilateral agreement of 1892 between Britain and Abu Dhabi, article I of which prevented the Sheikh from 'entering any agreement or correspondence with any party other than the British government' (Lorimer 1908). The Sheikh of Abu Dhabi was cautioned and his correspondence with the Iranian Darya-Begi ceased. The success of this exercise of inducement on the British representatives in the region encouraged the Qasemi Sheikhs of Sharjah to try to salvage as much as possible of the territory formerly administered by their tribal cousins.

Correspondence between officials of the Iranian and British governments confirms Iran's undisputed sovereignty over Bandar Lengeh and its dependent ports and islands, and the fact that the Qasemi Sheikhs of Lengeh were subjects and officials of the government by William Doria, British Charge daffier in Tehran in 1858 in which he complains of the conduct of the Sheikhs of Lengeh and Moghu and asks the Iranian government 'to prevent them, especially the Sheikh of Lengeh from bothering His Britannic Majesty's subjects in those vicinities (23).

These complaints did not, however, produce satisfactory results, and the British therefore decided to stir up local troubles against the Qasemis of Lengeh. A certain Hajji Mohammad, apparently a British paid agent, began encouraging the Lengeh population to leave for Basaidu on Qeshm Island. By early 1863 about 200 families were reported to have left Bandar Lengeh, effectively abandoning Iranian sovereignty for that of Britain in the occupied Basaidu (24). Disturbed by this event, Naser ad-Din Shah suggested to his prime minister that:

> *The Foreign Minister should negotiate with the British Minister (in Tehran) on this subject, arguing why should the British agent behave like that and move Arab inhabitants here and there, and send the text of this letter to Qavam ad-Dauleh and to write (instruct) Qavam ad-Dauleh to assign a good governor for Bandar Lengeh. It is not necessary that the governor should be an Arab, a very good governor must be appointed.* (25)

However, Naser ad-Din Shah's instructions do not appear to have been carried out, as the Qasemi Sheikh of Lengeh was still in position four years later, when he assisted Sheikh Al-Khalifah of Bahrain against the will of the British in 1284/1867. Almost immediately after being appointed ruler of Bahrain in place of his brother Sheikh Mohammad, Sheikh 'Ali bin Khalifah Al-Khalifah sought military and political support from the Iranian governors of Fars (Prince Hesam as-Saltaneh) and Bandar Lengeh (Sheikh Hassan Khan al-Qasemi) against the policies of the British Resident in the Persian Gulf, Colonel Pelly. The former failed to respond, but the Qasemi Sheikh and the people of Bandar Lengeh extended assistance to Sheikh Ali and the people of Bahrain. This act deeply hurt and angered British officers, who sent a warship to Lengeh and threatened the people there with punishment. The ship caused considerable damage to people and property in Lengeh resulting in strong protests from the government of Iran (26).

Recent Development

In April 1992 the Iranian authorities were reported to have prevented a group of non-nationals from Sharjah from entering Abu Musa Island. These were Pakistani, Indian and Filipino labourers and technicians and Egyptian teachers. Iran denied that its officials in Abu Musa had expelled UAE nationals and its permanent representatives at the United Nations, Kamal Kharrazi, stated at the time that "those (varying nationals) who have not lived on the island.... have no right to stay there...." (27). Some interpreted this statement as implying that only Sharjah nationals with proven connections to the island would be allowed to reside there in future (28). Iran's Minister of State for Foreign Affairs, Dr. Ali-Akbar Velayati, stated at the same time that the 1971 Memorandum of Understanding gave only Sharjah nationals the right to reside on the island (29).

The High Council of the United Arab Emirates met on May 12th to discuss the issue of Abu Musa Island and agreed at the end of the meeting that commitments of each member of the Union before 1971 were to be treated as commitments of the Union as a whole. A UAE representative visiting Tehran prior to this meeting had suggested that a joint commission of representatives of Iran and the UAE should be formed to study the issue, but Iranian authorities rejected this on the grounds that there was no such thing as the 'issue' of Abu Musa (30).

Then it was reported on 24 August that Iranian authorities refused entry to Abu Musa to a party of over one hundred people of different nationalities (mainly Egyptian) some of whom had also been refused entry to the island in April that year (31). Iranian sources made it clear that the reason for their action was that 'in recent months suspicious activities were seen in the Arab part of Abu Musa island', namely the Sharjah-controlled section, involving a number of individuals from third countries, including Western states:

> *Observers believe Iranian guards and agents were watching the comings and goings of foreigners in the island for some time. Reports from military sources in Tehran say that without the permission of the Iranian Government, the United Arab Emirates was building new establishments in the non-military part of the island. It seems that with the agreement of certain Arab countries, a number of non-native Arabs are to become residents on the island ... Iran's worst fears were realised when the GCC foreign ministers at the end of their Jeddah meeting declared that they will support UAE in regaining sovereignty over the three islands belonging to Iran* (September 10, 1992). (32)

President Rafsanjani of the Islamic Republic of Iran announced in his Friday prayer of 18th September 1992 that the Iranian authorities had arrested a number of 'armed third party nationals' who were trying to enter Abu Musa illegally, of whom a Dutch national was in prison in Tehran. He then added: *"Iran's policy in the Persian Gulf is not creation of enemies and conflicts, but defence of its territorial integrity and we will act seriously to ensure this"* (33).

The United Arab Emirates on the other hand, without officially denying these serious charges of breach of the spirit and the letter of the 1971 MOU, accused Iran of preventing UAE nationals from entering Abu Musa, demanding visas from them. The UAE also accused Iran of gradual encroachment in Abu Musa by building roads and an air-strip, and of intending to expand its military presence in the island; in short, occupying the island; in short, occupying the island (34). Commenting on the *incident, The Times* claimed that 'Iran unilaterally reneged on that [MOU] deal, convincing many Western observers that it planned to use the island in the shipping lane which carries half the world's oil as a base for three submarines that it is now purchasing from Russia.' The newspaper repeated the allegation made in Abu Dhabi and Cairo that Iran had asserted her full sovereignty over the whole of Abu Musa (35).

Tehran denied all these charges and sent representatives to Abu Dhabi to find a peaceful end to the problem. There were unconfirmed reports that Iran and Sharjah were prepared to reaffirm the provisions of the 1971 Memorandum of Understanding in their entirety, but talks came to an abrupt end when the leaders of the United Arab Emirates intervened and the UAE Foreign Minister unexpectedly decided to tie any agreement on Abu Musa to a demand for the 'return' of the two Tunbs to UAE sovereignty (36). Shaikh Zayid bin Sultan Al-Nahyan, President of the United Arab Emirates, was reported to have noted in London in September 1992 that his government *"was taking the dispute to international arbitration."* The media campaign intensified, and in October, the UAE government distributed a position paper amongst permanent representatives at the United Nations, highlighting what was claimed to be the historical facts about the islands.

As for the would-be visitors to Abu Musa, when they had proved that they were teachers and their families, going there to complete school examinations - the aboriginal inhabitants of Abu Musa village are under Sharjah sovereignty according to the 1971 Memorandum - the Iranians allowed them to enter the island in November 1992. Iran's Foreign Minister reportedly ascribed the incident to a misjudgement by 'junior Iranian officials' (37).

After the Iranian authorities had admitted the Arab teachers to Abu Musa, other factors helped the easing of tension between the two sides towards the end of 1992: border conflict flared up between Qatar and Saudi Arabia; UAE and Iranian academics had frank exchanges at a round-table discussion in London on 18 November; George Bush (perceived as a defender of UAE claims) was defeated in the United States presidential election. But in late December, the closing statement of the 13th summit of the Gulf Co-operation Council, announced in Abu Dhabi, called on Iran to *"terminate its occupation of Greater and Lesser Tunb islands,"* which belong to the United Arab Emirates (38).

This new and surprising treatment, from the Iranian point of view, of the arrangement arrived at between Iran and Great Britain on behalf of the emirates some 21 years earlier, upheld by the UAE since its creation in 1971 and by the GCC since its creation in 1981, provoked a strong reaction from Tehran in the form of a statement by President Hashemi-Rafsanjani on 25 December, dismissing the claim as totally invalid and warning the GCC that *"to reach these islands one has to cross a sea of blood"* (39). Yet the GCC reaffirmed the claim in the closing statements of its subsequent summits, and was the dispute between Iran and the United Arab Emirates.

Matters were not improved when King Fahd of Saudi Arabia, in his message to participants in the 1994 Hajj ceremony, asked Iran to give the islands of Tunb and Abu Musa to the United Arab Emirates. This was unprecedented, but the Arab league also came out in late 1995 on the side of UAE.

References

1- James Morier Esq., "A Second Journey through Persia, Armenia and Asia Minor", Longham, Hurst, Rees etc., London 1818, p.30.
2- J. G. Lorimer, "Gazetteer of the Persian Gulf", Vol. IIB, Geography and Statistical, India 1908, p.1276.
3- For more details of the geographical description of the island of Abu Musa, see; Pirouz Mojtahed-Zadeh, Masud Mohajer, Admiral Ebrahim Shah-Husseini, Malek-Reza Malekpour, "Special Report on Abu Musa", San'at-e Haml-o Naghl (Transport Industry) Monthly of Tehran, No.1474, November 1992.
4- Arnold T. Wilson, op. cit., page 55.
5- Wilson, op. cit., pp.245-6.
6- Article 3 of General Treaty for the Cessation of Plunder and Piracy by Land and Sea, dated 5th February 1820, as appears in Donald Hawley's "The Trucial States", London 1970, p.314.
7- J.G. Lorimer, "Gazetteer of the Persian Gulf", Vol. I India 1908, p.625.
8- J.B. Kelly, "Eastern Arabian Frontiers", London 1964, p.18.
9- Rupert Hay, "The Persian Gulf States", Washington 1959, pp.3 & 4.
10- Lorimer, op. cit., p.625.
11- From Reverend G P Badger to the government of Bombay, No.10, dated June 5th 1861, FO 60/385.
12- See Pirouz Mojtahed-Zadeh, "Sheikh-Neshinhay-e Khalij-e Fars = Sheikhdoms of the Persian Gulf", Ataei Publications, Tehran 1970.
13- J.C. Wilkinson, "Water and Tribal Settlement in South-East Arabia", Oxford Research Studies in Geography, Oxford 1977, p.6.
14- Donald Hawley, op. cit., p.93.
15- Esmail Naurizadeh Bushehri, "Iran-e Konuni va Khalij-e Fars", Tehran 1946, p.129.
16- Dr Dukes apparently died before reaching Tehran (Nayer-Nuri 1968: 316).
17- Donald Hawley, op. cit., p. 114.
18- A great-grandfather of the author.
19- Jahangir Qaem-Maqami, "Bahrain va Masael-e Khalij-e Fars", Tehran 1462, p.117.
20- Bombay Selection XXIV.
21- Kazem Vadiei, "Moqadameh-I bar Joghrafiyay-e Ensani-e Iran", Tehran University 1974, p.192-3.
22- J.G. Lorimer, "Gazetteer of the Persian Gulf", Bombay 1908, p.2086.
23- Extract from the Persian text of letter from William Doria to Iranian Foreign Minister, 3 Shavval 1275 (7.5.1858), *Iranian Government Documents* (Vol.6180).
24- Colonel Jahangir Qaem-Maqami, op. cit., pp. 120-1.
25- *Iranian Government Documents* (Vol. 6044: 108)
26- Iranian Government Documents (Vol. 6044: 263)
27- Foreign Broadcast Information Service, FBIS-NES-92-076, 20th April 1992.
28- See for example; R.N. Schofield, ed., "Territorial Foundation of the Gulf States", UCL Press, London 1994, pp.71-2.
29- Ibid.
30- *Echo of Iran* 40 (5, 52), London, 13.5 1992, p.9, quoting *Abrar* 13.5.1992.
31- BBC Persian Service, *News Bulletin,* 25.8.1992.

32- *Echo of Iran*, 30 (8/9, 55/56), London August/September 1992, pp.3-4.
33- Ibid.
34- Dr Hassan Al-Alkim's presentation in the Round Table Discussion on the Dispute over the Gulf Islands, London, January 1993, p.32.
35- The Times, London, 22, 9, 1992, p.11.
36- Press release, Embassy of the UAE, London, October 1992.
37- Iran Focus, November 1992.
38- Summary of World Broadcasts: the Middle East ME/1573/A/7, 29.12.1992.
39- Middle East Economic Survey, C3, 11.1.1993.

Chapter XIX

Legal and Historical Arguments on Tunbs & Abu Musa
Pirouz Mojtahed-Zadeh

A – A Look at Some of the UAE Arguments

The outstanding points in arguments put forward by the British in the past and by the United Arab Emirates at present, and Iran's counter arguments, are as follows:

1-Priority in Occupation

One of the first arguments put forward by the British in the past and adopted by the UAE is the argument of priority in occupation.

The British Minister in Tehran wrote to the Iranian Foreign Ministry in 1904 arguing: *"What he* [the Shaikh of Sharjah] *had done was only to hoist his flag in the islands still not occupied by any one of the governments"* (1). This claim is vague and ignores the following facts:

(i) Iran was the only government in the vicinity of the islands at the time and the statement *"still not occupied by any one of the governments"* makes little sense.

(ii) Sharjah was not, at the time, a state or 'one of the governments' in the Persian Gulf. The Shaikh was a tribal chief (probably of Iranian origin) under British protection, with a tribal dominion still without territorial dimensions. This is confirmed by all British official documents relevant to the affairs of the emirates, and by several former British political representatives in the Gulf (2) & (3) and authoritative British academics (4). The British also ignored the fact that their own pretext for taking control in the Gulf was to suppress the activities of these same tribes, then referred to by them as 'pirates' of no political entity, let alone territorial dimension.

(iii) In the nineteenth century, Iran had lease arrangements with Oman, according to which Fath 'Ali Shah in 1811 and Naser ad-Din Shah in 1856 granted the Sultan of Oman lease title to Bandar 'Abbas, Minab and southern Gulf coastal regions from east to west as far as Bahrain. If all these areas belonged to Iran, the islands of Abu Musa and the two Tunbs situated in its geographical centre, could not have been 'unoccupied'.

(iv) Marking occupation or ownership of territory by hoisting flags was a new concept introduced to the Persian Gulf region by European powers, whereas Iran's sovereignty and ownership of these islands, as well as all other offshore territories and inland areas of the Gulf region, were traditionally established without the display of flags of identity.

(v) In 1887 Iran hoisted her flag in Sirri and Abu Musa to mark her ownership of these islands in the wake of the dismissal of the Qasemi deputy governor of Bandar Lengeh (5).

(vi) All descriptions of the Persian Gulf region by Arab and Islamic geographers and historians of the post-Islamic era confirm that all islands of that sea belonged to Iran. The British had only to look at Hamdollah Mostoufi's Nozhat al-Qolub, for instance, to find statements such as the following: *"Island situated between Sind and Oman and in the Persian Sea belong to Persia, the largest of which are Qis (Qeshm) and Bahrain"* (6). He also mentions 'Kond' island which can be assumed to be 'Tunb' island.

(vii) When the Iranian Prime Minister, Haji Mirza Aqasi, officially proclaimed Iran's ownership of all islands in the Persian Gulf in 1840, it was not officially challenged by Britain or any other government at the time, or at any time thereafter.

2- Prior Control

The British also maintained that: 'Qasemi control of the southern Gulf and the islands had been established long before the Persian coast was settled' (7).

Such a claim defies the historical facts of the region, mainly because of lack of clarity as to which branch of the Qasemi family is meant to have established control over the two Tunbs, Abu Musa and Sirri islands 'long before the Persian coast was settled' (i.e. the 1887 settlement of affairs of Lengeh). If the Qasemis of Lengeh are meant, no doubt they 'controlled' Lengeh Governorate and its dependent ports and islands as Iranian subjects and officials long before they were dismissed in 1887. Otherwise, if it is claimed that the main branch of the family 'established control' over the islands before or after 1887, firm evidence is needed to clarify how this 'control' was established, and which country the islands belonged to before being brought under their control. Here other British official documents enable a better understanding of the situation. British, French and Russian official maps of the enghteenth and nineteenth centuries confirm that the islands belonged to Iran. Moreover, the British Minister in Tehran, writing to the Iranian Ministry of Foreign Affairs in 1904, claimed the contrary by stating that what the Sheikh of Sharjah had done 'was only to hoist his flag in the islands still not occupied by any one of the governments' (see No.1 - Priority in Occupation, second paragraph). If the islands were not occupied by any government in 1904, claims that the Qesemis' control of these islands was established 'long before the Persian coast was settled' (in 1887) cannot be justified.

Another British government document (8) verifies that, after the establishment of one branch of the Qasemi family at Lengeh or thereabouts, the family occupied the Iranian islands, probably in the 'confused period subsequent to the death of Nadir Shah', but it does not clarify which branch of the family did so. This story, if true, is only another admission that the Tunbs, Abu Musa and Sirri islands belonged to Iran and were illegally occupied by the Qasemis at a time when Iran in practice was leaderless and deeply sunk in confusion. Nevertheless, the British did not in practice recognise the presumptive occupation of the islands by the main branch of the Qasemi family (of Sharjah) until 1903, when they advised them to place their flag there.

3- Arab Origins of the Population

Both the British in the past and the UAE today vaguely refer to the "Arab origin" of the native population of Greater Tunb and Abu-Musa as a factor determining Arab ownership of these islands. Indeed, during the confusion of August/September 1992, the UAE was accused by some Iranian media of trying to move nationals from various Arab countries to the Sharjah controlled sections of Abu Musa in order to create an Arab majority there.

It is noteworthy, first of all, that the natives of Greater Tunb and Abu Musa islands are of mixed origin. They are partly Iranians of Bandar Lengeh, and partly Arabs from the Sudan tribe of Sharjah (in the case of Abu Musa) and from the Bani Yas of Dubai (in the case of Greater Tunb), with no tribal link with Ras al-Kheimah (see Chapter VII for details). At least one inhabitant of

Greater Tunb was reported in the official correspondence between Sheikh Yusof al-Qasemi of Lengeh and Mohammad Hassan Khan, Governor of Bandar Abbas and Lengeh in 1885 to be of Iranian descent by the name of Ahmad Tunbi of Lar origin (9).

Secondly, Iranians were the first inhabitants of all areas of the Persian Gulf. Arab migration to the Persian Gulf began shortly before the advent of Islam, and the process of Arab-Iranian admixture continued in the Persian Gulf for centuries. It is now impossible to say who in the Persian Gulf is of 'true' Iranian origin and who is of 'true' Arab origin.

Furthermore, groups of people known for their Iranian origin are still in the majority in southern Iraq, Hasa and Qatif of Saudi Arabia, and in Dubai, Sharjah, Ras al-Khaimah and Ajman of the United Arab Emirates. Accordingly, presumed origins of the population cannot be the basis for an argument over the ownership of localities in the Persian Gulf, including the islands of Tunb and Abu Musa.

4- *Iran's Late Claim*

British sources, on the other hand, have been implying that Iran claimed the islands of Greater and Lesser Tunb in 1877 and the island of Abu Musa in 1887 or '88. What these sources conveniently neglect is the fact that Iran was at this time reminding the British of Iranian ownership of the islands and that the insinuation of earlier Sharjah or Ras al-Khaimah ownership was unfounded.

5- *Nineteenth-Century Correspondence*

Apart from resorting to these old and long exhausted arguments put forward by the British of India during the colonial era, the United Arab Emirates bases its claims over the islands of Tunb and Abu Musa on a number of letters exchanged between Sheikhs of Sharjah and Ras al-Khaimah on the one hand, and British political agents and rulers of various tribes of the southern coasts of the Persian Gulf, and the Qasemi Sheikhs of Bandar Lengeh on the other. Some of these letters date as far back as 1864. They contain numerous inconsistencies and contradictions, and make fanciful claims on various localities up and down the region. The validity of these claims was not even admitted by the Shaikhs of Dubai, who in most cases did not find them worthy of reply.

The most important of these letters was written by Shaikh Yusof Al-Qasemi of Bandar Lengeh to the Shaikh of Ras al-Khaimah (see Fig. IV).

It is misleading to quote this letter in isolation. An examination of the document in the context of the circumstances in which it was written will clarify the nature of its contents. In 1873, when a dispute broke out between the Qasemi Shaikhs of Lengeh and Ras al-Khaimah over the issue of grazing local livestock in Greater Tunb, they sought the arbitration of British political agents (10). On 10 February, Shaikh Hamid Al-Qasemi of Ras al-Khaimah complained to Hajji Abol Qasem, British Political Agent in Lengeh, that Bu-Samaith tribesmen from the Iranian ports of Aslaviyeh, Charak and Lengeh, encouraged by Shaikh Khalifah Al-Qasemi of Lengeh, had prevented his subjects from entering Tunb to graze their animals. Hajji Abul Qasem ruled that Tunb island belonged to Lengeh (Iran) and the Bu-Samaiths had traditional rights to the grazing there.

As further enquiries into the dispute became necessary, the Political Resident in Bushehr, Edward C. Ross, empowered Hajji Abdul Rahman, Political Agent in Sharjah, to carry out more extensive enquiries. Having visited the island and interviewed the Qasemi Shaikh of Ras al-Khaimah and the Qasemi Shaikh of Lengeh, Hajji Abdul Rahman concluded his report by stating that Tunb island belonged to the Iranian province of Fars and was administered by the governor of Lengeh. On the basis of this report, Mr Ross wrote to Shaikh Qasemi of Ras al-Khaimah on 19 April 1873, stating that Tunb belonged to Lengeh, that the inhabitants of Ras al-Khaimah should refrain from annoying Iranian livestock breeders there, and that they should remove their horses from Tunb (11). It is intriguing that while in his book on the United Arab Emirates Muhammad Morsy Abdullah describes Hajji Abdul Rahman's opinion on the status of Abu Musa island 'being an Iranian possession' as accurate, he criticises him for his opinion on the status of Greater Tunb 'as belonging to Lengeh (Iran)' alleging that this opinion was motivated by economic self-interest, a desire to avert an Arab-Iranian war (a highly unlikely possibility at the time) and a reluctance to appear as favouring the Qawasim (12).

Ten years later, when relations were normalised, Shaikh Yusof al-Qasemi of Lengeh, having been encouraged to establish friendly relations with the Qasemi Shaikhs of Ras al-Khaimah, wrote the above letter to the Qasemi Shaikh of Ras al-Khaimah. The statement, 'the island of Tunb actually or in reality is for you,' leaves little doubt about the nature of the letter: it is the standard oriental courtesy or compliment, essential for relations to remain friendly.

A few lines below this statement, Shaikh Yusof adds a further compliment: 'and the town of Lengeh is your town' (marked 2 on Figure IV). No one has ever been under any illusion, then or at any other time, that Port Lengeh belonged to any country but Iran; it has always been and still is an indivisible Iranian territory. When this reference to Lengeh as belonging to the Shaikh of Ras al-Khaimah has never been and cannot be taken as anything other than a courtesy compliment, one must ask, how could a similar reference to Tunb island have been, and continue to be, taken literally? Certainly the expression *mi casa es su casa* ought not to be.

When in 1929 Abdul-Aziz Al-Saud, King of the new Saudi State in Arabia wrote to Sheikh Hamad Al-Khalifa of Bahrain complaining about the treatment of his subjects in Bahrain, he received a letter of compliments from the Sheikh who states that "Bahrain, Qatif, Hasa and Nejd were all one and *"belong to Your Majesty"* (13). Certainly inclusion of Bahrain in that list could not have been but pure compliment.

On the other hand, reports for the years 1881-89 from the Qasemi deputy governor to the new governor of Lengeh clearly acknowledge undisputed Iranian ownership of Lengeh and Tunb and Abu Musa islands. This is also shown in letters of 1885-6 from Shaikh Yusof al-Qasemi, Deputy Governor of Lengeh, to Sa'd al-Molk, Governor of Bandar Abbas and Lengeh, on various aspects of the administration and tax payments, of Lengeh and the dependent ports and islands (14).

Figure 20

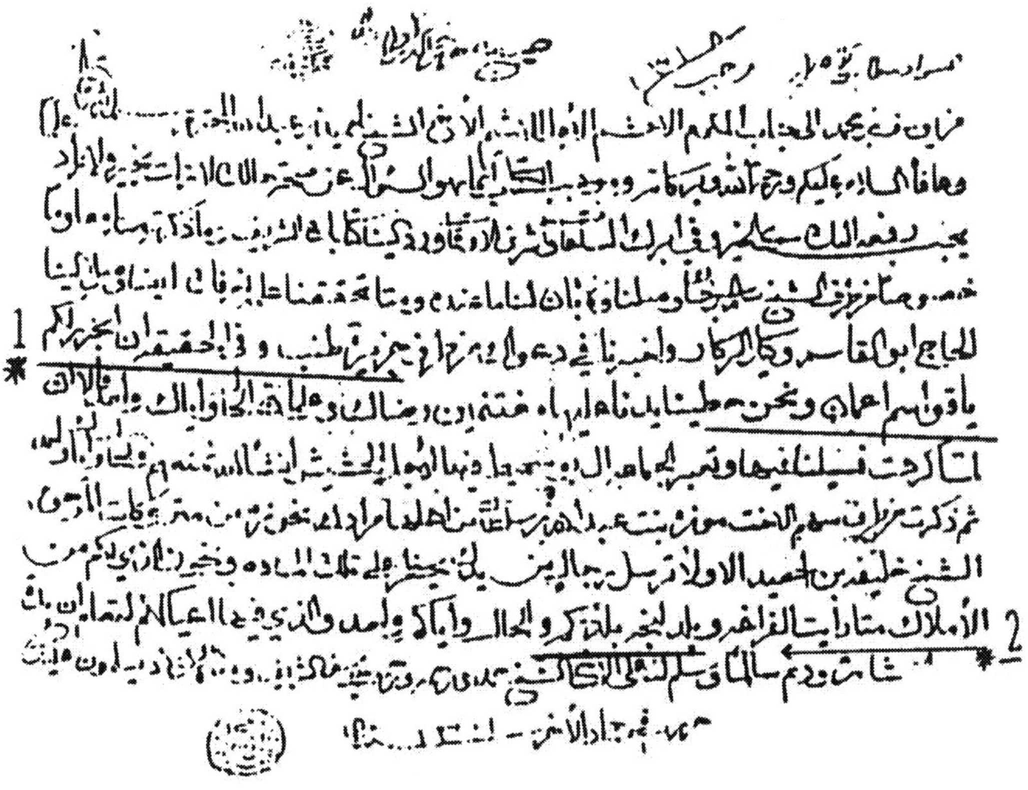

*Letter of 1 Jamadi al-Akhar 1301 (29 March 1884) from
Shaikh Yusof al-Qasemi of Bandar Lengeh to Shaikh
Hamid al Qasemi of Ras al-Khaimah*

The sentence marked _1_ in the text translated means:
"the island of Tunb is actually (or in reality) an island for you'.

The sentence marked _2_ in the text translated means:
'the town of Lengeh is your town'.

6- *Dual Legal Status*

The British claimed that the islands had been ruled by the Arab governors of Lengeh in their capacity as Qasemi Shaikhs rather than as Iranian officials. But how was this 'dual legal status' worked out? How could the governor of Lengeh rule dependent islands of the governorate, not as governor but as holder of another official and legal title?

Apart from masses of British and Iranian documents confirming the legal status of the Qasemis of Lengeh as 'Iranian officials of the Lengeh governorship and loyal subjects of the Iranian government', the British appear not to have taken all the facts into consideration when making the 'dual status' claim. How could they explain what happened when individual Qasemi governors of Lengeh were changed, dismissed or appointed by the Iranian authorities? Would this affect the governor's other mysterious legal or traditional status as 'hereditary Qasemi ruler' vis-a-vis Lengeh and its dependent islands? When the Iranian authorities abolished the Qasemi governorship of Lengeh in 19887, what then happened to their other legal or traditional status vis-à-vis Lengeh and its dependant islands, and why did the British not protest against continuing direct Iranian jurisdiction over Lengeh and also these islands between 1887 and 1903 (1908 in the case of Lesser Tunb)? Presumably it was on the strength of such questions that when Sir E. Beckett, the legal expert of the British Government at the Foreign Office (who later served as a member of the International Court of Justice at the Hague) was asked to evaluate the legal validity of the claims of dual status for the Qasemi Sheikhs of Bandar Lengeh respecting ownership of the islands of Tunbs and Abu Musa, he ruled in 1932 that:

> *My conclusion is that unless further evidence is forthcoming that it can be proved that during the period 1880-1887 the (Qasemi) Sheikh at Lingah ruled the islands under some title different from that under which he ruled the mainland (I doubt if it will be easy to show this), the Persians did possess sovereignty over Tamb and Abu Musa during those years.* (15)

It is important to remember that it was not the first time that the British claimed dual legal status for the Qasemi Shaikhs of Bandar Lengeh. They had done the same in respect of Sirri Island after 1887, but as can be seen from the correspondence described in Chapter VII, the British abandoned this futile argument shortly afterwards, and Iran's ownership of and sovereignty over Sirri Island continued relatively unchallenged until 1962, when the Iranian flag was officially hoisted on that island once and for all.

7- *The Factor of Prescription*

One of the legal arguments hinted at by the UAE is the factor of prescription, that is to say that, since 68 years passed between 1903, when Sharjah's flag was hoisted in these islands, and 1971, when they were returned to Iran, and since the rulers of Sharjah and Ras al-Khaimah had, during this period, constructed buildings there and installed official representatives on the islands, the factor of prescription should have overcome any Iranian claim of sovereignty.

According to international regulations, the factor of prescription stands when occupation of a territory is continued 'uninterrupted', 'undisturbed' and 'unchallenged'. Now, as discussed in previous chapters, it was less than a year after the Emirates occupied the Tunbs and Abu Musa in 1903 that the government of Iran began protesting against and challenging the occupation, and it has done so every year since 1904. Further, not only did Iran exhort Britain to negotiate on several occasions over recognising Iran's rights to the islands, but she physically interrupted the occupation on several occasions, and even succeeded in regaining Greater Tunb at the beginning of 1935, albeit for a brief period. There is no doubt that Iran's consistent and vigorous campaign over the 68 years of the occupation of the islands by the Emirates allows little room for the argument of prescription.

Some UAE sources urge that historical facts be ignored in such discussions, because if a historical approach is followed, 'with which we [the UAE] don't agree in international relations, a number of Middle Eastern countries will disappear, will cease to exist' (16). However, this argument has no relevance to the case of the islands of Tunb and Abu Musa, which are not countries.

Territories parted from the Persian or Ottoman empires, which appeared as new countries in the 19th and 20th centuries, were sizeable and populous areas which opted for or achieved independence under some kind of legal facade, and were not occupied and annexed by other states. In the case of the islands in question, they were almost uninhabited at the turn of the twentieth century when they were seized from Iran and annexed by Sharjah. Greater Tunb and Abu Musa are still sparsely populated - the former had 250 inhabitants and the latter 300 in November 1971, when they were returned to Iran- whereas Lesser Tunb was and still is completely uninhabited. These were chunks of Iranian territories seized by Great Britain at the turn of the twentieth century for reasons to do with their perceived security needs at the time. Furthermore, at least two articles of the Memorandum of Understanding of 19 November 1971 between Iran and Sharjah explicitly confirm Iran's sovereignty over Abu Musa island. Article 2 allows Iran to maintain military units in the northern parts of Abu Musa with full sovereignty - military units with full sovereignty over the areas concerned can only be established in a country's own territory. Article 3 recognises the Iranian law of territorial waters for Abu Musa, whereas the width of Sharjah's territorial waters was, at the time, 3 nautical miles, in accordance with the British law (17).

8- Duress

The UAE claim now that they accepted the 1971 Memorandum under duress, and recognised the new status of Abu Musa only de facto. However, Iran was neither negotiating with Sharjah, nor in a position to impose anything on her under duress. In fact, at the time of the Memorandum, Sharjah was a British protectorate and her foreign affairs were, according to the 1864 and 1892 agreements, the responsibility of the British government. It was Great Britain with whom Iran had arrived at the Memorandum of Understanding, when the former was still a major power in the world, much stronger than Iran, and would in no way have accepted such an arrangement from Iran under duress.

In fact, the reverse argument would be more convincing. Iranians could argue that, by imposing upon Iran an agreement on shared sovereignty over Abu Musa, Britain, a major power acting for the Emirates, prevented implementation of Iran's full sovereignty for the whole of the island. Under duress, Iran had to give the new status of the island 'de facto' recognition. Moreover, the UAE contradicted itself (in its position paper of 27 October 1992, distributed in the United Nations):

> *According to law, any contract or agreement signed under duress by either party is invalid and considered null and void....at times the Emirates government has considered this agreement imposed upon and signed under duress; yet at the same time it has called on Iranian government to execute precisely (her) parts of the document.* (18)

This contradiction renders the argument of 'duress' completely null and void. A point in international law suggest *allegans contraria non est audindus*, that is to say: he whose statements contradict each other ought not to be heard (19).

UAE officials also choose to ignore the high level of welcome extended to the Iranian forces on their arrival in Abu Musa by the Ruler of Sharjah's representative, which hardly suggests Sharjah's acceptance of the Memorandum under duress.

9-*Temporary Administrative Arrangement*

The United Arab Emirates also claim that the 1971 Memorandum of Understanding was a 'temporary administrative arrangement'.

There is no time limit on the application of the specifications contained in the Memorandum. On the contrary, no arrangement or agreement defining sovereignty rights, such as the Memorandum specifies for Iran and Sharjah in Abu Musa, can be considered temporary.

In fact, the Iranian side could argue the opposite. Great Britain, acting on behalf of Sharjah, was seeking to put Iran in a tight corner by prolonging the negotiations and playing for time. With time running out, and anxious to avoid the possibility that the emerging federation of the United Arab Emirates would inherit the dispute from the British, a source of friction which would be detrimental to the prospects of regional cooperation for peace and security in the wake of British withdrawal, Iran, despite 68 years of consistent attempts to reassert full sovereignty over the whole of Abu Musa, was left with no alternative but to agree to the British formula for recognising her rights of sovereignty.

Iran accepted this solution only in order to defuse the volatile situation created by the time shortage. Britain was due to leave the Persian Gulf two days later, on 1 December, officially terminating her one and a half centuries of responsibility for the territorial defence and foreign affairs of the tribes which became the Emirates. By accepting the Memorandum, Iran must have hoped that she could later reassert her full sovereignty rights over Abu Musa. This is clearly demonstrated in the preface to the Memorandum, which affirms that Iran (like Sharjah) had not abandoned her claim to full sovereignty over the whole of the island. In other words, while considering the existing Memorandum as valid and legally binding, Iran would have no alternative but to resume, whenever she deemed it expedient, the campaign for recognition of her full sovereignty rights over Abu Musa.

Finally, it is important to note that the ruler of Ras al-Khaimah had returned the island of Greater Tunb to Iran once before, in January 1935, when Iran vigorously demanded its return, but the British intervened and reversed the move. In other words, the British had imposed the occupation of these Iranian islands upon the Emirates, without Ras al-Khaimah being really committed to it. For other (political) UAE arguments see appendix to this chapter.

B – A Look at the History of Iran's Claims

In the nineteenth and first half of the twentieth centuries the British occupied and used a number of Iranian islands in the northern Gulf, either directly or through an assumed sovereignty of the Trucial Emirates. Apart from the Tunbs and Abu Musa, the British disputed Iranian ownership of Qeshm, Hengam and Sirri.

Qeshm was the first Iranian island in the Persian Gulf to be used by the British. As we saw earlier, having crushed the power of Arab 'pirates' of the southern Gulf in 1819, General Grant Keir moved a force, originally 1,200 strong, to Qeshm. The Iranians strongly protested this move, and called on the British to evacuate the island. The British appear to have ignored this protest, and in 1823 they established a naval supply depot as Basidu on the northwestern tip of the island (20).

When the British decided to establish the Indo-European telegraph line, which had to pass via the coast and islands of the Gulf, they negotiated with the Iranian authorities in 1868 for a cable station on Hengam. For reasons of their own, they closed the station in 1880, but re-occupied the old site 24 years later (21).

The history of Sirri Island is linked with that of the two Tunbs and Abu Musa. In 1887, when Amin as-Soltan appointed Hajji Mohammad Mehdi Maled at-Tojjar Bushehri as governor of Bandar Lengeh, the latter dismissed the Qasemi Shaikhs from the deputy-governorship of Bandar Lengeh. He hoisted the Iranian flag in Lengeh and on the dependent islands of Sirri and Abu Musa (Ashtiani 1949: 144). The British protested on the grounds of the 'dual legal status' of Sirri. On 11 March 1888, the British Minister in Tehran wrote to the Ministry of Foreign Affairs asking that, since the Qasemi Shaikhs' rule in Sirri island 'was hereditary and not because of their status as Iranian deputy-governors of Bandar Lengeh, why should Iranian authorities hoist their flag in Sirri Island after dismissing the Qasemis in Lengeh?' (22). Replying on the same day, the Iranian Foreign Ministry wrote:

> *In reply to the note of the exalted embassy, dated 26 Jamadi ath-Thani, asking for reasons and evidence proving that Sirri Island belongs to the government of Iran; firstly, it is profoundly surprising that the exalted British embassy, being perfectly well informed and aware of [Iranian possession of] all places and areas of the Sea of Oman, specially of the ports of the Persian Gulf (23), assumes that this matter (of Iranian ownership of these places) needs production of evidence, believes baseless claims of the Jawasim [Qasemi] Shaikhs and asks for presentation of evidence; secondly, in complying with the request of the embassy, it is to be stated that according to all laws of progressive countries the strongest evidence of ownership (of places or territories) of a government is 'occupation' and 'possession', and hence there is no need for presentation of any other evidence. The exalted embassy and agents of the government of India should in good faith and in their own eyes witness that Sirri Island has always been and still is a dependent of Bandar Lengeh and under its governorship have been (and are) assigned by the government (of Iran) to Bandar Lengeh...hoisting of flags in the ports of the Persian Gulf has not, from the ancient times, been deemed necessary, but not that hoisting them is sometimes deemed necessary, flags were (therefore) hoisted in all those ports. Similar action was accordingly taken in Sirri Island which is a dependent of Bandar Lengeh. (24)*

Shortly after, the British Legation wrote back:

> *It is correct that the deputy-governors of Bandar Lengeh administered Sirri Island, but it was not because (they) were governors of the said Bandar, but because they were the Jasemi (Qasemi) Shaikhs that they had control of that island. In consequence, the Government of Iran will note that the Jasemi Shaikhs' rule on behalf of Iran was only in Bandar Lengeh. The Jasemi Shaikhs had traditional inherited rights to Sirri Island, and no doubt has ever been cast on these rights....H.B. Majesty's embassy will be grateful if leaders of the Government of Iran produce evidence proving that Sirri Island belongs to Iran. (25)*

Having read this letter, Naser ad-Din Shah Qajar made the following note in the margin: 'evidence [of Iran's ownership of Sirri Island] is the same as that written previously. What other more important evidence is there to be written?' (26). On 21 July, the Ministry of Foreign Affairs replied that what the embassy had written about the fact that 'the Qasemi Shaikhs ruled in Bandar Lengeh on behalf of the government of Iran and that their rule extended to include Sirri island' was evidence to be added to that already indicated in the Ministry's letter of 26 Jamadi ath-Thani.

> *If the embassy were to review those (previously introduced) evidences, it would justly and rightly confirm that a territory having been in possession of a government and under the governorship of its representatives and agents for years will naturally be (considered as) the undisputed territory of that government and there is no need for evidence to prove this. (27)*

While this correspondence was taking place between Iranian and British government officials, the Qasemi Shaikhs made no claim to Sirri and offered no argument in that respect. At the same time, the British appear to have acknowledged Iranian claims:

> *A War Office map, presented by the British Minister [in Tehran] to the Shah in 1888, showed all the islands [the two Tunbs, Abu Musa and Sirri] in Persian colours: the Persian case was further strengthened with the publication in 1892 of Curzon's two-volume Persia and the Persian Question in which the map, prepared by the Royal Geographical Society under Curzon's own supervision, also showed the islands as Persian territory. (28)*

Nevertheless, the British continued arguing with the Iranians over what they believed to be the 'rights of the Qasemis to Sirri island'. In 1894, one of their last communications in this regard provoked the following response from the Iranian Ministry of Foreign Affairs:

Your letter of 10th Rabi al-Avval 1312 [11 Sept 1894] on the issue of Sirri Island has been received and noted. Your statement that governors of the governorate of Bandar Lengeh were Jawasim [Qasemi] Shaikhs and that exercise of their rule in Sirri Island was in respect of their family representation and thus the ownership of the island cannot be of the government [of Iran] is an acceptable argument only if extension of the Bandar Lengeh governorate in Sirri Island was restricted to those times when the governorship of Bandar Lengeh was in the hands of the Jawasim Shaikhs and the inhabitants of the island were exclusively from the Jawasim clan, whereas neither was the case, and when the governors of Bandar Lengeh were not Jawasim Shaikhs, [the Lengeh governorship] extended to [the island]. The Jawasim Shaikhs' deputy-governorship (of Lengeh) was overthrown in early 1306 (late 1887). Two [ten] years before that and since their overthrow, the [non-Qasemi] governorship of Bandar Lengeh has been in power. As you will subsequently see, since the governors listed below were in charge of the Bandar Lengeh Governorate [both before and after the overthrow of Qasemi deputy-governorship], they exercised their rule and right of administration in Sirri Island (as well as other dependent territories of Bandar Lengeh) and the inhabitants of the said island have not been exclusively from the Jawasim clan, but are from different clans, but are from different clans who have always obeyed the governors (listed below), and the said governors administered affairs there with authority.

- Governorship [in Bandar Lengeh] of Nasir al-Molk, under the governorship [in Fars] of Hajj Mo'tamed ad-Dauleh in the year 1293 AH (1876).
- Governorship of Sa'd al-Molk [in Bandar Lengeh] on behalf of Mo'tamed ad-Dauleh in the year 1294 (1877).

- Governorship of Farajollah Khan on behalf of Nasir al-Molk in the years 1295 to 1297.
- Governorship of H.E. Nezam as-Saltaneh until the year 1299 (1881-2).
- Governorship of H.E. Sa'd al-Molk, 1300 to 1301 (1882).
- Governorship of H.E. Navvab Mohammad Hosein Mirza, 1302 (1884).
- Governorship of Hajji Mohammad Mehdi Malek at-Tojjar Bushehri, 1303 to 1304 (1885-6).
- Second term of Governorship of H.E. Sa'd al-Molk, 1305 to 1307 (1886-7 to 1888-89). (It was at this time that the Qasemi Shaikhs' deputy governorship of Bander Lengeh was abolished).
- Governorship of H.E. Nezam as-Saltaneh, 1308 to 1309 (1889-1 to 1890-1).
- Third term of governorship of H.E. Sa'd al-Molk 1310 (1891-2).
- Governorship of Qavam al-Molk 1311 (1893-4).

Apart from all these....the embassy will justly confirm that Iran's possession of the said island is in no doubt, and in this case, it is clear that the government of Iran will never remove its flag (29).

This appears to be the last of the correspondence between British and Iranians on the subject of the ownership of Sirri, and Iran's ownership of and sovereignty over Sirri island continued relatively unchallenged until 1962, when the Iranian flag was officially hoisted on that island once and for all.

Anglo-Russian Rivalries and Occupation of Iranian Islands

British fear of a Russian encroachment in the Persian Gulf intensified at the turn of the twentieth century. In anticipation of such a development, the British decided to occupy Iranian islands of the Strait of Hormuz, or, at least, fear of Russian designs was the pretext for the occupation of these islands by the British who, brought some of them under their direct control and put some others under the assumed sovereignty of the Qasemi Sheikhs of Musandam whose rule in those coasts had not as yet assumed territorial dimension. In a letter to the Foreign Office in November 1900, the British India Office indicated:

> ... *In the early part of this year a report was received to the effect that the Russians might land men or hoist their flag at Bandar Abbas. As the outcome of my letter to you, dated the 13th February 1899, authority was given on 14th February .... under certain conditions, for hoisting British flag on Hormuz, or Henjam, or Kishm, or whatever island might be considered by the Naval authorities to offer the best advantages for a naval base in that neighbourhood.* (30)

In a reply, the Foreign Office wrote to the India Office on 23rd November suggesting that *"The islands of Henjam, Kishm and Hormuz"* were found most suitable for the said purpose (31).

Two years went by and the British were still debating the matter of occupying Iranian islands at the Strait of Hormuz in the event of a Russian intrusion in the Persian Gulf. The Russians signed in 1902 an agreement with the Iranians which increased Russian influence in Iran. In a memorandum on Sir A. Hardinge's letter of October 14, 1902 on the subject of Russian threats in the Persian Gulf, the War Office concluded that in the event of a Russian design against Iran:

(a) If Persia is broken up, we must at least, secure Seistan, and keep Russia out of the Persian Gulf.

(b) It would be dangerous for us to risk war with Russia and France... (32).

Early in the same year, a secret meeting at the British Foreign Office decided that in anticipation of a Russian aggression in the Persian Gulf, the strategic islands at or near the Strait of Hormuz should be occupied. This decision was made known to British political administrators in India and the Persian Gulf in the form of a memorandum, dated July 14th 1902 (33).

An intriguing aspect of these moves was the fact that the islands of Hengam and Qeshm had partially been under British occupation for some years.

The fact that the British had their flag flying in Qeshm and Hengam islands during the time of these debates leaves little doubt that the true aim of their strategic moves was occupation of other Iranian islands in the vicinity of the Strait of Hormuz, i.e. the islands of Tunbs and Abu Musa. This ultimate aim manifested itself in about a year later when the government of India sanctioned in a letter in June 1903 occupation of the islands of Tunb and Abu Musa in the name of the Sheikh of Sharjah (34).

British Foreign Office documents suggest that occupation of these islands took place in late June/early July 1903 in the form of an advice from the government of India to the Sheikh of Sharjah to hoist his flag on the Greater Tunb and Abu Musa islands (35). Ironically, Lord Curzon, Viceroy and Governor-General of India at the time, himself produced a map in 1892 clearly showing the islands of Tunb and Abu Musa as belonging to Iran(36).

Knowing that these islands belonged to Iran, British Indian authorities made an excuse of tribal relations between the Qasemis of the former governorate of Bandar Lengeh to which these islands belonged, and the Qasemis of Sharjah.

The fact that the British authorities were fully aware that Tunb and Abu Musa islands were Iranian owned and belonged to Iran was reflected in a later date, in the form of a Foreign Office confidential document on the "Persian Frontiers" which uses without reservation, the term "occupation" of these islands by the Qasemis. This document indicates:

In the second half of the XVIIIth century the Arabs of the pirate (later called the Trucial) Coast of Arabia occupied the islands of Tanb (also called Tunb, Tamb and Tomb), its dependency Nabiyu Tanb, Abu Musa and Sirri, it seems probable that they did so in the very confused period subsequent to the death of Nadir Shah... (37)

Donald Hawley, British Political representative for the Trucial States between 1958 and 1961, asserts in his book "The Trucial States" that: *"Abu Musa. This island is in the effective control of ruler of Sharjah, and has been occupied by the Qawasim for several generations...."* (38).

The week and uncertain nature of British claim to and occupation of these islands on behalf of the Sheikh of Sharjah can also be seen in a telegram from the British Minister in Tehran to the British Foreign Office, dated April 1904. He states:

The Government of India's telegram of 18th June 1903 does not appear to have been received here with reference to Tamb and Abumusa, but invalidity of Persian claims to these islands is, I presume, established by it. However, they are coloured Persian in India Survey Map of 1897 and Viceroy's unofficial Map of 1892.

> *It is clear on this presumption, that rights acquired by Sheikh of Shargah must be supported: but before Persian flag is hauled down it would be courteous to give Persian Government chance themselves removing it. We could say, if they refused, that we had shown more consideration than they had for Sheikh of Shargah, and could carry out proposal of Government of India. M. Naus might be induced to remove quietly his flag and guards, and Arab flag then could be re-hoisted after a convenient interval without ostentation. A suggestion that we are acting in a high handed way or to give rise to any violent incident I think is to be avoided.* (39)

This suggestion was adopted by British Foreign Office and use of a gun-boat in hauling down the Iranian flag, suggested by the Indian government (40), was avoided, whereas threats of use of a gun boat against Iran's position in Tunb and Abu Musa islands was made during British officials' contacts with the Iranians.

This policy was put in action and the Iranian government and M Nauz were persuaded to lower the Iranian flag on these islands. In a later report to the British Foreign Office, Sir A. Hardinge informed that:

> *I accordingly called to-day at the (Iranian) Foreign Office to be informed of His Majesty's decision. M. Naus was present at our interview, and showed me a telegram which he was just sending to Bushire informing M Damberian that the question of sovereignty over Tamb and Abumusa was a disputed one, and ordering him with the least possible delay to remove the Persian flag from those islands.* (41)

Having occupied the islands of Tunb and Abu Musa in 1903, the British continued for about two years still arguing about the need for the occupation of Iranian islands of Hengam and Qeshm in the event of a Russian threat, both of which had already been under partial British occupation. Iran was on the brink of civil war in those years and the authority of the central government was at its weakest. It took the Iranians about one year to realise what had happened to the islands of Tunb and Abu Musa. It was reported in April 1904 that Monseigneur Damberian, a director of the Iranian Customs, of Belgique origin, found out, during his tour of the ports and islands of the Persian Gulf on board Iranian ship "Mozaffari", that the Iranian flag was replaced in the islands of Tunb and Abu Musa by the flag of the Sheikh of Sharjah. He lowered that flag and ordered the Iranian flag to be hoisted again in those islands. He also commissioned two Iranian Tofangchi (armed guards) at Tunb and Abu Musa islands (42). The British Resident in the Persian Gulf despatched the Royal India Marine Steamer "Lawrence" to visit Tunb island (43), and having confirmed the news of the action of the Iranian Director of Customs, he suggested to the British Indian officials that the Iranian flag should be hauled down in those islands by use of gun-boats and replaced by the flag of Sharjah. He saw in such an action a double blessing as not only would such an action teach Iranians whom they were dealing with, but also:

> *This unwarranted infringement by Persia of rights of a chief under British protection may prove useful, should the removal of flag-staff - which stood on Plinth of old Henjam telegraph-station - give rise to a remonstrance on the part of the Persian Government.* (44)

When the Qasemis of Sharjah hoisted their flags in Greater Tunb and Abu Musa in 1903 and re-hoisted them in 1904, the island of Lesser Tunb escaped their attention and the attention of the British. The Anglo-Russian agreement of 1907 recognised British encroachments against Iranian territories in the Persian Gulf and removed Russian threats in the Persian Gulf. Yet, when in 1908 the British company Franc C. Strick strove to obtain red-oxide exploitation concessions in Faror, Sirri and Lesser Tunb, the British found it necessary to claim Lesser Tunb also. Major Percy Cox, British Political Resident in the Persian Gulf, suggested in October 1908 that: since Lesser Tunb is of the same name as Greater Tunb, its status would automatically be the same as that of the larger island. This formulation was adopted by the British Foreign Office and the company was advised to contact the Sheikh of Sharjah for concession (45) in spite of the fact that the company had, in its initial studies, reported that the Iranian flag had been in place in Lesser Tunb for years. Hence, Lesser Tunb was occupied by the British proteges in Sharjah in 1908 and their flag was hoisted there.

This transfer of the Iranian possessions in the Persian Gulf over to the Qasemis of Musandam was done on the basis of justification that the islands of Tunb and Abu Musa "had formerly been ruled by the hereditary Arab governors of Lingeh in their capacity as Qasemi Sheikhs rather than as Persian officials" (46).

This British undertaking was not taken by the outside world as a serious and lasting arrangement. The German Woenckhaus company, for instance, first obtained a concession from the Iranian authorities and began his work in Abu Musa (1907). The Sheikh of Sharjah stopped its work and the company was directed by the British to negotiate a new concession from the Sheikh of Sharjah.(47)

Recovered from the constitutional revolution, Iran found it too late and herself too weak to influence a reversal of the British decision of giving these islands to the Qasemis of Musandam. The Iranians remained unhappy about the whole affair, especially as illegal trade through these islands to the Iranian mainland increased.

The Iranian customs office made representations to the government in July 1927, demanding action against illegal trade by establishing observation posts on the three islands (48). A small fleet of the newly founded Iranian navy was sent to recover Abu Musa and the two Tunbs and to put an end to the problem there.

The Anglo-Iranian Negotiations of 1928-9

In the summer of 1928, the Iranian Customs Department began operating a motor-boat service from Greater Tunb. This was the outcome of a series of secret contacts with the Sheikh of Ras al-Khaimah, who was prepared to return the two Tunbs to Iran. In August that year, the motor-boat seized a sailing boat belonging to the Emirate of Dubai at anchor in the territorial waters of Greater Tunb. The British protested, but the Iranian Foreign Ministry declared that Tunb was under Iranian sovereignty and thus the action was in keeping with international regulations (49).

When Iran prepared, in 1928, to take her territorial disputes with Britain in the Persian Gulf, especially the issue of Bahrain, to the League of Nations, the British reminded the Iranians of their 1892 treaties with all the chiefs of the Trucial coast. The Iranians protested that 'the Persian government could not recognise as valid any (British) agreement with the Trucial chiefs which injured or limited the rights and interests of Persia' (50). The two sides agreed, however, that the status of the Tunb, Abu Musa and Sirri islands should be the subject of negotiations that winter. Protracted negotiations began in January 1929; Sir Robert Clive, British Minister in Tehran, represented Great Britain on behalf of Sharjah, and Taimurtash, Reza Shah's powerful Court Minister, represented Iran.

At the start of negotiations, the British officially claimed compensation of 5,000 rupees for the damage alleged to have resulted from the Iranian motor-boat action in seizing the sailing boat of the emirates. When the Iranians ignored this claim, the British concluded that 'owing to the effect produced on the Arab coast by the failure to obtain compensation, His Majesty's government should pay the sum at once in anticipation of a settlement of the claim (51).

The matter was never settled, as the Iranians continued to argue that their action was legal according to international law. Taimurtash offered to refer the case to international arbitration. Reporting on their initial discussions, Clive wrote to Foreign Secretary Sir Austin Chamberlain:

> *Then we talked about the islands of Tunb and Abu Musa and I asked the Court Minister what benefit did the government of Iran deem to have in taking these islands other than claiming that smugglers in the Persian Gulf are using them as their base for storing goods and smuggling them into Iran. Teimurtache answered that the government of Iran did not see this matter in the same way we do, but their main point is that these islands are the indivisible parts of Iran and were occupied by others by force. I answered Teimurtache in accordance with the guideline that you had sent me. The Court Minister said in that case there is no other way but to refer the matter to an international arbitration. Replying to His Excellency I expressed hopes that the two sides could settle the differences without having to refer the case to international arbitration. (52)*

The negotiations continued until mid-spring 1929 without much progress. Baldwin's Conservative government was replaced in May that year by a Labour government, and Arthur Henderson replaced Chamberlain as Foreign Secretary. Henderson showed a more protective line towards Britain's colonial role in the Persian Gulf and brought Clive's negotiations with the Iranians on the issue of the Tunbs and Abu Musa to an abrupt end. This led the Iranians to try to recover the island in the 1930s through a series of actions.

On 24 February 1930 the Iranian Ministry of War wrote to the Ministry of Foreign Affairs informing them of a report by the Commander in Chief of Iranian forces in the south that:

> *A number of flags have been hoisted by the British in the two islands of Tunb and Abu Musa which belong to Iran. Agents were also posted there. This has come as a real surprise to the inhabitants [of the islands]. I beg you to pass on this message to His Imperial Majesty. (53)*

On receiving this report, the Ministry of Foreign Affairs wrote to the British Minister in Tehran, Sir Robert Clive, stating:

> *Here I would like to inform your excellency that according to information received here the British flag has been hoisted in the islands of Tunb and Abu Musa. The Government of Iran considers these islands as belonging to them and find themselves with no alternative but to protest against this action. As far as the Ministry of Foreign Affairs is informed, the Government of His Britannic Majesty had no claim to the ownership of these islands, and hoisting of a flag,*

which is the manifestation of claim of ownership, has no precedence; your excellency is expected to act for the restoration of status quo. (54)

Attached to his letter of protest, the Ministry of Foreign Affairs sent the British Legation a copy of Moshir ad-Dauleh's letter of 14 June 1904, quoted above, to the British Minister in Tehran.

The British denied having hoisted their flag on the islands; but in June 1931 they were said once again to have done so, though the headman of Hengam reported that the Shaikh of Ras al-Khaimah had prevented the hoisting of the British (or his own) flag on Greater Tunb (55). The Ministry of the Imperial Court wrote to the Ministry of Foreign Affairs at the same time informing them of reports from Bushehr that the British had leased Greater Tunb from the Shaikh of Ras al-Khaimah for a period of fifty years (56).

On the whole, British Ministers' negotiations with Taimurtash from 1928 onward can be viewed as an attempt to change Iran's protest at Anglo-Qasemi occupation of Tunb and Abu Musa islands, into a position of satisfaction with a legal settlement in favour of the Shaikhs of Sharjah and Ras al-Khaimah. To this end, British authorities in the region prepared a general treaty of the Persian Gulf in fifteen articles, within the framework of which a reciprocal deal was offered to Iran.

The outstanding feature of this proposed deal was Iranian withdrawal of claims to Bahrain, Tunb and Abu Musa in return for Britain's recognition of Iranian sovereignty over Sirri Island and her withdrawal of claims to Basaidu (Qeshm) and transfer to Iran of telegraph stations in Lengeh, Bushehr and Hengam island (57). The Iranians rejected this package deal on the grounds that Iran's full sovereignty over the places mentioned was undisputed. Consequently, the whole idea of a general treaty of the Persian Gulf collapsed. Finally, during July 1932, Taimurtash told Hoare, British Minister in Tehran, that Iran would renounce her claims to Bahrain in return for British recognition of Iran's sovereignty over Abu Musa and Tunb islands, a proposal which the British rejected (58). The Anglo-Iranian oil crisis of 1932 intervened and the draft treaty was abandoned by 1934 (59).

Some British sources suggest that, in the latter parts of these negotiations, Teimurtash sent out feelers to test the British position vis-a-vis claims of the emirates to Tunb and Abu Musa, by hinting that Iran would renounce her claims to Abu Musa in return for Ras al-Khaimah's dropping its claims to and administration of the Tunbs (60). This hint was, in fact a repetition of what Teimurtash had murmured at the start of the negotiations, which had met positive reactions in the British Foreign Office, as can be seen in a minute by G.W. Rendel of Eastern Department, dated 10 December 1929

Sheikh of Ras al-Kheimah Returns the Tunb Island

In 1934 the Governor of Bandar Abbas and other Iranian officials visited Greater Tunb in a dhow. This visit was the result of a secret Iranian arrangement with the Sheikh of Ras al-Kheimah according to which the Sheikh lowered his flag in Greater Tunb and the Iranian flag was hoisted instead. Earlier, a Trucial Coast dhow was seized by an Iranian warship in Tunb's territorial waters. On two occasions in 1934, an Iranian warship visited the island in that year and landed a party of Iranians there. These activities attracted the attention of the British who vigorously protested against what was going on in that island. The Iranian government was also orally informed that the British Government would as a last resort protect the interests of the Trucial

Sheikhs by force (61). Reporting these events to his government, the British Minister in Tehran stated:

> *Some mysterious happening took place at Tamb in the early part of the year following on the action of the Sheikh of Ras al-Khaimah at the end of 1934 in having his flagstaff removed. There being grounds for suspicion that the Sheikh had been intriguing with the Iranians, the senior naval officer landed a small guard and, though this was later withdrawn, for some weeks a sloop visited the island at frequent intervals.* (62)

However, the British intervened at the end of this episode and reversed that development.

UAE and British sources have endeavoured to justify this action of the Sheikh of Ras al-Kheimah as an undertaking designed to embarrass the British, because he wanted "to draw attention to the fact that no rent was received from the British for the use of the lighthouse of Tunb" (63). This justification is not comprehensible as never before or after this incident did a ruler give part of his territory to a third country because of financial differences between the colony and the colonial power. The only acceptable explanation of this move can be that the Sheikh of Ras-al Kheimah being aware of unauthorised occupation of these islands, returned the two Tunbs to their rightful owners as a result of a disagreement with the colonial power and as a result of secret arrangements with Iran. Furthermore, whatever the explanation, the undisputed fact is that Ras al-Kheimah returned the two Tunbs to Iran in the mid-1930s when Iran was vigorously campaigning for the recovery of these islands. He did not give these islands to Saudi Arabi, Oman, Sharjah, Abu Dhabi or any other neighbouring Arab states. He gave them back to Iran.

Further Developments and Negotiations

The Iranians assumed that, while the sovereignty issue remained unresolved, neither side should engage in the exploitation of the iron oxide mines on Abu Musa. The British made no such assumption, and the Iranian Ministry of Finance wrote to the Iranian Ministry of Foreign Affairs on 9 March 1937 reporting that the British were working Abu Musa's red-oxide mines (64). When, at the end of 1948, the Iranians expressed a wish to place administrative offices on Tunb and Abu Musa, the British ignored it. In 1949 there were rumours, first that Iran was preparing to refer the case to the United Nations, later that they intended to occupy the islands by force. The Iranian government subsequently received a note from the British Embassy in Tehran expressing the British government's 'clear attitude' in that respect (65). The Iranians in return erected a flagstaff on Lesser Tunb in August that year, which the Royal Navy promptly removed.

In 1953, during Mosaddeq's second term of Premiership, there were reports in the Iranian press that an Iranian commission was to be sent to Abu Musa. An Iranian warship landed a party on that island to seek information from the inhabitants. Once again the British notified the Iranians that Abu Musa was subject to the Shaikh of Sharjah. Early the same year the British received reports that the Iranians were contemplating the despatch of troops to occupy the two Tunbs, Abu Musa and Sirri, and for several weeks RAF planes made reconnaissance flights over the islands (66). On 18 May 1961, during 'Ali Amini's Premiership, a single-rotor helicopter landed on Greater Tunb. As the British authorities made no protest, an Iranian launch made a second landing on 9 August. On the first occasion, the helicopter brought in an Iranian and two Americans, who photographed the lighthouse and adjacent buildings and talked to the lighthouse-keeper, but entered no building and accepted no hospitality (67). On the second occasion, according to a report by British naval officers, the Iranian launch approached the island from the east and landed a party on the eastern coast, but soon withdrew and went round to the south, where they landed a party at the village. The locals described two of the visitors as Americans; the second landing was thought to have been connected with the first, with the purpose of conducting an oil survey (68).

Confused by these incidents, the British first decided to protest, then to limit their reaction to making it clear to the Iranians that they knew about the incidents and would like an explanation. Finally, on 5 September, the British Embassy in Tehran handed the Iranian Ministry of Foreign Affairs a protest note, on behalf of the Shaikh of Ras al-Khaimah, against the Iranian landings on Greater Tunb (69).

The Iranian Government responded to the protest note on 21 September:

> *As the Embassy are aware, the Imperial Iranian Government have never accepted the claim that the island of Tunb is a part of the Shaikhdom of Ras Al Khaimeh or that any other state has a right over it. As has been officially declared to the Embassy on many occasions the Imperial Government of Iran consider the island of Tunb to be part of their own territory over which they have sovereignty. The Imperial Government's sovereignty over the island of Tunb is based on the rules and principles of International Law, and they have never given up their right to it. In the above circumstances the Imperial Ministry of Foreign Affairs do not consider the Embassy's protest as contained in the note under reference to be justified. (70)*

The Foreign Office deemed it necessary to repeat the protest in the hope that 'the Iranians will get tired of this sort of exchange before we do' (71). The British Embassy wrote again to the Iranian Ministry of Foreign Affairs on 13 January 1962, reserving the rights of the Ruler of Ras al-Khaimah in regard to the island of Tunb. In reply, the Iranian Foreign Ministry 'confirmed the contents of their note No. 3052 of the 21st September 1961 reserving all the Iranian rights in respect of the Iranian island of "Tunb" in the Persian Gulf' (72).

While continuing their arguments and negotiations with the British government on the subject of ownership of the islands of Tunb and Abu Musa in the early 1960s, the Iranian government began a policy of improving friendly relations with the emirates of the Arab coasts of the Persian Gulf (73). This policy entered a very active phase in 1962 and continued until 1971.

The British had suspected that the helicopter which took a party of Iranians and Americans to Greater Tunb was American, but investigation showed the helicopter to be British owned and hired by Iranians (74). A year later, during the premiership of Amir Assadollah Alam, Iran successfully completed the task of restoring her full sovereignty over the island of Sirri, in spite of opposition from the British and the Shaikh of Sharjah.

References

1- British Minister in Tehran to Iranian Ministry of Foreign Affairs, 26 Rabi ath-Thani 1322 (10.7.1904), Persian text, document 84 in "Gozideh-e Asnad-e Khalij-e Fars = A Selection of Persian Gulf Documents", Iranian Ministry of Foreign Affairs, Tehran 1989, p.268.
2- J.B. Kelly, "Eastern Arabian Frontiers", Faber & Faber, London 1964.
3- Rupert Hay "The Persian Gulf States", George Allen & Unwin, London 1959.
4- J.C. Wilkinson, "Water and Tribal Settlement in South-East Arabia", (Oxford Research Studies in Geography), Oxford Clarendon 1977, p.6.
5- Abbas Eqbal Ashtiani, "Motaleati dar bareh-e Bahrain va Jazaier va Banader-e Khalij-e Fars = Some studies on islands and ports of the Persian Gulf", The Majlis Printing House, Tehran 1328 (1949), p.144.
6- Hamdollah Ahmad ben Abi-Baker Mostofi, "Nozhat al-Qolub", ed. Guy le Strange, Leiden, Brill 1928 (original 730s AH), pp.171, 186, 234.
7- L/P & S/18/B397: Memorandum of 24th August 1928, pp.4512-28.
8- FO 371/45507, 171546: E10136/34, 'Persian Frontiers', Confidential document (17188) of H.B.M. Government, 31.1.1947, Section VI, paragraph 72, p.13.
9- FO 371/13721, Arabia E982/52/91, Letter No. F160 - N/28 of 29 January 1929 from the secretary of the Government of India to the India Office, Enclosure 3, reports of private letters of Sheikh Yusof of Lengeh to Mohammad Hassan Khan, Governor General at Bandar Abbas and Lengeh.
10- D.H. Bavand, "Bar-rasi-ye Mabani-ye Tarikhi va Hoghughi-e Jazayer-e Tunb va Abu Musa = The Study of Historical and Legal Backgrounds to the Islands of Tunbs and Abu Musa", Jame'eh-e Salem monthly, Vol. II, No.7, Tehran December 1992 - January 1993, pp.6-19.
11- FO 60/451: Persia and Arab States, Order in Consul Jurisdiction 1857 to 1882, part II, Further Correspondence respecting Consular jurisdiction in Persia 1874-76, Mr. Reilly's Correspondence and Memoranda, p.19.
12- Abdullah Mohammad Morsy, "The United Arab Emirates", Croom Helm, London 1978, pp. 234-5.
13- Document No.53 of "Gozideh-e Asnad-e Khalij-e Fars", op.cit., Vol. I, Tehran 1989, pp.168-9.
14- Abdullah, op.cit., pp.234-5.
15- FO 371/18901, Sir E. Beckett's Memorandum, dated March 12, 1932.
16- Hassan H. Al-Alkim's contribution to "Round Table Discussion on the Disputed Gulf Islands", Farid et al., November 1992, Published by Arab Research Centre, London, January 1993, pp.28-38.
17- The United Arab Emirates expanded its territorial sea to 12 miles in 1993.
18- Mohammad Reza Dabiri, "Abu Musa: a binding understanding or a misunderstanding?", Iranian Journal of International Affairs, Vol. V, Nos. 3 & 4, Fall 1993/Winter 1994, pp.575-583.
19- A.D.McNair, "The Law of Treaties", Oxford, Clarendon Press, Oxford 1961, p.185.
20- Sir Denis Wright, "The English Amongst the Persians", London 1977, p. 66.
21- Ibid., p. 67.
22- Abbas Eqbal Ashtiani, "Motaleati dar Bab-e Bahrain va Jazayer va Savahel-e Khalij-e Fars, Tehran 1949, p. 144.

23- The term 'Banader-e Khalij-e Fars' (ports of the Persian Gulf), in official documents of the Qajar period, normally included the islands of the Gulf.
24- Iranian MFA to British Legation, letter no. 26, 26 Jamadi ath-Thani 1305 (10.3.1888), Persian text in *Iranian Government Documents* (Vol. 6180).
25- British Minister to Iranian MFA, letter of 5 Rajab 1305 (18.3.1888), Persian text in *Iranian Government Documents* (Vol. 6180).
26- Qaem-Maqami, op. cit., p. 125.
27- Iranian MFA to British Legation, letter no. 44 of 12 Ziqadeh 1305 (21.7.1888), Persian text in *Iranian Government Documents* (Vol. 6180).
28- Sir Denis Wright, op. cit., p.68.
29- Iranian MFA to British Minister, letter of 24 Rabi ath-Thani 1312 (30.11.1894), Persian text in *Iranian Government Documents* (Vol. 6180).
30- Confidential from India Office to Foreign Office, dated 1st November 1900, enclosure No. 2, FO 60/733.
31- From George Hamilton to the Governor-General of India in Council, dated 23rd November 1900, secret No.30, FO 60/733.
32- Most secret Persia, War Office Memorandum on Sir A. Hardinge's letter of October 14, 1902, signed by Alton A.Q.M.G., FO 60/733.
33- Confidential Memorandum by Sir T. Sanderson, July 14, 1902, FO 416/10.
34- See Government of India to Mr Brodrick, Inclosure in No.130, April 16, 1904, No.154, FO 416/17, p.191.
35- See Horace Walpole of India Office to Foreign Office, dated April 16, 1904, No.154, FO 416/17, p.191.
36- See Lord G. Curzon "Persia and the Persian Question", London 1892, map enclosed in Vol. I.
37- Extract from the Confidential Document (17188) of H.B.M. government "Persian Frontiers", January 31, 1947, F0 371/45507, par. 72.
38- Donald Hawley, "The Trucial States", London 1970, p.287.
39- Telegram No.49, from Sir A. Hardinge to the Marquess of Lansdowne, dated Tehran April 20, 1904 enclosure No.165, FO 416/17, P.197.
40- From Foreign Office to India Office, No.174, dated April 23, 1904, FO 416/17, p.201.
41- Extract from A. Hardinge's telegram to Foreign Office, dated May 1904, FO 416/18, p.160.
42- Government of India to Mr Brodrick, dated April 13, 1904, inclosure No.130, FO 416/17, p.142.
43- Ibid.
44- Ibid.
45- From India Office to Foreign Office, dated 2 December 1908; to Viscount Morely of India Office, dated 24th November 1908; in reply to the inquiry of India Office of 20th October 1908, Enclosure to No.1: G.I., Persia E 34/42315, FO 371/506.
46- Hawley, op. cit., p. 162.
47- From First Agency of the ports of the Persian Gulf and coasts of Baluchistan to the Ministry of Foreign Affairs, dated 14 Shavval 1328 (1910), No. 64, in A Selection of Persian Gulf Documents, Foreign Ministry of the Islamic Republic of Iran's Institute of Political and International Studies, Tehran 1989, No. 91, p.280.
48- From the Customs Office of Ministry of Finance to the Ministry of Foreign Affairs, No.11469, dated Mordad 5, 1306 (27th July 1927).

49- FO 416/113: 49, Annual Confidential Report of British Legation in Tehran for the year 1928, paragraph 147, pp. 23-4.
50- Op. cit., paragraphs 150-4.
51- FO 416/113: 91, Annual Confidential Report of British Legation in Tehran for the year 1929, paragraph 156, p. 23.
52- Extracted from Sir Robert Clive to Sir A. Chamberlain, Confidential Report of 8.1.1929, Collection of British Political Documents No. 420; quoted in Shaikh al-Eslami (1988: 213).
53- Ministry of War to MFA, enclosure in confidential despatch of 5 Esfand 1308 (24.2.1930), in MFA (1989: 351).
54- MFA to British Legation, same date, in MFA (1989: 355).
55- MFA to War Ministry, 26 Khordad 1310 (16.6.1931), quoting Hengam headman's report No. 182, in MFA (1989: 363).
56- Minister of Imperial Court (Taimurtash) to MFA, 29 Khordad 1310 (19.6.1931), No. 113 in MFA (1989: 269).
57- FO 371//13776: Persia E/284/19/34, Sir Robert Clive to Austen Chamberlain, No. 1.0 of 16.2.1929.
58- FO 371/16070: Hoare to Oliphant, 15.7.1932.
59- FO 371/157031: FO Confidential Report, Status of the island of Tunb (Tamb) Sirri and Bu Musa, (1961).
60- FO 371/18980: Knatchbull-Hugessen to FO, 9.4.1935.
61- Foreign Office confidential report (1961), FO 371/157031.
62- From Mr. Knatchbull-Hugessen to Mr. Eden, Confidential Annual Report, 1935, E 1147/1147/34, dated Tehran January 28, 1935. See also the same to Foreign Office, dated 9th April 1935, FO 371/18980.
63- See for example; statement made by Richard Scholfield and Hassan Al-Alkim at the Arab, Iranian, British seminar of 18th November 1992 - "Round Table Discussion on the Disputed Gulf Islands", Arab Research Centre, London January 1993.
64- Ministry of Finance to MFA, 18 Esfand 1315 (9.3.1937), in MFA (1989: 379).
65- Captain R.M. Owen, "Confidential Report on Visit of HMS Lash Insh to Tunb Island, on 24.8.1961, FO 371/157031, p1.
66- Ibid.
67- Ibid.
68- Ibid., p.2.
69- FO 371/157031: FO to British Political Resident Bahrain, No. 227 of 24.8.1961; British Political Resident Bahrain, to FO, No. 1085/1 of 25.8.1961; British Embassy, Tehran to Iranian MFA, Note No. 487 - 1084/61 of 5.9.1961.
70- FO 371/157031: Sixth Political Department of MFA to HM Embassy, Extract from Note 3052 of 21.9.1961.
71- FO 371/150731: FO to Millard, No. BT 1083/7 of 2.11.1961.
72- FO 371/163032: Millard to Geven, Confidential of 13.1.1962; First Political Department of MFA to HM Embassy in Tehran, No. 5724 of 20.1.1962.
73- Persia Seeks New Links', The Scotsman, 7.9.1962.
74- FO 371/157031: British Embassy Tehran, to FO, No. BT 1083/10-1084/61 of 20.11.1961.

CHAPTER XX

Seizure of the Two Tunbs and Restoration of Sovereignty in Abu Musa

Pirouz Mojtahed-Zadeh

Determined to prevent the Arab Emirates inheriting from the British the dispute over ownership of Tunbs and Abu Musa islands which would prevent cooperation between Iran and her Arab neighbours in the Gulf, government authorities in Iran resumed demands for the "returning of Tunbs and Abu Musa to Iran" as from early 1970. After the settlement of the Bahrain issue that year, there were rumours that Iran had withdrawn its historical claims to Bahrain principally because it believed, at the time, that its greater interest centred on the strategic Strait of Hormuz, and in the islands at the mouth of the Persian Gulf, and that Iran was reassured by the British, in conjunction with "some" Arab governments, of getting Abu Musa and the two Tunbs, in return for Bahrain.

No doubt that Iran had been endeavouring to connect the two issues of sovereignty over Bahrain and the three islands of the Strait of Hormuz. The Shah of Iran visited Saudi Arabia in November 1968, a month after the signing of the continental shelf delimitation agreement between the two countries. This visit ended in the rapid improvement of bilateral relations in all aspects. Friendship and cooperation became so close and productive which led many to suspect that the two sides made a secret deal on the issue of Bahrain islands.

Although these rumours were baseless, the parallel secret negotiations between Iran and Britain on the Anglo-Iranian territorial disputes in the Persian Gulf which were taking place at the same time, gave rise to the rumours that the two sides, in conjunction with some Arab governments (1), agreed on a trade off deal by giving Abu Musa island to Iran in return for Iran's withdrawal of claims to Bahrain (2). This rumour was more credible because of its background history. The British had endeavoured since 1928-9 to come to a similar arrangement with Iran on the issue of Sirri Island and the islands of Tunb and Abu Musa.

The announcement by the Iranian government of the policy of withholding official recognition of the emerging federation of Arab emirates which would include territories belonging to Iran severely complicated the task of creating this federation. Saudi Arabia had similarly declared that she would not recognise the federation owing to her territorial disputes in Buraimi and Liwa regions with Abu Dhabi while Iraq's hostile attitude towards British designs concerning those small monarchies in the Persian Gulf was known. The British had, therefore, concluded that creation of the union of the small emirates without goodwill of the regional powers would put this powerless union in a risky position. Recognition of this fact was the main driving force behind the British decision of trying to reach some kind of compromise with Iran, the most powerful country of the region, by reluctantly recognising her rights to the three islands.

From the Iranian point of view, time was running out and British intransigency forced her to come to an arrangement of shared sovereignty with Sharjah clearly against her declared policy concerning Abu Musa. The Iranian government, nevertheless, officially declared that Iran's rights of sovereignty over the whole of Abu Musa was not to be affected by the terms of the Memorandum of Understanding which could be a mere instrument of a *de facto* recognition of status quo in Abu Musa and thus a temporary measure which would only postpone finalisation of restoration of Iran's full sovereignty over the whole of Abu Musa.

A vigorous campaign of legal, political and historical arguments was launched by Tehran aiming at making it known both to Great Britain and Arab quarters in the neighbourhood of the Persian Gulf that she had resolved to leave no stone unturned in making her repossession of the three islands a reality. This campaign appears to have made the intended impression as sympathy for Tehran increased internationally. Even the British seemed to recognise the fact that Iran's rights to these islands could not be ignored completely. In his confidential diary for 18th February 1969:

> *... British Ambassador (Sir Denis Wright)..... told me very confidentially that the case of Tunb Island is practically settled and will definitely be given to Iran, for we have told the Sheikh of Ras al-Kheimeh that if you don't come to some sort of arrangement with Iran - as these islands are situated above the median line (of the Persian Gulf) - Iran will lawfully, and if that was not possible, will forcefully take these islands, and the Sheikh agreed to make a deal over them. I said: what about Abu Musa? He said: this island is situated below the median line. I said: and our power is sufficient enough to put a step below the line... He said: (if you resort to force) your relations with the Arabs will be harmed. I said: to hell with it...* (3)

Even at this stage some former British officials in the Persian Gulf would express doubt about Sharjah's and Ras al-Kheimiah's "legal" and "legitimate" ownership of these islands. While using clearly positive terminologies in describing varying ownership of the islands of the Persian Gulf, Donald Hawley, British Political Agent for the Trucial States between 1958 and 1961, describes the ownership of the islands of Tunbs and Abu Musa in his book as having "been occupied by the Qawasim" (4).

By comparison, the Iranian press were putting forward a vigorous argument on Iran's "indisputable" ownership of these islands. Kayhan International of May 30, 1970, for instance, put forward a legal argument on Iran's sovereignty of the three islands, adding:

> *The three islands have belonged to Iran since time immemorial and have always formed an integral part of the country. About eighty years ago, the British government, for imperialistic considerations, unlawfully and temporarily separated them from Iran by preventing Iran from exercising its established sovereign rights over them.* (5)

These arguments were reiteration of the points that the Shah himself made earlier in 1970 and repeated thereafter. In an interview which took place during his flight to Switzerland in early February 1971 for instance, he stated:

These islands belong to the nation, and we have British Admiralty maps and other documents which prove this. We will - if necessary - regain them by force, because I don't want to witness my country to be put up to auction. (6)

In a second interview with the Indian magazine "Blitz" on June 24th, 1971 the Shah declared that: the islands belonged to Iran; they had been "grabbed some eighty years earlier at a time when Iran had no central government". And that his "father had sent gunboats to recover them, but the British assured Iran that no flag of sovereignty would be hoisted until the question was settled". The Shah then added: "I hope this happens now. Otherwise, we have no alternative but to take the islands by force" (7). A further warning of the use of force in "returning" the islands of Abu Musa and the two Tunbs to Iran came on June 27, 1971 by Amir Abbas Hoveida, the then Prime Minister, who told the people of the strategic Gulf port of Bandar Abbas that:

Iran was by no means indifferent to the future of the Persian Gulf, because it constituted its vital access route. Iran needed these islands for its security and prosperity, a goal for the attainment of which Iran would fight with all its might should it fail to settle this problem by peaceful means. (8)

Earlier having emphasized Iran's sovereignty rights to the islands, Foreign Minister Ardeshir Zahedi expressed similar concerns by drawing attention to the activities of Communist elements in the south of the Strait of Hormuz:

Look to the Chinese Communists in Aden. If these islands go, all our (regional and Western) interests will be damaged. Iran, therefore, is determined to seize the islands (if necessary) for the following reasons:
  1- Freedom of navigation in this waterway at all times is essential, for Iran, unlike Saudi Arabia and Iraq, depends upon the Persian Gulf as the only outlet for its oil exports.
  2- Iran needs to exploit its offshore oil resources and to protect not only its extensive oil installations at Kharg Island and elsewhere, but its oil cargoes for the entire length of the waterway. (9)

By the summer of 1971 the Iranian authorities began vociferously warning that they would use force if peaceful settlement of the question was not made possible.

Despite these warnings of the use of force, Iran continued negotiations with the British as the year 1971 was drawing to its close.

Some sources suggest that on November 21st, 1971 it was believed in Tehran that the last round of negotiations would not take place (10). Iran's chief negotiator, Amir Khosro Afshar (then Iran's Ambassador in London), confirmed to this author on Sunday 10th April 1994 that negotiations between him and Sir William Luce of Great Britain continued to the full, the last round of which took place in London only a few days before the landing of Iranian forces on the islands. On the method of negotiations he explained:

Sir William Luce and I used to negotiate in London. Having reached certain points of understanding, we would go to Tehran and discuss them before the Shah. Having heard the Shah's views, Sir William Luce would go to the emirates discussing the points with rulers of Sharjah and Ras al-Kheimah, from there going to London to brief his government. We then resumed the talks in London, repeating the same procedure.

Mr Afshar also disclosed to this author on the same date that, Saudi Arabia and Egypt were aware of the negotiations. He said:

I met and discussed our intention of repossessing the three islands once with King Faisal, and three times with Prince Fahad (now King Fahad) in London. I had also discussed the matter with Mahmud Riyadh, Egyptian Foreign Minister, during a meeting at the United Nations. Several times I discussed the matter with Sheikh Zaied of Abu Dhabi who was to become the President of the Emerging UAE. My last talks on the subject with him took place at the Iranian Embassy in London in the summer of 1971. Sheikh Zaied's suggestions included prosecution of this Iranian intention after the formation of the UAE was officially announced. I explained that Iran wanted cooperation with the emerging UAE and other neighbours in the Persian Gulf in the wake of British withdrawal from the region. This issue constituted long standing disputes between Iran and the British and had to be settled with them before they left the region. Should we allow this matter to remain unsettled after the departure of the British, the UAE inheritance of the dispute will prevent regional cooperation. He had nothing to say to this argument. Moreover, six hours before landing troops on the three islands, on the instruction of the Shah, I informed King Faisal, through Saudi Ambassador in Tehran, of our imminent move to repossess the three islands.

Mr Afshar also disclosed that he met Sheikh Saqar of Ras al-Kheimah and his heir apparent separately in London discussing the issue of the two islands of Tunb. No agreement was reached on the subject he said, but some months after Iran's move into the islands, the Saudis intervened asking him to meet the Sheikh and to see to his financial needs. He stated:

I met Sheikh Saqar in the Iranian Embassy in London and told him that we were prepared to extend financial assistance to Ras al-Kheimah provided that he officially renounced his opposition to the reassertion of Iranian sovereignty on the two Tunbs. He said he saw no sense in not doing so, but such an official declaration would put his life in jeopardy with the fanatics.

Equally important is the fact that some twenty four hours before the Iranian military action took place, Sharjah announced an agreement with Iran, according to which Iranian forces were to take possession of the strategic areas of Abu Musa.

The announced Memorandum of Understanding between Iran and Sharjah included the following points (11):

Neither Iran nor Sharjah will give up its claim to Abu Musa nor recognise the other's claim. Against this background the following arrangements will be made:

1. *Iranian troops will arrive on Abu Musa. They will occupy areas the extent of, which have been agreed on the map attached to this memorandum.*
2. *(a) within the agreed areas controlled by the Iranian troops, Iran will have full sovereignty and the Iranian flag will fly.*
    (b) Sharjah will retain full jurisdiction over the remainder of the islands. The Sharjah flag will continue to fly over the Sharjah police post on the same basis as the Iranian flag will fly over the Iranian military quarters.
3. *Iran and Sharjah recognise the breadth of the island's territorial sea as twelve nautical miles, (according to Iran's law of territorial waters).*
4. *Exploitation of the petroleum resources of Abu Musa and the seabed and sub-soil beneath its territorial sea will be conducted by Butes Oil and Gas Company under the existing agreement which must be acceptable to Iran. Half of the governmental oil revenues hereafter attributable to the said exploitation shall be paid directly by the company to Iran and half to Sharjah.*
5. *The nationals of Iran and Sharjah shall have equal rights to fish in the territorial sea of Abu Musa.*
6. *A financial assistance agreement will be signed between Iran and Sharjah.*

November 1971

The financial agreement referred to in the above MOU concerned payments by Iran to Sharjah of one and a half pounds sterling annually for a period of nine years. This was to cease should Sharjah's oil revenue reach £3 million per annum (12). Other sources, however, incorrectly imply:

The statement concluded a provision that one half of the oil revenues from the island and its continental shelf, should be allocated under special arrangement for the welfare of the people of Sharjah. (13)

Since Sharjah was still a British protectorate at the time and, in accordance with the terms of her special treaties of 1864 and 1892 with Great Britain, did not have the right to sign an official agreement or treaty with any foreign power except Great Britain, it is noteworthy that the above Memorandum of Understanding between that emirate and Iran cannot be considered but as a British sponsored pact between the two sides.

Sharjah gained its independence, within the framework of the United Arab Emirates two days later (December 1st, 1971).

An Iranian Foreign Ministry official who wished to remain anonymous told this author on 26th April 1972 of a letter signed by Dr Abbas-Ali Khalatbary, then Foreign Minister of Iran, and addressed to Sir Alec Douglas Home, British Foreign Secretary, warning that if Iran felt, at any time, activities occurring in the Sharjah controlled section of Abu Musa aimed at threatening Iran's interests and sovereignty and security in that island, the government of Iran will reserve for themselves the right to implement their full sovereignty over the whole of Abu Musa. Replying to this letter, the British Foreign Office informed Iran that the contents of the above letter were communicated to the Sheikh of Sharjah. A similar letter to the President of the UAE (December 1971) motivated a positive response.

Abu Musa's 12 mile territorial waters overlapped those of the Emirate of Umm al-Quiwain. In a settlement between Iran and Sharjah on the one hand and Umm al-Quiwain on the other, it was arranged for the latter to receive a 15% share of the oil revenue from the overlapped areas.

The understanding between Iran and Sharjah, declared by the ruler of that emirate on November 29th, 1971 was undoubtedly one of the most positive results of the Anglo-Iranian negotiations going on prior to Iran's repossession of the three islands.

The Memorandum of Understanding with Sharjah, however, left the overall matter of ownership of Abu-Musa undefined. In an interview with Al-Ahram correspondent in Sharjah, on December 7th, 1971, the then ruler of the Emirate of Sharjah stated that: "Sharjah did not believe that its agreement with Iran adversely affected its sovereignty over the island", and that "the agreement was temporary and was an instrument for overcoming crisis and preventing bloodshed" (14). This statement totally contradicted an earlier statement by the Iranian Premier to the Iranian Majlis (Parliament). Premier Hoveida had stated on November 30th, 1971:

> *The Iranian flag was unfurled on Mount Halva, the highest peak on the island of Abu-Musa. I deem it necessary to declare on this occasion that the government of H.I.M. has in no conceivable way relinquished or will relinquish its sovereign rights and incontestable jurisdiction over the whole island of Abu-Musa, and hence, the presence of local agents (i.e. Sharjah - officials) in a segment of the island of Abu-Musa should in no way be viewed or interpreted as contradictory to this declared policy.* (15)

Arab reaction to the Iranian action was mixed. Radical Arab states adopted vociferous policies both domestically and in the United Nations, while the moderates preferred prudence. The Arab League was urged by the radicals to lodge a collective Arab complaint with the United Nations Security Council, signed by all 21 member states of the time. The proposal was opposed to by the majority of the member states. Instead, they agreed to condemn Iran's action individually by issuing statements in their own capitals. All Arab states issued this statement of condemnation except Jordan, while leaders of Egypt, Morocco, Tunisia, Lebanon, Saudi Arabia, Oman, Qatar and Bahrain apologised privately to the Iranian leadership for having to issue such statements.

The radical Arab states: Algeria, Iraq, Libya and former South Yemen took their complaint to the United Nations Security Council. The Council met on December 9th, 1971 to examine the case. Representatives of these four countries were joined by representatives for Kuwait and the United Arab Emirates, the latter becoming a member of the United Nations on the same day (16).

Talib al-Shibib, representing Iraq, alleged in his account of the event that *"Iran had claimed the whole Gulf, but 'such ludicrous blanket claims' had been reduced to claims on Bahrain and later to the Tunbs and Abu Musa"* (17).

He asserted that his government had received a cable from the Sheikh of Ras al-Kheimah claiming that the two Tunbs had belonged to Ras al-Kheimah since ancient times (18).

Whereas the UAE representative made a very mild and conciliatory statement (19), Abdullah Yaccoub Bishara, representing Kuwait, claimed that the islands of Greater Tunb and Lesser Tunb belonged to Ras al-Kheimah "for centuries" (20). A similar statement made by UAE Foreign Minister at the United Nations General Assembly on September 30, 1992, also alleged that islands of Tunbs and Abu Musa belonged to the emirates "since the beginning of history" (21).

It is worth observing, however, that the tribal entity of Sharjah was created in 1864, the tribal entity of Ras al-Kheimah was created in 1921 and the United Arab Emirates came into being in 1971.

In his statement to the UN Security Council meeting of December 9th, 1971 Abdellatif Rahal of Algeria presented a more rational historical account of this case by saying:

> *There had been conflicting claims to those islands over the years, but it was undeniable that during the whole period of British control the islands had been part of the territory that had become the United Arab Emirate.* (22).

This statement, albeit more rational than those made by representatives of Kuwait, Iraq and Libya, was not in complete harmony with the facts of history. That the British control of the lower Gulf territories began in 1820 while Abu Musa and the two Tunbs were seized from Iran and given to the Qasemi tribal entity of Sharjah by the British in the year 1903.

For his part, Amir Khosro Afshar, representing Iran in the hearing, made a relatively short statement rejecting the charges against Iran as baseless, and said the question was essentially an internal matter for his country (UN 1972: 48).

Finally, Abdul Rahman Abby Farah, representative of Somalia, a member of the Arab League, proposed that the Council should adjourn consideration of the complaint allowing third-party efforts of mediation taking place. The Council agreed without objection to that course, and thus the case was let at rest.

Notes and References

1- Saudi Arabian government was suspected to have been involved.
2- Al-Ahram of Cairo, November 10, 1968.
3- Alinaghi Alikhani, Ed. *The Shah and I, Confidential Diary of Alam*", Vol. I - 1347 and 1348 (1969 and 1970), Text in Persian, published in USA 1992, p.130.
4- D. F. Hawley, *The Trucial States*, London 1970, pp.287-8.
5- Iran, Foreign Policy Series, No. 2, January 1973, The Echo of Iran, p.26.
6- Mohammad Reza Shah in interview with the Associated Press, Kayhan No. 8278, Tehran February 20, 1971, p.27.
7- Kayhan of Tehran, No. 8381, June 25th, 1971.
8- *Amir Abbas Hoveida in Bandar Abbas*, Ettlelaat of Tehran, June 27th, 1971.
9- *Middle East Journal* (MEJ), Vol. XXV, No. 2, 1971, pp. 234-5. Quoting Ardeshir Zahedi.
10- R. K. Ramazani, *The Persian Gulf*, USA, pp.56-8.
11- Extract from the text of the original copy of the Memorandum of Understanding as appears in Appendix III of this book.
12- Pirouz Mojtahed-Zadeh, *Political Geography of the Strait of Hormuz*, op. cit., p.12.
13- Alvin J. Cottrell, Iran *Diplomacy in a Regional and Global Context*, Washington, 1975, p.6.
14- Pirouz Mojtahed-Zadeh, *Political Geography of the Strait of Hormuz*, op. cit., p.12.
15- Alvin J. Cottrell, "Iran Diplomacy in a Regional and Global Context", Washington, 1975, p.6.
16- See: UN Monthly Chronicle, January 1972, Vol. IX, No.1, Record of the Month of December 1971, p.46.
17- Ibid.
18- Ibid.
19- Ibid, p.50.
20- Ibid, p.47.
21- International News Agencies as quoted by *Kayhan* (London) Thursday 8th 1992.
22- UN Monthly Chronicle, op. cit., p.48.

CHAPTER XXI

A Look at Some of the More Recently Propagated UAE Arguments
Pirouz Mojtahed-Zadeh

Territorial Claims for Nation-Building Exercise

The United Arab Emirates has been experiencing difficulties in creating real and true national cohesion in that federation of the seven political entities of Arab tribal identity (Arab Emirates). Lack of any real challenge of political geography nature to this identity seems to have deprived the UAE of the notion of nation-building process; the necessary stimulant that would bear the fruit of national cohesion. By contrast, Abu Dhabi's vociferous claims on the Islands of Greater and Lesser Tunbs and Abu Musa, seems to have worked inadvertently to strengthen the Iranian national unity instead of its intended results for the UAE. This was to act as a hot subject of the UAE's territorial dispute with the only non-Arab state (Iran) of the region, but it seems to have failed to play the magical role of a *cause celebre* at a regional and Middle Eastern level as a symbol of Arab nationalist resistance to the myth of spreading Iranian influence in the Persian Gulf (1). Domestically, it was expected to become the symbol of a foreign territorial challenge that would stimulate growth of the sense a 'nationhood' that would be particular to the UAE.
Failing to achieve any real results from the above strategy seems to have lead Abu Dhabi to adopt a more fundamental undertaking of a massive cultural project aimed at creating a new historical identity for the region by trying to re-write regional history. The ultimate aim in this cultural venture seems to be complete denial of all aspects of the history of the region that would one way or another relate to Iran and her ancient sovereignty of the southern coasts of the Persian Gulf. Supported by more radical nationalists (pan-Arab) quarters in places like Qatar, Kuwait, and to some extent Saudi Arabia, Abu Dhabi has benefited from many obliging regional and Anglo-American academics. In addition to declaring in the title of his book (2) the three islands of Tunbs and Abu Musa in the Persian Gulf as being owned by the United Arab Emirates, Thomas R. Mattair, for instance has argued that these islands belonged to the emirates of Sharjah and Ras-al-Khaimah for many centuries, without being able to address the fundamental issue of these emirates' existence prior to the 20th century as independent territorial states with spatial dimension that could enable them to claim any territory as representing their legal dominion. In fact when the idea of determining territorial dimension for the tribal entities of Eastern Arabia and defining boundary lines among them was expressed by the authorities of Indo-European telegraph line in 1864, British Political Resident in the Persian Gulf, Colonel Lewis Pelly, opposed it on the basis that implementation of these European concepts in Eastern Arabia was 'inexpedient' at the time (3). Pelly's officially recorded view was echoed later by J. B. Kelly who said:

> *The concept of territorial sovereignty in the Western sense did not exist in Eastern Arabia, A ruler exercised jurisdiction over a territory by virtue of his jurisdiction over the tribes inhabiting it. They in turn, owed loyalty to him...* (4)

These words were echoes of what many Western scholars and diplomats like Professor John Wilkinson of Oxford University and Sir Rupert Hay, a former British Political Resident in the Persian Gulf, had stated before and after him. John Wilkinson described the British attempts of 1960s for introducing the concept of territoriality to the local tribes and boundary making amongst them in Eastern Arabia as:

> *This ludicrous partitioning of territory is of recent origin and stems in large measure from the imposing of European notion of territorialism on a society to which they were foreign......Britain sought to develop an exclusive influence in the Gulf and, later still, to favour the claims of particular companies to act as concessionaries for oil exploration, she was forced first into defending the protégé coastal rulers from attack from the hinterland and then of proclaiming their authority over the population and resources of greater Oman...* (5)

Sir Rupert Hay states: *"Before the advent of oil the desert was in many ways similar to the high seas. Nomads and their camels roamed across it at will..."* (6).

In its endeavor to establish a new historical identity for the UAE in addition to their pan-Arab tendencies, the UAE Government seems to have opted for the adoption of the same strategy of political ideology devised in 1950s and 1960s, and implemented by the former Baath Party of Iraq in 1970s to 1990s.

Since its emergence in 1968 the second Baath regime in Iraq launched a massive and long-lasting anti-Iranian propaganda campaign, which became the central theme of its promotion of Baath philosophy. This was an expected geopolitical strategy contrasting the demographical features of Iraq. Almost 80% of the population of what has become the state of Iraq in early 20th century is made up of peoples of Kurdish and Shiite origin with strong cultural and ethnic ties with Iran. Moreover, like the emirates of southern shores of the Persian Gulf, Mesopotamia was part of what was the Iranian federative system (Persian Empire) for the greater part of the past three thousand years. These historical and geographical factors did not offer a comfortable prospect to the former Baath ideologues to work out a completely Arabic identity for Iraq that would enable it to play the role of a leading Pan-Arab power in the region. Hence, the Baath Party had to shed all layers of Iraq's cultural image that in any way represented Iran or its Persian civilization. A massive anti-Iranian campaign that had begun by the first Baath party of Iraq in 1959 was boosted by the re-emergence of that party in 1968.

A major feature of this endeavor was attempts to change the name of the Persian Gulf to *Arabian Gulf*, changing the ancient name of Iran's Khuzestan province into *Arabistan* and trying to sever that province from Iran by creating a terrorist group of a few elements related to the Iranian Arab tribes living in Khuzestan who occupied Iranian Embassy in London in 1980 in a terrorist action and even now is heavily involved in terrorist activities in Khuzestan and Tehran (7). Other features of this anti-Iranian racially inclined ideology include changing the name of the islands of Kish and Lavan off the Iranian coasts near the straits of Hormuz, hundreds of miles away from any where near Iraq or any other Arab state.

The Baath party and its political philosophy, which symbolized their peculiar way of shaping a national identity, had aimed at proving that; not only was Iraq a fundamentally Arab nation, but a leading one. This whole argument was to be consolidated on the basis of compensating for the goepolitical weakness: that the Baath party and its ruling class were from the Sunni Arab population of that country which has always been in minority there, and it was this weak geographical foundation of the argument that drove the Baath regime to a dictatorship of a most severe kind, vis-à-vis 80% of the people of Iraq, and to a belligerent approach in their relations with Iran.

The Baath policy of nation-building was not to follow the path of a normal process of settling the crisis of identity. All philosophers and thinkers of political, geographical and social sciences, including famous Arab thinker Edward Said, in his famous book *Orientalism* (8) concede that one normally constructs one's identity by comparing the notion of 'us' with the notion of 'them'. But in the case of the Baath party of Iraq, this mechanism worked differently. In their theory Baath party was to construct an extreme form of Pan-Arab identity for Iraq by destroying the identity of 'them', which in this case was represented by *Persia* (Iran). This was because what constitutes Iraq now had been a part of the Iranian federal system known in the West as *Persian Empire* for centuries both before and after Islam. To the Baath party thinkers, Cyrus the Great's conquer of Babylonia in the mid six century BC was not to be forgiven because, no matter how emphatically the holy books in Islam, Christianity and Judaism condemned Babylonian tyranny and its inhumanity, to them Babylonia was an Arab state that represented Iraq's glorious past upon which Iraq's new Pan-Arab identity had to be constructed.

It was on the basis of this peculiar way of reading history that a mind-boggling anti-Iranian (anti-Persian) campaign began which lasted for 35 years, causing the eight-year war of attrition with more than one million people dead, and hundreds of billions of dollars worth of destruction to both countries. The cultural aspects of this incessant campaign involved a furiously fought anti-Iranian propaganda throughout the Arab world. Even in their school books *Persia* (Iran) was presented as a pure evil. In a research work entitled *Sourat al-Iraniyn fi al-kotob al-madresiyat al-Arabiyat* (the image of Iranians in Arab school books), Talal Adrisi, an Arab scholar points out that the image of Iran (al- Faresi = the Persians) presented in the Iraqi school books is quite clear. He then quotes an Iraqi history book of the time of the former regime as saying (9):

> *Verily the Iranians are always the same low-down racist Persians who have, since the time of Rashedin Caliphate until the glorious Qadesiyah* (10) *of noble Saddam Hussein been against the Arab nation and its unity, against its Arabic-Islamic civilization and against its language.... All problems of the Arabs and the Muslims, and all conflicts and agitations, and ethnic wars, and all efforts for the destruction of its (Arab's) civilization are the result of Persian conspiracies.*

After the fall of Iraq's Baath regime in 2003, many indications suggesting that the Baath brand of ideology for nation-building by re-writing the history and revising the geography of the region is being questioned in the Arab world. Yet, this new trend appears to have started in a reverse direction in some Arab parts of lower Persian Gulf. In addition to rejecting many calls by Arab scholars and Arab newspapers asking Arabs to abandon the campaign of changing the name of the Persian Gulf (11) for instance, the UAE Government has increased its anti-Iranian campaign.

They have started to return sea-going vessels from their shores if happened to produce their cargo-bill bearing the name 'Persian Gulf'; they hugely increased financial support for any journalist, academic, or politician in the West that would adopt the term *Arabian Gulf* instead of the historical name of the Persian Gulf, the 2005 case of geographical controversy by National Geographic was an example; they began to support any activity that aimed at hurting Iran, the case of financial support for the creation of the Taliban regime in Afghanistan and its anti-Iranian activities in late 1990s and early years of the 2000s is one example and its critical stance, encouraged by US Secretary of State Condoleezza Rice, against Iran's nuclear energy program and attempts to formulate a pan-Arab opposition to it on the argument that close proximity of Iran's nuclear sites would pose a danger to the Arab countries of the Persian Gulf in the events of accidents, is another example. The UAE in putting forward this argument ignores the fact that they have never criticized Israel's nuclear arms program and the danger of Israeli nuclear sites proximity to the "brother" Arab nations of Lebanon, Jordan, Syria, and Egypt.

Writing and broadcasting undocumented allegations against Iran as *Persian Empire* and its founder, Cyrus the Great increased once again both locally and in the West. Appearance of an amazing piece of slur against Iran and its history of civilization, particularly against Iranian federative state (the so-called *Persian Empire*) of the pre-Islamic era, calling it *'The evil empire'* in one of the most unlikely forums, "the Guardian" daily of London (Thursday September 8, 2005) perhaps is a good example of revival of Baath-style campaign of nation-building in an Arab state through expression of hatred for Iran, which had for over 35 years brought the Arabs and Iranians nothing but wars and devastation.

It might, however, be understandable that these newly formed states would concern themselves with the task of nation-building within the framework of their desired Arab identity, but construction of one's identity cannot be achieved through destruction of the identity of others. In their identity seeking efforts when some of these emirates face the reality that the lands on which they are building their new nations formed the southern flanks of the Iranian federative system (the so-called *Persian Empire*) for thousands of years and, therefore, like the former Baath regime in Iraq, they too see their options limited to destroying the Persian (Iranian) identity. While, denying in many of their texts in history and geography the existence of such a political entity as Iran or Persia, in many other of their texts they try to reshape the history in a manner that would justify their anti-Iranian arguments. In a friendly exchange with an academic colleague in the United Kingdom, who, in reply to my invitation to a televised academic debate (for an Iranian television), wrote on Thursday 5 January 2006; *...my relations and interests are entirely tied up with the Arab side of the Gulf...* Nevertheless, he stated:

> *Archaeological evidence (notably by Walid al-Takriti in Buraimi area) is showing that the Dawudi qanat go back well before the Achaemanid period and that on the contrary, there is no firm evidence of an Achaemanid occupation of Oman. Indeed the argument is that Oman was the original site of the qanat development and was taken by the Persians and spread by them..... Some of the major qanat of Oman on the western side of the mountains predate the Achaemanid period.* (12)

Neither the author of the above nor the source he refers to seem to have paused and asked the question; considering that defining the existence of a real and actual civilization is the pre-requisite condition for any academic claim of the discovery of constructed infrastructure in any given area of the world, how could *qanat* (underground water channel system) have been constructed in Eastern Arabia and Oman before the Achaeminid period? They do not seem to be concerned that before making that claim, they have to establish existence of a civilization in that part before the advent of the Achaeminid Iranian civilization. This is an old practice, and attempts to attribute some of the better known and well-established features and samples of ancient Iranian civilization to modern countries like Turkey, Iraq and other Arab states of the region, is not new. There are always those in countries of more recent emergence who endeavor to work out an old and historical identity for the new nations through re-writing the history. There are claims that *qanat* was first constructed by ancient Turks who did not even live in southwest Asia before 12th century AD. Some others who are more concerned about purifying their Western identity of any Eastern cultural features, have attributed to Rome almost all of the well known ancient Iranian inventions such as the *qanat* underground water channel system, coinage (gold *Daric* and silver *Ziglus*), road system (*the Royal Road*) etc.

A closer look at the terminologies used in the above quoted letter is more revealing. In another part the author refers to the lack of "firm evidence of an Achaemanid occupation of Oman". This sentence represents lack of care in the use of the term "occupation" in reference to the presence of Achaeminid Iran in southern coasts of the Persian Gulf and what is now Oman and Emirates. The term occupation is normally used in reference to the legal or illegal act of taking over a piece of land from a previous owner. But in the case of Oman and southern coasts of the Persian Gulf the authors do not bother to identify an owner-occupier of those areas prior to the advent of the Achaeminid state. The existence of the *qanats* in those areas is the evidence of Achaemanid presence there. On the other hand, they seem to have difficulty in contemplating that no much evidence of the Achaeminid presence are to be found in many areas of the interior of Iran, but that does not suggest that a civilization and a political system (federative state) that had ruled and administered over the largest part of the civilized world of 6th to 3rd centuries BC, did not exist in its core areas (lands between and around the Caspian Sea and the Persian Gulf).

All local historical evidence, all Arab texts of history like Tabari, Masudi, Yaqubi, Maqdasi, Ibn Huqal etc. confirm what Sir Arnold T. Wilson asserted in his highly acclaimed publication in 1928 on the Persian Gulf that:

> *There are myths dating the origin of the people of the Persian Gulf to the meeting of three branches of mankind on the shores of the Gulf in about 10,000 BC: the Drividian of the Makran coasts (Iranian) absorbed by their Baluchi conquerors (Iranian); the Semites of the Arabian highlands who displaced or absorbed the original Hamitic Euro-African aborigines; and the proto-Elamites of southwestern Iran (Iranian).* (13)

The political geography of Eastern Arabia (southern coasts of the Persian Gulf) followed the same pattern of political development in that entire region since the dawn of history. This region first experienced the existence of 'state' in the modern sense of the word, in the mid-sixth century BC when the Achaeminid (559 to 330 BC) consolidated their federative system, which included most of the civilized world of the time. Iranian settlement and political domination of these areas were consolidated under the Sassanids (224-651 AD) (14). All Arab and Islamic sources of history of human movements in that Part of the lower Persian Gulf indicate that the first of any migratory movements of Arab tribes to those parts began in a few decades before the advent of

Islam according to all Arab sources of ancient history and to firm local evidence used by Dr. John Wilkinson of Oxford University who discloses that:

> *The main Shanu'a groupings of Arab immigrants from the interior of Arabia were established in the mountain of Musandam and Oman proper in the early sixth century AD, when the Kawadh (Qobads) ruled the region. It was probably in association with this migration into Oman that elements of the Kinda also came to settle in the mountain areas of jabal Kinda near Buraimi Oasis. Other Arab migration who settled in the desert and border areas of Oman formed the Azd Federation. Faced with this massive new tribal union of migrant Arabs, the Iranian rulers of the region had no alternative but to accord the newcomers a degree of autonomy under their own tribal leadership.* (15)

Re-Writing History to Formulate National Identity

In addition to the necessity of being familiar with the evolution of legally inclined concept of territoriality and territorial ownership in South East Arabia and southern shores of the Persian Gulf, and before speaking of "centuries of Sharjah and Ras al-Kheimah's history of ownership of territories in and around the Persian Gulf, Thomas R. Mattairs of our time aught to establish first; what is the history of statehood in that part of the world; second, how long these emirates have been in existence as political entities of legal and territorial dimension, and third; what was the role of the British in 19th and 20th centuries in allocating lands to various emirates at will. In this context, in order to avoid repetition of issues and instances of historical and legal arguments, I would refer these authors to carefully study the previous chapters in this book for matters related to history of statehood in The Persian Gulf, history of the existence of the Arab Emirates of the Persian Gulf, and the role the British played in allocating territories to various state or tribal entities at will in 19th and 20th century. The agents of British colonial rule in the region in 19th and early 20th century, who were the instruments of colonial interference in the political geography of the Persian Gulf and allocated various territories to different entities in the region, conveniently denied all aspects of Iran's traditional dominion and her sovereignty connections with the southern coasts of the Persian Gulf, but several British scholars and academics like Sir Arnold T. Wilson, Dr. John C. Wilkinson, Sir Rupert Hay, Donald Hawley, J. B. Kelly etc. have made reasonable references to these traditional realities of the region in their scholarly works.

Figure 21

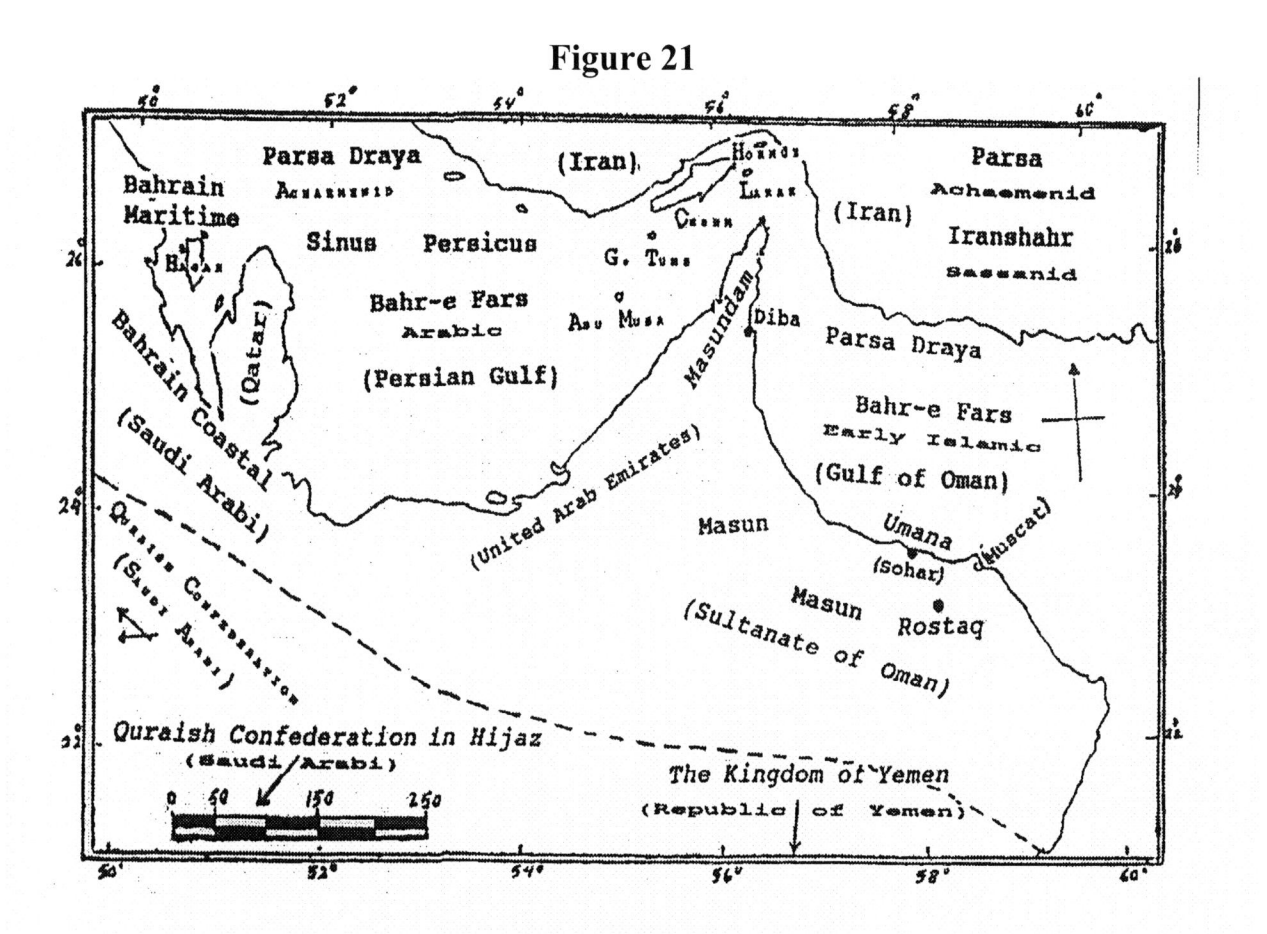

Approximate limits of Iranian dominions on the southern side of the Persian Gulf, in the pre-Islamic centuries. Iran's post-Islamic sovereignty exercise became vague until British colonization of these areas in 19th century put a complete and final end to the remaining Iranian territorial influence in those offshore areas

Here, it suffices to briefly state that even the name Ras al-Kheimah is a reminder of Iran's age-old sovereignty presence in southern coasts of the Persian Gulf. Iran's pre-Islamic dominion and sovereignty over these areas were well defined and well documented. The term Ras al-Kheimah is an Arabic construction of two parts: *Ras* is head (the tip of), and *Kheimah* means tent in both Arabic and Persian. *Ras al-Kheimah* therefore, means the 'tip of tends', and that is in reference to the tip of the tented headquarters of Iran's military camp in that vicinity during the time of Nadir Shah Afshar (first half of the 18th century). Iran's post–Islamic sovereignty and presence were defined in terms of Islamic territorial description, and continued albeit vaguely until the arrival in the Persian Gulf of British colonialism and start of their interference in the political geography of the region as from 1820 when they signed their first treaty of peace with the tribal entities therein. They continued this task and by 1899 signed many similar treaties that brought all major tribal entities under British protection and sovereignty. The Iranian Government protested against this process of colonization of Iranian dependent entities in the south of the Persian Gulf and Iranian premier in mid-1840s, Haji Mirza Aghasi issued a warning, reminding the British that all ports and islands in and around the Persian Gulf belonged to Iran, but they preferred to ignore his warnings (16). Here, it might be worthwhile to bring to the attention of the authors at the service of the UAE government claim to the three islands in question, one of many historical documents verifying acknowledgement by rulers of tribal entities of southern coasts of the Persian Gulf of historical tradition of Iranian sovereignty over those areas. The following is the text of articles I, II, and IV of a formal letter from Sheikh Sultan Bin Saqar of Ras al-Kheimah to the Iranian authorities most relevant to the status of Ras al-Kheimah as a dependency of Iran like other tribal entities of southern coasts of the Persian Gulf which had enjoyed the same status vaguely throughout the post-Islamic history of the region. In this letter, which is dated 17 of Sha'ban 1272 H.Q. (23 April 1865), the ruler of Ras al-Kheimah principally requests from the authorities in Tehran to grant him the lease of Bandar Abbas on the northern coasts of the Persian Gulf (northern coasts of the Strait of Hormuz); for that he argues that as Ras al-Kheimah was an Iranian dominion, its leasing of Bandar Abbas would benefit Iran without even encountering any legal problem:

Articles 1, 2 and 4 of the Statement of His Highness the Sheikh of all Sheikhs, His Excellency Sheikh Sultan Bin Saqar (17)

***Article 1**; The first issue is that I am grateful to you, and like my ancestors from the oldest time, we have been your servant, companion, and subject, and today also I am your servant, companion and subject, and I am ready for your command and instructions so that whatever command you might have will be carried out with our lives, by myself, my children, my clan and my tribe. We are all your subjects and citizens and servants and abide by your instructions. And Ras al-Kheimah has been your (territorial) dominion since the oldest time and is now an Iranian territory.*

***Article 2**; The second issue is that if I were to have a representative in Bandar Abbas, I will see to all affairs of Bandar Abbas perfectly and completely as might be asked of me. But if the forces of Sayyed Saeed (Sultan of Oman) come and position themselves before Bandar Abbas, I could not see it and keep silent. It would be inevitable that I challenged him and chased him out of that place. If I were to challenge him at sea the English will be the obstacle, and they would say that they are the lord of the sea; on whose permission and on whose authority am I quarrelling in the sea? You get a letter from the English or issue an order to the English not to challenge me at all in the sea so that not only could I see to the service of your maritime affairs to the best of my ability, but also I could add all coasts and islands in Oman to your dominion.*

***Article 4**; the fourth issue is that should I stay in Bandar Abbas, the province of Ras al-Kheimah is a vast province; some of the time there are disturbances and your support is essential. As I have become in your charge, your subject, and have accepted citizenship of the Iranian Government and my children, my tribe and clan request you to send 4 divisions of soldiers with a commander and ten canons and a sufficient amount of Qur-Khaneh (a 19th century Persian word for armory, arsenal, shot guns, or ammunition) and all expenses to Ras al-Kheimah where they could be stationed permanently... (18)*

Even as late as 1969 Arab scholars verified that the issue of territorial sovereignty in the southern coasts of the Persian Gulf was of an Arab-Iranian mixture. In an interview with the Iranian press, Dr. Sayyed Mohammad Nufel of Egypt, visiting Tehran in his capacity as Deputy Secretary General of the Arab League, stated:

> *I ridicule the efforts for changing the name of the Persian Gulf and condemn these futile efforts... I have made some studies about the region of the Persian Gulf and published a book in 1952 in which I used the term Persian Gulf, only saying that the Sheikhdoms were neither Arab nor Iranian, but a mixture of both...* (19)

The Iranian Government had as from the year 1950 imposed visa requirement for the inhabitants of the lower Persian Gulf traveling into Iran. Before that date, they carried an Iranian identity document that allowed them to travel freely between the opposite coasts.

The Anglo-Iranian territorial contention, which began in 1840s with Haji Mirza Aghasi's declaration of opposition to the British annexation of ports and islands of lower Persian Gulf, the most prominent of which in the twentieth century were the issues of Iran's claim on Bahrain and Britain's claim on Tunbs and Abu Musa on behalf of its client emirates, continued throughout the 19th and early 20th centuries until in 1965 when negotiations began between the two for a north-south maritime divide in the Persian Gulf. Though these negotiations did not produce conclusive agreements on the subject, it established in 1966 the median line of the sea as a principle upon which the continental shelf between Iran and her Arab neighbours was to be divided. It was on the basis of this principle that the subsequent maritime delimitation agreements were achieved. This was a decision on an *ad hoc* basis that the median line of the Persian Gulf would become the term of reference on which the maritime areas of the sea would be delimited and delineated between Iran to the north, and Arab Emirates and Saudi Arabia to the south (20). This was a general understanding on the basis of which the Iranians accepted that the southern limits of their sovereignty rights retreated to the median line of the Persian Gulf and therefore, relinquished claims on Bahrain archipelago in 1970. The British also decided, after intensive negotiations throughout the 1970 and 1971 to return the three islands of Tunbs and Abu Musa, situated in the northern half of the Persian Gulf and on the median line respectively, to Iran.

Doubting Validity of Official British Government Documents

Another issue of significance to be noted by all observers is the fact that in addition to hundreds of British government documents verifying Iran's ownership of the Islands of Tunbs and Abu Musa, there are numerous official British maps also confirming Iran's sovereignty rights to these islands (21). In a round table discussion between Iranian and Arab academics in London in November 1992 this author produced 24 maps, mostly compiled officially by the British government in the 18th and 19th centuries that proved Iranian possession of the islands in question. Prior to the said meeting it was widely believed in Iran, the Arab World and In the West that only a single official British map, produced in 1886, clearly recognized Iranian sovereignty over the islands. Even that single map became the subject of controversy in that meeting as Mr. Richard Schofield, a British academic at London Kings College of no apparent connection to UAE attempts to re-write the history of the region, responded positively to a question put to him by the Ambassador of the Arab League in London, that the 1886 official British map was compiled by mistake. Responding to this allegation, this author (Dr. Pirouz Mojtahed-Zadeh) explained that the map in question is a huge drawing in several sheets, the sheet containing the vicinity of the three islands in the Persian Gulf is as big as 2 by 1 square meters, each of the three islands of Tunbs and Abu Musa appearing on it in a size larger than a dinner plate with the term 'IRAN' printed inside each of them from side to side. He then questioned how a map as big as this and as simple as this could be compiled by mistake on the part of the War Office of Great Britain, a highly professional colonial office whose success in helping the establishment of world's greatest empire was the result of its thoroughness. Nevertheless, Mr. Schofield repeated this allegation in another meeting of academics discussing the 'international boundaries of Iran' (London School of Oriental and African Studies, 9-10 October 2002) (22) without being able to present any evidence that could in any way substantiate the allegation.

T*he Map of the Persian Gulf* as the 1886 map is called, was compiled by the Intelligence Division of the War Office of the United Kingdom. A copy of this map was presented to Nasr ad-Din Shah Qajar of Iran in 1888 on the instruction of Lord Salisbury, British Foreign Secretary at the time. Seeing the map, the Shah rightly concluded that the map barred any other argument on Anglo-Sharjah sovereignty over these islands. When Sir Drummond Wolf, British Minister plenipotentiary in Tehran, expressed regrets over the embarrassment that the map had been presented to the Iranian monarch, precisely because it confirmed Iran's territorial possessions in the Persian Gulf, including the islands of Tunbs and Abu Musa, Lord Salisbury remarked: *take note that maps shall never be presented in future* (23). Yet, as it was already too late, the map was published again in 1891 in colour, showing the three islands in the colour of Iran. Mr. Schofield alleges that the embarrassment over presentation of map was because it was compiled 'by mistake' and that was the reason for Lord Salisbury's remarks on the margin of British Ambassador's report, instructing the banning of presentation of official maps to foreign heads of states. This is clearly to overlook the simple and straight forward fact, and that was that the British government was embarrassed over the discovery by the Shah of Iran of their double dealing on the issue of sovereignty on these islands: On the one hand they had been corresponding with the Shah's government claiming Sharjah's ownership of these islands while, on the other hand, they officially and in their official documents (1886 map) acknowledge the truth about authenticity of Iranian sovereignty over the same islands.

Other British academic or diplomats of note who have discussed the issue of the three islands of Tunbs and Abu Musa and have made references to this map, have not even hinted to any possibility of it being compiled by mistake. Sir Denis Wright, a veteran British diplomat who studied the issue of Anglo-Iranian relations in details in two volumes has made references to the 1886 War Office map and its presentation to Nasser ad-Din Shah without even making any suggestion or hinting any question about the validity of the map being doubted. Rather he implies that presentation of this map to the Shah strengthened Iran's case. He states:

> *A War Office map, presented by the British Minister [in Tehran} to the Shah in 1888, showed all the islands [the two Tunbs, Abu Musa and Sirri] in Persian colour: the Persian case was further strengthened with the publication in 1992 of Curzon's two-volume Persia and Persian Question in which the map, prepared by the Royal geographical Society under Curzon's own supervision, also showed the islands as Persian territory.* (24)

When in the symposium on Iranian boundaries (9-10 October 2002) Mr. Schofield was reminded of the fact that the 1886 *Map of the Persian Gulf* was reprinted in 1891 by the British Government which is an official verification of the authenticity and validity of the map, he argued that as it was too late to do anything about it being compiled by mistake, the British authority decided to compile all subsequent publications with the mistake. Certainly this cannot be but an unnecessary admission of wrong doing on the part of the British Government. Moreover, this could also cause doubt about validity of other official maps of British Government, published subsequent to the publication in 1886 and 1891 of the *Map of the Persian Gulf*, including the *Official Map of Persia* (in six sheets): compiled in 1897 in the Simla Drawing office, Survey of India, Administration of topography of the Indian Foreign Office, in which the islands of Tunbs and Abu Musa are shown in the colour of the Iranian mainland.

Moreover, in an unlikely situation should Mr. Schofield's far fetched insinuation be accepted that all official maps of *Iran* or *Persia* and/or the *Persian Gulf*, published by the British Government subsequent to the 1886 map, were compiled deliberately with mistake on the issue of verification in those maps of Iranian ownership of the three islands, then he will not be in any position to question authenticity and correctness of the official British Government maps compiled and published before publication of the 1886 map, which could not have been affected in any way by possible problems that might have occurred in the completion of the 1886 map. Here, at least six examples of such maps, compiled and published before 1886 can be introduced, and they are as follow:

1- Map of The Persian Empire; compiled in 1813 by John Macdonald Kinner, Political Adviser to Sir John Malcolm, British Envoy, in his mission to Iran, in black and white; printed in colour in 1832 by J. Arrowsmith, showing the islands in the colour of Iranian territories

2- Map of *The Gulf of Persia*; compiled in 1829 by Captain G. B. Brucks on the instructions of East India Company, in which the islands of Tunbs and Abu Musa are coloured as Iranian territories and named in the covering note as Iranian owned.

3- Map of *Central Asia Comprising Cabool, Persia, the River Indus and countries eastward to it*: compiled in 1834 by Lieutenant Alexander Burnes on the basis of 'Authentic Maps', printed by Arrowsmith in colour, showing the islands of Tunbs and Abu Musa in the colour of Iranian territories.

4- Map of *Limits of the activities of the Tribes of Pearling Coasts*, compiled in 1835 by Captain S. Hennell, showing the islands of Tunbs and Abu Musa within Iranian jurisdiction.

5- Map of *Limits of the activities of the Tribes of Pearling Coasts*, compiled in 1838 by Major Morrison, British Political resident in the Persian Gulf, showing the islands of Tunbs and Abu Musa within Iranian jurisdiction.

6- Map of The Persian Gulf, compiled by Captain C.B.S. St. John, under the auspices of the Indian Government, Bombay 1876, in which the Tunbs and Abu Musa are depicted in the same colour as the Iranian mainland.

Gun Battle at Greater Tunb

There are those who describe the process of actual transfer of sovereignty control of the islands of Tunbs and Abu Musa to Iran by means of hoisting Iranian flags on them by an Iranian naval unit in the morning of November 30, 1971, as "Iran's military occupation" of these islands. What these individuals conveniently ignore is the fact that hoisting the flags of the recipient state over the territory, the sovereignty control of which is being transferred from one state to another, is a normal legal practice. For instance the district of Alaska was ceded to the United States by Russia on March 30, 1867, but it was the US Navy that started governing the territory by hoisting US flag there in 1879.

The Iranian flag was unfurled on the two Tunb islands and Abu Musa Island in the morning of November 30, 1971 in an official arrangement with the British authorities and the authorities of the emirates of Sharjah and Ras al-Kheimah. An Iranian Naval unit arrived in Abu Musa Island first and was officially welcomed by H. H. Sheikh Saqar Bin Mohammad al-Qassemi, brother of the ruler of Sharjah.

Figure 22

Having welcomed Iranian Naval representatives to the island of Abu Musa on November 30, 1971, on behalf of his brother H. H. Sheikh Khalid Bin Mohammad al-Qassemi, the then ruler of Sharjah, H. H. Sheikh Saqar Bin Mohammad al-Qassemi, is welcomed on board the Iranian naval vessel at anchor in Abu Musa waters.

Unlike the peaceful transfer of sovereignty control of northern half of Abu Musa Island to Iran, an unexpected incident at Greater Tunb disturbed peaceful transition.

On their arrival at Greater Tunb the Iranian naval representatives noticed the absence of welcoming party but the small island seemed to them peaceful enough. On the approach to the island Iranian officials on board naval vessel *Artmiss* heard gun shots from the inside of Ras al-

Kheimah's police station in the island. In an interview with this author on 21 June 2003, Iranian journalist Mr. Ali-Reza Taheri, who represented the daily Ettelaat of Tehran in the Iranian delegation on board Artmiss to the three islands, stated:

> *It had been arranged that like in Abu Musa, the Iranian delegation would be welcomed at Greater Tunb ceremonially..... The Iranian delegation would not even contemplate that peaceful process and their security would be threatened by the gunmen inside the police station (of Ras al-Kheimah at the Greater Tunb). Captain Suzanchi headed four navy personnel who attempted to investigate the source of disturbance. They were so sure of their safety that none of them had a naked gun in their hands when they were killed. On his martyrdom Captain Suzanchi's gun was still in its case fastened on his vest. At the time of the gun shots he had only his walky-talky in his hand.*
>
> *The Iranian delegation had no knowledge of the number of police officers in the station. The two individuals, who had come out of the station initially, had raised their guns over their heads indicating their intention to surrender. Evidently assuming wrongly that these two were the only personnel there and that there would not be anyone else in the station, Captain Suzanchi and his company approached the individuals surrendering themselves to the Iranian delegation. As soon as they reached the fire range of the station, they were showered with bullets coming from the inside of the station..... Captain Suzanchi and two of his fellow officers were killed on the spot; the forth officer was wounded with only one of them survived unscathed.*
>
> *Facing that unexpected situation which was later blamed on the British officer in command of Ras al-Kheimah's police station in Greater Tunb and a few Iraqi elements, the Iranian naval unit reacted in the defense of the lives of the rest of the delegation and the safety of the local residents and brought the police station under fire. Three of the rebels inside the building were killed and the rest were arrested and transferred to Ras al-Kheimeh...*

This incident that was not anticipated at all and was blamed on the lack of competence on the part of the British and Ras al-Kheimah authorities at Greater Tunb has apparently provided those opposed to the Anglo-Iranian settlement of the case of these islands with excuses to accuse Iran of having occupied the islands in question by force of arm. This accusation has been repeated many times in certain Arab and Western circles without the offer of any credible explanation or evidence to support the allegation and/or being aware of what had exactly happened in Abu Musa and in Greater Tunb on the day these islands were lawfully returned to Iran.

Finally, on the legality of UAE (Abu Dhabi's) claims on these Iranian islands the following arguments are worth noting (25):

> *1- The islands of Greater Tunb, Lesser Tunb and Abu Musa were returned to Iran on November 30th 1971 through legal processes, including the signing of a Memorandum of Understanding, before the state of the United Arab Emirates was created and the Aal Nahyan of Abu Dhabi took its leadership. According to international regulations no state can defy the agreements that had come into being before its creation unless such agreements had been officially declared as*

null and void by the newly created state. Not only did not the United Arab Emirates declare the arrangements arrived at by Iran and Great Britain (acting as the government of emirates of Sharjah and Ras al- Kheimah at the time) on the return of the three islands, but also the Supreme Council of the Union decided in its meeting of 12 May 1992 that foreign obligations of the emirates prior to the formation of the United Arab Emirates will be the obligations of the Union itself. Moreover, in its circular of 27 October 1992, distributed among the representatives of member states of the United Nations, Abu Dhabi asked Iran to observe the terms of its November 1971 MoU with Sharjah. Hence, laying claims on islands returned to Iran before the formation of the United Arab Emirates through legal process is an illegal act by Abu Dhabi.

2- The MoU of November 1971, signed between Iran and Sharjah, is a legal instrument which gives no right of interference to any third party. Also the return of the two Tunb islands to Iran by Great Britain took place on the basis of unwritten understanding between the two as Iran deemed that any written agreement would put her absolute sovereignty over these islands in doubt. Nonetheless, the permanent representative of the United Kingdom at the United Nations declared in the Security Council meeting of December 9, 1971 that the arrangement arrived at between his country and Iran on these islands constituted a model arrangement for the settlement of similar territorial issues elsewhere in the world. Hence, Abu Dhabi's lack of respect for these arrangements renders its claims on these islands illegal.

3- In the meeting of 12 may 1992 of the Supreme Council of the United Arab Emirates the Emir of Sharjah who is Iran's original partner in the 1971 MoU, refused to pass his Emirate's authority over the issue of Abu Musa island to the UAE leadership and left the meeting. Hence, Abu Dhabi's action in assuming authority for the case of Abu Musa Island in the absence of the ruler of Sharjah and without his consent renders any claim by Abu Dhabi on that island illegal.

4- In an insincere manner Abu Dhabi is trying to present the practice of the return of Abu Musa and Tunb islands to Iran on November 30th 1971 as a military occupation. In its scenario the visit to Abu Musa island of an Iranian naval vessel that went to hoist the Iranian flag on the island was enough a reason to manufacture the accusation of an Iranian military occupation of the island, disregarding the fact that Iranian naval representatives were welcomed officially by the brother of the Emir of Sharjah in the island. Hoisting flag of the recipient state on the territory changed hands between two states is a legal practice as US navy hoisted that country's flag at Alaska when that territory was transferred to US sovereignty from Russia.

At Greater Tunb a misunderstanding between the English commander of the police station and some Iraqi elements therein resulted in shooting between them. In a swift response, the Iranian naval vessel that had just arrived to hoist Iranian flag there arrested those involved and sent them back to Ras al-Kheimah. Clearly the attempt by Abu Dhabi in portraying this local incident at Greater Tunb and the official welcome extended to the Iranian representatives at Abu

Musa as Iran's *military occupation* of the three islands will demonstrate the falsehood upon which Abu Dhabi pursues its claims on these islands.

Letter of Clarification from Sharjah

In a letter to this author, completely unrelated to Abu Dhabi's efforts in re-writing the history and geographical description of the region in order to give some kind of legitimacy to their illegitimate claims on the Iranian islands, dated 8 May 2006, the Dewan Al-Amiri, the Court of His Highness Dr. Sheikh Sultan Al-Qassemi the Ruler of Sharjah clarified that the Sheikh Yusof of Bandar Lengeh mentioned in pages 69 and 70 of my book *The Islands of Tunb and Abu Musa* (SOAS, University of London Publication 1995) and on pages 184 and 185 of my book *Security and Territoriality in the Persian Gulf* (Curzon Press publication – London 1999), who ruled Bandar Lengeh since 1878, did not belong to the ruling Qassemi families of the emirates of Sharjah and Ras Al Kheimah. The letter reads:

> *With reference to your Documentary study about the Arabian Islands, you mentioned the name of Sheikh Youssuf Al Qassimi, who ruled Lingeh since 1878*
>
> *We would like to inform you that Sheikh Youssuf does not belong to the Ruling Family neither in Sharjah Emirate nor in Ras Al-Khaimah Emirate; rather, he was descending from a humble tribe and was a follower and servant of Sheikh Ali Bin Khalifa Al-Qassimi, who murdered the latter and became himself the ruler of Lingeh.* (26)

This author welcomes the above letter of clarification from the office of His Highness the Ruler of Sharjah with due respect and implements it in its future research works, but finds it necessary to explain that the nature of the said Sheikh Youssef's family connection with the Al-Qassemi families of Sharjah and Ras Al-Khaimah and/or the lack of it does not alter the facts described in the said pages of my above mentioned books.

Notes and References

1- Keith McLahlan, *The boundaries of modern Iran*, The SOAS/GRC Geopolitics Series 2, UCL Press, London 1994, p. 9.
2- Thomas R. Mattair, *The Three Occupied UAE Islands: The Tunbs and Abu Musa*, The Emirates Centre for Strategic Studies and Research, in English and Arabic, Abu Dhabi 2005. This is a UAE Government publication and the UAE Government emblem appears on its cover page.
3- J. G. Lorimer, Gazetteer of the Persian Gulf, Vol. I, India 1908, p. 625.
4- J. B. Kelly, *Eastern Arabian Frontiers*, London 1964, p. 18.
5- John C. Wilkinson, *Water and Tribal Settlement in South-East Arabia*, Oxford research Studies in Geography, Oxford 1977, p. 6.
6- Rupert Hay, *The Persian Gulf States*, Washington 1959, pp. 3-4.
7- This terrorist group (Al-Ahwaz) has, with the permission of British Government, placed its headquarters in London where they had in 1980 carried out their well known attack on the Iranian Embassy and were defeated by the British special anti-terrorist squad.
8- Edward Saeed, *Orientalism*, Vintage Books, New York 1979).
9- Talal Adrisi, *Sourat al-Iraniyn fi al-kotob al-madresiyat al-Arabiyat* (the image of Iranians in Arab school books), in Khair ed-Din Hasseeb ed., *Al-Alaghat al-Arabiyat-al-Iraniyah Relations*, Beirut 1996, p. 304.
10- Saddam Hussein's 8-years war on Iran (1980 – 1988) was named by the Baath regime after the last of Muslim Arabs' wars fought against Iran in 7th century AD.
11- See for example the following instances:
    Magdi Omar's interview in Al-Ahram of Egypt on 21/6/2001
    Abdul Monim Saeed in Al-Ahram of 23 December 2002.
    Al-Anba' daily of Kuwait wrote on 7 October 2003
    Mohammad Abu Ali in Al-Sharq al-Owsat of London 16/12/2004
    Abd or-Rahman Rashed in Al-Sharq al-Owsat on 1/1/2005
    Sad Ibn Taflah former Kuwaiti Minister of Culture and Information in Sharq al-Owsat of 1/1/2005 and in 15/1/2005
    Dr. Hesham Al-Asmar in Al-Ahram of Egypt 18 January 2005
    Dr. Yaseen Suwaid in An-Nahar of Lebanon and Morocco on 7/1/2005
    Dr. Foad Haddad in The Qods al-Arabi of London on 26/1/2006
    Sad Ibn Taflah former Kuwaiti Minister of Culture and Information in Sharq al-Awsat of 4/3/2006.
12- J. W??????@free.fr, 09 January 2006 20:03:42`+0100
13- Sir Arnold T. Wilson, *The Persian Gulf*, George Allen & Unwin Ltd., London, 2nd publication, 1954, p. 22.
14- For details of evidence and references on these developments see; Pirouz Mojtahed-Zadeh, *Security and Territoriality in the Persian Gulf*, Curzon/ Routledge, London 1999.
15- John C. Wilkinson, *The Julanda of Oman*, in the Journal of Oman, Vol. 1, London 1975, p. 98.
16- For a thorough account of the early developments of British colonial interference with the political geography of the Persian Gulf, see British references such as: Arnold T. Wilson, op.

cit., Sir Rupert hay, op. cit., Donald Hawley, *The Trucial States*, George Allen & Unwin, London 1970, J. B. Kelly, *Britain and the Persian Gulf*, 1795-1880, classic and recent reprinted work, Oxford University Press 1968, etc.

17- Document 15 of *Majmueh-e Asnad-e Farrokh Khan Amin ad-Doleh*, The collection of the documents of Farrokh Khan Amin ad-Doleh, the documents of the year 1274 H. Q. (1867), edited by Karim Esfahanian, Tehran University Press, Tehran 1979, pp. 24-5.

18- It is noteworthy that in a similar attempt for leasing Bandar Abbas from Iran's central authorities, Saiyid Saeed bin Ahmad, Sultan of Muscat (Oman) wrote on 20 Shaban 1272 (26 April 1856) to the Shah declaring himself as a subject of the Government of Iran. He renewed Oman's traditional sovereignty linkage to Iran in terminologies as obscure as it had been throughout the ages. For Persian and Arabic texts of this letter, see: *Majmu'eh-e Asnad-eDolatiy-e Iran* = A Collection of Iranian Government Documents, Vol. 6156.

19- Dr. Sayyed Mohammad Nufel, deputy Secretary General of the Arab League and representative of the Egyptian Government in the Human Rights Conference of 1969 in Tehran, in interview with Kayhan Daily of Tehran, No. 7420, Wednesday 4, 2, 1347 H.S., corresponding with 22 April 1969.

20- For details of these maps see; Appendix 1 of *The Islands of Tunb and Abu Musa: An Iranian Argument for Peace and Co-operation in the Persian Gulf*, by Pirouz Mojtahed-Zadeh, SOAS University of London publication, London 1995, pp. 86-88. This list is reproduced in; Pirouz Mojtahed-Zadeh, *Security and territoriality in the Persian Gulf: A Maritime Political geography*, Curzon Press, London 1999, New York 2002.

21- For more details see: Pirouz Mojtahed-Zadeh, *The Islands of Tunb and Abu Musa; An Iranian Argument in Search of Peace and Co-operation in The Persian Gulf*, occasional paper No. 15, CNMES, SOAS, London University, London 1995, ch. III.

22- Payvand Iran News, 10/015/02, *Report of the International symposium on Modern Boundaries of Iran "Problems and practices of Iranian boundaries"*, http://www.payvand.com/news/02/oct/1053.html.

23- Denis Wright, *The English Amongst the Persians*, Heinemann, London 1977, p. 68.

24- Payvand News Network, http://www.payvand.com/news/04/jun/1102.html, Report of the author's letter to Javier Solana of the European Union, 06/16/2004.

25- Official letter of clarification received electronically from Mr. Rashid Ahmed Al-Sheikh, Director General of Sharjah Ruler's Court, Al-Dewan Al-Amir, Government of Sharjah, addressed to Professor Pirouz Mojtahed-Zadeh, dated 8 May 2006.

26- Official letter of clarification received electronically from Mr. Rashid Ahmed Al-Sheikh, Director General of Sharjah Ruler's Court, Al-Dewan Al-Amir, Government of Sharjah, addressed to Professor Pirouz Mojtahed-Zadeh, dated 8 May 2006.

APPENDIX TO CHAPTER XXI

Other UAE Arguments*

In their propaganda campaign for regaining possession of the two Tunbs and Abu Musa islands, the UAE Government put forward a number of other (political) arguments on various occasions in international arena during 1990s until 2002, mostly responded to by the author. The following is an example of the kind of academic-political exchanges that have taken place between various Arab academic and/or political personalities and the author in US, Europe, and the Middle East.

Reported by Payvand Iran News Network, the following exchange had taken place on 10th of October 2002 during the proceedings of an international symposium which was organized at the University of London School of Oriental and African Studies on 9th and 10th October 2002 by the Centre of Near and Middle Eastern Studies/SOAS, in association with the Society for Contemporary Iranian Studies/SOAS and Urosevic Research Foundation/SOAS London*:

Session on Iran's boundaries in the Persian Gulf (10 October 2002)

Chaired by Dr. Pirouz Mojtahed-Zadeh, Professor of geopolitics at London and Tarbiat Modarres universities, the session on territoriality and boundary issues in the Persian Gulf proved to be the most important, the liveliest, the most fruitful, and the longest session of the symposium. Mr. Sohrab Asgari of Tehran University stated that Iran's maritime boundaries in the Persian Gulf have all been settled except in two areas: one is with UAE where territorial claims on islands of Tunbs and Abu Musa by the United Arab Emirates have prevented delimitation of relevant maritime areas. The other area is the north- western end of the Persian Gulf where Iran, Iraq and Kuwait have not been able to define their realms and boundaries. This is mainly because of Iraq is unable to define a starting point for maritime division, owing to its continued claims on Iranian and Kuwaiti border areas.

Although some measures have been foreseen in the existing boundary arrangements to prevent horizontal drilling for extraction from cross-border oil fields, no measure exist to regulate the use of energy from the newly discovered cross-border gas fields. Sizeable gas fields such as South Pars and Arash between Iran on the one hand and Qatar and Kuwait on the other, are the subject of controversies between Iran and these states. However, unlike some areas mentioned previously, cross-border cooperation here can lead to a just and equitable settlement of these controversies.

Having briefly examined the role of the British in the issue of Iran-UAE differences on the islands of Tunb and Abu Musa, Dr. Richard Schofield of GRC, King's College – London gave an impartial account of some historical and legal aspects of the dispute.

This talk left a vague impression with the audience that the reason for British Foreign Secretary's decision of writing on the side of British Government's 1886 map that official maps should no longer be presented to other heads of states was that the map was compiled by mistake and presentation of a mistaken map would be embarrassing. To cast this doubt out, chairman of the session, Dr. Pirouz Mojtahed-Zadeh explained that the map we are talking about is a 16 square meters document and could in no way be compiled by mistake. The reason for foreign secretary's decision of prohibiting future presentation of official maps was simply to stop the embarrassing display of the hypocrisy of official verification of Iran's ownership and sovereignty over the two Tunbs and Abu Musa islands on the one hand, and claiming the same territories for the rulers of their protectorate emirates on the other.

Inclined to support the position of the UAE vis-à-vis these islands, H. E. Ali Muhsen Hamid, the Ambassador of the Arab League in London put some questions to the chairman on the subject. The answer to each and every question raised by him was extensive, categorical and backed by irrefutable legal, historical, and geographical documents. Briefly, the Ambassador said that the MOU on Abu Musa between Iran and Sharjah was imposed on Sharjah and as it was signed two days before the creation of the UAE, it was not legal. In his reply Dr. Mojtahed-Zadeh said, first of all Iran did not negotiate with Sharjah and/thus could not impose anything on her. Iran negotiated the MOU with Great Britain acting on behalf of Sharjah, and Britain was much stronger than Iran at the time and Iran could not impose anything on Britain. In fact, the idea that Britain imposed the MOU on Iran and/thus prevented Iran from taking the whole of Abu Musa Island would sound more realistic. Furthermore, the fact that the UAE was created 2 days after the signing of the MOU makes no difference whatsoever, because, firstly Britain was the legal guardian of the emirates at the time and its agreement with Iran was perfectly legal and internationally accepted. Secondly the UAE high Council declared in 1992 that foreign and international undertakings of each member emirate before the creation of the UAE was the legal obligation of the UAE as whole. The Ambassador then said that the UAE asks Iran for negotiation on the subject and Iran does not, and UAE asks Iran to go to the International Court of Justice on the matter, but Iran refuses to do so. Dr. Mojtahed-Zadeh replied: first what your excellency is referring to is but a proof of UAE's hypocrisy, because it asks Iran for negotiations but when Iran goes for negotiations the UAE runs away. Five time so far Iran tried to negotiate with the UAE on the subject, but UAE did not come forward: twice former Iranian foreign minister Dr. Velayati went to Abu Dhabi for talks, but they declined to respond positively, and twice current foreign minister Kamal Kharrazi went to Abu Dhabi for talks with the UAE and they failed even to meet him. For the fifth time, as a result of mediation by Qatar, the two sides sent delegations to Doha for negotiations in 1998. The delegations met in the morning and introduced themselves to each other and went for lunch to get back to start the negotiations. In the afternoon the Iranian delegation went back to the negotiating room, waiting for their UAE counterparts, but instead of returning to the negotiating room they went to the international media declaring that the negotiation had failed because of the Iranian's intransigence. This is how the UAE politicians have been behaving in the past ten years. What failure? The negotiation had not even started to have failed. You see! The UAE talks about wanting to negotiate with Iran but whenever Iran goes for the negotiation they run away because they have nothing to negotiate about. Moreover, it is about a month now that rumors indicate that secret negotiations are taking place between the two parties. Normally in such a situation all those concerned with peaceful settlement of such disputes tend to keep quiet in order to allow the two sides to settle the matter in peace and with free hands. While, not only the authorities in Iran, but also I have asked everybody to be silent on the subject in order to help the talks progress, the Gulf Cooperation Council issued support for Abu Dhabi's claims against Iran. I ask you, is this the time for the GCC to interfere? If the GCC or other Arab's were sincere in wanting a peaceful settlement to UAE claims to these islands, they would, like the Iranians, keep quiet in this particular situation. The problem is that there is no sincerity on the part UAE and GCC. The Arabs have been behaving the same during Iraq's claim to the whole of Shatt al-Arab and parts of Khuzestan. Nothing is new, but I wish you Sir, and other scholars in the Arab world while judging Iran, think about Arab behavior in such matters against Iran as well. On the subject of going to the ICJ, we must know that going to the international courts is the last resort and is used when all other ways have been exhausted. The first way to be examined is direct negotiations for peaceful settlement. How could the UAE refuse to negotiate the matter with Iran but ask Iran to go to the international court? Moreover Iran went to the UN Security Council with the Arabs on this issue and the United Nations turned down the Arab complaint. How could you expect Iran to go to the international bodies twice as soon as her territories are claimed by another state?

The Ambassador subsequently denied that the UAE has ever tried to Arabise and/or internationalize the issue of its claims to these islands, and said that it was former Iranian President Rafsanjani who talked about the "sea of blood" not UAE leaders. Dr. Mojtahed-Zadeh replied that by distributing its position paper in the United Nations on 27 October 1992, the UAE started its efforts for internationalizing of the issue and you and I know very well the UAE has used Arab forums like the GCC and Arab League to habitually issuing statements of support for its claim. Isn't this internationalizing the issue? On the subject of President Rafsanjani's comment about the "Sea of Blood", the Arabs have misunderstood the statement and have been distorting the message for so many years. What President Rafsanjani said was this "those who want to take these islands from Iran must cross a sea of blood". You see the message is quite clear. This message is not about creating a sea of blood for attacking UAE or any Arab country, but it says that if UAE and its Arab friends want to attack Iran to take these Islands, the Iranians will create a sea of blood in "defending" their country. Moreover what Mr. Rafsanjani had in mind when saying this was how Iraq attacked Iran to take her territories, and how Iraq's Arab comrades supported its aggression against Iran. Hence, Mr. Rafsanjani's statement was not offensive; it was defensive, saying if a similar action were to take place against Iran again, the Iranians would defend their country the same way that they did in the case of Iraqi attack.

As the exchange was conducted in a very friendly atmosphere and with mutual respect, the Arab League Ambassador privately expressed hopes that similar friendly academic exchange with larger Arab audience in an Arab country could help broadening mutual understanding between the two sides.

---

* Payvand Iran News Network, http://www.payvand.com/, *Report of the International symposium on Modern Boundaries of Iran "Problems and practices of Iranian boundaries"*, Payvand Iran's News 10/15/02.

Contributors

Mohammad Ali. Ala

Dr. M. Ali Ala received his Ph.D. in Petroleum Geology from the London Imperial College in 1972 where he has been teaching as a Senior Academic and Director of the MSc Petroleum Geoscience course since 1994. This was after a few years of consultancy works internationally and affiliation to Imperial College's teaching staff. He has been a member of the editorial board of the Journal of Petroleum Geology since 1992. Dr. Ala is affiliated to the American Association of Petroleum Geologists since 1968 and the Petroleum Exploration Society of Great Britain since1973. He has published more than 50 research papers and review articles, mostly on the petroleum geology and oil industry of Iran. His research interests include source rock studies, sedimentary basin analysis and petroleum occurrence worldwide; politics and economics of oil with special reference to the Middle East and OPEC matters.

Bahram Amirahmadian

Dr. Bahram Amirahmadian received his Ph.D. in Political Geography from the University of Tehran in 1996 where he has been teaching political geography since 2000. He also lectures at the Islamic Azad University. His 10 books and 130 papers and articles include valuable research works on the political geography of the Caucasus region. In addition to participating many national and international seminars on geographical issues in Iran, Russia, and countries of the Caucasus, he has done much consulting works for the Iranian Ministry of Foreign Affairs, where he is a member of the editorial board of two quarterlies: "Central Asia and Caucasus" in Persian and "Amu Darya" in English and Russian. He has also been an adviser to the Central Asian and Caucasus Studies of the Institute of Political and International Studies of the Iranian Ministry of Foreign Affairs since the year 2000.

Hossein Askari

Dr. Hossein Askari received his Ph.D. in International Economics and Finance, from the Massachusetts Institute of Technology. He was Professor at the University of Texas at Austin. He served for two and a half years on the Executive Board of the International Monetary Fund representing Saudi Arabia, after which he came to the School of Business at the George Washington University in 1982 and is now the Iran Professor of International Business and International Affairs. He was the Director of an international team of energy experts that designed a long-term energy plan for Saudi Arabia in the mid-1980s. His research and teaching interests are focused on international trade and finance, and Middle East economic, financial and oil developments. He is the author or co-author of sixteen books and over one hundred professional journal articles.

Mohammad Hassan Ganji

Professor Emeritus Mohammad Hassan Ganji, who is originally from eastern Iranian borderlands, received his Ph.D. in geography from Clark University, Mass., 1954. During the half century of teaching at Tehran University he served as Vice-chancellor and adviser to the chancellor of that university. He also served as Chancellor of Birjand University. Among Professor Ganji's non-academic posts and positions his distinguished service as Deputy Minister of Road and Communication and Director General of the Meteorological Organization and stands out at national level, and his position as President of world Meteorological Organization, Asia Division at international level. He also was a member of the United Nations' Group of Experts on Geographical Names (UNGEGN). His publications include 13 book in Persian and more than 110 articles in Persian and English in various books and reputable Iranian and international journals and encyclopedias.

World Meteorological Organization announced on 15 June 2001 in Geneva that it attributed its prestigious IMO Rize to Professor MH Ganji.

Mohammad Reza Hafeznia

Dr. Mohammad Reza Hafeznia has received his Ph.D. in political geography from Tarbiat Modares University of Tehran on the "Strategic position of the Strait of Hormuz". He has completed a period of local research and study in India in 1980s and is now Professor of political geography at Tarbiat Modares University, where he also chairs the Centre for African Studies. His publications include 11 books, all in Persian and 37 articles of which a number has appeared in reputable English language journals outside Iran. Dr. Hafeznia has attended numerous international conferences on various subjects of political geography and has presented papers in many of them including the international symposium on Iranian Boundaries; London University, 9th and 10th October 2002.

K. S. McLachlan

Professor Emeritus Keith S. McLachlan is a highly respected expert of development-conservation issues in oil economies of North Africa, the Middle East, Central Asia and the North Sea. He has a long-term applied interest in planning for change in oil economies. For many years he studied and lectured on the economic and political geography of Iran and neighbouring countries, but has recently been involved in projects in Algeria, Kuwait and the Faroes.

Professor McLachlan served as President of the British Institute of Persian Studies for many years. He founded the Geopolitics and International Boundaries Research Centre at SOAS, University of London. Together with Dr. A. N. Alikhani and Dr. Pirouz Mojtahed-Zadeh he founded The Society for Contemporary Iranian Studies. To the students of Iranian Studies, among Professor McLachlan's numerous and valuable publications, his book on The Neglected Garden: Politics & Ecology of Agriculture in Iran (London, Tauris, 1988) stands out.

Pirouz Mojtahed-Zadeh

Dr. Pirouz Mojtahed-Zadeh has completed his Ph.D. at the universities of Oxford and London. He is Associate Professor of political geography and geopolitics at Tarbiat Modares postgraduate University in Tehran and Chairman of Urosevic Research Foundation in London. He was a senior research associate of Geopolitical and International Boundaries Research Centre at SOAS, University of London until 2001 when this centre was moved to King's College London. He has been a research adviser of the UN University and has lectured extensively in North America, West Europe, Middle East and the Far East. His publications include 18 books in Persian, 6 books in English apart from this, and 2 in Arabic as well as about 400 articles and research pieces published in English, Persian, and Arabic in reputable newspapers, magazines, and specialist journals around the world.

Masud Moradi

Dr. Masud Moradi has received his Ph.D. in European history from the University of Strasbourg in France, on the Rivalry of European Powers in Balkan 1875-1914 and its impact on the world of Islam. He is Assistant professor in geography at the University of Zahedan and dean of the Faculty of Literatures and Human Sciences. His publications include "The origin of Balkan Crisis" in French 2004, and a number of articles in Persian and English, especially in the Historical Journal in Iran. Dr. Moradi has completed a research and study sabbatical year in India and has attended many international conferences including the international symposium on the Iranian Boundaries, London University, 9 and 10 October 2002.

Farzad Cyrus Sharifi

Mr. Farzad Sharifi-Yazdi obtained his BA from Queen Mary College, University of London, and received his MA in International Boundary Studies & Dispute Resolution from the Geopolitics and International Boundary Research Centre at King's College, London University in 2002. He is currently working for his PhD in the field of *"Arab-Iranian territorial disputes in the Persian Gulf between 1958 to the present date"*. In the same London college Farzad works as a Part Time Lecturer, Planning, writing and organising lecture and presenting notes, presenting 1 hour lectures/presentations to undergraduate students on monthly basis.

Ms. Roshanak Taghavi

Ms. Roshanak Taghavi received a Bachelor of Science in Business and Economics from the Carroll School of Management at Boston College, during which time she also studied French literature and history, 20th century Middle Eastern history, and Medieval Islamic history at the Sorbonne (University of Paris IV). She recently completed a Presidential Internship at the American University in Cairo and works as a freelance writer for *Al-Ahram Weekly*. Her first co-authored publication in a professional journal will appear in *The British Journal of Middle Eastern Studies* in late 2005. She will begin graduate school in fall 2005, where she will obtain a Master of Arts in International Relations and Economic Development.

Lightning Source UK Ltd.
Milton Keynes UK
UKOW010810300912

199827UK00008B/447/A